Dictionary of Sex

The Wordsworth
Dictionary of Sex

—

Robert Goldenson Ph.D.
and Kenneth Anderson

Wordsworth Reference

First published in the UK as *Sex A-Z* by Bloomsbury
Publishing Limited, 1987.

This edition published 1994 by Wordsworth Editions Ltd,
Cumberland House, Crib Street, Ware, Hertfordshire SG12 9ET.

ISBN 1-85326-320-6

Printed and bound in Finland by UPC Oy.

Foreword

This is a dictionary of sex and more. Its 5,000 terms were selected to provide basic understanding of the nature of the human reproductive process, and to satisfy the reader who seeks information about the strange and the incredible. Besides technical terms, this dictionary includes colloquial expressions and background material drawn from leading contributors to this vast and varied aspect of life.

The following is a partial list of the contents of this unusual and comprehensive work: Anatomy and physiology; the physical mechanisms of sex. Erotic techniques, including the variety of intercourse positions. Physical and physchological disorders, aberrations and paraphilias, venereal diseases and remedies (including 30 entries dealing with latest data on AIDS). Unusual sexual practices around the world, and throughout history; forms of sexual behaviour in our own society. Sex and marriage therapy; heredity; genetic counselling. Sex related surgery. Sexual devices, from contraceptives to 'marital aids'. Sexual folklore and superstition; sex stimulants and alleged aphrodisiacs. Scientific sex studies, from Krafft-Ebbing to Masters and Johnson. Freudian terms and concepts; sexual phobias. Pregnancy; abortion; childbirth; sexual development. Sex and the law; sex and religion; sex in literature and the arts; historical references of sexual interest. Concise biographies of great contributors, from antiquity and the Middle Ages to the 1980s. Unexpected but apt quotations from literature and all walks of life. Sexual 'taboo' words and their origins; the richness of Shakespeare's sexual terms; obsolete but fascinating sex words; the inventiveness and humour of sexual slang today; social change reflected in the language of sex . . .

Together, these thousands of terms, explained in easy-to-understand language, will give the reader an insight into every area of human sexuality. This dictionary covers all key elements of the new scientific discipline of sexology, which includes the sexual aspects of anatomy, physiology, anthropology, sociology, psychoanalysis, psychotherapy, genetics, medicine, linguistics, and the legal and moral issues of our time – a vital subject that affects all people of all ages.

The Authors

Acknowledgements

The authors and editors of *The Wordsworth Dictionary of Sex* take pleasure in acknowledging the contributions of specialists who have made numerous helpful suggestions and have taken the trouble to review portions of the completed work, especially Ernest Lowenstein, M.D., Fellow of the New Jersey Academy of Obstetrics and Gynecology, and Edgar A. Gregersen, Ph.D., Professor of Anthropology at Queens College and the Graduate Center of the City University of New York, author of *Language in Africa* (1977) and *Sexual Practices* (1982).

We are also grateful to Mary S. Calderone, M.D., and other members of SIECUS (Sex Information and Education Council of the United States), and to members of the staff of the Institute for Advanced Study of Human Sexuality.

The British edition has been edited by John Ayto and Suzanne Ellis.

Aaron's rod an old euphemism for penis. The reference is to the biblical patriarch's staff, which blossomed and yielded almonds (Numbers 17:8).

abactio partus a legal term for unlawful abortion, used chiefly in Europe.

abbesse in medieval France, the officially appointed and sworn-in madam of a brothel; also called magistra (mistress). The English term *abbess* is less specific, referring to any madam of a brothel.

abdominal abortion a tubal pregnancy that is terminated spontaneously by the ejection of the embryo from the open end of the fallopian tube into the abdominal cavity. Depending on the degree of development of the aborted conceptus, it may be absorbed by tissues within the mother's abdominal cavity or it may have to be removed by surgical methods.

abdominal ostium the opening of the fallopian tube, surrounded by the fimbriae.

abdominal pregnancy an extrauterine pregnancy that develops in the abdomen. An abdominal pregnancy may be carried to term, with delivery by caesarean operation. The placenta becomes attached to tissues within the abdominal cavity as an alternative to implantation on the inner wall of the uterus. An abdominal pregnancy is uncommon, and delivery of a normal infant is even more rare. As with a tubal pregnancy, there is a high risk of fatal bleeding by the mother.

abdominal testicle a testicle that remains in the abdomen, above the inguinal ring. It atrophies, and therefore cannot produce sperm.

Abélard, Pierre (1079-1142) an eminent French philosopher who is best known today for his star-crossed love affair with his 17-year-old pupil Héloïse. They fled, were secretly married, and had a son. But her father had Abélard castrated and put in a monastery, and Héloïse was forced to become a nun. Their correspondence, maintained for several decades, is among the most famous love letters of all time.

aberration a deviation from what is considered normal sexual behaviour. Aberrant sexual behaviour is traditionally regarded as any sexual practice that is not intended to reproduce the human race and may include any act from autoeroticism to voyeurism. The Kinsey interviews revealed that nearly every adult uses one or more sexual aberrations occasionally or habitually, particularly if masturbation is included among sexual aberrations.

Abkhasians a people living in the Caucasus who are noted for their remarkable longevity and their sexual vigour in old age. They believe that regular sexual relations should start late in life, and that abstinence during their youth explains why some Abkhasians are said to have maintained their sexual interest and potency past the age of 100.

ablatio penis the surgical removal (Latin *ablatio*) of the penis or a part of the penis. The procedure is performed in treating cancer, as part of a sex-change plan, or in the treatment of gangrene that may result from interruption of normal blood flow in the penis during an episode of priapism.

abominable crime in 19th-century England, a legal term for anal intercourse; in the United States, today, a legal term for bestiality and/or anal intercourse.

aboratorium a slang term for abortion clinic.

abort a homosexual slang term meaning to defecate after anal intercourse.

aborticide the killing of a foetus; also, any agent—such as a saline solution—that may be used to destroy a foetus.

abortifacient any agent or procedure that is deliberately used to produce an abortion, especially measures that are medically accepted, such as ergot, saline solution, vacuum aspiration, and dilatation and curettage.

abortion the premature or untimely expulsion of a foetus (usually before the 28th week of gestation), whether induced or natural. An abortion that occurs before the fourth month of pregnancy is sometimes called an embryonic abortion; after the fourth month, the event is identified as a foetal abortion. A complete abortion is one in which the products of conception are expelled intact; if the membranes or placenta are not expelled with the foetus, it is an incomplete abortion. If one foetus of a multiple pregnancy is expelled prematurely while the remaining foetus is carried to term, the event is labelled a partial abortion. A missed abortion is one in which an embryo or foetus dies within the uterus. The term habitual abortion is applied to a condition in which two or more successive pregnancies are terminated by natural abortion.

Causes of natural abortion are many and include accident, a fever that may be only 1°F (0.5°C) above normal, an infection that inflames the lining of the uterus or of the foetal membranes, or the termination of an ectopic pregnancy, as in the rupture of a fallopian tube during a tubal pregnancy.

Historically, abortion epidemics have occurred during periods of starvation or similar general suffering, or from community-wide ergot poisoning.

See also ABDOMINAL ABORTION; ARTIFICIAL ABORTION; FRENCH ABORTION; INFECTIOUS ABORTION; JUSTIFIABLE ABORTION; LAWFUL ABORTION; PREEMPTIVE ABORTION; SELF-INDUCED ABORTION; SPONTANEOUS ABORTION; THERAPEUTIC ABORTION; TUBAL ABORTION.

abortionist a person who performs abortions. The term is generally applied to a person who performs abortions illegally, as distinguished from physicians or other trained health professionals employed by legitimate abortion facilities.

abortion laws laws governing the application of abortion procedures for the deliberate termination of pregnancy. The Abortion Act of 1967 authorized the legal termination of a pregnancy when two doctors certify that continuation of the pregnancy would involve the risk of the mother's life or would threaten the mental or physical health of the mother or any of her existing children, or if the child might suffer a serious mental or physical handicap if the pregnancy is carried to term. The act also required that all abortions must be reported to health-department authorities.

abortion procedures techniques used to perform abortions. Three basic techniques are used to induce abortions in the first trimester: menstrual extraction; dilatation and curettage (D & C); and uterine aspiration. All are usually administered after two missed periods. Four methods are employed for second-trimester abortions: intrauterine injection of a saline solution; injection of a urea solution after amniocentesis; intrauterine injection of prostaglandins; and surgical removal of the uterus. The surgical procedure, either hysterotomy or hysterectomy, also may be used in the third trimester with the risk of removing a uterus containing a premature viable infant. The prostaglandin technique is preferred by many obstetricians for women who are not hypersensitive to the effects of prostaglandins. Administration of the natural chemical, which is found in menstrual fluid and many body cells, requires only a few minutes, contractions usually begin within 30 minutes, and recovery is rapid.

abortus a foetus so undeveloped at the time of expulsion that it has no chance of survival. Abortus is also the Latin term corresponding to the English word abortion, as in *abortus artificialis*, artificial, or induced, abortion, *abortus completus*, complete abortion, *abortus imminens*, imminent, or impending, abortion, *abortus incipiens*, inevitable abortion, abortion in progress, *abortus incompletus*, incomplete abortion, *abortus septicus*, infectious abortion, and *abortus spontaneus*, natural, or spontaneous, abortion.

absence of gonads a congenital anomaly in which a person is born with neither testes nor ovaries, a very rare situation.

absinthe a bitter, aromatic liqueur made with wormwood and other herbs, and alleged to have an aphrodisiac effect: As the song goes, 'Absinthe makes the heart grow fonder.' This effect is probably nonexistent or exaggerated, but in any case overuse is risky because it may induce cerebral convulsions of an epileptic type.

absolute inversion Freud's term for extreme homosexuality characterized by complete disinterest in or even aversion towards the opposite sex.

abstinence refraining from sexual intercourse as a religious requirement or as a contraceptive measure. Periodic abstinence during the fertile period of the woman's menstrual cycle is the basis for the method of birth control known as natural family planning. Permanent abstinence (chastity, celibacy) is practised in some religious orders, for example, in early Buddhism and today among Roman Catholic priests and nuns. Temporary ritual abstinence is required of Muslims during the daylight hours of Ramadan, the month of fasting; and the East Indian Tantric cult advocates short periods of abstinence to concentrate sexual energy and increase sexual sensitivity and response.

abstinence rule the Freudian rule that patients should refrain from all types of gratification that might lower their anxiety level and drain off instinctual energy that could be used as a driving force in the analytic process. Examples of such gratifications are frequent sexual activity, smoking, conversing or acting out during sessions, or pursuing pleasurable activities outside the sessions. Also called rule of abstinence.

academy an older euphemism for brothel.

acceleration a speculative term referring to the observation that in the last two centuries human sexual maturation has been setting in earlier and earlier whereas intellectual maturation seems to begin later and later.

accessory gland an alternative term for prostate.

accessory urethral canal a second urethra that is found occasionally in the male penis. It is a birth defect and in most instances is nothing more than a blind pouch that extends a fraction of an inch along the shaft of the penis. Medical records show that some men have been born with two complete urethras extending to the bladder. An accessory urethral canal is often the site of a severe gonorrhoeal infection, requiring surgical removal of the extra urethra.

accidental homosexuality male or female homosexuality in which the partner is chosen when no person of the opposite sex is available.

accouchement a technical and now rather dated term for the process of giving birth, and also for the period leading up to this (confinement).

account executive a slang term for a pimp who caters to successful businessmen and/or offers high-class prostitutes.

Accu-Jac the perhaps most sophisticated male masturbation device, consisting of an electrically operated vacuum pump connected to a sleeve that fits over the penis for a gently sucking, adjustable movement. It comes with 'buddy' attachment, allowing two men to use it simultaneously. *Accu-Jac II*, in addition to having sleeves, is equipped with dildos for vaginal or anal insertion, permitting, for example, two men and two women to masturbate as a group.

AC-DC a colloquial term for bisexuality, from the initials of the two types of electricity, *a*lternating current and *d*irect current. Also spelled *AC/DC*.

acey-deucey a variant term for AC-DC.

achnutshik in Greenland, a transvestite boy who is brought up like a girl to become the quasi-legal spouse of a man when reaching the age of 10 to 15.

acid phosphatase an enzyme regarded by some authorities as a chemical secondary sexual characteristic of the male. Acid phosphatase is normally present in the male urine and is found in high concentrations in the prostate gland. It is closely associated with the production of the male androgenic hormone.

Ackerman Types a system of classifying breast tumours. An Ackerman Type I identifies cancer cells that have not penetrated a membrane and can be removed by simple surgical methods. Ackerman Type IV cancer cells have an invasive character and have spread through the bloodstream to attack organ tissues in other parts of the body. About 15 percent of all breast cancers are Ackerman Type IV tumours. The majority of breast cancers, however, are Ackerman Types II and III, which involve the ducts and alveolar membranes.

acme (ak'mē; Greek, 'point') a term used in psychoanalysis for the peak, or summit, of pleasure reached in intercourse.

acne syphilitica the Latin term for syphilitic acne, characterized by pustules or pimples with sharp peaks. The lesions are a sign of secondary syphilis and may be scattered over the body.

acne vulgaris a transient condition characterized by any of various comedones (blackheads), papules, pustules, and cysts that appear on the skin of adolescent individuals, particularly on the face, neck, and back, often causing acute embarrassment. The acne lesions involve the oil glands found around hair follicles and are probably caused by an increased production of androgenic sex hormones. Among the treatments are certain antibiotics, benzoyl peroxide, and retinoic acid.

acorn a colloquial term for the glans of the penis, describing its most common shape.

acorus a grasslike herb found in marshy places. One species, sweet flag, was once known as Venus' plant because of its reputed aphrodisiac qualities. It was used as a sexual stimulant from the days of ancient Rome through the Middle Ages.

acrai an obsolete Arabian term for nymphomania and satyriasis.

acromegaly an abnormal condition of bone overgrowth resulting from a pituitary gland disorder, usually a tumour. Although patients with acromegaly may have very large skeletons and internal organs, and often large external genitalia, the tumour that produces the condition is somewhat self-limiting. Pressure of the expanding tumour destroys the portion of the gland that stimulates sexual functions. Women develop amenorrhoea, gonads of both sexes shrink, and men become impotent and lose their sex drive.

acrosome a minute organ located at the tip of a spermatozoon. It is formed during differentiation of the spermatid from the Golgi complex as a fluid-filled vesicle. It then loses its fluid and fits over the anterior end of the spermatozoon as a head cap. During fertilization, the acrosome releases enzymes that break down the protective membranes of the ovum.

acrotomophilia the sexually arousing fantasy that one's lover is an amputee.

act the act: a term often used by Shakespeare with the meaning of sex act—which it still has today. Shakespeare sometimes modifies the term, as in '... served the lust of my mistress' heart, and did the act of darkness' (*King Lear*, III).

action a Shakespearean euphemism for sexual intercourse, still employed colloquially in this sense.

activating effects the results of hormonal stimulation that activate or deactivate behaviour. An example is sexual behaviour that results from increasing the levels of the sex hormone testosterone in a male. Injections of testosterone in female laboratory animals may activate masculine sexual behaviour such as mounting other members of the species.

active castration complex the totality of

fantasies and feelings associated with castration anxiety, as contrasted with the passive castration complex which consists of the belief that castration has already taken place, or the wish to lose the penis.

actual failure rate the failure rate of a contraceptive in typical normal use, including improper application of the device or technique. For example, the theoretical failure rate of an oral contraceptive may be 0.5 percent, but the actual failure rate is much higher because of defects in the pill itself or because the woman forgot to take the pill every day. The actual failure rate for a condom is about 15 percent, compared with a theoretical failure rate of about 5 percent.

actual intercourse a term sometimes used by interviewers trying to determine the real frequency of coitus between sexual partners. It reflects a common tendency by wives to overestimate the frequency of intercourse and by husbands to underestimate the frequency when asked to recall the number of times per week or month that the pair actually had intercourse.

actus brevis a medical term for premature ejaculation (Latin, 'brief act').

acute prostatitis an inflammation of the prostate gland that begins suddenly with chills, fever, and urinary pain or difficulty. The infection is caused by bacteria, which may be transmitted by sexual contact. Treatment is with antibiotics, but severe cases usually require hospitalization.

acute skeneitis an inflammation of the Skene's ducts of the female urethra. The inflammation is usually accompanied by accumulations of pus. Skene's ducts may be reservoirs of gonorrhoeal bacteria for a long period of time in an infected woman who has not been treated for the sexually transmissible disease.

acyclovir a drug used to treat herpes simplex infections. The antiviral drug is converted in the body to a form that interferes with the ability of the virus to replicate itself. Originally developed to treat HSV I (herpes simplex virus I) infections, the drug was found in the 1980s to be effective also against genital herpes. However, it must be used continuously to maintain suppression of the herpes virus already in the body tissues.

acyesis nonpregnancy or nonfertility (Greek *kyesis*, 'pregnancy').

ad a homosexual slang term for a graffito that gives name and telephone number, typically in a men's public lavatory or a bar.

Adam a homosexual slang term referring to a man's first male lover.

adamite an individual who follows the proverbial lead of Adam by going about unclothed. The *Adamites* were an ascetic Christian sect in Holland and Germany during the early modern era. They not only practised ritual nakedness in secret gatherings but engaged in sexual intercourse without being married, because they believed they had been reborn into a state of celestial innocence.

Adam's apple a projection of the thyroid cartilage of the larynx at the front of the neck. Because of its prominence in men, a sex-change operation from male to female may involve plastic surgery to reduce the size of the projection so that it will give the neck of the transsexual person a female appearance.

Adam's arsenal a jocular term for the male genitals (penis and scrotum).

Addison's disease a progressive atrophy of the adrenal cortex as a result of cancer, tuberculosis, inflammation, amyloidosis, and, most frequently, unknown causes. The disease results in a loss of normal production of several hormones, including the androgens, or male sex-hormone sources. Considerable amounts of other hormones, such as cortisol, also are lost, with symptoms of weakness, fatigue, skin-pigment changes, and low blood pressure. Although both men and women may be afflicted with Addison's disease, women tend to be affected most often by the sex-hormone deficiency, experiencing a persistent decline in libido and, occasionally, ovarian failure.

adelphogamy a form of marriage arrangement in which brothers share a wife or several wives. Adjective: *adelphogamous*.

adenosis a condition of the female breast marked by the presence of nodules on the outer surface. The nodules range in size from about one-half inch in diameter to less than a quarter inch. They tend to occur in childless woman around 40 years of age.

adiposogenital dystrophy a form of obesity associated with abnormally small external genital organs, as is observed in cases of Frölich's syndrome. The condition, caused by impaired function of the pituitary and hypothalamus glands, also may be accompanied by symptoms of diabetes mellitus. In some cases the disorder may be triggered by a central-nervous-system tumour or infection, such as encephalitis.

adjustment the establishment of a satisfactory relationship with one or more other persons so that the desires of each party can be accommodated in a mutually satisfactory manner. The process has been likened to a situation in which each participant has a basic scenario to be played and the objective of adjustment is to find a partner whose own scenario matches, or nearly matches, and their role playing is therefore compatible.

adnexa uteri a Latin term for the appendages of the uterus, particularly the fallopian tubes and ovaries.

adnexitis an inflammation of the ovaries and fallopian tubes.

adnexopexy a surgical procedure in which the fallopian tubes and ovaries are repositioned at a higher level in the pelvic cavity and are sutured to the inside of the abdominal wall. The procedure may be performed to correct an infertility problem.

adolescence the period between childhood and adulthood (roughly 12 to 21 in girls and 13 to 22 in boys), when dependence and immaturity gradually give way to independence and maturity. It is a time of emotional stress and strain, identity crisis, changes in sexual characteristics and body image, experimentation with different sex roles and different self-concepts, and high sex interest.

adolescent changes characteristic physical changes occurring during puberty, including accelerated development of the sex organs and secondary sex characteristics such as growth of pubic and underarm hair in both sexes, the first ejaculation of sperm and growth of facial hair in boys, and the first menstruation and development of breasts in girls.

adolescent homosexuality homosexual contacts, usually involving orgasm, during adolescence. Surveys by Kinsey and others have indicated that about 17 percent of homosexual women and about 18 percent of homosexual men experienced their first coitus before the age of 15. In most cases, however, homosexual contacts during adolescence are occasional and experimental, and may not lead to a pattern of homosexuality in adult life.

adolescent pregnancy pregnancy occurring during adolescence, roughly the period from 12 to 21. Surveys indicate that most unmarried pregnant girls had little or no sex education, and more than 75 percent stated that they do not use contraceptives at all, or only occasionally, and usually do not insist that their partners do so.

adolescent sterility a period of relative infertility that is believed by some sexologists to occur during the early stages of sexual maturity. As evidence, they point to the low incidence of pregnancy in societies that permit or encourage sexual activity as soon as puberty is reached, e.g., the Trobrianders and the Ifugao, in the Philippines. There is, however, evidence to the contrary in the growing number of early teenage pregnancies in Western society.

adoption a legal process in which a child (often a child born out of wedlock) becomes an integral part of a family into which he or she was not born. The adopting parents agree to assume all the normal responsibilities of the natural parents. Arrangements for adoption are usually made by a specialized agency, private or governmental, after thorough investigation, and approval from the local authority. The major reason for adoption is childlessness, usually because of infertility. Step-parents may also adopt the children of the partner they marry.

adrenal-cortical hyperfunction a condition of overactivity of the adrenal cortex, resulting in masculine sexual characteristics in women. Also called adrenogenital syndrome.

adrenal-cortical tumour a tumour of the cortex, or outer layer, of the adrenal gland. The tumour has a virilizing effect resulting in some signs of precocious puberty in a boy. The child may develop pubic hair and an enlarged penis, but the testes remain infantile. If the tumour is 'autonomous,' it remains independent of such influences as may be used to treat precocious puberty resulting from adrenal-gland hyperplasia, or overgrowth. Administration of cortisol or dexamethasone has no effect.

adrenal rest a clump of adrenal tissue cells that becomes displaced into the ovary or testis during embryonic development. An adrenal rest is an occasional cause of sexual precocity. In a male, it may result in premature enlargement of one or both testes.

adrenal virilism the appearance of masculine mental and physical traits in a woman as a result of abnormal production of male sex hormones by the adrenal glands. In severe cases, a woman may develop facial hair in addition to an enlarged clitoris, deep voice, and masculine hairline.

adrenarche a sign of puberty, marked primarily by the growth of pubic hair and sometimes menstruation. When it occurs before the normal age of puberty, it is usually caused by a tumour of the adrenal glands.

adrenogenital pertaining to the adrenal glands (the source of androgenic sex hormones) and the genitalia.

adult a recent euphemism for sexual or pornographic, as in *adult language, adult films, adult entertainment.* See also ADULT BOOKSHOPS.

adult bookshops a euphemism for shops specializing in the sale of books and periodicals that display stories or illustrations containing scenes of explicit sex. The publications also include the so-called 'girlie' or 'musclemen' magazines. Surveys indicate the vast majority of books sold in the shops are written for heterosexual males, who also represent the average customer.

adultery sexual intercourse between a married person and an individual other than the legal spouse. In many countries adultery has in the past been the principal and often the only ground for divorce. In earlier periods adultery was even punishable by death. Various published surveys indicate that at least 50 percent of married men and women admit to having sexual intercourse after marriage with a person other than their spouse. Despite legal and cultural prohibitions, adultery apparently has persisted throughout history and in communities with strict moral controls. In the People's Republic of China in the 1980s, for example, adultery was given as a reason for nearly 25 percent of divorces. H.L. Mencken defined adultery as 'democracy applied to love.'

adventure a euphemism for a preadolescent or adolescent manifestation of the sex drive. Boys and girls may seek the excitement of games with members of the opposite sex, including mutual body examination, observing the lovemaking of adults from a concealed position, or indulging in play that requires masculine competitiveness. For adolescent girls, the thrill of adventure may be found in making themselves visible to older boys or young men on the beach, at sporting events, or at similar sites where they might be 'picked up.'

aeromammography a form of mammography that is performed after the space behind the breast has been distended by an inert gas, such as carbon dioxide.

aesthetic pleasure pleasure associated with the contemplation or appreciation of beauty. The term is sometimes used in contrast to sexual pleasure, although according to Freud a sexual component may be present in many works of art, such as paintings or sculptures of nude men and women.

affair a euphemism for the male or female genitals. Also spelled (French) *affaire*. See also LOVE AFFAIR.

affection feelings of attachment, fondness, or love for another human being (or animal). Affection is a vital component of a full sexual relationship, but many men and some women who have been raised in cold homes may never have learned to express, or even experience, warmth and tenderness.

affectional attachments feelings of affection toward family members, friends, or family pets. The primary attachment is usually formed in the first year between the infant and the mother, and is encouraged by cuddling, kissing, nurturing, and demonstrations of affection between the parents.

affectional drive the urge to give and receive affection, both of which most psychologists believe to be innate, because infants respond to being held from the beginning of life and express love and affection as soon as they are able to pat or stroke their mother or others with whom they are in close contact. Studies have shown that when infants and small children are deprived of giving and receiving affection, they usually show signs of grief and may even fail to thrive. Moreover, later in life they may be deficient in sexual responsiveness.

affectional system an alternative term for love bond, or the attachment between individuals based on love.

Affenliebe (German, 'monkey love') a term sometimes used to characterize the tendency of some mothers to shower their offspring with affection and to anticipate their every desire.

affiliation a close association with a group or individual, based on the need to form attachments and become involved with other people. Totally unaffiliated persons usually feel lost and lonely. Sexual and marital relationships are forms of affiliation.

affinity strong attraction, often including a sexual relationship, between two persons; also, a relationship by marriage, such as the relationship established between a husband and his wife's blood relatives.

afterglow the stage of physical relaxation, emotional warmth, and peaceful sensations that usually follows the successful completion of sexual intercourse. In this phase, the pressure and tension produced by the sex urge, and the intense physical activity of coitus, subside. As the heart slows down and muscular contractions cease, a feeling of languor takes over and the partners—usually, at least—experience a sense of communion and closeness.

afterpains cramping abdominal pains that are experienced after childbirth. The pains are caused by contraction of the uterus muscles, which had become distended during pregnancy.

afterplay a continuation of erotic gratification after a climax has been reached. A recent book on sexual practices in the East states that 'Afterplay is equally as important as foreplay.... After the intense physical exertion of lovemaking and the release of orgasm, the body finds itself in a unique state which is highly conducive to meditation and mutual absorption' during which the couple should 'caress each other, play, talk, laugh, or meditate.' (*Sexual Secrets,* by Nik Douglas and Penny Slinger, 1979)

agamy the absence of the institution of marriage in a society.

agape (ä'gəpā'; Greek, 'love') in ancient Greece, spiritual, unselfish love of one person for another without sexual implications. In the Christian tradition, agape also encompasses the love of God for humankind, as well as the love of humankind for God.

agapemone a 19th-century term for a mate-swapping, free-love group, derived from the name of a community in England, where this practice was common around 1850.

agate a colloquial term for a small penis.

âge critique (äzh krētēk'; French, 'critical age') the menopause or climacteric period when readjustments to life and sexuality must be made.

age of consent a legal term meaning the age at which a person may consent to having sexual intercourse. In Britain the age of consent is 16. In Britain 21 is the age of consent between two consenting men in a homosexual relationship. A man can be charged with 'unlawful sexual intercourse with a girl under 16' if he has intercourse with an underage girl or rape if consent is lacking. The term also denotes the age below which marriage is illegal even with parental consent.

ager naturae Latin, 'field of nature') an archaic term for the uterus, in which the seeds (ova, sperm) of offspring are 'sown'.

agfay a pig-Latin euphemism for 'fag', an American slang term for 'male homosexual'.

agglutination test a chorionic gonadotropin hormone test for pregnancy in which a sample of the woman's urine is mixed with certain chemical reagents. If the woman is not pregnant, the mixture will agglutinate, or form clumps, in the test tube. If she is pregnant, the clumping will not occur. The test is claimed to be 97 per accurate when performed at least 2 weeks after the menstrual period is missed. The test is much faster than others, with results sometimes available within minutes.

aging actress a slang term for an elderly male homosexual.

aging and sex a term referring to the persistence or decline of sexual interest and ability in the later years of life. Though there is an undeniable decline in the capacity for intercourse, the decline is slow and may be counterbalanced by greater emphasis on skill and experience, and on tenderness, stroking, kissing, and masturbation. For women, aging and menopause may actually increase sexual desire when the fear of pregnancy is eliminated. For men, and women too, the quality of sexual experience becomes more important than the quantity. Even if their sexual capacity declines to zero, as occasionally happens, men and women are free to pursue other ways of maintaining their sense of adequacy.

agonadal pertaining to the absence of gonads, either male or female.

A-hole an American semieuphemism for the vulgar slang term arsehole.

aidoiomania an abnormally strong desire for sexual intercourse (Greek *aidoion*, 'vulva,' and *mania*, 'madness').

aidoitis inflammation of the vulva.

AIDS (ādz) abbreviation for acquired immune deficiency syndrome, a disease caused by a human T-cell leukaemia-lymphoma virus called the human immunodeficiency virus (HIV) and transmitted by intimate contact between humans. The condition is marked by swollen lymph nodes, a respiratory disorder called pneumocystitis carnii pneumonia, and Kaposi's sarcoma, a type of skin cancer. The disease is generally fatal; there is no known cure. See also ANSAMYCIN; ANTI-MONIOTUNG-STATE; ARV; COFACTORS; COMPOUND S; ELISA; FOSCARNET; GAY PNEUMONIA; GRID; HIV; HPA-23; HTLV-III; HUMAN IMMUNODEFICIENCY VIRUS; HUMAN T-CELL LEUKEMIA VIRUS; IMREG-1; INTERLEUKIN-2; ISOPRINOSINE; KAPOSI'S SARCOMA; KILLER T LYMPHOCYTES; LAV; LYMPHADENOPATHY; NON-OXYNOL-9; ONCOGENES; PENTAMIDINE ISETHIONATE; PHOSPHONOFORMATE; PNEUMOCYSTITIS CARNII PNEUMONIA; RETROVIRUS; RIBAVARIN; SUR-

AMIN; T-CELL; T-CELL HELPER DEPLETION.

aitas in ancient Greek, a mature man's young lover, usually still a boy, whom he also educates (literally, 'one who listens'). He is the opposite of an EIPNELUS. See this entry.

Albright's disease a bone disease that affects both men and women and is associated also with pigmentation changes, hormonal dysfunction, and precocious puberty in females. In many cases, the signs of sexual precocity lead to diagnosis of the disease. The girls have high levels of oestrogens, develop pubic hair and breasts at an early age, and begin menstruating prematurely. Although sexual precocity is observed in males with Albright's disease, appearing years before the bone deformities are detected, the early changes in sexual maturation are less common than in female patients.

alcahueta in Spain, a female matchmaker or procuress, a term that has been used since the 13th century. An *alcahuete* is a (male) pimp.

alcoholic jealousy a persistent form of jealousy experienced by chronic alcoholics. Typically, the jealousy is directed towards a rival and is usually accompanied by suspicion of infidelity towards the loved one.

alcoholic paranoia a paranoid state in which an alcoholic spouse or lover develops a pathological form of jealousy and the illusion that the partner has been unfaithful—an irrational conviction that is maintained despite all evidence to the contrary.

aleydigism an absence of male sex-hormone production in the Leydig (interstitial) cells of the testis.

algolagnia the psychiatric term for the psychosexual disorder, or paraphilia, in which sexual excitement is derived from inflicting pain (sadism), experiencing pain (masochism), or both (sadomasochism).

algomenorrhoea painful menstruation. See also DYSMENORRHOEA.

algopareunia physical or psychological pain during intercourse.

algophilia a morbid desire to experience pain during sexual intercourse or a need to suffer pain, as by flagellation, in order to be sexually stimulated.

alibido the absence of libido.

alimentary orgasm a psychoanalytical term proposed by Sandor Rado for the peak of gratification and alleviation of tension experienced by infants during breast feeding. According to his theory, this early experience is a prototype for the adult sexual orgasm, and the desire to recapture this early experience may lead to alcoholism and drug abuse.

allele one of a pair or group of related genes that can replace another of the pair or group on a chromosome as each represents the same genetic trait, such as eye colour. Each body cell contains an allele for each inherited characteristic from the mother and a matching but often differing allele from the father.

all-nighter a man or woman who is capable of many orgasms for hours on end; also, a night-long lovemaking session.

alloerotism a psychoanalytic term for the phase of psychosexual development in which the libido, or sex drive, is directed away from the self and towards another person. This is the phase of adult or genital sexuality in which the individual is capable of forming a mature love relationship. Also called *alloeroticism.*

alloiophilia an older term for heterosexuality.

alloplasty a psychoanalytic term for the capacity of the libido to be directed outwards towards the environment, and to provide the energy for adapting to reality as opposed to focussing on the self and immediate pleasure.

all the way a euphemism referring to intercourse, to actual penetration of the vagina by the penis (used mainly by teenagers); also, a term referring to the achievement of orgasm.

almanach an 18th- and 19th-century euphemism for a list of local prostitutes and their fees.

altogether, in the a colloquial term for naked.

altrigenderism the tendency to be attracted to members of the opposite sex and to engage in nonsexual, socially approved activities with them, such as playing games. Children begin to take an interest in the other gender in the late infantile period.

altruism concern for the needs and interests of others. In Freudian theory, the libido is directed towards the self at the beginning of life, and the child is essentially egoistic and narcissistic. As he or she develops ties with the parents and other persons, the libido is gradually directed towards their interests, and the child begins to derive satisfaction from altruistic behaviour, as in sympathy, cooperation, and being of help to others.

amasius a male prostitute in ancient Rome (literally, 'lover').

amastia an abnormal female physical condition in which either the breasts or the nipple are absent.

amateur night a colloquial term referring to an unfulfilling sexual encounter with an inexperienced partner; also, referring to such a partner himself or herself—who may be a virgin or simply without skill.

amazon a tall, strong, warriorlike woman, from Greek mythology. The word is of unknown origin, although many sources, including most reference works, erroneously state that amazons were named from the Greek term for 'without breasts.'

ambidextrous a jocular variant of the homosexual slang term ambisextrous, meaning bisexual.

ambierastia a seldom used term for bisexuality.

ambiguous genitalia external sex organs that are not fully differentiated, as in women with a large clitoris that may be mistaken for a penis, or with fused labia that resemble a scrotum. Similarly, some males develop feminine breasts, or an opening beneath the penis that resembles a vagina. Some of these individuals may be reared as members of the opposite sex.

ambisextrous a homosexual slang term for bisexual.

ambisexual another term for bisexual.

ambisexuality a possession of personality characteristics that can be associated with either masculinity or femininity, or with both; also, the capacity to respond sexually to both males and females.

ambivalence contradictory feelings, attitudes, or wishes towards the same person, situation, goal, or activity. Many children have conflicting attitudes towards their parents, and many young adults develop conflicting attitudes towards marriage. In the sexual field, many people have ambivalent feelings towards such practices as fellatio and cunnilingus.

ambosexual another term for bisexual.

amenorrhoea the stoppage or absence of normal menstrual discharge for reasons other than pregnancy, menopause, or lactation. Absolute or primary amenorrhoea may be the result of a congenital defect in the reproductive organs. Secondary amenorrhoea is a term that identifies the suspension of menstruation after it has become established and may be caused by removal or irradiation of the uterus or ovaries, by an illness, or by a change of environment. Physiological amenorrhoea is a term used to identify an interruption in the menses as a result of pregnancy, lactation, or menopause. Other forms of the disorder include emotional amenorrhoea, caused by a psychological problem; pituitary amenorrhoea, caused by a disorder of the pituitary gland; pathological amenorrhoea, caused by a disease such as gonorrhoea; and ovarian amenorrhoea, caused by a disease or abnormality of the ovaries.

See also HYPOTHALAMIC AMENORRHOEA; POSTPILL AMENORRHOEA; PRIMARY AMENORRHOEA; SECONDARY AMENORRHOEA.

American Association of Sex Educators, Counselors, and Therapists (AASECT) a professional organization in the U.S.A. that sets standards in the field of sex education and therapy; maintains a directory of sex educators and therapists, and conducts national, regional, and local training workshops.

amica a Latin term for female friend or mistress.

amicus a medieval term for pimp (Latin, 'friend').

amixia absence of interbreeding; restriction of marriage to members of the same 'race,' caste, religion, or cultural group to preserve the 'purity' of the stock.

amniocentesis a test procedure in which a sample of the amniotic fluid is extracted by a hollow needle inserted through the abdomen of a woman usually around the sixteenth week of pregnancy. Analysis of this fluid can be used in determining the sex of the child and, more important, in detecting disorders such as severe spina bifida, sickle-cell anaemia, phenylketonuria (PKU), and Down's syndrome. Unless there are special indications such as the mother's age or the possibility of chromosomal abnormality, the test is not used, because it involves some risk of infection, damage to the foetus, and induced miscarriage.

amniography a technique that has been used to diagnose placenta praevia by injecting a radiopaque dye into the amniotic sac to see the outline of the structure on an x-ray film.

amnion a smooth thin but strong membrane that covers the entire foetal surface and contains the amniotic fluid. It becomes the inner of two membranes surrounding the foetus, the other being the chorion.

amniotic fluid a clear but slightly yellowish liquid in which the developing foetus floats. At about full term, the foetus is immersed in 1,000 ml, or 1 quart, of the fluid which contains—in addition to water—traces of albumin, urea, fat, epithelial cells, inorganic salts, lecithin, various enzymes, and a few white blood cells. The fluid protects the foetus from temperature fluctuations, acts as a source of oral fluid, allows freedom of movement and development within the uterus, and reduces the risk of injury from any impact the mother may receive in the event of bodily trauma.

amniotomy the deliberate puncturing of the amniotic sac to induce labour also called 'breaking the waters.'

amoebas the microscopic, one-celled animals who started it all—according to the Austrian-American poet Arthur Guiterman (1871-1943): 'Amoebas, at the start, / were not complex—/ they tore themselves apart / and started sex.'

amor a Latin word for love; usually used with the meaning of sexual love.

AMOR ROMA spelt backwards—a pun on the fact that in ancient Rome (Roma) anal intercourse enjoyed great popularity.

amoral behaviour acts performed without knowledge or appreciation of accepted social standards. In the sexual sphere, a 2-year-old child or a profoundly retarded individual who exhibits his or her genitals is considered amoral rather than immoral or mentally ill.

amor ereos a synonym of love, coined by Bernhar l of Gordon (Bernard de Gordon de Montpellier), a 14th-century physician. Bernhard was an extreme mysogynist, who considered love to be a kind of mental disease, and who generally anticipated many of the Victorian attitudes by five centuries.

amor insanus an obsolescent Latin term for erotomania.

amorist a colloquial term for a gigolo or playboy, but also simply for a skilled lover of either sex.

amor lesbicus a Latin term for lesbianism.

amorosa a Latin colloquial term for a female lover.

amorous paranoia an obsolete term for delusional jealousy.

amor sui a Latin term for self-love.

amour a love affair, usually one involving a premarital or extramarital sexual relationship; also, love in general, and sexual love in particular. A lover or mistress is sometimes termed an amour.

amourette a transient or trifling love affair, not intended to last; also, a woman involved in such an affair.

amour fou (ämōōrfōō'; French 'mad, foolish

love') a literary expression for infatuation or obsessive love.

amour socratique (ämōōr' sōkrätēk'; French, 'Socratic love') an older euphemism for homosexual or for platonic homoerotic love.

ampallang bamboo or metal balls implanted in the penis shaft or glans for increased stimulation, as of the clitoris. The practice is common in different parts of the world, especially in Indonesia. At the beginning of puberty, smaller balls may be placed in artificial openings along the penis, to be replaced by increasingly larger balls later.

amphierotism a term coined by the Hungarian psychoanalyst Sandor Ferenczi for a psychological disorder in which the individual can conceive of himself, erotically, as a male or female, or both at once.

amphigenesis a form of sexuality in which a predominantly homosexual individual is able to have normal sexual relations with members of the opposite sex. *Amphigenic inversion,* as this is sometimes called, contrasts with absolute inversion.

amphimixis the merging of the germ plasm of both parents in sexual reproduction, so that each contributes to the inheritance of the offspring. Amphimixis is also the psychoanalytical term for the union of oral and anal components in the development of genital sexuality, as indicated by the involvement of these erogenous zones in foreplay.

amphiphilia the ability to love persons of either sex; bisexuality.

ampulla a broad, dilated segment of the fallopian tube that curves over the adjacent ovary.

ampulla ductus deferentis an alternative term for Henle's ampulla, a dilated portion of the ductus deferens near the point at which it terminates in the ejaculatory ducts.

ampulla tubae uterine the midportion of the fallopian tube that curves over the ovary.

amputation fetishism a type of fetishism in which sexual gratification depends on arousal by a partner with one or several amputations. An example is MONOPEDOMANIA. See this entry.

amulet a charm, sometimes inscribed with an incantation, worn to protect the wearer against evil or to enhance sexual potency. Many Romans wore amulets in the form of the male genitals, and in medieval times, mandrake roots were tied round the waist to prevent or cure impotence.

Amy-John American slang term for a lesbian, especially one who plays the 'male' role.

Anabaptists a Christian sect that originated in Europe in the 16th century. The members believed that baptism should be limited to believers and therefore should not be performed on babies. They also practised polygamy as well as common ownership of property based on religious principles.

anabolic steroid hormones hormones that contribute to the building of tissues, as distinguished from those that break down tissues or food substances into smaller units. Testosterone is a strong anabolic hormone that diverts protein substances into muscle tissue and reproductive organs, such as the penis. The oestrogens are mildly anabolic, helping to preserve bone tissue and contributing to muscle development.

anaesthesia sexualis Krafft-Ebing's term for frigidity. The term has also been used for permanent or temporary lack or weakness of sexual sensation or feeling (Greek *anaisthesis,* 'lack of sensation').

anal pertaining to the anus.

anal-aggressive character according to psychoanalysis, a defiant, obstructive, obstinate personality type that stems from the anal stage of psychosexual development, during which the individual has repeatedly asserted himself or herself by withholding the faeces.

anal birth a term of Freud's referring to dreams or fantasies in which anal erotism takes the symbolic form of a wish to be reborn through the anus.

anal-castration anxiety the revelation, in the course of psychoanalysis, that the patient's toilet phobias are actually an expression of castration fear. Such phobias include fear of being flushed away or the fear that a demon will emerge from the bowl and crawl into the patient's anus.

anal character a pattern of personality traits believed to originate in fixations at the anal stage of psychosexual development. Pleasure in expulsion of the faeces may lead to a personality characterized by generosity, conceit, and ambition, while pleasure in retention may lead to the 'anal triad' of obstinacy, stinginess, and orderliness. Also called anal personality.

anal coitus an alternative term for anal intercourse.

anal erotism the psychoanalytical theory that beginning in the second year of life the child derives sexual pleasure from expulsion, retention, or observation of the faeces. If psychosexual development is 'fixated' at this stage, the individual will experience special gratification from activities associated with the anal region, such as elimination, and masturbation, and anal intercourse. Also called *anal eroticism*.

anal fantasies images and dreams of anal intercourse, anal rape, or anal birth. Such fantasies may begin in childhood.

anal fetishism sexual fixation on the anus instead of the genitalia. It may be passive, directed towards one's own anus, or active, directed towards another persons's anus.

anal fixation a psychoanalytical term for the persistence of erotic needs and character traits stemming from the anal stage of psychosexual development. Anal needs are believed to lead to a desire for anal intercourse. According to Freud, anal traits comprise a pattern of obstinacy, frugality, and orderliness, which has been called the 'anal triad.'

anal humour various forms of humour—jokes, stories, limericks—involving defecation, 'breaking wind,' or anal coitus. According to psychoanalytical theory, preoccupation with such humour may indicate a fixation at the anal stage when the child derives sexual pleasure from retention or expulsion of the faeces.

anal intercourse coitus in which the penis is inserted into the partner's anus, usually after lubrication and stretching with the fingers. Anal intercourse is practised by homosexual couples, and sometimes by heterosexual couples. This technique is legally termed sodomy and is outlawed in a number of countries. Also called anal coitus; anogenital intercourse; coitus analis; coitus per anum; intercourse per anum.

analipsation a seldom used term for anal self-masturbation.

analist a person interested in the anus and/or practising anal intercourse.

anal itching a condition of pruritus, perianal soreness, and rectal burning, which also may be accompanied by diarrhoea and other symptoms. The causes may include the use of tetracycline antibiotics which allow an overgrowth of fungi in the area, pinworms, allergies, or a moniliasis infection that can be traced to anal intercourse with an infected male partner.

anality localization of the libido in the anal region; the anus as an erogenous zone.

anal masturbation achievement of sexual excitement by stimulation of the anus through manipulation or by means of an object or mechanical device such as a vibrator.

analogous pertaining to sex organs that appear to be different in the male and female although they have the same or similar functions. Examples are the female ovaries and male testes, which are the sources of gametes and sex hormones.

anal personality an alternative name for anal character.

anal phase according to psychoanalytic theory, the stage of psychosexual development during which the young child experiences erotic pleasure from expulsion or retention of the faeces. Also called anal stage.

anal-rape fantasy the image or fear of being raped through the anus, which is not uncommon in the dreams and fantasies of both men and women.

anal response the reactions of the rectal sphincter to sexual activity. Involuntary contractions may occur at approximately the same rate as those of the female orgasmic platform and the penile urethra, at 0.8 seconds intervals. The contractions do not always occur or may occur only a few times.

anal sadism the psychoanalytical theory that the young child goes through an 'anal sadistic stage' characterized by aggressive, destructive, and negativistic behaviour. One expression of these tendencies is in deliberately withholding the faeces in defiance of the parents, and another is the wish to defecate on them as a means of punishing or humiliating them. Fixation at this stage may give rise to an aggressive personality.

anal stage an equivalent term for anal phase.

anal stimulation a form of sex play in which the anal orifice is manipulated, or a finger is inserted into the rectum. Though common among homosexuals, these methods of stimulation may also be used during masturbation or heterosexual activity. Anal entry with the entire hand is colloquially known as fist fucking.

anal triad a pattern of obstinacy, stinginess, and orderliness, which are the prime traits of the anal character.

anal violin an anal masturbation device of the Orient consisting of a hard-boiled egg or a wooden or ivory ball to which a catgut string is attached. The egg or ball is inserted in the anus, the string is made taut, and a sex partner uses a violin bow to make it vibrate. The device was especially popular among eunuchs of the Ottoman Empire. Today, electric equivalents are used, too, as in Europe, the United States, and Japan.

Anadrynes a lesbian secret society of the 18th century in Paris, with chapters in London and other European cities. Founded by Madame de Fleury, it included members in the highest aristocratic circles. (Greek *anandre*, 'sexless,' and *gynandre*, 'female-male')

Ananga Ranga 'Theatre of God,' an illustrated sex manual dating back to 15th-century India. Its contents include an appreciation of the beauty of women, a description of the erogenous zones of men and women, the cycle of erotic passion as related to the phases of the moon, a systematic compilation of lovemaking postures, and a classification of male and female sex organs.

anaphrodisia the absence or weakening of sexual desire; also, frigidity.

anaphrodisiac a drug or other agent that suppresses sexual desire or performance. Examples are heroin, Ismelin (guanethidine sulphate), treatment of males with oestrogen, cyproterone acetate, potassium nitrate (saltpetre), and the bitter herb, rue (Ruta graveolens). Most of these drugs have undesirable side effects, and alleged effects on sexual desire may be more psychological than physiological.

anaspadias an alternative term for epispadias, a congenital deformity in which the urethra opens on the top of the penis.

Andamanese monogamous inhabitants of the Andaman Islands in the Bay of Bengal. The men are reported to be almost universally homosexual, and sexual arousal is achieved by nose-rubbing and sniffing rather than kissing. Rear entry has been said to be the position used with women, but this report seems to be false.

Andrade's syndrome a form of amyloidosis (starch degeneration) characterized by flaccid paralysis and impotence. Other effects include sensory-nerve disorders and, in the female, premature menopause. The condition has been identified as one of the heredofamilial amyloid syndromes, transmitted as an autosomal dominant genetic disorder, which is marked by progressive autonomic-nervous-sytem complaints.

androgamone a chemical produced by spermatozoa that helps attract the female gamete to increase the chances of fertilization.

androgen deprivation failure of the male to secrete the androgenic hormones necessary for development of masculine sexual characteristics. An androgen-deprived male may be born with such pronounced feminized characteristics as to be raised as a girl without, in some cases, even the parents being aware that the individual is genetically a male. The true nature of the problem unfolds as the person approaches sexual maturity.

androgen hypersecretion a condition of overproduction of androgenic hormones, marked by a virilizing effect. In women, the effects include clitoral enlargement, growth of facial and general body hair, and male balding patterns or hairlines. They also may develop an abnormally deep female voice. The condition may be caused by disorders of the adrenal glands or ovaries and can result in amenorrhoea and decreasing breast size.

androgenic flush an area of reddish pigmentation that appears around the neck of males as a result of the influence of 17-ketosteroids. When present in a female, it is a sign of excessive production of 17-ketosteroids.

androgenic hormones a group of hormones produced mainly in the testicles and the adrenal cortex, and in smaller amounts by the ovaries. The androgenic hormones include dehydroepiandrosterone, testosterone, epitestosterone, and androstenedione. Effects of the androgens are virilizing activity, penile and prostate development, pubic hair growth, facial-hair development, bone maturation, and development of sweat and sebaceous glands. Normal male growth and development of the secondary sexual characteristics of the male body are dependent upon the androgenic hormones, primarily testosterone. Androgenic hormones are sometimes used in the treatment of breast cancer.

androgenic urinary compounds the metabolic by-products of male sex hormones that appear in the urine. Their presence and amounts in the urine are used in laboratory tests of sexual functioning.

androgyny originally, sexual ambiguity of body build that is neither distinctly masculine nor distinctly feminine. In present usage, androgyny may mean exhibiting the physical, behavioural, dressing, or personality characteristics of both sexes. It may or may not refer to erotic bisexuality, that is, sexual attraction to either male or female, with frequent switching back and forth between them. Adjective: *androgynous*. See also HOLLYWOOD ANDROGYNY.

andrology the study of male fertility. It is a subspeciality of the medical practice of urology.

andromania a little-used term for nymphomania.

androphilia a man's or woman's sexual

attraction to a mature male.

androphobia an intense pathological fear of men.

androsterone one of the male sex hormones found naturally in the urine of men and of women who are afflicted with the virilizing effect of ovarian or adrenal abnormalities. Androsterone is less potent than testosterone in influencing male sexual characteristics, but it has a greater effect on normal male prostate-gland development and function.

anerotism a seldom used term for frigidity.

aneuploid a condition in which an individual has a set of chromosomes that is less or more than the normal diploid complement. Examples include the sex-chromosome aberrations, such as Turner's syndrome in which a female has only 45 instead of the normal 46 chromosomes because of the absence of one X chromosome.

angel a slang term for a male homosexual partner who supports and buys gifts for a more effeminate partner.

angioneurotic oedema a sudden swelling of the genitalia and other body parts as a result of an allergic reaction or minor infection. The fluid accumulation that causes the genital swelling is usually temporary.

angoisse du toucher (äNgô·äs′ dētooshä′) a French term for compulsive aversion to touching or being touched. It is the opposite of délire du toucher.

anhedonia an incapacity to experience pleasure in acts or situations that would normally be pleasurable, including sexual relations. In extreme form anhedonia may be a symptom of schizophrenia or depressive reaction.

anilingus stimulation of the anus with the tongue or lips, a form of sexual activity that is common among male homosexuals but less common in heterosexual relationships. It is colloquially known as rimming. Also called *aniliction; anilinctus*.

anima the feminine component of the male personality, which Jung believed is stored as an 'archetype' in the collective unconscious.

animalist a term occasionally used for a person who engages in sex with animals, but mainly used to refer to a hedonist or someone who is uninhibited in pursuing his or her sensual pleasures.

animal tamer a slang term for a person who commits bestiality.

animus the masculine component of the female personality, which Jung believed is stored as an 'archetype' in the collective unconscious.

Anlage (an′lägə; German, 'disposition') the primordium, or period of embryonic or foetal development of an individual.

annular hymen a hymen that is partially perforated before the initial coitus by natural forces to permit the discharge of menstrual fluid. Such a hymen is likely to be ring-shaped, or annular.

annulment a judicial or ecclesiastical declaration that a marriage is invalid. Grounds for annulment vary from country to country but may include existence of a prior marriage that has not been legally dissolved, impotence, insanity, refusal to have intercourse, concealed pre-marital syphilis, marriage under duress, and illegal consanguinity (blood relationship).

anogenital intercourse another term for anal intercourse.

anomaly any individual, organism, or structure that varies significantly from the normal, e.g. a person with an extra X or Y sex chromosome or a male with three testicles; also, a person whose sexual practices are outside the society's norm.

anorchia a condition in which a male (the *anorchus*) lacks testicles, either because they are congenitally absent or because they have failed to descend from the abdomen. Also called *anorchism*. Adjective: *anorchid*.

anorexia nervosa a pathological lack of appetite or refusal of food, leading to severe weight loss and, in women, to absence of menstruation, besides other serious consequences. This serious condition is most often found among teenage girls who have an incorrect perception of their body image, i.e. they incorrectly believe themselves to be fat. It is associated with low self-esteem and can be linked with a desire to escape the burdens of growing up and assuming a female sex role.

anorgasmia inability to reach orgasm. Also called *anorgasmy*.

anovaria the congenital absence of ovaries in a female. The condition occurs in patients with Hunter's syndrome.

anovular pertaining to a uterine bleeding that occurs independently of its normal relationship to the ovaries, such as menstrual bleeding without ovulation.

anovular stage the period of life in a female between the first menstrual period and the start of ovulation. Medical records indicate that ovulation may begin as early as 1 month after the first menstrual period to as late as 7 years after menarche.

anovulation the interruption of normal ovulation or the cessation of ovulation.

anovulatory menstrual cycle a pattern of menstruation that occurs independently of normal cycles of ovulation and menses. The pharmacological principle of oral contraceptives is that of producing anovulatory menstrual cycles in which ovulation is suppressed but controlled menstruation occurs at normal periods.

ansamycin an antiviral drug developed in Italy and used experimentally as a possible cure for AIDS. See this entry.

antaphrodisiac anything that lessens sexual desire; an anaphrodisiac.

antenuptial contract an agreement or contract made by a man and a woman before marriage, in which the interests and property rights of either or both parties are spelled out.

anterior pituitary the anterior portion of an endocrine gland located near the base of the brain. The anterior pituitary, or adenohypophysis, secretes at least six hormones. They include the thyrotropic hormone, which controls thyroid function; adrenocorticotrophic hormone, which acts on the adrenal gland; the somatotrophic, or growth, hormone; and the gonadotrophic hormones, which act on the ovaries and testes.

anterior pituitary gonadotropin a hormonal substance secreted by the anterior pituitary gland to act on the male and female reproductive systems. In the male, an interstitial-cell-stimulating hormone stimulates functioning of the interstitial cells of the testes to produce male sex hormones. A corresponding hormone in the female body is the lutein-stimulating hormone which stimulates the production of luteal cells and formation of the corpus luteum. The follicle-stimulating hormone of the anterior pituitary gonadotropins stimulates maturation of the ovaries in the female and production of spermatozoa and cells of the seminiferous tubules in the male.

anterior urethritis an infection of the lining of the urethra in the portion of the male urogenital system between the bulb and glans of the penis.

anthropophagy (Greek, 'eating of humans') an alternative term for CANNIBALISM. See this entry.

antiandrogenic agent a substance such as cyproterone acetate that is administered in the treatment of androgenic hyperactivity. It has been used to control hirsutism (excessive hair) in female patients with excessive levels

of androgens. In males, such drugs can have a demasculinizing effect, marked by impotence, infertility, and enlarged breasts.

antiandrogen therapy the use of antiandrogenic drugs to counter the effects of male hormones, as in cases of precocious puberty in boys or virilization of women. The antiandrogen-cyproterone acetate also has been used to reduce the sex drive in males charged with sexual offences. Because it can block normal testicular development, it is used with caution in immature males.

antiaphrodisiac another term for anaphrodisiac.

antibiotics antibacterial drugs that have been associated with birth defects when taken by women during pregnancy. Tetracycline may cause tooth and bone abnormalities. Several of the 'mycin' antibiotics may cause deafness.

anticonceptive an alternative term for contraceptive.

antieroticism the view that erotic films, plays, advertisements, and publications should be strongly opposed, or even censored, on the theory that they overemphasize the importance of sex in our lives or cheapen sexual relationships and activities, or that too much sex is morally wrong.

antigonadal action any interference with normal gonadal development or function. Such action may result from a pituitary gland tumour, a lesion in the amygdala, or the use of natural or synthetic sex hormones for therapeutic purposes. Included are certain anabolic steroids and hormones used to control breast or prostate cancer. Many diuretics can depress normal sexual functions.

antigonadotropin a substance found in the blood serum of some individuals that neutralizes the effects of one or more sex hormones. It tends to appear most frequently in the blood of individuals who have received repeated therapeutic injections of gonadotropic hormones to correct an infertility problem.

antiluetic any medicine used in the cure of syphilis (lues). Also called antisyphilitic.

antimoniotungstate an antiviral drug developed in France for the treatment of AIDS and other sexually transmitted viral infections. The drug was still experimental at publication time. See also AIDS.

antisex indoctrination the instilling of negative attitudes towards sex, especially in children. Many parents, as a result of their own inhibitions, hang-ups, or, in some cases, religious beliefs, raise their children in a cool atmosphere in which cuddling, caressing and touching (including touching themselves) are discouraged or even punished. They may also keep their children in total ignorance of sexual matters and oppose sex education not only at home but in school. Attitudes of this kind are believed to lay the groundwork for sexual conflicts, frigidity, and impotence in many instances.

antisyphilitic any remedy that may be used to treat a syphilis infection.

antivenereal any medicine used in the prevention or cure of veneral diseases.

antrum any cave or cavity, such as the space within an ovarian follicle as it grows and matures before releasing an ovum.

anus the opening of the rectum.

anxiety a pervasive feeling of apprehension, impending danger, and powerlessness accompanied by various signs of tension including increased heart rate, rapid breathing, sweating, and trembling. In contrast to fear, which is a response to a known, external threat, anxiety stems from internal, unconscious sources, and in the case of sexual anxiety usually originates in intrapsychic conflicts, forbidden impulses, insecurities, and feelings of guilt or shame instilled by parents.

apache (epash') a Parisian pimp of around 1900, often romanticized in fiction and on the stage.

apandria a feeling of aversion towards the male sex.

apareunia inability to engage in sexual intercourse; also, abstinence from intercourse.

apertural hypothesis the concept that ideas and fantasies associated with the prime instincts are focussed on the orifices of the organs that serve them. In the case of sex, these orifices are the mouth, vagina, urethra, and anus.

Apgar test a system of expressing the condition of a newborn by a series of rapid assessments of certain characteristics at 1, 5, and 15 minutes after delivery. The test covers five items: skin colour, heart rate, respiratory effort, muscle tone, and reflex irritability. Each item is scored from 0 to 2, so that skin colour that is blue to pale is scored 0, pink body but bluish arms and legs is scored as 1, and a completely pink body is scored as 2 (in a white baby). A perfect score, thus, would be a 10. The test was named after Dr. Virginia Apgar.

aphanisis an obsolete term used by the psychoanalyst Ernest Jones for the 'extinction of sexuality'—that is, for the inability to enjoy sex—which he believed to be the root of all neuroses.

aphephobia a morbid fear of touching or being touched by people or objects.

aphoria (Latin, 'nonbearing') a condition of female infertility. The word is usually accompanied by a term that specifies the reason, such as *aphoria impercita*, for barrenness resulting from a physical aversion to sexual intercourse.

aphrodisia an archaic term for sexual excitation. The term is derived from Aphrodite, the goddess of love in Greek mythology.

aphrodisiac a substance that is alleged to stimulate sexual desire and activity, especially certain roots (mandrake, ginseng, licorice), barks (yohimbine), foods (oysters, fennel), hormones (testosterone), tonics made from such substances as sarsaparilla, hops, or asafoetida, and perfumes. Claims for these substances and scores of others have never been scientifically established, but it is probable that suggestion plays a major part when they appear to have an effect.

aphrodisiomania a seldom used term for extreme sexual desire, or erotomania.

Aphrodite the ancient Greek goddess of love and the mother of Priapus, the god of procreation and phallic worship.

aplastic head sperm a spermatozoon that consists mainly of a filament, possessing little or no head or body.

apotemnophilia sexual satisfaction through fantasizing oneself as an amputee.

appeasement behaviour a term used by some psychologists to describe the increase in submissiveness associated with an increase in sexual arousal. The impulse in both partners to submit rises faster than the desire to dominate.

appendix testis a small bit of flesh attached to the testis near the head of the epididymis. It is a vestige of the mullerian duct, or the paramesonephric duct of the embryonic stage of development. Also called hydatid of Morgagni.

aprication the exposure of the body to sunlight, as in nude sunbathing (Latin *apricatio*, 'basking in the sun').

apricot brandy a drink with a reputation as an aphrodisiac beverage that dates back at least as far as Shakespeare's *A Midsummer Night's Dream*, where the fairies are instructed as to the erotic effects of the fruit. Some anthropologists have suggested that the famed apple of the Garden of Eden was actually an apricot.

Aranda hunters and gatherers of Central Australia, who are generally polygynous, with the sororal type of marriage preferred. The Aranda are one of the few societies whose members appear to be ignorant of the fact that males are necessary for procreation.

arbor vitae (Latin, 'tree of life') a 17th-century euphemism for penis.

arbor vitae uterina the medical term for the palmate folds of the uterine cervix.

ardor urinae a burning sensation when urinating.

areola of the breast the pigmented area that surrounds the nipple. The colour varies from pink to brown to black, depending upon the individual. After pregnancy begins, the areola becomes larger and the pigmentation deepens. When lactation begins, the pigmentation diminishes. The colour changes are sometimes used to distinguish a woman who has borne a child from one who has not been pregnant. Also called *areola papillaris*.

areola umbilicus an area of pigmentation around the navel that appears during pregnancy.

Aretino, Pietro (1492-1557) a serious Italian writer who is better known as a pornographer. His most famous works are *Figurae* (postures) and *Ragionamenti* (dialogues). His friend Titian portrayed him many times. Aretino is said to have blackmailed Michelangelo for his homosexuality.

Arioi a Tahitian religious order made up of men and women who travelled around the Society Islands as singers, dancers, athletes, and sexual exhibitionists. The society was established as a means of worshipping the god of fertility, but when the islands were colonized by the French, the practice was abandoned because of opposition from Christian missionaries.

armour an old slang term for a condom.

aromatherapy a term applied to the capacity of sweet-smelling herbs, oils, and incense to harmonize the internal forces of body and mind, as well as to soothe and heal the distraught spirit, and enhance sexual satisfaction. Natural substances such as essence of lotus, rose, jasmine, lavender, sandalwood, and rosemary are said to be far more effective than synthetic perfumes.

around the world a colloquial term referring to kissing the partner's entire body or, more narrowly, to kissing penis and testicles—or the clitoris and the entire vagina—and the anus.

arousability the capacity to be sexually excited, or 'turned on.' Erotic arousal is a prelude to sexual activity, especially intercourse, and can result from direct physical contact, as in foreplay, from self-stimulation, or from erotic fantasies and images evoked by films, dreams, dancing, and romantic situations, as well as music, perfume, or revealing clothes.

arousal techniques activities that tend to be sexually stimulating. Most common are the various forms of mouth-to-mouth kissing (with or without insertion of the tongue), kissing and mouthing the genitals and other parts of the body (earlobes, neck, buttocks, inside of thighs, breasts, glans, vulva, clitoris), and tactile stimulation (fondling and caressing) of the erogenous zones, including if desired the anal orifice.

arrested tail sperm a spermatozoon that is mainly head, with only a vestigial tail or filament.

arrested testis an undescended testicle, that is, one that lies within the inguinal canal but is unable to descend into the scrotum.

arrheno- a combining form meaning male (from Greek *arren*, 'male'). An example of its use is 'arrhenogenic,' which means 'producing only male offspring.'

arrhenoblastoma a masculinizing tumour of the ovary. It apparently evolves from cells that may have started to develop as testes during the embryonic period when reproductive organs appear to be bisexual. The arrhenoblastoma is the most common of the various tumours in the female body that can have masculinizing effects.

ars amandi although literally meaning 'the art of love,' a Latin term that refers primarily to advice on exciting and diversified ways of having sex. *Ars Amandi* is also the title of several classical works on this subject.

arse a slang term for the buttocks or anus. In addition it is used for a foolish person (particularly in 'silly arse') and as a collective term for women viewed as sexually available objects (especially in the phrase 'piece of arse'). There tends to be more of a taboo against its use in British English than there is in American English against its equivalent, *ass*, which is used relatively freely. See ASS.

arse-blow a vulgar slang term meaning to perform anilingus.

arse-fuck a vulgar slang term meaning to engage in anal intercourse.

arsehole a vulgar slang term for anus; also, for a person looked upon with contempt. The term ranks number 10 in the TABOONESS

RATING OF DIRTY WORDS. See this entry.

arse man a vulgar slang term meaning (a) a habitual and skilled seducer of women (usually said admiringly by other males), (b) a homosexual who favours anal sex, as the active partner, or, mainly, (c) a heterosexual who is attracted to a woman primarily through the contours and the movements of her buttocks. In the last sense, the arse man is often distinguished from the 'tits man' or 'breast man,' who favours the female breasts, and from the 'leg man,' who favours the female legs as primary turn-on. See also LEG MAN.

arse peddler a vulgar slang term for a male or female prostitute.

arse queen a vulgar slang term for a male homosexual who is either attracted primarily to the buttocks of other males or who loves to display his own buttocks so as to attract the sexual attention of other males.

ars musica (Latin, 'the art of music') a pun—very popular in the 18th and 19th centuries—referring to the act of breaking wind audibly, which was also referred to as 'playing the bum fiddle.'

articles de voyage (ärtik'lə dəvô·äyäzh') a French term, literally meaning 'travelling utensils' and referring to any masturbation devices taken along on trips where familiar sex partners are not available.

artifical abortion an abortion deliberately induced by artificial means, such as drugs or mechanical devices, as opposed to a spontaneous abortion.

artificial aids for the disabled devices designed to be used by individuals who have handicaps or disabilities as a means of achieving a measure of sexual satisfaction. They include pillows or cushions which help them adjust their position or control involuntary movements, as well as vibrators, dildos, lubricants, and penile splints.

artificial hymen a membrane that is fashioned to seal the vagina before marriage so that the woman will appear to be a virgin. This type of plastic surgery is commonly practised in cultures, such as Japan, where an intact hymen is regarded as a virtue for a bride.

artificial insemination the fertilization of an ovum other than through sexual intercourse, with the objective of inducing a pregnancy. Procedures usually followed include heterologous insemination, in which semen is contributed by an anonymous donor, and homologous insemination, in which the semen is provided by the partner. Heterologous insemination, also called *artificial insemination donor* (AID), is used when the husband is sterile, while homologous insemination (AIH) is employed when the partner is impotent, has a low sperm count or is physically incapable of coitus. Heterologous insemination also may be recommended in cases in which the man is the carrier of a serious genetic defect. To legitimize artificial-insemination pregnancies, written consent by all parties may be required, followed by formal adoption proceedings after birth of the child. Assuming normal female fertility and proper timing of ovulation, tested donor semen results in a pregnancy in as many as 70 percent of first attempts. Fresh donor sperm is obtained by masturbation and is introduced into the vagina rather than directly into the uterus, which would increase the risk of cramping and infection. An additional semen sample is usually deposited in a cervical cap or contraceptive diaphragm to be worn by the woman for about 1 hour.

artificial penis a substitute penis made of rubber, plastic, or other material and used by women or men for erotic or autoerotic purposes; a dildo.

ARV abbreviation for AIDS-related retrovirus, a term sometimes applied to an organism identified as a cause of acquired immune deficiency syndrome. See also AIDS.

asceticism a philosophy and way of life characterized by extreme self-denial, renunciation of physical pleasure, austerity, and in some cases withdrawal from society, martyrdom, and dedication to unworldly ideals. The ascetic pattern almost always includes sexual abstinence, which may arise from a fear of sexuality or a defence against sexual urges.

ascetic monasticism an austere, secluded way of life characteristically led by monks who live in a monastery and have taken religious vows of poverty, chastity, and obedience. The same vows are taken by nuns who live in convents or nunneries.

Ascheim-Zondek test an obsolete pregnancy test.

asexual nonsexual, or lacking in sexual interest or activity, as in a so-called platonic relationship. The term also refers to reproduction that does not involve the union of sex cells, as in certain animals and plants.

asexualization the process of sterilization, as in castration of the male or removal of the ovaries of a female. The term also is applied to vasectomy of the male or ligation (tying) of the fallopian tubes of the female.

ASMFR abbreviation for age-specific marital fertility rate.

asocial molester a person who may become a child molester simply because it is one of many antisocial crimes in which he involves himself during a lifetime of irresponsible behaviour.

aspermia an abnormal condition in which a man is unable to secrete or ejaculate seminal fluid. Causes can include a hypoandrogenic state, a neurological dysfunction, or a bladder-neck abnormality resulting from bladder surgery.

asphyxiophilia an alternative term for AUTO-EROTIC ASPHYXIA. See this entry.

aspro a vulgar American slang term for a professional male homosexual prostitute ('pro').

ass the American English equivalent of the British slang term *arse*. It shares the same basic range of meanings, but there tends to be less of a taboo against its use than there is against 'arse' in British English, and it is used much more widely. The term 'ass' ranks number 22 in the American TABOONESS RATING OF DIRTY WORDS. See this entry.

assignation an appointment for a meeting, especially a lover's rendezvous or 'tryst.'

assigned gender the gender in which a person is raised, regardless of chromosomal, gonadal, or other gender-determining factors. Generally, assigned gender is based on the external genital appearance of the individual. The individual may reassign his own gender as an adult, as occurs in sex-change cases.

assortive mating selective mating of persons (or animals) with similar mental or physical characteristics to perpetuate specified traits in the offspring. Also called *assortative mating.*

asterisks in amorous literature, a device indicating omission of an 'obscene' passage. While satisfying the moral standards, especially in the Victorian era, asterisks were also likely to stimulate the imagination. Lawrence Sanders noted: "'They went into the bedroom, closed the door and ***." To this day, I can't see an asterisk without getting aroused.'

astringent treatment the practice of applying alum or other chemicals to the vaginal wall to shrink the mucous membranes. In the West, astringents are occasionally used in brothels to give the pretence of virginity because some clients are 'turned on' by deflowering young women. In the East,

especially in the Marquesan Islands in the Pacific, the treatment is applied even before puberty and is believed to enhance the sexual desirability of women by narrowing the vaginal passage.

astyphia an alternative term for impotence, characterized by an inability of the male to achieve erection (Greek *a-*, 'not,' and *styein*, 'to stiffen').

asymmetric hypomastia a congenital abnormal condition in which one breast of a woman is significantly smaller than the other. The condition is correctable with a breast implant.

asymptomatic neurosyphilis a form of neurosyphilis in which there are the usual pathological tissue effects of the disease but without signs or symptoms of nervous-system involvement. The manifestations of neurosyphilis may not appear until many years after the asymptomatic stage of the infection.

Athenian an older term for male homosexual.

atocia female sterility (Greek *atokos*, 'without offspring').

atresia folliculi the cessation of function of a graafian follicle because of the failure of an ovum to become fertilized and implanted.

atresia uteri a congenital abnormality of the uterus marked by the absence of an opening into the vagina.

atresia vaginae the closure of the vagina so as to make normal penetration of the penis impossible. It may be the result of an unbroken hymen, or occasionally, of the growing together of the walls of the vagina; in either case, it can be corrected by surgery.

atrium vaginae the vestibule of the vagina.

atrophic condition of the vulva an abnormal condition marked by a loss of fatty tissue in the labia and mons pubis and a loss of skin elasticity. Other effects include a diminution in size of the clitoris and labia minor and a tendency for the skin of the vulva to develop inflammation and abrasions. The condition may be accompanied by a foul-smelling vaginal discharge.

atrophic vaginitis an inflammation of the mucosal lining of the vagina that occurs in postmenopausal women after oestrogen levels fall below physiological minimum levels.

atrophy the wasting and shrinking of an organ or tissue, such as the testicles.

attachment bond a strong affectional bond, particularly a bond established between an infant and its mother or mother surrogate, as indicated by such attachment behaviour as clinging, smiling, following, calling, or crying if the mother leaves the child. Behaviour of this kind is the prototype for later emotional attachments.

attachment disorder a pattern of apathy, unresponsiveness, lack of interest in the environment, and failure to thrive, as observed in infants who are emotionally neglected or socially isolated. These reactions are frequently found in children in institutions and in children who are ignored or unloved at home. In extreme form the condition is termed reactive attachment disorder of infancy. Its counterpart in adulthood is found in lonely, isolated, depressed individuals.

attractiveness the appeal of one person for another based on such factors as physical appearance, sexual characteristics, intelligence, understanding, social qualities, or any other characteristics that arouse interest or admiration, or satisfy the individual's special needs. Some people are attracted to frail, dependent, ineffectual individuals who need guidance or mothering; others, to strong, decisive persons who can stand on their own two feet. Also, some people are attracted to superficial charm, others to quiet sincerity.

atypical paraphilia an American Psychiatric Association category comprising the more unusual psychosexual disorders and preoccupations. Examples are coprophilia, frottage, klismaphilia, mysophilia, necrophilia, telephone scatalogia, and urophilia.

atypical psychosexual dysfunction an American Psychiatric Association category comprising sexual disorders outside the standard specific categories such as premature ejaculation and functional vaginismus. Examples are the female equivalent of premature ejaculation, and absence of erotic sensations despite physiologically normal sexual excitement and orgasm.

aulophobia a morbid fear of any wind instrument resembling a flute. It is believed to be the fear of a phallic symbol.

au naturel (ō nätYrel') a French term for naked, literally 'in natural state.'

aunt an 18th- and 19th-century term for a procuress.

auntie a colloquial term referring either to an aging but flamboyant male homosexual or to an aging female prostitute.

aural sex a pun on 'oral sex,' referring to obscene telephone calls or to sexually arousing recordings on records or tapes. (Thus the term does not imply attempts at physical sexual penetration via the ear).

Australian a slang term for a person who performs anilingus (kissing from 'down under').

autoassassinatophilia the staging or imagining of one's own murder for sexual arousal.

autocunnilingus a woman's use of her mouth or tongue to stimulate her own vulva.

autodermatophagia the eating of one's own skin as a form of autoerotism or automasochism.

autoerastia a seldom used term for self-love or autoerotism.

autoerotic asphyxia a dangerous sexual practice engaged in mainly by adolescent males (and occasionally females) who attempt to heighten the pleasure of masturbation by near asphyxiation. Currently the FBI has estimated that between 500 and 1,000 unintentional deaths occur each year in the United States, and are usually misdiagnosed as suicides or homicides. Many male victims are found hanged by the neck, sometimes wearing women's underclothes. Various techniques of asphyxiation were described by the Marquis de Sade, and are vividly depicted in pornographic literature and films. See also EROTIC HANGING.

autoerotism a term coined by Havelock Ellis for solitary activities that produce sexual excitement, especially masturbation, 'genital excitement during sleep' (nocturnal orgasms), and erotic dreams, daydreams, and fantasies. Also called *autoeroticism*.

autofellatio a man's use of his mouth or tongue to bring himself to orgasm by sucking or licking his penis.

autofetishism an extreme form of narcissism in which one's own body is adored, as a sexual obsession. A similar term is automonosexualism.

autoflagellation the whipping of oneself for sexual pleasure.

autogenital stimulation any form of stimulation of one's own genital organs, such as pelvic thrusts, masturbation, or self-stimulation before intercourse (for example, stroking one's nipples or fondling one's testicles).

autohedonia a seldom used term for autoerotism or masturbation.

automasochism self-torture for sexual arousal.

automonosexualism a term coined by Magnus Hirschfeld to describe the behaviour of men who are so self-centred and narcissistic that they can achieve sexual gratification only from their own bodies, through masturbation and, rarely, autofellatio.

automutilation self-mutilation, usually for sexual arousal.

automysophobia a morbid, neurotic fear of being dirty or smelling unclean, a fear that may inhibit sexual activity because the sex organs are close to the organs of defecation and urination.

autonecrophilia the seeking of sexual satisfaction by imagining oneself to be a corpse (Greek *nekros*, 'corpse').

autopaedophilia the seeking of sexual satisfaction by imagining oneself to be a child and by being treated as a child in a sexual relationship.

autoplasty a psychoanalytical term for directing the libido towards changing the self as a means of adapting to reality. The goal of psychoanalytical treatment has been described as *autoplastic adaptation*.

autosadism an alternative term for automasochism.

autoscopophilia a sexual variance in which gratification is achieved by looking at one's own body, particulary one's genital organs.

autosexuality a general term for deriving sexual satisfaction from oneself, usually through masturbation. If autosexuality is the only or preferred means of gratification and is practised because of fear of heterosexual relations, it is usually considered a sexual disorder, or paraphilia.

autosome any chromosome other than a sex chromosome. Humans normally possess 22 pairs of autosomes, plus the sex chromosomes (XX for women and XY for men) that are responsible for determining the male or female sexual characteristics of the individual.

autospermatoxin a spermicide produced in the blood serum of a male that renders his own spermatozoa immobile by agglutinating the sperm.

autosuck vagina an artificial vagina that makes sucking motions, powered from the cigarette-lighter outlet in a car.

autotomy self-mutilation, usually for sexual arousal (Greek *tomein*, 'to cut').

aversion therapy a form of behaviour therapy based on negative conditioning—that is, association of undesired symptoms or behaviour with unpleasant or painful experiences to which the individual reacts with avoidance. Examples in the sexual sphere are association of fetishistic objects with electric shock or noxious odours, and association of homosexual behaviour, as depicted on film, with nausea or vomiting induced by drugs.

avisodomy sexual intercourse between a human male and a bird (from Latin *avis*, 'bird', and sodomy). Commonly used—perhaps because of their accommodating anatomy—are chickens, ducks, geese, and turkeys. The practice seems to be worldwide, old as human history, and still quite current.

axillary hair hair that develops in the armpits of males and females during puberty. Axillary hair growth generally accompanies the appearance of pubic hair.

axillary intercourse another term for coitus in axilla.

azoospermia the lack of spermatozoa in the seminal fluid or a deficiency in the normal activity of the spermatozoa. Azoospermia may be the result of an obstruction in the seminal tract or a testicular abnormality. Various types of studies, such as endocrinal and chromosomal analyses, are performed to determine a testicular disorder. A biopsy may be required and x-rays may be used to define a possible obstruction after injection of a contrast medium into the vas deferens and ejaculatory ducts.

B a common abbreviation for black in 'personal' ads. It may be used in combinations, such as DB/F, meaning divorced black female, or MB/M, meaning married black male.

baby pro an American slang term for a young teenage prostitute. A baby pro often is in demand at resort hotels and conventions.

baby swingers an American slang term for couples who are participating in open spouse swapping for the first time.

bacchanalia orgies in ancient as well as late-medieval Rome. The term, however, was not in use before the 16th century.

bachelor mother a woman who is by choice an unmarried mother, or the mother of an illegitimate child.

backdoor a slang term for anus.

backdoor man a slang term referring either to a man who loves anal intercourse or to a woman's secret lover.

backdoor work a slang term for anal intercourse.

backgammon player an obsolete term for a person who practises anal intercourse. Also called *backgammoner*.

bacterial prostatitis a form of inflammation of the prostate gland that is characterized by repeated urinary infections. It is difficult to treat, but the usual procedure is warm baths accompanied by a long course of antibiotics that penetrate the prostate.

bad breast a controversial theory of the American psychoanalyst Melanie Klein that during the first year of life part of the breast is experienced as a bad object reflecting the death instinct.

bad object the theory of Melanie Klein that the superego, or conscience, is focussed on good and bad objects, and that the bad object represents something sexual or dirty and, in the unconscious, the devil.

Baer's cavity the fluid-filled cavity of the blastula or morula in early embryonic development.

bag a colloquial term referring either to the scrotum or to an unattractive and usually promiscuous woman.

bagnio (ban'yō) a type of Turkish bath popular in Elizabethan times (Italian *bagno*, 'bath').

bag of waters the foetal membranes containing the amniotic fluid.

Bala a polygynous society in Zaïre. Among the sexual practices of this people are cicatrices in artistic designs extending from the chest to the groin in women; circumcision for hygienic reasons; side-by-side intercourse with the couple facing each other; adultery considered sufficient grounds for punishment of the husband but not of the wife; and numerous male transvestites who are not considered homosexuals.

balance position a coital position in which the man and woman face each other while lying on their sides with legs outstretched. According to Hindu texts, lovemaking in this position is 'both gentle and focusses on rhythm and breathing.'

balanitis an inflammation of the glans penis or the glans clitoridis, often involving the foreskin. The tissues may become swollen, tender, and pruritic (itchy) with signs of ulcerations, venereal warts, and clefts or grooves in the surface. Kinds of balanitis include amoebic, diabetic, gangrenous, monilial, and trichomonal. One form of the disorder, xerotica obliterans balanitis, is caused by a constriction of the opening of the urethra, resulting in atrophy and shrinking of the glans penis. Infantile balanitis involves effects of organisms under the foreskin that thrive on urea. *Entamoeba histolytical* balanitis is a type of infection acquired by anal intercourse with an infected partner. The sugar in excreted urine contributes to diabetic balanitis. Monilial balanitis is caused by an infection of a *Candida* species. A spirochaete infection often results in gangrenous balanitis which can lead to ulceration and eventual destruction of not only the glans penis but of all external genitalia. Certain chemicals and drugs also may contribute to the disorder. Phimosis is a common early effect of balanitis.

balanitis gangraenosa a rapidly destructive infection believed to result from a spirochaete, producing erosion of the glans penis and often destruction of the entire genitals. The spirochaetal infection may be sexually transmitted. Also called gangrenous balanitis.

balanocele the herniation of the foreskin resulting in a protrusion of the glans penis through the ruptured tissue.

balanoplasty any kind of plastic surgery performed on the glans penis (Greek *balanos*, 'gland,' and *plassein*, 'mould').

balanoposthitis a disease of the penis in which adhesions form between the foreskin and the glans. The condition may result from a wide range of causes, including chemical balanitis; metabolic disorders involving the urine, such as diabetes; fungal infections; vaginal secretions; and bacterial or viral infections, such as syphilis or measles.

balanorrhoea a type of balanitis that is accompanied by a copious flow of pus.

Balinese the one million inhabitants of Bali Island off the coast of Java. Their customs include exposure of the breasts; marriage of adult twins, based on the idea that they have already been intimate in the womb; a taboo against teacher-student marriage, which is regarded as a form of incest; and preference for a variation of the Oceanic position in which the woman reclines and the man kneels between her legs.

ball to have sex—a widely used American colloquial term.

balls a Shakespearean euphemism for testicles (also written 'bawls')—still in use today as a slang term. Also called *ballocks*.

banana a colloquial term for penis.

bananas an alleged aphrodisiac, perhaps because of their shape.

bang a colloquial term for intercourse, used as a noun or a verb.

barber's shop in Britain, a traditional place where condoms could be bought. If a British

barber asks, 'Will there be anything else, Sir?' it is to avoid embarrassing a customer who may want to purchase condoms. The customer may then reply with either a polite 'No, thanks' or a grateful 'Yes, there is.'

Barr body the sex chromatin material in the female body cells. The Barr body is associated with the inactivated second X chromosome of the normal female complement of two X chromosomes. When the nucleus of a female body cell is stained with a particular material, the Barr body appears at the periphery. The Barr-body test can be used to determine if a woman is a 'superfemale' with more than two X chromosomes, in which case more than one Barr body will take the stain.

barrenness sterility; the inability to have children. The term is somewhat archaic, dating from the period when childlessness was attributed only to the woman.

barrier contraceptives contraceptive devices or substances designed to prevent sperm from coming in contact with the female egg, or ovum. They include condoms, caps or diaphragms, vaginal creams, jellies, foams, suppositories, and sponges.

bartholinitis an inflammation of the Bartholin's glands of the vaginal orifice. The glands are the most common site for infection around the external female genitalia. Although these glands normally secrete mucus into the vaginal canal, their presence is generally noticed only when they are diseased. Originally, bartholinitis was regarded as evidence of a gonorrhoeal infection, but recent clinical studies show the glands may be the site of infections by *Trichomonas vaginalis* and many other kinds of pathogenic organisms. An infection usually obstructs the ducts of the glands, which become tense, tender, and swollen. The effects can involve the entire labia, requiring surgical drainage and antibiotic therapy.

Bartholin's glands glands located on either side of the entrance to the vagina, producing in most cases a mucus secretion that serves as a lubricant during sexual excitement.

basal-body-temperature method (BBT) a birth control method based on changes in body temperature. The basal body temperature is usually very slightly below normal during the week before ovulation but rises to slightly above normal just before ovulation occurs. When it remains relatively higher for 3 consecutive days, it is a sign that the safe days have begun.

bashfulness timidity and shyness, often the

result of feelings of inferiority. Sexually speaking, bashfulness often reaches a peak in the early adolescent years when young people are likely to be self-conscious and embarrassed about physical irregularities such as overdeveloped or underdeveloped breasts, acne, early or late menstruation, lack of pubic hair, or anxieties over masturbation, petting, or nocturnal emissions.

bastard an illegitimate child. Though the term is basically descriptive and not judgmental, it is often used as a derogatory label (or even an abusive epithet), implying that the child himself is inferior, unacceptable, and a product of poor breeding. In some communities, the birth may be declared legitimate if the parents marry after the child is born. Also called love child. The term bastard is derived from the Old French expression *fils de bast*, 'son of a pack saddle,' that is, a child begotten on a pack saddle, which mule drivers used for a pillow. The term bastard ranks number 8 in the TABOONESS RATING OF DIRTY WORDS. See this entry. See also EMOTIONAL BASTARD.

bastardy proceedings legal proceedings undertaken to establish the paternity of an illegitimate child.

bat an American slang term for a prostitute, usually applied to a streetwalker who prostitutes herself in order to raise money for a drug or alcohol habit.

baths steam baths or similar public bathing facilities located in most large cities and used as meeting places for male homosexuals. In America it may be the gay equivalent of a heterosexual massage parlour, offering a dance floor, television or video films, a swimming pool, lockers where clothing can be kept, and small rooms with beds for sexual activity.

battered-child syndrome a pattern of child abuse and injury carried out by parents or parent substitutes, including not only spanking, but fracture of bones or burning with a cigarette or gas flame. This practice is an extreme means of punishment or an expression of anger, hostility, or frustration. The syndrome may include sexual abuse as well.

battered-wife syndrome wife beating or other acts of physical assault by the husband, believed to occur in all social classes. Battering may include physical abuse for purposes of sexual gratification: whipping, breaking bones, burning, mutilation, and other sadistic acts.

battyman a West Indian slang term for a male homosexual, probably derived from *batti*, a Jamaican word for buttocks.

bawdyhouse an old slang term for a house of prostitution or a brothel.

Bayle's disease a form of neurosyphilis marked by atrophy of the cerebral cortex and deterioration of the meningeal membranes that normally protect the brain and spinal cord. The central-nervous-system destruction results in loss of ability to concentrate, apathy, delusions, disorientation, and emotional instability. The disorder also is known as dementia paralytica or general paralysis of the insane.

B.C. an abbreviation for birth control.

B & D an abbreviation for bondage and discipline. Sometimes written as *B/D*.

beans a vegetable that has been used as an alleged aphrodisiac for centuries. Saint Jerome is reported to have forbidden nuns to eat beans because of the belief that they stimulated the genitalia.

beast fetishism a term coined by Krafft-Ebing for the fact that contact with animal furs or skins may have an aphrodisiac effect, producing 'peculiar and lustful emotions.'

beast with two backs, to make the an old literary term meaning to have face-to-face intercourse. Shakespeare, for example, wrote: 'your daughter and the Moor are making the beast with two backs' (Iago to Brabantio, *Othello*, I, 1, line 117). Also the French version is cited in literary English-speaking circles: 'Faire la bête à deux dos.'

beating fantasies the psychoanalytical theory that fantasies involving beatings have a hidden sexual meaning. For example, if a girl fantasizes that her father is beating her, this may mean that she is being punished for incestuous feelings towards him; and if she fantasizes that he is beating another child, it means 'He only loves me.' If a boy fantasizes being beaten by the father, it is also an unconscious expression of the father's love for him, but a mother's beating is interpreted as a defence against homosexual impulses.

beat the meat a slang term meaning to masturbate.

beauty contests competitions between young women based on physical attractiveness and, in some measure, on talent, sex appeal, and personality. Though largely accepted by the general public such competitions are anathema to women's liberation groups, who maintain that the contestants are treated as 'sex objects.' The Greeks, but not the Romans, held such contests for both men and women; however, they are practically nonexistent in Asian, African, and Oriental societies.

beaver a slang term meaning (a) the vagina or vulva, (b) a woman's pubic hair, and (c) a woman.

beaver shot a colloquial term for a photograph of a woman with open legs, showing vagina and pubic hair. Also called a spread beaver. A split-beaver shot is another synonym, which, however, may also refer to a closeup photograph or film scene showing the spread labia of the vagina.

bedding in the buff sleeping in the nude. Studies show that in the U.S.A. 19 percent of men and 6 percent of women prefer to sleep with nothing on at all. The studies also found that young affluent adults were the most likely to sleep in the buff. Nude sleeping was most popular among people in the western United States, 20 percent, and least popular among Southerners, 9 percent. In the colder northern states, nude sleeping was admitted by 11 percent.

bed-hop to have sex with a large number of short-term partners; to sleep around.

bedmates a slang term for an unmarried couple who live together or who share a bed for sexual purposes at a location other than the home of either partner. The term may also be used to identify partners in a common-law marriage.

bed-presser an old term for fornicator or womanizer—used, for example, by Shakespeare.

bedroom eyes a term usually used in the phrase 'make bedroom eyes at someone,' meaning to look provocatively at them, as if suggesting or inviting sexual intercourse.

bedswerver an archaic term for a person who is unfaithful to the marriage bed.

beefcake a photographic display of sexually attractive men, typically with well-developed musculature minimally covered by clothing. See also CHEESECAKE.

behaviour therapy the application of techniques aimed at modifying faulty or undesirable behaviour or symptoms, as contrasted with psychotherapy in which the patient's thoughts, feelings, and unconscious conflicts are explored. This general approach applies learning techniques such as conditioning, aversive therapy, and systematic desensitization to the elimination of sexual inadequacy, excessive inhibitions, sexual phobias, and undesired sexual orientation. In the aversion

technique, for example, the patient may be repeatedly exposed to photographs of homosexual behaviour while undergoing an electric shock or induced vomiting. In the Masters and Johnson technique, a patient may learn to overcome impotence or frigidity by developing a step-by-step relationship with his or her marital partner or a trained surrogate, and sexual anxiety may be overcome through the use of relaxation techniques.

Behcet's disease an inflammatory disorder that involves the genitalia, mouth, eyes, and other body structures. The cause is unknown but may be a viral infection or an autoimmune disease. The onset of the disease is marked by the appearance of ulcers of the mouth followed by similar ulcers on the penis and scrotum or on the vagina and vulva. Lesions also appear on the eye, skin, blood vessels, or joints. Blindness, paralysis, thrombosis, and aneurysms are among the complications. It was first identified by the Turkish physician Hulusi Behcet.

being love a term applied by the psychiatrist Abraham Maslow to a form of love that emphasizes mutuality and concern for the welfare of others, in contrast to 'deficiency love,' which is characterized by possessiveness, dependence, and limited concern for the welfare of others.

BEM Sex Role Inventory (BSRI) a recent (1981) masculinity-femininity test in which the subject checks statements selected by judges according to the degree to which they represent sex roles in Western society. In addition to masculine and feminine scores, there is a score for persons high in androgynous traits, such as warmth plus assertiveness.

benign orgasmic cephalgia a type of headache on both sides of the head that starts at the time of orgasm and may last for an hour or longer. This specific kind of headache is only associated with orgasm. It affects more men than women.

benign prostatic hyperplasia (BPH) an abnormal condition in which multiple fibrous nodules develop out of tissues of the prostate gland, resulting in an obstruction of the urethral outlet of the urinary bladder. The condition is marked by increasing urinary frequency and urgency, including a need to urinate during the night, because of the difficulty in emptying the bladder completely. The size and force of the urinary stream becomes diminished. The condition is easily complicated by urinary infection, resulting in a burning sensation during urination and chills and fever. The inability to completely empty the bladder also can lead to the formation of urinary stones and kidney impairment. Involvement of the blood vessels can result in the appearance of blood in the urine. Treatment includes temporary catheter drainage and surgery, usually by a procedure called transurethral resection in which the prostate is reached through the urethra and an incision into the pelvic area is not required. Also called *benign prostatic hypertrophy*.

bent a slang term for homosexual, indicating the person is not 'straight' (heterosexual).

berdache a term used in certain Native American nations, particulary in the North West U.S.A., for a male transvestite who not only dresses as a woman but performs women's tasks and adopts the feminine role in sexual behaviour with male partners.

bestiality sexual relations with animals through intercourse, masturbation, fellatio, frottage (rubbing), anal penetration, or having one's genitals licked. According to Kinsey, 17 percent of farm men have reached orgasm through sexual activity with animals. The term may also include deriving sexual pleasure and excitement from observing the sexual activities of animals, and from a fetish based upon animal furs or skins.

best leg of three an older euphemism for penis.

beta subunit HCG radioimmunoassay a highly sensitive pregnancy test that can detect conception nearly a week before the menstrual period is missed.

betrothal a legally binding promise or contract in which a man and a woman agree to marry. If one of the partners refuses to keep the promise, the other has the legal right to sue for damages in a breach-of-promise suit. Today such suits are increasingly rare (or dismissed by the court) because of opposition to forced marriages.

B-girls an American term for prostitutes who seek their clients in bars or cocktail lounges.

Bi a common abbreviation for bisexual in 'personal' ads. It may be used in combinations, such as BiW/M, meaning bisexual white male, or BiC/F, meaning bisexual Catholic female. Not capitalized, *bi* is a generally used abbreviation for bisexual.

bi bar an American term for a bar used as a meeting place by bisexual persons. Men may dance with men or women with women or men with women at a bi bar.

bidet (bē'dā) an oval basin equipped with hot and cold running water on which a person

sits while washing the genital and anal areas before sexual intercourse and after defecation. Bidets are common in Europe.

bi-gaited a colloquial American term for bisexual.

bigamy the statutory offence of being married to one person while still legally married to someone else. In Western society men practise bigamy more often than women, but it has become less common as a result of easier divorce and greater acceptance of extramarital affairs. The law against bigamy does not, however, apply where the spouse is missing from home for a certain number of years, and is presumed or legally pronounced dead.

big brother a slang term for penis.

big O, the a slang term for orgasm, used mainly by a woman, referring to her own orgasm.

bike a derogatory term for a promiscuous woman. It is usually used in compounds, such as 'town bike,' meaning a woman who has had sex with many men in town.

bilingual a colloquial, punning term for bisexual.

Bilitis a Greek courtesan to whom Sappho wrote love poems. In 1956 the first large-scale lesbian organization in the U.S.A. was named Daughters of Bilitis (from the name of the lesbian poet in *Chansons de Bilitis* by Pierre Louÿs around 1900).

Billig exercises a treatment of women with dysmenorrhoea by a technique of posture training. It was developed during World War II as a means of reducing absenteeism because of menstrual cramps and discomfort.

bilobular having two lobes. This medical term is applied, for example, to describe a form of prostatic hypertrophy in which the overgrowth of prostate tissue appears in the form of two lobes.

bint a British slang term for woman.

biogenesis a theory advanced by T.H. Huxley that living forms can only be derived from matter that is already alive and life cannot be produced artificially.

biogenetic basic law the rule that ontogeny repeats phylogeny, or that during embryonic and foetal development each individual passes through stages that are similar to the body structure of each type of animal ancestors of humans. Thus, each person begins life as a single cell, a zygote, and displays briefly the features of various lower animals as it progresses towards those of a basic mammal and finally a human being.

biological clock the internal mechanisms

that determine periodic changes in bodily functions—not only in respiration, heartbeat, temperature, hunger, sleep, elimination, and energy level, but also in sexual processes such as the menstrual cycle, the rhythmic change from erection to flaccidity of the penis during sleep, and the oestrus cycle, or heat cycle, in animals. Clear evidence of rhythmic fluctuations in the sex drive are lacking for men, but in women sexual desire appears to be most intense just before and just after menstruation.

biological mother in recent usage, a term that refers to both the genetic mother and the gestational mother of a child. See GESTATIONAL MOTHER.

biological rhythm any of a number of patterns of physiological or psychological activity that repeat in more or less predictable cycles. Examples include sexual response, menstruation, and body-temperature fluctuations. Most animals experience diurnal rhythms with activities that repeat in more or less 24-hour cycles.

biovular pertaining to the release of two ova from the ovaries, as in the development of biovular, or dizygotic, twins.

bipartite ovary an ovary that develops as a pair of attached segments of ovarian tissue.

bipotentiality of the gonad the tendency of gonads of mammals towards a bisexual organization. The first set of sex cords in the embryo constitute the medulla of the ovary, which is the equivalent of the seminiferous tubules of the testis. At the same time, the testis may exhibit for a short while in embryonic life the structural equivalent of the ovarian cortex. The double potentiality is the basis of sex reversal in humans.

bird a colloquial term for woman or girl, used mainly in Great Britain.

birds and bees a euphemistic term for the 'facts of life,' that is, the facts of sex.

bird's-nest soup an Oriental dish prepared from a kind of gelatine extracted from the nests of swallows. Bird's nests are rather tasteless without proper seasoning but make a good thickening for other soup ingredients. In China, bird's-nest soup is considered quite an important aphrodisiac. Coincidentally, salep, made from orchid bulbs, has been served in Europe as bird's-nest soup.

birth the act of being born, usually as the culmination of a successful pregnancy.

birth adjustments the abrupt, drastic adaptations that must be made by a newborn infant during the transition from a parasitic

existence within the womb to a relatively independent existence in the outside world. Among the adjustments are adaptation to a temperature of 70° instead of 100° F, obtaining oxygen through inhalation, taking nourishment by mouth and elimination of waste products through the proper organs. The sudden change is so great that the infant shows many signs of behaviour disorganization for several days (gasping, coughing, sneezing) and, according to Freud and Otto Rank, experiences its first, basic feelings of anxiety.

birth canal the passage through the uterus, cervix, vagina, and vulva through which a foetus passes during normal childbrith.

birth control regulation of the number and spacing of offspring by devices and techniques that prevent conception, including the pill, condoms, IUDs, diaphragms, spermicides, sponges, as well as the rhythm method, withdrawal, natural family planning, sterilization (salpingectomy, vasectomy), and termination of pregnancy through abortion.

birth cry the reflexive wail of a newborn infant marking the onset of respiration.

birth date the date on which a child is born. Because the exact date of conception is usually unknown, this date can be computed in advance with fair accuracy by adding 280 to the date on which the woman's last menstruation started.

birthday party a euphemism for orgy.

birthday suit a humorous colloquialism for a state of complete nakedness.

birth defect a physical deformity, intellectual defect, sensory defect, or disease process that is present at birth and is the result of such factors as prenatal conditions, birth injury, chromosomal abnormality, biochemical aberration, or heredity. Examples are clubfoot, cerebral palsy, deafness, Down's syndrome, Tay-Sachs disease, hypothyroidism, and cleft palate. Studies indicate that over 5 percent of children are born with a congenital disorder of some kind.

birthmark a congenital tumour or pigmentation that is present at birth or appears shortly afterwards. It may be flat or raised, as a mole or collection of fragile capillaries that may cause extensive bleeding beneath the skin. Many birthmarks gradually disappear during childhood.

birth order the position of the child in the family: first born, second born, middle, or youngest. According to Alfred Adler this position is a significant factor in personality development; he held, for example, that the youngest child will come to expect special attention and will develop a strong competitive drive. Adler's views have been questioned by various research studies, and today the emphasis is on parental attitudes and the child's psychological rather than ordinal position in the family.

B

birth positions the position in which the infant is 'presented.' About 96 percent of deliveries are head-first, or cephalic, presentations. The head is bent down, the chin resting on the breast bone so that the face or brow appears first. Breech or buttocks presentations constitute 4 percent of births, usually with the legs bent over the abdomen, but sometimes with the legs presenting first, and very occasionally with the baby sitting cross-legged. If the foetus is in the breech position, it can usually be manipulated by the obstetrician into the cephalic position.

birth rate the number of births each year per 1,000 population, which was 14.7 in the United States and 49.3 in Nigeria in 1980. When compared with the death rate, the net population increase for these two countries was 8.9 and 22.7 respectively. The birth rate per couple needed to maintain the world's population is 2.1, but in the United States during the early 80s, the birth rate dropped to less than one per couple for the first time in recorded history, primarily because of the more widespread use of birth control.

birth ratio a proportion of approximately 105 boy babies to 100 girl babies that is believed to occur constantly throughout the world. An exception is the birth ratio of offspring resulting from artificial insemination, which is much higher in male representation, a fact attributed to the likelihood that doctors take the sperm for injection from the top of a container, where 80 percent of the sperm contain the Y chromosome.

birthroom a room in a hospital's maternity unit in which comfortable homelike surroundings are provided so that women can give birth in a relaxing non-threatening environment.

birth trauma the physical and emotional stress experienced by the newborn child during the abrupt change from the warmth and security of the womb to the new conditions imposed by the external world. According to the psychiatrist Otto Rank this change arouses 'primal anxiety' and if that anxiety is not effectively 'worked through,' it may create a deep longing for the peace of the

womb, an inability to adjust to the rigours of life, and a predisposition to neurosis or psychosis. This theory is considered highly controversial.

bisexous an older (17th-century) term for bisexual.

bisexuality sexual attraction to both sexes, not merely in fantasy but in performance. Bisexual persons can achieve orgasm with either sex, though at times they may be preponderantly active with males, and at other times with females. Bisexuality has been found in many societies including New Guinea and the Pacific Islands. The term is also applied to hermaphroditism, in which both male and female genitals exist in the same person. Adjective: *bisexual.*

bit a derogatory term for a female.

bitch a slang term meaning (a) a person looked upon with contempt, primarily a female, (b) a prostitute or a lewd woman, and (c) a blatant male homosexual. The term ranks number 17 in the TABOONESS RATING OF DIRTY WORDS. See this entry.

biting the use of the teeth in expressing anger, aggression, tension release, or sexuality as in 'love bite.'

bit on the side a euphemism for clandestine sexual activity carried on without the knowledge of one's usual partner.

blastocele the fluid-filled cavity of a blastula or morula, a stage between the zygote and embryo.

blastocyst a hollow ball of cells that forms from the morula, the tiny ball of dividing embryonic cells, after it enters the uterus. The blastocyst evolves from the morula on or about the fourth day after fertilization of the ovum. The cellular outer wall of the blastocyst implants itself in the lining of the uterus after floating freely in the womb for a day or two.

blastomere any one cell or group of cells of a morula. The initial division of a zygote results in two blastomeres. Each of the original blastomeres divides into smaller blastomeres. The morula stage represents a ball of 16 blastomeres.

blastula a primitive stage of embryonic development in which the morula becomes a fluid-filled cavity surrounded by a single layer of cells. The blastula later develops into the gastrula in the embryological processes of many vertebrate and invertebrate animals. (Greek *blastos,* 'germ.')

blennorrhagia a condition of profuse

gonorrhoeal discharge from the penis or vagina.

blind an American slang term pertaining to a male who has not been circumcised. In this usage, 'the blinds' are the foreskin.

blind canals a term sometimes applied to vestigial structures of the embryonic female reproductive system.

blindfolding a fairly common practice in 'bondage games' designed to increase erotic pleasure. The woman is usually the mock victim, and the blindfold serves the double purpose of increasing the man's power over her, and of providing the added stimulus of surprise.

blood group any of several types of classifications of genetically determined red-blood-cell entities. The most commonly used system, introduced in 1900 by Karl Landsteiner, is the ABO system in which blood cells of individuals are classified as A, B, AB, and O, according to their ability to produce specific antibodies. The ABO blood-group system became a method for establishing nonpaternity in cases of disputed fatherhood.

blood test analysis of blood to determine blood type or the presence of such disorders as diabetes, leukaemia, mononucleosis, or venereal infection. In most states of the U.S.A. a certificate based on a laboratory test for syphilis is required of both applicants for a marriage licence.

blow a vulgar slang term meaning to perform fellatio—to give a *blow job*. The term blow ranks number 24 in the TABOONESS RATING OF DIRTY WORDS. See this entry.

blow stick a slang term for penis.

blue a colour associated with sex or pornography, as in 'blue movie.' At one time, blue was the colour of romanticism. At other times, it has been associated with homosexuality.

blue balls a colloquial term for the pain in the testicles that may result from sustained or repeated sexual arousal without ejaculatory release. Also called love nuts.

blue discharge a form of dishonourable discharge from the U.S. Army during World War II on grounds of homosexual behaviour.

blue vein a slang term for penile erection. It derives from the vein that runs along the penis and becomes distended during an erection.

blushing an involuntary flushing of the face produced by embarrassment, modesty, confusion, or self-consciousness. The reaction is common after puberty when young people are especially concerned about their second-

ary sexual characteristics and sexual relationships. Persistent blushing may be a conversion symptom produced by feelings of shame or guilt, especially over sexual reactions or behaviour.

blushing of the penis the engorgement of blood in the penis during erection.

body exploration a precopulatory activity in which various parts of the partner's body are touched, stroked, and manipulated. The emphasis is usually on the erogenous areas, such as the breasts, nipples, vulva, and penis.

body-fat trigger a gonadostat set point for the onset of menarche in females. Studies indicate a relationship between body-fat proportions and the start of sexual maturity in which menstruation will not begin until at least 17 percent of the body weight is fat. It has been suggested that oestrogen production is dependent on body fat. Also, an appropriate body weight and composition may be required for the basal metabolic rate to become reset for the sexual maturation stage of life.

body image the way we picture our body and its competence. Our body image is an important ingredient of our self-concept, helping to determine whether we accept or reject ourselves, whether we feel confident in social relationships, and whether we have an idealized or realistic idea of our attractiveness, strength, skills, and sex appeal.

body language communication of feelings, desires, and attitudes through gestures, posture, movement, or facial expression. Body language is an important aspect of the relations between the sexes. A wink, a smile, a 'come-hither' look, and a provocative posture often 'speak volumes' though not a word has been said.

body monitoring a reaction pattern characterized by closely observing one's body functions, especially increased awareness of changes in sexual responsiveness, vigour, strength, or general health during middle and old age. As a result, various attempts are made to maintain performance and appearance.

body narcissism overconcern about the body and particularly the erotic zones. According to psychoanalytic theory this tendency is especially evident in early childhood when boys and girls begin to explore their bodies, become preoccupied with bodily functions (elimination, sexuality, and sexual response as in masturbation), and experience a dread of body injury.

body of the penis the main portion of the penis that lies in front of the pubic symphysis or that is observable from the outside of the body of the male. Also called corpus penis.

body stalk a primitive embryonic structure that grows at the lower end of the embryo and eventually evolves into a part of the umbilical cord when the placenta develops.

boff a slang term meaning to copulate.

bollocks another slang term for balls or ballocks.

bondage a form of sexual gratification involving the physical restraint of one partner.

bondage and discipline (B & D) a type of erotic bondage in which the emphasis is on 'training' of the victim or 'breaking the victim's will' through such methods as flagellation or applying a bridle to the victim. The object is to produce sexual excitement in both the dominant and the submissive partner. Such 'games' can be dangerous and may be a symptom of sadomasochistic disorder.

bondage harness a more or less elaborate harness, usually of leather and similar to the halter and bridle of a horse, used to 'break in' a mock victim in sexual bondage games.

bonding development of a close attachment between two persons. See PAIR BONDING.

bone an American colloquial term for penis, especially the erect penis, as in the expression 'to get a bone on.'

bone marrow a substance that has been consumed in alleged aphrodisiac patés and as a powder for centuries. According to the epicurean poet Horace, bone marrow was a standard aphrodisiac in Rome during the 1st century B.C.

bone metastases bone cancers that have developed as a result of the spread of tumour cells from cancer of the prostate. They occur most frequently in the pelvis and sacrum, spinal column, and upper leg bone, in that order. It is estimated that approximately 30 to 90 percent of cases of cancer of the prostate eventually involve the bones, depending on the stage in which treatment is started.

bone queen an American homosexual slang term for a person who is extremely fond of performing fellatio.

boner an American colloquial term for erection.

boobs a colloquial term for the female breasts.

boondagger an American slang term for an aggressive lesbian, particularly one who dresses in a masculine style.

bordello a house of prostitution. Among variations in several old European languages the word has appeared as bord, borda, and bordel. The term has been used since the 16th century and means 'little house' in Italian.

bosom a genteelism for the female breasts. It is standardly pronounced bōoz'əm, but for those who found even this too risqué there was once a vogue for the yet more euphemistic pronunciation bazōom'.

bottie a euphemism for the buttocks, used by or to children.

bottom man the passive male homosexual partner in anal intercourse—the opposite of the 'top man.'

boudoir (bōod'wä) a lady's private room, which may be her bedroom or private sitting room. The literal meaning of this French word is 'sulking place.'

bouillabaisse the famous French fish soup, often considered an aphrodisiac. According to a legend, it was created by Venus herself, to stir the erotic feelings of her husband, Vulcan.

bowdlerism a term referring to 'cleaning-up' efforts of persons who are self-appointed guardians of the public morals. The word is derived from the name of Dr. Thomas Bowdler, the ultimate Victorian, who produced *The Family Shakespeare* in 1818, with all sexual references removed from the original version. See also GENTLEMAN COW.

box a colloquial, often derogatory, term for vagina.

box lunch a slang term for cunnilingus.

boy a male child.

boy-girl identical twins a pair of monozygotic twins in which one of a pair of boy twins became a female as a result of an accident. In the case reported in the *New York Times* (March 12, 1985), one of a pair of identical twin boys was castrated shortly after birth and injected with female sex hormones. The castration was requested by the parents after the infant boy was injured during circumcision. The castrated boy was raised as a girl.

boy in the boat, the a euphemism used by lesbians for the clitoris.

boy marriage marriage between a boy of 12 to 18 and a male adult. 'Pederastic marriage,' as it is also called, has been reported in the Egyptian oasis of Siwa early in this century, and among the Australian Nambutji, where every young man becomes the boy-wife of the man who has performed circumcision and subincision on him during initiation. Sometimes the boy performs the active homosexual role, and sometimes the passive role, and later he marries the daughter of his 'husband.'

BPH an abbreviation for benign prostatic hyperplasia.

brahmacarya a Hindu philosophy of sexuality in which celibacy is practised early in life and late in life while normal marriage and sexual activity is acceptable between the periods of asceticism.

braid cutting a rare type of sadism in which a hair fetishist cuts off the hair of the victim. Some psychoanalysts interpret the practice as a symbolic form of castration, involving the reassurance that castration need not be final because the hair will grow back.

brank a medieval device consisting of a helmet with an iron bit or gag with which to restrain the tongue. Branks were formerly employed to punish scolding women, but are now used in 'modern' form in erotic bondage games. Also called scold's bridle.

brass a British slang term for a prostitute, typically one who has seen better days.

breach of promise a breach of marriage contract which may become grounds for a lawsuit if both parties had mutually agreed to enter into marriage and one party refuses to complete the agreement. Laws vary in different communities, but in general a minor may not be held liable in an agreement to marry an adult whereas an adult may be held liable for breaking an agreement to marry a minor. Courtship without a firm commitment to marry is usually not considered grounds for a breach-of-promise suit.

breadwinner a euphemistic term for a prostitute's vagina.

break and enter a slang term referring to anal rape, the term as well as the practice being common in prisons. An alternative term, also in prison slang, is to force-fuck.

breast the mammary gland, the organ located on the surface of the female chest that is concerned with the function of lactation. The term also is used to identify the surface of the chest per se, female or male. See also BAD BREAST; BROKEN BREAST; PENDULANT BREASTS; SUPERNUMERARY BREASTS.

breast amputation an alternative term for mastectomy.

breast augmentation a surgical procedure for enlarging the female breast. The technique, which is performed 75,000 times a year in the United States, involves making an incision in the breast and inserting an implant of polyurethane or silicone gel. A

container of salt solution also may be used as a breast implant. An adverse effect is the tendency for the implant to harden.

breast binder any device applied after mammoplasty to support the female breasts following reconstructive surgery. A breast binder may be a commercial product or a pressure dressing made of standard bandaging materials.

breast complex a psychoanalytical concept based on the idea that the penis becomes a substitute for the mother's breast after weaning. One consequence may be breast envy, which may lead to homosexuality, with the penis of the homosexual and that of his partner unconsciously representing the breast.

breast feeding the process of nourishing an infant during the first months of life by allowing the child to suck human milk through the nipples of the mother's breasts. The infant stimulates the mother's nipple with its mouth, enhancing milk ejection through the nipple. The mother usually finds the nipple stimulation pleasurable; it leads to nipple erection. Some women also report that unexpected sexual sensations are produced by breast feeding. Nursing may also be associated with uterine contractions that have been described as similar to those sometimes experienced during orgasm. The woman may be disturbed by the uncontrollable reaction at first and needs to be assured that the feelings are normal.

breast lift a surgical technique for raising sagging breasts by tightening the skin and other tissues above them. More than 1,000 breast-lift operations per month are performed in the United States.

breast man another term for TITS MAN. See this entry.

breast phantom the feeling that an amputated breast is still there, based upon persistence of an intact body image. The illusion is usually accompanied by tingling, itching, or burning sensations, and in some cases a woman may deny that the breast has been removed.

breast ptosis (tō'sis) a medical term for a drooping female breast. The condition often follows middle age, particularly in women who have breast-fed their children. There is a loss of breast bulk, partly from atrophy, and a loss of elasticity of the breast skin tissue. The condition can be corrected by any of several surgical procedures.

breast reduction a surgical procedure for

reducing the size of the breasts by removing part of the inner tissues. About 35,000 breast-reduction operations are performed annually in the United States.

breast self-examination a procedure for early detection of breast tumours, consisting of palpation of each breast and armpit, usually performed immediately after menstruation. If any lump is felt, it is reported to a physician.

breeder a homosexual slang term for a heterosexual.

brewer's droop a British slang term for the inability to achieve an erection of the penis owing to having consumed too much alcoholic drink.

bridal night the first night a married couple spend together after the wedding, when anticipation is high and the afterglow of the wedding celebration is still having its effect. Studies show, however, that unless the couple have been living together (which is increasingly the case), the sexual relationship may be disappointing for one or both partners, and a period of adjustment may be required.

bridal sheets a term referring to the archaic practice of publicly displaying bloodstained bedsheets on the day after the consummation of marriage, as proof of the bride's premarital virginity.

bride capture marriage by abduction, a declining custom in certain societies, notably the Tikopia of Polynesia. The suitor kidnaps the girl from her father's house, participates in a ritual feast, issues a formal proclamation of marriage, and then forces the girl to consummate the union in public—a form of 'ritual rape.'

bride price money, goods, or property given to the family of the bride by the bridegroom or his family. This custom is found primarily in primitive societies in which the bride herself is regarded as property for which payment must be made. The dowry, which is still found in the West, is an echo of this ancient practice.

bring off a colloquial term meaning to bring to sexual climax.

bristols a slang term for the female breasts, deriving from British rhyming slang 'Bristol Cities' for 'titties' (Bristol City is a Bristol soccer club).

broad a colloquial, often derogatory, American term for a female.

broad-bean soup an alleged aphrodisiac that apparently originated in the Mediterranean area. Long popular in Italy, it was alo

used in Africa where some men claimed it was superior to yohimbe bark as a sexual stimulant.

broad ligament a relatively wide fold of peritoneum that extends from the pelvic wall to the uterus and contains the ovaries, fallopian tubes, and ligaments suspending the reproductive structures.

broken breast a mammary gland that has developed an abscess.

brood cell a cell that divides to produce two or more daughter cells. Also called parent cell; mother cell.

broody an adjective to describe a woman's desire to have a baby.

brothel a house of prostitution; a house or similar in which prostitutes reside and ply their trade either as employees or on a commission basis. Brothels have been traced as far back as the 6th century B.C. in Greece, 650 B.C. in China, the 12th century in Japan, and a little later in Rome, where they were licensed. Attempts were made to abolish them in medieval Europe, but they flourished nevertheless. The term brothel is derived from an Old English word for a worthless person. Also called bawdyhouse.

brother-sister marriages socially recognized exceptions to the universal prohibition against brother-sister marriage. Outstanding examples have been found in the royal families of ancient Egypt, in Hawaii, and among the Incas. Half-sibling and occasional full-sibling marriages occurred among the ancient Persians and Greeks; and among the Balinese and the Aymara of South America, marriage between a twin brother and sister is permitted.

brown boy a slang term for a male who derives sexual gratification from the eating of his or another person's faeces—an extreme case of coprophilia.

brown job a slang term for anilingus.

Brown-Sequard, Edward a 19th-century rejuvenationist who claimed he had restored his own virility with injections of an extract of dog testicles. Brown-Sequard, a French physician, apparently received a small amount of testosterone. However, authorities believe there may have been more of a placebo effect than an actual increase in his own testosterone blood levels.

btm a euphemism for the buttocks, used particularly to children.

bubbies a rather old-fashioned euphemism for the female breasts.

bubble-gum machine a euphemism for a

vending machine for condoms.

buccal intercourse a term occasionally used for oral-genital intercourse, in which the mouth is applied to the male genitals (fellatio) or to the female genitals (cunnilingus). Buccal is derived from the Latin word for 'cheek,' or oral cavity.

buccal onanism archaic term for fellatio, the use of the mouth in sexual stimulation of the penis.

Buck's fascia a sheet of connective tissue that binds the corpora of the shaft of the penis into a single structure. It extends from the glans penis to the bulb of the penis, where it continues as part of the fibres of perineal and related pubic-area muscles.

bud a colloquial term for clitoris.

buggery a legal, and often colloquial, term for sexual analism, or sodomy. The word is derived from 'Bulgarus' because Bulgarian heretics were reputed to practise sodomy at one time. The slang term *bugger* is used as either a noun or a verb.

bulbitis an inflammation of the urethra in the area of the bulb of the penis.

bulb of the penis an enlarged oval part of the corpus spongiosum portion of the penis at its terminus in the lower surface of the perineal membrane. It is a part of the penis that is not observed outside the body of the male and hence is not a part of the body of the penis. Also called *bulb of the urethra.*

bulbospongiosus muscle a muscle that encircles the back of the penis and adjacent parts of the corpus spongiosum and corpus cavernosum. It acts to empty the urethra of urine after the bladder has been emptied, and its fibres also contribute to erection of the penis by compressing the erectile tissue and the deep dorsal vein of the penis during sexual excitement.

bulbourethral pertaining to the bulb of the penis.

bulbourethral glands two small pea-sized glands adjacent to the bulb of the urethra near the prostate gland in the male. They secrete an alkaline fluid into the semen to protect it against the acidity of the urethra and vagina (which could kill the sperm). Also called Cowper's glands.

bulimia nervosa an eating disorder involving repeated episodes of uncontrollable consumption of food (binge eating) followed by self-induced vomiting. Among the causal factors are relief of emotional tension, use of food as a substitute satisfaction when sexually frustrated or disappointed, and an unrecogni-

zed need to escape the risks and responsibilities involved in social and sexual relationships.

bulldyke a slang term for an aggressive lesbian, particularly one who is muscular, has masculine traits, and prefers to play the 'male' role in homosexual relationships.

bullet bubo a hard swelling of the lymphatic glands in the anatomic region of a syphilitic chancre. The name is derived from the size, shape, and firmness of the swelling. Also called syphilitic bubo; indolent bubo.

bull's eye a colloquial term for vagina.

bum a euphemism for the buttocks. It is rarely used in American English, where it more standardly means a tramp or a contemptible person.

bumboy a derogatory slang term for a male homosexual.

bumfuck a vulgar slang term for anal intercourse.

bundling an early American custom of courting in which a man and woman shared a bed but were required to remain fully clothed. In some cases, they also were separated by a board installed between the head and foot of the bed. A practical purpose of bundling was to conserve heat in homes that lacked central heating in winter. A boy and girl were thus allowed to become acquainted in a cold room under warm circumstances. Despite the restrictions, however, pregnancies did result from bundling.

bunny-fuck a vulgar slang term for a 'quickie.' The term is used as a noun or a verb.

buns a colloquial term for (a) the buttocks, (b) the female breasts, (c) the vagina and vulva.

burdock a garden green that has been popular in love potions for at least 500 years. Burdock and goat testicles were recommended in a 14th-century formulation.

bush a colloquial term for the pubic hair, especially a woman's; also, by way of extension, a term referring to the woman herself.

business girl a euphemism for prostitute.

bustle punching a slang term for the male practice of standing very close to women in crowded trains, buses, etc. so as to press their penis against them.

butch a colloquial term for a female homosexual who tends to dress and behave in a masculine manner, and may be employed in a typically male occupation such as lorry driving. She usually but not always takes the active role in sexual relations.

buttered bun a slang term for a woman who has just had sexual intercourse with one man and is about to have it with another.

butterfly a flat, nonpenetrating latex vibrator that is mounted against a woman's pubic area, with straps going around her legs and waist. It may be positioned to give general stimulation or may be directed against the clitoris. It is designed to touch all the erogenous zones simultaneously.

buttfuck a vulgar American slang term for anal intercourse.

buttock the part of the body at the backside of the hip, composed mainly of tissues of the gluteal muscles. The term is derived from the Middle English word *but*, meaning the 'end.' Technically, use of the singular, buttock, refers to one side of the *buttocks*.

button a colloquial term for clitoris.

caesarean section the delivery of a foetus through a surgical incision in the abdomen. The purpose of the procedure is to preserve the life and health of both the mother and the child, particularly when delivery of a foetus through the vaginal birth canal is not feasible. Caesarean delivery has traditionally been an emergency operation, but in recent years the procedure has become increasingly an elective procedure. A contributing factor to the increased popularity of caesarean delivery has been the development of more sophisticated foetal monitoring devices that indicate well in advance that a breech presentation or other type of vaginal or pelvic difficulty may threaten the welfare of the mother or child, or both. There are a half-dozen methods of performing a caesarean delivery, including a total or subtotal hysterectomy, a traditional approach that is still regarded as questionable because of the risk of haemorrhage and damage to other visceral organs. The so-called classic method involves a vertical incision through the abdominal skin, from just above the pubic area to near the umbilicus and then through the wall of the uterus. A third method and one preferred by many experts requires a transverse incision through the skin just below the crease made by the protruding abdomen. It is followed by a vertical incision through the lower uterine segment. This method results in less maternal bleeding and a lower risk of scar rupture later. Still another method, the peritoneal exclusion technique, involves the suturing of the peritoneal layers before an incision is made into the uterus, the objective being to reduce the risk of peritonitis as a result of contamination by fluids or tissues removed in the operation. In addition to the approach of making a transverse incision through the skin, followed by a vertical incision through the wall of the uterus, some surgeons also make a transverse cut through the lower portion of the uterus. (Many believe erroneously that the procedure was named after Julius Caesar, who, according to the legend, was delivered by this method: but it is likely that the term is derived from the Latin word *caedere*, meaning 'to cut.' It is also argued that the caesarean section was instituted by early Christians who wanted to baptize the foetus of a mother who died before or during labour.)

caesarean scar rupture a rupture of the uterus through the scar of a previous caesarean section. The incidence of such ruptures is small, but it tends to occur most often in women who have undergone the classic caesarean procedure in which a vertical incision was made through the abdominal wall and then, also vertically, through the wall of the uterus. The risk also increases with women who have had more than one caesarean operation.

Calderone, Mary Steichen (born 1904) American physician, cofounder of SIECUS (Sex Information and Education Council of the United States) and its executive director and president from 1964 to 1982. Dr. Calderone is the author of many important books about sex and the family and is the recipient of half a dozen honorary degrees and of many distinguished awards for her work in the field of sexuality. Still immensely active in her ninth decade, she holds that 'Children feel and behave sexually from even before birth. They should be allowed to be sexual.' 'You don't have to teach your children to masturbate. Just don't interfere with it.' '...from year 1 to the age of 5, the development of sexual behaviour and thinking will parallel closely with the rapid development of language during the same years.'

calendar method a birth-control method that requires the woman to keep a continuous record of the length of her menstrual cycles over a period of 6 to 9 months, and then to follow a detailed formula for calculating fertile days and 'safe' days. The method is not considered reliable because of possible irregularities in the menstrual cycle.

calf love another term for puppy love.

call boys male homosexual prostitutes with whom appointments are made by telephone. These young men tend to rate higher with their clients than prostitutes who solicit in public.

call girls female prostitutes who accept appointments by telephone. Because these women usually live in well-furnished apartments and do not solicit clients in pubs or on the street, they are considered higher class than 'common prostitutes.' They cater to business and professional men who pay a high price for their services and may take them to dinner to boot.

callomania a pathological delusion of having extraordinary personal beauty.

camp an adjective describing overtly or outrageously effeminate behaviour in a male homosexual. 'To camp it up' means to behave in a camp way.

canal of the epididymis the beginning portion of the epididymis formed by the openings of the spermatozoa ductules of the testis.

Candida albicans a yeastlike fungus commonly found in the genital tract, particularly of women, causing vaginitis, vulvitis, and often thrush. In men—particularly homosexuals—the fungus may occasionally take the form of balanitis, or inflammation of the penis, especially beneath the foreskin.

candida infection an infection of the skin or mucous membranes caused by a yeastlike fungus, usually identified as *Candida albicans*, although other Candida species may be involved. The fungus is normally found in the digestive tract but commonly infects the vagina, particularly in women afflicted with diabetes mellitus because the fungus thrives on carbohydrates. Proliferation of Candida also is encouraged by the use of steroid or antibiotic medications. Symptoms may include a thick vaginal discharge that is irritating and causes itching. Thick, white cheeselike patches form on the vaginal mucosa, and the woman is likely to experience dyspareunia (painful intercourse) with a concomi-

tant loss of interest in sexual activity. See also CANDIDIASIS.

candidiasis a genital infection of the vulva or vagina resulting from *Candida albicans* fungus. The infection may be acute or subacute and marked by a vaginal discharge, pruritus, and vaginal membranes that are inflamed and red but coated with white thrushlike patches. Treatment requires scrupulous cleanliness, application of medication, such as Nystatin, and abstention from sexual intercourse unless the male partner wears a condom. The risk of reinfection by a male partner does exist. See. also CANDIDA INFECTION.

candy pants an American commercial term for edible panties—bikini pants that are made out of sweet material, for example, cherry-flavoured 'fabric' with licorice string ties.

cannibalism a rare sexual disorder, or paraphilia, characterized by a compulsive urge to devour human flesh. This impulse is occasionally observed in psychotic individuals who seek sexual gratification in digging up and mutilating corpses. Some psychoanalysts trace cannibalistic urges and fantasies to fixation at the oral biting stage of psychosexual development.

cannibalistic phase a psychoanalytic term for the second half of the oral stage in which the infant first expresses anger and aggressiveness by biting the mother's breast or the nipple of the bottle during feeding. Fixation at this stage may give rise to impulses or fantasies centring on biting, chewing, or swallowing, later in life.

cantharides (kanther'idēz) a technical name for dried Spanish flies, *Lytta vesicatoria*, which contain a white crystalline substance capable of producing blisters on sensitive human tissues. The chemical, cantharides, has been used medically as a counterirritant and as a scalp stimulator. When taken internally, it produces an irritation of the genitourinary system that is regarded by some as an aphrodisiac effect. See also SPANISH FLY.

cap a rubber contraceptive device which fits over the cervix. See DIAPHRAGM.

capote allemande (käpôt' äləmäNd'; French.' 'German hood') an obsolete euphemism for condom.

capote anglaise (käpôt' äNglās'; French, 'English Hood') an obsolete euphemism for condom—equivalent to the English term 'French letter.'

caput epididymis the head of the epididymis, which is frequently the site of nodules or other causes of epididymitis.

cardinal ligament of the uterus the transverse cervical or Mackenrodt ligaments that suspend the uterus from the walls of the pelvis.

career molester a person who habitually and systematically molests children, usually using deliberate means to find children unknown to him. A career molester often uses a repeated technique to lure children, such as carrying a pet animal to attract a child. The career molester avoids the use of force.

caritas (Latin, 'charity') the Christian idea of brotherly love and the transcendent love of God. Caritas, like the Greek concept of agape, is nonsexual, but also embraces feelings of benevolence.

carnal abuse a form of 'carnal knowledge' in which an adult has genital contact with a child without actual intercourse.

carnal knowledge term for performance of the sex act. For example, a man who has raped a young woman is said to have had carnal knowledge of her.

carpopedal spasm muscular spasms of the hands and feet as generally occurs during orgasm. The stiffened posture of carpopedal spasm is sometimes represented in Oriental erotic art.

caruncula any small piece of torn flesh or fleshy elevation. The term is sometimes applied to protuberances around the vaginal orifice that represent bits of the ruptured hymen of a woman who is no longer a virgin (also called *carunculae hymenales*).

Casanova, Giovanni Giacomo, Chevalier de Seingalt (1725-1798) Italian adventurer, diplomat, historian, mathematician, chemist, composer, playwright, etymologist, but best known for his 12-volume *Memoirs*, because they include frank accounts of his innumerable sexual encounters. Despite his fear of emotional commitment, Casanova (quite unlike the fictitious Don Juan) was not sexually exploitive; he respected the individual personalities of his loves and put emphasis on the spiritual side of a relationship—and this hundreds or thousands of times: a perhaps unparalleled phenomenon not only of sexual prowess but of emotional resources. And, while Casanova was undeniably obsessed with women, he was constantly concerned with intellectual matters, writing dozens of works and befriending or intimately conversing with nearly all the notables of his century (of whom he gives vivid accounts), including Voltaire, Boswell, D'Alembert, Frederick the Great, Benjamin Franklin, Goethe, and Catherine the Great of Russia.

cassolette (French, 'small saucepan,' or 'incense pan') a term sometimes applied to the odour of the vulva, which is sexually stimulating to men. Many women, however, seek to eliminate this natural odour with soap, sprays, and perfume. It is considered a basic component of sexuality in Eastern manuals such as the *Kama Sutra*.

castrati males who were castrated before puberty so that they could be trained to play feminine roles in plays and operas in the 18th century. The tonal quality of the castrati was so pure that the castrated youths were in great demand as performers. Many famous composers of the era wrote operatic parts especially for the voices of the castrati.

castrating woman an epithet sometimes applied to a woman who attempts to emasculate her son or husband psychologically through a domineering, often derogatory, attitude.

castration surgical removal of the sex glands, that is, the testicles in the male or the ovaries in the female. At one time the castration of males was used as a method of sterilization, but it has been replaced by vasectomy. It was also used as a punishment for sex criminals, and still is in some societies. Today the operation is performed in cases of cancer of the testicles, prostate, or ovaries. Its effect on men is to reduce sexual desire, raise the voice level, make the beard sparser, and produce a weight gain. It renders both man and woman incapable of reproduction.

castration anxiety apprehension concerning loss of or injury to the sex organs. Also called *castration fear*.

castration cell a signet-ring shaped cell that is found in the anterior lobe of the pituitary gland of men who have been castrated. Also called signet-ring cell.

castration complex in psychoanalytical theory, the unconscious fear that the genitals will be cut off or damaged as punishment for forbidden sexual desires towards the parent of the opposite sex. In boys, the complex is focussed on loss of the penis, and may be aggravated by threats of castration as punishment for masturbation. In girls, it may take the form of a fantasy that the penis has already been removed as a punishment, for which they blame the mother.

catamenia a medical term for menstruation or menses.

catamite an archaic term for a boy kept for purposes of pederasty, that is, anal intercourse.

catapygon a male homosexual in ancient Greece (Greek *pyge*, 'buttocks').

catasexuality a rarely used term for sexual interest in corpses or in humans with animal-like characteristics.

catheter any hollow tube, made of materials such as rubber, glass, metal, plastic, or fabric, that can be inserted into a body organ or cavity for diagnostic or therapeutic purposes. Most familiar is a urinary catheter that is inserted through the urethra to drain the bladder and prevent the complications of urinary retention, as after surgery. Catheters also are inserted into an arm or leg artery or vein and threaded into heart chambers to diagnose heart diseases and to inject radiopaque substances into the urinary tract for x-ray studies of organs and tissues in the genitourinary tract.

cat house a colloquial term for brothel. See HOUSE.

caul a portion of the foetal membranes that sometimes cover the face and head of the foetus during childbirth. At one time, sailors carried pieces of caul in the superstitious belief that the membrane would protect them from drowning—as it apparently protected the foetus from drowning in amniotic fluid. In reality, the caul must be removed quickly from the face of the foetus so that it can breathe when no longer dependent upon the umbilical cord for oxygen.

cavernitis an inflammation of the erectile tissues of the penis or clitoris. The term is derived from the name of the cylinder of erectile tissue, the corpus cavernosum.

cavernosum pertaining to the corpus cavernosum, the erectile tissue of the penis and clitoris. The term, derived from Latin, means literally 'full of hollow.'

caviar the prolific fish eggs of sturgeon, and other fishes—a dish that is both exotic and erotic, and which is considered an aphrodisiac. In Europe, caviar was not only eaten as a sexual stimulant but as food that presumably would ensure pregnancy as a result of the stimulation. Because of its scarity and price, caviar is regarded as a precious gift from one lover to another.

cavity of the uterus a flat space about 6 centimetres in length extending from the cervical os to the fundus of the interior of the uterus. The cavity loses its flatness when it contains a foetus and placenta. The fundus of the nonpregnant uterus forms the base of a triangle between the two fallopian tube openings, narrowing to an apex at the isthmus of the uterus.

CBI abbreviation for close-binding-intimate, a term applied to mothers who appear emotionally attached to a son, and just one son in a family of several. The mother may appear to favour the son over her husband and use the son to act out imaginary romances. One study found that many homosexuals came from family backgrounds with a *CBI mother*.

CBR abbreviation for crude birth rate.

celery one of the better known alleged aphrodisiac foods, bearing the endorsement of none other than Madame Pompadour. Celery, and particularly celery soup, has been praised in literature for many years as a food that is necessary to maintain, extend, or restore sexual vigour.

celibacy a condition of total abstinence from sexual activity involving another person. Although some religious groups demand total abstinence from any sexual activity, some self-professed celibates admit to masturbation. The practice is frequently associated with holiness, as with Catholic nuns and priests and the vestal virgins of ancient Rome. (Latin *caelebs*, 'unmarried.')

cellular therapy a highly controversial rejuvenation treatment developed in Montreux, Switzerland, by Paul Niehans, whose clientele included kings, popes, Hollywood stars, statesmen, and wealthy businessmen. His technique consisted of injecting cells taken from embryonic sheep which, he believed, would extend the patient's life and prolong all biological functions including sexual activity.

censorship the concept that the law should control what is regarded as obscene. Historically, censorship of sexual relations and attitudes was based on the need to prohibit any practices that tended to limit the population of a culture or community. Ancient Hebrew law forbade adultery, onanism, masturbation, and homosexuality, while at the same time indicating approval of polygamy. Solomon, the ultimate polygamist of Judaeo-Christian culture, was honoured for his many wives and concubines. The ancient Greeks, by contrast, who were less concerned about maintaining a strong population for survival against their enemies, had laws permitting adultery, fornication, male homosexuality, and lesbianism. Obscenity laws followed the development of the printing press and the spread of literacy among the populations of the Western world. The laws originally were intended to control the publishing of political or religious opinions that varied from those of the ruling government, beginning in Venice and Paris and spreading to Britain where an effort was made to control 'mischievous printers and authors.' One of the first recorded cases of censorship on grounds of obscenity in England involved the conviction of Richard Curl, who had published a book entitled *Venus in The Cloister*, in 1725. The determination of what may or may not be obscene has remained an important and controversial issue of public debate and government legislation.

centre of bliss a euphemism for vagina.

centromere the part of a chromosome that is associated with the spindle fibres during cell division. The centromere appears microscopically to function as a belt that holds two chromatids together during the metaphase stage of human cell reproduction.

centrosome a subunit of most but not all animal cells, consisting of a sphere of clear cytoplasm with two centrioles at the centre. The centrosome is usually located in the centre of the cell, near the nucleus. During mitosis, the centrosome divides into two parts which migrate to opposite sides of the dividing cell.

cerebral-type sexual precocity a form of sexual precocity that is linked to an abnormality of the hypothalamus, which controls the release of sex-stimulating hormones by the pituitary gland.

ceremonial defloration a religious rite practised in certain societies of Africa, and in India, where a girl's hymen or maidenhead is ruptured by squatting on a 'lingam,' or artifical penis, which symbolically represents the sex god, Shiva. The ceremony may take place in front of a whole group, and is followed by a celebration. It may also be performed by an older woman, as often occurs in Africa.

cervical canal the spindle-shaped passage through the uterine cervix (neck), particularly the area between the internal cervical os and the external cervical os. It is lined with numerous folds of mucous membrane.

cervical erosion an inflammatory condition of the cervical canal marked by swollen and congested cervical mucosa. The epithelial tissues are altered by the erosion, which usually is the result of a chronic irritation or infection. The condition can be a cause of infertility as the disorder creates an unfavourable environment for movement and survival of spermatozoa.

cervical evaluation a laboratory study of the condition of the cervix and the cervical mucus, usually recommended in cases of infertility. During the preovulation phase, the cervical mucus ranges from dry to a clear, watery, and slippery mucus with increasing spinnbarkeit. During the time of ovulation, cervical mucus is abundant and egg-white in appearance, with spinnbarkeit that ranges between 4 and 10 centimetres. The condition is considered highly favourable for fertilization. Two days after ovulation, the cervical mucus becomes cloudy and sticky, forming a barrier that is impenetrable to sperm. Instead of drying in a fernlike pattern, representative of good spinnbarkeit, the mucus dries in a granular pattern.

cervical-mucus method a birth-control method based on the change in the vaginal mucus from a thick, yellowish discharge to a thin, clear liquid. This change detectable by the woman occurs when ovulation is about to take place, and the chances of impregnation are high.

cervical-os method a birth-control method based on changes in the position and texture of the opening (os) of the cervix. Just before ovulation occurs, the os becomes soft and retreats farther into the vagina. By learning to detect these changes, the woman can tell when ovulation is about to occur.

cervical pregnancy a pregnancy in which the fertilized ovum becomes implanted in the uterine cervix instead of the inner wall of the uterus. A cervical pregnancy is marked by abnormal bleeding and is terminated by surgical removal of the conceptus.

cervicectomy the surgical removal of the uterine cervix.

cervicitis an inflammation of the uterine cervix.

cervicovaginitis an inflammation that involves both the uterine cervix and the vagina.

cervix (Latin, 'neck') the neck of the uterus and a passageway between the uterine cavity and the vagina. In a woman who has never been pregnant, the cervix is almost conical in shape with an external diameter of approximately 1 inch (2.5 cm). It protrudes from the uterus into the vault of the vagina. It has been described as having the firm feel of the tip of a nose. After one or more pregnancies, the cervix acquires lacerations, and the opening, which appears more or less like a small circle before a pregnancy, looks more like a wide slit after one or more births. The cervical lacerations are a source of haemorrhages and infection immediately after delivery. Cancer of the cervix is a major cause of death among women.

C-film a square piece of film containing spermicide used as a method of contraception. The film must be applied to the cervix before it melts. It is not recommended by the Family Planning Association as it is not reliable.

chain sex a group-sex practice in which a number of people engage in sexual contact at the same time; for example, A has intercourse with B while B performs fellatio on C, who engages in cunnilingus with D, etc. They thus become links in what is colloquially called a 'daisy chain.'

chancre an ulcerous lesion usually appearing in the genital area as a sign of a sexually-transmissible-disease infection. A chancre of the lip or tongue may be identified as an extragenital chancre. A concealed chancre may be one that is concealed beneath the foreskin. A hard chancre is usually a sign of syphilis while a soft chancre, or chancroid, is caused by an infection of *Haempophilus ducreyi*, a strain of bacteria.

chancroid a sexually transmitted bacterial disease that is common in the tropics but rare in the United States. It is found more frequently in men than in women, although they may be carriers. The symptoms appear 1 to 5 days after intercourse with an infected person, and consist mainly of swollen lymph glands in the groin and small, painful chancres (inflamed papules and ulcerations) in the genital region. Also called soft chancre; soft sore; ulcus molle.

change of life an alternative for menopause.

charlie an Australian slang term for both a prostitute and a lesbian.

charlies an Australian slang term for the female breasts. It derives from rhyming slang 'Charlie Wheeler' for 'Sheila' (Sheila being Australian slang for 'woman').

chastity the abstention from sexual activity, usually meaning a state of celibacy or virginity. The term also has been applied to avoidance of any type of sexual contact. Historically, the concept of chastity had an economic basis in the sense that a monogamous woman would not become the mother of children fathered by a man other than her hus-

band. The husband, thus, would not be expected to support children other than his own.

The French writer Remy de Gourmont (1858-1915) held that 'Chastity is the most unnatural of the sexual perversions.' This thought is shared by the Nobel Prize winner Anatole France (1844-1924), who wrote: 'Of all sexual aberrations, chastity is the strangest.' Also Aldous Huxley (1894-1963) called chastity 'the most unnatural of the sexual perversions.'

chastity belt a lock-and-key device allegedly worn by some women in the later Middle Ages to cover their genital organs and prevent sexual intercourse during the husband's absence. (Similar devices, sometimes called *chastity corsets*, have been found in the Caucasus, and among the Cheyenne Indians.) There seems to be evidence that chastity belts were never worn but merely represent a hoax, deliberately or unwittingly perpetuated through their exhibition at places like museums and castles.

cheesecake a photographic display of sexually attractive usually scantily-clad women. Compare BEEFCAKE.

chemical balantis an inflammation of the glans penis resulting from irritation by chemicals. A common cause of such irritation is the application of antiseptic medications to the penis, with iodine, phenol, or similar substances.

chemical vaginitis inflammation of the vagina caused by corrosive or irritating chemicals in the treatment of vaginal disorders. A common example is the use of a douche preparation in a strength that is much higher than recommended. The inflammation may be followed by vaginal adhesions and dyspareunia.

cherry a slang term for the hymen—supposedly a sign of virginity.

chicken a colloquial term for a boy prostitute who is patronized by older adolescents and men (*chicken hawks*), usually in a large city.

chicken ranch a brothel, particularly a large isolated one in a rural area.

child abuse a form of child molestation that involves not only physical injury to the child by an adult or adults, as in the battered-child syndrome, but may also include sexual abuse.

childbirth the delivery of an infant at the end of a pregnancy.

childbirth fear an English translation of the technical term maieusiophobia, a pathological fear of giving birth.

childless without children. Currently abut 25 percent of all marriages in the United States are childless because of infertility on the part of the husband, wife, or both. Voluntary childlessness, usually coupled with contraception or abortion, may stem from lack of interest in children, psychological tension, or career goals.

child marriage marriage between an adult (usually male) and a minor (usually female). At one time it was not uncommon for American parents to permit their young daughters to marry older men as a means of providing for their support, but this practice has been curbed by age-of-consent laws, and at present is allowed only in a few states. In India, where child marriage was once quite common, a minimum age of 15 (later 16) was enacted into law in 1955. However, the practice still exists in a few societies such as the Australian aborigines, the Yanomamo of South America, and the Kadar of Nigeria. In most cases, though betrothal or marriage takes place while the girl is very young, even in infancy, sexual consummation does not occur until she reaches puberty.

child molestation sexual abuse of children between infancy and adolescence by such acts as fondling or stroking the child's genitals, exhibitionism, and intercourse. The offence usually consists of brief contact and is distinct from rape or other violent acts, though in some cases it includes incest or anal intercourse. The average age of molesters is 35, and they are usually men (occasionally women) whom the child knows: a family member, a friend of the family, a neighbour, or a child-care worker. The fact that the problem is widespread is now being more generally acknowledged, and several organizations now help children at risk.

child-penis wish the psychoanalytic theory that the little girls' desire for a penis is replaced by their wish to have a child by their own father.

child prostitution a form of prostitution in which children below the age of consent provide sexual services in exchange for money. Most, but not all, are runaways who find themselves desperate for money, and therefore easy prey to pimps and other exploiters who not only promise them a 'cut' but assistance in finding and furnishing a place to live. In a few cases, child prostitutes operate from home or are compelled by their parents to sell their services.

Children's Defense Fund a U.S. organiz-

ation that collects information and publishes periodic reports on teenage pregnancies. In 1982 the number of children born to adolescents in the United States was 523,531, representing 14 percent of all births that year.

chlamydia an infectious disease caused by the organism *Chlamydia trachomatis*. Initial symptoms (which may occur in both sexes) include a simple infection, accompanied by mild pain and a minor discharge. If the disease continues to develop in a woman, it may result in infertility in some cases; but if pregnancy does occur, the disorder may pose a serious threat to the foetus and newborn infant, producing lung and eye infections.

Recent statistics indicate that chlamydia infection is the fastest-growing sexually transmitted disease in the United States, with an estimated 3 million new cases per year.

Chlamydia trachomatis an organism that may cause several sexually transmitted diseases, especially chlamydia, lymphogranuloma venereum, nonspecific urethritis, and nongoncoccal urethritis. Various strains may also cause salpingitis, trachoma, inclusion conjunctivitis (eye infection in a newborn), proctitis, and sterility in some 11,000 women annually. Antibiotics are usually prescribed when chlamydia pus cells are found in the urethra.

chloasma gravidarum temporary pigment changes that occur in women during pregnancy, such as skin colour alterations of the face, abdominal area, and nipples.

chocolate probably the original alleged aphrodisiac of the Western Hemisphere. Aztec Emperor Montezuma reportedly consumed 50 cups of chocolate a day for its reputed sexual stimulation. The scientific name, *theobroma*, translates literally as 'food of the gods.' By the 18th century, the aphrodisiac reputation of chocolate had spread over Europe and North America. Today, a gift of chocolate has replaced the valentine as a symbol of love.

chocolate cysts small cysts of endometrial tissue in the ovaries. The colour is the result of blood produced during the hormonal cycles that affect endometrial tissue in the lining of the uterus, where it normally occurs. Ectopic or misplaced endometrial tissue may be found in more than 20 areas of the female body, from the umbilicus to the perineum.

chorda spermatica a Latin term for spermatic cord.

chorda umbilicalis a Latin term for umbilical cord.

chordee (kō′dā) a painful condition of the penis that becomes bent at an angle during erection. It may be caused by an anomalous tendon that pulls the shaft of the penis laterally or downwards. The condition may also result from a gonorrhoeal infection involving the corpus spongiosum or the corpora cavernosa. Chordee associated with abnormal fibrous tissue along the shaft may also occur with hypospadia, requiring surgical correction.

chorditis an inflammation of the spermatic cord. In acute chorditis, the ductus deferens may be tender and swollen, usually as a secondary effect of an infection or other disorder that has spread from neighbouring structures. In chronic chorditis, the ductus deferens may be thickened and hard or fibrous with beadlike nodules along its length, the result usually of syphilis or tuberculosis.

chorea gravidarum a disorder of pregnancy in some women characterized by irregular involuntary movements that may involve any muscles except those of the eyes. The woman may feel clumsy and have trouble in dressing or feeding herself. The condition usually occurs in the first trimester of the first pregnancy and follows a pattern similar to that caused by a streptococcal infection. The same effects have occurred in some women using oral contraceptives.

chorioangioma a tumour that can develop in the uterus from placental tissues. It evolves from blood capillaries of the placenta and may appear as a solitary red nodule in the placenta. It is not cancerous.

choriocarcinoma a cancerous tumour that develops in the uterus. A choriocarcinoma commonly follows the formation of a hydatidiform mole, but also may develop after an abortion.

chorion a double-membrane structure that forms a protective covering for the fertilized ovum. It becomes the outer layer of foetal membranes, the amnion serving as the inner layer.

chorionepithelioma a tumour that orginates in the uterus and spreads to the vagina where it appears near the cervix as a clump of purple wartlike tissue. It bleeds easily, and the blood accounts for its coloration. The presence of the growth in the vagina often is the first clue to the presence of uterine cancer.

chorion frondosum the villi of the chorion that represent the foetal portion of the future placenta. The villi extend into the decidua basalis, thereby tapping into the sources of nourishment for the embryo.

chorionic-gonadotropin-hormone test a human pregnancy test based on the presence of a specific subunit of a human chorionic gonadotropin molecule in the blood. With this test, it is possible to predict within 98 to 100 percent accuracy a pregnancy within 6 to 8 days after conception.

chorionic villi the fingerlike projections from the surface of the blastocyst that reach into the blood and glycogen-rich lining of the uterus at the time of implantation. The outer surface will evolve into the chorion, the outer layer of the placental membranes, hence the name of the blastocyst structures.

chorionic-villi sampling a technique used to detect chromosomal defects in an unborn child. The technique depends upon a biopsy sampling of a bit of placenta obtained through the cervix of the mother rather than by drawing a sample of amniotic fluid, as in amniocentesis. Advantages of chorionic biopsy are that the test can be performed as early as the eighth week of gestation and that results are available a day later, whereas amniocentesis is not performed before the fifteenth week and the results usually are not available until 3 weeks later. The risk of miscarriage resulting from chorionic biopsy, however, is substantially higher than when tissue sampling is done by amniocentesis.

chorionitis an inflammation of the chorion membrane of the placenta, which may result from a viral, bacterial, or other infection.

chromosomal disorders rare disorders resulting from abnormal chromosome patterns. The most common symptom in these disorders is mental retardation, usually severe. In addition, practically all cases are afflicted with physical anomalies: XXXX females may have minor physical defects, but menstruate and can bear children; the extremely rare XXXXX syndrome involves ocular anomalies, microcephaly, and abnormalities of the limbs; XXXXY males are characterized by abnormally small genital organs, a short, broad neck, and muscular hypotonia (weakness); XXXY males have a normal penis but small testes and prostate, and about half develop enlarged breasts; XXYY males are born with skeletal deformities and genital anomalies, and later develop enlarged breasts and eunuchoid abdominal and hip fat; and XYY cases are physically and intellectually normal but were once thought to have criminal tendencies as a result of the presence of an extra Y chromosome—but later studies have cast doubt on this theory, because the same abnormal pattern has been found in many normal, nonviolent males.

chromosomal gender the normal sex-chromosome combination that determines genetic gender, as XX for a female and XY for a male.

chromosome the nuclear material of a cell, consisting of coiled strands of deoxyribonucleic acid (DNA) molecules. The chromosome also contains ribonucleic acid (RNA) and chemicals called histones and nonhistone proteins. Chromosomes carry the genes, or hereditary traits, of the individual. For a given individual, all the specifications for every structure and function are contained in the codes formed by sequential arrangement of four molecules within the DNA molecule. The four subunits, called nucleotide bases, are adenine, cytosine, guanine, and thymine. The four bases are believed to serve as four character codes from which genetic information is derived according to the 'words' formed by the linkages of the bases. Because of the various possible arrangements of the nucleotide bases and sequences of arrangements, any trait of any living organism can be accounted for by the nucleotide templates of chromosomes.

chromosome map a graphic representation of a chromosome showing the location and arrangement of various genes and their relative distances from each other.

chronic hyperoestrogenism a continued excessive level of oestrogen, a female sex hormone, in a man. The condition is one of the most common causes of gynaecomastia, or abnormal breast enlargement in a male. It may result from treatment with certain drugs that may have an oestrogenic influence on the male body.

chronic hyperexcitability of the penis another term for satyriasis.

cicatrization the process of decorating the skin with scars deliberately produced by knife wounds. The practice is found particularly among dark-skinned peoples, as in the Sudan.

cicisbeism a 'ménage à trois' practice in which a sexually dissatisfied wife arranges to have an official lover (Italian *cicisbeo*), with the cognizance of her husband. The custom was not uncommon among society families in Italy during the 17th to 19th centuries.

cilia the minute hairlike projections on the inside of the fallopian tube. Their function is to help sweep the ovum along towards the uterus. The fallopian tube also contains both circular and longitudinal muscle fibres which can produce a peristaltic, wavelike motion to assist in the transport of the ovum.

cinaedus the most common term in ancient Rome for a male homosexual.

cinnamon a spice prepared from the bark of any of several related trees of the *Cinnamomum* genus. Some spice that is marketed as cinnamon is actually cassia, a close cousin of true cinnamon. Whatever the true vintage, cinnamon has been cited as an aphrodisiac in poems, plays, and ballads since ancient times.

circle jerk a group of men in a circle with each one masturbating his neighbour or with each one masturbating himself.

circumcision surgical removal of the foreskin, or prepuce, of the penis, for hygienic, medical, or religious reasons. The operation is usually performed on the second day after birth, and in traditional Jewish families on the eighth day after birth. In some societies, however, circumcision is a puberty rite and a prerequisite for marriage. The practice dates back to the Egyptians, and it is estimated that over half of all men living today have been circumcised. In one type of procedure, the foreskin is pulled forwards over the glans and slit so that it can be retracted behind the glans. The prepuce is then pulled forwards again and held with a clamp while the excess tissue is excised with a scalpel. An alternative method uses a Yellen clamp, a cone-shaped device that slips over the end of the glans penis while the foreskin is sutured and pulled over the surface of the cone toward the vertex, where pegs on either side are used to anchor the other ends of the sutures. The foreskin is held in that position for several minutes to reduce circulation in the foreskin and thus diminish the risk of bleeding. The part of the foreskin over the cone is then removed with a scalpel. A yellowish thick fluid appears on the glans for several days, but it is not a sign of infection and no special effort is made to remove it immediately.

circumcision clamp any of several clamping devices applied to the foreskin to hold it in a specific position while cuts are made with a scalpel. An example is the Yellen clamp. See also FEMALE CIRCUMCISION.

cissy a derisive term applied to an effeminate boy or man who apparently identifies with females rather than males. A so-called cissy avoids rough-and-tumble activities, aggressive sports, and rowdiness, which are still associated with masculinity in the Western world. Instead, he prefers quieter and gentler activities such as artwork, knitting, and cooking. Little if any evidence can be found that most effeminate boys are basically homosexual.

cisvestism a term coined by Magnus Hirschfeld for the practice of wearing inappropriate clothes that have sexual significance. Male homosexual sadomasochists, for example, may dress up as cowboys, policemen, marines, or motorcyclists with leather jackets and boots (even though they may not own a motorcycle).

civilian a homosexual slang term for a heterosexual.

clap a slang term for gonorrhoea.

clap thread a slender filament composed of mucus, white blood cells and tissue cells that is extruded from the urethra of a person with chronic gonorrhoea.

cleavage the division of the zygote after fertilization and before the stage of blastulation. Cleavage usually begins on the second day of gestation and continues until the future human consists of a tiny ball of 16 blastomeres. It is during the cleavage stage that monozygotic multiple births begin with the separation of blastomeres.

Cleavage is also the division between the female breasts, especially as revealed by a low-cut neckline.

cleidorrhexis a procedure that has been used in child delivery in which the shoulder bones are fractured to reduce the diameter of the foetus at the level of the shoulders, thereby making delivery through the birth canal possible.

climacteric the pattern of physical and psychological changes that occur in women during the menopausal period when menstrual flow gradually diminishes and reproductive capacity declines and finally ceases. The changes occur over a period of 2 to 3 years between the ages of 40 and 55, and include more or less severe reactions such as hot flushes, chills, palpitations, irritability, depression, and fatigue. Some men also undergo a similar period about 10 years later—the so-called male menopause—during which they react to reduced sex-steriod production by experiencing decreased sexual desire and potency, as well as such symptoms as flushes, fatigue, and in some instances depression and a desperate attempt to prove

their sexual capacity. Also called climacterium.

climacteric melancholia a term occasionally applied to depressive symptoms in women, and sometimes men, developed during the climacteric period.

climacteric psychosis an alternative term for involutional psychotic reaction or involutional psychosis.

climax orgasm; or the peak of sexual excitement during intense orgasm. It may be manifested by carpopedal muscle spasms and vocal utterances ranging from screams or groans to meaningless monologues or crying jags. The expressions of sexual excitement generally last longer than the orgasm itself.

climbing a colloquial term for an unusual coital position in which one partner is supported on the erect body of the other, and appears to be mounting that partner while copulating.

clipping a British term for the practice of posing as a prostitute but absconding without providing the services paid for.

clitoral hood the prepuce of the clitoris that forms a cap over the glans from external fold tissues of the labia minora. In a prepubertal girl, the clitoral hood may be afflicted with adhesions between the prepuce and the glans clitoris, a condition that may result in inflammation and a local abscess. The condition disappears spontaneously in most cases after puberty, but before that period it may require surgery.

clitoral hypertrophy an enlargement of the clitoris, which may be associated with precocious puberty or a similar abnormal effect of sex-hormone production.

clitoral orgasm an orgasm induced by direct stimulation of the clitoris, the main source of sexual excitement and pleasure in the human female. The clitoris may be stimulated manually by the partner or by the woman herself, by the contact and motion of the penis, by the partner's tongue or mouth, by an object introduced into the vagina, or by an instrument such as a vibrator.

clitoral stimulation stimulation of the clitoris as a means of increasing sexual excitement. The clitoris normally is quite sensitive to tactile stimulation, containing a nerve net that is three times as large as that of the penis in proportion to its size. Because the prepuce of the clitoris is a part of the labia minora, stimulation of the labia minora may have the same effect as direct stimulation of the clitoris.

clitoridectomy the surgical removal of the clitoris. The procedure was relatively common in the past when it was assumed that a girl with an enlarged clitoris might become sexually active. Clitoral amputation may be performed today for cosmetic reasons in a case of clitoral enlargement, because of a disorder of continuous clitoral erection, or as a result of a neoplasm or other serious medical problem involving the clitoris. In the 19th century, clitoridectomy was used as a means of controlling masturbation and nymphomania (with dubious effect), and in many African societies, Islamic groups, and among the Pano Indians of Ecuador this form of genital mutilation is being practised as a social or initiation rite. The reason for this male-imposed cruelty is often the (largely mistaken) belief that the absence of the clitoris will prevent a woman from experiencing orgasm—which is considered the male prerogative.

clitoriditis an inflammation of the clitoris. Also called clitoritis.

clitoridotomy the surgical excision of the prepuce of the clitoris, a procedure equivalent to circumcision of the male.

clitoris an erectile organ of the female external genitalia that is homologous with the male penis. It is partly concealed by the labia minora, but a free extremity appears as a rounded tubercle. It is composed of two corpora cavernosa held in a fibrous membrane and, like the penis, provided with a suspensory ligament and two small muscles. The term clitoris was not in use before the 17th century; in fact, Shakespeare and the Elizabethans had no word for this organ. (Greek *kleiein*, 'to shut, close.')

clitorism the prolonged erection of the clitoris, a painful and dangerous condition similar to priapism in the male. Because of the disruption of normal blood circulation to the clitoral area, the tissue cells may die. The condition is associated with the female practice of tribadism.

clitorize a seldom used term meaning to masturbate—said of a woman.

clitoromania an alternative term for nymphomania.

clitoromegaly a medical term for an enlarged clitoris, usually caused by an excessive level of male sex hormone in a woman.

clitty a colloquial term for clitoris.

cloaca (Latin, 'sewer') a common urogenital and rectal opening found in the human embryo and in the adult stage of some lower animals. A cloaca may persist in some humans as a congenital anomaly in which the bladder, rectum, and vagina share a common opening.

cloaca theory the Freudian doctrine that very young children fantasize that babies are born through the anal aperture, following the same course as faeces, and that both sexes can perform this function.

clomiphene-stimulation test a pituitary-hormone test employed to determine gonadotropic function in males. Clomiphene, a chemical analogue of oestrogen, is administered to a male who shows signs of abnormal sexual development. Ordinarily, clomiphene stimulates the release of follicle-stimulating hormone and luteinizing hormone by the pituitary gland. If the gonadotropic hormones are not secreted, the results are interpreted as indicating a disorder in either the pituitary gland or in the hypothalamus, which stimulates or inhibits the release of the pituitary hormones through an oestrogenic negative feedback system. The cause frequently is found to be a pituitary tumour.

clone organisms or groups of cells that are genetically identical because they are derived from the same organism or cell. Clones may develop from sexual reproduction methods, such as mitosis. Monozygotic twins would be considered clones. (Greek *klon*, 'slip, twig'.) See also HUMAN CLONING.

clonic spasm alternate contractions and relaxations of muscles, as in the urogenital floor muscles that aid in the process of semen ejaculation by the male.

closed swinging extramarital sex in which the husbands and wives trade partners who pair off and go to a separate site to have intercourse in privacy. The couples usually agree to return to a particular place at a certain time so that the husbands and wives can return home with their own spouses.

closet, come out of the to acknowledge openly one's homosexuality—no longer being 'in the closet.'

closet queen a slang term for (a) a male who dresses in female clothing, and who is usually a secret transvestite, or (b) a male who has homosexual sex but tells himself, and sometimes others, that he is not a homosexual.

clothing and sexuality a term referring to the capacity of certain types of clothing to stimulate sexual fantasy and excitement. The revealing costumes of 'bunny girls,' can-can dancers, belly dancers, and topless and bottomless waitresses, as well as slit skirts, bikinis, and skin-tight jeans (on men and women) are familiar examples. It is a well-known fact that partial nudity is more sexually provocative than complete nudity. Less familiar examples of suggestive practices are decorated codpieces, penis sheaths, and pubic wigs.

clubbing an abnormal condition of a fallopian tube that follows a course of chronic inflammation resulting in a closure of the open end of the tube. The fimbriae may fuse to form a solid club-shaped end to the fallopian tube, or there may be a small dimple, or navel, to mark the original opening.

club sandwich a slang term for a sex act in which a woman lies between two men.

clumping test for pregnancy a test based on the presence of chorionic gonadotropin hormone that is found in a woman's urine 10 to 14 days after conception. A sample of urine is mixed with chemicals that will form a clumping precipitate if she is not pregnant. The test also is called agglutination test.

cluster-fuck party a vulgar slang term for orgy.

cluster marriage an unconventional lifestyle in which several married couples live together and have sexual access to each other.

Clytemnestra complex an emotional pattern in which a wife kills her husband in order to 'possess' one of his male relatives. The complex is based on a classical myth in which Clytemnestra fell in love with the cousin of her husband, Agamemnon, then killed Agamemnon, and was herself later killed by her son, Orestes.

cobblers a British slang term for testicles, deriving from rhyming slang 'cobbler's awls' for 'balls.' Nowadays it is more commonly used as an expletive meaning 'Nonsense!' than literally as 'testicles.'

cock a vulgar slang term for penis. The term ranks number 7 in the TABOONESS RATING OF DIRTY WORDS. See this entry.

cockeater a vulgar slang term for fellator or fellatrix.

cocksman a vulgar slang term for a man who is obsessed with copulating with as many women and as often as possible, and who usually thinks of himself as possessing great sexual prowess.

cocksucker a vulgar slang term for a fellator or a fellatrix; also, a derogatory term for a person held in contempt. The term ranks number 2 in the TABOONESS RATING OF DIRTY WORDS. See this entry.

cock teaser a vulgar slang term for a woman who acts as though she wants sex but has

no real intention of following through with the act. A colloquial abbreviation is C.T.

codpiece a bag or flap hiding the opening in front of men's hose in the 15th and 16th centuries (*cod*, 'testis,' and *pese*, 'piece'). The term became also a euphemism for the penis itself.

cofactors other viruses that are frequently present in AIDS patients and which complicate diagnoses and studies of the condition. Cofactor viruses include cytomegalovirus (CMV), hepatitis-B virus, and the Epstein-Barr virus that is associated with certain cancers and forms of herpes infections. See also AIDS.

cohabitation the act of living together in one domicile as applied to a man and a woman who may or may not be married, and also to homosexuals who live with each other. The term implies the performance of intercourse. See also LASCIVIOUS COHABITION.

cohabitation contract a legal document in which sexual partners living together although unmarried agree as to certain specified rights and responsibilities of their arrangement, such as proportions to be paid by each partner towards rent or other expenses. The terms and legal costs are similar to those of a prenuptial agreement.

coil a contraceptive device in the form of a coil, inserted by a physician in the uterine cavity, where it prevents the fertilized egg from implanting itself in the uterine wall.

coit a colloquial term meaning to perform coitus.

coital anisertia an inability to insert the penis into the vagina, for whatever reason.

coital death death as a result of a heart attack or respiratory failure experienced during intercourse, an event that occurs (very rarely) among male coronary patients who engage in prolonged and highly active intercourse involving fatiguing coital positions whch raise the heartbeat and blood pressure to an excessive peak. In one study of 34 fatalities, 27 occurred during or after extramarital intercourse.

coital frequency usually, the frequency with which married couples have intercourse per week. Kinsey and his associates found that the age of the husband is a major factor, and reported an average frequency of four times per week between 15 and 20 years of age, three times at the age of 30, two at the age of 40, and slightly less than one at 60. The range of individual differences was found to be large, with some younger husbands reporting more than 30 copulations per week. Ford and Beach report that in most of the societies studied by anthropologists the average for adults is once a day, ranging from once a week among the Keraki of New Guinea to three to fives times nightly among the Aranda of Australia and the Thonga of Africa, and as many as 10 times a night for the polygamous Chagga of Tanzania.

coital gamesmanship the use of intercourse for nonsexual purposes, such as an expression of dominance or self-esteem.

coital movements movements performed during intercourse. Male and female movements can both be extremely varied, but in general the basic 'pelvic thrusts' begin with slow, shallow penetration on the part of the man and become progressively deeper and faster, with or without temporary withdrawal and rotation. Simultaneously, or shortly after, the woman's thrusts begin to follow the same general pattern. Some partners follow a regular rhythm, such as nine shallow thrusts followed by one deep thrust, but this is not common. With practice, pleasure can be prolonged by withholding orgasm, and some couples prefer simultaneous, or mutual, orgasm to separate orgasms.

coital positions a variety of positions assumed during intercourse for purposes of enhancing or maintaining sexual pleasure and excitement, novelty, interest, or comfort, or improving or reducing the chances of conceiving. Different positions are found to have different advantages, and there is no single 'perfect' position, although the 'missionary position' (man above) is most common. Varying the position can not only combat monotony but is a way of discovering preferences of both partners. One investigator attempted a complete inventory, and came up with 521, many of which are only slight variations of common erotic postures such as face-to-face, man or woman above, side-by-side, sitting, standing, kneeling, and rear entry. Also called coital postures; intercourse positions; figurae veneris.

coition an Anglicized form of the Latin word coitus.

coitophobia an intense, pathological fear of intercourse.

coitus an act of intercourse usually but not always involving penetration of the penis into the vagina. The term is derived from the Latin coire, 'to go together.' Also called coition; copulation; intercourse, sexual intercourse.

See also ANAL COITUS; ORAL COITUS; PERINEAL COITUS; STANDING COITUS.

coitus à la vache (ä lä väsh; French, 'in cow fashion') heterosexual intercourse in which the woman assumes the knee-chest position and the man kneels behind her and enters the vagina from the rear.

coitus analis a Latin term for anal intercourse.

coitus ante portas (Latin, 'coitus before the door') intercourse or sex play in which the penis is wedged between the woman's thighs instead of penetrating the vagina. This method is common among adolescents as a contraception technique (which does not always work) or as a way of preventing rupture of the hymen. It is also used by male homosexuals. Also called interfemoral intercourse; coitus inter femora; intracrural intercourse.

coitus a tergo (Latin, 'coitus from behind') heterosexual intercourse from the rear, as in coitus à la vache. Also called coitus a posteriori.

coitus condomatus intercourse with the use of a condom.

coitus fear another term for coitophobia.

coitus in ano (Latin, 'coitus in the anus') anal intercourse. Also called coitus per anum; coitus in anum; coitus analis.

coitus in axilla (Latin, 'coitus in the armpit') intercourse in which the penis is inserted in the armpit of the partner.

coitus incompletus an alternative term sometimes used for coitus interruptus or withdrawal, a doubtful contraceptive technique in which the penis is withdrawn before ejaculation.

coitus in os (Latin, 'mouth coitus') another term for fellatio, especially if ejaculation takes place inside the mouth.

coitus inter femora another term for coitus ante portas.

coitus interruptus withdrawal of the penis from the vagina just before ejaculation. This is the oldest method of contraception, and is mentioned in the Book of Genesis. The failure rate is above 15 percent because withdrawal may not be complete and semen may be emitted before orgasm.

coitus intra mammas (Latin, 'coitus between breasts') intercourse in which the penis is inserted between the woman's breasts, which she may hold together with her hands. Also called coitus intermammarius.

coitus more ferarum (môr′ə ferä′rōōm; Latin, 'coitus in the manner of beasts') an obsolete term for intercourse from the rear.

coitus oralis an obsolete term for fellatio or coitus in os.

coitus prolongatus prolonged coitus; also, coitus reservatus, such as Karezza.

coitus representation the psychoanalytic view that the act of intercourse may be represented or symbolized by unconscious behaviour such as the movements of the tongue in stuttering or the rise and fall of the voice in singing.

coitus reservatus deliberate suppression of orgasm in the male, achieved through practice in approaching ejaculation without completing it. The technique has long been practised in the Orient as a means of achieving the equivalent of many orgasms. An opium paste is sometimes applied to the penis to reduce its sensitivity. The technique was also practised in the 19th-century Oneida community, where young men were often trained in continence by older women. Also called coitus prolongatus.

coitus saxonicus a method of avoiding unwanted pregnancy, in which the male squeezes the root of his penis just before orgasm so that the semen flows back, into the bladder. It is named after the Saxons, who favoured this practice.

coitus sine ejaculatione a type of intercourse in which penile erection is normal but ejaculation of semen fails to occur. The cause is generally an organic disorder and a sign of male infertility. The condition should not be confused with impotence, or with coitus reservatus in which ejaculation does not occur because it is suppressed.

coitus wheel a coital position in which one partner is bent backwards in a circular manner.

cold bath an ancient anaphrodisiac still viewed as a method of decreasing sexual desire. Actually, the idea of taking a cold bath to reduce one's sexual drive was recommended by Plato and Aristotle. The notion also has been given as a source of the old masculine argument that to prevent infidelity a woman should be barefoot in winter or pregnant, the cold feet being the equivalent of a cold shower.

cold punch a method of removing obstructive tissue in the prostate area by a transurethral surgical approach. A metal tube containing a sharp knife blade is inserted through the male urethra from the end of the penis and as far as the urinary bladder. The end of the instrument contains a light and a lens so that the surgeon can see the inside of the bladder and the tubular knife as it snips off bits of tissue. The bits of prostate tissue fall back into the bladder and may be removed by applying suction through the tube.

collaborative victim a term applied to victims of sex offences in which there is evidence, particularly among children, that they did not resist the offender.

colliculitis an inflammation of the seminal colliculus of the male.

colliculus seminalis a small elevation in the wall of the prostatic portion of the male urethra. It is the site of the openings of the prostatic utricle, a vestigial cul de sac, and the ejaculatory ducts. Also called urethral crest.

colpitis a alternative term for vaginitis, or inflammation of the vagina. The word may be modified by another identifying the cause of the condition, as *colpitis mycotica*, for a fungal infection of the vagina. (Greek *kolpos*, 'vagina.')

colpocystitis an inflammation that involves both the vagina and the urinary bladder.

colpopathy any disease of the vagina.

colpopoiesis a Greek word meaning literally the making of a vagina. The term is applied to the plastic surgery techniques of constructing an artificial vagina.

colposcope a device used to examine the interior of the vagina and the surface of the cervix.

colpotomy any surgical incision into the vaginal tissues, as in colpoplasty to correct vaginal disorders by plastic surgery techniques.

combination pill oral contraceptive containing both an oestrogen and a progestogen to mimic the normal female menstrual cycle.

come a Shakespearean euphemism meaning to have an orgasm which is now in general use. Shakespeare also used 'to come over' in the sense of 'to have sexual intercourse.' As a current slang term, 'come' is also used as a noun, referring to the ejaculate. Also spelled cum.

come freak a homosexual slang term for a person who is extremely fond of performing fellatio.

coming out a term used by homosexuals of both sexes to indicate that they no longer conceal their homosexuality. *Coming out of the closet* implies that they have accepted themselves and, in most cases, have publicly disclosed their sexual orientation.

commasculation an obsolete term for male-male intercourse.

commoner a homosexual slang term for a heterosexual.

common-law marriage a form of marriage between a man and a woman based on an agreement to live together as man and wife without a civil or religious ceremony. In some U.S. states, after a certain number of years, they may be considered legally married, although the burden of proof rests with the claimant on such legal rights as inheritance, alimony, 'palimony,' and pensions.

commune an alternative life-style in which individuals of both sexes pool their resources and share such tasks as preparation of food, household chores, child rearing, do-it-yourself activities, and food production. Sexual sharing may or may not be part of communal living.

community-producing deviance a type of activity that is usually regarded as illegal or immoral because it involves the mores of the community rather than an individual or consenting couple in a sexual activity. An example is operation of a house of prostitution.

companionate marriage a controversial form of marriage advocated by Judge Ben Lindsay of Denver in 1927, and recommended by Bertrand Russell and Havelock Ellis. The concept was presented as a means of recognizing already-existing relationships among young people and as a means of avoiding failures in the selection of marriage partners. It was based upon the legalized practice of birth control, the right of childless couples to a divorce by mutual consent, and renunciation of any financial claim by both parties.

complete Oedipus the presence of both a positive and negative Oedipus situation—that is, a child may simultaneously have an incestuous desire for the mother and at the same time identify with the father, and may also desire the father while identifying with the mother.

complete precocity precocious puberty in a male in which there are interstitial-cell tumours in both testicles. In the complete-precocious-puberty case, the male-sex-hormone levels are excessive for the age of a prepubescent male and in many cases may be at levels normally found in an adult man.

complex literally, an 'embrace.' The word was introduced by Neisser as a psychological term in 1906 and was made popular by Freud and Jung. See also COMPLICATED.

complicated literally, 'in embrace,' especially sexual embrace—an older mean-ing of the word (from Latin *com-*, with and *plicare*, 'to fold'). John Donne wrote, in 1631: '... enwrapped and complicated in sin.' See also COMPLEX.

Compound S an antiviral drug developed in Britain by the Wellcome Foundation, as a potential cure for AIDS. Early test results indicated that Compound S may cause liver damage and bone-marrow suppression but that it can cross the blood-brain barrier to attack pockets of infection in the brain, which other experimental AIDS drugs are unable to do. See also AIDS.

comprehensive physician a slang term for proctologist—who sees his patient as a (w)hole. See also REAR ADMIRAL.

compulsive masturbation an obsessive urge to masturbate even in the absence of sexual feeling or gratification. The individual is usually unaware of his or her motivation, which may be to substitute this activity for missing social satisfactions, to compensate for shyness and inability to establish heterosexual relationships, or to relieve inner tension or anxiety.

compulsive sexual activity a persistent, irresistible impulse to engage in sexual acts, whether or not these acts lead to full gratification.

conception union of an ovum, or egg cell, with a spermatozoon, resulting in the start of a new life. Once the ovum is fertilized, no other sperm can penetrate its cell wall. Also called fertilization; impregnation. See also MAGNETIC CONCEPTION.

conceptional weeks a term referring to a system of calculating the length of a pregnancy from the approximate date of conception, or 38 weeks. Using conceptional weeks, the second trimester begins 12 2/3 weeks after conception. The differences between conceptional and menstrual weeks is sometimes important in determining when an abortion and what type of abortion may be performed.

conception ratio the proportion of Y to X chromosomes in sperm, about 160 to 100, that succeed in fertilizing an ovum in the fallopian tube. The numbers of X and Y sperm produced by the testis are presumed to be equal.

conceptive capable of conceiving, or of becoming pregnant.

conceptus the products of conception, including the embryo or foetus, the foetal membranes, the amniotic fluid, and the foetal portion of the placenta.

concubine a woman who cohabits (lives and has intercourse) with a man to whom she is not legally married; a mistress, or secondary wife. *Concubinage* is mentioned in the Old Testament and has been a common custom of wealthy Muslims and Turkish Sultans. (Latin *concubitus*, 'lying together.')

concupiscencia (Latin, 'lust') a term referring to an early Christian belief that sex is the root of all evil since the fall of Adam and Eve. Saint Augustine, who helped promote the concept of sex as a sinful act, believed that intercourse between husband and wife was evil and children were begotten 'by lust.' Some observers have noted that Augustine probably overreacted to guilt feelings about his own youthful escapades, much as some leaders of more recent antipornography campaigns have been found to be overreacting to guilt feelings about their own sexual activities.

condom a contraceptive device used by males consisting of a thin rubber or gut sheath that is drawn over the erect penis before intercourse. Though used primarily to prevent conception, condoms may also be used to prevent venereal infection (and are therefore often called prophylactics), as well as for the control of premature ejaculation, because they usually slow up the orgasm. The failure rate from tearing, slippage, or bursting is nearly 15 percent. Among the many colloquial terms for condom are French letter and, in American English, rubber.

The device is occasionally referred to in a figurative sense. Over a hundred years ago, Gustave Flaubert wrote: 'Let us always have a vast condom within us to protect the health of our soul amid the filth into which it is plunged.'

condylomata acuminata another term for genital warts.

conflict-habituated referring to a type of male-female sexual relationship that appears superficially hostile but which can actually be exciting, compatible, and .satisfying because the apparent hostility is a part of the couple's own mating dance or sex scenario.

confinement a technical and now rather dated term for the time preceding and during childbirth.

congenital existing at birth. The term is applied to constitutional tendencies and predispositions or defects acquired during prenatal development, or during the birth process, and is used by some authorities to include genetic, or inherited, conditions as long as they are present at birth.

congenital adrenal hyperplasia a condition of adrenal gland overgrowth that is one of the causes of sexual precocity. The condition can result in pseudohermaphroditism in a girl but produces no gross abnormalities in boys. However, the boy usually has an excessively large penis for a child and the penis may continue to increase in size, and pubic hair may appear during childhood. But pituitary-gonadotropin secretion remains suppressed so that the testicles remain at an infantile stage.

congenital hypertrophy of the verumontanum an overgrowth of tissue of the verumontanum, in the floor of the male urethra near the prostate. It develops from remnants of the embryonic mullerian ducts. This congenital disorder is attributed to an excess of female sex hormones during the foetal stage. The hypertrophy can block the urethra, causing bladder distention and, if not treated early, kidney damage and death.

congenital syphilis a form of syphilis that is acquired by a foetus in the uterus of a mother infected by the disease. The condition is characterized by snuffles, rashes, bone disorders, and a general wasting in infancy, followed in later childhood by interstitial keratitis of the corneas, deafness, and a type of notching of the incisor teeth that is identified with the disease. It is not unusual for a victim of congenital syphilis to escape the infantile symptoms, only to develop the effects in adolescence. The risk of a foetus acquiring congenital syphilis is related to the stage of the mother's infection. If a mother is treated for syphilis before the end of the fourth month of the pregnancy, it is unlikely that her offspring will become infected.

congested ovaries an abnormal condition in which unrelieved sexual tension in a woman causes a concentration of blood in the ovaries and other areas of the reproductive system, such as the vulva. The condition may follow a period of prolonged sexual foreplay which does not reach the stage of sexual intercourse and orgasm.

congested testicles a condition that occurs in the testes of a man who engages in prolonged foreplay without the sexual activity culminating in ejaculation. The disorder is caused, physically, by an accumulation of blood in the testicles and may be marked by pain and swelling.

congress an obsolete literary euphemism for sexual intercourse.

coning medical jargon for the round shaping of a female breast during mammoplasty, or surgery to correct the size or shape of the breast.

conizing the cervix a technique for obtaining tissue samples of the uterine cervix for microscopic examination. The cone-shaped tip of the cervix is removed with a scalpel for biopsy study. Conization is considered more thorough than some other methods in obtaining biopsy material that might otherwise be missed. It is particularly important in cases of carcinoma in situ, to be sure that no areas of potential cancer have been missed.

conjugal pertaining to a marital relationship or both partners in a marriage (Latin *conjugere*, 'to yoke together').

conjugal infidelity another term for adultery.

conjugal paranoia delusional jealousy stemming from an unfounded conviction that the partner has been unfaithful. False 'evidence' of infidelity is usually cited, such as an unsigned note or phone calls in which the other person hangs up.

conjugal rights the rights and privileges implied in the marriage relationship, particularly the right to intercourse. Current law does not stipulate how frequently this right should be exercised, but refusal to have intercourse with one's husband or wife within a reasonable period of time may be grounds for divorce if construed as unreasonable behaviour.

connection juncture the symphysis pubis, or point at which the pubic bones meet at the lower front side of the pelvis and the area from which tissues of the deep fascia of the penis arise.

connubial related to the lawful marriage state, or *connubium*, as in the phrases *connubial love* and *connubial bliss*.

consanguineous matings intercourse or marriage between persons who are descended from the same ancestor or who are considered closely related. The closeness of the relationship varies from society to society.

consanguinity literally, having the same blood; more accurately, a genetic relationship between individuals who have a common ancestor.

consensual sex sexual relations undertaken by mutual consent. Today many if not most authorities on criminal law advocate the abolition of laws prohibiting certain sexual behaviour of consenting adults, such as orogenital contacts and anal intercourse, when carried out in private.

consent to agree or accept voluntarily, as in to consent to marry. If a party to a marriage is a minor, parental consent is required, if there are no other legal obstacles. In most communities, there is a legal age limit below which a marriage is illegal even with parental consent.

consolateur an old French term for dildo, especially when it is used for masturbation—as a substitute or 'consolation' for intercourse.

constrictor vaginae one of the muscles of the female urogenital system. It surrounds the orifice of the vagina and has fibres that pass on either side to be inserted in the clitoris. The action of the muscle is to reduce the size of the vaginal orifice while simultaneously contributing to the erection of the clitoris. When the muscle thus grips the penis, it usually enhances male pleasure and excitement.

consultori familiari public family-planning centres in Italy. The consultori issue medical certificates required for an abortion, in addition to providing birth-control information, gynaecological care, and prenatal and postnatal services.

consummation of marriage the completion of marriage by intercourse. Studies by Masters and Johnson and others have shown that failure to consummate almost always stems from both husband and wife. The man may be afraid of hurting his wife, may ejaculate before penetrating, or may be too shy or clumsy to complete the act. The woman may be afraid of being hurt or suffer from vaginismus, which tightens the muscles at the entrance to the vagina, or may be emotionally resistant because of a frightening sexual experience in the past.

consummatory act the final stage in a series of complex responses, such as the fertilization of the eggs of a female fish after the stages of nest establishment and courtship or, more relevantly here, the act of coitus that follows the stage of foreplay in human sex. Also called *consummatory response*.

consummatory behaviour the relatively stereotyped copulatory pattern for human beings and other mammals. The essential male acts are mounting, thrusting, inserting the erect penis, and ejaculating. The essential female acts are assumption of the mating posture, which facilitates the male's insertion, or intromission, plus the maintenance of this position until intra-vaginal ejaculation has occurred.

continence self-restraint, especially in controlling the sex drive; also, the ability to control the urge to defecate or urinate.

continuity of germ plasm the self-replicating property of gametes that transmits from one generation to the next the hereditary substance of the genes.

continuum of sexuality a Kinsey term for the gradations in choice of sexual partner, ranging from exclusively heterosexual through bisexual to exclusively homosexual. The variations were graded from 0 for persons exclusively heterosexual to 6 for persons exclusively homosexual.

contraception the prevention of conception, especially through the use of devices and medications or through such procedures as withdrawal, natural family planning, the rhythm method, abstinence, and sterilization.

contraceptive a device or medication used to prevent conception, including diaphragms, condoms, IUDs, vaginal spermicides, or the pill.

contraceptive charms magical incantations, amulets, or devices that are believed to have the power to prevent conception. Examples are the 'snake girdle' made of beaded leather and worn over the navel by some Plains Indians of North America, and the ancient Roman custom of tying an ivory tube containing either the liver of a cat or a part of a lioness's womb to the left foot.

contraceptive effectiveness a statistical method of determining the real birth-control benefits of a particular contraceptive. It is calculated by subtracting the actual failure-rate percentage from 100. Thus, if the actual failure rate of a particular oral contraceptive is 2 percent, the actual effectiveness is 98 percent, or the pill is 98 percent effective. When the theoretical failure rate is used instead of the actual failure rate, the effectiveness is inevitably higher.

contraceptive jelly a spermicidal chemical applied to a mechanical device, such as a diaphragm or condom, for the prevention of conception. When used alone, jellies have proved unreliable. Also *contraceptive cream, contraceptive foam.*

contrasexual a term applied by Jung to the portion of the psyche that represents the opposite sex, based on his belief that everyone has both a male side (animus) and a female side (anima) but that one side is usually dominant and the other repressed. Before the term acquired this Jungian meaning, contrasexual was used to mean homosexual (for example, by J.A. Symonds, 1887, or E. Irenaeus Prime-Stevenson, 1911).

contrectation a technical term for sexual stimulation by manipulating the sex organs of another person (Latin *contrectare*, 'to handle, fondle').

Coolidge effect the observation that when a male is too 'spent' sexually to be turned on by the same female, he nevertheless will usually be 'ready for action' if a fresh partner is available that moment. According to the anecdote, U.S. President Calvin Coolidge and his wife were visiting a chicken farm, which they toured separately; and when Mrs Coolidge wondered how often a cock can mount a hen and the farmer told her it's about (say) 40 times a day, she said: 'Please tell this to my husband.' The farmer did so; but when Mr Coolidge asked whether the cock did it all with the same hen and was told it's a different hen every time, the 30th President said: 'Please, tell *this* to my wife.' (Casanova—who *would* know about this—wrote 200 years ago; 'Three quarters of love is curiosity.')

cooperative birth control a method of contraception where both partners agree to abstain from sexual intercourse during the woman's fertile days.

cooperative interaction an arrangement between sexual partners in which they actively assist each other in overcoming sexual inadequacies in performance, particularly in matters that are mental or emotional in origin, such as premature ejaculation, or impotence resulting from fear of failure.

coprography the impulse to write or draw obscene material, particularly words and expressions concerning excrement or sexual activities involving the anus. Graffiti are common examples of this impulse.

coprolagnia a sexual disorder, or paraphilia, in which an individual repeatedly derives sexual excitement from handling faeces, as well as from the sight, smell, and thought of faeces.

coprolalia an irresistible impulse to utter obscenities, particlarly slang words involving faeces (faecal speech). From a psychiatric point of view, involuntary coprolalia is a symptom in latah, Tourette's disorder, and many cases of schizophrenia. Also called coprophrasia.

coprology an older term for obscenity.

coprophagia the eating of faeces, a symptom occasionally found in deteriorated schizophrenics, who have apparently regressed to the anal stage of psychosexual development.

coprophemia a sexual disorder, or paraphilia, in which obscene speech is an essential prelude or accompaniment to sexual arousal.

coprophilia a sexual disorder, or paraphilia, characterized by pathological preoccupation with excreta or filth, including such reactions as constantly joking about defecation, hoarding faeces, faecal fantasies, sexual excitement during evacuation, and, in some schizophrenic patients, smearing faeces on the walls or other objects. According to psychoanalytic theory, a morbid interest in faeces is associated with fixation at the anal stage of development. Also called anal eroticism.

coprophobia pathological fear of excrement, often expressed sybolically as an extreme fear of dirt, contamination, or infectious disease. In the Freudian view, these reactions represent a defence against anal eroticism, or coprophilia.

coprophrasia a synonym for coprolalia.

copula carnalis a legal term for intercourse between husband and wife.

copula fornicatoria a legal term for intercourse between a man and a prostitute.

copulation intercourse, or coitus. The term is applied to the mating of humans and of animals. Verb: *to copulate.*

copulatory behaviour a general term for behaviour patterns associated with intercourse of human beings and of different species of animals. In humans the term refers to activities that vary widely from culture to culture and individual to individual, such as different types of foreplay and different coital positions.

corditis an inflammation of the spermatic cord.

core gender identity the basic physical characteristics that identify an individual as male or female (and, in some cases, as a hermaphrodite), resulting from the influence of sex chromosomes and the development of foetal gonads and hormones secreted by these glands, which determine the development and functioning of the external genitals.

cornholer an American slang term for a person practising anal intercourse. Verb: *to cornhole.*

corona glandis the raised edge of the glans penis, forming a rounded border at the junction with the neck of the penis.

corpus albicans a white-to-yellow scar that forms on the ovary at the site of the corpus luteum at approximately the start of the menstrual cycle.

corpus cavernosum one of two cylindrical masses of erectile tissue that form the major portion of the shaft of the penis. At the pubic symphysis, the two lateral corpora appear to diverge as tapering crura and converge above the smaller corpus spongiosum to become embedded in the glans penis. Although the three cylinders of flesh—the two corpora cavernosa and the corpus spongiosum—have the superficial appearance of being a single structure, they are held together by several layers of tissue, including the dartos tunic and the deep (Buck's) penile fascia. And a septum penis divides the two corpora cavernosa for the length of the complete shaft.

corpus cavernosum urethrae an alternative name for the corpus spongiosum, which contains the terminal portion of the male urethra.

corpus fibrosum a small collection of fibrous tissue marking the site of a graafian follicle that failed to produce a mature ovum.

corpus haemorrhagicum the blood-tinged empty graafian follicle after an ovum has been expelled. It is a stage between the graafian follicle containing the ovum and the corpus luteum that develops from the cells lining the follicle. The corpus haemorrhagicum lacks the rounded surface of the follicles, having collapsed under the pressure of neighbouring follicles.

corpus highmori a structure than runs vertically along one side of the testis. It supports various vessels and ducts with processes that radiate towards the side of the gland, dividing it into lobules. (It is named after the 17th-century anatomist Nathaniel Highmore.)

corpus luteum a yellow hormone-secreting body that forms in an ovary at the site of a ruptured follicle. The corpus luteum develops immediately after ovulation in response to stimulation of the luteinizing hormone released by the pituitary gland. Cells lining the corpus luteum develop into granulosa-lutein cells which produce the hormone progesterone. Other cells within the corpus luteum, theca-lutein cells, secrete a second female sex hormone, oestrogen. If the fertilized ovum becomes implanted in the lining of the uterus, the corpus luteum becomes much larger and functions as a ductless gland, secreting progesterone and oestrogen to support the pregnancy. If pregnancy does not occur, the corpus luteum degenerates and leaves a scar, called a corpus fibrosum, at its site. Menstruation usually begins within 4 days after the onset of corpus luteum degeneration.

corpus mammae the parenchyma or functional tissues of the breast. Included are the mammary ducts, tubules, and acinar, or secretory, cells.

corpus spongiosum one of the three cylinders of flesh that constitute the shaft of the penis. It is smaller than the corpora cavernosa and is located beneath and in a median position with respect to them. The corpus spongiosum also contains the male urethra. It begins near the pubic symphysis as a conical enlargement, the bulbus penis, and expands at the anterior end into the mushroom-shaped glans penis.

cortical inductor substance a hormone or hormonal substance that usually becomes active around the sixth week of gestation to convert the undifferentiated embryonic gonad into an ovary. The cortex of the gonad undergoes proliferation and pushes strands of secondary sex cords into the interior of the future ovary. Bits of the sex cords break off in the interior to become primordial ovarian follicles.

cortisol a natural hormone produced by the cells of the adrenal cortex. It has an effect like that of dexamethasone in reducing the excretion of 17-ketosteroids and other sex hormone substances and is administered in some cases of precocious puberty to slow the rate of maturation of the reproductive systems of children.

cotherapists a pair of sex therapists in the Masters and Johnson system of treating cases of sexual dysfunction. One therapist is a man and the other is a woman, an arrangement that encourages inputs from both the male and female points of view in discussing sexuality problems that involve a married couple. The male cotherapist interviews the wife, and the female cotherapist interviews the husband.

cottage a British homosexual slang term for a public lavatory, viewed as a place of homosexual assignation. *Cottaging* is the practice of frequenting cottages in hopes of sexual adventure.

coupling a genetic phenomenon in which various hereditary traits become combined on chromosomes so that future generations may receive combinations of traits. It is also possible that none of the coupled genes will be transmitted to offspring.

courtesan fantasy a fantasy in which a woman imagines she is a concubine or court-esan, or a fantasy in which a man imagines that he is having sexual relations with a courtesan. Also called hetaeral fantasy (based on the Greek word for courtesan, *hetaera*).

courtship behaviour among human beings, as opposed to animals, the attitudes and behaviour characteristics of different societies or social strata during the courtship period. There is little correspondence between practices such as night crawling or mate selection by the chief of the tribe in certain societies, and courtship in other societies that emphasize going out with someone and engagement as a lengthy testing process in which the couple explore each other's interests, values, and personalities, express their feeling for each other through presents and shared activities, and discover how responsive they are to each other emotionally and sexually.

cousin marriage marriage between cousins of first, second, or other degree. A study of 762 societies reported by Murdock shows that two thirds forbid marriage to any kind of cousin. Roman Catholics permit second-cousin marriages, and also first-cousin marriages with special permission. The Bible does not prohibit cousin marriages of any kind, and Judaism follows this tradition. Marriage between first cousins is permitted by Islam and many Protestant churches.

couvade (kōōväd') a custom found in a number of non-Western societies in which the father takes to bed before and during delivery of the child, and may even exhibit pregnancy symptoms and pangs of childbirth. The custom has been interpreted as a sympathetic reaction and as a means of drawing evil influence away from the wife and baby.

covert homosexual a homosexual who conceals his or her homosexuality from fellow workers and many social contacts although other homosexuals are aware of the person's true sexuality.

covert sensitization a form of aversion therapy employed in the treatment of some sexual aberrations. The patient is taught to utilize an unpleasant fantasy to serve as 'punishment' for a fantasy related to an undesirable behaviour.

Cowper's cyst a cyst of the bulbourethral glands.

Cowper's glands the bulbourethral glands embedded in the sphincter of the urethra and immediately in front of the prostate.

COYOTE a U.S. trade union for prostitutes.

The letters of the acronym stand for Call Off Your Old Tired Ethics.

crab louse a louse that is generally specific to humans, infesting areas of coarse hair in the anogenital area and also hair of the chest, eyebrows, and armpits. The scientific name of the louse is *Phthirus pubis*, and the infestation is called pediculosis pubis. Although relatively large for lice, crab lice may be difficult to find, particularly in hairy areas of the body, where they attach their eggs to the bases of hair shafts. On areas of open skin, they may appear as tiny blue specks. At other times they may resemble small crustlike skin lesions. Crab lice also leave their mark, literally, as specks of their own faeces on the undergarments of hosts. The crab louse is transmitted by sexual contact with an infested person in most instances. It is not an important disease vector like the body louse that transmits typhus. A common hazard is an overdosage of medication in an effort to eliminate the pest.

crack a fat an Australian slang term meaning to have a penile erection.

crackling a collective British male slang term for sexually attractive women. It is most commonly used in 'a bit of crackling,' meaning a sexually attractive woman.

crack saleslady an American slang term for prostitute.

crack salesman an American slang term for pimp.

cradlesnatcher a derogatory for a woman who has a sexual affair with, or marries, a younger man.

cramps a popular term for the uterine spasms that are a major cause of menstrual pains.

craniopharyngioma a congenital pituitary-gland defect in the form of a tumour that interferes with normal functioning of the hypothalamus and pituitary gland, sometimes affecting various brain areas, such as the visual tracts. In children the tumour cells result in infantile genitalia. Development of the tumour after puberty results in impotence for men and amenorrhoea for women.

crap a vulgar term meaning to defecate; also, to ejaculate. In addition, as a noun it can mean nonsense.

cream a euphemism for semen.

cremasteric muscle a muscle that is an extension of the internal oblique abdominal muscle and which spreads out in loops over the spermatic cord. The longest of the loops extend as far as the testis and are attached

to the tunica vaginalis. There is a similar but vestigial muscle in the female.

cremasteric reflex a reaction in which the testis is retracted when the skin on the front and inner surface of the thigh is stimulated. The retraction occurs on the same side of the body as the area of stimulation.

cribiform hymen a hymen that is essentially intact although it contains numerous pinpoint openings that permit drainage of the menstrual flow.

crime against nature a legal euphemism that has been applied to any sexual activity other than efforts directed towards procreation. For example, sodomy and homosexuality have been identified as crimes against nature.

criminal assault a euphemism for rape.

crossbreeding the theory that it is possible for human beings to crossbreed with infrahuman animals such as apes. There is no evidence for this theory. Interbreeding is also impossible among the genera of lower animals, such as an ape and a tiger, although two members of the same genus, such as the cat family, may crossbreed. The theory of interbreeding between humans and lower animals probably originated with the centaurs, mermaids, satyrs, and sphinxes of Greek and Roman mythology.

cross-dressing the practice of wearing the clothes of the opposite sex, as a paraphilia (transvestism); as an attempt at transformation into the opposite sex (transsexualism); as a way of dressing up for a 'drag ball'; for stage performances (male or female impersonation); or for the purpose of achieving sexual excitement (fetishistic cross-dressing).

cross-gender behaviour playing the social role of the opposite sex, for example, by adopting the clothes, hair, gestures, speech patterns, or general personality characteristics commonly associated with the other sex. Such behaviour may be based upon upbringing (stemming, for example, from disappointment that the child is not a boy or a girl) or may reflect homosexual or bisexual tendencies.

cross-sex parent the parent of a child who is of the opposite sex, as the mother is the cross-sex parent of a son.

cross-sex toys toys that attempt to break the sex stereotypes of games and play activities. An example of a cross-sex toy is a football for girls.

crotch a slang term used in referring to the

genital area and sometimes applied specifically to the vulva.

crotch cheese a slang term for smegma
around the clitoris and labia minora. Compare
HEAD CHEESE.

crotch watchers a slang term for women
who like to observe the genital bulges in the
trousers or other garments of men.

croupade (krōōpäd'; French, 'buttock position') a group of coital positions involving
entry from the rear. This type of intercourse
can be accomplished with the woman kneeling, lying, standing straight, or bending over,
or with the man sitting or kneeling behind
her. The variant in which the man positions
himself astride the woman's thighs is sometimes called cuissade (from French *cuisse*,
'thigh').

crowning the point in child delivery when
the head of the foetus appears at the external
opening of the vagina. Technically, the head
crowns when its widest part distends the
vulva, just before the forehead appears.

crown jewels a rather dated humorous British euphemism for the male genitals—the
reference being to their pricelessness as far
as their owner is concerned.

crude birthrate (CBR) the number of live
births per 1,000 population in a given year.
The CBR depends on the level of fertility and
the age distribution of a particular population; the higher the percentage of high-
fertility age groups in a population, the
higher the CBR.

cruising a term used among homosexuals
for the practice of going into pubs, men's
public lavatories, and the like, in search of
one-time sexual encounters.

crumpet a British collective slang term for
sexually desirable females. A 'bit *or* piece of
crumpet' is a sexy young woman.

crush infatuation of a preadolescent or adolescent girl or boy with another young person, or with an older person such as a teacher.

crus of the clitoris a portion of the corpus
cavernosum of the clitoris that is attached to
a projection of the bones of the pubic region.

crus penis the portion of the corpus cavernosum of the penis that is attached to the
ischiopubic ramus, or bar of bone located at
the junction of the ischium and pubis.

cryptomenorrhoea the entrapment of the
products of menstruation within the uterus
or vagina. The condition is frequently associated with an imperforate hymen. It also can
result from a blockage of the uterine cervix.
The symptoms include severe abdominal

pain and a scant or absent menstrual flow.
A possible complication is a reflux of the
menstrual products through the fallopian
tubes and into the pelvic cavity, causing
peritonitis, endometriosis, and painful
adhesions.

cryptorchid a male whose testicles have not
descended into the scrotum. In a true case of
cryptorchidism, the testicles remain in the
abdomen or in the inguinal canal and have
not become ectopic. A cryptorchid usually is
at a high risk of developing testicular cancer.

C-section an abbreviation for caesarean
section.

C.T. an abbreviation for the vulgar slang
term cock teaser.

C-20 block a medical term used to identify
a deficiency of an enzyme needed for the
normal production of sex hormones from cholesterol. The metabolic failure occurs at the
C-20 position of the cholesterol molecule.
Although both males and females may lack
the enzyme, males are more likely to be affected because the foetus will develop without
androgenic hormone influence and a person
with the normal male chromosome (XY) combination will be born with external female
genitalia.

cuckold an old-fashioned term for a man
whose wife has been unfaithful; a term of
mockery sometimes applied to the husband
of an adulteress.

cuissade a variant of CROUPADE. See this
entry.

culdoscope an instrument with an attached
light that is inserted through the vagina as
part of an inspection of the pelvis. A small
incision is made in the vagina and the peritoneum while the woman is in the knee-chest
position so that the examining physician can
visualize structures throughout the pelvic cavity. The procedure is called *culdoscopy*.

cultures a euphemism for various sexual
techniques. Examples are 'French culture' for
oral-genital sex, 'Greek culture' for homosexuality or anal sex, 'Roman culture' for orgies
and swinging, 'Italian culture' for anal sex,
'English culture' for spanking to increase
sexual pleasure, or 'Oriental culture' for experimentation with all possible intercourse
positions.

culture-specific syndromes mental disorders peculiar to individual societies
throughout the world, some of which involve
one or more sexual aberrations. Examples
are sexual anxiety as a major symptom of
echul, a disorder found among the Diegueno

Indians; coprolalia, observed in latah victims in Malaya and Congo; vivid sexual dreams among victims of kimilue, a disorder found among Native Americans in lower California; and an Eskimo disorder known as piblokto in which women tear off their clothes and run out into the ice and snow for release of tension and as a protest against their inferior status. For a more detailed example, see KORO.

cum an alternative spelling of come.

cunnilinguist a person who performs cunnilingus. A jocular variant is 'cunning linguist'.

cunnilingus sexual stimulation of the external female genitalia (vulva, clitoris) with the tongue or mouth. Also called *cunnilingham*. (Latin *cunnus*, 'vulva,' and *lingere*, 'to lick.')

cunnophile a colloquial term for a person who loves vulvas, especially one who loves to perform cunnilingus.

cunnus a Latin term for vulva.

cunt a vulgar term for (a) the vagina or the vulva and (b) a male or female person held in contempt. The term may derive from Old English *cwithe*, 'womb,' or from *quaint* (*queynte* in Chaucer's 'Miller's Tale'). 'Cunt' ranks number 5 in the TABOONESS RATING OF DIRTY WORDS. See this entry.

cunt curtain a vulgar slang term for the female pubic hair.

curettage the scraping of material fom the inner wall of an organ, usually to remove a tumour, polyp, or other unwanted material or to obtain a biopsy sample. Curettage may be a part of an abortion procedure in which products of conception are removed from the cavity of the uterus with a *curet* or by suction.

curled-tail sperm a spermatozoon with a tail or filament that is wrapped in concentric circles about the head, rather than stretching out in a more or less linear manner.

curse, the an informal euphemism for menstruation.

curtains a slang term for foreskin.

Cushing's syndrome a disorder of adrenal-cortex functioning associated with chronic exposure to an excess of corticosteroids. Causes may include an overdosage of ACTH (adrenocorticotropic hormone), oversecretion of the hormone by the pituitary gland, or secretion by a nonpituitary tumour, such as oat-cell cancer of the lung. Effects on the patient include obesity, pigmented streaks on the skin of the abdomen and flanks, hypertension, osteoporosis, bruising, and amenorrhoea in women, although all of the signs and symptoms may not appear in any individual patient. In addition to menstrual

difficulties, female patients may experience balding about the temples, excessive growth of body hair, and other physical traits associated with the male sex as a result of androgenic hormone production.

cutting repetitive wrist-cutting by so-called 'slashers,' occurring primarily in women and frequently associated with menstrual irregularity, depression, and problems of sexual identification. Some authors interpret the cutting as a distorted autoerotic activity used both as a defence against sexual impulses and a gratification of these impulses.

cyesis (sī-ē'sis) a medical term for pregnancy.

cypridophobia an intense, morbid fear of contracting venereal disease. The term is derived from Cypris, a Greek name for Venus, who is reputed to have been born on the island of Cyprus. Also called *cypriphobia*.

cyproterone an antiandrogenic drug that may be used to counter the effects of an excess of male sex hormones, particularly in women, who may develop facial hair and other masculine features as a result of an adrenal gland disorder or by the use of hormonal therapy for cancer. Cyproterone also has been used to control precocious puberty in boys and to reduce the sex drive in sexual offenders.

cyst any cavity in body tissue lined with degenerating, inflamed, or other abnormal tissue substances, such as a blue-dome cyst in a mammary gland caused by bleeding in a milk duct, a milk cyst caused by obstruction of a milk duct, or a nabothian cyst of the cervix caused by a uterine mucous-gland disorder.

cystitis an inflammation of the urinary bladder. The cause may be an infection, injury, or foreign body, which may be a stone, a catheter, or a chemical irritant. Symptoms usually include pain and the production of urine that may be discoloured by pus or some other substance. See also HONEYMOON CYSTITIS.

cytogenic a Greek-derived term meaning literally 'producing cells,' as in the reproductive process or formation and development of new tissue cells.

cytogenic gland a gland that produces living cells or cytogenes, such as a testis or ovary.

cytomegalovirus (CMV) a herpes virus characterized by production of unique large cells containing 'inclusion bodies.' CMV infection is often, and some say usually, transmitted sexually, and in the adult leads to enlargement of the liver or spleen, a rash, aches and pains, sore throat, and general malaise. The most severe consequences, however, occur in infants infected in utero. Such infants are frequently afflicted with such disorders as mental retardation, blindness, deafness, blood abnormalities, or cerebral palsy. See also HERPES.

C

daisy a slang term for a homosexual.

daisy chain a slang term for group sex involving a number of individuals performing the same or varied acts of sex. Although the term originally was applied to group sex involving male homosexuals, it later became a term used to describe group sex involving either homosexuals or heterosexuals or both.

Dalkon shield an intrauterine contraceptive device that was marketed during the 1970s when it was implicated in a number of cases of pelvic inflammatory disease (PID) and spontaneous abortions. More than a dozen deaths were attributed to its use.

dammed-up libido a Freudian term for the inhibition or frustration of the sexual drive by such factors as lack of opportunity for gratification, inability to be sexually aroused or to achieve a climax (impotence, frigidity), or unconscious blocks stemming from parental or religious admonitions.

danzanol a male hormone that is used in the treatment of endometriosis in women. The hormonal therapy is intended to suppress the menstrual cycle for 6 to 9 months, thereby diminishing the amount of abnormal uterine lining in the woman's fallopian tubes or abdomen.

dartos muscle a layer of loosely organized muscle tissues immediately beneath the skin of the scrotum. They are involuntary muscle fibres but react to temperature and sexual stimulation.

date of menarche the average age at which a girl experiences her first menstrual period. British studies show that the average age is now 13, compared with 15 in the last century.

date rape a sexual assault that develops during a date.

dating the process of making social appointments with members of the opposite sex. It is ordinarily the first overt form of heterosexual behaviour, marking not only the awakening of sex interest, but also the end of the period when the boy's associates are primarily male and the girl's primarily female. The dating period varies greatly in time, sometimes starting as early as 12 or 13 years or age (girls start earlier than boys). In any case, dating gives young people an opportunity to learn about each other physically, emotionally, and socially. Sexual relationships begin with holding hands, arms round the waist, and a goodnight kiss, and go on from there with varying speed.

Daughters of Bilitis a lesbian organization named after BILITIS. See this entry.

D & C abbreviation for dilatation and curettage. See DILATOR.

D & E abbreviation for dilatation and evacuation, a commonly used abortion technique. It also is reported to be the safest abortion method for pregnancies terminated in the second trimester. The uterus is dilated, and the contents are evacuated. Also called vacuum suction or vacuum curettage.

dead-end street a slang term for vagina.

de-analize the transfer of sexual impulses from the anal region to other objects and forms of expression, such as mud, smearing, paints (finger painting), money, cleanliness, obscene jokes, and coprophilia.

death in the saddle a slang term for death setting in during intercourse—an extremely rare occurrence. See also COITAL DEATH.

debauchery extreme, intemperate indulgence in sensual pleasures, especially sexual activities of all kinds, such as seduction of innocent individuals, and sexual orgies.

decidua basalis the portion of the endometrium, or lining, of the uterus that underlies the chorionic vesicle during the implantation period of embryonic life. The portion that overlies the embryo is called the *decidua capsularis*.

de Clérambault's syndrome a form of erotomania first described by the French psychiatrist G.G. de Clérambault. The disorder is almost entirely confined to women, who suffer from a fixed delusion that an older man of great wealth and rank is passionately in love with them. Some authors interpret the delusion as a defence against homosexual impulses, while others regard it as a defence against feelings of rejection. Also called psychose passionnelle.

deep fascia of the penis an alternative term for Buck's fascia, a sheet of connective tissue that surrounds the three separate cylinders of the penis, forming the shaft of the penis.

deep kiss a sexually stimulating kiss in which the tongue explores the inside of the partner's mouth. Also called soul kiss; French kiss; tongue kiss.

deep throat a form of fellatio in which the penis penetrates deeply into the woman's mouth and throat. Named after the film *Deep Throat*, this technique is rare because most women gag when it is tried, and they also have difficulty breathing because of the fact that the nose may be pressed against the man's pubic hair and bone.

deep vaginal penetration a form of sexual intercourse reported by Kinsey researchers as particularly satisfying for some women. It involves total body tactile stimulation and intimate involvement with another person, plus pressure of the body weight and genitals on the clitoris, labia, and other areas equipped with tactile sensory nerve endings.

deerotization an equivalent term for delibidinization.

defloration the rupture of the hymen, which usually occurs during the first experience of intercourse. There may be slight bleeding, but with little if any pain. 'Deflowering' implies that the woman is deprived of the 'flower' of virginity. In some Hindu, Indonesian, and South American Indian societies, infant girls are subjected to 'finger defloration' at about 1 month of age. See also CEREMONIAL DEFLORATION; FINGER DEFLORATION; RITUAL DEFLORATION.

degenerate a person whose moral standards and social behaviour have deteriorated. The term is often applied to an individual who persistently commits sexual offences such as rape or sodomy.

degree of potency a measure of the relative risk of impotence in men as correlated with age. While an average of about 2 percent of all men may suffer from impotence at the age of 35, the risk increases to 10 percent at the age of 55 and 22 percent at the age of 65. Between the ages of 65 and 90, the proportion of men who are impotent gradually increases to nearly 100 percent, although there always have been exceptions of men able to father a child regardless of their age.

delayed ejaculation, the opposite of premature ejaculation. Deliberately delayed ejaculation often requires the use of drugs or devices to reduce the sensitivity of the penis. A drug used for delayed ejaculation is Nupercainal, a local anaesthetic that deadens the nerve endings in the penis during intercourse. Some men achieve a similar effect by wearing multiple condoms, and some men through self-control.

delayed male pubescence puberty that does not begin until after the normal upper limit of about 16 years of age. In some reported cases, pubescence in males has been delayed until the age of 22. Such individuals may be of normal height for their age, but obese, and have genitalia that appear underdeveloped during their teen years. However, normal genitalia develop later when pituitary-hormone stimulation begins.

delay of gratification the psychoanalytical term for the ability to tolerate frustration and tension generated by unsatisfied instinctual drives such as hunger, thirst, and especially sex, as well as to postpone gratification of these urges.

DelCastillo syndrome an alternative term for germinal-cell aplasia, a condition in which the testes lack germinal epithelium although Sertoli cells are present.

delibidinization a psychoanalytical term for elimination or sublimation of the sexual impulse or libido. An example is the removal of the sexual aspects of voyeurism when that impulse is diverted to curiosity about intellectual matters. Also called deerotization; desexualization.

Delilah syndrome a pattern of promiscuity among women stemming from the desire to control their partners and render them weak and helpless. According to the biblical story, Delilah took over the role of her father who had exploited and controlled her earlier life, and used her wiles to destroy Samson and the Philistines, who had dominated her.

délire du toucher (dālēr'dētōō'shā) a French term for a compulsive desire to touch or be touched. It is the opposite of angoisse du toucher.

delusional jealousy a paranoid type of jealousy marked by the false conviction that the patient's spouse or other loved one is unfaithful. He, or she, is constantly suspicious, watching for any possible sign of infidelity, such as lateness for an appointment, and manufactures evidence if it does not exist.

demimonde (dem'ēmond'; French, 'half-world') a class of women who lived in the 'twilight zone' of cafés and music halls during Victorian times, providing companionship and sexual excitement to 'respectable' men without engaging in open prostitution. Such a person was called a *demimondaine* (dem'ē mondān').

demivierge (demēvyerzh'; French, 'half-virgin') an old-fashioned term for a girl who, though technically a virgin, engages in a wide range of sexual activities with men short of actual intercourse.

denidation the sloughing off of the superficial layers of the lining of the uterus, as occurs with the endometrial layers during menstruation.

Denonvillier's fascia a fibrous layer of connective tissue that covers the prostate and seminal vesicles and separates them from the wall of the rectum.

deorality the transfer of satisfaction connected with the oral region to some other region or activity. For example, pleasure and gratification experienced in breast feeding may later take the form of pleasure derived from dependence on a maternal figure.

depilation the removal of body hair, especially hair on the face, hands, arms, legs, and armpits. Excess hair is often considered unsightly and unattractive in women. Some women attempt to increase their sexual attractiveness by shaving the pubic area or the pudenda as a whole (the genital, groin, and anal areas). The resulting extreme and unexpected nudity may be sexually stimulating.

deprivational homosexuality an alternative term for situational homosexuality, or homosexual behaviour that develops because of an absence of heterosexual outlets.

dermatitis medicamentosa a type of scrotal dermatitis that represents a reaction to a drug to which the person is allergic.

dermatitis venenata a type of dermatitis of the scrotum that results from exposure to an irritating agent, such as a fabric dye. The

skin usually appears swollen, red, and marked by pimples or blisters. The scrotum may be painful or cause itching.

dermatophytosis a fungal infection that may involve the genital area. It is characterized by reddened skin surfaces with sharp raised borders and pinpoint blisters. It may be caused by any of a dozen species of fungi that are specific to humans.

dermoid cyst a noncancerous ovarian tumour composed of assorted bits of embryonic tissue, including hair, teeth, bone, cartilage, skin, and sweat glands. The tumour may be tiny or more than 12 inches in diameter. Various theories have been offered for the occurrence of dermoid cysts, including the arrested development of an embryo in the fallopian tube. It also has been suggested that a dermoid cyst may represent an attempt by an unfertilized ovum at parthenogenesis.

derrière (deryer'; French 'behind') a euphemism—popular mainly in the late 19th century—for the buttocks.

De Sade, Marquis Donatien-Alphonse-François (1740-1814) an aristocratic Parisian whose life as well as writings revolved around a single dominant theme: cruelty of every kind performed for the purpose of achieving sexual excitement. This practice, which Krafft-Ebing later named 'sadism,' was spelled out in lurid detail in several books, notably *120 Days of Sodom, Justine* and *Juliette*. In his own life, Sade's chronicle of sadism began at the age of 26, when he repeatedly abused, whipped, poisoned, and knifed prostitutes. Later, he corrupted and abused children of both sexes, and held orgies in which pain and degradation were the chief preoccupation. There is little wonder that he spent 12 years in the Bastille, and was then transferred to the 'lunatic asylum' at Charenton for the last 13 years of his life.

desexualization a psychotherapeutic process whereby the libido is directed towards goals other than sexual desires, thus desexualizing the person's emotional frustration.

destructive phase the third of three stages of the female menstrual cycle, manifested by the breakdown of the lining of the uterus and the menstrual flow of blood, fragments of endometrium, and mucus.

determinate cleavage the division of a zygote into blastomeres that are destined to develop as specific parts of an embryo. Damage to or destruction of any of the cells results in a deformed foetus. Isolation of any of the cells results in an incomplete individual.

detumescence the reduction or diminution of a swelling, as when the penis returns to a flaccid condition after orgasm. The term also has been used by some authors to identify the ejaculatory event itself.

detumescence of the clitoris the reduction of erection and engorgement of the erectile tissues of the clitoris after orgasm. The female phase of detumescence is much slower than the male, requiring anywhere from 5 to 30 minutes. If orgasm is not achieved, clitoral detumescence may not occur for 12 to 24 hours, resulting in considerable discomfort.

deuterophallic phase a rarely used term applied by the psychoanalyst Ernest Jones to the second stage of the phallic phase of psychosexual development (between 3 and 7 years of age), when the child first suspects that people are divided into male and female, each with different genital organs.

developmental arrest a teratomorphic (malformation) condition involving a foetus. The condition occurs because a temporary embryonic or foetal stage of a body part is accidentally retained permanently. Examples of developmental arrest include imperforate anus and cleft palate.

developmental excess a condition of embryonic or foetal development that leads to a malformation because growth is exaggerated or normal numbers of body parts are increased. Examples include gigantism, polydactylism (extra fingers or toes), and supernumerary (extra) breasts.

deviant sexual behaviour a derogatory term for sexual activities that many people consider abnormal. Examples are exhibitionism, voyeurism, paedophilia, incest, zoophilia, fetishism, sadism, masochism, homosexuality, orogenital contact, anal intercourse, group sex, transvestism, and rape. Today the term variant sexual behaviour or sexual variance is preferred by many sexologists because it is purely descriptive and not judgmental. Also called sexual deviation. See also RESPECTABLE DEVIANT.

deviate a term applied, often pejoratively, to a person whose sexual behaviour is in sharp conflict with the standard accepted by a particular society or simply by the user of the term.

devitalized relationship a sexual relationship which has become increasingly passive with time. It is a relationship commonly observed in couples who are middle-aged and whose life-style has been altered by pregnancies, the loss of privacy, and a redirection of interests away from each other and towards parental responsibilities. The partners may or may not accept their roles in such a relationship.

dewberry a member of the blackberry family that usually produces mature fruit early in the summer. It is one of the fruits recommended in *A Midsummer Night's Dream* as a sexual stimulant.

dexamethasone a drug used to control signs of precocious puberty in a boy. The drug reduces the excretion of 17-ketosteroids and other hormonal substances and leads to normal physiological development of the male reproductive system.

DHEA abbreviation for dehydroepiandrosterone, a steroid hormone that has been promoted in health food stores as a natural substance that can enhance sexual performance. The U.S. Food and Drug Administration has prohibited the sale and marketing of the product because of unsubstantiated therapeutic claims made by the distributors. [7]

diabetic vulvitis an inflammation of the vulva affecting women with diabetes mellitus. Because of the high sugar content of urine in diabetic patients, the genital areas are vulnerable to the growth of fungi. In a diabetic woman, the vaginal vestibule, labia, and adjacent areas may acquire a beefy-red inflamed appearance. Scratching the tissues to relieve an itching sensation caused by the fungi leads to complications.

Diana complex the psychiatric term for the deep-seated wish of a woman to be a man, probably based on the Roman deity Diana who played a masculine role as goddess of hunting and protector of women.

diaphragm a dome-shaped rubber contraceptive device that is filled with a spermicidal jelly or cream and placed in the vagina to fit over the cervix and prevent sperm from entering the uterus. Also called a cap.

dick a slang term for penis.

die a slang term meaning to reach orgasm. Many writers, from Shakespeare to our time, have used the term in this sense.

diesel a slang term for a very masculine lesbian.

diet and breast cancer a term referring to the relationship between foods eaten by women and their risk of developing breast cancer. Statistical studies show that Japanese women have a much lower risk of breast cancer than North American women, a factor attributed to the greater dependence of Japanese on seafood and low-cholesterol meals. In the United States, women of the Seventh Day Adventist and Mormon faiths, which advocate dietary restraints, have a lower incidence of breast cancer than other American women.

digitate a slang term meaning to masturbate—said of a woman.

dilator a device used to overcome vaginismus, a condition in which the muscles surrounding the vagina prevent it from dilating enough to permit intercourse. A series of dilators of graded sizes is used to stretch the vagina. Dilators of a somewhat different kind are also used in the procedure known as *dilatation and curettage* (D & C).

dildo an artificial penis, available in various sizes and materials (usually rubber or plastic). These devices are used in autoerotic and other practices. Also called godemiche; lingam; olisbos. The term seems to derive from the Italian word *diletto*, meaning 'delight.' Shakespeare uses the word dildo freely, for example in *The Winter's Tale*.

Dionysian attitude a state of mind that is irrational, sensuous, frenzied, and disordered (from Dionysus, the Greek god of wine, orgiastic religion, and fertility). Friedrich Nietzsche, in 1872, introduced the word *Dionysian* with the meaning of creative-passionate in contrast to Apollonian, or critical-rational.

dip one's wick a rather dated British euphemism meaning, of a male, to have sexual intercourse.

dippoldism the flogging of children, usually for sexual gratification. It is named after a sadistic German school teacher, Dippold, who was convicted of manslaughter after the death of one of the children.

dipstick a slang term for penis.

dirty jokes jokes involving the use of words and expressions that are considered obscene or salacious in 'polite' society—especially 'street' words for sexual anatomy or sex activity, and words for elimination processes and products. Jokes of this kind are sexually stimulating to some people.

dirty old man a colloquial derogatory term for a man whose sexual preferences are for women much younger than him, especially one who leers at young women, makes sexual suggestions to them, etc. It is sometimes abbreviated to *DOM*.

dirty words a colloquial term for 'obscene' words for sexual anatomy or sexual acts (pussy, prick, fuck) sometimes used by chil-

dren and others for their shock value or merely because they hear them in the neighbourhood and have only a vague idea of their meaning. Many adults also use such words as epithets, or during sexual activities. See also TABOONESS RATING OF DIRTY WORDS.

discharge a colloquial term meaning to ejaculate.

disinhibition in the sexual sphere, the loss of rational control for one's impulses; unrestrained sexual activity frequently following the use of alcohol or drugs.

displaceability of libido the psychoanalytic view that the 'partial impulses' stemming from each of the four phases of psychosexual development (oral, anal, phallic, genital) can substitute for each other in adult sexual life, especially in the foreplay stage of intercourse.

display behaviour verbal or nonverbal behaviour exhibited by animals or human beings in order to convey a message. Examples in the sexual sphere are a rooster's strutting, a bird's display of plumage, or the body language used by a woman who bares her legs or bends over to exhibit her breasts or a man who wears tight trousers or a shirt unbuttoned to the navel.

dissociated virilism the development of secondary sexual characteristics at an unequal rate, usually as the result of a hormonal disturbance such as an adrenal tumour. Androgenic hormones, for example, might cause a premature enlargement of a boy's penis without affecting the testicles, which might remain normal in size for the boy's age but appear small by comparison with the penis.

distillate of love an archaic term for the droplets of clear, sticky fluid that are secreted by Cowper's glands and form at the tip of the penis during sexual excitement. There is not enough of this fluid to act as a coital lubricant, but because it is alkaline, it helps to neutralize the acidity of the urethra, which may impair sperm. However, the fluid itself contains some sperm and may in rare instances lead to pregnancy.

diurnal rhythms biological activities, such as hunger and elimination, that repeat themselves at approximately the same time every day. It has been suggested that the tendency of men to awaken with an erection and a sex urge stems from the fact that the male sex hormones are produced in larger quantities in the morning. Increases in the female sex drive in the morning may also be hormonal.

dive a slang term meaning to perform cunnilingus. Also called to muff-dive.

diverticula bulges or pouches in the male urethra, some of which may be caused by the use of catheters. Urethral diverticula may develop at any point along the penis from the bulb to the glans, and the pouch hanging from beneath the penis can in some instances become nearly as large as the scrotum. Diverticula are often encountered in persons with spinal-cord injuries who develop urethral abscesses without being aware of the problem because of a loss of pain or other sensation in the region.

divine monosyllable a 19th-century euphemism for 'cunt.'

divorce the legal dissolution of a lawfully contracted marriage. Grounds for divorce vary from country to country, but among the most common are incompatibility, adultery, desertion, physical or mental cruelty, nonsupport, mental incompetence, and physical incapacity (sterility, impotence). In Britain the 'irretrievable breakdown' of the marriage for a variety of reasons including adultery, separation for two years etc, is grounds for divorce. See also EMOTIONAL DIVORCE.

divorce counselling the professional counselling process applied to divorced persons either on an individual basis or in a group. The individual approach is useful if the partners need special reassurance, a high degree of privacy, and an in-depth approach to emotional problems. The group approach provides support from others 'in the same boat,' a feeling that one's problems are not unique, a sense of belonging when the clients feel lost and cast adrift, and an opportunity to learn from the experiences of others.

dizygotic twins a medical term for fraternal twins, which develop from separate fertilized ova.

DOB abbreviation for Daughters of Bilitis. See BILITIS.

doctor game a common children's play activity in which boys and girls pretend to be doctors or nurses in order to examine each other's bodies, including the sex organs.

doctrine of signatures a discarded theory that the outward appearance of a substance represents its inner properties, especially its capacity to heal or perform magic. According to this concept, certain objects that outwardly resemble sexual organs (for example, rhinoceros horn or oysters) have aphrodisiac effects.

Döderlein bacillus a species of *Lactobacillus* found in the human vagina. It grows anaerobically (without oxygen) and apparently has a protective function in its ability to produce lactic acid by acting on glycogen (body-starch) molecules in the cells of the vagina. The lactic acid in turn destroys some of the potentially dangerous bacteria, such as staphylococcus organisms, that may be present in the vagina. The Döderlein bacillus accounts for the acid condition in the vagina.

doggie fashion a colloquial term referring to coitus a posteriori, also to coitus in ano. See also TV STYLE.

Dogiel's corpuscles sensory nerve endings found in the skin of the genitalia and also in the mucous membranes of the nose and mouth. They are named after the 19th-century anatomist Jan Dogiel.

doing it a Shakespearean euphemism for having sexual intercourse—still being used in this sense. See also IT.

DOM abbreviation for the colloquial term 'dirty old man.'

dominatrix the dominating (female) member of a bondage-and-discipline couple. The term also applies to a woman acting thus 'professionally,' as in a brothel.

domineering father a father who establishes unattainable goals for his children, thereby damaging their own self-confidence.

domineering mother a mother who dominates the family and tends to undermine the self-confidence of the other members of the family, especially the men.

dong a slang term for penis, especially a large one.

Don Juan the legendary Spanish libertine whose insatiable sexual drive exemplifies erotomania and satyriasis to the nth degree, and whose innumerable conquests inspired artistic works by Molière, Mozart, Lord Byron, Richard Strauss, George Bernard Shaw, and others. In many of these works he is depicted as a ruthless seducer who has no personal interest in his victims and is driven only by an urge to prove his virility—but ultimately pays the price for his profligacy by being condemned to hell.

Don Juan syndrome another term for satyriasis.

donovania granulomatis bacterial organisms associated with granuloma inguinale, or granuloma venereum.

Donovan's body a rod-shaped bacterium found in large numbers in ulcerating lesions of granuloma inguinale.

door-to-door condoms a term referring to the sale of condoms in Japan, a practice that is conducted by saleswomen who account for 20 percent of all Japanese condom sales. The use of condom saleswomen is sponsored by the Japanese Family Planning Association. The condoms are sold in a variety of packages designed to appeal to feminine tastes because the merchandising is done on a woman-to-woman basis.

Dorian love an archaic term for male homosexuality and pederasty reputedly practised by a tribe that conquered the Peloponnesus in the 12th century B.C.

dose a euphemism for a veneral infection, particularly of gonorrhoea or syphilis.

double creatures the prehuman beings of a Greek myth used to explain heterosexuality and homosexuality. According to the myth, people were originally double creatures with twice the number of limbs and organs they now possess. Some were double males, some double females, and some half male and half female. When the gods split them in half, the male-female creatures became the heterosexuals of the world while the double-male and double-female creatures became the homosexuals.

double entendre (dub'əl äntän'də, dōō'bəl äNtäN'də; French, a 'double understanding') a word or expression with two meanings, one of which is often a sexual or otherwise risqué allusion.

double-gaited a colloquial term for bisexual.

double-head sperm a (relatively rare) spermatozoon that bears two heads attached to a single tail.

double-lumen implant a breast implant that contains two compartments. One compartment consists of a silastic gel implant of a fixed size, and the second is an outer inflatable sack that can be filled with a saline (salt) solution to the desired size.

double standard the traditional view that sexual freedom is acceptable for males but not for females, and especially that premarital sex is expected of young men who may 'sow their wild oats,' but that 'nice girls' must maintain their virginity until marriage. This view is considered sexist today. See also TRANSITIONAL DOUBLE STANDARD.

double-tail sperm a (relatively rare) spermatozoon that has one head attached to two filaments.

double vagina a congenital anomaly caused by failure of the mullerian ducts to fuse during embryonic development. A double vagina is usually accompanied by a double cervix, each with a uterus. In most cases, the vagina, cervix, and uterus on one side will be larger than on the other side.

doubling time the time required for a cancer to double its size. The term is used in estimating the time required for a cancer of the reproductive system to reach a detectable size. Breast cancer cells, for example, double in size in 50 to 150 days, depending upon other factors. Counting backwards, a physician may determine that a breast cancer the size of a marble probably required 3 years to reach that diameter from the original cancer cell.

douche bag a syringe with detachable nozzles for the injection of fluids, used mainly to rinse the vagina and give enemas. The term is also applied in American English to a nasty, sloppy, and usually foul-mouthed person.

douching rinsing the vagina with a jet of water (sometimes containing vinegar, alum, soap suds, or even Coca-Cola) after intercourse. As a contraceptive measure douching is almost totally ineffective, and can even increase the chances of pregnancy by propelling the sperm towards the cervix. The practice is more common in the U.S.A. than Britain.

dowry the property or money that a woman brings to her husband when they marry, usually considered a contribution for support, but in some cases a price exacted by the husband (or his family) for the privilege of marrying him. The concept is archaic in this day of feminine liberation. Also called dower; marriage portion.

drag a colloquial word for female clothing worn by either a male transvestite or a female impersonator during a stage appearance. Not all transvestites are homosexuals, but those who are 'cross-dress' sometimes in an attempt to pass as women, or wear elaborate female costumes and dresses when they attend a *drag ball.*

drag queen a male homosexual attired in spectacular women's clothes, hairstyle, and jewellery for a 'drag ball' or party.

draw the blinds a slang term meaning to pull the foreskin back; also, to pull it over the glans penis.

Dreadnought the trademark for the first rubber condom with a reservoir end, introduced in the U.S.A. in 1901.

dressing patterns the idea that the clothes we wear are a major indication of our sexual role and gender identity. Originally males dressed as males and females as females, but unisex or androgynous (bisexual) clothes have become a fashion. Transvestites, on the other hand, dress in the clothes of the opposite sex, and studies show that they were often encouraged to cross-dress in childhood.

dressing ring a metal ring about 1 inch in diameter inserted through the glans, or tip, of the penis as a means of achieving greater sexual excitement during intercourse. During the Victorian era, the ring was also used to secure the organ in the right or left trouser leg (also called Prince Albert).

droit du seigneur (drô·ä′ dē sānyoer′) a term referring to the traditional belief that feudal lords in certain countries had the 'right of the lord' to 'deflower' the bride of a serf during the first night after marriage. This old literary theme was perpetuated by Voltaire and the authors of the French *Encyclopédie*, with variations on the Broadway stage and the Hollywood screen. The significance of this myth lies in its use as a symbol of authority and an expression of the prevailing conception of woman as sexual property. Also called virginal tribute, also ius prima noctis (Latin, 'right of the first night').

dry day a day in a menstrual cycle when cervical mucus is scant and thick. It occurs in the first days after the end of menstruation and is considered a 'safe day' for women who follow a birth-control method of avoiding intercourse around the time of ovulation.

dry fuck a vulgar slang term for a type of quasi-intercourse in which one goes through the motions without penetration of the vagina by the penis, usually with both partners keeping their clothes on. Verb: *to dry-fuck.*

dry hump an alternative—somewhat less vulgar—term for dry fuck.

dry orgasm a sexual disorder in which ejaculation does not occur in spite of adequate erection and stimulation. The failure is caused either by emotional factors or by a prostate disorder that produces retrograde (backward) ejaculation into the posterior urethra or bladder. Also called coitus sine ejaculatione; ejaculatio deficiens; ejaculatory incompetence.

dry vagina a vagina that does not become moist or wet during sexual excitement, and therefore does not lubricate itself. This condition is normal but not usual, and may make intercourse somewhat difficult and even painful.

dual masturbation an equivalent term for mutual masturbation.

dual orgasm a term referring to the orthodox

psychoanalytical view that the clitoris is the prime site of sexual excitement and orgasm in young women, but as psychosexual maturity is reached, the focus shifts to the vagina and clitoral orgasm is then a mark of immaturity and at least partial frigidity. Studies by Kinsey and by Masters and Johnson have revealed that the vaginal walls are relatively insensitive to touch and that many women do not have full vaginal orgasms. Their view, which is widely accepted, is that the vagina and the clitoris respond in identical fashion regardless of which is stimulated, though some women prefer stimulation focussed on one of these organs rather than the other.

dual-sex therapy the team approach to therapy for sexual inadequacy as developed by Masters and Johnson, based on the theory that two therapists are needed, one male and one female, because men acting alone cannot be expected to fully understand the feelings and reactions of a woman, and women acting alone cannot be expected to fully understand male sexuality—but when they collaborate in the process, therapy will be more effective and of lasting value.

DUB abbreviation for dysfunctional uterine bleeding.

ductless glands a term applied to any gland that empties its secretions directly into the bloodstream, such as the endocrine glands that secrete sex hormones.

ductus deferens (def′erens) an excretory duct of the testis and an extension of the epididymis. Anatomically, the ductus deferens, or vas deferens, begins at approximately the point at which the tubule of the epididymis becomes less twisted and begins moving upwards towards the prostate and its associated structures, particularly the seminal vesicles. Near the prostate, the ductus deferens becomes somewhat twisted again and enlarges into an ampulla before joining its seminal vesicle. The ductus deferens has a total length of about 18 inches and has a rather firm muscular structure. The inner lining of the duct is ciliated in some areas, apparently to help move spermatozoa along the route from the testes to the prostate.

duelling scars facial scars resulting from wounds acquired in fencing matches. Such scars were considered a badge of distinction and courage, and a sexual attraction among upper-class Germans in the 19th and early-20th centuries.

dugs an archaic term for the female breasts.

duration of foreplay the number of minutes spent in foreplay before actual coitus. The Kinsey study showed an average of 12 minutes in the 1940s; the Playboy Survey 30 years later found an average of 15 minutes. The Kinsey study showed that foreplay was longer among college-educated partners; the Playboy Survey found no difference in length of foreplay related to education.

duration of motility the movement of spermatozoa in a sample during the first 24 hours after ejaculation. In a fertility clinic, the sample may be checked every 2 hours for the first 6 hours and again at the end of 24 hours. A drop of 10 percent per hour in motility is considered normal, with possibly a few sperm still moving about a day later.

Dutch cap the name of a contraceptive device consisting of a rubber diaphragm fitted with a semirigid ring that is filled with a spermicide and inserted in the vagina. See also DIAPHRAGM.

dydo a gold, steel, or silver rod with small metal balls screwed on at each end. One or several rods are inserted in holes made in the rim of the penis to increase sexual excitement for both the man and the woman during intercourse.

dyke an alternative term for bulldyke. In the 19th century, dyke was a slang term referring to the female genitals.

dysfunctional uterine bleeding an alternative term for uterine bleeding, or abnormal loss of blood from the uterus in the absence of a tumour, pregnancy, inflammation, or detectable anomaly.

dysgerminoma a solid ovarian tumour that may be associated with pregnancy. It may also occur before or during adolescence and has been associated with some cases of female precocious puberty. It develops from primordial germinal tissue cells of early embryonic life, before the germ cells become differentiated into male or female sex cells.

dysmenorrhoea pain and cramps in the back and lower abdomen associated with menstruation. Primary dysmenorrhoea is menstrual pain that is experienced in the absence of any observable pelvic lesion and is probably caused by a uterine disorder. Secondary dysmenorrhoea is menstrual pain that is probably caused by a pelvic disorder. Mechanical dysmenorrhoea is a form of the problem that results from an obstruction, such as cervical stenosis (narrowing) that prevents a normal menstrual flow from the uterus. Primary dysmenorrhoea is often associated with menarche, or the onset of puberty. Spasmodic dysmenorrhoea is pain associated with the commencement of menstrual flow and may stem from an underdeveloped uterus or the presence of clots in the cervix, or both. Spasmodic dysmenorrhoea pain usually increases over a period of several hours, then subsides. This condition may decrease after the first pregnancy. Functional or congestive dysmenorrhoea is also known as psychogenic dysmenorrhoea and tends to increase during periods of emotional disturbance or anxiety. See also ESSENTIAL DYSMENORRHOEA; FUNCTIONAL DYSMENORRHOEA.

dyspareunia a medical term for coitus that is difficult or painful for the woman, regardless of the cause of the problem. See PAINFUL INTERCOURSE.

dysuria a condition in which urination is painful or difficult, usually because of an organic disorder such as a spastic bladder. Psychic dysuria is a term applied to an inability to urinate in the presence of other persons.

early ejaculation an alternative term for premature ejaculation, sometimes defined as ejaculation that occurs within 10 seconds after penile penetration of the vagina. Some experts would extend the time limit to at least 60 seconds after penetration.

ear piercing the most common form of body perforation, primarily for insertion of earrings often for sexual adornment. In some quarters, a single ring in the left ear of males is a sign of homosexuality.

ear pulling a habit that is interpreted by Freudians as a 'masturbatory equivalent,' and by others, such as Leo Kanner, as a substitute for thumb sucking.

easy rider a colloquial term meaning a man who marries a prostitute and lives off her earnings.

eat a slang term meaning (a) to perform cunnilingus or (b) to perform fellatio. In Shakespeare's use, the term refers to sexual intercourse generally, as in *Timon of Athens* (I, 1, lines 206-209): '*Apematus*: No; I eat not lords ... they [women] eat lords; so they come by great bellies. *Timon*: That's a lascivious apprehension.'

eat at the Y an American slang term meaning to perform cunnilingus (a woman's open legs forming the letter Y).

eat out a slang term meaning to have oral-genital sex. The term is used by itself or in phrases such as 'to eat someone out.'

effie a slang term for an effeminate man, who may be heterosexual or homosexual.

ecdysiasm a compulsion to take off one's clothes in public as a means of arousing sexual excitement in others. H.L. Mencken coined the term *ecdysiast* for striptease performers.

echinococcus cyst an infestation of the connective tissue of the fallopian tubes and ovaries by tapeworm larvae. Although rare in the United States, the condition is not uncommon in parts of Latin America, Australia, and Europe. The tapeworms enter connective tissue of the pelvis by travelling from the intestinal tract through the lymphatic system or bloodstream. The disorder is named after the species of tapeworm, *Taenia echinococcus*.

eclampsia a condition marked by convulsions and coma and associated with high blood pressure, fluid accumulation, and the excretion of proteins in the urine. It occurs in pregnant women or in women who have just given birth. In some cases, eclampsia is associated with uraemia, caused by the failure of the kidneys to excrete certain products of protein metabolism.

eclamptic symptoms the physical effects of an attack of eclampsia, which typically begins with a severe headache and may end in a coma. Symptoms reported by patients include dizziness, epigastric pain, vomiting, visual disturbances, mental confusion, and muscle twitchings. The muscle contractions and relaxations may become particularly severe, and the patient can experience loud breathing sounds and cyanosis, in which the skin acquires a bluish tinge because of a lack of oxygen reaching the blood in the skin. Coma follows, and the woman eventually regains consciousness with no memory of the episode.

ecouteurism a psychosexual disorder, or paraphilia, in which the preferred or exclusive method of achieving sexual gratification consists of listening to stories of sexual encounters or to the sounds produced during intercourse, either 'live' or on tape.

ecstasy the state of extreme euphoria experienced at the moment of orgasm, often considered to be the peak of human pleasure.

ectoderm the outer layer of the hollow ball of cells, the blastocyst, that develops from the zygote. Later it gives rise to the skin, nails, and hair.

ectopic anus an anus that is normal in structure and function but which is located in the abnormal site, such as side-by-side with the vagina.

ectopic pregnancy a pregnancy in which the foetus develops outside the uterus—in an ovary, a fallopian tube, or the abdominal cavity.

ectopic testis a testis that has become trapped in some abnormal area of the body, particularly a testis that has lodged in a location outside its normal route of descent, as in the thigh, perineum, or groin. An ectopic testis is distinguished from an undescended testis in that it has descended, but not into the scrotum.

ectopotomy a surgical procedure in which an incision is made through the abdominal wall to remove a foetus or other products of conception outside the uterus.

effeminacy a personality pattern among males that is considered typical of females. However, current studies of feminine attitudes and behaviour do not conform to the traditional concepts of femininity, and the definition of effeminacy is therefore in flux. Today, men who show a high degree of sensitivity and aesthetic perception, or an interest in homemaking and child care are not necessarily regarded as effeminate. But an urge to wear women's clothes, and a preponderance of female hormones are still regarded as indicators of effeminacy.

effeminate homosexuality a male homosexual pattern characterized by adoption of the gestures, voice inflections, and mannerisms often associated with femininity. Effeminate homosexuals may also dress in women's clothes (transvestism) and assume the passive role in intercourse.

efferent ducts the vasa efferentia through which the spermatozoa move from the testis to the epididymis. They are assisted in the migration by waves of peristalsis, caused by alternate contractions of circular and longitudinal smooth muscle fibres, much as food is moved through the digestive tract.

egg cell the immature ovum of the human.

ego-dystonic homosexuality a psychiatric term for a psychosexual disorder characterized by a persistent pattern of homosexual arousal that the individual (male or female) finds extremely distressing, distasteful, and a source of shame—yet, despite these negative feelings, the individual finds that he or she cannot eliminate the homosexual pattern and establish heterosexual relationships.

ego-syntonic homosexuality active homosexual behaviour that the individual, male or female, considers acceptable and in keeping with his or her personality and emotional needs.

eipnelus in ancient Greece, a young man's older male lover, who also teaches him (literally, who 'breathes into' him; from Greek *eis*, 'in,' and *pneein*, 'to breathe'). He is the opposite of an AITAS. See this entry.

ejaculate the semen expelled from the urethral meatus of the penis during intercourse; also, to expel semen in this manner. The average amount of semen per ejaculation has been calculated to be 4 cubic centimetres, with a weight of about 4 grams. For details on sperm, see SEMEN ANALYSIS; for details on substances and calories, see SEMEN CONTENT.

ejaculatio deficiens failure to ejaculate during intercourse. Also called ejaculatory incompetence; coitus sine ejaculatione.

ejaculation a phase of the male orgasm in which semen spurts outwards from the glans penis. According to Masters and Johnson, ejaculation is actually the second stage of a physiological action in which emission is the first stage, ejaculation being a subjective response to emission, which is marked by contractions of the ductus deferens, prostate, and seminal vesicles. See also DELAYED EJACULATION; EARLY EJACULATION; FEMALE EJACULATION; PREMATURE EJACULATION; RETARDED EJACULATION; RETROGRADE EJACULATION.

ejaculation centre an area of nerve cells believed to be in the sacral region of the spinal cord. The nerve centre controls ejaculation and other genital activities.

ejaculation physiology the process whereby the various nerves, muscles, and blood vessels produce a coordinated series of actions causing semen to spurt from the glans penis. The process involves four spinal nerves and, emanating from the spinal cord in the lower back, a system of autonomic nerves that react to erotic thoughts, which may also be stimulated by olfactory and tactile sensations. Sex hormones in the bloodstream help sustain the process, and the blood flow itself becomes a part of the activity by contributing to the swelling and turgidity of the penis and clitoris. According to Masters and Johnson, the ejaculatory event occurs in two stages. In the first stage, there is a spasmodic contraction of the seminal vesicles, and ampulla of the ductus deferens, and the ejaculatory ducts that moves the spermatozoa and seminal fluids to the urethra as it passes through the prostate. In the second stage, a series of rapidly successive contractions and relaxations of muscles near the base of the penis cause the semen to spurt through the urethra and out of the penis. The sensation of the second stage is associated with the pleasurable feeling in the male that is identified as orgasm. According to some experts, control of the second stage of ejaculation is at least partly subjective, and control of the action by suppressing or delaying the orgasmic phase makes coitus interruptus possible. The intensity of ejaculation and orgasm are influenced by a number of factors, such as the degree of sexual excitement and the age and health of the individual. After ejaculation, blood flows from the spongy tissue of the penis at a faster rate than fresh arterial blood flows in, until the penis is flaccid again.

ejaculation proper an alternative term for second-stage orgasm, when seminal contents of the male sexual accessory organs have released their contents into the urethral bulb and spasmodic contractions expel the semen forcefully through the urethral meatus of the glans.

ejaculatio praecox a medical term for premature ejaculation.

ejaculatio retardata a medical term for excessively delayed ejaculation during intercourse, often because of emotional factors such as anxiety or insecurity, or aging. The delay may also be achieved by training in self-control as a means of extending the pleasure of intercourse.

ejaculator seminis an alternative term for the bulbocavernosus muscle, or ejaculator urinae, in the male. The fibres of the muscle encircle the shaft of the corpus spongiosum and join with fibres of the corpora cavernosa. The muscle acts to empty the urethra after the contents of the bladder have been voided, and the fibres also participate in producing an erection of the penis by compressing the erectile tissue.

ejaculatory canal the duct about 1 inch in length that appears just outside the prostate gland, at the junction of the ductus deferens and the seminal vesicles.

ejaculatory control the ability to inhibit or delay ejaculation in order to prolong sexual foreplay or to postpone orgasm until the female partner is 'ready.' Ordinarily some measure of control is achieved by mental distraction (thinking about another subject) or by muscular relaxation (slowing or ceasing pelvic thrusts). Masters and Johnson have developed various special methods, such as squeeze technique, to increase control and to overcome premature ejaculation. In some Eastern cultures, Taoist and Tantric treatises advocate such techniques as closing the eyes, opening the eyes wide, holding the breath, pressing the acupuncture point above the right breast, gnashing the teeth, and firmly pressing the area between the scrotum and anus, because the semen duct is located there.

ejaculatory duct a duct on either side of the prostate, each slightly less than 1 inch in length, through which seminal fluid passes from the seminal vesicles into the male urethra. They join the outlets of the ductus deferens ampullae before reaching the urethra so that seminal fluid and secretions of the testes are combined at the junctions of the ducts.

ejaculatory incompetence the most commonly used term for coitus sine ejaculatio, or ejaculatio deficiens. The condition may be caused by a variety of factors, for example, fear of impregnating the partner, a traumatic emotional experience, and conscious or unconscious feelings of rejection towards the partner.

ejaculatory inevitability the moment during the sexual response cycle when the ejaculatory urge becomes irresistible, and ejaculation unavoidably occurs.

ejaculatory urge the impulse of the male to expel semen via the urethra during orgasm. In the sexual response cycle the man arrives at a point of 'ejaculatory inevitability,' when the ejaculation reflex is abruptly triggered.

Electra complex the female counterpart of the Oedipus complex in the male, in which the daughter falls in love with the father, becomes jealous of the mother, and blames the mother for depriving her of a penis. The term is based on a Greek myth in which Electra induced her brother Orestes to kill her mother Clytemnestra and her lover Aegisthus after these two had murdered her father Agamemnon and married each other. The term has been all but replaced by Oedipus complex which covers both a son's and daughter's attachment to the parent of the opposite sex.

elephant a British slang term for anus. It is short for 'Elephant and Castle,' which in turn is rhyming slang for 'arsehole.'

elephantiasis scroti a medical term for a gross swelling of the scrotum resulting from an obstruction of the lymph structures serving the scrotum.

See also FEMALE ELEPHANTIASIS; FILARIAL ELEPHANTIASIS; NONFILARIAL ELEPHANTIASIS.

11-ketoandrosterone a sex hormone that occurs in the urine and is measured in laboratory studies of testes and adrenal-gland functions.

11-ketoetiocholanolone a sex hormone secreted by the testes and adrenal glands and measured in urine samples to evaluate hormonal functions.

ELISA an acronym for enzyme-linked immunosorbent assay, a medical test system that is used to determine exposure of a person to the AIDS virus. The test detects an antibody to the virus, which indicates the person has been exposed to AIDS and may carry the virus, but it does not necessarily mean the individual who shows a positive test result is an AIDS victim. See also AIDS.

Ellis, Havelock (1859-1939) an English physician who devoted himself wholeheartedly to the psychology of sex and the science of sexology in direct opposition to Victorian inhibitions. Among the areas discussed in his seven-volume work *Studies in the Psychology of Sex* were recognition of erotic love as an art; the importance of touch, smell, sight and hearing in lovemaking; the nature of erotic dreams; and the prevalence of masturbation, exhibitionism, fetishism, sadism, masochism, and narcissism. He was also noted for his vigour and open-mindedness in advocating experimental premarital relations, early sex education of children, birth control, changes in the divorce laws, and elimination of criminal laws against homosexual acts between consenting adults.

emancipation of women another term for the feminist or women's liberation movement, in which women seek to free themselves from the demands and prohibitions imposed on them by a male-dominated society.

emancipatory striving a behaviour pattern occurring primarily among adolescents who assert independence from their parents and other adults by (a) seeking constructive experiences such as involving themselves in community work, or (b) turning against society by defying school rules, joining motorcycle gangs, taking drugs, or engaging in risky sexual practices such as bondage and discipline.

embarrassment dream a type of dream cited by Freud that usually takes the form of undressing in public. He believed this dream stems from similar experiences that aroused shame in childhood.

embracing behaviour a term applied to nonsexual embracing used by persons (and higher animals) as a means of reaching out for comfort and relief from anxiety in stressful or fearful situations.

embryo the developing organism between the stage of a fertilized ovum and the foetal state. In humans, an organism is considered an embryo from approximately the 14th day of gestation until the 55th day. An embryo at 55 days may measure about 3 centimetres from crown to rump and will possess all its principal organ systems, at least in rudimentary form. It will have a distinctly human appearance.

embryonic axis a theoretical line through the centre of an embryo, indicating an existing or future bilateral symmetry and determining which organs and tissues are on the left or right side.

embryonic disc a thickened plate of cells at one end of the blastocyst that emerges about the time the ball of cells becomes implanted in the wall of the uterus. It gives rise to the embryo proper.

embryonic growth rate the change in size and weight of an embryo or foetus during the period of gestation. During prenatal life, the body weight of an individual increases six billion times, compared with a 20-fold increase between birth and maturity. Between the fourth and ninth weeks of gestation, body length increases at an average rate of 1 millimetre per day, after which the sitting height increases at a rate of 1.5 millimetres per day. If the body continued to grow at the same rate after birth, it would be several million times the size of the earth at maturity. Fortunately, the rate of growth slows during the last foetal month and after birth so that 95 percent of the final weight is acquired between the end of gestation and adulthood.

embryonic period a span of approximately 7 weeks in the life of a new human organism, beginning approximately 2 weeks after conception and continuing until the start of the foetal stage. During this period, the embryo will be most vulnerable to viruses, radiation, drugs, or other external agents that can have teratogenic effects, resulting in a congenital abnormality. Embryonic life begins about the same time that the mother may realize she is pregnant because she has missed her menstrual period. At about the 22nd day, or a week later, the embryo's heart begins to beat. By the end of the fourth week, the embryo has acquired the limb buds that will develop into arms and legs. Around the 31st day of the embryonic period, the eyes, mouth and nose begin to appear. The external genitalia are also distinguishable.

emission an alternative term for first-stage orgasm of the male ejaculation process.

emmenology a specialized branch of medical science that studies the physiology and abnormalities of menstruation (Greek *emmena*, 'menses').

emotional divorce a marital relationship in which husband and wife live parallel lives with little communication or normal give and take. Studies show that this situation is more common among parents of schizophrenics than among other married people.

empty-nest syndrome a colloquial term for a reaction pattern frequently observed in one or both parents after their children have reached maturity and have established homes or families of their own. The 'syndrome' is characterized by feelings of emptiness, loss, mild depression, and sometimes grief, and is especially prevalent among parents who have been excessively dependent on their children and are unprepared for a life on their own.

endocervical insemination artificial insemination in which the semen is deposited in the canal of the uterine cervix, instead of or in addition to the deposit of semen in the vagina.

endocrine basis of homosexuality the concept that homosexuality is derived from an abnormal balance of sex hormones. Studies by Masters and Johnson and others have produced equivocal results, one experiment showing lowered testosterone levels and impaired spermatogenesis in males who were predominantly homosexual but no significant difference between heterosexual men and bisexuals. But the finding could not be explained as to cause and could not be demonstrated to be true of a majority of homosexuals.

endocrine-type sexual precocity sexual precocity in a male that results from a tumour or from hyperplasia (overgrowth) of the sex-hormone-secreting tissues of the adrenal cortex or testes.

endoderm the inner layer of cells of the blastocyst. It gives rise to tissues that form the linings of most of the cavities and passages of the body, such as the linings of the trachea, lungs, gastrointestinal tract, and urinary bladder.

endogamy the practice of limiting marriage to members of the same ethnic, kinship, cultural, or religious group. Endogamy has been particularly prevalent in societies where marriages were arranged by tribal chief, feudal lord, or the parents.

endometrial cycle the menstrual pattern as it affects the lining of the uterus, progressing in more or less monthly cycles from proliferation to erosion of the pars functionalis layer. The cycle is controlled by secretions of the female sex hormones oestrogen and progesterone in response to the release of ova from the ovaries.

endometrial hyperplasia an overgrowth of the endometrial lining of the uterus. The condition is a common cause of functional uterine bleeding.

endometriosis the presence of endometrial tissue, normally found in the lining of the uterus, outside the uterus in areas such as the urinary bladder, intestine, ovary, or the outer surface of the uterus.

endometritis an inflammation of the endometrium. Acute endometritis usually is the result of a bacterial infection of the tissue. Chronic endometritis usually is related to products of conception retained in the uterus, the use of an intrauterine contraceptive device, fibroids, or an infection that has spread from the fallopian tubes. Specific causes include effects of an abortion, spontaneous or induced; an infection acquired during labour; gonorrhoea; tuberculosis; infiltration of the uterine lining by placental cells; and aging. Senile endometritis is produced in part by changes in the endometrium that accompany aging; the normal columnar epithelial cells become thin and stratified, and thus more susceptible to infection as a complication of atrophy.

endometrium a specialized form of mucous membrane that lines the uterus. It is divided into two main types of tissue. One is the pars functionalis, which is shed during menstruation, and the pars basilis, which is associated with the myometrium, or muscular portion of the organ. The pars basilis is not shed and serves as a base for the proliferation of cells for the layers of pars functionalis that develops during the next menstrual cycle. The pars basilis is responsive to oestrogen but not to progesterone. The functional zone consists of a compact layer (stratum compactum) and a spongy layer (stratum spongiosum). The endometrium also contains glands, stroma, lymphoid follicles, and blood vessels. The stroma represents the supporting tissue of the endometrium. During the proliferative phase, the stroma, or covering, becomes enlarged with fluid, blood vessels, and actually increases in the size of the cells. During menstruation, much of the stroma is sloughed off and a denser, more compact stroma remains until proliferation begins again.

end pleasure a psychoanalytical term for the pleasurable release of tension that occurs during the culmination of the sex act, as contrasted with the 'forepleasure' experienced during foreplay.

enema addiction extreme dependence on the use of enemas and laxatives, especially among obsessive-compulsive individuals who associate regular evacuation with cleanliness and health. Sexually speaking, the sensations provided by enemas can be so enjoyable and exciting to some individuals that 'high colonic irrigation' is offered by many 'massage parlours'—and the interest in enemas can be so strong that it takes the form of a cult with its own magazines.

engagement the period in which a man and woman have come to an understanding that they will be married, usually formalized by the gift or exchange of rings. It is viewed as a period when the couple get to know each other better and test their relationship, including sexual responsiveness. Legally, engagement (or 'betrothal') is regarded as a binding contract, although today breach-of-promise suits are rarely undertaken, and may actually be banned.

engagement ovaries a term sometimes applied to painful swelling and congestion of the internal female genitalia because of prolonged, sexually stimulating petting without release of tension through orgasm. A similar condition, popularly called 'stoneache,' occurs in men.

English Collective of Prostitutes a 'trade union' that looks after the interests of prostitutes in England.

English vice a slang term for flagellation, derived from the popularity of the practice of whipping in British brothels. An alternative term is *English culture*.

engorgement filling with blood to the point of congestion; especially the process in which the caverns (corpora cavernosa) of the penis fill with blood during sexual excitement, pro-

ducing an erection. The labia majora, labia minora, and the outer third of the vagina also become engorged during the sexual act.

engrossment preoccupation or absorption in a book or activity. But in psychiatry the term is used in particular for the tendency of the father to be deeply involved in holding, playing with, and admiring his newborn child. Involvement of this kind is a source of pride, self-esteem, and elation.

enjoy a euphemism meaning to have sex. The term has been popular since the 16th century.

envy a complex emotion compounded of discontent with one's lot and a jealous desire to obtain the advantages (for example, wealth, position, or beauty) of another person. Competition among siblings (sibling rivalry) is probably the first expression of this emotion, but it may also take the form of penis envy, vaginal envy, and womb envy.

eonism a term introduced by Havelock Ellis to identify transvestism. The word was derived from the name of a French nobleman, Chevalier Charles Eon de Beaumont (1728-1810), a physically normal male and proficient swordsman who preferred wearing women's clothing. His parents had dressed him as a girl, and he often wore female clothing as part of his career as a secret agent. His transvestite life-style was so convincing that for 49 years he was believed to be a woman who sometimes dressed as a man.

ephebiatrics the study of changes that occur in a person during puberty and adolescence, including the causes and effects. It also may be a medical speciality that deals with the diagnosis and treatment of disorders peculiar to teenagers and young adults. (Greek *ephebos*, 'adolescent boy.')

ephebophilia a man's love for a boy who has barely reached puberty—common in ancient Greece.

epicene having characteristics of the other sex, as with an effeminate man or a masculine woman; also, lacking the characteristics typical of either sex, or 'sexless,' as in the case of Peter Pan. Jeans may be described as epicene since both sexes wear them.

epididymis (-did'imis) an elongated convoluted tubule that extends from the testis to the ductus deferens. It transmits sperm produced in the testis towards the ejaculatory mechanisms near the prostate. It consists of a body or central portion, an enlarged head, sometimes identified as the globus major, and a lower pointed tail that is continuous with the ductus deferens. At the testis or head end of the epididymis are from 12 to 20 ducts that provide passageways for the sperm to the epididymis from the interstitial cells of the testis, where the sperm develop. Although the epididymis occupies a small amount of space in its tortuously twisted form behind a testis, it may reach a length of about 18 feet if stretched out.

epididymitis any inflammation of the epididymis. The cause may be an infection or injury with symptoms of painful, tender swelling and fever. Epididymal nodules may be caused by tuberculosis, which results in adhesions between the epididymis and the wall of the scrotum, or by syphilis, which usually involves the globus major portion first. The cause of epididymitis also may be a tumour, which is rare but possibly cancerous, or a spermatocele in the globus major, usually in the form of a retention cyst. A retention cyst is characterized by the presence of a milky fluid in the epididymis, with or without spermatozoa. A spermatocele is translucent, but a tumour is opaque, when the scrotum is examined by transillumination.

epigenesis a theory in embryology that organ systems develop anew in the embryo and are not performed as such. The individual develops from a simple to a more complex form through progressive differentiation from less differentiated cells according to instructions encoded in a DNA template.

epimenorrhagia a menstrual flow that is profuse but which occurs at short intervals, a condition that often is an early sign of menopause.

epimenorrhoea a menstrual flow that occurs at abnormally short intervals.

episiotomy a surgical incision made at the perineum to permit delivery of the foetus. An episiotomy may be performed when the foetus is large, delivery is more rapid than expected so that there is not enough time for normal stretching of the tissues, and more room is needed for insertion of forceps or to manipulate a foetus away from a breech or other awkward presentation that would be difficult to handle.

equisexuality an older term for homosexuality (Latin *aequus*, 'same').

epispadias a development defect of the penis resulting in the urethral orifice on the upper side of the penis. The opening may be on the glans, the shaft, or the penoscrotal junction. Like hypospadias, the condition is a congenital deformity that can be corrected by sur-

gery. A similar defect can develop in the female urethra which may be marked by a cleft in the upper wall of the urethra.

epithelioma the type of cancer that most often involves the penis. It develops as a thickening of the epithelial cells on the surface of the penis and a downward spread of the cancerous cells through the lower tissue layers where the cancer cells enter lymph vessels. The cancer cells then travel through the lymph system to the presymphysial and inguinal lymph nodes, where the new cancers grow rapidly so as to form bulges under the skin at the base of the penis and in the inguinal areas. Untreated, the cancers erode through the skin.

epoophoron duct the vestigial wolffian duct sometimes found in the female pelvic cavity. It represents the remains of the embryonic mesonephric duct from which the bladder, urethra, and ureters develop. In the male, the tissue also forms the vas deferens and the duct of the epididymis. It normally degenerates in the female but may persist in a rudimentary form as the epoophoron.

erectile dysfunction inability of a male to achieve penile erection. The causes may be physical or psychic. Generally, if a man experiences an erection while sleeping but is unable to achieve an erection as a part of normal sexual activity, the cause is assumed to be psychic. Physical causes may include low testosterone levels, which can be caused in turn by a disorder of the hypothalamus or pituitary gland. Alcoholism, drug abuse, diabetes mellitus, syphilis, multiple sclerosis, stroke, and prostatectomy also are among possible physical causes of erectile dysfunction. Nearly any drug that affects the autonomic nervous system may also affect sexual functioning. Diuretics taken for high blood pressure are a common contributing factor. Depression, sexual guilt, and fear of intimacy are common psychic reasons, and in many cases a single episode of erectile dysfunction may result in a 'fear of failure' mental attitude in which anxiety about a possible repetition of the episode becomes the psychic cause for erectile dysfunction. Despite myths that aging is a common cause, studies of senior citizens demonstrate that while ejaculatory potency may diminish in later years, erectile function is usually retained. Psychic erectile dysfunction often is situational in cause and can be corrected by changing the place, or time, or some other factor that contributes to inability of the male to initiate or complete intercourse. Some experts have suggested that a change of sexual partners can have a therapeutic effect. A Masters and Johnson approach suggests that treatment be nondemanding, beginning with 'nongenital' pleasures, such as merely touching or fondling, rather than assuming that erectile function and intercourse will be expected of the male partner. The therapeutic foreplay is continued for several sessions that build towards normal intercourse, but without making any demands on the male that he must perform coitus in a satisfactory manner. For some physical causes of erectile dysfunction, hormone injections are recommended.

erection the swelling, rigidity, and elevation of the penis and, analogously but to a lesser extent, of the clitoris. See also FALSE EREC-TION; MORNING ERECTION.

erection centre a nerve complex located in the sacral or lumbar segments of the spinal cord that transmits impulses resulting in erection of the penis.

erection time the amount of time required for a male to achieve erection after the start of sexual stimulation. Studies of younger men show that an erection can usually be produced in less than 10 seconds. The time actually varies with different individuals and with the same person in different circumstances. Older men generally require a longer time to achieve erection, but again there will be exceptions.

erithraicon one of the mythical aphrodisiac plants of the ancient world. Erithraicon was said to be such a powerful sexual stimulant that merely holding the plant in one's hand would produce uncontrollable sexual desire. Women in particular were warned that erithraicon plants should not be touched unless the person was under the influence of an anaphrodisiac.

erogenous zone a region or part of the body that is exceptionally sensitive to sexual stimulation, including the clitoris, vagina, penis, mouth, anus, scrotum, and urethra, all of which are considered primary areas, as well as the breasts (especially the nipples), buttocks, the area adjacent to the sex organs (and to some extent the entire skin surface), and other orifices of the body (nose, ears). Also called erotogenic zone.

Eros the Greek god of love; a term used in psychoanalytic theory for the basic drive, or instinct, that comprises both the sexual instinct, which is aimed as preservation of the species, and the life instinct, or instinct

for self-preservation and individual survival. Also called life instinct.

erosive balanitis a form of balanitis that tends to occur as a secondary effect of a sexually transmissible disease. It is encouraged by phimosis which produces anaerobic conditions under the foreskin, leading to the incubation of certain disease organisms acquired during sexual activity. It blossoms into painful erosions of the glans and foreskin, accompanied by swelling and secretion of a yellowish, foul-smelling fluid. Surgery often is required to prevent gangrene and loss of the penis.

erotic sexually stimulating, as in erotic films, novels, or paintings; also, arousing feelings of love, as in romantic poetry.

erotica a category of literature or other artistic works (plays, films, illustrations, sculptures) dealing with erotic themes, especially in a manner that stimulates sexual responses. The term may also include 'obscene' and 'pornographic' material.

erotic aids artificial devices used to enhance or extend sexual excitement. Major items include dildos, vibrators, extension sheaths, variously shaped condoms, 'finger tinglers,' 'French ticklers' (clitoral stimulators, or love rings), vaginal balls, penile splints, plastic vaginas, and inflated dolls, and various pills, potions, and creams that are supposed to have an aphrodisiac effect. Also called sex aids; marital aids.

erotic apathy very limited interest in sex.

erotic-arousal pattern a combination of stimuli or a series of actions that produce a sexual response. Among humans the pattern is not so fixed as in animals, and may include many types of erotic behaviour: wearing provocative clothes and perfumes, romantic settings and music, flirting, and especially all the components of foreplay.

erotic art artistic productions based on sexual themes. Erotic art originated during the dawn of history or before, and was usually associated with magic and religious rituals. Sexual symbols, such as the phallus, were frequently depicted or sculpted, but there was less emphasis on the pleasures of sex than on fertility. Sexual activities, including different types and positions of intercourse, began to be depicted in the later Greek and Roman period, but were suppressed during the Middle Ages. It was not until the Renaissance that sexual themes were revived in the work of Botticelli, Michelangelo, Romano, Rubens and Rembrandt. During the 19th century, the Japanese and Chinese produced woodcuts and paintings of the most explicit sort, and during the early 20th century many Impressionist painters again returned to erotic themes and it is still a common focus of art.

erotic bondage restraint of various kinds applied for the purpose of inducing sexual excitement—for example, tying up the 'victim' with ropes, straps, chains, thongs, or bridles; also, limiting movement by applying manacles, gags, heavy masks, and blindfolds. Individuals or couples who practise bondage as a form of stimulation are frequently passive or timid souls who derive a sense of power from controlling others and living for the moment in a fantasy world of medieval torture and slavery.

erotic character the pattern of visible features that constitute sexual attractiveness, especially a person's figure, hair, voice quality, and skin texture.

erotic code according to William H. Davenport, the 'signs and acts which, in appropriate contexts, convey special erotic meanings that arouse sexuality and enhance its expression.' The code varies widely from culture to culture, including, for example, specific rules of sexual modesty (hiding or exposing sex organs) and specific physical features that constitute erotic beauty (slimness, obesity, or 'curvaceousness').

erotic dancing dancing as a sexual stimulant. Social dancing may be sexually exciting, especially if the bodies of the partners are in close contact (including frottage) or if they mimic sexual movements (for example, pelvic thrusts) while dancing apart. The rhythm of the music may also enhance the eroticism of the dancing. Erotic dancing also plays an essential role in non-Western societies such as African cultures, and early Greek and Dionysian rites, and the mystic love ceremonies of Tantrism.

erotic delusion a persistent symptom of erotic paranoia consisting of a false belief that another person is in love with the individual and is having an affair with him or her.

erotic festivals periodic festivals characterized by public rites, ceremonial dancing, and uninhibited sexual activity. Some Australian aborigines worship a 'spirit of sex' called Knaninja and conduct a ritual exchange of wives which they believe to be 'purifying'. Many societies in Oceania—for example, the Trukese, Yapese, and Trobrianders—hold feasts followed by ceremonial orgies, public

copulation, and sex expeditions in which groups of young men (and sometimes young women) seek out sex partners wherever they can find them. These practices are diminishing under Western influences.

erotic films films designed to elicit sexual interest or sexual arousal. Films of this type range widely from romanticized eroticism without focussing on actual sexual relations, to explicit depiction of sexual acts of all kinds, and, in some cases, bizarre activities such as flagellation, bondage, and sexual asphyxia. These latter films are known as 'blue films,' in contradistinction to 'art films' which are less explicit and pornographic.

erotic hanging hanging oneself, or being hanged by others, as a means of enhancing sexual excitement, often during masturbation. This aberration is based on the theory that partial suffocation increases sexual response by interfering with the flow of oxygen to the brain. A study has shown that 'erotized repetitive hangings,' as they are technically called, result in the death of at least 50 teenagers and young adults in the United States every year. See also AUTOEROTIC ASPHYXIA.

erotic hunger strike a term applied by Alfred Adler to a fear of eating among adolescent girls who seek to maintain a boyish figure as an escape from the normal feminine sex role.

erotic image a mental picture, based on visual or narrative stimuli, that arouses sexual interest or desire.

erotic instinct a Freudian term for the libido, or sex drive; also, another term for Eros, the life instinct, which is aimed at individual and species survival.

eroticism preoccupation with sexual arousal not only through direct stimulation of the genital organs or nongenital areas such as the mouth or anus, but also through sex-oriented materials such as erotic photographs, films, or magazines. Also called erotism.

eroticization another term for erotization.

erotic odours a term referring to the relation of odours to sexual activity. In Western society, odours directly associated with sex (especially body odour, bad breath, and vaginal secretions) appear to be often distasteful, judging by the widespread use of deodorants, perfume and after-shave. However, genital and other body odours, such as urine odour, have been found to have an aphrodisiac effect on some people. Perfumes may be used for the double purpose of covering body odours and enhancing sexual attractiveness. Eastern treatises such as *The Perfumed Garden* emphasize not only the erotic effect of odours emanating from the sex organs but the use of pleasant-smelling flowers, perfumes, aromatic oils, and incense in love rituals.

erotic paranoia a mental disorder in which the most prominent feature is a fixed erotic delusion. For example, a woman may believe she has had a secret affair with a man of great wealth and social status; and a man may insist that a great movie star is in love with him, finding 'evidence' for this conviction in newspaper photographs or even in the flight of birds.

erotic pyromania another term for pyrolagnia.

erotic response level the amount and kind of stimulation required to produce sexual arousal. In most people the erotic response level varies considerably from time to time and is contingent on such factors as the situation (highly romantic or less romantic), recent sexual satisfaction or deprivation, the skill of the partner, and the nature of the stimuli (such as explicit sexual material, or the attractiveness of the partner and the amount and kind of foreplay).

erotic transference the redirection of erotic feelings from one person to another, especially from an individual in one's past life to someone in the present. In psychoanalysis this process is termed libidinal transference and takes the form of transferring feelings of love from the patient's parents to his or her analyst.

erotic type one of three basic libidinal types described by Freud. In the erotic type the individual is preoccupied with loving and being loved.

erotism a synonym for eroticism.

erotization in psychoanalytic theory, the process of associating sexual pleasure and gratification with various parts of the body and their functions, including the mouth (kissing, oral sex), the anus (defecation, anal intercourse), the nose (olfactory sensations associated with sex), and the eye (voyeuristic pleasure in looked at nudity or sexual activity). According to Freud, many activities such as scientific inquiry and dancing may also be expressions of erotic drives. Also called eroticization; libidinization.

erotocrat a man of surpassing virility with a strong effect on women. See CASANOVA.

erotogenesis Freud's term for the origin of

sexual impulses or instincts, which in his theory are derived from several sources, especially the oral, anal, phallic, and urethral zones of the body.

erotogenic characterizing any impulse that stems from the libido and has the capacity to arouse sexual excitement. Also called *erotogenetic.*

erotogenic masochism an alternative term for primary masochism.

erotogenic zone another term for erogenous zone.

erotographomania a morbid preoccupation with writing love letters, usually anonymous and frequently expressed in religious symbolism.

erotolalia use of obscene words and phrases as a means of expressing sexual impulses, or to enhance sexual excitement during intercourse.

erotologist a semieuphemism for a collector of pornographic material, corresponding to *erotology* as a semieuphemism for pornography. The term erotology has recently assumed the additional meaning of a subfield of lexicology that deals with sex-related vocabulary. In addition, the term tends to be a synonym for sexology.

erotomania a psychiatric term with two meanings: a preoccupation with sexual thoughts and fantasies; and a compulsive, insatiable desire for sexual activity which, in some cases at least, arises from inner doubts about sexual adequacy or latent homosexual tendencies. Prime examples of erotomaniacs ('sex maniacs') are the historic Casanova and the legendary Don Juan. Also called, technically, aidoiomania.

erythroblastosis foetalis a severe form of foetal anaemia in which the blood of the foetus contains large numbers of immature red blood cells, and characterized by overactive bone marrow, cirrhosis, and enlarged spleen. Death frequently occurs in the uterus or shortly after birth. The case is an Rh blood incompatibility between the mother and the foetus. The mother's blood produces antibodies that destroy the red blood cells of the foetus. The mother's antibodies can cross the placental barrier to destroy the foetal blood cells. In addition to the Rh-factor incompatibility, various degrees of erythroblastosis foetalis can result from a conflict between the blood groups of the mother and foetus. The most serious may occur when the mother has group O blood and the foetus has blood type A_1, which is more reactive with O-type blood than other type A blood groups or type B.

erythrophobia an intense, morbid fear of the colour red as well as red objects. In sexual terms the fear is often associated with the fear of blushing aroused by sexual thoughts or exposure of sexual features, for example, the breasts or the crotch.

erythroplasia of queyrat a lesion on the glans of the penis consisting of red flat shiny plaques. Because of the tendency of the lesions to become cancerous and spread through the shaft of the penis, they are usually removed by surgery or other means as early as possible.

escutcheon a shield or plate depicting a coat of arms, but also the pattern of pubic hair that develops during puberty.

Eskimos a people with considerable variation among its different groups, but who have certain practices in common: sex hospitality; wife exchange as a means of changing the individual's identity and confusing the evil spirits during a catastrophe; institutionalized homosexuality; seed raising (a father has intercourse with his underage son's wife, and raises any offspring that result); a very low copulation and conception rate during the summer; and the belief (particularly among Asiatic Eskimos) that contact with a menstruating woman may be contaminating, and may cause a man to drown at sea. Other customs include multiple wives and, in one group at least (the Netsilik), multiple husbands; the use of powdered bird beaks as an aphrodisiac (Greenland Eskimos); and belief in the vagina dentata myth (also Greenland).

essential dysmenorrhoea a form of dysmenorrhoea in which menstrual pain occurs in the absence of any detectable pelvic lesion, and which is probably caused by factors involving the uterus itself. In some cases, the pain may be caused by uterine contractions and obstruction of normal blood flow to the uterine tissues. The condition may be characterized by low abdominal pain that may range from colicky and crampy to dull and constant. It may be accompanied by nausea, headache, diarrhoea and increased urinary frequency. The symptoms may begin immediately before the start of menstruation, reaching a peak a day later, then subsiding in 2 days. Essential dysmenorrhoea is most common among younger women. Also called period pain.

eternal suckling Freud's term for an individual who demands constant care, attention, and protection throughout life.

euchromatin the portion of the chromosome material that is actively involved in gene expression, as distinguished from heterochromatin, which represents a part of the chromosome involved only in the maintenance of cellular functions.

eugenics the scientific study of measures designed to improve hereditary characteristics, a well as the application of such measures through social control. The term positive eugenics is applied to measures that promote reproduction of individuals with desirable traits; and negative eugenics, to the prevention of reproduction of individuals with undesirable traits.

Eulenspiegel Society a predominantly heterosexual U.S. organization founded in 1971 to promote 'masochistic liberation.' It has since been broadened to include sadists and other 'sexual minorities.' (Tyll Eulenspiegel was a semifictitious prankster in 14th-century Germany. The German word *Eulenspiegel*, or Dutch *Ulenspegel*, may be read to mean, literally, 'Sweep me the mirror,' with the understanding of 'Sweep my backside.')

eunuch a male whose sexual glands (testes) have been removed before puberty; a castrated male. Eunuchs, or 'castrati' develop many of the secondary sex characteristics of females, especially a higher voice, absence of a beard, and scanty body hair. At one time, castration was performed to preserve the soprano voice of young choir boys, and also to provide harem guards who could not seduce their charges. (Greek *euoukos*, 'guardian of the bed.')

eunuchoid a male who resembles a eunuch in manifesting female sex characteristics such as a high voice and absence of facial and body hair. The condition involves impotence, and is caused by deficient production of male sex hormones.

eunuchoid habitus a body build in which the lower length of the body is greater than the upper length, when measured from the symphysis pubis as the normal median line of one's height. Also, the distance between the fingertips of the outstretched hands exceeds the standing height of the individual. Normally, the breadth of the outstretched arms should equal the standing height. The eunuchoid habitus is a physical characteristic of some individuals with a sex-hormone deficiency. The condition is much more common in males than females.

eunuchoid Turner's syndrome an exception to the general rule that females with an

XO sex chromosome complement are less than 5 feet tall. Some girls with the chromosomal aberration may be taller than normal with the eunuchoid disproportions of arm and leg length.

euphemism an inoffensive term used instead of a term that is considered offensive or embarrassing. Euphemisms are especially common in the areas of sex and bodily eliminations—such as the expression 'adult' for 'sexual' or 'pornographic,' or Boswell's and his contemporaries' tortured way of saying 'to copulate with a woman': 'to pour a libation of procreative juice into the proper orifice.'

eurotophobia a morbid fear of the female genital organs.

evirate (ēvī'rət) an archaic term for a man who has been emasculated and therefore feminized; also, a term applied to a man who is under the delusion that he has turned into a woman. (Latin *ex-* and *vir*, 'man, male.')

exaltolide phenomenon the ability of only mature women to perceive the odour of exaltolide, a synthetic chemical. Exaltolide reportedly has a musk-like odour, but studies show it cannot be detected by men or by females who have not yet reached puberty. Sensitivity of adult women to the odour of exaltolide varies with the menstrual cycle and peaks around the time of ovulation.

excitement a state of general arousal and emotional tension involving a pattern of physiological reactions that usually includes increased heartbeat and raised blood pressure.

excitement phase the first stage of the sexual response cycle, during which the individual, male or female, reacts increasingly to stimulation in the form of fantasies, dreams, erotic art or films, body odours, and especially viewing and caressing the partner's body, particularly the genitals. In the male, excitement begins with erection, and in the female, with secretions that lubricate the vagina. As sexual activity continues, tension and pleasure mount until the stages of plateau and orgasm are reached.

excrement fear another term for coprophobia, a morbid fear of faeces and contamination.

exhaust pipe a slang term for anus.

exhibitionism a psychosexual disorder, or paraphilia, characterized by a compulsive need to expose one's body, particularly the genital organs, as a means of achieving sexual excitement. The act is usually performed by a male in the presence of female children or unsuspecting adults, and may be accompanied or followed by masturbation. The surprise, fear, and horror aroused in this act gives him the extra thrill he needs to achieve erection and ejaculation.

exhibitionistic need an urge to attract attention or impress others by displaying one's wit, knowledge, beauty, or body.

exogamy a type of marriage in which the partner is chosen from outside the individual's social, ethnic, or cultural group. Today such marriages are almost as common as the endogamous types.

exoleti male prostitutes, usually rough and hairy, in brothels in ancient Rome. They were the opposite of the effeminate pueri.

experimental marriage an arrangement in which a man and a woman agree, verbally or in writing, to live together to test their compatibility and to determine if they should enter into a formal marriage. Seven-year experimental marriages were common in 10th-century England, and marriages of 1 year were permitted in Scotland before the Reformation. More recently they have been permitted in rural Latin America to determine the ability of the couple to produce children.

explicit sexual materials verbal and visual materials (stories, articles, photos, films, drawings) that describe or depict sexual anatomy or sexual activities in unreserved and unambiguous detail. Material of this kind may be designed to be educational or sexually provocative.

exposure the act of displaying one's sexual features to entertain or attract the interest of others. Common means of exposure among women are slit skirts, plunging necklines, striptease performances, belly dancing, and 'bunny' and topless costumes. Men go shirtless to display a hairy chest or engage in nightclub or theatrical performances in the nude.

external genitals the visible sex organs. In the female these include the vulva, labia minora, labia majora, mons veneris, clitoris, hymen, and the vestibule of the vagina. The external organs of the male comprise the penis, glans, prepuce, scrotum, and testicles.

external migration a phenomenon whereby an ovum released from the ovary on one side travels through the peritoneal cavity and enters the fallopian tube on the opposite side to be fertilized.

external sphincter one of the two bundles of circular muscle fibres that control the flow of fluid through the male urethra. It is located below the openings of the ejaculatory ducts, near the base of the prostate. In retrograde ejaculation, the external sphincter closes and the internal sphincter opens so that semen is forced into the bladder rather than through the penis—a technique used by some men for birth control.

extragenital effects the physiological effects of sex hormones beyond their sexual functions. For example, extragenital effects of testosterone include nitrogen, phosphorus, and potassium retention, water balance, and bone and muscle growth.

extragenital reaction responses to sexual stimulation in parts of the body other than the sex organs—(a) the breasts: erection of the nipples and engorgement of the areolae, especially in women; (b) the skin: flushing of chest and neck in women, feelings of warmth, perspiration; (c) the cardiovascular system: increased heart rate and elevated blood pressure; (d) the respiratory system: faster and deeper breathing, holding the breath and gasping during orgasm; (e) the digestive system: increased salivation and rectal spasms; and (f) the urinary system: closing of urinary sphincter in men, and the urge to urinate after orgasm in some women.

extramarital sex sexual relations with someone other than one's spouse; 'adulterous' intercourse. Kinsey found that by the age of 40 about 50 percent of men and 25 percent of women have had at least one extramarital affair, often attributed to unhappy marriage or to a search for variety and excitement.

extrauterine pregnancy another term for ectopic pregnancy.

extravaginal intercourse intercourse in which the erect penis is inserted in a body area other than the vagina. Types of extravaginal intercourse include coitus inter femora, coitus intra mammas, and coitus in axilla.

eye an old slang term for (a) anus or (b) vagina. In this sense, an *eye opener* may mean (a) the active partner in anal intercourse or (b) the penis.

F a common abbreviation for female in 'personal' ads.

face fucking fellatio in which the fellator lies on his or her back.

face man a slang term for a man who loves to perform cunnilingus.

face massager a euphemism for vibrator.

face-to-face intercourse coital positions in which either the man or the woman is above, or both sit facing each other. The advantages are an opportunity to look at the partner's face, to kiss, to carry on a conversation, to stimulate the clitoral area with the male pubic hair and bone, to stimulate the partner's breasts and nipples, and to adjust the angle and degree of penetration.

facial, to get a an American slang term meaning to be fellated.

fade an American slang term for a black person who seeks sexual partners who are nonblack.

faecal freak a person who derives sexual gratification from the eating of his or another person's faeces—an extreme case of coprophilia.

faeces-child-penis concept the psychoanalytical theory that an association exists in the male infant's mind between faeces as a part of the body that is eliminated and the later concern about loss of the penis during the Oedipal stage (that is, fear of castration).

faggot an American slang term for a male homosexual, usually derogatory. This usage apparently has no connection with the original meaning of faggot, which denotes a bundle of sticks or twigs used for fuel. Also called *fag*.

fag hag a slang term applied to a woman who seeks the company of homosexual men because such a relationship may offer protection from male sexual aggressiveness. Also called fruit fly.

fairy a slang term for a male homosexual, often derogatory.

fairy lady a slang term for the feminine partner of a lesbian couple.

fallectomy the surgical removal of a fallopian tube, or a portion of a tube. The procedure may be performed on either or both of the fallopian tubes. A common reason for the surgery is to prevent future pregnancies. A fallectomy also may be done to remove a cancer. Also called salpingectomy.

fallopian-tube pregnancy an ectopic pregnancy caused by implantation of a fertilized ovum within a fallopian tube. It often occurs as a result of a previous fallopian-tube infection. The woman's first symptoms usually include spotting and cramping pain in the lower abdomen shortly after missing a menstrual period. The symptoms may be similar to those of a threatened abortion, and some tests for pregnancy may be positive, although the uterus may appear smaller than expected for the length of gestation. There may be haemorrhage, shock, and peritonitis, which may be particularly severe and threatening if the fallopian tube ruptures before the disorder can be corrected surgically. Also called tubal pregnancy.

fallopian tubes two small tubular structures, about 4 inches long, that extend from either side of the anterior of the uterus. At the opposite end, near the ovaries, the fallopian tubes are bell-shaped with fingerlike (fibriated) edges. At this end, a fallopian tube is somewhat less than a half inch in diameter, but the calibre narrows to approximately 1/25 of an inch where it joins the uterus. Some of the cells lining the inside of the tubes project hairlike cilia that help move an ovum towards the uterus after ovulation. The fimbriae become turgid at the time of ovulation, apparently to help the fingers catch the ovum released by an ovary. As the ovum moves through the fallopian tube, it is most likely to encounter spermatozoa about halfway along the route to the uterus, the usual site of fertilization. If all conditions are favourable, the fertilized ovum, or zygote, will reach the fundus of the uterus and become implanted about 4 days later. An infection or lesion can interfere with normal transit of the fertilized ovum by partial closure of the tube, and the zygote may become trapped, developing as a fallopian-tube pregnancy. Obstruction of the tubes also may result in sterility because the spermatozoa and ovum are prevented from meeting. Also called oviducts.

Fallopius, Gabriello a 16th-century Italian anatomy professor at the University of Padua, after whom the fallopian tubes are named.

false erection the normally erect position of the nipples of the female breast, as distinguished from the erection that develops in more than half of all women during the excitement phase of sexual response.

false labour a not uncommon condition occurring in pregnant women when childbirth is imminent. Uterine contractions may occur once or twice an hour, but instead of increasing in frequency, they may cease or disappear completely for a period of time, after which they become increasingly frequent and regular.

false ovary a congenital anomaly in the form of a segment of ovarian tissue attached to a normal ovary by a band of fibrous tissue.

false passage medical jargon for injury to the penile urethra or corpora cavernosa by the insertion of foreign objects, including catheters, into the urethra. The urethra is easily punctured by solid objects. In addition to the initial injury, the wound in the posterior urethra often results in a pocket that becomes the site of an abscess.

falsies a slang term for a padded brassiere.

familial hormonal disorder an apparently hereditary condition in which sex-hormone levels are abnormally low, genitalia do not develop normally, and females may never menstruate. The impaired sexual characteristics are often accompanied by mental retardation, deafness, and poor muscular coordination. Also called Koennicke's syndrome.

familiarism a sociological term for the tendency to maintain extremely close relationships within the family, and to transmit this sense of solidarity to the next generation. Members of these families form such close attachments that they often have difficulty in establishing independent, mature relationships in adult life.

family as an adjective, a recent euphemism referring to the absence of sexual terms or scenes, as in 'for family viewing' or 'family entertainment.'

For other meanings see MATRIFOCAL FAMILY; NUCLEAR FAMILY; PATRIARCHAL FAMILY; PSEUDOFAMILY.

family counselling provision of professional guidance, advice, and face-to-face discussion of personal and family problems, including sex-related difficulties encountered by marital partners, ways of dealing with a homosexual family member, adjustment to sexual trauma such as rape or child sexual abuse, questions relating to abortion and genetics, and discussion of family planning.

family jewels a slang term for testicles.

family planning voluntary control of the size of the family, including the number and spacing of children, through planned pregnancies and the use of contraceptive measures.

family romance a psychoanalytical term for children's fantasies about their family. For example, they may picture themselves as children of other, more important, parents possibly because of disillusionment with their real parents; or they may imagine saving the life of their father or mother, or of a king or queen, who represents the parent, and in this way discharge their debt to their parents for having given them life.

family therapy group psychotherapy in which all members of the immediate family participate. The therapeutic process focusses on the interactions between these members, the improvement of relationships within the family and between the family and the outside world, the promotion of better communication between members of the family, and constructive solutions to difficulties, including, in many instances, sexual problems.

fancy man a slang term for a pimp, or a procurer.

fancy woman a slang term for mistress.

Fang an African society exhibiting a number of characteristic beliefs which may be shared with neighbouring societies: a taboo against daytime copulation (violating this taboo is bound to result in sickness); a contemptuous attitude towards all homosexuality, and the belief that the practice will be punished supernaturally with leprosy; fellatio as grounds for divorce if performed either by the husband or the wife; the most extreme use of aphrodisiacs ever recorded: over 100 plants and other objects such as the teeth of chiefs, the bones of albinos, and the sex organs of women who have been mothers-in-law; and holding 'love medicine' festivals to renew the sexual life of the young people. Also, many Fang believe that a boy will become impotent if milk from his mother's breast drips on his penis.

fanny a colloquial term meaning primarily the buttocks in the United States and primarily the female genitals in Great Britain. The term may be derived from *fundament*, and seems to have been in use since the 13th century.

fantasy a mental image that may take the form of imagined events, daydreams, or night dreams based on wishes and unfulfilled impulses. Sexual urges are often disguised or expressed in symbolic form. Examples are anal fantasy, anal-rape fantasy, courtesan fantasy, and incest fantasy. Also spelled phantasy.

See also ANAL FANTASIES; ANAL-RAPE FANTASY; BEATING FANTASIES; COURTESAN FANTASY; HETAERAL FANTASY; INCEST FANTASY; MASOCHISTIC FANTASIES; MASTURBATION FANTASIES; NECROPHILIC FANTASIES; POMPADOUR FANTASY; PREGNANÇY FANTASIES; PRIMAL FANTASIES; PROCREATIONAL FANTASY; REBIRTH FANTASY; SEXUAL FANTASIES; WOMB FANTASY.

fare a slang term for a prostitute's client.

fart a slang term meaning to expel intestinal gas through the anus. While the term is considered vulgar, it does not appear among the 28 terms in the TABOONESS RATING OF DIRTY WORDS. See this entry.

fartarse a slang term meaning to behave in an annoying or time-wasting fashion, usually in the expression *fartarse around*.

fascia a sheet or layer of connective tissue that may enclose or separate various parts of the body, such as the fascia clitoridis.

father-daughter incest sexual relations between a father and daughter, which is one of the most common forms of incest, exceeded only by the brother-sister form. The incest victim is often a young girl and the trauma can have life-long effects.

father figure an alternative term for father surrogate.

father fixation an inordinate, abnormal attachment to the father as experienced by either a son or a daughter. Freud attributes this type of fixation to inability to resolve the Oedipal situation satisfactorily.

father surrogate an uncle, stepfather, or family friend who takes the place of the actual father, performing typical paternal functions and serving as a model or 'father ideal' for the child. Also called father figure.

faute de mieux (fōt də myœ´) in psychiatry, the term for accidental homosexuality, especially a male's choice of another male as a sexual partner when no women are available—that is, 'for want of anything better' (which is the literal meaning of this French term).

fear of rejection the dread of being socially excluded or sexually refused. When sexual rejection is accompanied by ridicule, feelings of inadequacy and insecurity may be so intense that further overtures may not even be attempted or, if attempted, may be completely unsatisfactory. Also called rejection fear.

fecundation an alternative term for impregnation.

fecundity the capacity to produce offspring, especially in great numbers; fertility. The term is more frequently used for animals than for human beings.

feed one's pussy a vulgar slang term meaning to have intercourse—said of or by a woman.

felch queen a slang term for a homosexual who is sexually aroused by faeces.

fellatio sexual stimulation of the penis with the mouth, lips, and tongue. Freud claimed that sucking the penis is a substitute for the original gratification of sucking the nipple and, later, the finger. Also called fellation. (Latin *fellare*, 'to suck').

fellator a person who performs fellatio. The female form is *fellatrix*.

female circumcision an inaccurate term for clitoridectomy because the clitoris itself, not merely the prepuce, is excised.

female ejaculation an inaccurate term sometimes used for the secretion of a lubricating fluid by glands adjacent to the vagina during sexual stimulation. The flow increases as sexual excitement builds, and in some cases sudden contraction of the vaginal walls causes the fluid to spurt out—which is the basis of the mistaken notion that women ejaculate as men do.

female elephantiasis a variation of the elephantiasis that affects the scrotum of males, causing an enormous enlargement of the scrotum. In females, it is the vulva that may become vastly enlarged for the same reason, a blockage of the lymphatic system resulting in an accumulation of fluid. The greatly enlarged vulva may have a surface that is pale and smooth or nodular and warty in appearance.

female-genitals fear another term for erotophobia.

female impersonator a male entertainer who dresses as a woman and performs in variety or nightclubs. Female impersonators are not necessarily transvestites or homosexuals.

female masturbation the use of masturbation among women of all ages as a means of reaching orgasm. According to Kinsey studies, masturbation was the main source of sexual orgasms among unmarried women before the age of 20. In adolescence, it accounted for nearly 85 percent of the orgasms. The figures declined gradually to 37 percent for unmarried women at age 40, then increased again to account for slightly more than half of all orgasms after age 45. Masturbation accounted for about 10 percent of all orgasms for married women of all ages and from about 15 percent to nearly 30 percent for the previously married. In the age groups between 36 and 50 years, the use of masturbation as a source of orgasms was approximately the same, around 10 percent, as extramarital sex among married women.

femaleness the typical anatomical and physiological features of a girl or woman, including the organs that control reproduction and nurturing of the child. The female sexual characteristics are derived from the sex (XX) chromosomes.

female orgasmic dysfunction a term proposed by Masters and Johnson to replace the loose term frigidity. It is applied to women who do not go beyond the plateau phase of sexual response and therefore do not attain orgasm. The two forms of dysfunction are primary orgasmic dysfunction and situational orgasmic dysfunction. Causative factors are of three types: (a) organic, including defective sexual apparatus, hormonal imbalance, nervous-system disorder, inflammation or lesion in sex organs, aging, or excessive use of drugs or alcohol; (b) relational, including the male partner's overeagerness, clumsiness, marital conflicts, or a sexually undesirable mate; and (c) psychological, including negative feelings about sex (shame, disgust,

guilt) implanted by parents, fear of pregnancy, homosexual tendencies, or overconcern about reaching a climax.

female orgasm frequency a relationship between female orgasms per week and age, as reported in the Kinsey studies. Like the studies of male orgasms, the Kinsey survey began at the age of 15. The teenage girls experienced an orgasm an average of once every other week. The peak of female orgasm frequency seemed to occur between the ages of 25 and 45, at between one and two orgasms per week. After 45, there was a steady decline with age until the age of 80. Among married females in their 20s, 5 percent reached orgasms five to seven times per week.

female sexual-desire peak the phase of the menstrual cycle when a significant proportion of women express a heightened sex drive. Of numerous studies, results indicate that 30 percent of women reach their peak of sexual desire just before menstrual flow begins, about half reach a sexual-desire peak after the start of menstrual flow, and the remainder prefer sexual intercourse around the time of ovulation.

female sperm a spermatozoon carrying a female, or X, sex chromosome. The X-chromosome sperm has a larger head than the Y-chromosome sperm. The head also is oval-shaped. The female sperm is heavier and slower. When a sample of sperm is allowed to stand for a period of time, the heavier female sperm settle to the bottom while the lighter male sperm float to the top.

feme sole (fem sōl) a legal term for a single woman, widow, or married woman who is divorced or legally separated from her husband. Also called femme sole (French, 'solitary woman.')

feminine hygiene the colloquial term for measures taken by women to insure sexual cleanliness and absence of body odour on a daily basis, especially during menstruation and pregnancy. Among these measures are bathing, powdering, and vaginal spraying. Many advertisers also use the term for sanitary tampons and towels, contraceptives, suppositories, and jellies.

feminine identification a tendency of some boys and men to adopt the female role and female behaviour characteristics of the particular culture, including gestures, verbal expressions, interests, personality traits, and, in extreme cases, women's clothes (transvestism). In some instances a masculine role model has been lacking during the individual's upbringing, or the mother 'has always wanted a girl.'

feminine identity an inner sense of belonging to the female sex. Among male transsexuals this sense of affiliation may be so strong that they feel they were 'meant to be' female, or actually are internally feminine in spite of external male characteristics.

feminine masochism a term applied by Freud to a pattern of receptivity, passivity, and acceptance which he considered to be characteristic of the 'feminine nature.' The term is also applied to the tendency of some males to gratify a need to be punished by fantasizing that they are women suffering the pangs of giving birth or serving as prostitutes against their will.

feminine traits personality characteristics of girls and women. Historically, women have been described as primarily interested in child rearing and homemaking, and as sexually submissive, highly emotional, illogical, noncompetitive, and non-aggressive. Currently the trend is to question whether such traits are innate and basic, and to emphasize the idea that in view of the wide variations from culture to culture and from time to time, such traits may be more socially conditioned and less universal than was claimed in the past.

femininity the pattern of physical, social, and sexual role characteristics that are considered typical of the female. Today the personality pattern associated with femininity in Western society is changing.

femininity complex the controversial theory of the psychoanalyst Melanie Klein that boys respond to castration fear by wishing they had breasts and a vagina (vaginal envy) but at the same time dread the feminine role and react to this dread by becoming excessively aggressive.

femininosexual an obsolete term for lesbian.

feminism a physiological disorder occasionally found in men who develop enlarged breasts, wider-than-usual hips, and a higher-than-usual voice because of undersecretion of androgens or oversecretion of oestrogens. The term is also applied to the FEMINIST MOVEMENT.

feminist movement a widespread and extremely influential movement by women against male-dominated society, a demand for equal pay for equal work, and the right of women to social and sexual equality including full power, responsibility and rewards in all aspects of life. More specifically, feminists demand an abolition of the double standard, a sharing of homemaking and child-rearing responsibilities, and elimination of the traditional stereotype of women as fragile, dependent, passive individuals who are governed by emotion rather than reason. Also called women's liberation movement; emancipation of women. Colloquial terms are women's lib and fem lib.

feminization a condition in which a male acquires female qualities or characteristics, with or without alteration or curtailed natural development of the male reproductive organs. In one form of feminization, a genetic male with normal XY chromosomes produces normal levels of male sex hormones, but the rest of the body fails to respond so that the individual has the superficial appearance of a female.

feminizing neoplasms tumours of the ovaries that may result in precocious puberty in a girl, or irregular uterine bleeding, breast enlargement, or endometrial hyperplasia in a sexually mature woman.

feminizing testes syndrome a form of pseudohermaphroditism associated with an inherited defect in testosterone response. The individual has a blind vaginal pouch and breasts. However, testes also are present within the labial folds. The patient is treated by surgical removal of the male gonads and administration of oestrogens. There is no uterus, and the patient does not menstruate and is infertile.

femme fatale (fäm fätäl') a woman who is reputed to have an irresistible attraction for men. Typically she wears seductive clothes, speaks in a throaty, 'sexy' voice, and makes a studied attempt to be mysterious and fascinating. The whole idea seems dated today, harking back to Pola Negri and other Hollywood sirens.

femoral testicle a testicle that descends from the abdomen but fails to reach the scrotum, becoming trapped instead under the skin of the thigh at about the level of the scrotum.

fence sitter a slang term for a bisexual woman.

fennel a tall green plant with tiny yellow flowers, used in soups, sauces, and other preparations that are claimed to provoke sexual desire. Its reputation as a sex stimulant is known throughout the world. The ancient Hindus mixed fennel juice with milk, honey, sugar, and licorice for an aphrodisiac.

ferning a pattern produced by mucus from

the uterine cervix at the time of ovulation. The mucus during ovulation becomes polymerized into elastic strands, called spinnbarkeit, which can be drawn into filaments 4 inches in length. When placed on a microscope slide, the mucus dries into crystals that form a fernlike pattern. If blood or an infection is present, the phenomenon will not occur. The spinnbarkeit mucus is believed to develop to help the spermatazoa move rapidly through the cervix towards a just released ovum. Shortly after ovulation, the character of the mucus changes again, because of the influence of progesterone, and dries into granules rather than a frondlike pattern when placed on a microscope slide.

fertile days the days during the menstrual cycle when the woman is most likely to conceive. To allow for individual variations, fertility is frequently considered to be highest between the 10th and 18th days after the beginning of the menstrual period.

fertility the ability to reproduce; the capacity for conception. See also NATURAL FERTILITY; POTENTIAL FERTILITY.

fertility awareness a woman's awareness that she is about to ovulate or has ovulated. The natural family-planning method of birth control involves a recognition of the signs and symptoms that indicate the days on which pregnancy may occur.

fertility cycle the menstrual cycle marked by the rise and fall of levels of female sex hormones, particularly oestrogen and progesterone, over periods averaging 4 weeks. There is no similar fertility cycle in men, who maintain a relatively stable fertility level throughout most of their adult years.

fertility drugs any of the hormonal medications administered to stimulate or restore fertility in a woman. When the hormone given to a woman is designed to stimulate follicle development of the ovary, the drug may unintentionally stimulate the development and release of more than one ovum at a time, resulting in multiple births. As many as 15 fertilized ova in a woman using fertility pills have been reported. Unfortunately, the fertility drugs tend to be self-defeating in that multiple births also have a high death rate.

fertility rate the number of pregnancies per year per 1,000 women of childbearing age. It has been estimated that if such women engage in regular intercourse without contraceptives, approximately 800 will be pregnant by the end of the year.

fertilization an alternative term for impregnation. See also INTERNAL FERTILIZATION.

fertilization membrane a membrane that surrounds the zygote after fertilization of the ovum by the spermatozoon. It is a viscous membrane formed by granules of the cytoplasm and serves to prevent the penetration of the ovum by any other spermatozoon. The membrane is formed by the stimulation of a substance, oocytin, that is carried by spermatozoa.

fetish a nonsexual object or part of the body (glove, foot, shoe, handkerchief) that is endowed with sexual symbolism and is capable of arousing sexual excitement. In psychoanalytic theory, a shoe may represent the vagina and a female foot may represent a penis. Another type of fetish is a talisman or amulet that is believed to embody a supernatural spirit and to possess magical powers, such as bringing luck. See also GARTER FETISH; LEATHER FETISH; NONSEXUAL FETISH; SEXUAL FETISH; RUBBERITES.

fetish forms the shapes of objects regardless of their texture, that have an appeal for certain fetishists. Shoes are a common example of a fetish form.

fetishism a psychosexual disorder, or paraphilia, in which sexual gratification is repeatedly or exclusively achieved through fondling, kissing, or licking inanimate objects such as women's shoes or undergarments, garters, or locks of hair. Handling these objects is often accompanied by sexual fantasies and masturbation. See also AMPUTATION FETISHISM; ANAL FETISHISM; BEAST FETISHISM; FOOT FETISHISM; SHOE FETISHISM.

fetishistic cross-dressing transvestism for the express purpose of achieving sexual excitement.

feuille de rose (fœ'ē də rōz' a French term for anilingus (literally, 'rose petal').

FF abbreviation for fist fucking, sometimes used in 'personal' ads.

F factor a fertility factor found in some primitive organisms that has the ability to reproduce by itself or as part of a chromosome. The F factor appears able to confer its reproductive ability on genetic material that otherwise may be unable to conduct the reproductive process. Also called sex factor F.

fiancé a man who is engaged to be married.

fiancée a woman who is engaged to be married.

fibroma of the vulva an overgrowth of connective tissue of the vulva, which may become an elongated pedicle, swollen with fluid if the condition is complicated by a circulatory disorder.

fibromyoma a type of tumour that is associated with overdevelopment (hypertrophy) of the prostate in older men. The tumour consists mainly of smooth-muscle and fibrous connective-tissue cells that suddenly begin to proliferate around the urethral ducts and glands. The tumours eventually compress the portion of the urethra passing through the prostate so that urination is difficult.

fibrous hymen a hymen that is abnormally thick and tough, requiring a surgical incision to permit the woman to consummate intercourse because the hymen resists penile penetration.

fig a fruit that was the symbol of the penis and the vagina in ancient Dionysian festivals, sharing the stage with grapes and wine. Plutarch recorded the use of the fig in ceremonies of the cult of Priapus. The Spanish explorers introduced the fig (one alleged aphrodisiac) to the Western Hemisphere and with the help of Cortes introduced chocolate (another alleged aphrodisiac) to Europe.

figurae veneris the learned (Latin) term for COITAL POSITIONS. See this entry.

filarial elephantiasis elephantiasis that is caused by an invasion of the lymphatic structures by tiny worms. *Filaria bancrofti*, transmitted by a mosquito bite. The worms cause a mechanical obstruction of the lymph vessels, resulting in a massive accumulation of fluid and swelling of the affected organ, which in men is usually the scrotum.

fille de joie (fē'ē də zhô·ä'; French 'girl of joy') the most common French term for prostitute.

fimbriae an anatomical structure that resembles a fringe, such as the fimbriae or threadlike processes of the upper opening of the fallopian tube, which help to guide the ovum from the ovary into the fallopian tube.

finger, to a colloquial term meaning to masturbate—said mainly of a woman.

finger, to give the a slang term referring to the American gesture of extending the middle finger of a hand upwards—which is considered obscene because it is meant to say 'Up your arse' or, for short, 'Up yours.'

finger defloration rupture of the hymen by insertion of a finger when the child is as young as 1 year of age.

finger fucking a slang term for manual stimulation of the clitoris and vagina or, amongst male homosexuals, the anus.

finger pie a slang term for manual stimulation of the clitoris and vagina.

first leg of three an older euphemism for penis.

first love the first experience of an adolescent girl or boy with an exclusive relationship that is usually based on a combination of physical attraction, a need to share affection and understanding, and a romanticized conception of love. Sexual activity other than handholding, kissing, and the like does not usually play an overt part, and the relationship is more akin to infatuation than to deep and abiding love.

first-stage orgasm the first of two phases of the male ejaculation of semen during sexual excitement. The first stage is marked by the release into the dilated urethral bulb of the contents of the prostate gland, seminal vesicles, and the ductus deferens.

first time the first experience of intercourse. In Eastern mystical teachings, the initial experience is fraught with more significance for the girl than for the boy, but for both it is regarded as a religious rite. The boy has usually been taught the art of lovemaking by an older or experienced woman, but for the girl the first experience of intercourse is regarded as a 'once-in-a-lifetime event,' and, as Douglas and Slinger point out in *Sexual Secrets*, 'the man should be aware of this and treat her as a goddess. Envisaging himself as a representative of Lord Shiva, the Supreme Yogi, he should initiate her into sex gently and in the spirit of service ... It is especially important to make the First Time a memorable and joyous occasion.'

first try a young man's first attempt at intercourse. If normal anxiety and tension can be overcome (usually with the aid of the partner) and he performs reasonably well, confidence increases and future attempts will usually be successful. But if he fails, and his partner does not give him the reassurance he needs, studies show that he may be laying the groundwork for further failures and even, in some cases, impotence. Young women are usually taught not to expect a full response on their first try, and are generally less affected than young men if it does not occur.

fish a derogatory slang term for (a) vagina or (b) woman, mainly in male homosexual usage.

fish and onions a culinary concoction designed to ensure an erotic reaction. The combination probably began with the Romans who believed that both fish and onions were aphrodisiacs. And serving them together doubled the chances for an amorous evening.

fishwife a slang term for a male homosexual's wife.

fist fucking a type of ANAL STIMULATION. See this entry.

fit end to end an obsolete slang term meaning to have intercourse. Also called *to fit ends*.

five-digit system a parity classification system used to record (a) the number of pregnancies, (b) the number of deliveries, (parity), (c) the number of premature deliveries, (d) the number of abortions, and (e) the number of living children. Thus, a woman pregnant for the first time is recorded as 1-0-0-0-0; if the pregnancy ends with a viable infant, the record shows 1-1-0-0-1. A second pregnancy is indicated as 2-1-0-0-1, but if the pregnancy ends in abortion, the record shows 2-1-0-1-1.

fixation a strong attachment to an idea, theory, or another person, usually one's father or mother. In psychoanalysis, fixation refers to the persistence in adult life of an early psychosexual stage or type of gratification, or a reaction to stress in which the individual regresses to the point where development was arrested in childhood. Examples are preoccupation with oral and anal sex, compulsive cigarette smoking, or thumb sucking in adulthood.

fixation patch a patch of woven plastic mesh that is bonded to a female breast implant to help hold it in place after mammoplasty. The plastic mesh becomes attached to the connective tissue of the underlying muscle and helps hold the breast implant erect; thus, the weight of the implant is not entirely supported by the skin of the breast.

flaccid an alternative term for limp, describing the condition of the penis before and after an erection.

flagellantism the religious doctrine of self-punishment, or punishment by others, particularly by flagellation, with the objective of doing penance, 'mortification of the flesh,' or self-discipline. The doctrine originated in the 12th century. Today the term is more often applied to a sexual disorder in which whipping or being whipped is practised for the purpose of sexual arousal and gratification.

flagellation the practice of flogging or being flogged as a means of producing sexual excitement or, in some cases, as an expression of sadistic or masochistic impulses. Beatings of various kinds, including flagellation (colloquially called 'fladge'), are sometimes provided as a service by houses of prostitution.

flanquette (French, 'flanking') a coital position in which the man's legs are astride one of the woman's legs, and her legs are astride one of his. This brings different areas of skin into contact, and changes the angle of entry into the vagina.

flapper a once-popular slang term for a young woman who tried to appear sophisticated and unconventional in dress and manner. (The term reportedly was derived from a fad of girls who wore their overshoes in wet weather unbuckled so that the unfastened sides would make a flapping noise.)

flap shot a slang term for a close-up picture of the female genitals in a pornographic film or magazine.

flasher a slang term for an exhibitionist, particularly a man who suddenly exposes his sex organs to women.

flat condyloma a large flat lesion often observed near the anus or on the vulva in cases of secondary syphilis. The lesion usually appears in clusters and may be associated with congenital syphilis patients under the age of 5 years.

flat fuck a vulgar slang term for lesbian intercourse.

flea-wort an aphrodisiac according to Pliny the Elder. In *Historia Naturalis* he wrote that the sap of the flea-wort plant not only would increase the sexual desire of a woman but would ensure the birth of male offspring.

fleece an older term for the female pubic hair.

flesh an obsolete term meaning to have intercourse—also *to flesh it*. The term was used approximately from the 16th to the 18th century.

fleshy excrescence an older term for clitoris.

flip-flop a slang term meaning to change roles in anal intercourse.

flip side a slang term for buttocks or anus.

flirt to behave amorously, or coquettishly, without serious intentions, as in winking or smiling to attract the other sex. *Flirting* is often a first tentative step towards a sexual relationship.

flogging repeatedly striking a child or adult with a whip or stick. Though originally a form of punishment or penitence, the practice is now more likely to be associated with erotic bondage and other sadistic means of sexual gratification.

floral arrangement another term for daisy chain.

fluorescent antibody technique a laboratory method of detecting the gonorrhoea organism in persons who show no outward signs of infection.

Fluorescent Treponemal Antibody Absorption Test (FTA-ABS) a type of fluorescent antibody test in which blood serum is treated with a fluorescent dye that makes the syphilis organism glow when examined under ultraviolet light.

fluoxymesterone an oral drug that is sometimes prescribed to increase testosterone levels in a man afflicted with impotence caused by low testosterone production.

foetal activity movements of the foetus in the uterus, which are usually strong enough to be felt by the mother around the fifth month, when it measures about 5 inches in length and weighs about one and a quarter pounds. At one time these movements were termed quickening, and were believed to mark the beginning of life.

foetal adrenal androgen a hormone secreted by the adrenal gland of the foetus that results in masculinization of the foetus. Excessive growth of the foetal adrenal gland before the 12th week of gestation can result in masculinization of external female genitalia, leading in some cases to female pseudohermaphroditism.

foetal alcohol syndrome a somewhat predictable pattern of mental and physical abnormalities among children of mothers who consume alcoholic drinks heavily during pregnancy. The anomalies include strabismus and other eye disorders, arm, leg, and joint abnormalities, poor muscular coordination and weak grasp, heart abnormalities, and mental retardation. Historically, knowledge about the possible effects of alcohol consumption on offspring dates back to early Greek and Roman periods when laws in some cities, such as Carthage and Sparta, prohibited consumption of alcoholic drinks by newlyweds so that they would not conceive children who would be born with mental or physical defects. Also called alcoholic mother syndrome.

foetal asphyxia a condition that can occur while the foetus is in the uterus if the carbon dioxide level rises while the oxygen level is inadequate. The imbalance of respiratory gases in the foetal circulation results in respiratory and metabolic acidosis. This results in turn in the foetal blood becoming acidic, which can produce brain damage or be fatal.

foetal blood vessels the blood vessels within the umbilical cord that transport oxygenated blood and nutrients from the placenta to the embryo or foetus and remove waste products from the embryo or foetus. The umbilical cord normally contains two arteries and one vein, but a small percentage of umbilical cords contain only one vein and one artery. The vein carries oxygenated blood and nutrients while the arteries return the deoxygenated blood to the placenta.

foetal circulation the circulation of blood between the foetus and the placenta. Circulation is through the umbilical cord which normally has two arteries and one vein. The vein carries freshly oxygenated blood to the foetus from the placenta and returns deoxygenated blood via the arteries. Because the foetus does not breathe, the placental blood supply is its source of oxygen, the oxygen having entered the blood supply from the mother's lungs. The placental blood supply also is the source of all the foetal nutrients needed for growth and development. The foetal heart begins beating around the 22nd day of gestation. The placental blood travels by several paths after reaching the liver, some flowing to the inferior vena cava through blood vessels from the liver or by a route through a vessel called the ductus venosus. The placental blood mixes in the vena cava with blood returning from the abdominal wall and the lower extremities, enters the right atrium of the heart and passes through a hole in the inner wall of the heart to the left atrium. It then flows into the left ventricle and is pumped into the aorta for delivery to the head and upper extremities. The complex pattern of circulation changes abruptly at birth when breathing begins and the umbilical cord is cut. The hole between the right and left sides of the heart must close, and some of the internal foetal blood vessels, no longer needed, atrophy. If the foramen ovale, the hole between sides of the heart, fails to close, the abnormal 'blue baby' condition results.

foetal distress the disordered functioning of a foetus whose life is threatened by such conditions as toxaemia of pregnancy, foetal alcohol syndrome, an infectious disease transmitted through the placenta, maternal drug addiction, or an injury that could produce a spontaneous abortion.

foetal erections erections of the male foetus in the uterus. Such erections, which can be observed in ultrasound images, occur regularly throughout the foetal development, beginning in early stages. 'The human sexual response system begins to function in utero

and continues throughout the entire life span'
(Mary Calderone).

foetal infection the transmission of an infectious disease from a mother to a foetus before or during labour. The foetus can acquire a disease organism by inhalation of infected amniotic fluid, by transmission of a pathogen across the placental barrier, or by contact while passing through the birth canal. Diseases most frequently acquired in the birth canal are gonorrhoea, herpes virus Type 2, haemolytic streptococcus, and *Candida albicans*. Rubella and syphilis are among diseases acquired in utero. A foetus is most vulnerable to rubella virus in the first 10 weeks of the pregnancy. The risk of foetal death from syphilis is about 25 percent if the mother is not treated by the 18th week of pregnancy. Herpes virus Type 2 can be transmitted through the placenta as well as by contact with the virus in the birth canal.

foetal-maternal exchange the transfer of substances between the mother and foetus across the so-called placental barrier. From the maternal side, oxygen and nutrients are supplied. In the foetal exchange, waste products of foetal life are passed into the mother's bloodstream. The foetal-maternal exchange differs somewhat during the first trimester and the second and third trimesters because the foetal and maternal bloodstreams are separated by a double membrane wall during the first 12 weeks of pregnancy. During the remainder of the pregnancy, the maternal and foetal bloodstreams are actually separated by only one layer of cells, increasing the vulnerability of the foetus to certain environmental hazards. Most drugs, including narcotics and anaesthetics, as well as viruses cross the placental membrane without difficulty, and some pathogenic bacteria have been known to infect foetuses by traversing the placental membrane.

foetal membranes the original membranes that form round the blastocyst and develop into amnion, chorion, and related structures during the second and third week of a pregnancy. They are also called extraembryonic membranes because they are not actually part of the embryo and will be separated from the embryo at birth.

foetal period the stage of prenatal development following the embryonic period, and extending from the beginning of the third month after conception until birth. Between the eighth and 12th weeks, the external genitals can be identified as male or female; the

length of the foetus increases to about 4 inches; the skin takes on a pinkish colour; the ears, arms, hands, fingers, and toes are completely formed; and the foetus clearly resembles a human being. From there on, development consists primarily of enlargement, further differentiation of such structures and internal organs already present, easily detectable foetal movements, descent of the testicles into the scrotum of the male, and opening of the eyes.

foetal response reaction of the unborn child to environmental conditions such as increased heart rate when the mother smokes and alleged increase in activity when the mother undergoes emotional stress.

foetal testicular androgen an alternative term for the masculinizing hormone secreted by the Leydig cells of the foetal testis, resulting in masculine external genital characteristics.

foetation the process in which the foetus develops within the uterus. The term also is used synonymously with pregnancy.

foeticide deliberate termination of pregnancy, or abortion, during or after the third month after conception. The term is used less frequently than abortion, which denotes any premature termination of pregnancy by either natural or artificial means.

foetus a human organism in the third stage of prenatal development, the first and second stage being the ovum and embryo. The embryo becomes a foetus at approximately the 57th day of gestation. The foetal stage continues until the pregnancy is terminated by birth or foetal death by abortion or failure to develop normally. See FOETAL PERIOD.

foetus at risk a foetus whose normal development is threatened by factors such as maternal health and life-style or unfavourable genetic traits. Studies show that a child born to parents with no background of mental disease has about 3 percent chance of acquiring a mental disorder, whereas a child born in a family with known mental disorders may have a 50 percent risk of mental disease. In any pregnancy in which one of the parents has a dominant genetic disorder, the chances are 50 percent that the child will be affected. If one of the parents has a recessive autosomal disorder, the chances are 25 percent, or one in four, that the disorder will be transmitted to the foetus, by Mendelian laws. Foetal risk also may be increased by a maternal disease, such as diabetes or hypertension, the use of alcohol, and exposure to certain diseases, such as syphilis, rubella, or herpes virus Type 2.

Foley-catheter bulb a catheter with an inflatable bulb that is sometimes used to remove an obstruction in the prostatic portion of the male urethra. The bulb of the catheter is not inflated until it reaches the prostate, where it is used as a sound to force an opening through the stricture. The bulb may be filled with sterile water.

follicle cavity the space left in the ovarian follicle immediately after it ruptures to release an ovum.

follicle-stimulating hormone (FSH) one of the pituitary gonadotropic hormones produced by basophilic cells of the anterior lobe of the pituitary. Its function is to stimulate ovarian-follicle growth in the female and spermatogenesis in the male. Production of the follicle-stimulating hormone begins to increase significantly at puberty, and in the male it is believed to influence the growth of the seminiferous tubules of the testes, in addition to its effect on the production and maturation of sperm. In the female after puberty and stabilization of the menstrual cycle, follicle-stimulating hormones fluctuate a bit, rising approximately 14 days before the start of the next menstrual period. The hormone also increases the secretion of oestrogen from the ovarian follicle in the female. The activity of the follicle-stimulating hormone is in turn regulated by a releasing hormone (RH) that is secreted by the hypophysis and transmitted to the pituitary as part of a complex biochemical feedback system within the body.

follicular phase a stage of the menstrual cycle that follows the menstrual period. The follicular phase usually lasts about 9 days, during which time the lining of the uterus, under the influence of the female sex hormone oestrogen, undergoes a regrowth. New cells, rich in blood and glucose, form on the walls of the uterus in preparation for the possible arrival of a fertilized ovum. The follicular phase usually ends with the ripening of an ovarian follicle.

folliculitis the inflammation of a hair follicle. The condition may be associated with acne, a staphylococcus infection, exposure to irritating chemicals, and many other factors. Some forms of the disease can result in a loss of hair. A staphylococcal infection of the hair follicles can be transmitted by close body contact with a person carrying the germ.

folliculitis gonorrhoeica an inflammation of the tiny cavities in the roof of the urethra, caused by a gonorrhoeal infection of the glands of Littre and the neighbouring pitlike recesses or lacunae.

follitropin a purified extract of follicle-stimulating hormone prepared from the urine of postmenopausal women and used in the treatment of anovulatory infertility. The product is reported to result in multiple births in about 30 percent of women receiving the preparation. When men with oligospermia are given follitropin, their sperm count increases and spermatozoa motility improves.

fondling in general, caressing or handling in a loving way. In sexology the term is specifically applied to body caresses, including touching and manipulating the sex organs for the purpose of sexual excitement. In treating impotence, Masters and Johnson recommend that the couple begin by fondling each other in ways that please both, while avoiding the genital areas; later they gradually extend this process to the sex organs.

food taboos the avoidance of foods that are somehow associated with virility because of their shape or other qualities. Polynesian women before the influence of European cultures were forbidden to eat bananas because of their penile shape. Also forbidden were coconuts because they resemble huge testicles.

foot binding a centuries-old tradition among upper-level Chinese women who had their feet bound until they became extremely small and deformed. The tiny, almost useless, feet were considered erotically stimulating. The practice probably originated as a leisure-class status symbol.

foot fetishism the use of the feet in achieving sexual excitement. The feet have been found to be sexually sensitive, and may contribute to arousal when they are stroked, or when the toes are used to stroke or massage the sex organs of another person. Foot fetishists can be 'turned on' by the sight or thought of a foot.

footsie a colloquial term for amorous caresses with the feet. If a couple are 'playing footsie under the table' they are using foot contact as a means of surreptitious flirting or petting.

foot worship in Hindu lore, obeisance to feet as 'microcosms of the body' with subtle connections to all its organs. The feet are washed, anointed with oils, and 'worshipped with incense and flowers' not only because of their basic function of bearing the weight of the body, but because of the part they play in sexual arousal by being kissed or by being brought into contact with the partner's genitals.

force-fuck an alternative term for BREAK AND ENTER. See this entry.

Fordyce's disease an acnelike condition marked by the appearance of sebaceous cysts widely distributed over the shaft of the penis.

foreign bodies a term referring mainly to mechanical or other objects that are inserted into the vagina for purposes including masturbation, sanitary protection during menstruation and attempts to correct displaced reproductive organs with pessaries. The foreign body may become lodged in the vagina or forgotten until inflammation or leukorrhoea causes the woman to seek medical attention.

foreplay sexual stimulation before intercourse involving kissing, caressing, or stroking any or all erogenous zones; the preliminary stage of coitus.

forepleasure the psychoanalytical term for the pleasure experienced during foreplay.

foreskin the prepuce, or fold of thin skin that overhangs the glans penis. A similar fold of skin is formed from the labia minor to overlap the glans of the clitoris. The foreskin covers a varying amount of the surface of the glans and is separated from it by a preputial space. It is a continuation of the thin skin that covers the shaft of the penis. It is hairless but does contain a number of small papillae on the surface. On the inner layer of the fold are preputial, or Tyson, glands that secrete an often odorous oily substance which, when mixed with discarded skin cells, becomes smegma.

foreskin tying the practice of tying the foreskin with cord, in certain cultures where circumcision is not practised—for example, among the Marquesans, Amazonian Indians, and ancient Greeks (during rituals or athletics). The object seems to be to protect the penis. The knot is loosened for urination and copulation.

forget-me-not a colloquial term for venereal disease.

fornication voluntary intercourse between two persons who are either unmarried or not married to each other. Fornication and *to fornicate* have been used in English for almost 800 years.

Foscarnet a trademark for a Swedish antiviral drug, phosphonoformate, that has been tested in Europe as a possible treatment for AIDS. See this entry.

fossa navicularis vulvae a shallow depression between the vaginal hymen and the folds of the labia. Also called vestibular fossa.

fourchette (fo͞oəshet'; French, 'fork') a fold of skin that joins the posterior ends of the labia minor. In a virgin the frenulum, or skin fold, usually joins the sides across the middle line. Also called frenulum of the labia.

four-eleven-fortyfour a British black slang term for the penis. It may be rhyming slang for 'score'. Also spelled *4-11-44*.

four-F method a male phrase meaning 'find'em, feel'em, fuck'em, and forget'em.' The term would be used by a *4-F'er*, a type of man who is interested only in a casual relationship, which he callously breaks off when this is convenient to him. An approximate equivalent of the four-F method is the 19th-century term THREE F'S. See this entry.

four-letter word a euphemism for 'dirty word,' used similarly to MONOSYLLABLE. See this entry. See also TABOONESS RATING OF DIRTY WORDS.

Fournier's gangrene a type of gangrene of the scrotum that may begin suddenly in a healthy male. Within a very short time the scrotum becomes painful and swollen, followed by the death of the scrotal skin and subcutaneous tissues. The condition is associated with urinary-tract infections, a streptococcus infection of the scrotal skin, or a circulatory interruption.

fox a colloquial American term for a very pretty—*foxy*—woman.

fractured penis a rupture of the corpora cavernosa and other tissues of the penis as a result of direct external trauma. Medical reports indicate that such injuries have occurred to men falling out of bed with an erect penis or through some other bedroom accident.

fraternal twins dizygotic twins, that is, two offspring that have developed from two ova that were simultaneously fertilized by separate sperms. Twins occur about once in 87 births, and of these, 75 percent are of the fraternal type. They may be of like or unlike sex, and each has its own assortment of hereditary traits and its own distinct personality.

freak a colloquial term referring to a person who is known to have unusual sexual preferences. Indulging in such preferences is *to freak off* in American English.

freckle an Australian euphemism for anus.

free love the freedom to 'make love' with any person one chooses, without sanctions or restrictions of any kind; complete sexual permissiveness, as advocated by such figures as George Sands, George Bernard Shaw, Bertrand Russell, and H.G. Wells, and, at one time, by the Oneida Community in New York State.

Frei test a skin test used in the diagnosis of lymphogranuloma venereum. An antigen of the virus cultured in eggs is injected under the skin of a suspected patient. The antigen is matched with the injection of a control substance, usually a mild saline solution, in another skin area. If a reddish area develops at the site of the antigen injection, it is positive for the presence of the lymphogranuloma virus in the body of the patient.

French abortion a slang term for spitting out the semen after having performed fellatio.

French bean a small bean that originated in Asia and found its ways to Europe in the 16th century, after which it somehow became identified as a sexual stimulant. The notion was fostered with the help of a popular song of the era in which it was identified as the 'love bean.'

French disease an older euphemism for syphilis. Also called *French crown*.

French kiss a kiss in which the mouths are open and the tongues are in contact. Also called soul kiss; tongue kiss.

French letter a colloquial term for condom. (The French call it *capot anglais*, 'English overcoat.') Also called *French cap*.

French tickler a condom with soft petal-like protrusions on the end to tickle the inner part of the vagina.

French way, the a colloquial term for oral-genital sex. Also referred to as *French culture*. Similarly used terms are *Frenching*, a *French job*, and *French tricks*.

frenulum any fold of skin or mucous membrane. The frenulum of the prepuce is a vascular fold of skin on the penis. The frenulum of the clitoris is a junction of the labia minora below the glans of the clitoris. The frenulum laborium is a connecting fold of skin between part of the two labia minora.

frenum the small portion of the shaft of the penis immediately behind the edge of the corona of the glans penis. It is an area of particular sensitivity to sexual stimulation.

frequency of total outlets based on Kinsey's studies, the number of orgasms achieved during an average week by means of six main types of sexual activity: coitus, masturbation, sexual dreams, petting, homosexual activities, and animal contact. Among (white) males the mean frequency between adolescence and 85 years of age is found to be nearly three per week (but with great individual variations), with the peak reached between the ages of 16 and 30, followed by a gradual decline. The average (white) female was found to be less active between puberty and the age of 15, and did not attain her peak until almost 30 years of age. Here the mean frequency is harder to estimate, but appears to be somewhat less than among males, and with greater individual variation.

frequency pattern a graphic representation, as on a chart, of the number of times an event occurs in a given time span. For example, a survey of the number of orgasms per week among male members of a population group showed a range of from 0 to 30, with a statistical mean of three per week. However, only 8 percent of the group actually had three orgasms per week and the highest percentage, 13 percent had only one per week. When plotted on graph paper, the frequency pattern shows a peak at one end (one per week) and a steep slope downwards to a long flat line extending to 30. The frequency curve reveals a more realistic pattern of the wide variations in individual sex behaviours than might be presented by other methods of statistical reporting.

Freud, Sigmund (1856-1939) the Austrian psychiatrist and neurologist who originated the theory and practice of psychoanalysis. Freud's approach focussed on the dominance of the unconscious in both normal and neurotic behaviour, the great influence of sexuality on personality development, and the use of free association as a therapeutic technique. His specific contributions in the field of sexology centred on the interpretation of sexual dreams, the analysis of unconscious sexual conflicts and repressions, the lasting effects of childhood sexual experiencés, the Oedipus complex, the relation between sexual guilt feeling and neurosis, the stages of psychosexual development, and, in general, the dominant influence of the libido, or sexual instinct, on our lives.

The American psychiatrist W. Bertram Wolfe wrote: 'Freud found sex an outcast in the outhouse, and left it in the living room as an honoured guest.'

frictation a homosexual practice in which two male partners achieve sexual gratifi-

F

cation by rubbing against each other while in a face-to-face position. Among female homosexuals a similar practice is termed tribadism.

frigging one of the oldest English expressions for masturbation. As an adjective it is less vulgar than 'fucking.'

frigidity a female disorder characterized by total unresponsiveness, or by various degrees and kinds of impairment of sexual response, such as mild lack of interest in intercourse, sexual activity and interest without reaching full orgasm, total lack of sexual feeling or pleasure (sexual anaesthesia), or active aversion to sexual relations. Among the many possible causes are distasteful experiences or sexual abuse in childhood, inhibitions instilled by parents, and hostility towards males.

Fröhlich's syndrome a condition characterized by genital underdevelopment and obesity in males sometimes, but not always, caused by a tumour of the cells of the anterior pituitary gland. Other disorders often associated with the abnormality include diabetes insipidus, visual impairment, and mental retardation. In cases not resulting primarily from pituitary tumours, the cause is believed to be a hypothalamic dysfunction.

front door a colloquial term for vagina. Also called *front window*.

frottage (frôtäzh'; French, 'rubbing') a sexual disorder, or paraphilia, primarily found in males who repeatedly attempt to reach orgasm by rubbing against women in crowded surroundings such as lifts or underground trains. The person who engages in this behaviour is termed a *frotteur* ('rubber').

fruit a slang term, often derogatory, for male homosexual. In earlier colloquial usage, a fruit was a loose woman (called 'fruitester' by Chaucer).

fruit fly a synonym for the slang term fag hag.

FSH an abbreviation for follicle-stimulating hormone.

F.U. (ef'yoo', ef' yoo ') abbreviation for fuck you. Both the full form and the abbreviation are extremely insulting.

fuck a vulgar term—*the* vulgar term—meaning (a) to copulate, (b) the act of copulation, (c) the partner in copulation (used mainly in 'a great fuck' and 'a lousy fuck'), or (d) the ejaculate. It is also used as an expletive as in 'what the fuck!') and in a variety of combinations: for example, *fuck-all* is nothing at all; a *fucker* is a contemptible person; *fucking* is

used as an all-purpose adjectival and adverbial intensifier; to *fuck about* is to act foolishly or annoyingly; to *fuck off* is to go away (usually used as an expletive) and also, in American English, means the same as fuck about; and *fuck up* means to botch or mishandle. In addition *un fuck-off* is Franglais for a British person; it derives apparently from the fondness for this expression shown by British tourists on the Continent. The word 'fuck' has been omitted for centuries in most dictionaries, although it was as early as 1598 that it appeared in an Italian-English dictionary. John Florio's *A Worlde of Wordes*. The sign of its return to the fold of acceptance, if not of respectability, was its inclusion in the *Supplement to the Oxford English Dictionary*, published in 1972. It is first found in written documents in the early 16th century, and may come from a Scandinavian word related to Norwegian dialect *fukka* 'to copulate' and Swedish dialect *focka* 'to copulate' and *fock* 'penis.' Beyond this it may go back ultimately to Latin *pungere*, meaning 'to prick or strike,' and Greek *pygmé*, 'fist.' Although fuck is an obscenity *symbol*, it does not rate number 1 in the TABOONESS RATING OF DIRTY WORDS. See this entry.

'fuckin' as infix a linguistic phenomenon that consists of the insertion of the intensifier 'fuckin(g)' before the accented syllable of polysyllabic words, as in 'fanfuckin-tastic,' 'il-fuckin-legal,' or 'unbe-fuckin-lievable.'

full house a slang term for simultaneous gonorrhoea and syphilis.

full penetration the maximum distance that an erect penis may penetrate into a vagina. Because of differences in individual anatomy, exact measurements can vary. But the depth of an average vagina is slightly less than 4 inches. For many sexual partners, full penetration is best achieved if the couple is in the female-superior position, that is, when the man is lying on his back and is mounted by the woman.

functional dysmenorrhoea psychogenic dysmenorrhoea stemming from emotional factors such as anxiety and stress.

functional impotence failure to achieve or maintain a penile erection because of circulatory or nervous-system disorders, effects of aging, anxiety, stress or excessive use of alcohol or drugs, including many medications taken for high blood pressure or other medical problems.

functional uterine bleeding any blood discharge from the uterus that is not associated with a tumour, inflammation, or pregnancy. Bleeding may be profuse, prolonged, or painless, but cannot be traced to any anomaly. Also called dysfunctional uterine bleeding (DUB).

functional vaginismus painful contractions of the vaginal muscles resulting from psychological factors such as fear, guilt, or traumatic experiences.

fundiform ligament one of the ligaments of the penis. It is formed from strong bands of tissue that extend from the front of the abdomen to the symphysis pubis and around the top and sides of the penis.

fundus the round, free upper end of the uterus, above the entrance of the fallopian tubes. In the nonpregnant woman, the fundus is the widest part of the uterus. Although generally portrayed as a vertically-oriented organ, the uterus actually has a horizontal position in a standing woman, with the fundus pointing forwards.

funicular encysted hydrocele a swelling of the scrotum caused by an inflammation of the spermatic cord. The superficial appearance of the scrotum resembles that of a hydrocele resulting from an inflammation of the tunica vaginalis except that the source of the disorder is higher in the scrotum.

fur a colloquial term referring to the female pubic hair.

furburger an American slang term for vagina, and in the context of cunnilingus— 'to eat a furburger.' See also HAIR BURGER.

furor amatorius a Latin term for an unrestrainable desire for sexual activity (*furor* meaning 'fury').

furor feminus a Latin term for nymphomania.

futz an American slang term for vagina.

galactopoiesis the maintenance of milk secretion in the human breast. The process involves the interaction of six hormones; prolactin, somatotropic growth hormone, adrenal-cortex hormones, oestrogen, progesterone, and oxytocin.

galactorrhoea a condition characterized by the production of milk in the breasts in the absence of a pregnancy. The condition is associated with discontinuation of the use of oral contraceptives, particularly after the woman has been off the pill for less than a year. The risk of the disorder appears to decrease with time.

Galgenmännlein an alleged aphrodisiac—a German version of mandrake that presumably grows spontaneously beneath a gallows from the semen of an executed man (German, 'little gallow's-man,' that is, hanged man).

gamete any sex cell that combines with a sex cell representing the opposite sex to form a zygote. Examples of gametes are ova and spermatozoa.

gamete intrafallopian transfer (GIFT) a technique for helping infertile woman to conceive in which the male and female gametes (sperm and ovum are implanted directly in her fallopian tubes by catheter, so that they are not exposed to the risks of their normal journey through the female reproductive system.

gamone a substance produced by the male and female gametes that attracts the germ cells of the opposite sex. The ovum secretes a chemical identified as gynogamone, and the spermatozoon produces a substance known as androgamone.

gamonomania an extreme, compelling desire to marry; pathological preoccupation with marriage.

gamophobia an intense, morbid fear of marriage, often stemming from hidden causes such as fear of sex or sexual failure, feelings of insecurity, or inability to take responsibility.

gang rape rape committed by a gang of men, who take turns violating the victim. The effect may be physical damage, serious psychological disturbance, or, in some cases, death. Gang rape has been reported as a means of social control in several societies—for example, as punishment for adultery among the Cheyenne and other Plains Indians of North America. Gang rape of men is common in prisons. Gang rape of men by women has been found in only one or two societies. A colloquial term is *gang bang*.

gangrene of the scrotum a severe abnormal condition in which scrotal tissues may die, usually because of interruption in the blood flow to the area. Gangrene also may result from injury or burns or from the seepage of infected urine into the subcutaneous tissues of the scrotum. Alcholics and men with diabetes are particularly vulnerable to scrotal gangrene as a complication of other disorders, such as infections.

gangrenous balanitis another term for BALANITIS GANGRAENOSA. See this entry.

gang sex sexual activities among a group of preadolescents, adolescents, or adults who act together and follow their own social and antisocial code. Such activities include homosexual contacts, mutual masturbation, intercourse of male and female gang members, sexual experimentation of all kinds, and, in some cases, gang rape.

gaolbait a slang term for an underage woman with whom it would be illegal to have sexual intercourse.

garden of Eden a once very popular term for vagina.

garter fetish the garter as a fetish—a traditional symbol of sexuality. The garter was for generations a standard part of a woman's wedding garments. Garters also were featured on the legs of dance-hall performers. In recent years, because of the popularity of tights, the garter has lost much of its fetish appeal.

gash a slang term for the external female genitals.

gastromenia a form of vicarious menstruation in which the bleeding comes from the stomach rather than the uterus.

gate swinger a slang term for a bisexual.

gay a male or female homosexual. The term is favoured by homosexuals themselves. It has lost its colloquial status and is in the process of making older meanings of the word obsolescent. Gay is used as a noun or an adjective, and is primarily applied to the male.

gay bar a city bar that caters mainly to homosexuals interested in making social and sexual contacts.

gaydom an alternative term for gay life-style or the gay community.

gay girl in Middle English, any girl, in contrast to a 'knave girl,' meaning a boy. See GIRL.

gaying it a 16th-century euphemism for having sex (usually heterosexual sex).

gay liberation a social movement in which homosexuals of both sexes assert their right to their own sexual orientation and seek to free society from prejudice and discrimination against homosexuals. They also demand that homosexuality be recognized as a normal variation in human relationships, and participate actively in gay organizations and gay causes.

gay man a term that in the 19th century meant a womanizer.

gay marriage a long-term monogamous or relatively monogamous relationship between two male or two female homosexuals who share the same flat or house. 'Marriages' of this kind are sometimes solemnized by special ceremonies, but cannot yet be legalized. They arise out of dissatisfaction with casual encounters and a need for a more permanent and intimate relationship as well as the need to combat loneliness.

gay pneumonia an alternative term for pneumocystitis carnii, a lethal respiratory complication of an AIDS infection. The term was first used by staff members of the Centers for Disease Control in Atlanta, Georgia, USA

in 1981 when doctors began ordering large amounts of CDC-controlled drugs to treat outbreaks of the AIDS form of pneumonia. See also AIDS.

gazungas a slang term for the female breasts.

geisha (Japanese, 'art person') a Japanese woman who has been specially trained to act as a professional hostess, entertainer, and companion for men. Her repertoire includes conversing, playing musical instruments, serving food, singing, dancing, conducting the traditional tea ceremony, and, in some cases, performing sexual services. Geishas, however, are highly respected and not considered prostitutes.

gel-filled implant a female breast implant that is filled with gel. The plastic breast implants are sold in sizes ranging from 75 millilitres to 450 millilitres, for women of different builds.

gender bender a colloquial term for an androgynous person.

gender change a semieuphemism for sex change.

gender dysphoria dissatisfaction or unhappiness with one's identity or role as male or female. These attitudes often stem from treatment by parents who wished for a child of the opposite sex and who may even try to force the child to behave and dress like a member of the opposite sex. Extreme dissatisfaction with one's gender may be reflected in transsexualism.

gender identification operation an alternative term for sex-change surgery.

gender identity the individual's sense of masculinity or femininity, as determined by biological, psychological, and social influences, including physical characteristics resulting from chromosomal factors, as well as attitudes and behaviour patterns resulting from family and cultural influences.

gender-identity conflict a psychological situation in which coitus occurs without use of contraceptives because the contraceptive is a threat to gender identity. A man may want to demonstrate his machismo by impregnating women or a woman may feel a need to become pregnant to prove that she is fertile.

gender-identity disorder of childhood an American Psychiatric Association category characterized by a persistent feeling of discomfort or dysphoria concerning one's anatomical sex, experienced before puberty. The child expresses a strong desire to be a member of the opposite sex, may insist that he or she is actually of the other sex, and rejects the anatomy and activities associated with his or her actual sex in ways that go far beyond ordinary tomboy or cissy behaviour.

gender-identity disorders a term applied by the American Psychiatric Association to rare psychosexual disorders in which there is a conflict between the individual's anatomical sex and his or her sexual identification as male or female.

Gender Identity Program in America, a programme at some hospitals that supervises sex-change operations and counsels men who want to become women or women who want to become men. The programme may include a year of psychiatric evaluation and therapy before surgery and a series of post-operative checkups.

gender role the pattern of behaviour characteristics of male or female in a particular culture. Gender roles are largely determined by the way the individual is reared, and usually conform to biologically determined sexual identity. They may change as social and sexual roles change.

general fertility rate (GFR) the number of live births per 1,000 women aged 15 to 49 in a given year.

general marital fertility rate (GMFR) the number of live births per 1,000 married women of a specific age in a given year.

general paresis a form of paralysis that is caused by cerebral syphilis. Also called dementia paralytica; general paralysis of the insane.

general paresis, depressed type a form of advanced paralytic syphilis in which the patient is deeply discouraged and despondent. Although considered psychotic, the patient appears aware of his failing condition, which may become the focal point of his despondency.

general paresis, expansive type a manifestation of advanced paralytic syphilis in which the patient expresses euphoria and grandiose delusions. Because of improved control of syphilis by public-health authorities, fewer cases of this form of psychosis are found today.

general paresis, paranoid type a form of advanced neurosyphiliticpsychosis in which the dominant symptom is a delusion of persecution.

generation gap the disparity between the attitudes and values of the old and new generations, as manifested particularly in difficulty in communication between· adolescents and

their parents. The generation gap is probably a perennial phenomenon, but is accentuated in rapidly changing societies like our own.

genesial cycle the reproductive period of a female's life.

genetic-balance theory the principle that each person possesses both male and female sex determinants in its chromosome assortment. And while genes give direction to sex in the early stages of male and female differentiation, what the genes actually control is the intensity of male or female hormone secretion. Thus, an individual may be a male or female genetically but display physical characteristics of the opposite sex.

genetic counselling the provision of information about genetic defects to prospective parents as a means of reducing the number of children born with physical or mental disorders. A second objective is to alert health professionals to the possibility of a genetic disease in a family. The information may be reinforced by offering biochemical or cytological tests. The counselling process usually involves development of a family tree, which may require compilation of as much health history of the family as possible, using family Bibles, photographs from family albums, or data about diseases and causes of death of all close relatives as well as ancestors. Ethnic information is elicited because of the tendency of certain inherited diseases to occur more frequently among families from particular cultural backgrounds. Mediterranean fever, for example, is more likely to affect Sephardic Jews while Tay-Sachs disease is found in Ashkenazic Jews but rarely in Sephardic Jews. If the family tree shows an apparent recurrence of a particular genetic disease among several relatives, the family history is regarded as positive for the disorder. Some genetic diseases have been determined by empirical evidence and Mendelian laws to be quite accurately predictable when a family history has been compiled. The statistical chance that a 'Caucasian' mother will give birth to a child with cystic fibrosis is 1:2,500. If a sibling of a cystic-fibrosis patient marries an unrelated person, the chances increase to 1:25. But if two apparently normal siblings of cystic-fibrosis patients marry, the odds of having a child with cystic fibrosis become 2:3.

genetic defect a congenital deformity or abnormality, either mental or physical, that stems from faulty genes or chromosomes.

genetic mother a recent term for a woman

whose fertilized ovum is implanted in another woman who bears and gives birth to the child. See GESTATIONAL MOTHER.

genetic sex determination the process whereby the sex of a zygote of humans and most other mammals is determined at fertilization according to whether the spermatozoon's sex chromosome is an X (for female) or Y (for male).

genital apposition a precopulatory activity or stage in foreplay in which the sex organs of each partner are in direct contact but without intromission (penetration). Apposition may or may not lead to actual intercourse.

genital character a psychoanalytical term for the pattern of personality traits that characterizes the adult phase of psychosexual development, when the individual focusses sexual energy, or libido, on the genital organs and on sexual activity and relationship with persons outside himself.

genital corpuscles another term for Dogiel's corpuscles.

genital eroticism sexual arousal produced by stimulation of the genital organs.

genital femoral nerve a branch of the lumbar plexus that supplies innervation to the cremaster muscle and the skin of the scrotum and labia majora. A femoral branch of the same nerve supplies the skin of the upper part of the thigh.

genital herpes an infection of herpes virus Type 2 that involves the skin and mucosa of the genital and anorectal areas. A moderately contagious disease, it is usually transmitted by sexual contact. Herpes lesions commonly appear within a week after contact, with a small area of reddened or inflamed skin or mucous membrane. Small blisters appear at the site, followed by a period of erosion of the vesicles. They are replaced in turn by round ulcerations. Several small ulcers may merge into a large ulcer. The ulcers are painful and become crusted, but they generally subside within 2 weeks, sometimes leaving scars. The lymph nodes in the inguinal region may become tender and swollen during the outbreak. The herpes lesions can develop on the glans, shaft or foreskin of the penis or on the vagina, clitoris, labia, and cervix. There is no know cure of genital herpes. Once infected, the individual becomes a carrier, and symptoms may recur at any time, usually causing outbreaks during fever, infection, emotional problems, and menstruation. An outbreak may be particularly severe during

pregnancy. The virus may be transmitted from the pregnant woman to the foetus through the placenta or during passage of the newborn through the birth canal. Also called herpes genitalis; herpes progenitalis. See also HERPES.

genitalia the male and female reproductive organs: the penis, testes, prostate gland, seminal vesicles and bulbourethral glands in the male; and the vagina, uterus, ovaries, fallopian tubes and related structures in the female. Also called genital organs; genitals; privates.

genital intercourse coitus in which the male genital organ (penis) is inserted in the female genital organ (vagina). This may be accomplished in a wide variety of positions.

genitality the capacity to concentrate sexual excitement in the genital organs, a process that begins with childhood masturbation and culminates in adult sexuality.

genitalization a psychoanalytic term for the process of transferring, or 'displacing,' sexual gratification from the genital organs to nonsexual objects that resemble or symbolize them, such as boots or stilettos.

genital jewellery jewellery of various kinds worn in or on the genital organs for adornment or sexual pleasure. The practice is found in a number of societies, particularly among the Trukese where women may perforate their labia and insert tinkling objects; in the Philippines, where penis bars are used to secure metal rings; and in Europe, America, and Japan, where some men wear rings around their genital organs (penis rings) as a decoration, but also to help them maintain an erection or to increase their partner's pleasure during intercourse.

genital kiss oral stimulation of the male or female genital organs as a means of achieving sexual excitement and gratification. Kinsey found that over half of college-educated males and fewer than 5 percent of gradeschool educated males in the USA reported using this technique with their wives. Among women the practice was found to be far less common: almost 60 percent had never attempted it, and the rest had done so only infrequently. These percentages seem to have increased considerably since Kinsey's time.

genital libido sexual desire concentrated on the genital organs, including the urge to masturbate and to engage in intercourse. According to psychoanalytical theory, the génital libido expresses itself after the oral and anal stages of psychosexual development. It starts with the pleasure experienced by the young child in touching his or her sex organs and comes to fruition during the 'genital phase,' which is reached at puberty.

genital love a Freudian term for sexually mature love, which is expressed in the final stage of psychosexual development, when the love object is another person.

genital modification alteration or mutilation of the genital organs in the male or female. The most common and widespread example is circumcision, which has been performed on an estimated 50 percent of all males in the world today. Other, rarer, male modifications are insertion of an 'ampallang' in the penis, superincision and subincision, hemicastration, total castration, and a form of infibulation involving the foreskin. Female modifications include insertion of bells in holes made in the labia, infibulation, clitoridectomy, and vaginal introcision.

genital mutilation severe damage inflicted on the genital organs by castration, cutting, or burning. Examples are mutilation of corpses by necrophiliacs, or self-castration practised by the Dervish and Skoptsy sects. The motivation may be masochism, religious penance, or extreme asceticism.

genital organs an alternative term for genitalia.

genital phase the culminating phase of psychosexual development, reached during puberty when a sexual partner becomes the focus of erotic interest and activity. Also called genital stage.

genital primacy the stage of mature psychosexual development, characterized according to Freud, by 'subordination of all sexual components under the primacy of the genital zone.'

genitals an alternative term for genitalia. See also EXTERNAL GENITALS.

genital stage an alternative term for genital phase.

genital stimulation excitation of the male or female sex organs by such means as fondling, licking, and sucking.

genital tubercle a phalluslike process that appears between the umbilical cord and tail of the human embryo and eventually becomes differentiated into either the male or female external genitalia.

genital tuberculosis tuberculosis that invades the reproductive systems of both men and women. In men, the areas affected are the prostate, testes, and epididymis. Among women, tuberculosis invades mainly the fallopian tubes and uterus. Although it is generally assumed that tuberculosis is a rare disease, about 2 percent of all disorders of the upper genital tract of women involve tuberculosis.

genital warts growths that tend to appear in multiple lesions of small moist pink swellings with tiny hairy processes extending from the surface. They tend to appear on the corona of the glans penis of the male or immediately behind the glans. Moisture tends to increase the chances of multiple warts, which may form a cluster. A solitary genital wart may be found occasionally. In women, the warts tend to appear on the vulva, the vaginal wall, and the cervix. The condition may be sexually transmitted in some cases, and is therefore also known as venereal warts. A mother can transmit them to her offspring.

genital zones the external sex organs and adjacent areas, all of which are sensitive to erotic stimulation.

genitive case a Shakespearean euphemism for vagina (punning on a case that houses the generative organs). Shakespeare also uses simply 'case' in this sense (a case that sheathes the man's sword), and he uses 'focative' and 'focative case' as a euphemism for 'fuck.'

genophobia an intense, morbid fear of sex.

genotype the genetic constitution of an individual, as distinguished from the phenotype, or physical appearance of the person. The term is also used to refer to the chromosomal alleles that are present at one or more places (loci).

gentleman cow a famous bowdlerism: Dr. Thomas Bowdler substituted the term for 'bull' in copies of Tennyson's *The Wreck of the Hesperus*. See BOWDLERISM.

gentleman of leisure a euphemism for pimp.

gentleman of the backdoor an obsolete euphemism for a man practising anal intercourse, whether heterosexual or homosexual.

germ cells the cells of an individual with the function of reproduction, such as the ovum and spermatozoon. The term also is applied to the immature stages of the male and female gametes. Also called initial cells; sexual cells.

germ disc an alternative term for embryonic disc, the cluster of cells within the blastocyst that develops into the embryo proper.

germinal cell any ovum or spermatozoon or the immature stage of an ovum or spermatozoon.

germinal-cell aplasia an abnormal condition in which the testes contain only Sertoli cells. The germinal epithelium of the tubules is absent. The condition is a cause of infertility.

germinal period the approximately 2-week time span between fertilization of the ovum and development of the first embryonic features of the implanted zygote. During the germinal period the zygote divides several times to form a blastocyst, develop a yolk sac, and establish a primitive placenta in the lining of the uterus. It is generally after the germinal period that the woman realizes she may be pregnant.

germ plasm a term introduced by the German biologist August Weismann as part of his theory that acquired characteristics are not inherited. The germ plasm, according to Weismann, is the reproductive and hereditary substance of individuals. It is passed on from the germ cells of one generation to the germ cells of descendants through a mechanism by which future persons develop and hereditary traits are transmitted.

gerontosexuality a sexual variance in which a young person has a distinct preference for an individual of advanced years as an object of sexual interest or activity. In such cases the reason for the choice may be merely economic, but it also may be an expression of a sexual desire for a parent substitute. Also called *gerontophilia*.

gestation the period of pregnancy. Synonyms include cyphoria, cyesis, and gravidity. (Latin *gestare*, 'to bear.')

gestational age the age of the foetus calculated from the date, or presumed date, of conception.

gestational mother a recent term for a woman who bears and gives birth to a child for whom another woman's—the 'genetic mother's' —fertilized ovum had been implanted. Both women are biological mothers of the child. See also SURROGATE MOTHER.

gestation period the period from conception to delivery of an offspring, which in the human is 266 days, or 280 days after the last menstrual period. From the last menstrual period, the pregnancy usually lasts 40 weeks, 9 calendar months, or 10 lunar months. For other animals, it ranges from 20 days for a shrew to 22 months for an elephant.

gestosis any toxaemia or disorder of pregnancy, including gestational oedema, gestational proteinuria, hypertension, eclampsia, and preeclampsia.

getting into a woman's pants a colloquial term for having intercourse with a woman.

getting it together a euphemism for having sex. Also getting it on.

getting laid a slang term for having sex, used both in an active and inactive sense.

getting off a slang term for reaching a sexual climax.

getting one's end away a British slang term for having sexual intercourse.

getting one's nuts off an American slang term meaning (a) ejaculating, climaxing, (b) masturbating to climax, or (c) obtaining sex, and climax from a partner.

getting one's rocks off a slang term for ejaculating.

getting partner the sex partner in dysfunctional therapy who is touched by the other partner. In the Masters and Johnson programme the getting partner helps guide the hands of the giving partner to body areas most responsive to sexual stimulation. The getting partner becomes the giving partner in another part of the sensate-focus therapy.

getting some a colloquial term for getting sexual satisfaction.

getting some round eye a slang term for being the active partner in anal intercourse.

GFR abbreviation for general fertility rate.

giant mammary myxoma a massive tumour of the breast that develops over a period of several years in some women as they approach menopause. The tumours are generally noncancerous but may reach a weight of more than 7 pounds before being removed with the breast itself in a simple mastectomy procedure.

gichigich a sexual technique employed by the Yapese, who live on a large island in the Pacific Ocean: The woman sits on the man's lap, and he enters the outer labia only, moving his penis slowly in different directions until she reaches climax after climax. The technique is so strenuous and tiring that it is only used before marriage; during marriage the 'missionary position' is employed.

GIFT the acronym for gamete intrafallopian transfer.

gigantism a variation of eunuchoidism usually resulting from a mild pituitary insufficiency. A deficiency of androgenic hormone results in a delayed closure of the areas of long bones in which growth normally occurs so that long-bone growth that normally ends before adulthood may continue for another 10 years or more. Not all eunuchoids are giants, and not all giants are eunuchoid, but in many cases the causes are the same. Pituitary insufficiency results in diminished activity of the various endocrine glands, as in acromegaly.

gigolo a man who is employed by a woman as a companion or escort, although in some cases he may also perform sexual services.

gin jockey an Australian slang term for a white man who has sex with Aborigine women.

ginseng the root of the ginseng plant (genus *Panax*), which is grown in China, Korea, and now in Apalachia. It is used as an alleged aphrodisiac as well as a stimulant and tonic with alleged physical and emotional effects.

girl a female child. The term has also been used to mean a young unmarried woman, a female servant or employee, or sweetheart, also, a woman in general; but this usage is now regarded as patronizing. In Middle English, a girl (*girle, gurle*, etc.) was a young person of either sex. To make a distinction, one could say *knave girl* to refer to the male and *gay girl* to refer to the female (spelled *gaye gerle* by Chaucer). See also B-GIRLS; CALL GIRLS; PHALLUS GIRL; REAL GIRL; WORKING GIRL.

girl fear another term for parthenophobia.

girlie magazines a popular term for periodicals featuring photographs or other illustrations of nude or seminude females.

give head a slang term that used to mean to have (ordinary) intercourse, but which in the 20th century came to mean performing fellatio or cunnilingus.

giving partner the sex partner in dysfunctional therapy who does the touching of the other partner. The giving partner may fondle or massage the getting partner in body areas found to excite the most pleasure. The giving partner will be the getting partner during part of therapy.

glandulae preputialis the smegma-secreting glands on the corona of the glans and on the neck of the penis.

glandular fever an alternative term for INFECTIOUS MONONUCLEOSIS. See this entry.

glans penis the terminal end of the penis, a mushroom-shaped structure that actually is the anterior end of the corpus spongiosum and which conceals the terminal ends of the corpora cavernosa. The corona of the glans penis, the corona glandis, marks the rounded border of the structure. A slitlike opening at the front of the glans is the external orifice of the male urethra. Immediately behind the corona is the neck of the penis. The retroglandular sulcus, a small furrow, is the point at which the foreskin, or frenulum, begins to extend over the glans. If the foreskin has an orifice too small to be retracted over the glans, the condition may lead to adhesions or infection, or both.

gleet an abnormal discharge of urethral mucus occurring in gonorrhoea. The term is also an alternative name for gonorrhoea itself.

glory hole a euphemism for vagina. Amongst homosexuals it also means a hole cut in the wall of a cubicle of a public lavatory, through which a man can put his penis for someone on the other side to fellate.

gluteus maximus the broad, fleshy buttock muscle nearest the surface. The term is used colloquially to refer to the buttocks themselves (pars pro toto).

GMFR abbreviation for general marital fertility rate.

godemiche an obsolescent term for dildo. The word is of uncertain origin, but it has variously been explained to come from Latin (meaning something like 'I enjoy myself') or from French (from *go*, with an earlier meaning of 'freely', and *miché*, a slang term for a prostitute's client).

go down on a euphemism meaning to perform oral sex on (a partner).

go-go girls scantily clad women who perform provocative dances in discotheques or night clubs. The establishment may have a rule against their dating clients, to avoid prostitution laws, but this rule is not always followed. Also called *go-go dancers*.

going steady a mainly American term for the stage in the dating process when the couple see each other regularly and usually exclusively. During this phase they establish an increasingly intimate emotional and physical relationship, which may or may not involve full sexual relations. As yet, however, they have not reached an 'understanding' that will lead to engagement or its equivalent.

go it alone a euphemism meaning to masturbate.

golden shower a slang term for urination, used in the context of sexual gratification obtained or sought from being urinated on or from drinking someone else's or one's own urine. A *golden-shower boy* is a male who enjoys being urinated on or drinking urine.

gonad an organ that produces either female or male gametes and the sex hormones. The female gonad is the ovary, the male gonad is the testis. Before differentiation, in the embryo, either of the gonads may be identified as an indifferent gonad. (Greek *gone*, 'seed.')

gonadal dysgenesis a gonadal development disorder, usually congenital, such as hermaphroditism and pseudohermaphroditism. A form of gonadal dysgenesis in males is the vanishing-testis syndrome in which the individuals are superficially normal males but lack testes, usually because of testicular destruction that occurred at some point in the foetal period after foetal testosterone secretion had started. In females, Turner's syndrome is the classic example of the disorder. Girls develop only juvenile external genitalia and rudimentary ovaries that cannot ovulate. They lack normal breast development and fail to menstruate. Turner's syndrome is associated with the complete or partial absence of an X chromosome.

gonadal gender gender as determined by the type of gonads in the individual, as ovaries in the female and testes in the male.

gonadal ridges one of the first signs in a developing embryo of the future internal reproductive organs. The gonadal ridges appear around the seventh week, on the border of the mesonephros, the primitive excretory organ. The external genitalia of the embryo begin to appear about the same time but are not distinguishable as male or female until early in the foetal stage.

gonadectomy a medical term for castration, or the surgical removal of the testes or ovaries.

gonadocentric characterizing the stage of psychosexual development beginning in puberty when the sexual drive becomes fully focussed on the genital organs.

gonadopause a diminution, and in some cases a cessation, of sexual activity with the onset of old age.

gonadostat theory a concept that the onset of puberty in humans is controlled by a feedback system involving the levels of circulating steroid hormones in the individual. According to the theory there is a 'set point' in the hormonal mechanism at which changes such as growth spurt, the appearance of pubic hair, and other sexual characteristics are triggered. The theory is based on experiments with intact and castrated animals.

gonadotrophin a substance that regulates the activity of the male or female gonads. Three types of gonadotrophins are sometimes identified as (a) pituitary gonadotrophin, present in extracts of the anterior pituitary glands, (b) serum gonadotrophin, which is found in the blood, and (c) chorionic gonadotrophin, which is found in the urine of pregnant women. They are variations of the follicle-stimulating and luteinizing hormones secreted by the pituitary gland.

gonadotropic hormones hormones that stimulate the gonads. The main gonadotropic hormones are the follicle-stimulating hormone (FSH) and the luteinizing hormone (LH). Both are secreted by the anterior pituitary gland, which in turn is stimulated by the luteinizing-hormone-releasing factor of the hypothalamus. The follicle-stimulating hormone develops the ovarian follicle and stimulates the growth of the seminiferous tubules, while the luteinizing hormone stimulates the Leydig cells of the testicles and prepares and ripens the ovarian follicle. Other sex hormones are concerned primarily with the development and maintenance of male and female sexual characteristics and functioning, such as penile development and breast growth.

gonococcal arthritis a condition of fever, severe pain and limited range of motion of a joint that has been affected by a gonorrhoea infection. The skin over the joint may be red and feel hot to the touch. The joint is swollen and contains a thick pus teeming with gonococci. If not treated immediately, the infection can destroy the joint. Unusually, gonococcal arthritis affects only one joint at a time. It affects women more often than men.

gonococcal conjunctivitis a form of inflammation of the conjunctiva of the eyes caused by an infection by *Neisseria gonorrhoeae*, the gonorrhoea germ. The condition is marked by a copious puslike exudate that may lead to blindness if not corrected. The condition tends to occur most often in infants who have acquired the infection while passing through the birth canal of a mother with untreated gonorrhoea.

gonorrhoea an inflammatory condition of the genitourinary tissues, usually marked by a pus-formed discharge and pain on urination. The causative disease organism is a bacterium, *Neisseria gonorrhoeae*, that is usually transmitted by sexual contact. The disease is found throughout the world and has been identified as the oldest of all known venereal diseases. In males, gonorrhoea may involve the epididymis, the prostate, and seminal vesicles, as well as the external genitalia. In females, the infection often spreads internally to the cervix, uterus, fallopian tubes, and ovaries. The rectum may be involved in both

G

sexes. There, it is usually without symptoms, but the victim may have perianal discomfort and a rectal discharge. An anal infection usually spreads to the lining of the rectum, which shows pus formation when examined with a proctoscope. Gonococcal pharyngitis also may be found in both sexes, with symptoms of a sore throat and difficulty in swallowing. Women are more likely than men to be infected for weeks or months without experiencing symptoms. Prepubertal girls frequently are found with gonorrhoea infections, reportedly from contact with infected bedding, and may experience vulvovaginitis and proctitis, although it is also suspected that the infection may be transmitted by sexual abuse. The infecting organism, a form of diplococcus, is easily identified in a medical laboratory although cultures are commonly made of specimens to ensure proper identification of the bacterium. All patients are advised to abstain from intercourse until the infection has been eradicated. Three basic types of treatment involve administration of antibiotics: penicillin G, ampicillin or amoxicillin, or tetracycline. It is recommended that the patient return twice, at 1-week intervals, for tests to determine if the antibiotic treatment was effective. Penicillin therapy may not prove effective against strains of gonorrhoea that have been contracted in Southeast Asia. Complications include gonococcal arthritis, which is most likely to affect females, and sterility, which may affect males if the infection spreads to the epididymis. In a pregnant woman, gonorrhoea can result in inflammation of the amnion, premature rupture of the foetal membranes, premature labour, a child that is small for its gestational age, or death of the infant shortly after birth from the disease or a related infection, such as pneumonia or respiratory distress syndrome. Ophthalmia neonatorum, an eye disorder, may be acquired by the offspring in passing through the birth canal of a mother infected with gonorrhoea.

gonorrhoeal arthritis a specific gonococcal infection of the body's joints. This condition may be acute or chronic and may be confined to a single joint or involve a number of joints. The condition is confirmed by the recovery of gonorrhoea organisms from the synovial (joint) fluid. Untreated, the infection results in a freezing of the joint.

gonorrhoeal bubo a swelling of the lymph glands of the inguinal region, and early sign of an infection of gonorrhoea.

good, to be a euphemism meaning to refrain from having intercourse. 'Be Good, And If You Can't Be Good, Be Careful' was the name of a song popular around 1907. 'Being good' in bed refers to the degree of sexual pleasure a person can give their partner.

goolies a British euphemism for testicles.

goose a slang term meaning to poke someone between the buttocks, especially in order to startle her or him, or as a sexual come-on. In older usage, a *gooser* was a male homosexual preferring anal intercourse.

gooseberry bush a location commonly invoked when explaining childbirth to young children. A standard answer to the 'awkward' question 'Where do babies come from?' is 'Behind the gooseberry bush.' See also STORK.

Gordon-Overstreet syndrome a variation of Turner's syndrome in which the individual shows the characteristics of short stature, webbed neck, and other features associated with the XO dysgenic female chromosome set but also develops hirsutism and enlargement of the clitoris. The condition is caused by virilization because of male-hormone production of the abnormal gonad.

go south a euphemism meaning to have oral sex.

go straight a colloquial term meaning to change from homosexual to heterosexual relationships. Also, occasionally, called 'to get straight.'

go to bed with a euphemism meaning to have intercourse with (a partner).

government-inspected meat a homosexual slang term for a soldier who is attractive to male homosexuals.

goy toy a slang term for an uncircumcised penis.

graafian follicle a small cavity or recess in an ovary, containing an ovum that is separated from surrounding tissue by a single layer of follicular cells.

Gräfenberg ring the first of the modern intrauterine contraceptive devices, invented in 1930 by a German physician, Ernst Gräfenberg. The Gräfenberg ring was a coil of silver wire. Intrauterine devices of various sorts have been used for both human and animal females since ancient times but have had limited success or have eventually resulted in uterine infections (as the Gräfenberg ring was known to have done).

graffiti obscene words or drawings scrawled on walls, lavatory cubicles, or other public places. The object appears to be to release inhibitions, or to protest against sexual conventions or society as a whole. Singular: *graffito*.

granuloma inguinale an infectious disease characterized by the presence of bright, beefy-red ulcerations of the skin of the genital, inguinal, and anal regions. The penis, scrotum, groin, and thighs of males are affected as are the vulva, vagina, and perineal area of females. The lesions appear around the anus and buttocks of homosexual males. Diagnosis of the disorder is confirmed by a finding of Donovan's bodies in the lesions, which, untreated, may spread over large areas, eventually covering all of the genitalia. Treatment is with antibiotics. But recovery is slow, and there is a risk of secondary infections, which may be fatal.

granulosa cells a layer of cells that forms a lining of the ovarian follicle. The granulosa cells respond to stimulation of the follicle-stimulating hormone by multiplying rapidly, producing the liquor folliculi, and by actually forming the follicle. As the ovum matures, it is the granulosa cells that begin the breakthrough of the ovary wall to release the egg cell.

granulosa-cell tumour a tumour of the ovary that resembles in structure the granulosa cells of an ovarian follicle. The tumour has a feminizing effect, accounting for the characteristics of precocious pseudopuberty in little girls and for irregular menstrual cycles of bleeding in postmenopausal women.

granulosa-theca-cell tumour a tumour of the ovary that may produce large amounts of the feminizing hormone oestrogen. It is composed of elements of the cell wall of a graafian follicle and can cause sudden and rapid signs of sexual maturity in a girl.

grapelike cystadenoma a variation of a serous ovarian cyst in which the growth has the appearance of a cluster of grapes. Instead of forming as a single spherical sac of fluid, it contains numerous small serous-filled sacs.

grapes the traditional fruit of sexuality, originally promoted by Dionysus, the Greek god of wine. According to the Greek legends, Dionysus travelled throughout the lands planting grapevines, always accompanied by sex-mad groupies known as maenads. He is portrayed as wearing a crown of grapeleaves, riding in a chariot pulled by a satyr.

gravida (grav′idə) a woman who is pregnant. The term usually is applied to the physical and mental effects of pregnancy combined and sometimes is used to indicate a particular health problem associated with pregnancy, as in gravidocardiac, meaning a heart condition induced by a state of pregnancy.

gravida I a woman who is pregnant for the first time. Also called primigravida. A woman pregnant for the second time is identified as a *gravida II*, or secundigravida; and so on.

gravidity another term for pregnancy.

Great Divide a slang term for the PENOSCROTAL RAPHE. See this entry.

Great Mother the universal, primordial mother or mother concept ('Magna Mater') in Roman mythology and Jung's theory of archetypes.

great imitator a characterization of syphilis based on the fact that its symptoms are so varied that they may deceive the patient into believing that he or she has a benign disease of one kind or another. Syphilis may be mistaken, for example, for hives, measles, indigestion, or headache. The symptoms usually go underground and disappear for a time, and the patient may think he or she is completely well.

Greek love an obsolescent term for male homosexuality. In current usage, anal intercourse is referred to in expressions like *Greek fashion, Greek culture,* the *Greek way,* or, simply, *Greek*—also as a verb: *to greek*. See also HOMOSEXUAL.

green discharge a form of dishonourable discharge from the US Navy during World War II on grounds of homosexual behaviour.

GRID an acronym for gay-related immune deficiency, a term used to identify AIDS before 'acquired immune deficiency syndrome' was adopted as the official term for the disorder in 1982. See also AIDS.

Griselda complex the reluctance of a father to give up his daughter to another man. The American psychiatrist James J. Putmam, who coined the term, interpreted this complex in terms of an unresolved Oedipus complex. Griselda was the name of the virtuous heroine in medieval romances.

grope a slang term meaning to fondle sexually in an unwelcome way. Thus a man groping a woman might be trying to put his hand inside her blouse or up her skirt.

gross indecency a 19th-century British legal term for anal intercourse.

group B streptococcal infection a type of strep infection that can cause significant complications, particularly in pregnant women and their offspring, sometimes resulting in abortion, perinatal death, premature birth, and severe neonatal illness such as septicaemia, meningitis, and pneumonia. The infection may be sexually transmitted in some cases, and is a cause of death in approximately 5,000 infants per year in the United States.

groupie a female fan, especially of a male rock star, whose devotion usually goes so far as to offer her body to her idol. Some groupies make themselves sexually available to the entire musical band. See also PLASTER CASTER.

group marriage an arrangement—not actually a legal marriage—in which several men and women live together as if they were actually married to each other, sharing a common sex life as well as household burdens and child rearing. Groups of this kind have been found in Australia, Brazil, Siberia, and, over a century ago, in the upstate New York community of Oneida.

group sex sexual activity by a group of people in the same place and at the same time, usually involving exchange of partners, observing each other, and different variations of intercourse. The groups may be entirely composed of heterosexuals or homosexuals, or a combination of the two.

guiche (gēsh) a metal ring about 1 inch in diameter inserted in the perineum, the area of skin behind the scrotum. By lightly pulling on the guiche during sexual relations, the male partner is said to increase arousal and prolong orgasm. The device originated in the South Pacific.

gut fucker a vulgar slang term for a male homosexual who practises anal intercourse.

Guttmacher Institute a private US research and policy organization that sponsors studies on reproductive health and publishes reports of its own research and those of other similar agencies.

gymnophobia a morbid fear of naked bodies (Greek *gymnos*, 'naked, bare').

gynaecological spread a euphemism for a photograph of a woman with open legs, focussing on the vagina.

gynaecomastia a condition in the male in which the mammary glands are overdeveloped and in some cases may secrete milk.

Gynaecomastia occurs as a part of the Klinefelter syndrome and is associated with the presence of an extra X chromosome. The male with gynaecomastia may be normal, eunuchoid, or infertile. See also INVOLUTIONAL GYNAECOMASTIA.

gynaecomastia-aspermatogenesis syndrome a form of Klinefelter's syndrome in which the male develops breasts and does not produce sperm, usually because of impaired Leydig-cell activity. The individual often has a chromosomal aberration with 47 or 48 chromosomes, such as an extra X chromosome or a double XY complement, instead of the normal 46 chromosomes including a single XY set, as in a normal male.

gynaephobia a morbid fear of women. Also spelled gynophobia.

gynaetresia a congenital anomaly in which the vagina is totally absent or abnormally shallow. The condition is often detected at birth, but correction by plastic surgery is delayed until puberty. One reason for the delay is that an artifical vagina must be dilated frequently, as by coitus, to be successful.

gynandroblastoma a rare ovarian tumour that produces both male and female sex hormones. It is generally benign although it may grow to a diameter of 8 inches, interfering with neighbouring normal tissues by its mass. The patient may experience an overgrowth of endometrial tissue with uterine bleeding while also showing signs of hirsutism. (Greek *gyne*, 'woman'; *aner*, 'man.')

gynandromorph a person possessing both male and female sexual characteristics. In humans, the condition is an anomaly associated with a sex chromosome error. In lower animals, it may be a normal condition.

gynogamone a substance secreted by the ovum that is believed to attract spermatozoa to facilitate their union.

gynomonoecism a genetic anomaly in which an individual who is female in appearance is able to produce spermatozoa in her ovaries.

haemacytometer an instrument used to count spermatozoa in male fertility studies.

haematocolpos an abnormal condition in which the vagina becomes engorged with blood because of an imperforate hymen.

haematometra an enlarged uterus caused by the entrapment of menstrual flow when the blood cannot be discharged through the vagina because of an imperforate hymen.

haematosalpinx a condition in which menstrual blood that cannot be discharged through the vagina because of an unbroken hymen backs up through the fallopian tubes and into the peritoneal cavity. The condition is most likely to occur in a girl who has begun to menstruate. The medical complications usually lead to examination by a doctor who will perforate the hymen to correct the situation.

haematropic metabolism the process whereby the placenta functions as a mechanism between the mother and her embryo to transport nutrients to the embryo and to carry away the waste products of the embryo's own metabolic functions.

haemospermia vera a benign condition in which there is a mixture of blood and seminal fluid in the seminal vesicles.

hair a secondary sex characteristic that marks the advent of puberty and helps to distinguish male from female. Though hair is distributed over most of the body in both sexes, males generally possess more profuse body hair than females, especially on the chest, face and eyebrows, and in the ears and nostrils. Their pubic hair extends both upward and downward farther than that of women. Also, men tend to become bald far more rapidly than women. Transsexual males who wish to become women may remove facial and body hair by electrolysis, and transsexual females may induce growth of facial and body hair through the administration of androgens.

hair burger a slang term for vagina, used in the context of cunnilingus—'to eat a hair burger,' also 'to eat hair pie.' See also FURBURGER.

haircut a slang term for a secondary stage of syphilis in which alopecia, or loss of hair, is a common effect.

hair genes the units of heredity affecting hair growth. Although androgenic sex hormones play a key role in the development of facial hair in humans, and account for the problem of hirsutism in females, the effect is moderated considerably by the structure and function of hair follicles, which is a genetic factor. As a result, some individuals, particularly Native Americans, may be unable to grow a beard despite an adequate level of androgenic hormones and otherwise normal sexual characteristics.

hair pulling a compulsive habit of pulling out hair from the head, and sometimes from the pubic region. This behaviour pattern is occasionally observed, but the motivation is often unclear. It may, however, be an expression of anger, tension, or frustration, or a substitute for masturbation. The psychiatric term for hair pulling is trichotillomania.

half-and half a colloquial term for bisexual.

half-mast a colloquial term referring to a semierect penis.

hallucinogens drugs that produce sensory and perceptual distortions and all types of hallucinations, such as visual, auditory, and tactile. Other reactions are palpitations, tremors, anxiety or depression, and fear of losing one's mind. The effects on sexual feelings and behaviour are unpredictable and appear to depend largely on the individual's state of mind, expectations, and the circumstances in which the drugs are used. Major hallucinogens include LSD, mescaline, psilocybin, bufotenine, dimethyltryptamine (DMT), and phencyclidine (PCP, angel dust).

Halotestin a trademark for a U.S. brand of fluoxymesterone tablets, used to improve sperm motility in infertile males.

hammartoma a noncancerous tumour of otherwise normal nerve tissue that is associated with some cases of premature sexual development in children. The tumours appear in the diencephalon portion of the brain, and are likely to affect the pituitary-gland function so that adult levels of gonadotropin hormones are secreted and a small boy with the central-nervous-system lesion may have mature, enlarged testes and penis, and pubic hair.

hammock a layer of connective tissue in the floor of the pelvic cavity that helps support or attach various genital organs of both sexes. The root of the penis, for example, is attached to the pelvic hammock fibres.

Hampton a humorous British euphemism for penis. It is short for Hampton Wick (a place to the southwest of London), which in turn is rhyming slang for prick.

hand job a slang term for masturbation.

haploid a cell or individual with only one set of chromosomes. This condition occurs in gametes and gametocytes after the first meiotic division. In humans, the haploid number is 23. After fertilization, the diploid number of 46 is restored.

haptephobia a morbid fear of being touched, in some cases stemming from a fear of sex. Also called haphephobia.

hard a Shakespearean euphemism referring to the penis in erection—which in today's slang usage is also referred to as having a *hard on*. A popular T-shirt of the mid-1980s worn by women, says 'A hard man is good to find', an aphorism attributed to Mae West.

hard chancre the primary lesion of syphilis, usually appearing on the corona or the glans penis or the inner layer of the foreskin, less commonly on the penile shaft, scrotum, or mouth area. It begins as a silvery pimple that gradually erodes to form an ulcer teeming with *Treponema pallidum* spirochaetes. It is usually painless, round or oval, with a slightly raised border. It tends to occur as a single lesion, rather than as multiple sores.

hard-core sex blatant, explicit sexual activity or material, as in X-rated films and sex magazines.

hard media a term pertaining to the texture and sometimes the colour of objects popular with fetishists. Hard-media objects include leather, rubber, and plastic materials that tend to have a smooth, metallic look and which as garments are tightly fitting. A popular hard-media colour is black.

harem (Arabic, 'reserve' or 'sanctuary') a secluded portion of a Muslim house or palace occupied by the master's wife or wives, concubines, and female servants, who are also known collectively as the harem. Harems have existed in Siamese, Babylonian, Peruvian, and Hindu societies, but have been most common in Islamic societies. The basic purpose has been to provide sexual outlets, companionship, and entertainment for the master, and to protect the marriage by keeping him from resorting to prostitutes. The harem, however, is usually also the place in which female members of the household in general—including the master's mother, sisters, and daughters—are confined, mainly to ensure male privacy.

haricot an Australian euphemism for a male homosexual. It is short for haricot bean, which in turn is rhyming slang for queen.

harlot an obsolete term for prostitute. In Chaucer's time, the word meant servant.

HCG radioreceptor assay a laboratory test of female urine used to detect pregnancy by measuring the presence of human chorionic gonadotropin (HCG). The hormone occurs only in the urine of pregnant women or in women afflicted by a type of tumour that produces HCG.

head cheese a slang term for smegma beneath the foreskin and around the glans of the penis. Compare CROTCH CHEESE.

head flattening a head moulding custom prevalent among the Northwest coast Native Americans and in other native societies, as well as parts of France in the early 20th century, based on their conception of beauty and sexual attractiveness. The head was flattened and pushed back to a point early in life by binding the infant to a board with another board pressing on his forehead.

head job a slang term for oral sex.

head-over-heels a synonym for the slang term sixty-nine.

health club often a euphemism for massage parlour (which itself is a euphemism).

heart disease any cardiovascular disorder, such as a congenital heart defect, heart-muscle abnormality, or valvular disorder resulting from rheumatic fever or another infection. Class III heart disease, requiring considerable limitation of activity, or Class IV heart disease, with symptoms of cardiac insufficiency even at rest, are regarded as indications for therapeutic abortions up to the 24th week of pregnancy.

heart-rate changes the change of rate of the normal heartbeat during sexual response. In the normal resting individual, the average heart rate is 60 to 80 beats per minute. During the plateau phase, it rises to 100 to 160 beats per minute. There is a corresponding increase in blood pressure during sexual response.

hedonophobia a morbid fear of experiencing pleasure of any kind.

Hegar's sign one of the signs of pregnancy, marked by a softening of the isthmus of the uterus. It occurs around the seventh week of gestation and is detected by the examining physician by digital (finger) examination of the outer surface of the cervix as it projects into the vagina.

Hellenic love an archaic term for male homosexuality as practised in ancient Greece.

Héloïse the 12th-century pupil and ill-fated lover of Pierre ABÉLARD. See this entry.

hemicastration the removal of one testicle, a practice believed to be limited to four societies, one in Ethiopia, two in Micronesia, and among the Hottentots in southern Africa, who are said to have performed the operation to prevent the birth of twins, which was thought to bring bad luck. The practice has all but disappeared. Also called semicastration.

hemihypertrophy an alternative term for unilateral sexual precocity, in which genitalia on the right or left side of the body develop at a faster rate than sexual organs on the other side.

hemispheric prosthesis a female breast implant that is designed to produce a rounded breast profile similar to that of a breast that has become reduced somewhat after childbirth, with a convex contour and cleavage.

hemizygote an individual who possesses only one of a normal pair of chromosomes or one of a pair of allelomorphic genes. Such an individual manifests the trait for the genes inherited, regardless of whether they are dominant or recessive. Examples are found among the X-linked genetic effects in a male because there are no matching genes on the Y chromosome.

hepatitis B a viral disease with a long incubation, caused by hepatitis virus B, and usually transmitted either by injection of infected blood through the use of contaminated needles, or by sexual contact, anal or oral. The first symptoms are vomiting, fatigue, and depression, which are usually followed by jaundice. Therapy is primarily designed to prevent complications. Also called serum hepatitis.

herm a square stone pillar surmounted with a bearded head of Hermes, the messenger of the gods. A prominent phallus was usually carved into the pillar, and the herm was used as a religious shrine marking the spot where Greeks paid homage to the power of reproduction and growth.

hermaphrodite a person affected with hermaphroditism, in which the sexual characteristics of both the male and female are found in one individual. The condition may be expressed in several ways. In true *hermaphroditism*, the individual has both ovaries and testes. Bilateral hermaphroditism is characterized by the presence of an ovary and a testicle on each side of the body. A lateral hermaphrodite may have an ovary on one side of the body and a testicle on the opposite side. A unilateral hermaphrodite is one who has both an ovary and testicle on one side and either an ovary or a testicle on the other side. A pseudohermaphrodite, or false hermaphrodite, may possess either ovaries or testes and external genitalia of the other sex, although the individual also may possess sexual characteristics that are a combination of male and female. However, classification is based on the identity of the gonads so that the person is considered male if the gonads are testes or female if the gonads are ovaries, regardless of the identity of the external genitalia.

hermaphroditus verus a medical term for true hermaphrodite, or an individual possessing both male and female gonads.

herpes a term generally applied to any 'herpetiform' eruption of skin or mucous membrane tissues resulting from an infection of one of the herpes-virus strains. The most common of the nearly half-dozen variations is herpes simplex, also called cold sore, which accounts for most of the acute vesicular eruptions that usually appear on the face in association with another infection, during menstruation, after a period of exposure to ultraviolet light, or as a result of an emotional disturbance. Varicella/zoster, Epstein-Barr, cytomegalovirus, and herpes B, all of which affect humans, are variations of herpes simplex. Herpes B virus is endemic among Asiatic monkeys but can be transmitted to humans, sometimes with fatal consequences. Herpes varicella is better known as the cause of chicken pox, and herpes zoster is the same virus that tends to return in later life to produce the symptoms of shingles. The Epstein-Barr (ES) virus is the cause of infectious mononucleosis, or 'kissing disease,' while cytomegalovirus, a herpes virus that is present in the salivary glands of about 50 percent of the adult population, rarely surfaces except in cases of loss of natural immunity when it may manifest itself as a form of mononucleosis or a variety of other diseases, including a form of viral pneumonia. See also GENITAL HERPES.

herpes gestationis a form of herpes simplex infection that appears on the skin of some women during the second or third trimester of pregnancy. The symptoms of a rash with small blisters and severe itching usually disappear after the pregnancy is ended. However, they recur with successive pregnancies. The viral infection is associated with a high incidence of miscarriages.

herpes progenitalis a herpes simplex infection of the penis or vulva.

herpes simplex encephalitis a complication of a herpes simplex Type 1 infection in which the viruses spread from the respiratory area of the nose along the olfactory nerve tracts to the frontal and temporal areas of the brain. The onset of the infection is marked by headache, runny nose, fever, nausea and vomiting. There also may be loss of appetite, sensitivity to light, dizziness, insomnia, and disorientation. Untreated, the encephalitis progresses to seizures, paralysis, coma, and death. In many instances proper diagnosis has been delayed because the patients were initially regarded as psychotics or alcoholics. Symptoms in advanced cases of infection may include urinary incontinence, hallucinations, personality changes, tremors, and loss of muscular coordination. Treatment is with antiviral medications.

herpes simplex Type 1 (HSV-1) a herpesvirus that usually is found in herpes infections of the eye, skin, nose and throat, and brain. It causes infections of the mouth and gums, rhinitis (inflammation of the nasal passages), conjunctivitis, a form of eczema, and various other diseases, including a skin infection peculiar to wrestlers and identified as herpes gladiatorum. The incubation period is about 1 week, although it may range from 2 days to 2 weeks, and the virus usually invades the skin and mucous membranes of the mouth and nose. The lesions begin as tense vesicles containing a clear fluid. The vesicles, or tiny blisters, are usually small, except in a form of the disease called Kaposi's varicelliform eruption, which can be fatal. It is characterized by large fluid-filled blisters. Within several days, the vesicles ulcerate and eventually disappear, usually without leaving a scar. Recent studies indicate that this type of herpes is frequently transmitted by kissing, and may be sexually transmissible, especially through orogenital contact.

herpes simplex Type 2 (HSV-2) a herpes virus that usually is transmitted by sexual contact. It is found in genital ulcers or blisters of women and in penile lesions of men. The HSV-2 virus is similar to the HSV-1 variety but distinguishable in laboratory tests; among other factors, the Type 2 virus has a greater density. Studies of the Type 2 infection have found that up to 50 percent of the patients are teenagers, although the mean age of the patients is between 25 and 30 years. Most have had the infection for from 4 to 5 years, and most experience outbreaks of the infection at least five times a year. Most of the patients also had been treated for gonorrhoea or other kinds of sexually-transmitted diseases, in addition to Type 2 herpes simplex. About two thirds of female patients experience relapses, with menstruation, emotional upsets, or other infections triggering the relapse. There is a statistical link between the virus and cancer of the cervix.

he-she a slang term for a male or female homosexual.

hetaerae a superior class of prostitutes in ancient Greece who provided intellectual as well as physical stimulation to their clients. Unlike common prostitutes, they were accomplished in the arts, conversation, and debate and paid taxes to the state in proportion to their income.

hetaeral fantasy another term for courtesan fantasy.

heterochromatin a type of chromosome material that is unique in that it is responsible for cellular metabolism and functions and is not involved in transmitting genetic characteristics from one generation to the next. It can be identified by a laboratory stain that it absorbs. The heterochromatin occurs in the inactivated X chromosome of the female sex chromosomes and is also detected in the male Y chromosome at certain stages of cell division.

heteroerotism a psychoanalytical term for

the attachment of the libido or sex drive to persons or objects outside the self. The achievement of such relationships is regarded as a major task of adolescence. Also called heteroeroticism.

heterogamous pertaining to the union of male and female gametes that are of unequal size, as occurs in human fertilization, the female ovum being much larger than the male spermatozoon.

heterologous artificial insemination artificial insemination in which the semen is provided by a donor other than the husband or partner.

heterosexism a label applied by homosexual leaders to the use in advertising illustrations of scenes in which men are paired with women, and vice versa. Guidelines for the elimination of heterosexism submitted to the Greater London Council in 1985 suggested that advertisements show some men paired with men and women paired with women in scenes of dancing or similar forms of socializing.

heterosexual anxiety anxiety aroused by attitudes or feelings associated with relationships to the opposite sex, such as inhibitions resulting from upbringing or religious beliefs, concern over sexual attractiveness, or fear of inadequate performance.

Heterosexual-Homosexual Behaviour Rating Scale an instrument developed by Kinsey and his co-workers in the U.S.A. for measuring the degree of heterosexuality and homosexuality by placing an individual into one of seven categories according to sexual behaviour and interest: exclusively heterosexual, predominantly heterosexual with incidental homosexuality, predominantly heterosexual with more than incidental homosexuality, equally heterosexual and homosexual, predominantly homosexual with more than incidental heterosexuality, predominantly homosexual with incidental heterosexuality, and exclusively homosexual.

heterosexualilty sexual attraction to members of the opposite sex, usually including sexual activity.

heterosexual precocity the development at an early age of the secondary sexual characteristics of a person of the opposite sex, such as adult masculine features in a girl. The abnormality may stem from an adrenal-gland tumour.

heterosociality the tendency to establish social relationships with members of the opposite sex, often but not always based on sexual interest.

hickey an American term for a mark made on the skin by biting and sucking during sexual play, usually on the neck. Also called love bite.

hieroduli male temple prostitutes of ancient cultures, particularly in Greece. The hieroduli were often priests who were also transvestites. The term means, literally, 'servants of the goddess.'

high levels of sexual activity sexual activity that ranges between above normal and remarkable. Some studies indicate that sexual hyperactivity is associated with neurotic behaviour, although it is not clear which is the cause and which is the effect. In statistical studies, such as the Kinsey data, the most sexually active men averaged seven orgasms per week, a higher frequency than the most sexually active segment of women. However, some women have experienced orgasm 12 or more times an hour. Among male prostitutes, some are reportedly able to ejaculate six or more times a day for years. Many individuals are historically famous for their sexual prowess, including Casanova, Catherine II of Russia, the Roman Emperor Nero, and the Roman Empress Valeria Messalina. See also SEXUAL PRODIGIES.

hilar cells one of three types of cells in the ovary that produce sex hormones. The hilar cells are involved in the production of androgenic hormones. The other types of hormone-producing cells in the ovary are the granulosa cells and the theca cells. Not included are the corpus luteum cells that periodically produce progesterone.

Hindu genital classification a classification of male and female sex organs according to their dimensions. The most celebrated typologies are described in the Hindu treatises *Kama Sutra* and *Ananga Ranga*. The three types of lingam (penis) are the hare, up to 5 inches long fully erect; the bull, up to 7 inches; and the horse, up to 10 inches. The three types of yoni (vagina) are the deer, up to 5 inches deep; the mare, up to 7 inches; and the elephant, up to 10 inches. There are three equal 'unions' such as hare and deer, which present no problems, and six unequal unions, in which 'positions should be used that create a balance.'

Hindu love postures the numerous and varied coital or intercourse positions described and illustrated in Hindu love manuals, especially the 4th-century *Kama Sutra*, and later texts such as the *Ananga Ranga*. These manuals were usually given to girls approaching puberty to prepare them for a full sexual life. Each posture is given a name, such as 'splitting a bamboo,' 'conjunction of sun and moon,' 'position of a cow' (or dog, elephant, tiger, horse, monkey, crab, or tortoise). Many of the positions were given poetic names such as 'playing the flute' (fellatio), 'tiger's tread' (rear entry), and 'fluttering and soaring butterfly' (woman above position).

Hirschfeld, Magnus (1868-1935) a German psychiatrist who pioneered in the study of homosexuality and advocated the reform of laws that penalized homosexuals. He also distinguished between transvestism and homosexuality and founded the first journal of sexual pathology and the Institute for Sexology. His major work was entitled *Sex Anomalies and Perversions*. Hirschfeld also preceded Alfred Kinsey in compiling data on sexual behaviour, obtaining interviews from 10,000 persons on a questionnaire covering 130 separate items. Most of Hirschfeld's pioneering work was destroyed by the Nazis.

hirsutoid papilloma of the penis a condition marked by the appearance of small white lesions around the corona of the glans penis. The lesions may be accompanied by the appearance of hair growth on the warty papules. Also called pearly penile papules.

Hite Report a survey of female sexuality conducted in the U.S.A. in the 1970s by author and historian Shere Hite. The study discussed responses to interview questions received from over 3,000 women on such subjects as how they best achieved orgasm. The *Hite Report* has been challenged as being biased because the questionnaire was distributed to members of feminist groups and readers of women's publications rather than to a representative sample of the general female population. The author has written other similar reports, including the *Hite Report on Male Sexuality*.

HIV abbreviation for HUMAN IMMUNODEFICIENCY VIRUS. See this entry.

holandric inheritance the acquisition of traits transmitted by genes on the Y chromosome, representing the paternal line of heredity.

Holland a Shakespearean euphemism for the buttocks or the anal area—Holland being a low-lying country (with an added pun on 'hole land'). See also NETHERLANDS.

Hollywood Androgyny a published Amer-

ican study of films featuring cross-dressing of characters. The study cited the 1959 movie *Some Like It Hot* as a pivotal cinematic production that led to the general acceptability of films in which men dressed as women, as in *Tootsie* or women as men, as in *Victor Victoria*.

hologynic inheritance the acquisition of traits transmitted by genes located on X chromosomes, thereby expressing characteristics of the maternal line of heredity. The tendency for multiple ovulation and dizygotic twin births is a hologynic trait.

home pregnancy test do-it-yourself test in which the presence of HCG (human chorionic gonadotropin) is detected by placing a few drops of the first urine passed early in the morning into a test tube along with certain chemicals.

homework a euphemism for sex-therapy exercises recommended by Masters and Johnson in treating a dysfunction. Homework assignments may involve stroking of bodies, with breasts and genitals as forbidden areas in early stages of therapy. Each partner helps train the other to find the body areas that are most or least pleasantly stimulated.

home wrecker colloquial term for the 'other woman.'

homicidophilia the seeking of sexual gratification through the murder—real or imagined—of one's partner or a stranger.

homo a derogatory term for a homosexual, usually a male one. Also called *homie* in American English.

homo- a prefix that is often misunderstood because it has two meanings. As a Latin term, it is derived from *homo*, meaning 'human being,' as in 'Homo sapiens' or 'homicide.' But as a Greek term, it is derived from *homos*, meaning 'one and the same,' as in 'homogenous' (of the same kind, uniform) or as in 'homosexual'—of the same sex.

homochronous inheritance the manifestation or expression of genetic traits or characteristics occurring at the same age in the children as they did in the parents.

homoerotism a pattern of erotic, or sexual, interest in members of one's own sex. Also called *homoeroticism*. Adjective: *homoerotic*.

homoerotophobia an intense fear of homosexuals and homosexual behaviour; also, a fear of being homosexual.

homogamy the reinforcement of hereditary traits as a result of the interbreeding of members of a population group that remains isolated for cultural or geographical reasons.

Examples include the condition of cretinism that developed in past centuries in Alpine valley communities or the tendency of certain disorders to recur more frequently among members of religious groups who seldom marry outside their own sect.

homogenesis reproduction by the same process in each generation of a species, resulting in offspring that are similar to the parents.

homogenic an obsolete term for homosexual.

homogenitality a pattern of interest in the genital organs of members of one's own sex, also, genital relations with persons of one's own sex. Also called *homogenitalism*.

homologous pertaining to male and female sex organs that develop differently from the same embryonic tissue, as the scrotum and labia both develop from the genital tubercle.

homologous artifical insemination artificial insemination in which the husband or partner provides the semen.

homophile a person who is sexually and emotionally attracted to members of his or her own sex; a homosexual.

homophilia another term for homosexuality.

homophobia another term for homoerotophobia.

homoseductive mother an overprotective mother who is also too intimate with her son and dominant in the family. The term was introduced by the psychiatrist Irving Bieber in his study of family backgrounds of male homosexuals versus male heterosexuals.

homosexual a person who is sexually attracted to someone of his or her own sex. The term (from Greek *homo*, 'same,' and Latin *sexus*, 'sex') was coined by the Hungarian physician Karoly Maria Benkert in 1869. (In ancient Greece, where it was common for men to be at least bisexual, no term existed for homosexuality, only a variety of terms referring to specific homosexual roles and attitudes.)

homosexual community a subculture composed of male or female homosexuals who share the same social and political organizations, meeting places, activities on behalf of gay rights, customs, special vocabulary, and, in some areas, pubs, beaches, park areas, and shops. Also called gay community.

homosexuality a pattern of sexual relationships between members of the same sex, based on mutual attraction that may be limited to sexual fantasies and feelings, but usually involves overt sexual activities ranging from kissing, fondling, frictation, and mutual masturbation to fellatio, and inter-course, and anilingus among men and cunnilingus and tribadism among women. Kinsey's data, now about 30 years old, indicate that in North America 37 percent of the adult male (white) population and 13 percent of the adult female (white) population have had some overt homosexual experience to the point of orgasm. Far fewer, however, are exclusively homosexual for an extended portion of their lives: 8 percent among men and about 1 to 3 percent among women.

See also ACCIDENTAL HOMOSEXUALITY; ADOLESCENT HOMOSEXUALITY; COVERT HOMOSEXUAL; DEPRIVATIONAL HOMOSEXUALITY; EFFEMINATE HOMOSEXUALITY; EGODYSTONIC HOMOSEXUALITY; EGO-SYNTONIC HOMOSEXUALITY; ENDOCRINE BASIS OF HOMOSEXUALITY; IATROGENIC HOMOSEXUALITY; LATENT HOMOSEXUALITY; MALE HOMOSEXUAL PROSTITUTION; MASKED HOMOSEXUALITY; MONOGAMOUS HOMOSEXUAL RELATIONSHIP; NATURAL HOMOSEXUAL PERIOD; OVERT HOMOSEXUALITY; PHYSICAL CHARACTERISTICS OF HOMOSEXUALS; PRIMARY HOMOSEXUAL; PSEUDOHOMOSEXUALITY; SITUATIONAL HOMOSEXUALITY.

homosexual marriage a lasting but not necessarily permanent relationship between male or female homosexuals who occupy the same living quarters and consider themselves married in fact if not in law. Also called gay marriage.

homosexual panic an acute, sudden anxiety reaction precipitated by fear of being attacked by a person of the same sex; fear of being considered homosexual by associates; fear of inadequacy or impotence in a homosexual relationship; an unconscious fear of being a homosexual or of engaging in homosexual behaviour; or loss of a long-term homosexual partner.

homosexual patterns three phases of homosexuality that include, according to some authorities, (1) an active role, in which the individual functions sexually as a male, (2) a passive role, in which the person plays a female role, and (3) a mixed role, in which the person alternates between active and passive roles. The mixed role is reported to be the most frequently followed pattern.

homosexual practices the variations in methods preferred by homosexuals in various cultures of the world. Studies indicate that American and British homosexual men prefer oral intercourse while Mexican homosexual men overwhelmingly express a preference for anal intercourse.

homosexual rape forcible assault by one person (or several) upon an individual of the same sex. This type of rape is usually committed by males, and occasionally by females, on younger members of a prison population.

homozygote an individual or organism with identical genes at any given location on a pair of homologous chromosomes. The individual will always manifest the characteristics produced by the genes. An example is the gene for eye colour.

homunculus a fully formed miniature human being that some theorists in the 16th and 17th centuries believed to be contained in the spermatozoon. Prenatal development was pictured primarily in terms of expansion in size. The doctrine on which this theory is based is termed preformism.

honeymoon assault violent defloration of the virginal bride on the wedding night, usually by forced penetration. Pain, bleeding, and lack of consideration on the part of the husband may prove traumatic and may inhibit both partners or even produce temporary frigidity and impotence.

honeymoon cystitis an inflammation of the bladder found among women who have just been married, or who engage in frequent and regular intercourse for the first time. The condition is uncomfortable and painful especially during urination, and is often caused by vaginal dryness resulting from nervousness and apprehension. An artifical lubricant and a considerate partner usually help. See also CYSTITIS.

honey pot a euphemism for vagina.

hooker a colloquial term for prostitute. The word has enjoyed popularity since the 1830s.

horizontalize an obsolete slang term meaning to have intercourse. A still popular term in France is *la vie horizontale*, 'the horizontal life,' referring to sexual activities, especially to the world of prostitution.

hormonal control the use of sex-hormone adjustments in the control of cancer of the prostate. The technique may include surgical removal of the testicles or the administration of female sex hormones, or both, as needed to reduce the levels of male sex hormones in the patient.

hormonal gender a term referring to the hormones normally associated with the male or female sex, as testosterone in the male and oestrogen and progesterone in the female.

hormone a chemical agent produced by an organ or cells of an organ and transported by the circulatory system to cells of another organ where it sets in motion or excites the target tissues. Most hormones are produced by endocrine glands, although there are exceptions. The human body's hormones vary widely in composition and function. The adrenal hormones and sex hormones are generally classified as steroid molecules. Some pituitary hormones are proteins, and neurotransmitters such as epinephrine are technically phenolic substances. All are extremely potent, requiring in some cases only a few molecules to trigger a response in a remote organ. They also are quite specific and usually are regulated by a complex bio-feedback system, as can be observed in the pituitary gonadotropin-hormone-secretion system. The hypophysis signals the anterior lobe of the pituitary to release follicle-stimulating hormone (FSH), which stimulates secretion of oestrogen in the ovarian follicle. When the oestrogen levels in the bloodstream reach a certain maximum level, the negative-feedback message results in the hypophysis secreting an inhibitory hormone that turns off the FSH-releasing mechanism of the pituitary.

horn a euphemism for the penis, especially the erect penis. This meaning of the word predates Shakespeare—who uses it repeatedly—and seems to be connected with the legend in which Jupiter assumes the shape of a bull when he is out for mischief. See also THREE-INCH FOOL.

horned pillow a pillow shaped like a half-moon and designed to be placed under a woman's buttocks to facilitate deep penetration and free movement during lovemaking. The pillow was first developed by the Chinese but is also used by the Hindus. In Western countries ordinary pillows may be used for the same purposes.

horny a colloquial term for being sexually aroused or in need of sexual satisfaction—said of (or by) a man or woman. See also HORN.

horror feminae the Latin term for dread of women.

hot flush a temporary sensation of warmth experienced by some women during and after menopause. The exact cause is unknown, but it is believed to be an autonomic-nervous-system effect on the blood vessels resulting in turn from neurohormonal activity of the hypothalamus and pituitary gland. Also called *hot flash* in American English.

Hottentot bustle a colloquial alternative to the medical term steatopygia.

hots a slang term for uncontrollable sexual desire, as in 'She's got the hots for him.'

house a colloquial term for whorehouse. Also called *house of ... delight, civil reception, assignation, sin, ill repute, ill fame,* and many other names beginning with 'house' (or ending with 'house,' such as cat house, call house, or bawdyhouse).

housegirl a colloquial term for a girl or woman who lives in a house of prostitution and serves male clients on a regular basis.

how's-your-father a humorous British euphemism for sexual activity, particularly sexual intercourse.

HPA-23 an antiviral drug developed in France at the Pasteur Institute and at Rhone-Poulence, S.A., for the treatment of AIDS. HPA-23 was given 'Orphan Drug' status by the US Food and Drug Administration in August 1985, allowing the drug to be used to treat AIDS patients in the United States without formal approval. Adverse effects include a drop in the body's normal level of blood platelets. See also AIDS.

HPV abbreviation for human papillomavirus, a cause of genital warts.

HTLV-III the former name for human immunodeficiency virus, the organism that in most cases causes AIDS. The initials represent human T-cell leukaemia virus (and in New York City they are the telephone number—H-T-L-V-1-1-1—for the AIDS hot line). Because the virus is believed to be the same as the French LAV strain, the term was frequently shown as *HTLV-III/LAV.* See this entry and also AIDS.

human chorionic gonadotropin (HCG) a hormone secreted by the fingerlike villi of the chorion, the outer layer of the two placental membranes. It stimulates the continued secretion of oestrogen and progesterone by the corpus luteum of the ovary after ovulation. This activity suppresses further ovulation or menstruation until after the newly established pregnancy has been terminated by loss of the foetus or birth of the infant. HCG is known to enter the foetal circulation and to help regulate some of the mechanisms of foetal development, although the exact role is not well understood.

human cloning a theoretical variation of parthenogenesis in which two or more genetically identical humans could develop by mitosis from a single somatic cell. Monozygotic multiple births represent a type of cloning in that each member has the same complement of genes. A study of several hundred

unfertilized human ova found that nearly 1 percent had started to develop into embryos without contact with spermatozoa, raising the prospect that parthenogenesis in a human might be possible, although there is no evidence that such an event has ever occurred, resulting in a true 'virgin birth.' However, if parthenogenesis could occur, the offspring would have to be a female child and a clone of the mother because it would possess only the X chromosome genes of the mother.

human immunodeficiency virus (HIV) a virus that causes an infection of acquired immune deficiency syndrome, or AIDS. It was formerly known as HTLV-III. See this entry and also AIDS.

human menopausal gonadotropin (HMG) a hormone that is used by intramuscular injection to stimulate ovulation in anovulatory women. It is a synthetic preparation of two natural gonadotropin hormones, follicle-stimulating hormone (FSH) and luteinizing hormone (LH), usually mixed half-and-half with a small amount of lactose.

human T-cell leukaemia virus a group of viruses that includes one strain identified as HTLV-III, the former name for human immunodeficiency virus, which casues AIDS. See also AIDS.

humiliation the process of degrading or deprecating another person, or the feeling of shame and loss of self-esteem associated with this process. Sexual sadism and masochism may take the form of humiliating a partner by such acts as spanking, chaining, torturing, and erotic bondage.

hump a slang term meaning to copulate.

hunger and love the most important expressions of the Life Urge, according to the psychiatrist Wilhelm Stekel. Stekel related hunger and love to Nietzsche's Will to Power, noting that the person with power is able to secure for himself the important gratifications in the forms of the best food and the most attractive sex partners. And 'hunger serves current life, love takes care of future life.'

hung up a colloquial term referring to penis captivus, or penis capture, which may occur in animals, such as dogs, that have a bone within the penis. But there is no scientific evidence that a human male gets 'hung up' in the same manner. The myth is probably based on the male experience of vaginismus during intercourse. (Vaginismus is a strong tightening of the muscles of the vagina that may occur during coitus.) But vaginismus is transient and spasmodic and in most cases would result in a loss of male erection.

hung up on someone a colloquial term meaning very attached to someone, especially in a sexual attachment.

Hunterian chancre the classic hard chancre of syphilis, described by 18th-century surgeon John Hunter. The Hunterian hard chancre requires about 1 week to evolve from the initial syphilitic lesion.

husband's pregnancy symptoms a variation of couvade, in which the father experiences signs and symptoms of illnesses associated with pregnancy, such as abdominal pains and 'morning sickness.' The symptoms disappear as soon as the child has been born.

hussy an obsolescent term for a lewd or shameless woman. The word is an abbreviation of 'housewife,' and a hussy was thus a perfectly respectable person in the 16th century. See also WOMAN.

hustler a male prostitute who sells his services (usually fellatio) to male homosexuals. He may be a homosexual or covert homosexual himself even though he may think of himself as a heterosexual. See also STREET HUSTLERS.

Hutchinson-Gilford syndrome a hormonal disorder in which the person shows signs of both premature aging and infantilism. The genitalia are normal until puberty but fail to develop beyond that point. There is an absence of pubic hair. The person becomes potbellied and bald, and the skin becomes elastic and atrophic with prominent veins in some areas.

hydatid mole a large mass of enlarged chorionic villi that may develop in the uterus, probably as a result of an ovulation defect. The tumour, which resembles a bunch of grapes, tends to occur most frequently in women younger than 20 or older than 40, and the incidence is particularly high among Oriental women. It creates some of the symptoms of pregnancy except for the absence of foetal heart sounds. Also called molar pregnancy.

hydatidocele a tumour of the scrotum or testis containing cysts formed by the larvae of a tapeworm, *Echinococcus granulosus*, which enters the body through the digestive tract.

hydradenoma a sweat-gland tumour that can develop on the labia majora or surrounding tissue of the female genitalia. The growth, which is noncancerous, can break through the skin and become a small bleeding ulcer.

hydrocele a collection of fluid in the spaces of the tunica vaginalis, a membrane that covers the testes. The cause may be an infection or an injury. A hydrocele also may be a congenital abnormality. A hydrocele of the epididymis is called a spermatocele.

hydronephrosis a complication of benign prostatic hypertrophy in which obstruction of the urinary tract by an overgrowth of prostate tissue results in a backpressure from the urinary bladder through the ureters to the kidneys. The kidneys gradually deteriorate, resulting in uraemia, with potentially fatal effects. The condition may also be caused by urinary stones or malignancies.

hydrophallus an abnormal condition in which the penis is distended because of an accumulation of lymph or other fluid in the tissues.

hydrops folliculi a large ovarian follicle cyst that is filled with fluid. It usually has a smooth surface and may be several inches in diameter.

hydrosalpinx a fallopian tube that is filled with a fluid accumulation, sometimes as a result of the contents of a pyosalpinx becoming liquefied. Like the pyosalpinx (an inflamed fallopian tube), the hydrosalpinx is distended to twice or greater than its normal size.

hymen a delicate membrane stretching over the entrance of the vagina and partially closing it. Many women have large openings in the hymen, and some have no hymen at all. The opening can be enlarged for intercourse by stretching with the fingers, or it may be excised by a simple surgical procedure. Also called the maidenhead, because its presence may (and in rare cases may not) indicate that the girl or woman is a virgin, that is, a 'maiden.' See also ANNULAR HYMEN; ARTIFICIAL HYMEN; CRIBIFORM HYMEN; FIBROUS HYMEN; PERFORATED HYMEN; RUPTURED HYMEN; SEPTATE HYMEN.

hyperemesis gravidarum severe vomiting episodes during pregnancy, often requiring hospitalization and, in some cases, therapeutic abortion. Mild cases of hyperemesis are usually associated with psychogenic factors, particularly in women who are 'stomach reactors' to stressful situations. In other cases, however, no psychogenic influence is observed. If uncontrolled, there may be haemorrhaging and loss of the foetus or embryo. When the condition is psychogenic, psychotherapy is recommended.

hypergenital type a constitutional body type

marked by exaggerated, premature development of primary and secondary sex characteristics, a large chest and skull, short arms and legs, emotional stability, strong artistic impulses, and, in the female, early menstruation, sensitive breasts and genitals, and exceptional fecundity.

hypergonadotropic hypogonadism a failure of the ovaries to react to secretions of gonadotropic hormones. There may be elevated blood levels of gonadotropins but little evidence of oestrogen secretion. It occurs normally in some women at menopause, but in a younger woman the condition may be a sign of inflammation or a tumour of the ovaries or the result of a psychogenic or neurological disorder. It also occurs as a symptom of Turner's syndrome.

hypermobile testes a condition in which the testes descend into the scrotum or ascend into the abdominal cavity intermittently, often because of an inguinal hernia that has not been repaired. The testes may move into the scrotum in a warm environment, as while taking a hot bath, then retract into the abdomen when the temperature of the environment drops.

hypernephroma a type of tumour found occasionally in the vagina as a secondary growth to a kidney cancer. The tumour is spawned by cancer cells carried from the kidney to the vagina. It appears as a nodular yellow mass on the mucous membrane of the vaginal wall. The vagina may be the site of tumours that originate in nearly any part of the body and are transplanted by metastasis, or the migration of cancer cells from the original tumour by way of the bloodstream.

hyperprolactinaemia a condittion caused by a pituitary-gland dysfunction resulting in an excessive level of prolactin in the blood. In women, the condition is associated with disorders of breast development and function and also with secondary amenorrhoea. In men, the condition, which may be an adverse effect of certain psychotropic medications, causes impotence and a decreased libido.

hypersexuality an excessive, insatiable need for sexual activity, often associated with inability to achieve complete gratification. The condition arises out of such factors as a need to disprove impotence, frigidity, or suspected homosexuality; or an urge to achieve self-esteem or superiority through unlimited sexual conquests.

hypogenital type a constitutional body type characterized by underdevelopment of the genital organs, somewhat female secondary sexual characteristics in the male, elongated legs, and small trunk and head. The condition is believed to be inheritable. It is also called eunuchoid type. A similar but less pronounced condition is occasionally found among females.

hypogonadotropic hypogonadism an abnormal condition in which the ovaries of a female fail to function normally because of the disorder involving the pituitary gland or the hypothalamus, such as a tumour or infection in either of these organs. The precise signs and symptoms depend upon the cause and the period of life in which the ovarian failure occurs.

hypoleydigism a condition in which the amount of testosterone secreted by the Leydig, or interstitial, cells of the testis has diminished.

hypomastia underdevelopment of the female breast, usually because of gonadal hormone disorder.

hypomenorrhoea menstruation that is characterized by an abnormally small flow. The term also is used to describe a very short duration of menstruation.

hypomorph a mutant gene that is able to affect the expression of a trait but at a level too low to cause an obvious abnormality. Also called leaky gene.

hypophysial cachexia a condition in which there is a general deterioration of health and bodily integrity as a result of pituitary gland dysfunction. With failure of the pituitary gland to secrete hormones stimulating the adrenal glands and gonads, hormones secreted by those structures also diminish in amount and effect. Female breasts atrophy, and gonads become nonfunctional. A form of progeria, or premature aging, occurs with atrophy of body tissues, loss of hair and teeth, and the onset of dementia. Metabolic disorders, such as diabetes insipidus and hypoglycaemia, develop. Symptoms of Simmonds syndrome and Sheehan's syndrome are associated with the cause and effects.

hypopituitary constitution a general bodily and mental-health condition characterized by a deficiency in functions controlled by pituitary hormones, such as hypogonadism. The male may possess small genitalia and have a low level of sex drive, along with low blood pressure, small stature, and gynandromorphic features. The female may have small breasts and hirsutism and be frigid or infertile, or both.

hyposexuality underdevelopment or total lack of sexual drive, interest, and activity. The condition may be organic (for example, a low sex-hormone level or a brain lesion) or psychological (extreme inhibitions or conflicts).

hypospadias a defect in the shaft of the corpus spongiosum so that the urethral orifice is located on the underside of the penis. The defect may occur at any point between the glans penis and the junction between the penis and scrotum. The condition may be complicated by anomalous fibres or tendons that tend to pull the penis downwards. The defect develops during the foetal period and can be corrected surgically.

hypothalamic amenorrhoea an interruption of the normal menstrual cycle by a mental or physical disorder that prevents the hypothalamus from signalling the release of gonadotropin hormones from the pituitary gland. Causes may include a sudden weight loss or an emotional disturbance, such as anxiety.

hysterectomy the surgical removal of the uterus. See SUBTOTAL HYSTERECTOMY; TOTAL HYSTERECTOMY.

hysteria a neurotic disorder characterized by emotional outbursts, histrionic behaviour, and conversion of unconscious conflicts into physical symptoms that do not have an organic basis. Among the common sexual reactions associated with hysteria are loss of sensation in the sex organs (sexual anaesthesia) and paralysis of the hands, which Freud interpreted as a defence against the guilty impulse to masturbate. Also called conversion disorder. The term hysteria is derived from the Greek word for uterus, *hystera*. Hippocrates believed that this disorder occurs in women whose uterus wanders to different parts of the body in search of a child.

hysterical character disorder in psychoanalytical theory, the classical outcome of an unresolved Oedipus complex among women: a seductive, exhibitionistic, dominating, 'castrating' woman whose sexual drive takes the form of manipulating and humiliating men.

hysterical pregnancy a false pregnancy or pseudocyesis, usually resulting from emotional conflict and immaturity.

hysterorrhoea any discharge from the uterus, particularly the menstrual flow.

hysterorrhexis a rupture of the uterus. The condition may develop either in a pregnant or in a nonpregnant state.

hysteroscopy the examination of the cervix and uterus with a *hysteroscope*, a lighted tube with lenses that permits direct visual inspection of the lining of the womb. It may be used in varied procedures, such as removing polyps or checking the position of an intrauterine device.

hysterotomy any surgical incision into the uterus, as when performing a caesarean section.

hysterosalpingography the x-ray examination of the uterus and fallopian tubes after they have been injected with a radiopaque dye to help identify the structural surfaces and any defects. The procedure usually is scheduled for the first week after the end of the last menstrual flow to avoid the possible irradiation of an ovum or zygote. In addition to introducing a dye that will enhance the appearance of structures on the x-ray film, the injection of the oil-based substance can have a therapeutic effect by forcing apart adhesions and dislodging any mucus plugs that might block the fallopian tubes. Hysterosalpingography is not without risks; fatal complications have resulted from the procedure. Also called the dye test.

iatrogenic homosexuality doctor-induced homosexuality: homosexual desires or behaviour resulting from the close relationship developed between doctor and patient during psychotherapy or psychoanalysis.

ichthyosis-hypogonadism a form of diminished sexuality marked by small genitalia and a scaly skin condition. The disorder is an inherited X-linked anomaly. The patient also may exhibit other abnormalities, such as mental retardation and absence of a sense of smell. The condition of ichthyosis—derived from Greek words for 'fish condition'—may be generalized or cover only certain areas of the body with the 'fish-skin disease.'

id the Freudian term for the totality of primitive, unconscious drives, or 'instincts,' that demand immediate, egocentric gratification. In Freud's view, human beings are at the mercy of these 'blind, irrational' urges (especially hunger, thirst, elimination, and sex) until they gradually develop a conscious ego that operates according to the demands of reality and the behests of the supergo, or conscience.

idealization the tendency to exaggerate the positive characteristics and overlook the imperfections of another individual such as a parent, teacher, or a person with whom one is romantically involved.

identical twins a common term for monozygotic twins.

identity disorder a disorder of late adolescence characterized by emotional distress and confusion on such issues as personal goals, moral and religious values, sex role, career choice, group identification, and relationship to the opposite sex.

idiogamist a person who is incapable of a full sexual response with anyone other than his or her spouse. The term is primarily applied to a man who is impotent with anyone except his wife or someone resembling his wife.

Ila inhabitants of Zambia who subsist on fishing, hunting, agriculture, and cattle raising. Polygyny is common, as in a large part of Africa, but there are a number of unusual sexual practices: A bride must remove all her husband's hair from his pubic region and chin the day after consummation of the marriage; there is a taboo against intercourse before a fishing expedition; and boys are required to masturbate and imitate sexual intercourse with one another as part of their initiation training. In addition, there is a prohibition against orogenital contact and a taboo against adult male homosexual activity, because they believe pregnancy might result. In general, Ila men have a distinct preference for women with enormously protruding navels.

ilioinguinal nerve (il′ē-ō-in′gwinəl) a branch of the first lumbar nerve that supplies both sensory and motor-nerve fibres to the skin and muscles of the inner surface of the thigh and the adjacent genitalia.

illegitimate child a child whose parents are not married. Illegitimacy used to be a major social stigma, but today the parents of many children born outside marriage are in long-term stable relationships so the problem of any stigma is reducing. Also called natural child; love child; bastard.

illicit relations a legal term for unlawful sexual relations such as intercourse between father and daughter or any other form of incest; intercourse between a man and a woman who are not married to each other; adulterous relations; oral-genital contacts; intercourse with prostitutes; intercourse with animals; and intercourse between adult and a boy or girl below the age of consent.

immissio penis a Latin term for the penetration of the penis into the vagina. The term may appear in legal documents relating to rape or other forms of illicit intercourse. The law sometimes regards penetration as having occurred if the glans penis passed beyond the labia majora in an effort at coitus.

impalement injury to the penis or scrotum or both by penetration from the outside by a sharp object. The effect is generally the same as that experienced in battlefield situations in which rupture of the perineal tissues as well as those of the penis and scrotum result from shrapnel or bullet wounds. As with similar injuries, there will be bleeding and swelling of damaged tissues, followed by scar formation and possible loss of erectability of the penis.

implantation the process whereby the zygote, after being fertilized about midway in its descent through the fallopian tube, extends fingerlike projections from its outer ring of blastocyst cells and anchors itself in the endometrial lining of the uterus. This generally occurs on about the sixth day of its existence and after it has been a free-floating blastocyst in the uterine cavity for a day or two. The implantation stage of the zygote's life is sometimes called the trophoblast phase. The trophoblast at this point has differentiated into two layers of cells, and it is the outer layer that invades the blood-rich cells of the lining of the uterus. The inner layer contains the germinal cells that will develop into the embryo. The outer layer will become the placenta. The villi, or projections of the outer layer of the trophoblast, also evolve into a miniature endocrine gland, producing human chorionic gonadotropin that induces a continuation of progesterone and oestrogen by the ovary, preventing the release of another ovum while the organism, of which the trophoblast is a part, has a good chance of becoming a foetus.

implantation ratio the proportion of Y to X fertilized zygotes that become implanted in the wall of the uterus. The ratio is 120 male zygotes to 100 female.

impotence a male sexual dysfunction characterized by inability to achieve or maintain an erection sufficient for performance of sexual intercourse. It may also take the form of coitus without ejaculation, orgasm without pleasure, and lack of interest in sex. Among the causes are anxiety over performance, internal conflicts, and emotional tension. Also called *impotency*. See also FUNCTIONAL IMPOTENCE; NEW IMPOTENCE; ORGANIC IMPOTENCE; ORGASMIC IMPOTENCE; PRIMARY IMPOTENCE; PSYCHIC IMPOTENCE; PSYCHOGENIC IMPOTENCE; SECONDARY IMPOTENCE; TREATMENT OF IMPOTENCE.

impregnation the process of fertilization or insemination. See also ORAL IMPREGNATION.

impuberty a physical state characterized by absence of primary and secondary sexual characteristics when they normally appear. The term is applied where puberty has not been reached because of delayed development, and is also used to indicate a continuation of childhood characteristics into adolescence or adulthood. Also called *impuberism.*

impulse rapist a man who commits rape simply because an opportunity presents itself. The typical impulse rapist has been described as a burglar who finds himself alone in a house with a sleeping woman and rapes the woman, although his original motive was neither sexual nor aggressive.

Imreg-1 an antiviral drug developed by the American company Imreg. Inc., for use as a possible cure for AIDS infections. See also AIDS.

inappetence a technical term for lack of appetite or, in some cases, lack of sexual desire.

in between a colloquial term for bisexual.

Inca a early Peruvian empire in which monogamy prevailed except for the highest social class. Other customs include severe punishment for homosexuality in most areas; extreme emphasis on chastity before marriage (girls were burned alive if they broke their vows); hanging as punishment for bestiality (such as sexual relations with llamas); and encouragement of brother-sister marriage between members of the royal family.

incarcerated fibroid a fibroid tumour of the uterus that may develop in the cervix and block the birth canal in a pregnancy so that normal delivery of a child is not possible.

incest sexual relations (usually heterosexual) between blood relatives such as a father and daughter, brother and sister, mother and son, uncle and aunt, niece and nephew, or cousin and cousin. Social taboos or laws against incest are found in practically all societies, but the degree of relationship may differ from society to society. (Latin *incestus*, 'impure.') One study found that more than three fourths of all cases of incest were father-daughter relationships. Mother-son incest cases accounted for about 1 percent, and brother-sister incestuous relationships were reported at 18 percent. However, some researchers believe that brother-sister cases of incest are actually the most common, but the least reported. See also FATHER-DAUGHTER INCEST; MOTHER-SON INCEST; MILK INCEST.

incest barrier in psychoanalysis, a psychological defence against incestuous impulses and fantasies. The barrier develops during the latency period as a result of the young person's recognition of social laws and customs that prohibit incest. It helps to free the growing child from incestuous wishes directed to one or the other parent, and therefore paves the way to the establishment of relationships outside the family.

incest fantasy the tendency of boys and girls of oedipal age (between 3 and 7) to dream or imagine that they are having sexual relations with the parent of the opposite sex. According to psychoanalytical theory, when boys entertain such fantasies towards the mother, they may develop a fear of castration, and when girls have such fantasies towards the father, they may develop severe sexual conflicts.

incest permissiveness the attitude that incest is permissible, or even required, under certain circumstances. Recent studies have shown that incest is more widespread in the United States than previously recognized, but it is usually performed sub rosa and not socially acceptable. On the other hand, the Kubao of South America *require* a boy to have intercourse with his mother to mark the beginning of his official sex life; and in Africa, a Watusi bridegroom must do the same as a cure for impotence experienced on his wedding night. Examples of this kind are extremely rare. There is apparently no society in which all types of incest are permitted.

incest taboo the social prohibition against sexual relations between persons of closer blood ties than the particular society allows.

incestuous molester sexual molestation that involves members of the same family, usually a relationship between a father and daughter.

incestuous ties a term applied by Eric Fromm to a pattern of close, dependent relationships within the family that may interfere with healthy, mature involvement with persons outside the home. The term incestuous as used by Fromm does not imply sexual relations among family members.

inclusion cyst a cyst that may form in the perineal area of a woman, at the fourchette or in the vagina. An inclusion cyst can result from a particle of skin tissue that becomes trapped beneath the surface during surgery of the perineum.

incomplete precocity a condition in which a prepubertal male has acquired some features of precocious puberty because of an interstitial-cell tumour in only one testicle. The testicle on the other side remains at the infantile stage.

incontinence lack of restraint or control, especially of sexual impulses; also, inability to control eliminative functions.

incubus a medieval term for an evil demon who assumes the shape of a man and has intercourse with a sleeping woman, or a nightmare in which this takes place. The incubus may have been invented to explain illegitimate pregnancies. See SUCCUBUS; SPECTROPHILIA.

indecent exposure a legal term applied to the public display of a part of the body normally covered by clothing. Laws in different countries vary, as in Florida where state law defines exposure of genitalia in public as indecent while in the community of Sarasota, Florida, laws also prohibit the public exposure of breasts and buttocks.

indeterminate cleavage the development of a fertilized ovum into blastomeres with similar developmental potential. If isolated at a stage of indeterminate cleavage, a separated blastomere may develop into another individual. Monozygotic twins may develop as a result of indeterminate cleavage.

Indian corn not the yellow maize sold tinned or frozen in supermarkets, but the traditional ears of red-to-brown-to-black grains grown by Native Americans. Although not popularly known as an aphrodisiac, the notion was suggested in Longfellow's *Evangeline*. While husking corn in the autumn, the maidens 'blushed at each blood-red ear, for that betokened a lover.'

indifferent period a time span in the fifth and sixth weeks of gestation in which the genitalia of the embryo appear but the sex cannot be determined by examination of either the external or internal features. In addition to a normal pair of generalized sex glands, all embryos are equipped at this indifferent stage with both male and female sex ducts. The sex-determining mechanism was established at fertilization, but sex recognition usually is not possible until the seventh week of pregnancy.

indisposed a euphemism for menstruating.

indoor sports a humorous euphemism for sexual activity, from petting to intercourse, carried on indoors.

indorser an obsolete slang term for the active partner in anal intercourse.

induced abortion any artificial abortion, or one produced deliberately, such as a therapeutic abortion.

infanticide the practice of killing infants as a form of child abuse, as a means of controlling population growth, or as a form of 'mercy killing' when the child is born with a severe deformity, a profound mental defect, or a disease deemed incurable. ('Right-to-lifers' usually characterize abortion as a form of infanticide.) In many primitive societies that practise infanticide for population control, more girl babies than boy babies are killed.

infantile masturbation self-stimulation of the sex organs during infancy and early childhood, an activity that not only affords pleasure but probably helps focus sexual reactions on the genital organs.

infantile seduction a term used in psychoanalysis for sexual relations with a young child, believed by some specialists to stem from an unresolved Oedipus complex.

infantile sexuality the Freudian theory that children of both sexes have the capacity for sexual feeling during the first months of life, as manifested by the 'investment' of the libido, or sexual energy, in the oral, anal, and early genital phases of development, as well as pleasure experienced in such activities as breast feeding, defecating, and self-stimulation of the genitals (masturbatory activities).

infantile tube a fallopian tube that has failed to develop normally. It is usually thin, weak, and lacking in a normal blood supply. Also called hypoplastic tube.

infarct of the prostate an abnormal condition in which an artery of the prostate becomes occluded, depriving an area of prostatic tissue of normal supply of oxygenated blood and nutrients. The disorder generally causes few if any symptoms but can result in the death of part of the prostate tissue. If the same artery mishap occurred in the heart or brain, the person would experience a heart attack or a stroke. An infarct of the prostate is frequently associated with hypertrophy or hyperplasia (overgrowth) of the prostate.

infatuation an extravagant, often shallow 'falling in love,' which may—if it lasts long enough—ripen into genuine love. It is likely, however, to be short-lived because it is usually based on superficial qualities such as sex appeal and physical attractiveness.

infection a term pertaining to an old superstition that a man acquires, as by infection, some of the traits of every woman with whom he has had sexual relations and that such traits can be transmitted to his children.

infectious abortion a spontaneous abortion that is produced by an inflammation of the uterus or foetal membranes, caused by an infectious disease. Placental infections may be caused by viruses, bacteria, protozoa, or rickettsial organisms.

infectious mononucleosis a generally mild but frequently prolonged febrile illness that is caused by a type of herpes virus and affects mainly young adults. The main symptoms include swollen lymph glands, fever, and a sore throat. The herpes virus, an Epstein-Barr virus, is found in diagnostic tests. Because the infection is often transmitted by mouth-to-mouth contact, it is colloquially known as the 'kissing disease.' It is also called glandular fever.

inferiority complex a pattern of insecurity and inadequacy which, according to Alfred Adler, originates in childhood dependence and helplessness and may be aggravated by physical deficiencies (organ inferiority) and social or sexual failures. To compensate for inferiority feelings, individuals become competitive or overcompetitive, and in the sexual sphere may develop an insatiable need to prove their superiority through conquest after conquest.

infertile period a term usually applied to the period in the menstrual cycle when a woman cannot conceive. The calendar method is used by many women in identifying their 'safe' days, though it is not fully reliable when used alone.

infertility the inability to have children, because of the female partner in about 60 percent of cases and because of the male partner in about 40 percent. Between 10 and 15 percent of couples in Britain have problems achieving pregnancy. Common physical causes in the male are low sperm count, failure to deposit sperm in the vagina, and obstruction of the epididymis, vas deferens, or ejaculatory ducts. Causes in the female are failure to produce a sufficient number of healthy eggs, partial or complete obstruction of the fallopian tubes, endometriosis, rejection of the fertilized egg, and pelvic tumours. Psychological causes, such as excessive tension, may also be operative in either the male or female.

infibulation prevention of intercourse before marriage by sewing or clasping together the labia majora, leaving a small opening for urination. This practice has been found, for example, in eastern Africa and among Peruvian Indians. The male equivalent—very rare—appears to be sewing together the prepuce of the penis. The term is derived from *fibula*, the Latin word for pierce or clasp.

infidelity unfaithfulness; sexual relations with someone other than one's spouse.

in flagrante delicto 'in the very act of committing the offence'; a term often applied to being caught in the act of adultery. At a time when a single act of adultery was considered adequate grounds for divorce, a husband would arrange to be caught by a private detective to provide his wife with evidence of unfaithfulness.

inflatable implant a female breast implant that consists of an empty plastic sac that can be inserted through a small incision in the breast and filled with a saline (salt) solution through a valve. The inflatable implant is not recommended for women with a minimum amount of natural breast tissue because it tends to be unnaturally firm and the valve may be detectable through the skin.

infundibulum the open end of the fallopian tube, which contains the fingerlike extensions, or fimbriae, that literally catch the ovum when it is released from the ovary.

ingler an obsolete term for the passive partner in anal intercourse. The term was in use from the early 17th to the 19th century.

ingravidation a medical term for impregnation or fertilization.

inguinal (in'gwinəl) pertaining to the groin or the area of the groin, an anatomical groove that generally marks the region where the lower abdominal wall meets the thigh.

inguinal adenopathy a clinical manifestation of syphilis in which the inguinal lymph glands are swollen, hard, and tender because of the syphilitic inflammation. The condition, usually painless, appears about 3 to 5 days after the chancre develops. The inguinal adenopathy is usually bilateral. It occasionally results from infections other than syphilis.

inguinal canal a passage between the deep inguinal ring and the subcutaneous inguinal ring, a pair of openings in the lower abdominal wall, through which the spermatic cord passes between the testicles and structures within the abdomen from which the cord originates. In the female, the inguinal canal is a tunnel through which the round ligament of the uterus passes.

inhibited female orgasm the American Psychiatric Association term for a psychosexual disorder involving persistent delay in or absence of orgasm after adequate sexual activity and a normal excitement phase. The condition results from psychological causes such as severe conflict or unconscious guilt feelings.

inhibited male orgasm the American Psychiatric Association term for a psychosexual disorder among males involving persistent delay or absence of orgasm after adequate sexual activity and a normal excitement phase, and stemming from psychological causes.

inhibited sexual desire the American Psychiatric Association term for a psychosexual disorder in either male or female that consists of persistent and pervasive inhibition of sexual desire, taking age, health, and style of life into account. The condition is not caused exclusively by medication or physical or mental disorder, but appears to be primarily or wholly psychological.

inhibited sexual excitement the American Psychiatric Association term for a psychological disorder characterized by persistent lack of sexual excitement after adequate sexual activity and not caused exclusively by medication, physical disorder, or another mental disorder. In males it takes the form of partial or complete failure to maintain erection (impotence), and in females, partial or complete failure to maintain the lubrication-swelling response until completion of the sex act.

inhibition restraint of impulses or behaviour resulting from such factors as emotional insecurity, fear of consequences, or moral qualms operating on a conscious or unconscious level. Inhibition of sexual impulses is frequently attributed by psychoanalysts to unconscious feelings of guilt implanted by parents.

Inis Beag a rural Irish community in the most conservative part of the country, believed to be one of the most sexually restrictive societies in the world. A rigid form of Catholicism is practised, and children are raised in total ignorance of sex, and are sexually segregated at an early age. Masturbation and mutual body exploration are severely punished, and nudity, even during marital intercourse, is taboo. Courting, premarital intercourse, and expressions of affection are unknown. Sexual advances are entirely the man's prerogative, and the purpose of marriage is solely economic and reproductive.

initiation the performance of rites, ceremonies, or ordeals on the occasion of an individual's acceptance into a group or club, or in celebration of a new status such as manhood. In the latter case, sex instruction may be given; for example, in Polynesia young boys serve an apprenticeship by being assigned to older married women for sex training, and in much of Latin America, and sometimes in Europe and in the United States, fathers take their sons to brothels to be initiated into the heterosexual world of the adult. Initiation into womanhood in many societies takes place at the onset of menstruation, marriage or the first birth.

inner controls internal forces, such as conscience and implanted values, that exercise control over our behaviour, often producing restraint and inhibition.

insemination the act of fertilization of an ovum by a spermatozoon. The term also may be used to identify the deposition of semen in the vaginal tract, as occurs in artificial insemination. See also ARTIFICIAL INSEMINATION; ENDOCERVICAL INSEMINATION; HETEROLOGOUS ARTIFICIAL INSEMINATION; HOMOLOGOUS ARTIFICIAL INSEMINATION.

insertee a slang term for the passive partner in anal intercourse.

inserter a slang term for the active partner in anal intercourse.

inside-worry an old euphemism for pregnancy (originating in the 17th century).

inspectionalism a psychiatric term for voyeurism.

instinct an inborn drive or behaviour pattern that appears in every member of a species at a certain point of development, for example, hibernation in animals and mating behaviour in birds. The existence of fixed instinctual behaviour in humans is not so evident as in animals. In psychoanalysis, the term is limited to basic biological drives (especially hunger, thirst, sex, elimination, and aggression) that must be met if physical and psychological equilibrium are to be maintained.

intercalary cells long slender cells found in the lining of the fallopian tube. They secrete a substance that is believed to supply nutrition to the ovum and spermatozoa in the vagina.

interception any technique for preventing implantation after fertilization of the ovum, as a method of birth control.

intercourse the commonly used term for coitus, or sexual intercourse between a man and a woman in which the penis is inserted into the vagina. Also used in expressions such as 'oral intercourse' or 'homosexual intercourse.' See also ACTUAL INTERCOURSE; ANAL INTERCOURSE; ANOGENITAL INTERCOURSE; AXILLARY INTERCOURSE; BUCCAL INTERCOURSE; EXTRAVAGINAL INTERCOURSE; FACE-TO-FACE INTERCOURSE; GENITAL INTERCOURSE; INTERFEMORAL INTERCOURSE; INTRACRURAL INTERCOURSE; POSTPARTUM INTERCOURSE; SEXUAL INTERCOURSE.

interfemoral intercourse a nonvaginal method of sexual intercourse in which the penis is inserted between the pressed thighs of the partner, frequently used during the last month of pregnancy.

interleukin-2 a substance produced by the T-cells of the body's immune system. It has been used to treat AIDS infections. T-cells, which resist viral infections, are manufactured in the thymus gland, which atrophies as one progresses from childhood to adulthood. See also AIDS.

intermarriage marriage between individuals belonging to different 'racial,' social, or religious groups, also between closely related individuals (consanguineous matings). In many societies intermarriage in the first sense has been prohibited to preserve the supposed 'purity,' superiority, or security of the group; in others, it has been based on overt or covert prejudice against certain groups.

intermediate sex an older term for homosexuality.

intermenstrual fever a small increase in temperature that occurs during ovulation. The temperature rise is used by some women in determining their fertile phase and to predict the onset of menstruation, which usually follows 14 days later.

internal cervical os an internal opening in the uterus at the isthmus that separates the body of the uterus from the cervix. The external cervical os is the opening in the part of the cervix that projects into the vagina.

internal fertilization the actual fusion of the ovum and spermatozoon within the body of the female, as distinguished from the union of gametes outside the body, the type of fertilization characteristic of fish and other lower organisms.

internal migration the passage of an ovum

from the fallopian tube on one side of the uterus through the uterine lumen and into the fallopian tube on the opposite side of the uterus.

internal sphincter one of two circular muscle groups that control the flow of fluids through the male urethra. The internal sphincter surrounds the urethra at the entrance to the bladder and closes during sexual excitement, thus preventing retrograde ejaculation into the urinary bladder.

intersex a general term for physical or psychological sexual patterns that lie between completely male and completely female. Among them are bisexual males and females (sexually attracted to both sexes), gynandrous males (male sex organs but deficient in male hormones and therefore exhibiting female characteristics such as lack of facial hair), gynandrous females (female sex organs but muscular appearance), transsexuals (physically male or female, but psychologically identified with the other sex), female or male homosexuals (appropriate physical identity, but attracted to their own sex), and transvestites (a male or female who wears clothes of the opposite sex).

intersexuality a state of incomplete sexual differentiation because of insufficient or delayed hormone production. The individual possesses secondary characteristics of both sexes, and in some cases partially developed internal or external sex organs of both sexes.

interstitial cells cells that are in the tiny spaces between the seminiferous tubules of the testis. The cells contain granules of a yellow pigment, but when stimulated by interstitial-cell-stimulating hormone, they produce the male sex hormone testosterone. Interstitial-cell activity usually begins around the age of 12, but medical records indicate it can start at least 4 years earlier or be delayed until after the age of 21. Also called Leydig cells, after the German histologist Franz von Leydig.

interstitial-cell-stimulating hormone (ICSH) a hormone secreted by the anterior lobe of the pituitary gland that stimulates the interstitial cells of the testis to secrete the male sex hormone testosterone. ICSH is essentially the same substance as the luteinizing hormone (LH) that is responsible for the preparation and ripening of the ovarian follicle in the female. A negative-feedback system in the male physiology, similar to the oestrogen-feedback mechanism in the female, regulates the production and secretion of testosterone

in the interstitial (Leydig) cells. The normal range of testosterone secretion by the interstitial cells is from 4 to 9 milligrams per day.

interstitial pregnancy an ectopic pregnancy, or one that occurs within body-tissue spaces outside the uterus.

interstitial tubal pregnancy a pregnancy that develops in the interstitial portion of a fallopian tube, the narrowest part of the tube as it approaches the uterus.

intertrigo a superficial inflammation of the skin of the genitalia, from a fungal infection. It appears as a reddish-brown discoloration of inner surfaces of the thighs and perineum where opposing skin surfaces rub together. In men it may spread over the scrotum and skin of the penis. In women, intertrigo often involves the labia and vulva areas. Particularly vulnerable are obese individuals in warm moist climates.

intimacy a close, trusting personal relationship between two people who are completely at home with each other and feel free to express their innermost feelings. Intimacy is a basic ingredient of marriage and a lasting, satisfying sexual relationship, though it is possible for people to be sexually involved without being intimate.

intimate with a euphemism meaning sexually intimate with (someone).

intracanicular fibroma a benign type of breast tumour containing glandular and fibrous tissue.

intracanicular papilloma a benign wartlike tumour that develops in the breast.

intracranial gumma a soft degenerating tumour of the brain that is characteristic of tertiary syphilis. Symptoms associated with the tumour include loss of memory for recent events, delirium, and emotional instability. The term gumma is derived from the Latin *gummi*, meaning 'gum,' which describes the texture of the syphilitic lesion.

intracrural intercourse an alternative term for interfemoral intercourse.

intraductal carcinoma a type of breast cancer that develops in the milk ducts.

intramural portion the segment of the fallopian tube that is within the wall of the uterus. The tissues lining the fallopian tube are continuous with those of the uterus.

intrapartal care the care of a woman from the beginning of labour until the expulsion of the placenta.

intrapreputial movement movement of the clitoris during the plateau phase of preorgasmic sexual excitement. The movements are synchronized with thrusting as a result of traction on the labia minor and clitoral prepuce during coitus.

intrauterine device (IUD) a major form of conception control consisting of a plastic, metal, or rubber device placed in the uterus by a trained professional to prevent pregnancy by interfering with implantation of the fertilized ovum in its wall. The device is usually in the shape of a coil, ring, T, Y, or loop, especially the Lippes Double-S Loop. In the United States, practically all production of IUDs has been discontinued because of legal complications.

intrauterine membrane (IUM) an experimental alternative to the intrauterine contraceptive device (IUD). The IUM reportedly has an advantage of being more flexible.

introcision a surgical procedure in which the vaginal opening is enlarged to make childbirth easier. The practice has also been found among Australian aborigines, where the husband is required to have intercourse with his wife while the womb is still bleeding, on the theory that this will hasten the healing process.

introitus the orifice of a body cavity such as the sensitive entrance to the vagina, which is ordinarily relaxed but may tighten during sexual intercourse.

intromission insertion of the penis through the introitus and into the vagina.

in utero the medical term for 'inside the uterus,' usually applied to an unborn child that is still within the womb.

inversion a term used by Freud and his followers for any of three types of homosexuality, which he called absolute inversion, amphigenous inversion, and occasional inversion. The term is also applied to assumption of the role of the opposite sex in intercourse. Also called sexual inversion. See also ABSOLUTE INVERSION; OCCASIONAL INVERSION; AMPHIGENESIS.

invert a homosexual, male or female. The term is seldom used today.

inverted nipple a breast nipple that is retracted as a congenital defect or because of changes in the breast tissue in later life. The cause generally is abnormally shortened milk ducts which pull the nipple inward. Reconstructive surgery, for cosmetic reasons or to make breast feeding feasible, often requires severing the ducts that draw the nipple inwards. An inverted nipple also can be a sign of breast cancer, particularly in an older woman.

in vitro (Latin, 'in a glass') occurring in labora-

tory apparatus, for example, the fertilization of an ovum by a spermatozoon.

involution a regressive change, or deterioration, in physical and psychological functions, such as occurs in the aging process; also, return of the uterus to its normal size after childbirth.

involutional pertaining to changes occurring during climacteric such as a gradual cessation of menstruation and reproductive capacity, menopausal symptoms, fatigue, and in some instances mild-to-severe anxiety and depression.

involutional gynaecomastia a type of breast enlargement in males that occurs in old age.

involutional melancholia an older term for a depressive condition that may accompany menopause. The disorder begins gradually and is usually characterized by pessimism, insomnia, loss of appetite, anxiety, irritability, and restlessness. Treatment may include psychotherapy and antidepressant drugs. Also called climacteric melancholia; involutional depression.

involutional psychotic reaction an emotional disorder that occasionally occurs in both sexes during the climacteric, and characterized either by (a) severe agitation, feelings of worthlessness and despondency, persisting insomnia, and loss of appetite, or less often, by (b) paranoid thinking in the form of persecutory delusions and in some cases hypochondriacal, self-condemnatory, or nihilistic delusions.

ipsation self-induced sexual excitement (from latin *ipse*, 'oneself')—an obsolete term for autoeroticism.

iris one or more of the species of a flower that has been said for generations to be a plant with aphrodisiac qualities. Most frequently mentioned is *Iris florentina*, also called *Iris germanica*, or German iris, with smooth red-to-purple coloured leaves. It is the source of a perfume and is sometimes associated with the satyrion flower which the ancients believed could lead to either a male or female offspring, depending upon whether one ate the root (male) or the leaves (female).

iron a British slang term for a male homosexual. It is short for iron hoof, which in turn is rhyming slang for poof.

irrumatio a term sometimes applied to a form of fellatio in which the penis makes in-and-out movements while in the woman's mouth, similar to those of vaginal intercourse. (From a Latin word for being sucked.) Also called *irrumation*.

ischomenia the arrest or holding back of the menstrual flow, as by the use of hormonal drugs.

isochrome a chromosome that divides transversely (across the middle) rather than longitudinally (top to bottom) during cell division. This results in one daughter chromosome that is smaller than usual (short arms) or larger (long arms). It may be expressed as a small x (for short arms) or large X (for long arms), and a standard female complement including an isochrome would be either xX or Xx.

isoimmune haemolytic disease of the newborn an alternative term for erythroblastosis foetalis, resulting from Rh or ABO blood group incompatibility.

isoprinosine a drug used to alleviate symptoms in the early stages of AIDS, although it has no effect on the syndrome itself. See also AIDS.

isosexual an obsolete term for homosexual (Greek *isos*, 'equal'). See, however, ISOSEXUAL PRECOCITY.

isosexual precocity precocious puberty that is accompanied by characteristics of the person's own sex, as may occur in a female infant with an ovarian granulosa-cell tumour that produces female sex hormones.

isthmus the middle third of the fallopian tube, where the tube narrows or becomes constricted before merging with the uterus.

The uterus also has an isthmus, a narrowing or constriction near the centre, when the woman is not pregnant.

it a euphemism for sexual intercourse, as in the 1928 Cole Porter hit 'Let's Do It.' The word also may mean sex appeal, as in 'This girl has got it.' (In this sense, the 1920s movie star Clara Bow was famous as 'the It Girl.') Until the middle of the 20th century, 'losing it' would refer to the loss of virginity (whereas in the 1980s this expression merely means losing one's control, temper, or cool). Shakespeare uses 'it' to mean both sexual intercourse and a woman. In the phrase 'to get it up,' reference is made to the penis. See also DOING IT.

Italian culture a slang term for anal sex. The *Italian habit* was Shakespeare's euphemism for this practice.

Italian letter a colloquial term for condom, analogous to 'French letter.'

ithyphallic pertaining to an erect penis (from Greek *ithys*, 'straight,' and *phallos*, 'penis'). The word is sometimes used to describe something that is sexually stimulating, such as an aphrodisiac that is alleged to produce an erection.

IUD abbreviation for intrauterine device.

IUM abbreviation for intrauterine membrane device.

ius primae noctis an alternative term for DROIT DU SEIGNEUR. See this entry.

IVF abbreviation for in vitro fertilization.

jack a slang term for semen. To *jack off* is to masturbate.

jacksie a British slang term for anus.

Jacquemier's sign a change of colour of the vaginal mucosa that frequently is a sign of pregnancy. The mucosa just below the urethra may acquire an almost purplish hue after the fourth week of a pregnancy.

Janjero an Ethiopian society in which hemicastration has been reported, as well as the custom of taking male genitals rather than scalps as war trophies. In addition, the nipples of adolescent boys were cut off during puberty rites ('nipple excision').

Japanese a generally monogamous society in which most married men have extramarital relations (as high as 90 percent among the wealthy), but such relationships are uncommon among wives (about 5 percent). The early Japanese were noteworthy for their erotic manuals depicting a wide variety of positions and practices, and emphasizing physical details such as luxurious pubic hair and exaggerated penises; for phallic shrines and processions among the followers of Shinto; and for the establishment of the Tokyo red-light district in 1627. Today open prostitution is being replaced by the equivalent of call girls and bar girls (and discriminating Geisha girls). The Japanese have also shown a special interest in sexual gymnastics, human-animal contact, and use of vaginal balls which they term rin-no-tama.

Jarisch-Herxheimer reaction a sudden reaction to the administration of penicillin and certain related antibiotics in the treatment of syphilis. The symptoms include a fever and exacerbation of skin lesions lasting about 24 hours. The effects are temporary and require no specific treatment.

J Arthur a British slang term for masturbation. It is short for 'J Arthur Rank' which in turn is rhyming slang for wank.

jealousy a painful emotion compounded of hostility or resentment against a rival, especially when he or she possesses enviable beauty, wealth, status, or sex appeal. The earliest form of jealousy is an older child's anger directed towards a new baby in the family. In adults, jealousy may take the extreme form of a 'crime of passion' or a delusion of infidelity. See also ALCOHOLIC JEALOUSY; DELUSIONAL JEALOUSY; PROJECTED JEALOUSY.

jelly roll an American slang term for the vagina, also applied to coitus, a lover, and a male with an abnormal sex appetite.

jerk off a slang term meaning to masturbate.

jill off a lesbian term meaning to masturbate—by analogy with JACK OFF. See this entry.

jimmy riddle a British slang term for urination, as in 'have a jimmy riddle.' It is rhyming slang for 'piddle.'

jissom a slang term for semen.

jive a slang term for intercourse.

Jobst breast support a type of elastic brassiere used to hold the female breasts in place during the initial healing process after mammoplasty.

John a slang term for the male client of a female prostitute.

John Thomas a British euphemism for penis.

joint a slang term for penis. By way of analogy, a *jointess* is a clitoris.

Jorgensen, Christine the female name taken by one of the pioneer subjects in sex-change surgery. The patient was originally a Long Island, New York, photographer and war veteran, George Jorgensen. At the age of 26, Jorgensen travelled to Denmark to undergo a sex change with hormones and surgery in a clinic run by Dr. Christian Hamburger. Jorgensen returned to the United States in 1962, a celebrity, and helped compile the first serious study of transsexualism.

joy to joy: an obsolete (16th-century) term meaning to have intercourse.

joystick a slang term for penis.

jugs an American slang term for the female breasts.

juniper an evergreen shrub that produces purple berries used in the preparation of medicines and alleged rejuvenants and aphrodisiacs. Juniper-berry juice is used as an ingredient in alcoholic drinks and in love potions.

justifiable abortion an abortion that is deemed necessary to protect the life or the physical or mental health of the mother. An abortion also may be considered justifiable if prenatal diagnosis indicates the child would suffer permanent physical or mental disability if allowed to be carried to term.

juvenile paresis a type of partial paralysis identified with congenital syphilis. If a woman infected with syphilis transmits the spirochaetal organism to the foetus during the fifth month of her pregnancy, the infection may be dormant in the offspring until around the age of 10 or 12, when neurological symptoms begin to appear. They may include failing memory and judgment, loss of muscular coordination, and visual difficulties. Although congenital syphilis can usually be prevented or controlled by penicillin, erythromycin, or other drugs, during or immediately after pregnancy, effects of the disease tend to resurface as much as 15 years after birth of the child. Although the mother may have acquired a syphilis infection before or very early in pregnancy, it is believed that the spirochaete, *Treponema pallidum*, is unable to cross the placental barrier until about the fifth month of pregnancy because it is blocked by a membrane, Langhans' layer. However, Langhans' layer begins to atrophy after the 16th week of pregnancy, permitting the syphilis organism to reach the foetus.

Kahn test a blood-precipitation test for syphilis in which a blood-serum sample is heated, mixed with a test solution, and incubated overnight. If clumps of precipitate appear the following day, the results are considered positive.

Kajaba a Colombian society with numerous sexual customs rarely if ever found elsewhere. Among them are gang rape of a man by women; confession of sexual misdeed to avoid harmful effects; sexual contact with animals by almost everyone in the society; preference for masturbation as a form of sexual release; ritual offerings of semen especially by boys who are required to have intercourse with widows. The society also believes that if the man's rhythm during intercourse is thrown off, his partner, his children, and he himself will be harmed; and that an incestuous relation must be repeated in order to expiate the crime by collecting the semen and vaginal secretions and giving them to a priest to sacrifice.

Kama Sutra a 4th-century Hindu manual on love and sex (based on earlier sources). The *Kama Sutra* is both mystical and sophisticated, and extols the sensual delights of poetry, music, and perfumes while describing a great variety of intercourse positions. It was translated into English and secretly published, in 1883, by Sir Richard Burton. (Sanskrit *kama*, 'love, lust,' and *sutra*, 'thread, string'—of aphorisms, rules, and the like.)

Kamchadal a hunting society in Eastern Siberia. As in other parts of this area, men are permitted more than one wife. However, the marriage ceremony is unique: to make the marriage legal, the groom must touch the bride-to-be's naked vulva—which may be easier said than done, because even though the parents may have given him permission to marry their daughter, he must 'capture' her first. This means that he must fight off the women of the village who try to protect her, and at the same time tear off layers of clothes in which she has dressed for further protection. If she wants him, she makes all this relatively easy; if not, she tries to discourage him.

Kantner and Zelnik Survey a pair of surveys of teenage American girls conducted in 1971 and 1976. The study was limited to girls between the ages of 15 and 19, and questions were directed towards obtaining data about premarital sexual behaviour and use of contraceptives. More than 4,600 girls participated, and the samples included girls from various ethnic groups. The surveys revealed that 42 percent of the teenage girls had experienced sexual intercourse.

Kaposi's sarcoma a type of malignant tumour that affects the skin, usually marked by purple or brown plaques or nodules on the legs and feet. The tumour involves blood vessels, so that there is some loss of blood, a complication that is often fatal when the lesions begin to appear in the gastrointestinal tract. Kaposi's sarcoma is a frequent manifestion of an AIDS infection. See also AIDS.

Karezza a coitus reservatus or coitus prolongatus technique long practised in India, where men are trained to withhold ejaculation through breath control, meditation, posture, and finger pressure. Karezza is practised not only as a means of birth control but devotees also claim that by repeatedly approaching ejaculation without completing it they extend their sexual pleasure and experience the equivalent of many orgasms. The practice has been found not only in various countries of the Orient, but in the Oneida community of upstate New York.

karyogamy the fusion of the nuclei of two gametes, as occurs during fertilization of an ovum.

karyomere the head of a spermatozoon.

karyotype a genetic portrait of an individual based on the chromosome complement in the nucleus of a cell. A chromosome picture can be made literally by photographing the chromosomes in a body cell through a microscope, then cutting the photographic images from the print and pasting them on a sheet of paper. The karyotype for a normal human male will contain 46 autosomes, or nonsex chromosomes, plus one X chromosome and one Y chromosome. A karyotype for a person with Down's syndrome will contain an extra chromosome No. 21.

keeping the census down a euphemism for masturbating.

Kegel exercises repeated contraction and release of the network of muscles that surround the opening of the vagina and support the woman's internal organs. Developed by Dr. Alfred Kegel in 1952, these exercises have the effect of strengthening the female orgasm (and the male orgasm as well, because they enable the woman to grip the penis more firmly) as well as preparing for childbirth, reducing urinary incontinence, and preventing prolapse of the womb. Also called pelvic floor exercises; vaginal exercises.

Kempf's disease a form of acute homosexual panic, described by the American psychiatrist Edward Kempf as anxiety based on a fear that the individual will be attacked by a homosexual or that he may be identified as a homosexual.

Keraki a New Guinea society in which young men are required to engage in anal intercourse as part of the puberty rites, based on the belief that they will not grow normally unless they have received the semen of older men. The Karaki also believe that boys can become pregnant, and a lime-eating ceremony is performed to prevent this. After the puberty rites, they graduate to playing active homosexual and heterosexual roles.

keratin the substance of horns, nails, and hair. It is formed of protein molecules and contains a large proportion of sulphur. Keratin is sometimes used as the substance of alleged aphrodisiacs derived from animal horns.

kerbcrawling the practice of driving along slowly at the side of the road trying to solicit sex from passing women (who may or may not be prostitutes).

khyber a British slang term for buttocks or anus. It is short for Khyber Pass, which in turn is rhyming slang for arse.

kiddieporn laws a colloquial term for laws and statutes prohibiting the distribution of books and other materials that show sexual performance by children—even though such materials may not have been found to be 'obscene.' Because of the latter aspect, such legislation has been challenged in U.S. state and federal courts.

kidney wiper an archaic euphemism for penis. Kidney in turn is an obsolete word for uterus.

kid stuff a slang term meaning (a) child abuse, especially sexual, or (b) paedophilia.

killer T lymphocytes white blood cells in the human immune system that normally combat cancer cells and viral infections. In laboratory studies of AIDS it has been observed that the AIDS retrovirus attacks the killer T lymphocytes, thereby reducing the body's immunity. See also AIDS.

kimilue a culture-specific syndrome among the Diegueno Indians of Lower California, characterized by extreme apathy, loss of interest in life, and vivid sexual dreams.

kinky a slang term referring to any sexual behaviour that is considered deviant or bizarre.

Kinsey, Alfred Charles (1894-1956) a zoologist at Indiana University, USA who made many lasting contributions to the study of insects but switched his major interest in 1937 when he was asked to give a course on marriage. Finding that existing knowledge of sexual behaviour was meagre and lacking in scientific validity, he developed data-gathering methods, chiefly in the form of interviews, that eventually provided the statistical basis for the study of such subjects as masturbation, homosexuality, premarital sex, and the nature of the female orgasm among white Americans.

Kinsey Report the first comprehensive empirical study of human sexuality, based on more than 16,000 personal interviews with white Americans. Among the many findings were the following: women are frequently capable of multiple orgasms, and usually retain their sexual potential longer than men; 96 percent of men and 85 percent of women masturbate; 37 percent of (white) American males and 13 percent of females have at least one homosexual experience; 85 percent of women who have had premarital experience have no serious regrets; one out of every six farm boys has had sexual contact with animals; about one in five single girls who have had intercourse become pregnant, and the overwhelming majority of these have abortions; and males experience an average of three orgasms per week before marriage, and the same after marriage, while the findings for women are 0.4 and 2.0 up to the age of 35.

The use of Kinsey's sampling has been challenged because it was not representative of the United States population in general. Persons of lower educational levels, nonwhites, and persons living in rural areas, for example, were not represented in the proportions in which they existed in the United States when the studies were conducted. See also PLAYBOY SURVEY.

kinship-model family group a family unit of biologically related members of two or more generations usually dominated by a maternal grandmother who makes the major decisions, assumes responsibility for raising the children, and supervises the appropriate sex roles of the members.

kinship system the network of blood relationships that determine membership in a family whose members are usually conceived as descending from a common ancestor. Kinship networks vary somewhat from society to society but generally include parents, grandparents, siblings, uncles, aunts, nieces, and nephews. Sexual relations are usually prohibited between members of the same kin.

kissing the act of making contact with the lips, as a form of greeting, expression of affection, sexual desire, love, friendship, or reverence. Kissing the mouth or other parts of the partner's body represents major steps in sexual arousal. However, kissing is somewhat less than universal because it is not generally found amoung the Ainu, Okinawans, Andamanese, Vietnamese, Somali, Lepcha, Cewa, and Siriono.

kissing disease a colloquial name for infectious mononucleosis (glandular fever).

kissing the bride the right of the best man and friends to kiss the bride after the wedding ceremony. This custom is said to be a vestige of the early Roman period when a captive bride was deemed to be common property of the males in a community.

Kiwai inhabitants of islands off the coast of Papua New Guinea, who are generally monogamous, though polygyny is permitted. Among their sexual myths is the belief that a woman would give birth to twins if she ate

bananas from a tree with two bunches; also, that a woman can overcome sterility by eating spiders and spider eggs.

kleptolagnia a variation of kleptomania characterized by a desire to steal because the act is accompanied by sexual excitement.

kleptomania a psychological disorder characterized by an irresistible impulse to steal objects that are not for immediate use or monetary value, and which in many instances are hidden away, given away, or returned surreptitiously. Severe tension is felt before committing the act, and pleasure, relief, and frequently sexual arousal are experienced while committing it.

Klinefelter's syndrome an abnormal condition of testicular dysgenesis (failure to develop) and aspermatogenesis (failure to produce sperm) sometimes accompanied by the development of female breasts in a male. There are several variations of the anomaly first described by the American physician Harry Klinefelter, the characteristics apparently influenced in part by the individual's chromosome complement. They have in common an extra X chromosome so that the usual complement may be 47,XXY, rather than the normal male complement of 46,XY, meaning a total of 46 chromosomes including one X (female) and one Y (male) sex chromosome. Some Klinefelter's-syndrome patients may have complements of 48,XXXY or 48,XXYY or even the normal female complement of 46,XX. Patients with more than two X chromosomes are usually mentally defective, and those with two Y chromosomes are likely to have traits associated with males possessing the extra Y chromosome, such as aggressive tendencies. Still other Klinefelter's-syndrome patients may have mosaic chromosomal patterns, such as 46,XY/47,XXY, indicating two or more gene combinations. Although males with Klinefelter's syndrome were originally thought to be mentally retarded, early research was based on examination of patients in mental institutions. More recent studies have found that many otherwise normal males could be classified as Klinefelter's-syndrome cases. They tend to be taller than the average adult male and to have normal intelligence and normal male physical characteristics except for the testicular dysgenesis and signs of gynaecomastia. The condition is usually not diagnosed until they are examined for possible causes of infertility.

klismaphilia a psychosexual disorder, or paraphilia, characterized by the persistent use of enemas for sexual arousal.

Kluge's sign a bluish colouration of the vulva and walls of the vagina during the second month of pregnancy. The colouration, which is normal, is caused by a congestion of blood in the tissues as a result of the pregnancy.

Klüver-Bucy syndrome a bizarre form of hypersexuality that is associated with lesions of the temporal lobes of the brain. The condition also has been observed in patients who have undergone bilateral temporal lobectomy, which severs fibres of the limbic system and may trigger a release phenomenon marked by a sudden lack of sexual inhibitions. In addition, the patient has a compulsion to examine objects orally and an unusual appetite for meat. The same effects are produced in experimental animals by administering lobectomy.

knackers a British slang term for testicles.

Knaus method an alternative term for the rhythm method of birth control, based on the fact that a woman is most likely to conceive midway between menstrual cycles.

knave girl in Middle English, a boy, in contrast to 'gay girl,' meaning a GIRL. See this entry.

knee-chest position a technique that has been used to force an undescended testicle into the scrotum. The patient is seated in a straight-backed chair, his feet on the seat of the chair and the knees held close to the chest. The position sometimes forces the testicle into the scrotum by pressure on the inguinal canal. The technique may be used by an examining physician in diagnosing a case of cryptorchidism.

knee trembler a slang term for intercourse in standing position.

knockers a slang term for the female breasts.

knocking shop a British slang term for brothel.

knock up an American slang term meaning to make pregnant, as in 'He knocked me up.'

knowledge an old (Biblical) euphemism for sexual intimacy. In this sense, *to know* someone means to have (or have had) sexual relations with her or him (only her in the Bible).

koro a sexual disorder observed primarily in southern China, Malaysia, and Borneo. Koro victims develop a morbid, obsessive fear that their penis is shrinking and will disappear into the abdomen and lead to death. To prevent this dreaded outcome, they usually tie a cord around the penis or encase it in a wooden splint. If that does not help, they call upon members of their family to take turns holding the organ in a tight grip. There is also a female form of the disorder in which a woman becomes convinced that her breasts are shrinking and her labia are being sucked inwards. In either case the disorder may be associated with guilt over masturbation or promiscuity. The male form is also called shook yong, which means 'shrinking penis' in Chinese.

Koryak fishers, hunters, and herders in northeast Asia. Sex hospitality is common in this society; the guest will be incensed if he is refused access to his host's wife, and the host will be insulted if the guest rejects his wife or daughter, and may even retaliate by killing him. Also unusual is the custom whereby some men 'marry' stones instead of women—putting clothes on the stone, taking it to bed, and caressing it as though it were a person.

Krafft-Ebing, Baron Richard von (1840-1902) a neurologist who specialized in forensic psychiatry, chiefly noted for his detailed and comprehensive studies of sexual aberrations under the title of *Psychopathia Sexualis*, published at a time when Victorian attitudes were dominant. Though personally opposed to sexual deviations in general, such as sadism and masochism (both of which he named), his clinical descriptions of sexual pathology are classic, and his investigation of general paralysis of the insane confirmed the fact that syphilitic disorders are caused by an organism that attacks the nervous system.

kraurosis penis a condition of shrinking and atrophy of the glans penis and foreskin associated with a stenosis, or narrowing, of the urethra.

kraurosis vulvae a dryness and atrophy of the tissues of the vulva, sometimes leading to cancer. It occurs mostly in aging women and is characterized by itching and dryness of the external genitalia.

Kurtatchi a polygynous society of the sororal type in Northern Bougainville, one of the Solomon Islands. This is one of the few human societies in which girls and women directly and intentionally expose their genital organs as a means of inviting sexual activity.

K-Y jelly a lubricant commonly used to reduce undesirable friction in intercourse or related activities.

labia majora the two 'major lips' that surround the vaginal orifice. They consist of longitudinal folds of tissue that extend downwards and backwards from the mons pubis, enclosing the labia minora, the vagina, the urethra, and the clitoris. The labia majora dilate and become engorged with blood during sexual excitement. Also called lips of the vulva. Singular: labium majus.

labia minora the two 'minor lips' of the vulva, which lie between the labia majora. They come together in the prepuce of the clitoris at the upper end, and in the hymen at the lower end. The labia minora, like the labia majora, swell during sexual excitement. Among the Marquesans, Trukese, and a few other societies, elongated labia minora are of special erotic interest, and attempts are made to stretch them. Singular: labium minus.

labioscrotal fusion an aspect of female pseudohermaphroditism that results when male sex-hormone stimulation occurs before the 12th week of gestation. The androgenic hormone production also inhibits the normal descent of the vagina. As the term suggests, the individual is born with fused labia that resemble the scrotum, which actually is a continuation of the embryonic urogenital sinus.

labioscrotal swellings a primordial anatomical structure in the embryo that differentiates into the male scrotum or the female labia majora.

labour in childbirth, the contractions of the uterine muscles that first dilate the cervix, and then with the assistance of the abdominal muscles gradually push the baby downwards through the cervix and birth canal until it emerges into the world. The first sign of labour is usually stronger and stronger contractions, a slight blood-stained discharge

from the vagina (the show), or rupture of the amniotic membrane with release of the amniotic fluid (breaking of the waters), although this usually happens later in the process. See also FALSE LABOUR; PREMATURE LABOUR.

lace curtains a slang term, mainly in homosexual usage, for foreskin.

lactation the secretion of milk, usually in the period immediately after childbirth.

lacunae the numerous small reservoirs of blood that develop in the lining of the uterus during the luteal phase of the menstrual cycle. The term is derived from the Latin and suggests 'small lakes' of blood within the endometrial tissues.

ladies' college an early-18th-century euphemism for brothel.

ladies' delight a colloquial term for penis. Also called *ladies' lollipop; ladies' treasure.*

Ladin's sign a sign of pregnancy observed in the fifth or sixth week of gestation, noted as a softening of the uterine tissues at their junction with the cervix.

lady killer a slang term for a man who is obsessed with his abilities to attract the attentions of women. The true lady killer is not necessarily sexually aggressive but instead suffers from feelings of inferiority about his sexual prowess and overcompensates by demonstrating that he is attractive to females.

lady of easy virtue a colloquial term for prostitute. Also called *lady of pleasure/the night/the evening/the street,* and many other names beginning with 'lady.'

La Leche League an organization which provides information and advice on breast feeding.

Lamaze method a natural childbirth technique developed in Russia and popularized by the French physician Ferdinand Lamaze during the 1950s. It involves a series of prescribed exercises through which the prospective mother learns to manage her contractions and to dissociate them from the experience of pain. The husband is encouraged to study the anatomy and physiology of childbirth with his wife, and to give her support during the birth experience. Also called psychoprophylaxis method.

Laminaria a genus of brown algae seaweed that has been used to induce abortion by forcing open the uterine cervix during pregnancy. The dried seaweed expands as it absorbs moisture, forcing open the birth canal.

lamprey an eel-like sea creature with a jaw filled with sharp teeth. Perhaps because of its phallic shape, it has been consumed for its presumed aphrodisiac effects for centuries. Among other claims, it is reported to increase the male production of seminal fluid.

laparoscopy an endoscopic examination of the abdominal cavity, performed by inserting a small lighted scope through a small incision in the abdominal wall. The procedure is used in the diagnosis of female infertility, unexplained abdominal pain, pelvic inflammatory disease, pelvic cancer, ectopic pregnancy, sterilization, and related situations. Laparoscopy may be performed under a general or local anaesthetic. Carbon-dioxide gas is injected into the abdominal cavity to lift the inner wall of the abdomen away from the organs within the pelvic area, creating an empty space for better visualization of the organs through the endoscope (also called a *laparoscope*). A blue dye may be injected into the uterus via the vagina during laparoscopy; if the fallopian tubes are not blocked, the dye will be visible as it flows from the open ends of the tubes near the ovaries. The procedure is relatively simple and painless. The opening in the abdominal wall is closed with one suture and an adhesive bandage, and the patient usually can return home a few hours later. Laparoscopy was introduced in 1910, but it was not until the 1960s that fibreoptic equipment made the laparoscopy a routine procedure.

lap lover a slang term for a person who loves performing cunnilingus.

Lapps a strictly monogamous society (properly called Saami) in Northern Scandinavia comprising hunters, fishers, and reindeer herders. At one time, the Lapps used sex organs such as penises of stallions in ritual magic,

but this practice has disappeared. However, they still sacrifice the uteri and penises of reindeer to the family gods.

largest baby the largest normal infant ever born, according to the *Guinness Book of Records*, was 24 pounds 4 ounces. The birth was recorded in 1961 in Turkey.

larynx the voice box. The larynx grows during puberty, particularly in males, resulting in a deepening of the voice.

lascivious cohabitation an old, usually legal, term for living together with 'sexual privileges,' whether or not the couple are married. (Lascivious means lustful or wanton.)

last favour a traditional euphemism for sexual intimacy—as seen from the woman's perspective.

latah a culture-specific disorder found in Malaya, Thailand, Siberia, the Congo, and the Philippines, in which dull, submissive women who have been subjected to a sudden fright develop such symptoms as extreme fearfulness, mimicking behaviour (echolalia, echopraxia) and a compulsion to utter profanities and obscenities.

late androgenic stimulation activity of male sex hormones in the body of a female foetus after the 12th week of gestation. The hormonal stimulation occurs too late to interfere with the normal descent of the vagina, but it does cause enlargement of the clitoris. The genitalia are normal otherwise.

latency in psychoanalytical theory, the stage of psychosexual development between the resolution of the oedipal phase and the onset of puberty, comprising approximately the ages 5 to 12. During this stage, sexual preoccupation appears to be repressed or transferred ('sublimated'), and boys and girls are primarily interested in skills, peer activities, and relationships with members of their own sex. Many theorists, however, deny that sexual interest is completely dormant, citing the prevalence of sex play and sex interests during this period.

latent homosexuality partially or completely repressed homosexual tendencies that may occasionally express themselves in fantasies, extreme criticism of homosexuality, or homosexual impulses. When these impulses threaten to break through—for example, under the influence of alcohol—they may precipitate an episode of acute anxiety.

laurel a shrub that produces leaves long associated with masculine prowess. In the ancient Orient, men were advised to use laurel leaves to enhance their virility. The Greeks used crowns of laurel to honour their athletic champions in the Pythian games.

Laurence-Moon-Biedl syndrome an abnormal condition of obesity, sexual underdevelopment, retinitis pigmentosa, mental deficiency, and anomalies of the hands and feet. Although the condition is hereditary, all of these symptoms are rarely seen in one individual, but they are likely to be found collectively in the siblings of one family or in one generation. The eye disorders, particularly retinal degeneration, are the most numerous of the abnormalities. The female patients reaching adulthood experience a significantly higher-than-average rate of abortions. They also are likely to have underdeveloped breasts and amenorrhoea. Gynaecomastia, impotence, azoospermia, and aleydigism are found in male patients.

LAV abbreviation for lymphadenopathy-associated virus, an organism identified in 1984 as a cause of AIDS (acquired immune deficiency syndrome) by doctors at the Pasteur Institute in Paris. Because LAV is believed to be the same as the virus identified by American researchers as HTLV-III, the term is often shown as HTLV-III/LAV. See also AIDS.

lavender a herb used as a medicine, a perfume, and as an alleged aphrodisiac. In *The Winter's Tale* hot lavender is suggested by Perdita as a rejuvenant for 'men of middle age.' Lavender was chewed, smoked with tobacco, and kept with clothing to give linens a pleasant aroma.

lay the perhaps most common slang term referring to sexual intercourse. The word is used (a) for the act, (b) for the partner, or (c) as a verb.

LBW abbreviation for low birth weight, generally established at less than 2,500 grams, or 5 pounds 8 ounces.

leather bar a slang term for a bar used as a meeting place for homosexual men.

leather clubs groups of male homosexuals who engage in sadomasochistic practices, ride motorcycles, and wear predominantly leather clothes. For sexual purposes, they divide themselves into masters and slaves. The masters wear black leather jackets, leather trousers, chaps, and boots, topped off with a leather cap decorated with the club's insignia. The slaves wear frayed jeans and bike jackets with a slave harness underneath, fitted with various restraint attachments such as chains and a 'cock ring.'

leather fetish an intense sexual preoccupation with articles of clothing made of leather, including jackets, boots, shoes, and caps. The fetish apparently represents supermasculinity and is common among male homosexual sadomasochists, who frequently meet in 'leather bars.' Some women also adopt leather attire.

leatherites a slang term for fetishists wearing leather garments, particularly erotic items.

Leboyer technique a method of child delivery introduced by the French obstetrician Frederick Leboyer in support of his theory that gentle handling during birth results in an infant who will have a stable, pleasing personality. The method prohibits any intervention that might be a painful stimulus, such as spanking the infant to stimulate breathing. Such violence, according to the theory, may cause emotional trauma that would affect the individual throughout its lifetime.

lechery inordinate indulgence in sexual activity or sexually provocative behaviour; lustfulness, lasciviousness, lewdness. Literally, a *lecher* is someome who 'licks' (from Old French).

lécheur (lāshœ' ; French, 'licker') a person who performs fellatio or cunnilingus. The female form is *lécheuse* (lāshœ').

left-handed wife an obsolete term for concubine or mistress.

leg man a man who is attracted by the female legs as primary turn-on, as distinguished from the 'arseman' and the 'tits man' or 'breast man.' See also ARSE MAN.

Lepcha a Sikkim society in the Himalayas. The Lepcha are hunters and fishers who permit polygamy, though monogamy is more common. They are said not to involve sex with love; intercourse is a cut and dried affair, without kissing, courtship, extended foreplay, or emotional involvement.

lepromatous leprosy a form of Hansen's disease, or leprosy, that tends to affect persons with a weakened immune system. One of the effects in males is atrophy of the testicles.

Leriche's syndrome a disease of the blood vessels that affects the lower part of the body, which is deprived of freshly oxygenated blood because of an arterial obstruction. The effects include pains in the gluteal muscles of the buttocks and impotence. Treatment requires surgery to remove the obstruction or to install a plastic prosthesis to replace the blocked artery.

lesbianism female homosexuality. The term is derived from the name of the Greek Island of Lesbos where many of the female inhabitants followed a homosexual life-stlye, and where the poetess Sappho wrote lyrical accounts of their activities around 600 B.C. Also called *sapphism*. Among the colloquial and slang terms for a lesbian are *leslie*, *lez*, *lesbo*, *lesbyterian*, and *lizzy*.

leukoplakia a precancerous disorder marked by the appearance of thick, white, slightly raised tumours or patches on the penis or vulva.

leukorrhoea a viscous white discharge from the uterus or vagina. It is sometimes associated with a local disease, such as moniliasis. It is usually composed of mucus and vaginal-lining cells that have been discarded. Leukorrhoea that occurs after a pregnancy may be caused by overactivity of the cervix, which produces copious amounts of mucus. It also may be an early sign of pregnancy, because of hormonal activity within the uterus or cervix.

levirate marriage marriage of a widow with her brother, or in some cases with the deceased husband's heir. The primary object is the domestic well-being of the widow. Among the early Hebrews this custom was compulsory if the deceased was childless and the brothers had lived together. The term junior levirate refers to marriage of the widow to the deceased husband's younger brother.

Leviticus a book of the Old Testament that associates menstruation with impurity and uncleanliness. It is the probable source of many cultural taboos regarding sexual relations or any other contact with menstruating women.

lewdness the quality of being obscene, or licentious. The term is frequently applied to sexually provocative drawings or paintings, pornographic films, or such behaviour as indecent exposure and fondling of children.

Leydig cells interstitial cells located in spaces between the seminiferous tubules of the testis. They function as endocrine glands, secreting androgens, particularly the male sex hormone testosterone, under the influence of a pituitary cell hormone. They are named after the German histologist Franz von Leydig.

Leydig-cell tumour a usually noncancerous growth in the interstitial cells of the testis

that is often the cause of precocious male puberty. The tumour may also result in gynaecomastia if it develops after puberty.

liaison an illicit sexual relationship between a man and a woman; a premarital or extramarital relationship. Unlike marriage, liaisons are not viewed as permanent, and do not involve legal or religious sanction.

libertine an old-fashioned word for a person—usually a man—who indulges in sexual activity without restraint. Casanova and the fictitious Don Juan, who made a career of promiscuity, were libertines par excellence. Other words for the same concept—equally old-fashioned—are rake, roué, and lecher.

libidinal development an alternative term for psychosexual development, as used in the psychoanalytical system.

libidinal transference in psychoanalysis, the transference, or displacement, of the patient's erotic drives from the parents to the analyst.

libidinal types Freud's threefold personality classification based on the distribution of libidinal or sexual energy in the psyche: In the erotic type, the libido remains invested in the id, and the individual is preoccupied with loving and being loved; in the obsessional type, the libido is concentrated in the superego, and the individual is dominated by conscience; and in the narcissistic type, the libido is invested primarily in the ego, and the principal interest is in self-love and personal gratification to the exclusion of others.

libidinization another term for erotization, or investment of bodily organs and functions with sexual pleasure.

libido (Latin, 'desire, lust') the psychoanalytical term for the energy of the sex drive or impulse in its physical and mental manifestations. In Freud's earlier theory, the libido was the single dominant instinct, governing development from infancy to maturity and the basic source of energy for all human activites. Later, in his 'dual instinct' theory, he recognized a second controlling force, the aggressive drive. Jung also offered a libido theory, but applied the term to a general life force expressed in all types of activities—biological, sexual, social, cultural, and creative. See also DAMMED-UP LIBIDO; DISPLACE-ABILITY OF LIBIDO; GENITAL LIBIDO; ORAL LIBIDO; SUMMA LIBIDO.

libido analogue a libido equivalent; an object that represents libidinal or life energy in a different form. Jung, who originated this term, cites as examples fetishes (such as a lock of hair), mythological figures of gods, and sacred objects used in primitive rites.

libido and premature sexuality a term referring to the relationship between precocious puberty or precocious sexuality and sex drive. One British study found a remarkable lack of interest in members of the opposite sex among boys and girls who experienced abnormally early development of sexual characteristics. Only three boys of a group of 19 and one girl in a group of 50 in the study of sexual precocity expressed interest in contact with members of the opposite sex. The study also found that pregnancies among girls experiencing precocious puberty were rare.

licentiousness sexual activity that is completely unrestrained; sexual behaviour that is uncontrolled by legal or moral codes.

lichenification an abnormal condition of the skin of the genital area, usually aggravated by scratching. It commonly is a complication of pruritus vulvae, or itching vulva, in women, and is characterized by thickened and leathery skin around the genitalia. A similar condition may affect the scrotum and neighbouring skin areas of males.

licking as a sexual practice, stimulating the partner's sex organs or other erogenous zones by stroking them with the tongue. Licking the entire body has been given the colloquial name 'going around the world.' It is interesting that the term lechery derives from a word meaning 'to lick.'

licorice a European herb with purple flower spikes and a root that contains a sweet substance used in confectionery and medicines. It is one of the herbs listed in Chaucer's 'Tale of Sir Thopas' as an aphrodisiac, along with valerian, clove, and nutmeg, that might be added to ale in order to stimulate allegedly the sexual desire of the person consuming the brew.

lie with a euphemism meaning to have intercourse with (a person).

life force a basically sexual source of energy that Wilhelm Reich believed to be suffused throughout the universe. Roughly equivalent to 'orgone energy,' this force was conceived to be the ultimate source of sexual gratification, health, vitality, and well-being.

life instinct in psychoanalysis, an alternative term for Eros.

ligament a thick band of fibrous tissue that connects joints or bones, supports soft tissue organs, or serves other structural functions in the body, such as the broad ligament of the uterus.

linea nigra a darkly pigmented line that runs vertically along the centre of the abdomen of some women as a sign of pregnancy.

lingam the Sanskrit word for penis. The lingam is often depicted in stylized form as a symbol of the Hindu god Shiva (Siva). Lingams of various sizes are used in Hindu phallic worship.

lingam ring an early Chinese and Hindu sexual aid, or 'love instrument,' in the form of a jade, silver, or ivory ring designed to fit around the base of the lingam (penis) as a means of stimulating the woman's clitoris during intercourse. Today's equivalent, called a 'cock ring' or 'love ring,' is made of latex rubber with protrusions designed to act as a stimulator.

linguist a colloquial abbreviation for cunnilinguist.

lip clap an obsolete term for kiss or kissing.

lip eroticism sexual stimulation through the use of the lips, as in kissing and sucking.

lipoid hyperplasia a disease in which a person lacks the enzymes needed to begin the conversion of cholesterol molecules into sex hormones. As a result, cholesterol rather than the sex hormones is distributed to the testes and ovaries.

lipoma of the vulva a fat tumour that may develop on one side of the vulva. It is noncancerous but, if untreated, can grow to a large size.

Lippes loop a type of intrauterine contraceptive device that works by altering the rate of an ovum's passage or by discouraging implantation of a fertilized ovum in the lining of the uterus. It is a nonmedicated type of IUD that is sold in various sizes, ranging form A for women who have never been pregnant to a larger D size for women who have had multiple pregnancies.

lip plate a large, decorated disc, or plate, used by women as a means of greatly enlarging the mouth. This fashion was once common in the Ubangi-Chari region of central Africa, but is currently dying out. The reasons behind this custom are obscure, but it has been suggested that the object was to make the women unattractive to slave raiders.

lips of the vulva the outer and inner folds of skin (labia majora and labia minora), which are part of the external female sex organs, and which dilate and become engorged during sexual excitement.

lip work an obsolete euphemism for cunnilingus.

lithopedion a medical term for a stone baby, or calcified foetus, that may form in the uterus after death in the womb.

lithotomy position a posture assumed by a patient who lies on his back with the hips and knees flexed and the thighs pulled away from the midline of the body. The position is used sometimes for medical examination of the male prostate. The position is also used for some internal examinations of women.

little brother a euphemism for penis.

little death a colloquial term for intense orgasm, especially referring to the partners' simultaneous orgasm. The term is a literal translation of the French *la petite mort*.

little friend a euphemism for period.

little shame tongue an obsolescent term for clitoris. 'Shame tongue' is a literal translation of the German *Schamzunge*.

Littre's glands a number of small glands that open into the urethra. They are mucous glands and occur in both the male and female urethral organs.

live-in a slang term referring to cohabitation by unmarried men and women. See also POSSLQ.

live in sin an obsolescent term meaning to live like husband and wife without being legally married.

living together the practice of sharing a home, including the same bed, without being married. Common objectives appear to be to insure companionship, test compatibility, share expenses and responsibilities, and experience a mutually satisfying sexual life. Such an arrangement is often taken more seriously than merely 'shacking up,' because it is similar to a trial marriage.

LMP abbreviation for last menstrual period.

load a slang term for the ejaculate, or for the quantity of sperm ejaculated in one orgasm.

loaded ship an old term referring to coitus during pregnancy. Throughout history, despite moral and sometimes legal prohibitions, many a wife and her lover have resorted to this practice to avoid an *unwanted* pregnancy. In ancient Rome, Agrippa (daughter of Emperor Augustus, wife of Emperor Tiberius) bragged that despite her uncountable lovers all her five children were her husband's 'because only as a loaded ship do I carry a passenger (numquam enim nisi navi plena tollo vectorem).'

loathsome disease an older euphemism for venereal disease.

local an American slang term referring to being masturbated by someone else, as in 'getting a local' at a massage parlour or by a prostitute.

lochia the vaginal discharge after childbirth. See also VAGINAL DISCHARGE.

lonely-hearts column personal ads in newspapers or magazines. See PERSONAL ADS.

longest menstrual life the greatest reported span of time between menarche and menopause. Beacause of a tendency to late menopause to be associated with precocious puberty, girls who began menstruating at an early age might be expected to have a long period of reproductive life. In lifetime studies of three girls who began menstruating at the ages of 2 and 3 years, it was found that menopause did not occur until the women were 52 and 53 years old respectively and were presumably fertile for approximately 50 years each.

loop-de-loop an older American slang term for the sixty-nine position.

loose a euphemism for sexually promiscuous, especially when referring to a woman.

loss of consortium a legal claim for damages in compensation for the loss of conjugal relations. Loss of consortium may be applied in cases of impairment or loss of sexual relations resulting from negligence or malfeasance of a physician or other person contributing to physical injury to a spouse, or of a person, such as a paramour, whose actions caused the dissolution of a marriage.

loss of erectability a condition that can result from true priapism in which the corpora cavernosa become engorged with blood but erection does not occur in the glans or corpus spongiosum. The erection occurs without sexual desire and may begin suddenly. Thrombosis develops in the corpora of untreated priapism cases, and the spaces become filled with fibrous tissue that obliterates the spongy tissue. The man is unable to achieve erection thereafter. See also IMPALEMENT.

loss of erection the failure to maintain a penile erection once it has been achieved. The cause is generally emotional, based on a fear of failure to perform the sex act adequately.

lotus-flower pollen an ingredient recommended in the Hindu sex manual *Ananga Ranga* for a concoction to be rubbed on the penis for improved erectile effectiveness.

love a complex emotion compounded of deep and abiding affection for another person, concern for his or her welfare, feelings of intimacy, trust, and tenderness, as well as pleasurable sensations experienced in the presence of that person. Love may be erotic or romantic, but may also be platonic or metaphysical, such as love of God. It may take many forms, including brotherly or sisterly love, parental love, self-love, and altruistic love. An exciting, satisfying sexual relationship is a major ingredient of love between the sexes (or within each sex), but there can be love without sex and sex without love.

See also BEING LOVE; CALF LOVE; FIRST LOVE; FREE LOVE; GENITAL LOVE; GREEK LOVE; HELLENIC LOVE; HUNGER AND LOVE; MONKEY LOVE; MOTHER LOVE; OBJECT LOVE; PHALLIC LOVE; PLATONIC LOVE; PREGENITAL LOVE; PRODUCTIVE LOVE; ROMANTIC LOVE; TRANSFERENCE LOVE.

love ads a euphemism for advertisements of a sexual nature in 'personal' columns.

love affair a romantic episode or relationship that usually involves sexual activity, not necessarily including intercourse.

love apples according to an interpretation of the Bible story, the 'apples' that Rachel received from Leah, whereupon she became pregnant with Joseph. The love apples were said to be the fruit of the mandrake plant. Leah traded them for a night in the bed of Jacob, the husband of Rachel. Rachel ate the love apples and became pregnant after having been barren.

Currently, love apples is a euphemism for testicles.

love at first sight a strong and immediate attraction to another person, usually of the opposite sex, more akin to infatuation than to genuine love. Such an attraction is often the result of sex appeal or romantic circumstances, as contrasted with such factors as shared experiences and matching of personalities and interests. However, so-called love at first sight may, when given a chance, slowly ripen into deep and durable love.

love bite a mark made on the neck, by biting and sucking during sexual play, usually on the neck.

love broker a euphemism for pimp.

love child a somewhat literary and euphemistic expression for an illegitimate child, or bastard.

love-in a colloquial term, used especially in the 1960s, for a gathering of people, mainly young people, with a share-and-share-alike attitude, who get together to 'let it all hang out' in displaying affection or singing or taking drugs.

love juice a euphemism for sperm.

love magic potions, spells, and charms meant to entice a partner into sexual activity. For example, a man may try to gain control over the desired woman by obtaining a lock of hair or her nail clippings, putting drops of his sweat or even his semen in her food, or giving her a betel nut over which he has said an incantation.

lovemaking in current usage, a colloquial term for sexual intercourse. The terms lovemaking and 'to make love' used to have a more generally erotic or courting sense, before gradually acquiring their almost exclusively sexual meaning in recent decades. See also MAKE LOVE; THERAPEUTIC LOVEMAKING.

love match marriage motivated primarily by love, as contrasted with other motives such as security, sex appeal, status seeking, or monetary considerations though any of these may also be involved.

love needs a term applied by the psychiatrist Abraham Maslow to the need for affection, acceptance, affiliation, and belonging, in his need-hierarchy theory.

love nest a flat or house used by an unmarried couple for purposes of living together or for periodic meetings between sexual partners who have permanent homes elsewhere.

love nuts another term for BLUE BALLS. See this entry.

love object the person towards whom feelings of affection, devotion, and sexual interest are directed. In psychoanalysis the term 'object love' is used for the investment of the libido or sexual energy in an object or person other than oneself.

love play the entire gamut of erotic activities ranging from teasing, hair pulling, wrestling, and fumbling exploration among children, to various ways of expressing tenderness and affection, such as love notes (billets doux), caresses and kisses, and all the forms of physical contact that lead more or less directly to sexual gratification—that is, foreplay, experimentation with different coital positions, and in some instances more unusual attempts to maximize sexual response, such as erotic bondage and flagellation.

love powder a drug or charm reputed to have the power to produce sexual excitement in general, or sexual interest in the particular person administering it. Also called love potion or love philtre (which derives from the Greek word *philein*, 'to love'). All of these expressions have been largely replaced by the common and current term aphrodisiac.

lover a man who is erotically involved with a woman who is not his wife. The term lover is often applied to a man and a woman who are having an affair. The term also is used by a male homosexual to identify a sex partner with whom he has a long-term relationship.

lovers' lane a tongue-in-cheek term used by the medical profession to identify the fallopian tubes, where the ovum and spermatozoon meet to form a zygote, or offspring of the parents.

love that dare not speak its name, the a late 19th-century euphemism for male homosexuality (probably coined by Lord Alfred Douglas, Oscar Wilde's lover).

love toys a colloquial term for erotic aids.

low-profile prosthesis a female breast implant that provides a contour that is intermediate between a tear drop and a hemispheric shape.

LSD and sex a term referring to the effect, or possible effect, of the hallucinogen, lysergic acid diethylamide, on sexual performance and sexual excitement. A few 'acid heads' claim that LSD enhances sexual potency and responsiveness, but most users have found that other reactions are far more common: transient or repeated delusions and hallucinations, perceptual distortions, feelings of unreality, paranoid thoughts, marked anxiety or depression, impaired judgment, and such physical symptoms as palpitations, rapid heartbeat, and tremors.

lues (lōō'əs; Latin, 'infection, plague') a synonym for syphilis. The word is often used with a modifying term, such as *lues nervosa*, indicating neurosyphilis, or *lues venera*, identifying syphilitic lesions of the genitalia.

luetin an extract of killed cultures of *Treponema pallidum*, the syphilis-disease organism, used in the Noguchi skin-reaction test for syphilis.

lumpectomy a local excision or partial mastectomy performed to remove a Stage I (not invasive and rarely spreading) breast cancer. The technique has been a subject of controversy, some surgeons arguing that a lumpectomy may be successful under optimum conditions although the chances of recurrence of the cancer are greater than with a simple mastectomy. A lumpectomy may be recommended for a small malignancy on the outer edge of the breast.

lupae (Latin, 'wolves') an obsolete term for prostitutes, especially prostitutes in the parks of ancient Rome (probably from their practice of getting their clients' attention with a wolf cry).

lust an intense desire, or craving, especially for sexual gratification.

lust dynamism a term coined by H.S. Sullivan for an active, powerful sex drive, such as the desire of the adolescent to reach orgasm.

lust murder an extreme form of sadism in which sexual gratification is achieved through raping, murdering, and mutilating the victim. In his book *Human Sexuality*, McCary states: 'in true lust murders, no coitus occurs; orgasm is the outcome of the act of murder and mutilation.' Murderers of this kind are usually if not always psychotic, and their hostile acts may be related to a fear of rejection. Also called sex murder.

luteal phase the stage of the menstrual cycle that begins with the release of an ovum from an ovary and the production of the female sex hormones progesterone by the corpus luteum, which forms in the just emptied ovarian follicle. The progesterone stimulates an accelerated buildup of the endometrium, which suddenly becomes thicker and more vascular in preparation for the possible implantation of a fertilized ovum.

luteinizing hormone (LH) a hormone secreted by the anterior lobe of the pituitary gland. In the female, it regulates the development of the ovarian follicles. In the male, it stimulates the secretion of testosterone by the Leydig (interstitial) cells of the testes. The luteinizing hormone also is believed to play a role in the sexual maturation of the female, but the activity is not well understood. During the menstrual cycle, after menarche, the luteinizing-hormone level rises gradually until ovulation is induced. If fertilization of the ovum does not occur, LH levels decline rapidly until the end of menstruation when secretion of the hormone again increases towards levels needed to induce ovulation.

luteoma a variation of the granulosa-theca-cell tumour composed of cells that resemble miniature versions of corpus luteum cells. A luteoma is capable of producing either masculinizing or feminizing effects in a female. A luteoma also may or may not be cancerous.

luteotrophic hormone a releasing factor of the hypothalamus (hypophysis) that stimulates the pituitary gland to release the gonadotropin hormones, the luteinizing and follicle-stimulating hormones. Also call luteotropin; luteinizing hormone-releasing hormone (LRH).

lying-in a dated term for the period during which a woman remains in bed prior to giving birth. Maternity hospitals used to be called 'lying-in' hospitals.

lymphadenopathy chronically swollen lymph nodes, an early symptom of an AIDS infection and a common effect of other sexually transmissible diseases. See also AIDS.

lymphogranuloma venereum (LGV) a sexually transmissible chlamydial disease prevalent in tropical and subtropical regions and usually characterized by a temporary genital lesion followed by inflammation of the inguinal lymph nodes. The first sign is a small blisterlike lesion at the point of infection, which ulcerates and disappears. Meanwhile, the inguinal lymph nodes on one side enlarge gradually, forming a large mass under a reddened skin area. The infected person also is likely to experience a fever, headache, pain in the joints, and nausea. The lymph nodes may develop pockets of pus, which may be blood-stained, and the matter may be discharged outside the body. Women who have acquired the disease through conventional intercourse may experience backache and sores on the vagina and cervix. If males or females acquired the infection by anal intercourse, the disease usually has been complicated by ulcerative proctitis. Blood-stained pus is then discharged through the anus. Genital complications include elephantiasis, which requires treatment by plastic surgery to restore the normal appearance of the groin. Abscesses and fistulas resulting from LGV also may require corrective surgery. Rectal strictures are usually corrected by dilatation techniques. Also called *lymphogranuloma inguinale*.

lymphoid tissue structures on the lymphatic system. Because of an inverse growth relationship between lymphoid tissue and genitalia, it was believed earlier in the 20th century that lymphatic tissue retarded sexual development. The notion was disproved by studies showing that surgical removal of the tonsils had no effect on the rate at which the patient reached sexual maturity.

Lyon hypothesis a theory that only one X chromosome per body cell will be active. In the female, born with two X chromosomes, the X chromosome selected to be inactivated is determined early in embryonic life. As both the mother and the father may contribute an X chromosome, either the maternal or paternal X chromosome genes may be inactivated by the random-selection process.

machines an obsolete American term for condoms made of sheep intestines.

machismo a colloquial term for exaggerated masculine pride and display of what is thought to be maleness (from Spanish *macho*, 'male'). But, as Zsa Zsa Gabor said so aptly, 'Macho does not prove mucho.'

Mackenrodt's ligaments the transverse cervical ligaments extending from each side of the pelvis to the neck of the uterus. They are the primary support for the uterus.

Mackintosh Society an organization of English rubber fetishists. The name is derived from the inventor of rubberized raincoats and other waterproof materials, Charles Macintosh, a Scottish chemist.

macrogenitosomia a congenital condition of enlarged genitalia resulting from an excessive secretion of androgenic hormones during foetal development. The condition is characterized by male infants being born with enlarged but immature external genitalia and female infants with signs of pseudohermaphroditism at birth.

macromastia overlarge breasts. The condition, which is usually irreversible, is associated with hypertrophied milk ducts and an abnormal increase in fat and fibrous connective tissue. The condition may occur on only one side or on both sides. A variation of the condition, precocious mammary hypertrophy, is caused by hormonal disturbances and results in symmetrical enlarged breasts on both sides. An extreme form of macromastia has been termed gigantomastia of pregnancy.

madam a colloquial term for the female manager of a brothel.

Magee, Mary an Irish woman whose campaign for access to contraceptives in the mostly Roman Catholic country in the 1970s led to Ireland's 1979 Family Planning Act, making birth control legal. Magee obtained contraceptives by mail order when advised by her doctor that her health would be damaged by a pregnancy. When Irish customs officials confiscated the contraceptives, Magee sued the government claiming her right to privacy had been violated. The Irish Supreme Court agreed.

Magna Mater Cybele, a nature goddess who symbolized primordial motherhood in Greek mythology. According to Jung, this symbol, or archetype, of the universal mother resides in the collective unconscious of humankind.

magnetic conception a term referring to a 17th-century theory that human fertilization was the result of magnetic energy produced by the friction of sexual intercourse. Once the female reproductive tract was magnetized, according to the notion, the male semen provided the spark of life needed to conceive a new individual.

maiden fear a colloquial term for parthenophobia.

maidenhead a colloquial term for hymen.

maieusiophobia (mā·ōō'sē·ōfō'bē·ə) an intense, morbid fear of childbirth.

maieutics a medical term for obstetrics (Greek *maieutikos*, 'skilled in midwifery').

main avenue an American euphemism for vagina.

main squeeze a slang term, mainly in black American usage, for one's regular girl friend, or one's wife.

make feet for children's stockings a colloquial expression meaning to procreate. The term has been in use for about 200 years, also as 'to make feet for children's shoes.'

make it with a slang term for sexual activity, either heterosexual or homosexual. A variant term in American English is 'to make (someone).' See also MAKING OUT.

make love a Shakespearean euphemism meaning to have sexual intercourse (analogous to the French *faire l'amour*). Curiously, after centuries of more general meanings, the term has reacquired, in our time, this immediate reference to sex. See also LOVEMAKING.

making out a colloquial American term used by young unmarried people for sexual contact that may include anything from necking to petting and even intercourse in some cases. In the heat of sexual excitement, the participants may ignore the risk of pregnancy.

malady of France Shakespeare's euphemism for syphilis.

male accessory organs reproductive-system structures that serve as adjuncts to intercourse. They include the prostate gland, the seminal vesicles, and the bulbourethral glands.

male anomalies congenital defects of the male reproductive system. Anomalies often go unnoticed unless the person is concerned about his lack of fertility, leading to close examination of the reproductive structures. Anomalies may include the complete absence of the vas deferens or a vas deferens that is a solid cord without a lumen (open area), the failure of one or both testes to descend into the scrotum, or absence of the seminal vesicle or failure of the seminal vesicle to secrete fluid.

male-breast carcinoma a form of breast cancer that affects a small percentage of men, usually when they are in their 50s. The cancer and breast tissue are similar to those occurring in women. However, men tend to tolerate the symptoms of pain and discomfort for several years, probably because they fail to realize the seriousness of the disorder or to accept the fact that a man may have breast cancer.

male chauvinism an aggressive assertion of male superiority coupled with attempts to 'keep women in their place' and deny them equal rights in the home, the work place, and society in general. A man who behaves in this way is a male chauvinist pig (MCP).

male climacteric the medical term for the so-called male menopause or climacteric.

male homosexual prostitution a form of prostitution in which boys or young men provide sexual services to other males for financial or other gain, such as favours or protection in prison. Unlike female prostitutes they do not depend on pimps, but solicit by themselves. The standard term for them

in British English is 'rent boys'; more specialized are 'call boys', whom clients contact by telephone.

male-identified a recent term for male homosexual. Also called male-oriented.

male member an alternative term for male organ.

male menopause a common, though inaccurate, term for the psychological and physiological changes experienced by some men during the climacteric.

maleness identity as a male based on the presence of the anatomical structures and physiological functions associated with the male sexual and reproductive role.

male oestrogen the oestrogen that appears in the urine of males with functionally active Leydig cells in their testes. The purpose of male oestrogen has been been questioned although some authorities assume it has an inhibiting effect on potential excesses of male sex hormone activity.

male organ the external organ for copulation and urination in the male; a nontechnical term for penis. Also called male member; member; organ.

male-oriented a recent term for male homosexual. Also called male-identified.

male pregnancy the idea that males can conceive under certain conditions. For example, the Keraki of New Guinea believe that anal insemination could occur among boys who submit to older men during puberty rites; some Navaho insist that a man can become pregnant if his wife is on top during intercourse; and some black homosexuals hold that the semen may itself develop into a 'blood baby' which makes the belly swell, followed by labour pains and a bloody 'delivery' from the rectum.

male prostitution the sale of sexual services by boys or men. Male prostitution is almost invariably homosexual, but there are occasional instances of heterosexual male prostitution in which women reward men for their services. In ancient China, and later in Japan, eastern Africa, and Egypt, male prostitutes were frequently transvestites.

male-reproductive-system assessment a medical examination that is conducted for evaluation of the male genitalia, including reproductive functioning and the presence of any diseases or defects. The examination includes studies of a series of semen samples, each specimen collected after a 3-day period of abstinence.

male sexual functioning the three natural

processes of the male contribution to reproduction: sperm production, penile erection to penetrate the vagina, and ejaculation to deliver the spermatozoa to the proper area of the vagina.

male sperm a spermatozoon bearing a Y chromosome. It can be differentiated under a microscope from a spermatozoon carrying an X chromosome by its smaller, spade-shaped head and longer tail. The male sperm also is lighter and faster, perhaps accounting for the higher male conception ratio.

malposition of testes any condition marked by failure of one or both testicles to enter the scrotum before birth or before puberty. Undescended testes are found in about 10 percent of infant boys and 2 percent of boys at puberty.

Malthus, Thomas (1766-1834) an English economist credited with initiating a birth-control movement in Great Britain. Malthus made the original predictions that the rate of population increase in the world would eventually result in general starvation and poverty because the earth would not be able to support a multibillion human population.

malthusianism a euphemism for masturbation.

mamma a Latin term for the female breast. Plural: *mammae*.

mammalingus sexual stimulation of the female partner by suckling her breast during foreplay or intercourse.

mamma-poppa position another term for missionary position.

mammarized society a culture in which both male and female members are intrigued by the female breast. Although both the male and female breast are basically identical and differ mainly in size, the female breast has been a symbol of womanhood since prehistoric times, as indicated by cave drawings and ancient mythology. For men, the female breast is often the first site of physical contact and sexual intimacy with a female. Women generally strive to conform to socially acceptable breast sizes and shapes. Although there have been brief periods in the 20th century in which unisex or flat-chested fashions were popular, the actual physical loss of the breast—as in surgical mastectomy—frequently is a traumatic experience for a woman. It has been compared to the psychological impact that castration may have on a man.

mammary abscess an abscess of the breast, which generally occurs during the period of nursing an infant or while weaning.

mammary amputation another term for mastectomy.

mammary gland the milk-secreting gland of the female. Rudimentary mammary glands are found on the chest wall of the male. The average female mammary gland is about 4 to 5 inches in diameter and protrudes about 2 inches from the chest wall. During lactation, the gland may double or triple in size, mainly from a proliferation of milk-secreting alveoli and milk ducts. A mammary gland contains between 15 and 20 lobes, each with its own duct leading to a tiny opening in the nipple. Each lobe is supplied by a number of milk-secreting alveoli. Most of the glandular tissue consists of fat deposits and connective tissue packed around the lobes. The mammary gland increases somewhat in size during the early phase of each menstrual cycle, then regresses after ovulation. A more obvious increase in size occurs during pregnancy. After menopause, the mammary gland regresses toward its prepubertal size.

mammography the examination of a mammary gland by the use of soft-tissue x-ray techniques that do not require the injection of a radiopaque dye. It may be performed in the diagnosis of a suspected lesion because the tumour may appear on the *mammogram* as a stippled area. However, a mammogram does not determine whether a lesion may or may not be cancerous and is regarded as of questionable use by some physicians.

mammometer a device that measures the volume of each breast of a female. The instrument contains a graduated cylinder that is filled with fluid and placed over each breast, one at a time. The amount of displacement of fluid by each of the breasts is measured precisely on the graduated cylinder, and the results for the left and right sides are compared to determine any deviation. The mammometer is used in plastic surgery of the breasts to ensure that both breasts will be the same size.

mammotrophic hormone an alternative term for prolactin, the pituitary hormone that stimulates milk production by the mammary gland.

Mandragoris an alternative name for Aphrodite, the goddess of love. The term is derived from a word for mandrake, the 'universal aphrodisiac'.

mandrake a herb, Mandragora officinarum, native to northern Africa and southern Europe, and used for centuries as a narcotic, analgesic, hallucinogen, and alleged aphrodisiac.

maneater a slang term for a male homosexual.

manhole a slang term for anus.

manhole inspector a slang term for the active partner in anal intercourse.

manhood a literary euphemism for penis.

Mann test a technique for testing the intactness of the female cervix by inserting into the uterus a rubber balloon that has been treated with a radiopaque dye that can be visualized on x-ray film.

mantra a sound, such as 'Om,' or a series of sounds, received from a guru, and repeated aloud or silently as a means of focussing the mind during meditation, as well as relaxing the body and releasing primal forces. According to Hindu teachings, when a mantra is repeated during lovemaking, it has the effect of awakening sexual energy and achieving the peak of passion.

Manus nonliterate inhabitants of the Admiralty Islands, north of Papua New Guinea, particularly noteworthy for their negative attitudes towards sex. According to Margaret Mead, sex is inherently shameful and sinful to them, and is particularly humiliating to women, most of whom are frigid and find intercourse painful. There is no word for love in the Manus language, and romantic stories, dances, and songs do not exist. Kissing, fondling of the breasts, and all other forms of foreplay are equally lacking, and the entire society appears to be (or perhaps to have been) very puritanical.

manustupration an obsolete term for masturbation.

maracas a humorous slang term for the female breasts.

maraichinage (märashinäzh') a form of prolonged kissing in which the lovers' tongues caress the insides of each other's mouths—a kiss that may last for hours. In its most extreme form this practice takes the place of genital intercourse, and it has been used as a form of birth control. Maraichinage seems to have originated among the Maraichins, the inhabitants of the Pays de Mont, in the Vendée in Brittany (France).

marbles a slang term for testicles.

Margulies spiral an intrauterine contraceptive device in the shape of a coil with a beaded tail. The beads protrude through the cervix into the roof of the vaginal canal, permitting the woman to feel whether the IUD is in place by checking for the beads in

the vagina. Introduced in 1959, the Margulies spiral was not popular with men who sustained injury to the glans penis during coitus.

marijuana and pregnancy a term referring to the use of marijuana by pregnant women, reported by the U.S. National Institutes of Health to range between 10 and 37 percent. The NIH has reported that its studies of effects of marijuana on foetal development are confounded by a number of variables such as the use of other substances, nutrition during pregnancy, changes in use of marijuana during pregnancy, and the trimester or trimesters during which it was used. Also confounding the results is the accuracy of recall of these factors by the women interviewed. The NIH has found suggestive evidence that marijuana use by a pregnant woman interferes with normal foetal growth and may affect the visual or other neurological responses of the offspring. The NIH reports add that women who use marijuana are also likely to use tobacco and alcohol, which are themselves harmful.

marijuana and sex hormones a term referring to the effects of marijuana and cannabinoids on hormones associated with the reproductive function. Studies reported by the U.S. National Institutes of Health have found that cannabinoids, the active ingredient in marijuana, inhibit the secretion of the luteinizing and follicle-stimulating hormones as well as prolactin in primates. The changes in pituitary hormones result in decreased production of sex-steroid hormones of the adrenal glands and cause changes in ovulation. The principal site of pharmacological action of cannabinoids is in the hypothalamus, at the base of the brain, which in turn controls the release of pituitary sex hormones. However, the effects are reversible in sexually mature animals when administration of the drug is stopped. There are reports that human female marijuana users have shorter menstrual cycles than non-users. In men, marijuana effects on the pituitary can result in reduced testosterone levels.

marital adjustment adaptation to the responsibilities and demands of marriage, including adjustment to the idiosyncrasies and wishes of one's spouse, the sharing and appreciating of each other's interests, the achieving of mutual sexual gratification, and cooperation in decision making, the raising of children, homemaking, and the solving of practical problems.

marital conflicts severe or relatively mild

but persistent disagreements between marital partners, often focussed on such areas as sexual relations, child rearing, the balance of power in the marriage, money matters, and life-style. Extreme and lasting conflicts are termed marital discord, and may lead to separation and divorce.

marital discord a severe, persistent form of marital conflict, often leading to separation and divorce.

marital rape forcible sexual assault by a husband against his wife, in many societies considered a husband's right of marriage since medieval days. Since 1979, as a result of feminist movements, new laws or court decisions have made it illegal for a husband to have sexual relations with his wife without her consent in more than half of the states of the United States. It is expected that by the end of the 1980s all or nearly all states will have enacted legislation protecting wives against sexual intercourse by their husbands if the wife is unwilling. In Britain this form of assault is still not considered to be rape.

marital relations sexual relations between marriage partners, as contrasted, for example, with premarital and extramarital relations.

marital-status distribution the composition of a given population in terms of the number or percentage of married persons in the population. The demographic term is extended in some countries to include persons 'living in union' but unmarried.

marital therapy a commonly used term for marriage therapy.

marking myths old wives' tales about the causes of birthmarks, which were attributed to an object of the same general shape seen by the mother while pregnant. Marking myths also try to give the false impression that physical features of a child may be caused by the mother being frightened by a wild animal or an incident such as a conflagration or seeing red blotches.

Marquesans inhabitants of mountainous islands in the Central Pacific who subsist on fish and tree crops. Their sexual culture includes slitting the foreskin, without anaesthetics, to promote cleanliness; erotic festivals in which public copulation takes place; sex hospitality; seated sex with the woman astride the man's lap; oral sex; great frequency of intercourse (generally up to five times a night); institutionalized transvestism; the obligation of a husband to have sex with his wife almost immediately after the birth of a child to stop the flow of blood; the custom of talking about the chief's genitals, giving them special names; the use of astringents to shrink the vaginal walls and, allegedly, to insure the superiority of Marquesan women; and the belief in the myth of vagina dentata.

marriage a relationship between a man and a woman formalized by the wedding ceremony and consummated by sexual relations and the establishment of a family. Traditionally, marriage has been preceded by a period of courtship, an engagement period, and an expression of approval by both sets of parents. Despite the fact that today many couples live together before marriage, and the fact that the conventional religious ceremony is often replaced by an informal gathering, as well as the fact that the rate of divorce is close to 50 percent, marriage still appears to be a viable and meaningful institution.

See also BOY MARRIAGE; BROTHER-SISTER MARRIAGES; CHILD MARRIAGE; CLUSTER MARRIAGE; COMMON-LAW MARRIAGE; COMPANIONATE MARRIAGE; CONSUMMATION OF MARRIAGE; COUSIN MARRIAGE; EXPERIMENTAL MARRIAGE; GAY MARRIAGE; GROUP MARRIAGE; HOMOSEXUAL MARRIAGE; INTERMARRIAGE; LEVIRATE MARRIAGE; MULTIPLE MARRIAGE; OPEN MARRIAGE; PLURAL MARRIAGE; RENEWABLE MARRIAGE; SYMBIOTIC MARRIAGE; SYNERGIC MARRIAGE; TRIAL MARRIAGE; UNCONSUMMATED MARRIAGE.

marriage certificate the document confirming the fact that a marriage has been lawfully contracted. It is usually given to the couple by the person who performs the ceremony, who must then submit a copy to a designated official for the purpose of recording the marriage.

marriage contract the legal concept of marriage and the contract whereby a man and a woman agree to enter into a union for life for their mutual benefit, to provide each other with companionship, sexual gratification, and economic help, and to procreate and raise children. The contract is binding even if none of these considerations is explicitly mentioned at the time of marriage.

marriage-enrichment groups groups of couples who meet regularly with a trained leader to discuss the marriage relationship, including sexual feelings and behaviour, as well as to air all types of experiences from childhood on that might be interfering with their relationship. The exchange of feelings and ideas has frequently been found to salvage weak marriages as well as to enrich relatively strong marriages. Also called *marriage-encounter groups*.

marriage fear a common term for the morbid fear of marriage, or gamophobia.

marriage guidance counselling to help married couples solve marital difficulties. In Britain marriage guidance is often carried out by the Marriage Guidance Council.

marriage of convenience a marriage that is not based on mutual affection or love, but on monetary or social advantages, such as gaining social position or keeping an estate within a family. In some cases the outward appearance of the marriage is maintained while both partners are free to enter into other alliances.

marriage therapy psychotherapy focussed on disturbances in the marriage relationship, usually conducted on a joint basis or with a combination of joint and individual sessions. The therapist (marriage counsellor, psychologist, social worker) usually conducts the sessions either on a problem-solving level, in which grievances and conflicts are aired and worked through, or on a more analytical level where the emphasis is on the underlying sources of the problem, which may include childhood experiences, deep-seated attitudes, and basic personality differences.

masculine habitus the general physical characteristics associated with an adult male. Included are a receding hairline, facial hair, body hair, masculine musculature, and a male escutcheon. These physical traits are produced by the stimulation of 17-ketosteroids and when present in a female lead to hirsutism and other masculine characteristics. The excess 17-ketosteroids also result in an enlarged clitoris and, in many instances, a stronger sex drive than is usual for a female.

masculine identity a strong sense of affiliation with males, or identification with masculine attitudes, roles, values, and personality characteristics as defined by a particular culture.

masculine protest a term coined by Alfred Adler and used in two senses: (1) rebellion of women against the traditional feminine role of submissiveness and dependence, and adoption of the so-called masculine role in which they become aggressive and domineering and attempt to usurp the male position, and (2) an excessive drive for power and superiority among men who have not recovered from early doubts about their masculinity. When carried to the extreme, each of these patterns was deemed neurotic by Adler.

masculinity role behaviour characteristic of a boy or man in a given society, as distinguished from anatomical or physiological sexual identity, that is usually termed maleness.

masculinity-femininity tests psychological tests designed to measure the degree of masculinity or femininity (as well as androgyny) in individual subjects. The Terman-Miles test of 1938 is outdated, but the MMPI (Minnesota Multiphasic Personality Inventory), the Guilford-Zimmerman survey, the Gough Femininity Scale, and the BEM Sex-Role Inventory are often used today.

masculinization the development of characteristics associated with the male sex. The term is ordinarily used with regard to women who show signs of virilism, such as hirsutism.

masculinizing neoplasms tumours of the pituitary or adrenal glands that result in masculine physical characteristics in women. The changes can include clitoral enlargement, hirsutism or masculine hair distribution over the body, a deep voice, and masculine muscular development.

masculinizing surgery sex-change surgery to correct the physical appearance of a person who is genetically a male but who was born with an androgen deficiency so that his physical appearance is that of a female.

masculinovoblastoma an adrenal-gland tumour that has masculinizing effects in females. Also called adrenal-rest tumour.

mask a covering for the face with slits for the eyes, usually made of cloth or papier mâché. Though worn today for masquerade balls or theatrical productions, masks are said to have been introduced in Europe by Venetian courtesans in the 13th century, probably as a sexually provocative disguise. They were also worn by many fashionable English women during the 17th century.

masked homosexuality unconscious homosexuality, which may take many forms: exclusive preference for sexual acts usually engaged in by homosexuals, such as anal intercourse with members of the opposite sex; also, according to the psychoanalyst Wilhelm Stekel, sexual relations with old women (gerontophilia) or sexual desire directed to children.

mask of pregnancy a popular term for chloasma, a condition of increased pigmentation that develops over the bridge of the nose and cheeks of some women who are pregnant. The condition also may occur in women using oral contraceptives.

masochism a psychological disorder in which the individual persistently derives pleasure from pain inflicted upon him or her by others or by himself or herself. In most instances the pain is a prelude to or accompaniment of sexual relations, or may itself produce orgasm directly. The term masochism may also be applied to experiences that do not involve sex—at least overtly—such as religious flagellation, self-sacrifice, humiliation, or martyrdom. In these cases the major motive appears to be relief from feelings of guilt over evil thoughts or misdeeds, which may include sexual fantasies or activities. See also EROTOGENIC MASOCHISM; FEMININE MASOCHISM; MENTAL MASOCHISM; MORAL MASOCHISM; PRIMARY MASOCHISM; SEXUAL MASOCHISM; VERBAL MASOCHISM; SADOMASOCHISM; SACHERMASOCH.

masochistic fantasies fantasies of being choked, whipped, starved, insulted, or otherwise mistreated and abused, as an expression of masochistic impulses, and especially as a means of achieving sexual excitement.

massage parlour a colloquial term for an establishment that purports to offer only body massage and perhaps a sauna but is usually a centre for sexual services of various kinds, including masturbation ('relief massage') or, for an extra fee, intercourse. Other 'services' might include 'assisted showers', enemas, and vibrator 'treatments'.

mastalgia a painful condition of the mammary gland. In a younger woman, mastalgia is usually the result of fibrosis or a cyst formation. In menopausal women, particularly if obese, the condition is associated with pendulous breasts. Also called mastodynia; mammary neuralgia.

mastectomy the surgical removal of the breast, or mammary gland, usually performed because of a cancer. Simple mastectomy is a procedure in which one or both breasts are removed but not the adjacent muscles or lymph nodes. A radical mastectomy involves the removal of the breast plus the pectoral muscles beneath the breast tissue and the axillary (arm-pit) lymph nodes. An extended radical mastectomy involves lymph nodes of the upper chest area in addition to the tissues removed by a standard mastectomy. A modified radical mastectomy removes the breast and axillary lymph nodes but leaves all or part of the pectoral muscles of the chest wall. Other procedures include local excision (also

called lumpectomy), partial mastectomy, and subcutaneous mastectomy, but they are limited to conditions in which the cancer is small and presumably has not metastasized (spread) to the neighbouring lymph nodes or other tissues of the area.

master gland a name sometimes used to identify the pituitary gland because it secretes hormones that in turn stimulate other endocrine glands to secrete hormones. For example, the anterior lobe of the pituitary releases a luteinizing hormone (LH) that stimulates the testis to produce testosterone.

Masters and Johnson the research and therapy team consisting of the American gynaecologist William H. Masters, M.D., and Virginia E. Johnson, who began as his assistant and later became his partner and, still later, his wife. Through in-depth interviews, observations, and laboratory studies of the physical aspects of sexual relations, this investigative team has confirmed many of Kinsey's findings, and has added many of their own, such as the fact that women are capable of multiple orgasms, that the size of the penis bears no relation to sexual performance, and that there is no such thing as a vaginal orgasm as contrasted with a clitoral orgasm. Since 1959 they have concentrated on the development of sex therapy for couples, starting with a thorough examination of their sexual history and interpersonal relationship, and continuing with the application of specific behavioural techniques that have resulted in success rates of nearly 98 percent in cases of premature ejaculation, 74 percent for male impotence that began after some sexual experience, and approximately 80 percent for female frigidity. Their work has been recorded in two major volumes; *Human Sexual Response* (1966) and *Human Sexual Inadequacy* (1970).

mastitis an inflammatory condition of the breast. Symptoms include soreness, fullness and hardness of the breast, which may be red from the inflammatory effects. A similar condition may be caused by a blockage of one or more milk ducts, resulting in engorgement of the breast with milk.

masturbation a form of autoerotism characterized by sexual arousal through manipulation or stimulation of the sex organs, especially the penis and clitoris. The act is usually accompanied by sexual fantasies and may involve the use of a mechanical device such as a vibrator. Studies indicate that about 95 percent of males and 85 percent of females

Ⓜ

masturbate, usually starting in the third or fourth year. Practically every type of physical or mental disorder has been attributed to this practice, but it is now regarded as essentially harmless. However, anxiety and guilt over excessive masturbation may interfere with adult sexual satisfaction. (The word comes from Latin *masturbari*, 'to masturbate,' and may be derived from *manu stuprare*, 'to defile oneself with the hand.')

See also ANAL MASTURBATION; COMPUL-SIVE MASTURBATION; FEMALE MASTUR-BATION; INFANTILE MASTURBATION; MUTUAL MASTURBATION; PREPHALLIC MASTUR-BATION EQUIVALENT; PSYCHIC MASTUR-BATION; SYMBOLIC MASTURBATION.

masturbation equivalents activities that appear to be psychological substitutes for masturbation—for example, nail biting, ear pulling, hair plucking, and gambling.

masturbation fantasies mental images experienced during masturbation, having the effect of enhancing sexual excitement. Ordinarily they consist of mental pictures of members of the opposite sex, usually in the nude, various variations on sexual intercourse, and scenes from provocative films. In many cases these fantasies are a key to unexpressed sexual tendencies and desires, such as sadistic, masochistic, or homosexual practices.

matchmaker an intermediate who brings a couple together for the purpose of marriage. In 19th- and 20th-century Europe and America, and among orthodox Jewish groups, the two young people meet only in the presence of a chaperone until betrothal takes place. Professional matchmakers, known as marriage brokers, are paid for their services. Today arranged marriages are rare in Western societies.

maternal age the age at which a girl or woman can bear children. Most women have their first babies between the ages of 20 and 24, but there are verified reports of childbirth at the age of 5 (in cases of puberty praecox) and as late as 57 years. A young woman cannot bear a child until ovulation starts and mature ova are released, which usually takes place about a year after menstruation first occurs. See also MEDINA.

maternal androgen a masculinizing hormone that may enter the foetal circulation by way of the placenta as a result of a virilizing tumour of the ovary. The maternal androgen may affect the external genitalia of the female infant, resulting in masculine sexual characteristics. The male hormones also may enter the foetal circulation via the placenta as a result of hormonal medications taken by the mother during pregnancy.

maternal instinct in human beings (as well as other mammals), the innate drive of the female to feed, protect, and nurture her offspring. The term instinct has been questioned on the ground that the drive is neither universal nor based on any clear cut organic mechanism. Nevertheless, some investigators maintain that the maternal behaviour is the result of the release of the hormone prolactin during pregnancy, and cite as proof the fact that female animals who are not pregnant, as well as some male animals, exhibit maternal behaviour when injected with the hormone. However, the currently preferred term is *maternal drive*, because it does not imply that this urge is always innate.

maternalism a concept that mothering is an instinct possessed by members of the female sex alone.

maternal nondisjunction the failure of the XX chromosomes to divide equally during gametogenesis so that one daughter cell acquires both X chromosomes and the other receives no sex chromosomes. During fertilization, a spermatozoon with one X chromosome uniting with the XX chromosome ovum will result in a zygote with an XXX complement. If the paternal X chromosome gamete unites with the other maternal cell, lacking an X chromosome, the result will be an XO zygote with only 45 chromosomes and an infant with gonadal dysgenesis (Turner's syndrome). If the paternal gamete contains the Y sex chromosome, which unites with the XX ovum resulting from maternal nondisjunction, the offspring will have the XXY karyotype of Klinefelter's syndrome. If the spermatozoon containing the Y chromosome unites with the maternal ovum lacking an X chromosome, the result will be a YO sex chromosome combination and will not survive. At least there is no documented evidence that a YO offspring has survived.

maternal virilization disorder an abnormal condition in which a pregnant woman transmits to a female foetus the virilizing effects of an ovarian tumour. If the mother is afflicted with an ovarian arrhenoblastoma, producing masculinizing effects, while pregnant, a female foetus may be born as a female pseudohermaphrodite.

maternity blues a colloquial expression for feelings of lethargy, dejection, and 'letdown' experienced by over half of all women during the first few days or weeks after childbirth. Also called postpartum blues; baby blues.

mating the process of copulating, breeding, or pairing off for purposes of reproduction. The term is usually applied to animal species, but sometimes to humans who 'join together' in marriage or outside marriage. Spouses may therefore be referred to as *mates*.

mating dance a euphemism for the scenarios men and women follow in preparation for sexual activity. Among married couples, both partners soon learn to recognize the various steps in their ritual.

Matlab a province of Bangladesh that has been used for health-research studies since the 1960s. Because it represents in many ways a cross-section of Third World populations and problems. Matlab was chosen in 1975 for a test of the effects of offering free oral contraceptives or condoms to families in 150 of the district's 233 villages. It was found the general fertility rate dropped 25 percent in villages where contraceptives were made available, compared with the rate in the 83 villages where contraceptives were not offered.

matriarchy a society in which lineage, or descent, is traced through the female (termed matrilineal); also, a society in which the mother is the head and ruler of the family or clan. Some authorities believe matriarchal societies precede patriarchal societies, just as the child's early life is dominated by the mother rather than the father.

matrifocal a family unit based on the mother and her children. The biological father has a temporary role in the family but actually is considered a permanent member of his own mother's family. In the matrifocal family, the mother is likely to be the breadwinner, and care of the younger children is delegated to the older female relatives.

matrimony the state of marriage, or wedlock; also, in the Catholic religion, the rite, ceremony, or sacrament of marriage.

matrix a structure within which something else originates and takes form; an archaic term for uterus or womb.

matron a mature married woman, especially one who carries herself with dignity and enjoys a recognized social position. In some areas she is expected to dress and behave in a more reserved manner than marriageable girls or women. A matron is also a woman who serves as a superintendent, manager, or guard in a hospital, prison, or school.

McDonald's sign a pregnancy sign detected by an examining physician in noting the suddenly easy flexion of the upper half of the uterus. The sign is noted during the seventh or eighth week of a pregnancy.

Mead, Margaret (1901-1978) an American anthropologist who pioneered in the study of non-Western societies. Among her best-known works are *Coming of Age in Samoa, Growing Up in New Guinea,* and *Male and Female.*

meatometer (mē'ātom'ǝtǝ) an instrument for measuring the size of a urethral meatus—the external orifice, or opening at the end (Latin *meatus,* 'opening').

meatorrhaphy a surgical procedure in which the mucous membrane of the urethra is sutured onto the surface of the glans penis after enlargement of the urethral opening. The purpose of the operation is to prevent a contracture of the enlarged meatus.

meatotomy a surgical incision into the urethral meatus for the purpose of enlarging it. The surgery is performed with an instrument called a *meatotome.*

meat rack a derogatory term for a stretch of road frequented by prostitutes soliciting for custom. A noted one in London, for example, is near Kings Cross station.

median bar a type of prostatic hypertrophy that can obstruct the flow of urine from the bladder above the prostate gland. The median bar is a mass of rapidly growing fibromuscular tissue that extends laterally across the urethral opening from the bladder like a toll gate.

median lobe a lobe of prostate tissue that develops as an overgrowth in the abnormal condition of prostatic hypertrophy. The median lobe tends to grow upwards into the urinary bladder as a rounded projection over the urethral outlet.

mediastinum testis a thickened portion of the tunica albuginea at the back of the testes. From the front and sides, septa spread out and subdivide the tests into conical lobes.

Medina, Lina a Peruvian girl who in 1939 became a mother at the age of 5 years. The 6 pound 8 ounce male child was delivered by caesarean section. The mother began menstruating at the age of 8 months, according to medical records. (The father was 8 years old.) See also MATERNAL AGE.

medullary referring to a form of cancer of the prostate that is usually more insidious than the scirrhus type because it is not hard and therefore more difficult to detect without surgery.

medullary inductor substance a hormonal influence that around the sixth week of gestation begins to convert the undifferentiated embryonic gonad into a testis. Sheets of cells condense into primary sex cords that become a collecting system and join with other tissues to form seminiferous tubules. Leydig cells form and secrete the male sex hormones needed to spur the formation of the penis and scrotum.

megalosperm an abnormally large spermatozoon.

Meigs' syndrome a disease complex involving a tumour of the ovary and fluid accumulation in the abdomen and chest cavities. The fluid originates in the tumour and passes from the abdominal cavity into the thoracic cavity.

meiosis a type of cell division in which the number of chromosomes is reduced from the number present in the body cells to half the total, or the number of chromosomes needed for a gamete to be mated with another gamete of the opposite sex. The process occurs in nearly all animals to reproduce their species. In the human male cells, the meiotic division of a diploid (46 chromosome) gametocyte leads directly to the formation of haploid (23 chromosome) gametes which will eventually mature into spermatozoa. In the female, meiosis involves a more complex system in which an oogonium (primitive egg cell) begins with a diploid complement of chromosomes but must evolve through stages of primary oocyte and secondary oocyte in two successive divisions before maturing into a ripe ovum with the diploid number of chromosomes.

Meissner's corpuscles an encapsulated sensory-nerve ending located in various body surface areas. It reacts to tactile stimuli and is associated with sexual arousal when the brain interprets the touch-sensory impulses as an erotic stimulus.

melatonin a hormone secreted by the pineal gland that appears to exert some control over the gonadotropin hormones of the pituitary gland. Calcification or a tumour of the pineal gland results in precocious puberty, particularly in boys, but it also may result in hypogonadism. The hormone has a diurnal rhythm, with blood levels of melatonin increasing tenfold at night compared with daytime levels.

member a common euphemism for penis. Also called male member.

membranous urethra the portion of the male urethra near the bulb of the penis, and between the prostatic and penile segments of the urethra.

membrum virile a Latin term for penis—literally, 'male member.'

Meme the brand name of a polyurethane plastic material used in operations to enlarge female breasts.

menacme the portion of a woman's life during which menstruation occurs (Latin *mensis,* 'month,' and Greek *akme,* 'highest point').

ménage à trois (mänäzh' ätrô·ä'; French, 'household of three') an arrangement in which a married couple and the lover of the husband or wife, or of both of them, form a 'household of three.' The arrangement may be made by the wife if she finds her husband inadequate, or if she is bisexual and wants a lover of the same sex in addition to her spouse. The arrangement may also be initiated by the husband for similar reasons. See also CICISBEISM.

menarche (mənä'kē) the first menstruation, which marks the onset of puberty in the female. The menarche usually occurs between the 11th and 16th year, averaging 13.0 in Britain and 12.5 in the United States. Also called first period.

menarche influences effects of climate or other factors on menarche. Various studies show that climate has little if any influence on the onset of puberty in females. Eskimo and African females have the same average age of menarche. However, altitude apparently has an influence, retarding the onset of menstruation by an average of 1 month for every 1,000 feet above sea level. The decline in the average age of menarche from 17 years in 1830 to 13 years in 1960 in the United States and six European countries is attributed to improved health and nutrition. Also important is the genetic factor, as daughters usually begin to menstruate at the same age as their mothers. Studies of female twins also indicate a strong genetic influence in menarche timing. An example of environmental influences on menarche is seen in the !Kung bushmen societies of Africa whose female members had late menarche and ovulation and did not become pregnant before the age of 19 until the societies abandoned their nomadic hunting life-style and adopted the sedentary agrarian life of the neighbouring Bantu nations. Within a very few years after the !Kung women adapted to the richer diet of an agricultural life-style, their average body weight increased and menarche occurred much earlier.

mendelian inheritance laws the principles of heredity established by the 19th-century Austrian monk Gregor Mendel. The first law states that recessive traits are neither lost nor blended in future generations because both recessive and dominant genes are transmitted and independently segregated. The second law holds that the distribution of recessive or dominant traits to future generations occurs randomly and independently so that it is unlikely that the genes of one parent will remain together in future generations. The mendelian laws have been modified somewhat since Mendel's early experiments with seeds of yellow and green peas. Human genetics is more complex with many more traits to be considered. Human skin colour, for example, indicates that some traits can be blended.

mendelian ratio an expression of the mathematical distribution of recessive and dominant traits that may be inherited from a set of parents. For the average distribution of two traits over two generations, the odds, according to mendelian ratios, are 9:3:3:1, assuming there will be 16 grandchildren. The ratios indicate that nine of the 16 grandchildren will inherit both of the dominant traits. One will inherit both recessive traits. Three will receive one dominant and one recessive gene for each of the traits. In a two-generation example of two heterozygous parents (having dissimilar genes at the same locations on their chromosomes) with four children, one child will receive a homozygous dominant trait and one will show a homozygous recessive trait while the other two will display a heterozygous dominant trait.

meningeal neurosyphilis an acute or subacute form of syphilitic meningitis that may occur within the first few years of an infection. Physical effects may include headaches, insomnia, fatigue or lethargy, neurasthenia, convulsions or epilepsy-like seizures.

meningovascular syphilis a localized or general inflammation of the supporting and nutrient tissues of the nervous system resulting from a neurosyphilis infection. Cranial-nerve tremors and visual disturbances are common symptoms; the patient acquires a small irregular eye pupil that reacts to accommodation, but not to light stimulus. Neck stiffness, headaches, dizziness, and mental confusion accompany the condition.

menopausal depression a mild-to-severe state of dejection or despondency occurring during the female climacteric, particularly among women with a prior tendency to depression, dissatisfaction, or feelings of inadequacy. The severe type may take psychotic form, characterized by delusions of sin, guilt, or poverty, or an obsession with death. Also called involutional melancholia.

menopausal myopathy a type of muscle disorder that affects some women during or after the menopause. It is characterized by atrophy of some muscle tissue and polymyositis, or a diffuse inflammation of the skeletal muscles.

menopause the period during which menstruation ceases and the female reproductive cycle comes to an end. Contrary to common fears, sexual desire and enjoyment are usually maintained, and may actually increase when pregnancy is no longer a concern.

menorrhagia a condition of excessive or prolonged menstrual bleeding. Causes may include a uterine lesion, such as polyps or fibroids, although a common factor since introduction of the oral contraceptive is the use of a drug that provides an excessive amount of oestrogen. The oestrogen in turn can lead to an abnormally thick proliferation of endometrial tissue in the uterine lining between menstruations. Still other causes may be blood disorders, such as leukaemia or aplastic anaemia.

menorrhoea the normal menstrual flow.

menostasis a suppression or interruption of the menstrual flow. The cause may be amenorrhoea, an obstruction to the discharge of menstrual flow from the cervix or vagina, or the onset of menopause.

menotropins a preparation of gonadotropic hormones obtained from the urine of postmenopausal women and used to stimulate ovulation in women and spermatogenesis in men. Side effects include the risk of multiple pregnancies in women and gynaecomastia in men.

menoxenia any irregularity in menstruation (Latin, *menses,* 'month,' and Greek *xenos,* 'strange').

menses a monthly discharge of uterine blood and tissue that is also called menstruation. (Menses is Latin for 'months.')

menstrual age the age of the foetus calculated from the start of the mother's last menstruation.

menstrual aids various devices worn by women to collect the menstrual flow, including a pad of disposable absorbent material held in place against the opening of the vagina; and a tampon shaped in the form of a small roll that can easily be inserted into the vagina to absorb the flow. Also called sanitary protection.

menstrual calendar a calendar on which the beginning and end of the menstrual cycle is marked month after month. This device enables the woman to establish the occurrence of ovulation (presumably the most favourable time for impregnation) as well as her safe period when intercourse is not likely to result in conception. It is also of use in detecting irregularities in the cycle, such as an exceptional delay or an extra heavy flow, that may be an indication of a physical ailment that needs attention.

menstrual cramps spasms in the pelvic region produced by contraction of uterine muscles during the process of shedding the lining of the uterine wall, or endometrium, during menstruation. The cramps cause discomfort or pain, especially in the lower back, but are usually less severe after childbirth.

menstrual cycle the female fertility cycle, which begins the first day of one menstrual period, followed in about 2 weeks by ovulation, then continues for another 2 weeks until the first day of the following menstrual period. The cycle occurs between puberty and menopause except for periods of pregnancy. On the average it lasts about 28 to 30 days but can vary from 27 to 35 or 40 (or, rarely, over 100) days.

menstrual disorders disorders associated with menstruation, resulting in many instances from a combination of physical conditions with emotional factors such as internal conflicts, inhibitions, and guilt feelings towards sex instilled by parents.

menstrual extraction an abortion procedure in which the contents of the womb including the fertilized egg are removed by suction. This method may be used when conception has just occurred or when it has not been fully confirmed.

menstrual flow the loss of blood, mucus, and discarded cells of the endometrium. During the fertile years of the life of a normal woman, she menstruates between 300 and 500 times (depending upon periods missed during pregnancies). Each menstrual period lasts between 3 and 7 days and the amount of vaginal discharge measures between 6 and 8 ounces. The actual amount of blood loss per day is seldom more than 15 millilitres, or

one-half ounce, the remainder being cellular debris and other substances.

menstrual fluid in whisky a term referring to the old wives' tale that a woman can win any man she wants by dropping a bit of her menstrual fluid in his whisky.

menstrual hut a shelter at the edge of a village reserved for women of the community who are menstruating. Menstruating women are thus isolated from the family and other members of the village for a period of about 1 week every month. The practice is followed in some Third World communities and at one time was used by some Native American nations.

menstrual migraines migraine headaches that tend to occur periodically in cycles that follow the menstrual cycles, beginning during the premenstrual days or just after the start of the menstrual flow.

menstrual period another term for menstruation.

menstrual regulation a euphemism for a very early abortion in which suction is used to clean out the contents of the uterus before the next period is due. It often is performed before the woman even knows if she is pregnant.

menstrual sponge a small natural or synthetic sponge tied to a string that is inserted into the vagina to absorb the menstrual flow. It is removed by pulling on the string and may be washed, squeezed dry, and used over again. Menstrual sponges are not commonly used in North America or Britain.

menstrual weeks a system of calculating the length of a pregnancy from the end of the last menstrual period (LMP), or 40 weeks. Technically, the second trimester begins 13fi weeks after the last menstrual period.

menstruation a discharge of blood and tissue from the lining of the uterus, which has been built up in anticipation of implantation of a fertilized egg. If pregnancy does not take place, the menstrual period usually occurs once a month and lasts from 3 to 6 days. Also called menses; monthly period; catamenia. See also PRECOCIOUS MENSTRUATION; VICARIOUS MENSTRUATION

mental masochism a form of sadomasochistic behaviour in which the individual seeks mental rather than physical suffering. It may be a means of showing submission and humiliation without experiencing physical pain.

meretrix an obsolete Latin term for prostitute (from *mereo*, 'I earn'). Derived from it is also the word *meretricious*.

merkin (mur'kən) a wig for the female genitals. It replaces missing hair or covers hair of one colour with hair of another colour. For example, in a country of mainly dark-haired people a prostitute may wear a blond merkin to be unusual and therefore more desirable to her clients. The term is of unknown origin; from the 16th to the 18th century, it was used to refer to a woman's natural pubic hair, and to the female genitals themselves.

mesoderm a third layer of primordial germ cells of the preembryonic conceptus, which develops between the endoderm and the ectoderm layers. It gives rise to tissues that become bone, muscle, blood and blood vessels, and connective tissue.

mesonephric duct a paired tubule of the embryo that forms a part of the urinary bladder and urethra. The ureter grows from the lower end. In the male it evolves into the vas deferens and the epididymis. In the female, the structure becomes a vestigial set of cordlike tissues near the ovary.

mesovarium a short fold of the broad ligament of the female pelvic cavity that helps suspend the ovary on either side.

Messalina complex another, seldom used, term for nymphomania—from the indiscriminate sexual appetite of Valeria Messalina, wife of Emperor Claudius.

metafemale another term for superfemale. See SEX-CHROMOSOME ABBERRATIONS: SUPERFEMALE

M.F. a common abbreviation of the vulgar slang term 'motherfucker.'

mibolerone a sex hormone used as a birth-control drug for dogs. The progesterone-like drug is given to female dogs to prevent oestrus.

microIF a microimmunofluorescence test used to identify specific antibodies in the diagnosis of certain types of sexually transmissible diseases, such as lympho-granuloma venereum.

micronucleus one of two nuclei found in the cells of some organisms in which one nucleus, the larger of the two, controls cell growth and metabolism and the smaller, the micronucleus, functions in reproductive activities.

microorchidism a congenital condition of abnormally small testes. The average size of the male testis is about 2 inches in length and 1 inch in width, with a weight of slightly less than one-half ounce.

microsperm an abnormally small spermatozoon.

micturition an alternative term for urination or the passing of urine (Latin *micturire*, 'to make water').

middle germ layer an alternative term for the mesoderm, or layer of embryonic germinal tissue that evolves between the endoderm and ectoderm.

middle leg a euphemism for penis.

midpain an intermenstrual pain, such as the pain experienced by some women about midway between menstrual periods when the ovarian follicle ruptures to release an ovum. also called Mittelschmerz.

midwife a person who is not a doctor but is trained to assist women in childbirth. Today midwives are usually female nurses, who work under the supervision of a doctor. Largely as a result of the emphasis on natural childbirth and the participation of the father in preparation for the birth process, there is a trend towards home deliveries by midwives, with a doctor in attendance.

MIF abbreviation for mullerian inhibiting factor, a substance secreted by the embryonic testis that helps determine the differentiation of the genital ducts into either male or female offspring.

Mignon delusion a child's false belief that he or she is living with foster parents and that the real family is rich and famous. This delusion is most often observed in children with schizophrenic tendencies, and is sometimes interpreted as a defence against aggressive impulses occurring in the oedipal period. Mignon was a child character who suffered from a similar delusion in Goethe's novel *Wilhelm Meister's Apprenticeship*.

migration of the ovum the passage of the ovum from the ovary to the uterus (through the tubes).

migratory gonorrhoeal polyarthritis a form of arthritis in which a number of joints are affected in succession before the condition finally settles in one or several specific areas. The disorder appears in patients with gonorrhoea a few days to a few weeks after the first signs of gonorrhoeal urethritis. The person has a moderate fever for a few days with pain, mainly in the larger joints of the body. In prolonged episodes, there is remission in sites previously affected as new areas become involved. After the swelling subsides in a joint, the skin over the joint may peel. The usual treatment is with antibiotics.

mikvah a Hebrew term for a ritual bath for a woman who has ended her menstrual period. In some Orthodox Jewish communities, a woman is expected to go to the mikvah after her menstrual period before she can resume sexual relations with her husband.

milk incest an incestuous relationship based on sharing the same milk. Among Muslims, marriage is forbidden between a man and his wet nurse and between a man and a woman who have been breast-fed by the same woman. The same incest taboo has been found among the Mende of West Africa, the Samaritans, the Kopts of Egypt, Eastern Orthodox Christians, and Italian Roman Catholics.

milking the penis a slang phrase sometimes used to describe the envelopment of the penis by the walls of the vagina during the orgasmic phase of sexual intercourse.

To milk a man is also a prostitute's slang term for trying to find out whether he has a venereal disease by massaging the penis to see whether a suspicious discharge might appear.

milk line a ridge of tissue that develops on the front of the embryo from the arm pits to the thighs around the sixth week of gestation. During the following 3 weeks, the milk-line ridge retreats from the original length to a small area of the chest from which the mammary glands evolve. The nipple buds form somewhat later on the primordial breasts. Any supernumerary breasts usually appear along the original milk line.

milky way a colloquial term for the female breasts.

minge a slang term for the external female genitals, ultimately of Romany origin.

minitheatres an American term for small cinemas that specialize in showing erotic films. One survey found that they attracted mainly young heterosexual couples. In the 1980s, the trend was towards renting videos of erotic films to be shown in the privacy of one's home.

mint an aromatic plant with reputed aphrodisiac properties when used as a flavouring for foods and beverages or when applied to the body. Its erotic value is mentioned in Shakespeare's *The Winter's Tale*.

misbegotten a derogatory term referring to an illegitimate child.

miscarriage spontaneous expulsion of the foetus before it is able to survive outside the uterus—usually before the 28th week of pregnancy. Miscarriages occur in 10 to 15 percent of pregnancies, and in about 50 percent of cases the foetus is found to be clearly defective.

miscegenation marriage or cohabitation between a man and a woman of different 'races'; a mixture of 'races' by interbreeding. Historically, miscegenation resulted from slavery and wars, as in the conquest of Spain by the Moors, and cohabitation between slave and master in Colonial America. (Latin *miscere*, 'to mix,' and *genus*, 'race.')

misogamy a morbid hatred of marriage based in many cases on a fear of sexual intimacy or inability to undertake the responsibilities of married life. Some psychoanalysts cite an unresolved Oedipus complex as a major cause.

misogyny a morbid hatred of women, an extreme mental state with many possible causes. Women may hate women because they wish to be men or because they detest effeminacy—attitudes that can sometimes be traced to their father's disappointment when the mother gave birth to a girl. Men may hate women because of a conflict or disappointment generated by homosexual tendencies or by a frustrated desire to become a woman. According to psychoanalysts, both types of hatred may be the result of an unresolved Oedipus complex.

misopaedia a morbid hatred of children, which some psychiatrists attribute to an unconscious tendency to regard the children as the consequence of incestuous relations.

missionary position the man-above position in intercourse. The term originated in Polynesia, where missionaries approved this position even though the Polynesians themselves preferred other postures. It is the most common position in Western societies and has the advantage of easy entrance and facilitation of kissing, caressing, and impregnation, though it restricts active participation on the part of the woman. (The old Latin term was *figura veneris prima*, freely translating as 'the primary position for sexual intercourse.')

Miss Xylophone a homosexual slang term for an extremely skinny male (whose rib cage is visible).

mistress a woman who provides sexual services and companionship to a man who may or may not be married, usually on a long-term basis and in return for financial support and a place to live. In some cases the relationship involves a deep and lasting exchange of affection, understanding, and sharing that resembles marriage. In the past, mistresses have been known as paramours and kept women.

mitogen a substance that causes cells to

divide by mitosis. The substance is related to lymphokine, a lymphocyte-transforming factor, or a chemical that induces white blood cells to produce clones to serve as antibodies in the person's immune system.

mitogenetic radiation a force produced by cells undergoing division by mitosis that is believed to radiate to nearby cells, inducing them to reproduce by mitosis. Also called Gurvich radiation.

Mittelschmerz (mit'elshmerts; German, 'middle pain') a type of abdominal pain that is experienced by some women midway between menstrual periods. It is caused by a reaction of the peritoneal membrane tissues lining the abdominal cavity to a chemical stimulation that may accompany the release of an ovum from an ovary. The peritoneum is quite sensitive to irritations caused by contact with misplaced body chemicals.

mixed chancre a genital sore resulting from more or less simultaneous infections of syphilis and the soft chancre germ.

mixed gonadal dysgenesis a condition in which a person is born with both male and female genitalia, although fertility as a male or female is rarely possible. In most cases, the child is raised as a girl. The testes are removed in childhood because of the risk of testicular cancer and of embarrassment to the individual if male sex hormones begin producing masculine characteristics at puberty.

mixoscopia a form of voyeurism in which orgasm is achieved by watching a loved one engage in sexual relations with another person.

mixoscopia bestialis a sexual disorder, or paraphilia, in which observation of intercourse between a person and an animal is the preferred or exclusive method of achieving orgasm.

mobility of libido a Freudian term for the transfer of sexual energy from one 'object' to another—that is, from one person or one part of the body to another. Sexual excitement may therefore be described as a 'movable feast' (to use Hemingway's expression).

modesty in the sexual sense, the tendency to conceal one's sex organs and other parts of the body such as thighs and buttocks from public view. In Western society this tendency usually reaches a peak at puberty, when young people are self-conscious and easily embarrassed about exposing their bodies. Societies vary greatly on this score—for example, though the Mundurucu women of

Brazil wear no clothing at all, they are taught to avoid any provocative or indecorous posture; and in the Kwoma society of New Guinea, boys are taught to fix their eyes on the ground in the presence of a woman, and are punished if they stare at a woman's genitals.

mohel a Hebrew word for the individual who performs the religious rite of circumcision on a male infant 8 days after birth.

moist warts an alternative term for condylomata acuminata, a venereal wart transmitted by the human papilloma virus.

molar pregnancy a pregnancy that results in the development of a hydatid mole from the trophoblastic stage of embryonic development. The chorionic villi undergo cystic degeneration, and the hydatid mole that develops must be removed because of the risk that it will evolve into a cancerous tumour. Meanwhile, the usual signs of pregnancy are present in the woman, but in an exaggerated form. The uterus grows rapidly, morning sickness occurs but is very severe, blood levels of chorionic gonadotropins are extremely high, and the woman's blood pressure is elevated.

molestation a sexual offence in which advances are made against the will of the victim, or, in legal terms, 'without lawful consent.' The advances usually involve sexual fondling and sometimes intercourse, and the victim may be a child or mentally retarded person.

Mollie houses clubs that existed in 18th-century England for men who met in women's clothing for homosexual parties.

molluscum contagiosum a skin condition caused by a large 'pox' virus and characterized by formation of raised, orange-pink papules containing peculiar encapsulated bodies (molluscous bodies) on the external genitalia, thighs, buttocks, and lower abdomen. The disorder may be treated by curetting or by applying an orange stick dipped in acid to the centre of the lesion. The predominant mode of transmission is sexual.

momism a colloquial term coined by the novelist Philip Wylie for a pattern of excessive care and attention showered on children by overprotective mothers (and in some cases fathers). Attitudes of this kind may deprive these children of a full chance to become emotionally independent and mature. In many cases momism may be a compensation for unspoken rejection of the child, or a substitute for sexual satisfaction in the marriage.

Ⓜ

Monilia a former name for a genus of fungi now called *Candida albicans.*

moniliasis a former name for candidiasis. Also called *monilial vaginitis.*

monkey love a tendency to express love for a child or other person by showering him with excessive attention, anticipating his or her every need or desire. (Monkey love is a literal translation of the German word *Affenliebe.*)

monogamous homosexual relationship an exclusive, sometimes lasting, sexual relationship between male homosexuals or, more frequently, female homosexuals. The difference seems to stem from the fact that male homosexuals tend to be more promiscuous than female homosexuals and that female homosexuals usually have a greater capacity to be faithful to a single partner.

monogamy marriage with only one person at a time. See also SERIAL MONOGAMY.

monopedomania a sexual variant in which gratification is sought through intercourse with one-legged partners, who are usually women. This type of amputation fetishism is widespread (judging by the amount of letters to the editor of publications such as *Forum*) and is not limited to our age. Montaigne wrote, 400 years ago 'It is a common proverb in Italy that anyone who has not lain with a limping woman does not know the perfect pleasure of Venus' *(Essays,* III, xi).

monorchidism a condition of having only one testis in the scrotum. The second testis may be undescended and therefore remaining in the abdomen or be missing entirely, either as a result of a developmental anomaly or because of surgical excision for testicular cancer.

monosexuality the state of having the physical characteristics of one sex only, which is normal for human beings and all other mammals. The term is sometimes used in contradistinction to bisexuality, ambisexuality, intersex, and hermaphroditism.

monosomy an individual possessing only one member of a pair of chromosomes. An example is a female with Turner's syndrome, characterized by the effects of only one X chromosome rather than the normal XX chromosome pair for a female.

monospermy the fertilization of an ovum by a single unaided spermatozoon.

monosyllable a euphemism for any offensive monosyllabic word, such as the numbers 3, 5, 6, 7, 16, 18, 22, and 26 in the TABOONESS RATING OF DIRTY WORDS. See this entry. See also DIVINE MONOSYLLABLE.

monotrophy a phenomenon in which a mother is able to bond to only one infant at a time. Studies by Klaus and Kennell show that if a mother leaves the hospital with one twin earlier than the other, she may not feel the baby taken home later is hers. The second twin may be abused or neglected and may fail to thrive. Monotrophy also is used to explain the tradition of dressing twins alike, making them seem as one in the mother's unconscious.

monozygotic twins identical twins that have developed from a single zygote. Monozygotic twins may develop in one of three different ways, each process following a single fertilization of one ovum. In one mechanism, the zygote may form two blastomeres that separate and form two implantations on the wall of the uterus with two placentas and two sets of foetal membranes. A second process allows one blastomere to form two separate cell masses with separate amnions but one chorion and one fused placenta. In the third alternative, one blastomere produces two inner cell masses with two embryos sharing one placenta, one amnion, and one chorion. In monozygotic twinning, both infants will be of the same sex, whereas dizygotic twins are formed from multiple ovulations and may be of the same or of opposite sexes. Monozygotic twinning is regarded as a random event, but dizygotic twinning appears to be asociated with an inherited trait that is carried by the female offspring of mothers of twins. Twins occur in about 1 percent of all births in North America, and approximately 30 percent of twins are monozygotic. The frequency of twin births is highest among black women and lowest among Oriental women. Monozygotic twins are usually smaller than dizygotic twins, have a greater incidence of congenital defects, and a higher risk of death as foetuses or newborn infants. While sharing a placenta, one monozygotic twin may grow more rapidly than the other and at the expense of the smaller twin, which becomes weaker and more likely to acquire birth defects. Maternal complications of anaemia, eclampsia, haemorrhage, and premature delivery occur much more frequently in multiple pregnancies. Like twins, triplets can develop from one or more than one fertilized ovum.

mons pubis a cushion of fat that covers the symphysis pubis, or bony prominence of the genital area where the left and right pubic bones of the human female meet.

monster myths old wives' tales and folklore regarding the causes of severe birth defects. A common misconception is that sexual intercourse during menstruation can result in deformed offspring, a notion possibly based on ancient sacred writings that 'menstrous women shall bring forth monsters.' The misshapen Vulcan of mythology was believed to have been sired during menstruation. Chiron the Centaur, according to mythology, was the result of intercourse between a human and an animal, thereby creating a hybrid being.

mons veneris an alternative term for mons pubis.

moon to expose one's buttocks to passersby as a form of exhibitionism. Car windows are a favoured frame for the picture thus presented.

moral masochism a psychoanalytical term for an unconscious need for punishment by authority figures representing the father. According to Freud, this need stems from the childhood desire for passive intercourse with the father, which has been blocked and transformed into a desire to be beaten by him.

morning-after pill a colloquial name for the drug diethylstilbesterol (DES), which is taken by mouth to cause the uterus to expel any ovum that has been fertilized. The drug must be taken within three days of unprotected intercourse. DES has been linked with cancer in the female offspring of women taking it. DES is used primarily to prevent pregnancy after rape.

morning drop a greyish-white drop of mucus fluid appearing at the orifice of the penis. If this occurs regularly within 3 days after intercourse, a medical examination is usually recommended, because it may be a symptom of gonorrhoea.

morning erection an erection commonly experienced by men upon awakening, usually because of the pressure of a full bladder.

morning sickness episodes of nausea experienced by some women in the morning, or sometimes all day, during the early months of pregnancy, and in some cases throughout pregnancy. The medical term is nausea gravidarum.

morphine a narcotic with actions that can aggravate symptoms of an enlarged prostate, leading to urinary retention and a need for repeated use of catheterization to drain the urinary bladder.

morphological sex the form and structure of the genital organs, which is usually used as a criterion of sex determination (male, female, hermaphrodite), because these morphological characteristics generally coincide with chromosomal, gonadal, and hormonal characteristics, and also with the individual's gender role.

mort douce (mô′do͞os′; French, 'sweet death') death occurring during intercourse. See DEATH IN THE SADDLE. The term is also used to describe the sense of blissful tranquillity that follows sexual orgasm, and it is sometimes a synonym for euthanasia.

mother the female parent. See BACHELOR MOTHER; BIOLOGICAL MOTHER; GENETIC MOTHER; GESTATIONAL MOTHER; GREAT MOTHER; HOMOSEDUCTIVE MOTHER; PHALLIC MOTHER; SURROGATE MOTHER.

Mother is also a common abbreviation of the vulgar American slang term 'motherfucker'.

mother archetype the primeval concept of the mother which, according to Jung, resides in the racial unconscious, as evidenced by the fact that the mother figure occupies an important place in ancient mythology.

mother complex a strong emotional attachment to the mother, usually with sexual overtones.

mother figure an alternative for the more technical term 'mother surrogate.'

mother fixation an inordinate attachment to the mother, sometimes so strong that the individual, male or female, is unable to establish sexual relations or fall in love with a woman.

motherfucker a very common vulgar American slang term that may be (a) an insult and expression of contempt, (b) an expletive of anger, not necessarily directed at an individual, (c) an affectionate or complimentary address, or (d) a synonym for a tough problem or a rough situation, but may have many other connotations. The term ranks number 1 in the TABOONESS RATING OF DIRTY WORDS. See this entry.

mothering a process in which the mother or mother surrogate (and the father as well) provides an infant or child with physical care, emotional warmth and support, and a sense of security and self-worth believed to be essential for normal development. Some individuals develop such a lasting need for mothering that they have an excessive urge to be mothered by their spouse or sex partner.

mothering one a term coined by H.S. Sullivan for a person—male or female—who provides the basic care, love, and protection required by an infant or child.

mother instinct an alternative term for maternal instinct.

motherliness a non-gender-related ability of an adult to show gentleness, love, and understanding in a relationship with another individual, usually applied in an adult-child relationship. The trait is acquired from the adult's own early experiences with a mother figure, and despite the sexist connotation it is not a characteristic only of women.

mother love the deep affection and 'tender loving care' displayed by the mother towards her children. Mother love is first manifested in meeting the physical and emotional needs of the infant, who is almost completely dependent on the mother. It later takes the form of providing support, encouragement, and guidance in helping the growing child to meet his or her changing needs.

mother-son incest sexual relations between mother and son, which seems to be considerably rarer than father-daughter or brother-sister incest. This form of incest may be associated with absence of a father, marital conflict, a morally defective home, alcoholism, antisocial behaviour, or mental illness on the part of one or both partners.

mother surrogate a mother substitute, or mother figure, such as a sister, aunt, nurse, teacher, foster mother, or father, who carries out the responsibilities of the natural mother.

motoro a term for night-crawling or sleep-crawling on Mangaia, a Polynesian island.

mount of Venus a term derived from the literal translation of the Latin *mons veneris*, a medical name for a cushion of fat covering the body of the female pubis. In some women, it is the most prominent part of the external genitalia.

mouse unit a unit of measurement of gonadotropins in humans. It represents the amount of gonadotropin in a sample of human urine that when injected into an immature mouse will cause the weight of the uterus of the mouse to double in 4 days. As the weight of the mouse uterus is not determined before the injection of gonadotropin hormones, the comparison is based on the known weight of an untreated immature mouse uterus.

mouth-genital contact sexual activity in which the mouth is used to stimulate the partner's genital organs—an alternative term for orogenital contact.

mouth music a slang term for oral sex.

mucus plug cervical mucus that is secreted by cells in the palmate folds. The amount and consistency of the mucus is influenced by sex hormones. During ovulation, the cervical mucus enhances the movement of spermatozoa into the uterus. At other times, as during pregnancy, the mucus forms a seal to protect the uterus against invasion from disease organisms.

muff diving a slang term for cunnilingus.

Mujerados male tranvestites, or 'men-women,' who often served as shamans in Native American nations living in New Mexico.

mullerian ducts the paramesonephric ducts of the embryo that evolve into the female reproductive system of fallopian tubes, uterus, and vagina. Vestiges of the ducts are found in the male as bits of tissue in the prostate gland and on the testes.

Muller's tubercle a fusion of two mullerian ducts that occurs in the ninth week of gestation in the female embryo. The fused portion evolves into the uterus and vagina while the attached, unfused portions develop into the fallopian tubes.

multipara (multip'ere) a woman who has had two or more pregnancies resulting in live births.

multiparous labia the labia of women who have borne children, which differ from those of women who have not given birth. Parous, or multiparous, labia are larger, more pendulous, and often contain varicose veins. During the plateau phase of sexual intercourse, multiparous labia majora become enlarged and oedematous or heavy with fluid. The multiparous labia minora undergo a colour change to a burgundy red during the plateau phase.

multiple family therapy a form of family therapy in which members of the family meet with two or more therapists at the same time.

multiple marriage any form of marriage in which there is more than one wife or husband, such as polygyny or polyandry. Also called polygamy; plural marriage.

multiple mothering care of children by several mother surrogates in an institution such as an adoption centre or a Kibbutz. Studies show that adopted children usually thrive as well as home-reared children if the surrogates are warm and caring.

multiple orgasm the ability to experience repeated orgasms without a refractory period between them. Usually, only women are physically capable of multiple orgasms without a refractory period; nearly all men require a recovery period of several minutes to several days between orgasms, depending upon the individual man. Women are most likely to achieve multiple orgasms after they reach the age of 35, the reputed peak of their sexual potency. Multiple orgasms also occur frequently in pregnant women in their second trimester when there is increased vasocongestion. In some women multiple orgasms appear to blend into one continuous response of up to a minute's duration.

murphy game, the a British slang term for the practice of enticing a customer with the prospect of a prostitute's services but then robbing him or beating him up.

muscle a euphemism for penis.

mushrooms fungi that have been believed to be a sexual stimulant—a belief that may have originated with the ancient Arabs. In the early 17th century, mushrooms simmered in oil were served as an erotic delicacy.

mutilation referring to genital mutilation by others or by oneself (self-mutilation).

muton the smallest portion of a DNA molecule whose alteration can result in a mutation.

mutual absorption a term referring to the Tantric and Taoist view that the man and woman should 'absorb each other's vital juices' during sexual intercourse. Absorption of the woman's secretions, or 'yin-essence', during prolonged sexual contact is said to counteract the weakening effect of loss of semen, or 'yang-essence,' in the male. Similarly a woman is believed to be strengthened by the 'yang-essence' when a man ejaculates.

mutuality the capacity to share erotic pleasure with another person, as in 'pleasuring' each other (mutual stimulation and arousal), mutual masturbation, and reaching a climax simultaneously (mutual orgasm). Mutuality also includes the sharing of feelings, affection, love, and thoughts that make the sexual relationship a meaningful and moving experience.

mutual masturbation sexual activity in which two or more individuals manipulate each other's genitals at the same time for purposes of sexual excitement and gratification. Mutual masturbation is common among both heterosexual and homosexual partners.

mutual orgasm orgasm reached by both partners at the same time. Many couples prefer mutual orgasm, claiming that it affords them the greatest enjoyment and satisfaction. However, preoccupation with this goal may

mar sexual enjoyment, and there may be some advantage in having the woman achieve several separate orgasms first, the last of which may be made to coincide with the man's ejaculation. Also called simultaneous orgasm.

mutual pleasuring a newer term for sexual activity in which each partner stimulates the other's genitals, usually manually, either as a prelude to intercourse or as a form of sex play that is gratifying in itself. The older term is mutual masturbation.

myoma a benign tumour of muscle tissue. One form of myoma, a fibromyoma, develops in the uterus of more than one fourth of all women over the age of 35. Myomas tend to grow rapidly during pregnancy or after oestrogen therapy and tend to atrophy with menopause. Uterine myomas are responsible for many complaints of excessive or erratic menstruation. They are commonly removed by D & C procedures.

myomectomy the surgical removal of a myoma.

myometrium the muscular tissue of the uterus, forming the bulk of uterine tissue. It is composed of bundles of muscle fibres intermingled with blood and lymph vessels and nerves. During pregnancy, the muscle fibres grow larger and become better developed. The myometrial fibres continue into the fallopian tubes. (Greek *mys*, 'muscle,' and *metra* 'womb.')

myotonia the increased muscle tension that accompanies sexual excitement. The condition affects both voluntary and involuntary muscles of the body. The muscles tend to contract rapidly but are slow to relax during a state of myotonia.

mysophilia a pathological interest in filth, often expressed as a paraphilia in which contact with a dirty partner or a partner wearing filthy clothes enhances sexual excitement.

myth of motherhood an argument supported by some researchers contending that motherhood is not instinctive but a result of the fact that the child becomes attached to the mother at infancy because she is the source of its milk, and the relationship, therefore, is frankly materialistic. This argument is reinforced by animal experiments in which males and virgin females exhibit maternalistic behaviour with pups in the absence of their mother.

M

nabothian cyst a cyst that can occur in the nabothian gland of the uterine cervix. The cyst, which is generally harmless, is firm and white. It tends to occur in the cervix of women who have borne children.

nail biting the compulsion to chew on one's fingernails, even down to the quick, as a means of discharging tension, releasing hostility, or in some cases as a masturbation equivalent.

nakedness fear an alternative for the technical term gymnophobia.

nameless crime an obsolete term for sodomy.

nancy boy a slang term for male homosexual.

narcissism extreme self-love based on an idealized self-image. The term is derived from a Greek myth in which a youth named Narcissus fell in love with his own reflection in a pool of water. The trait is common among the immature and neurotic. See also BODY NARCISSISM; PRIMARY NARCISSISM.

narcissistic object choice a Freudian term for the tendency to choose a sexual or marital partner who is a mirror image of oneself. A choice of this kind is an expression of self-love.

narrotophilia obsession with sexual stimulation through the reading of erotic narrations.

nates an alternative term for the pair of buttocks.

National Childbirth Trust (NCT) an organization that runs classes to prepare parents physically and emotionally for childbirth and offers informal postnatal support and advice.

National Fertility Studies surveys conducted in 1965 and again in 1970 of approximately 5,000 American women. One of the results showed that the overall frequency of intercourse per month increased during the 5

years between interviews.

national indoor game a colloquial American term meaning intercourse—usually as 'to play the national indoor game.'

nativism the theory that sexual variations, such as homosexuality, stem from inborn rather than learned or conditioned influences.

natural child an old-fashioned term for an illegitimate child, implying that the child is produced by a natural, though illicit, sexual relationship.

natural childbirth a method of delivery described by the British physician Grantly Dick-Read in his book *Childbirth Without Fear* (1942). He held that the pain experienced in giving birth is almost entirely the result of fear and tension, and therefore advocated education and training based on an understanding of the process of childbirth, learning to coordinate breathing with relaxation, and exercises that would develop the muscles used in the final stage of labour. The result was a 'natural' process in which drugs and anaesthetics were completely eliminated.

natural extension a euphemism for an unnatural, that is, artificial extension of the penis, consisting of a reusable rubber sleeve that extends the penis by 2 or 3 inches. Also called medical extension or, plainly penis extension.

natural family planning (NFP) controlling the number and spacing of pregnancies through natural procedures as distinguished from artificial contraceptive devices or drugs. In the past, the principal natural procedures were the rhythm and calendar methods, but today the emphasis is on various physical signs, such as body-temperature changes and consistency of the cervical mucus, which indicate when ovulation is about to occur, so that the woman can avoid sexual intercourse during the fertile days.

natural fertility the reproductive performance of a person or group of persons in the absence of contraceptives, induced abortion, or any other form of birth control.

natural homosexual period a term occasionally applied to the stage of psychosexual development preceding the onset of puberty, when boys tend to socialize with boys and men, and girls frequently have crushes on girls of their own age or on adults of the same sex, such as teachers. The period ends with the awakening of heterosexual interest in adolescence.

naturism a health movement with an emphasis on nude sunbathing, sports, and club activities. The term naturism was first adopted in Germany at the beginning of this century to distinguish the movement from the cult of nudism, which had come to have sexual connotations. Naturist clubs (also called sun clubs or open-air clubs) are organized on a family basis.

nausea gravidarum the so-called morning sickness associated with pregnancy. The symptoms are not necessarily a sign of pregnancy, and they do not always occur in the morning. Some women experience nausea and vomiting in the evening or late afternoon rather than the morning, and some encounter the problem at any time of the day. Various factors that may contribute to the feelings of nausea include hormonal changes, allergies, viral or other infections, emotional disturbances, and reactions to the sight or smell of certain foods or certain nonfood odours, particularly tobacco smoke and petrol. Nausea gravidarum is rather common during the first trimester. However, severe protracted vomiting during pregnancy, a condition known as hyperemesis gravidarum, requires hospitalization.

navel the depression near the centre of the abdomen that is a vestige of the umbilical cord to which the offspring was attached during foetal life.

naviculans an old Latin term for clitoris (*navicula*, 'boat').

necking milder forms of petting, consisting of such activities as hugging, light kissing, and manual stimulation of the girl's or woman's breasts through her clothes. Necking is approximately equivalent to light petting.

neck of the womb the cervix, which means neck in Latin,—that is, the narrow portion

of the uterus or womb that opens into the vagina.

neck stretching a Burmese custom in which women of the Padaung society placed ring after ring round their necks until the necks were double their normal length. The object was to increase a woman's sexual attractiveness.

necromania a pathological desire for sexual relations with a corpse, usually accompanied by a morbid interest in everything related to dead bodies, such as autopsies, funerals, morgues, and cemeteries. See also NECROPHILIA.

necrophilia a severe but rare sexual disorder, or paraphilia, in which sexual excitement is derived from contact with female (and sometimes male) corpses removed from graves. Necrophiles are almost always psychotic males who have no interest in normal sexual relations. In some cases they themselves kill the victims before assaulting or mutilating them. See also NECROMANIA.

necrophilic fantasies mental images of corpses or of sexual relations with a corpse. Necrophiles frequently depend on such fantasies as a means of achieving sexual excitement. Some prostitutes simulate a lifeless appearance in order to satisfy necrophilic clients.

necrospermia an abnormal condition in which a sample of male sperm contains spermatozoa but a high percentage of the sperm lack motility.

negative-feedback loop a natural physiological system that maintains sex hormones at a relatively constant level in an individual. The level of testosterone in a male is controlled by the luteinizing hormone which in turn is regulated by the luteinizing-hormone-releasing factor of the hypothalamus. The hypothalamus monitors the testosterone level in the blood and is thus guided in the amount of luteinizing-hormone-releasing factor to produce.

negative nuclear sex a term used to describe the absence of chromatin material in a normal female tissue cell. When there are two X chromosomes present, one usually is inactivated and appears as a Barr body, or easily stained chromatin material, on a microscope slide. Most, but not all, patients with Turner's syndrome show a negative nuclear-sex pattern because they possess only one X chromosome per cell. The reason that some test as positive nuclear sex is unexplained.

negative Oedipus a psychoanalytical term for an Oedipus complex in reverse: The son experiences erotic feelings towards his father instead of his mother, and the daughter becomes erotically attached to the mother instead of the father. Also called inverted Oedipus.

negative sexual conditioning a cultural indoctrination about sexual activities, particularly during the formative years of a person's life, with emphasis on evil, painful, or other adverse aspects. Negative sexual conditioning is associated with sexual inadequacies in adult life.

neonatal period the period from birth to 2 to 3 weeks of age, during which the newborn must make the transition from the warmth and security of the womb to independent survival. It is a period when the infant must be well protected from infection, and from anxieties as well, through the loving and nurturing care of both the mother and the father.

neoplasm of the ovaries any tumour, cancerous or noncancerous, involving the tissues of the female ovaries. The tumour can result in a change in hormonal secretions that causes changes in the sexual characteristics of the individual, either primary or secondary.

nervi erigentes sacral nerves that when stimulated produce an erection of the penis.

nether eyebrow a 19th-century slang term for pubic hair.

Netherlands a Shakespearean euphemism for the vaginal area. See also HOLLAND.

nether mouth an obsolete slang term for (a) anus or (b) vagina.

neuroendocrine pertaining to an effect on an organ of the body produced by the interaction of nerve fibres and hormones. Many of the sexual activities of humans involve neuroendocrine functions because of the close links between the hypothalamus of the brain and the pituitary gland. The hypothalamus can literally turn off and on the sex hormones of the pituitary gland.

neurosyphilis syphilis infection that has spread into the nervous system, which occurs in about 10 percent of all untreated cases. The first signs of neurosyphilis are usually detected before the patient experiences any symptoms. Laboratory analysis of cerebrospinal fluid shows a significant increase in white blood cells and proteins and a positive reaction to a syphilis blood test. If the spinal cord becomes infected, the patient will usually experience a gradual weakness and wasting of the shoulder and arm muscles, progressing to a condition of paraplegia with loss of sphincter control. Other effects include tremors of the mouth and tongue, visual disturbances, loss of tendon reflexes, pain, and loss of muscular coordination. Pain in the lower limbs is followed by a loss of feeling in the legs so that walking is difficult. Loss of bladder sensation results in either urinary retention with infections or incontinence, or both. Impotence is a common penalty for this sexually-transmissible disease.

new-father blues another term for paternity blues.

new impotence a reported increase in impotence among young men that has been attributed to a feeling of sexual insecurity among males as a result of women's liberation. The reasoning is that 'liberated women' are more sexually demanding, an effect that threatens some men. Authorities believe that the incidence of male impotence has not changed but that more men are admitting they are afflicted and are seeking professional help as a result of the general atmosphere of sexual liberation.

NGU an abbreviation for nongonococcal urethritis

nice a euphemism meaning 'pure' and, especially, abstaining from intercourse—said mainly of a woman. But in Middle English 'nice' meant 'foolish,' from the Latin *nescius,* 'ignorant' (based on *nescire,* 'not to know').

nidation the process whereby a blastocyst burrows into the endometrial lining of the uterus for implantation of the embryo.

night courting a practice in which two people of opposite sex share the same bed without engaging in sexual intercourse. The custom appears to have originated in cold climates, as in Scandinavia, England, and Scotland and preceded the practice of bundling in Colonial America. Somewhat similarly, many Kikuya of Kenya permit the girls of the society to visit their male friends in a special hut, where they eat and sleep together but without full intercourse.

night-crawling a sexual practice in which a young man crawls into bed with a young woman and copulates with her. The custom has been called surreptitious rape by Margaret Mead, but in many cases the visit is invited by the girl in order to get a husband. It has been found in Polynesia and the Philippines, but also among North and South American Indians, where it is usually limited to fondling the girl's genitals. In some of these societies the women are the night-crawlers. Also called sleep-crawling and motoro.

99 a slang term for anal intercourse (patterned on '69'). Also written *ninety-nine*. A synonymous term is '66'.

nipped in the bud a slang term for circumcised as an infant.

nipple bud the embryonic mammary-gland nipple, which begins as a mass of epithelial cells on the milk-line ridge. The nipple bud sends cords of tissue cells downwards into the underlying chest tissue. The 15 to 20 cords eventually become the milk ducts.

nipple cancer a tumour of the nipple and areola of the breast. It usually is associated with a cancer deeper within the breast tissues.

nipple graft the transposition of the nipples of female breasts. The nipple may be moved as part of surgery to correct breast ptosis, or drooping breasts, or in reducing the size of hypertrophic, or over large, breasts. The nipple may be excised and removed separately to a more aesthetic location on the breast, or it may be moved without detaching it from underlying and nearby skin tissue.

nipples the cone-shaped tips of the breasts in both male or female, composed of erectile tissue. In women the nipples are the outlet for the milk ducts, but are also a sensitive erogenous zone, responding to touch, licking or sucking, and become erect during sexual arousal. In men the nipples also become erect during arousal, but there is wide variation in the capacity of pleasure when they are stimulated. See also INVERTED NIPPLE.

nob a slang term for penis.

nocturnal emission involuntary ejaculation occurring in about 80 percent of young males during an erotic dream. Popularly called wet dream.

nocturnal orgasm orgasm reached during a sexual dream. Kinsey has found that 70 percent of the women he sampled have dreams of sexual content, but only 50 percent of that number reached orgasm. Almost 100 percent of the men in his sample had experienced erotic dreams, with nearly 85 percent culminating in orgasm. The incidence of sexual dreams to orgasm reaches a peak in women during their forties, and in men during their teens and twenties.

nocturnal pollution an alternative term for nocturnal emission.

Noguchi's reaction a skin test for syphilis developed by the Japanese-American pathologist Hideyo Noguchi. An extract of killed cultures of several strains of *Treponema pallidum*, the bacterium responsible for syphilis, is injected into the skin. The appearance of a red pimple at the site of the injection is considered a positive reaction to the test.

noma a disease marked by ulcerations of the mucous membranes of the genitalia and other body areas. It affects mainly youngsters but spreads rapidly, causing tissue destruction that results in a disfigurement when healing finally occurs. The tissue destruction is painless.

nonage the period when a person is legally underage for various activities such as driving a car, buying alcohol, making a contract, or getting married.

nonbacterial prostatitis a chronic inflammation of the prostate gland that is not caused by any known microorganism. It is believed to be an autoimmune disease in which the person's own immune system attacks the cells of the prostate. While no cure is known, the condition is often treated with drugs that relieve symptoms, such as ibuprofen, a nonsteroidal anti-inflammatory medication, and drugs that prevent urinary-tract spasms. The patient is advised to drink plenty of water and no alcohol.

nonconscious ideology a term applied to subtle and often unintentional thoughts or comments that may be regarded as 'sexist', such as thinking that a boy may become a doctor but a girl would have to settle for becoming a nurse.

nonconsummation failure to achieve full penetration during attempts at sexual intercourse. The condition, which is bound to cause great distress, may result from muscular spasms on the part of the woman (vaginismus), inability of the man to maintain a lasting erection, or both. The causes are almost always psychological—for example, the man may be afraid of hurting the woman, or may be afflicted with premature ejaculation, and the woman may be afraid of being hurt, which in some cases stems from a former traumatic sexual experience. Treatment involves relaxation of tension, exploration of parental attitudes towards sex, stretching of the vagina, and, in some instances, extended psychotherapy.

nondisjunction an accidental misplacement of a chromosome during either meiosis or mitosis, resulting in a daughter cell with an extra chromosome and a second daughter cell with a missing chromosome. The mishap occurs as the errant chromosome migrates to the wrong side of the dividing cell. Nondisjunction accounts for a number of sex chromosome aberrations, such as Turner's syndrome or Klinefelter's syndrome, or the supermale or superfemale karyotypes.

nonfilarial elephantiasis a swelling of the leg, scrotum, labia, breast, or other part of the body resulting from an obstruction of the lymphatic circulation stemming from a cause other than a filarial infection. A common nonfilarial cause of the disease is a streptococcal infection.

nongonococcal urethritis (NGU) a nonspecific type of urethritis that may be caused by *Chlamydia trachomatis, Ureaplasma urealyticum*, or some pathogen other than *Neisseria gonorrhoeae*, the causative bacterium of gonorrhoea. In men, the symptoms of urethral inflammation usually occur within a week to a month after sexual contact with an infected partner. There also may be difficulty in urination and a pus-formed discharge from the penis. In severe cases, there may be signs of blood in the urine. In women, there may be a vaginal discharge, inflammation of the cervix, pelvic pain, pain on intercourse, and painful, difficult, or frequent urination. Both men and women also may report symptoms of anal or throat inflammations after rectal or oral sex contact. The organisms are usually resistant to penicillin but may respond to other antibiotics, such as tetracycline. Untreated, the disease can progress to urethral strictures and involvement of the bladder, epididymis, and prostate. Complications for women patients may include bartholinitis and infections of the reproductive tract up to and including the fallopian tubes. Children born to women with nongonococcal urethritis often acquire an eye infection of the disease organism while moving through the birth canal. Nongonococcal urethritis is essentially the same as nonspecific urethritis (NSU).

nonmarital sex a term covering both premarital sex and extramarital sex.

nonoxynol-9 a chemical that is present in some vaginal foam spermicides. The substance is reported to be effective in killing the virus responsible for acquired immune deficiency syndrome (AIDS) in laboratory tests. However, it has not been tested on humans and would not be helpful in treating the disease in persons already infected. See also AIDS.

nonreactive phase a term sometimes applied to the phase of the male sexual-response cycle after ejaculation, when there is no response to sexual stimuli of any kind. This period usually lasts for 15 to 30 minutes in younger men, but increases with age. Women do not experience a clearcut nonreactive phase, and may have repeated orgasms.

nonsexual fetish a fetish that is associated with a part of the body that is not directly involved in sexual activity, such as the feet. A nonsexual fetish item may also be inanimate.

nonspecific urethritis (NSU) a painful inflammation of the genital tract often but not always associated with sexual contact. The bacteria involved may be unidentified, and though some of the symptoms resemble those of gonorrhoea, it is not classified as a sexually transmissible disease. Common female symptoms are slight burning or bleeding during urination, and common male symptoms include a discharge from the penis and urinary bleeding. The condition is essentially the same as nongonococcal urethritis (NGU).

nookie a slang term for (a) vagina or (b) intercourse.

nookie bookie a slang term for pimp.

norethindrone a progestin that is used in the treatment of endometriosis and abnormal uterine bleeding. Use of the drug during pregnancy has been reported to result in masculinization of a female foetus.

norgestrel a progestin that has been used in some oral contraceptive formulations. It has been reported to cause masculinization of a female foetus.

norks an Australian slang term for the female breasts. It is thought that the name may come from Norco Co-Operative Ltd. of New South Wales, a company whose brand of butter had a pack with a picture of a generously-uddered cow on it.

normal sexual behaviour a term of varied meanings based on behaviour that is (a) statistically average or usual, (b) customary in a particular culture, (c) desirable or acceptable in a given society, or (d) not abnormal in the sense of not associated with physical or mental illness. It seems true that there is a wider range of what is considered normal (in the sense of acceptable) in our society than there was a generation or so ago (for example, oral sex). Studies such as Kinsey's have also revealed that there is a wider variation in statistically average behaviour than in earlier periods.

NORWICH an acronym formed from 'knickers *o*ff *r*eady *w*hen *I* *c*ome *h*ome', written at the foot of a letter or on the back of an envelope. It seems to have originated with

British soldiers abroad writing home to their wives and girlfriends.

nose rubbing the practice of rubbing noses as a form of greeting or sexual expression, particularly in societies where kissing is not the custom, such as the Trobrianders, Eskimos, Tamil, Andamanese, Thai, and Vietnamese.

NSU an abbreviation for nonspecific urethritis.

nth orgasm the final orgasm in a series of orgasms reported by experienced women who claim that sexual excitement increases with each in the series. After the 'nth,' which may be any number after two or three or 20 orgasms, the female genitalia may have become so sensitive that further intercourse becomes painful rather than pleasurable.

nubile an adjective applied to a girl or young woman who is suited for marriage and sexual relations by reason of age and physical development; marriageable.

nuchal cord an umbilical cord that becomes wrapped around the nucha, or neck, of a foetus. It can occur during life in the uterus or during delivery of the infant. The condition occurs in about one fourth of all deliveries and is remedied by slipping the cord over the head of the infant or by clamping and cutting it to prevent a hazard to the infant.

Nuck canal cyst a cyst that may form in the inguinal region of a female. The site, the canal of Nuck, is a peritoneal pouch that exists in the area of the inguinal canal. The cyst may develop as an inflammation in the upper portion of the labia majora and spread into the canal.

nuclear family the basic family, consisting of parents and children. Studies show that today only about 30 percent of families fit the traditional nuclear pattern, and that nonnuclear families include many types, such as married couples without children or whose children have left home, single persons living alone, single-parent families with children, extended families, and couples living together without being married, and with or without children.

nude-group therapy a controversial form of group therapy based on the notion that emotional release and 'disclosure' can be enhanced by the removal of clothes.

nudism a social movement in which men, women, and children gather in the nude usually for short periods of time, on the theory that exposure of their bodies to air and sunlight promotes health and well-being.

As a general rule, nudity of this kind is not sexually motivated, and sexual activities are pursued in private.

nudity the state of being naked, or unclothed. In the Western world partial or complete nudity is well-accepted in the field of art, but may also be used as a sexual stimulant or enticement, as in the striptease and topless bars. Among religious sects, the Dukhobors expressed disapproval by removing their clothes, even in church. During the 70s, 'streaking' was practised for a time as a form of public protest. Among nonliterate societies, various parts of the body may be exposed (breasts, genitals, or both), but complete nudity has been found in only a few societies such as among the Mundurucu women of Brazil and the Dinka men of the Sudan.

nug an obsolete term for intercourse.

nulliparous labia the labia of women who have not given birth. Such labia differ from those of women who have been mothers, both during sexual excitement and in ordinary circumstances. Nulliparous labia are thinner, flatter, and more widely separated than in the parous woman. During sexual intercourse, the nulliparous labia virtually disappear except that they may become swollen if the plateau phase is prolonged. The nulliparous labia minora acquire a bright red colour during the plateau phase.

number three a 19th-century euphemism for sex ('number one' being urination and 'number two' being defecation).

nunnery a euphemism for brothel, stemming from the early 17th century.

nurturance the provision of nourishment, care, comfort, and protection for the young and helpless.

nuts an American slang term for the scrotum with testes.

nymphae a little-used term for the labia minora, or lesser lips, of the external genitals in the female. In some cultures a *nymphectomy* is performed on the labia minora to reduce sexual responsiveness of women and to ensure faithfulness to their husbands. The operation, however, has been shown to have little effect. Singular: *nympha*. (Greek *Nymphe*, 'bride, nymph.')

nymphitis an inflammation of the labia.

nymphokick a slang term for erotic excitement.

nympholepsy sexual ecstasy or frenzy.

nymphomania a compulsive, insatiable need for sexual stimulation and gratification in women, frequently leading to promiscuity or to masturbation performed several times a day. The disorder may stem from such factors as emotional tension, an inordinate need to be accepted by men, and attempts to deny homosexual tendencies or to disprove frigidity. Many men falsely label any woman a 'nympho' simply because her sexual drive is stronger than their own.

N

O the big O: a slang term for orgasm. The term is used mainly by a woman, referring to her own orgasm.

oats a euphemism for sufficient sexual satisfaction, usually used in the phrase 'get one's oats.'

obesity and breast cancer a term referring to a statistical relationship between female body size and cancer of the breast. Studies indicate that obese women are more likely to develop breast cancer than thin women. Although the cause is unknown, it has been suggested that a hormonal relationship is involved, with fat cells increasing the levels of female sex hormones.

obesity and sexuality a term referring to the relation between overweight, sexual attractiveness, and sexual performance. In our society, obesity in either men or women usually has little sexual appeal. Some grossly overweight individuals, especially men, avoid prolonged intercourse because they find it too tiring. In some African societies obese women are prized to such an extent that girls are placed in 'fattening huts' before marriage.

object cathexis a psychoanalytical term for the investment of sexual, or libidinal, energy in persons, activities, or goals outside the self. Also called object love.

object finding a Freudian term for directing the sexual impulse, or libido, away from the self and towards external 'objects' such as a person, activity, interest, or fetish.

object loss a psychoanalytical term for the actual or threatened loss of love by reason of the death, illness, rejection, or removal of the loved one.

object love an alternative term for object cathexis.

object relations a psychoanalytical term for relationships to persons, activities, or things

through which gratification of sexual or aggressive impulses may be achieved. The gratification may occur directly, as in intercourse, or through indirect expression (sublimation), as in erotic art productions or identifying with a toreador in the bullring.

obscene publications books and especially magazines that specialize in pornographic pictures and articles dealing with the more extreme forms of sexual variance, such as fetishism, bondage, flagellation, urolagnia, and coprophilia.

obscene telephone calls generally anonymous and random phone calls, usually to women, in which the caller obtains sexual gratification by making obscene remarks or, in some cases, simply by heavy breathing. Recipients of these calls generally find them emotionally upsetting as well as revolting. This deviant pattern is termed telephone scatalogia in psychiatry.

obscenity language, gestures, graffiti, pictures, jokes, films, or sexual behaviour (such as exhibitionism and voyeurism) that grossly violate the standards of 'good taste' in a particular society, and are therefore considered repulsive and revolting. See also TABOONESS RATING OF DIRTY WORDS.

obscenity-purity complex an alternative term for puritan complex.

obstetric auscultation a technique for listening to foetal heart sounds or the placental blowing sounds (souffle) by placing a stethoscope on the abdomen of a pregnant woman.

obstetric canal the tunnel through which the foetus passes from the uterus to the vulva during childbirth.

occasional inversion Freud's term for homosexual activity occurring when an individual has no access to the other sex for an extended period, as in prison or in the army.

occupy an obsolete euphemism meaning to have intercourse (with someone, mainly a woman).

Oceanic position a coital position in which the woman lies on her back and the man squats or kneels between her spread legs, and usually embraces her while engaging in intercourse. The position is prevalent in the islands of the Pacific, second only to the missionary position, but variants are also found in Africa, Asia, and South America.

odalisque a female slave or concubine in a harem, especially in the entourage of the Sultan of Turkey. Though he was free to have sexual relations with any odalisque, etiquette required him to limit himself to those who were chosen for him by his mother or presented to him by state officials. (Turkish *oda*, 'room,' in a harem.)

oedema an abnormal amount of fluid in the tissues of a body area. The fluid usually results from inflammation and accumulates in areas between tissue cells. Oedema not infrequently occurs in pregnant women. Face, hands, legs and/or feet may swell, usually towards the end of the day. Oedema of the scrotum is a not unusual result of injury, allergy, a circulatory problem, or an insect bite. Scrotal oedema can cause the scrotum to swell to an enormous size.

oedipal phase an alternative term for oedipal stage.

oedipal situation a term sometimes used in referring to the Oedipus complex.

oedipal stage a psychoanalytical term for the phallic phase of psychosexual development, usually between the ages of 3 and 7, during which the Oedipus complex manifests itself.

Oedipus complex the psychoanalytical doctrine that between the ages of 3 and 7 the son develops a strong incestuous desire for the mother and a feeling of intense rivalry and hostility towards the father. During this period the daughter develops a sexual attachment to the father and rivalry towards the mother. The name is derived from the Greek tragedy by Sophocles in which the hero, Oedipus, unwittingly kills his father and marries his mother. The son and daughter both repress their incestuous desires because they fear retaliation by the parents. In the normal course of events the male Oedipus complex is resolved by the boy's fear of castration and gradual identification with the father, and the female Oedipus complex is resolved by the threat of losing the mother's love, and by

finding fulfilment in the feminine role.

OERT abbreviation for oestrogen replacement therapy, comprising the administration of oestrogen pills, injections, or vaginal creams to counter effect of menopause or postmenopausal problems.

oestradiol a naturally occurring female sex hormone produced by the ovarian follicle. This oestrogenic hormone also can be produced synthetically. It also is produced by the foetal tissues. In the woman, oestradiol plays an important role in the development of female sexual characteristics beginning at puberty. During the menstrual cycle, oestradiol is responsible for the increases in endometrial enlargement before ovulation. The growth of the ducts of the mammary glands depends on the woman's blood levels of oestradiol. In the male, oestradiol is given by injection in the treatment of cancer of the prostate. It also causes atrophy of the male reproductive organs and inhibits the production of spermatozoa. The therapeutic uses of oestradiol in the female include treatment of ovarian insufficiency during menopause, termination of lactation, and building the resistance of young women to vaginal infections.

oestrin an ovarian hormone, subordinate in function to Prolan A and Prolan B, two sex hormones produced in the anterior lobe of the pituitary gland, or hypophysis. Injection of oestrin results in an enlargement of the genitals and an accompanying sexual response. Also called folliculin.

oestriol a placental hormone with oestrogenic effects similar to those of oestradiol. It is synthesized in the liver, placenta, and uterus from oestradiol and other female sex hormones. Oestriol has been used in the treatment of menopause, dysmenorrhoea, and some types of haemorrhages. Efforts to develop an oral contraceptive based on oestriol have not been successful.

oestrogen a term applied to many substances possessing the pharmacological and physiological effects of the ovarian hormone oestradiol. Oestrogens in varying degrees of potency stimulate the development of and maintain the functions of female secondary sexual characteristics. Among the most important natural oestrogens are oestradiol, oestrone, and oestriol. A number of synthetic oestrogens are used in the manufacture of oral contraceptives. The oestrogens are secreted by the ovaries, corpus luteum, adrenal cortex, placenta, and testis. Oestradiol is the most active of the natural oestrogens. In addition to their role in female sexual characteristics, oestrogens help stimulate the proliferation of endometrial tissue during the first half of the menstrual cycle, stimulate the growth of breast tissue, and play an important part in sustaining a pregnancy.

oestrone a female sex hormone and the second most active form of oestrogen, after oestradiol. Oestrone is produced by the oxidation of oestradiol but reportedly has only 30 percent of the potency of oestradiol when used therapeutically.

oestrus a recurring period of sexual excitability and receptivity in most female mammals. The condition can be produced in laboratory animals by injecting them with female sex hormones, which also cause changes in the genitalia. Also called heat; rut.

oestrus behaviour sexual activity manifested by female animals during the fertile period of their particular reproductive cycle. The animal displays a willingness to mate with males of the same species, usually without discriminating among the possible candidates. The period of oestrus behaviour may range from a few hours in some livestock animals to more than a week in cats and dogs. Unlike human fertility cycles that repeat approximately once a month in the female, oestrus cycles in animals may repeat only once or twice a year. Animals that experience oestrus only once a year are designated as monoestrous while those that are in heat more often are polyoestrous.

offshore drilling a slang term for extramarital sex.

Ogino-Knaus rule a method of predicting fertile and infertile periods of a woman's menstrual cycle based on the idea that conception is most likely to occur midway between menstrual periods and is least likely in the days immediately before or after a menstrual period.

olfactory eroticism sexually exciting sensations associated with the sense of smell. The slight odour of vaginal secretions may have a stimulating effect on a male partner. Certain foods such as garlic, onions, and truffles have long been considered aphrodisiacs primarily because of their odour.

oligohydramnios an abnormally small amount of amniotic fluid, usually an amount designated as less than 1,000 millilitres. The condition is associated with certain foetal anomalies, such as a failure of the ears to develop normally. It also is a sign of a foetal disorder, such as a kidney malfunction.

oligomenorrhoea a less-than-average frequency of menstrual periods. The interval between menstruations is sometimes set at cycles of more than 38 days but less than 90 days. Some gynaecologists define oligomenorrhoea in terms of menstrual cycles with intervals of between 42 days and 1 year, particularly in adolescent girls whose menstrual cycles have not yet become regular. In at least 50 percent of cases of oligomenorrhoea, the abnormal menstrual cycles are synchronized with abnormal ovulatory cycles and fertility is not otherwise diminished. In other cases, however, oligomenorrhoea may be caused by a deficiency of pituitary hormones, an excess of androgenic hormones, or a sign that amenorrhoea is becoming established, particularly if the condition follows a relatively long period of regular, normal menstrual cycles.

oligospermia a condition in which the male semen has a deficiency of spermatozoa or an abnormally low sperm density. The suggested minimum sperm density for a male to be considered fertile is 20 million spermatozoa per millilitre of semen. The condition is sometimes associated with a circulatory disorder of the testicles, marked by a swollen scrotum.

olisbos an artificial phallus used by ancient Greek practitioners of tribadism, commonly made of leather.

Ombredanne's operation a surgical procedure developed in France for the repair of hypospadias. A new urethra is constructed from skin of the scrotum and the underside of the penis. The foreskin is then transplanted to the underside of the penis.

onanism an obsolescent term for coitus interruptus (sexual withdrawal) and masturbation, based on an Old Testament passage (Genesis 38:9) in which Onan went to his brother's widow and 'spilled his seed on the ground' rather than impregnate her.

oncogenes segments of certain genetic molecules that are capable of inducing cancer. The HTLV virus associated with AIDS carries oncogenes, a factor that has been used to explain some effects of the disease, such as Kaposi's sarcoma. See also AIDS.

one-eyed monster a slang term for penis.

one-eyed trouser snake a euphemism for penis, popularized by the Australian humorist Barry Humphries.

one-hand book a colloquial term for a sexually arousing book, namely, a book that is held in one hand while the other hand is busy masturbating. The term originated with the French literary critic Charles Augustin Sainte-Beuve (1804-1869) who remarked that even 'books that one reads with one hand' may have literary merit.

Oneida Community a 19th-century utopian community located in northwestern New York state. It was noted for its liberal sexual attitudes during a period better remembered for Victorian conservatism. Men of the Oneida Community were trained to practise coitus reservatus, or control of ejaculation. Postmenopausal women, free of the risk of pregnancy, volunteered to help young men practise the technique, regardless of how many sessions were required to perfect their ability.

oneirogmus ejaculation during a sexual dream.

one-night stands transient sexual encounters usually lasting no more than one night, between heterosexuals, male homosexuals, or lesbians, and sometimes involving male or female prostitutes, who usually meet in singles bars, at parties, in shops, in the street, on beaches, or practically anywhere else.

onion a plant praised almost universally, and for centuries, for its alleged sexual stimulus. Arabs recommended onion omelettes. Chinese vouched for the effects of stir-fried onions, and an ancient Roman poet wrote of onions as the answer to the questions of what to do 'if your wife is old and your member is exhausted.'

onion skin a colloquial term for foreskin.

on the game, to be a euphemism meaning to be a professional prostitute.

on the job a euphemism for in the act of intercourse, as in 'The chambermaid walked in while they were on the job.'

on the rag, to be a slang term meaning to menstruate.

ontogeny repeats phylogeny the concept that the development of the individual human from fertilization involves passing through the various phases of human evolution during life in the uterus. Thus, at certain stages of embryonic life, the human may resemble the embryo of a bird or four-legged animal and may acquire and then discard certain anatomical structures important to lower animals.

oocyte an immature ovum, or egg, at a stage when it is not yet ready for fertilization. A primary oocyte contains the full number of chromosomes (46) but must undergo meiotic

division, resulting in a secondary oocyte and a polar body, each with 23 chromosomes, and divide a second time, yielding a mature ovum and a second polar body before it is ripe for fertilization.

oocytin an enzymatic substance in spermatozoa that is released during fertilization to stimulate the formation of a new membrane around the zygote.

oogenesis the series of steps a human egg cell must go through to mature into a ripe ovum that can be fertilized by a spermatozoon. In the series of steps, the immature ovum loses half of its complement of chromosomes so that the zygote will receive 23 chromosomes from the female parent and an equal number from the male parent.

oogonium a primordial ovum that is ready to evolve into an oocyte.

oophorectomy the surgical removal of an ovary. The operation may be for the removal of one or both ovaries—for ovarian cancer or cysts or for hormonal dysfunction (Stein-Leventhal syndrome).

oosperm a zygote, or fertilized ovum.

open laparoscopy a technique for examining the pelvic organs of a female by making a small incision in the umbilical region for direct visual inspection. It is an alternative to closed laparoscopy in which a small puncture is made in the abdominal wall through which a laparoscope is inserted.

open marriage a marriage based on mutual agreement that both partners are free to have intimate friendships, including sexual relationships, with others outside the marriage. The arrangement is undertaken on the theory that the emotional and sexual needs of the partners cannot be fully satisfied within a monogamous relationship. Studies show that most marriages cannot sustain this degree of openness.

open swinging a form of consensual extramarital sex in which two or more couples engage in sexual activity in the same room. Open swinging is most likely to occur at parties for swinging couples.

ophthalmia neonatorum a discharge of pus from the eyes of a newborn infant, usually occurring within the first 3 weeks after birth. The cause in more than half of all cases is a gonorrhoea infection acquired while passing through the vagina of an infected mother. The condition also can be caused by an infection of streptococcus or some other disease organism.

opportunistic sex sexual intercourse that

occurs simply because the opportunity presents itself. Because of the opportunity the participants often do not take time to ensure that pregnancy or a sexually transmissible disease will not result.

opposite sex a commonly used term that identifies males from a female perspective or females from a male perspective. Author Dorothy Sayers once commented on the semantic riddle, 'What is the neighbouring sex?'

oral-biting period another name for the oral-sadistic phase during which the infant expresses anger through biting, and gains pleasure from chewing on objects.

oral changes the reactions of the digestive tract to sexual excitement. Most obvious are changes in the mouth, where saliva secretion increases rapidly to the point where some individuals may literally drool by the time the orgasmic phase is reached. Erotic kissing also is usually characterized by increased salivation.

oral character in psychoanalysis, personality patterns based on experiences during the oral stage of psychosexual development. According to this theory, the child who experiences adequate sucking satisfaction and attention from the mother during this period will develop a cooperative, generous, optimistic outlook on life. If, however, he or she does not get enough satisfaction during the oral sucking and biting stage, the individual will become aggressive, critical, and overcompetitive.

oral coitus a term sometimes used to refer to fellatio or cunnilingus.

oral contraceptive a birth-control method in which a pill ('the Pill') is taken by mouth.

oral dependency a psychoanalytical term for a tendency to be dependent on other people and to seek the same type of security, care, and protection from them that was experienced during the oral stage at the beginning of life.

oral eroticism a psychoanalytical term for pleasurable activities involving the mouth, including suckling, eating, smoking, kissing, biting, thumb sucking, talking, and oral sex. Many psychoanalysts believe gratification associated with such activities is sexual in origin, dating back to the first, or oral, stage of psychosexual development, when the infant derives his or her greatest pleasure from sucking on the nipple or bottle. Also called *oral erotism*.

oral fixation a psychoanalytical term for persistence of behaviour associated with gratification experienced during the oral stage of psychosexual development, especially thumb sucking, baby talk, nail biting, and dependence on others for care and protection.

oral-genital contact a synonym for orogenital contact.

oral impregnation the myth that pregnancy can occur as a result of oral contact, as in kissing. This belief may be a childhood attempt to explain the way conception occurs, or may be an attempt to instill a fear of impregnation that will block sexual contact of any kind among young people.

orality a general term comprising all types of oral activity or gratification, including oral sex, 'love bites,' kissing, smoking, verbosity, chewing food or tobacco, and oral character traits such as excessive generosity or aggressiveness.

oral libido a psychoanalytical term for concentration of sexual energy in the oral zone. This first occurs during the oral phase of psychosexual development, and is characterized by gratification obtained through nursing, exploring objects with the mouth, and sucking on a blanket or thumb. Oral satisfactions continue in such forms as kissing and orogenital contact.

oral phase a synonym for oral stage.

oral progesterone test a pregnancy test in which there is a presumptive sign of pregnancy because of a missed menstrual period. The woman is given an oral dose of progesterone. If she is not pregnant, the increased progesterone should cause menstruation to begin within a few days. If she is pregnant, menstruation does not occur.

oral sadism a psychoanalytical term for the primitive impulse to use the mouth, lips, and teeth as instruments of aggression, hostility, or sadistic sexual satisfaction. This impulse is believed to originate in the oral-sadistic phase of the infantile oral stage.

oral-sadistic phase the second phase of the oral stage according to the psychoanalytical account of psychosexual development. During this stage, which lasts from about the eighth to the eighteenth month, the child begins to feel like an independent person, expresses anger by biting the mother's breast, or the nipple of the bottle, and derives sexual pleasure from chewing on anything he or she can put into the mouth. Also called oral-biting period.

oral sex a general term for the use of the lips, mouth, tongue, and throat cavity in sexual stimulation and gratification. The various types of oral sex include kissing, sucking, biting, licking, exploring the partner's genital organs and erogenous zones with the tongue, and swallowing the partner's sexual secretions.

oral stage according to Freud, the earliest stage of psychosexual development, lasting throughout the first 18 months of life, when the mouth is the principal erogenous zone and when the most important source of gratification is sucking during the feeding process and, towards the end of the period, biting and chewing. Also called oral phase.

orchestras a humorous British euphemism for testicles. It is short for orchestra stalls, which in turn is rhyming slang for balls.

orchidopexy the surgical correction of an undescended testicle by any of several procedures for relocating the testicle in the scrotum.

orchiectomy the surgical removal of the testis. The procedure may be performed in cases of testicular cancer, which is rated as the most common type of solid malignancy for males under the age of 30. Since testicular cancers are usually associated with cryptorchidism, the testis may be removed through the abdominal wall.

orchipexy a surgical procedure in which an undescended testis is moved into the scrotum. The testis may be anchored to the lining of the scrotum so that it will not retract into the abdomen.

orchis a synonym for testis (Greek *orchis*, 'orchid, testicle'). Orchis is also a botanical name for orchids of the woods, swamps, and moist areas; various species grow in Europe, Asia, and North America. Perhaps because of the etymological relationship between the name of the plant and the Greek word for testis, various orchis varieties have been used as alleged sexual stimulants since ancient times.

orchitis an inflammation of the testis. The symptoms usually include a swelling and feeling of heaviness, accompanied by pain. The condition may be associated with gonorrhoea, syphilis, or tuberculosis, but is most commonly caused by mumps.

organ a common euphemism for penis.

organ eroticism sexual interest or excitement associated with a particular body organ or part, such as the nipples, buttocks, penis, vulva, or ears.

organic impotence an inability to achieve and maintain an erection because of a physical defect in the genitalia or the nervous-system tracts that control erection.

organizing effects the results of hormonal stimulation that produce changes in tissue structure, such as prenatal sex hormones that result in the creation of genitalia.

organ of Giraldes an alternative term for the paradidymis, an embryonic vestige found on the spermatic cord of the male.

orgasm the peak, or climax, of sexual excitement and pleasure during which ejaculation of semen occurs in the male and vaginal contractions in the female. The peak period lasts less than 1 minute for most males and females and is accompanied by increased heart rate and blood pressure, a mild clouding of consciousness, and release of tension. The male orgasm is nearly always followed by a refractory period in which sexual excitement cannot occur, but if stimulation continues, the female orgasm may be repeated several times. Studies show that the orgasm potential reaches its height in men at around the age of 18, and in women around the age of 35. (Greek *organ*, 'to grow ripe, swell, be lustful.')

See also ALIMENTARY ORGASM; CLITORAL ORGASM; DRY ORGASM; DUAL ORGASM; FEMALE ORGASM FREQUENCY; FIRST-STAGE ORGASM; INHIBITED FEMALE ORGASM; INHIBITED MALE ORGASM; MULTIPLE ORGASM; MUTUAL ORGASM; NOCTURNAL ORGASM; NTH ORGASM; PHARMACOGENIC ORGASM; SECOND-STAGE ORGASM; SIMULTANEOUS ORGASM; STATUS ORGASMUS; VAGINAL ORGASM.

orgasm frequency among males a term referring to the relationship between male orgasm frequency and age, as revealed by the Kinsey studies. The Kinsey data showed a relatively consistent frequency of between two and three orgasms per week from the age of 15 to the age of 25, after which there was a sudden upward peak to about the age of 30, followed by a steady decline with advancing age. However, occasional orgasms were reported by men in their 70s and 80s.

orgasmic dysfunction inability or difficulty in reaching a normal orgasm, stemming in the male from such conditions as ejaculatory incompetence, premature ejaculation, delayed ejaculation, or inhibited response; and in the female, from such conditions as frigidity, inhibited response, painful intercourse (dyspareunia), and involuntary contractions of the vaginal muscles (vaginismus). The causes of orgasmic dysfunction may be organic (defective sexual apparatus, hormonal imbalance, disorders of the nervous system, genital inflammations or lesions, excessive use of drugs or alcohol) or psychological and relational (resentment towards the partner, finding the partner unattractive or undesirable, feelings of shame or guilt towards sex instilled by parents, or strong emotional ties to one or both parents). See also FEMALE ORGASMIC DYSFUNCTION; PRIMARY ORGASMIC DYSFUNCTION; SECONDARY ORGASMIC DYSFUNCTION; SITUATIONAL ORGASMIC DYSFUNCTION; ORGASM.

orgasmic inadequacy failure to achieve orgasm during sexual relations for reasons that are primarily psychological, such as a conscious or unconscious expression of hostility.

orgasmic peak the moment of orgasm or climax when sexual excitement and gratification reach their maximum intensity.

orgasmic platform the outer third of the vagina, which becomes congested with blood during the plateau phase and contracts rhythmically during the orgasmic phase of the female sexual-response cycle. The more frequent and intense the contractions, the more intense the subjective experience of climax, and the more actively the vagina participates in coitus. 'Platform' refers to the fact that the physiological changes that occur during orgasm appear to emanate from this area.

orgasmic reconditioning a behaviour-therapy technique used with individuals who fail to reach orgasm. Sexually provocative photographs or films are shown to the patient, who masturbates while looking at them. These stimuli, however, are replaced by more conventional heterosexual pictures just before orgasm is reached, and at progressively earlier points, in order to develop a normal pattern of arousal. Also called *orgasmic reorientation*.

orgasmic stage the third phase of the sexual response cycle, in which the tension and pleasure experienced in the plateau stage increase to a point where a peak, or climax, of excitement is triggered. The orgasm is a sudden release of sexual tension during which the male ejaculates and both the male and the female experience a series of six to 15 muscular contractions, each lasting slightly less than one second. Though the whole body may be involved, the focus of the male orgasm is the penis, prostate gland, and seminal vesicles, while the focus in the female appears to be in the muscle and tissue surrounding and deep within the vagina.

orgastic impotence the incapacity of the male to reach orgasm in spite of normal erection and ejaculation. Inability to achieve full gratification may result in a decline in sexual interest. The condition may be caused by immature psychosexual development, an unconscious fear of 'letting go,' or anxiety over losing an important product of the body.

orgastic potency the capacity of males or females to reach full orgasm during sexual intercourse or masturbation.

orgone box an enclosure made of wood and metal resembling a telephone box. Wilhelm Reich, who developed this device, claimed that it captures orgone energy, and that by sitting in it, the patient could learn to direct this energy to the sex organs for the purpose of restoring potency, and to ailing parts of the body, such as the lungs or joints, for therapeutic purposes. Also called *orgone accumulator*.

orgone energy a primal force that permeates the entire universe according to Wilhelm Reich. He believed this reservoir of energy could be tapped by various means such as the 'orgone box' and body massage. He also held that this form of energy could be used to increase 'orgastic potency,' and cure human ills ranging from the common cold and impotence to cancer.

orgone therapy a controversial form of therapy developed by Wilhelm Reich on the theory that 'full orgastic potency' is the key to psychological well-being. According to Reich, potency can be enhanced by cosmic orgone energy through body therapy and the use of the orgone accumulator. The orgasm itself, he held, serves to regulate the emotional energy of the body and to relieve sexual tensions that would otherwise be transformed into neuroses.

orgy uninhibited revelry characterized by group indulgence in drinking, singing, dancing, and unrestrained sexual activity. The term has been traced to the wild behaviour of ancient Greeks during ceremonies honouring the god Dionysius. (Greek *ergon*, 'work'!)

orgy room a room in a homosexual men's bath that is used for group sex.

Oriental culture a colloquial term referring to experimentation with all possible intercourse positions.

orifices openings or apertures in the body, all of which may be erogenous for some people; the mouth, vagina, urethra, anus, ears (meatus), and possibly the nostrils.

original sin in Roman Catholic theology, the doctrine that as a result of intercourse with

Eve, Adam violated their original innocence and created a state of depravity that has been transmitted from generation to generation. According to St. Augustine and other church fathers, as a result of the original sin (termed the Fall) coitus became tainted with guilt, and was transformed into 'shameful lust'; it should therefore be limited to propagation of the species and should not be performed for pleasure.

orogenital contact sexual activity in which the mouth and usually the tongue are used to stimulate the genital organs of a sexual partner. (The two major types, fellatio and cunnilingus, are defined in separate entries.) Many couples, both heterosexual and homosexual, practise orogenital sex, although others consider it distasteful. In several countries there are still laws against these practices. Also called buccal intercourse; mouth-genital contact; oral-genital contact; oralism; oral sex; orogenital activity.

orolabial stimulation a technical term for cunnilingus or fellatio.

oscarize a slang term meaning to have homosexual intercourse. An *Oscar* is a homosexual. Both terms are derived from the name of Oscar Wilde.

oscheo (os'kē-ō) a term that pertains to the scrotum and is usually combined with a modifying term, such as oscheoma, for a scrotal tumour (Greek *oscheon,* 'scrotum').

oscula me Latin for 'kiss me'—popularized in America on T-shirts. The back of some of these shirts may say, *ego loquor latinam,* 'I speak Latin.' (Another T-shirt legend, popular in the early 1980s: *quis amat te, infantis?* 'Who loves you, baby?') *Osculation* and *to osculate* are mock-learned ways of saying 'a kiss' (*osculatio*) and 'to kiss' (*osculari*). *Osculatory* means 'related to kissing.'

osmolagnia sexual arousal that is caused by certain odours. Osmolagnia is believed by some experts to be an important factor in oral sex.

os penis a bone found in the fibrous tissue dividing the corpora cavernosa of many species of animals, from bats to rats and including primates. However, it does not exist in the human penis. Also called baculum; os priapi.

Ota IUD the first plastic intrauterine device, developed by the Japanese physician T.Ota. Ota's IUD was first introduced around 1959 and had a failure rate of only 2.3 percent in 20,000 women, compared with a failure rate of 2.4 percent with the Gräfenberg silver IUD.

Othello syndrome a form of sexual paranoia in which a husband or wife is suspicious of the spouse's infidelity. The condition may be characterized by jealous rage and violence.

other, the a British euphemism for sexual activity, especially sexual intercourse.

other woman a colloquial term for a woman whose lover is a married man. Depending on the speaker's perspective, the other woman may be referred to as a 'home wrecker.'

OTR an abbreviation for 'on the rag.'

out an adjective describing a person who is open about his or her homosexuality.

outbreeding the mating of unrelated individuals, sometimes leading to a superior hybrid strain, as contrasted with inbreeding that may result in an increased risk of inheritance of defective traits by the next generation.

outlaw a slang term for a prostitute who does not work through a pimp.

ovarian agenesis a congenital lack of functional female gonads, as occurs in Turner's syndrome. The condition also may be associated with a failure of normal development of secondary female sexual characteristics.

ovarian calculus an abnormal concretion of protein and inorganic matter, usually calcium, that may form in a corpus luteum after ovulation.

ovarian cycle the cycles of changes that affect the ovary between menarche and menopause.

ovarian cyst any of several types of cystic enlargements of the ovary. One form of ovarian cyst is a fluid-filled follicle, usually a follicle in which ovulation failed to occur on schedule, as when the ovum is too deep within the ovary for normal spontaneous rupture of the follicle. The follicle may be small but the cyst—which is rarely malignant—can be large enough to cause pain and menstrual irregularities. The malignant cysts of the ovary include the mucinous and serous cystadenocarcinomas and, occasionally, a serous cystadenoma. However, serous cystadenomas of the ovary also can be noncancerous.

ovarian fossa a small recess on either side of the pelvic wall where the ovaries are located.

ovarian ligament a rounded tube of tissue that lies within a broad ligament supporting the ovary.

ovarian pregnancy an ectopic pregnancy in which an embryo becomes implanted in an ovary instead of in the uterus. An ovarian pregnancy always ends in the rupture of the ovary and absorption of the conceptus or by degenerating into an ovarian tumour. (An abdominal pregnancy may survive by implanting itself on the outside of an ovary.)

ovariectomy the surgical removal of an ovary.

ovaries the female gonads or sex glands located on either side of the uterus that release egg cells or ova at the rate of about one per month between menarche and menopause. The ovaries also produce the sex hormones, oestrogen and progesterone, which contribute to the level of sexual maturity, regulation of the menstrual cycle, and the achievement and maintenance of pregnancy. See also CONGESTED OVARIES; BIPARTITE OVARY; ENGAGEMENT OVARIES; FALSE OVARY; SENILE OVARY.

ovariotomy the surgical removal of an ovary or a portion of an ovary, as in the excision of a diseased portion of an ovary. Removal of an ovary through an abdominal incision may be identified as an abdominal ovariotomy; the term vaginal ovariotomy identifies a procedure in which removal is made through the vagina. Oophorotomy usually refers to an ovariotomy performed to remove an ovarian cyst.

overnight sensation a slang term for nocturnal emission.

oversexed a colloquial term for a man or woman whose sex drive appears to be abnormally strong, and in some cases insatiable. Though frequently, and erroneously, attributed to a physical condition, it is far more likely to be caused by normal variations that do not match the partner's expectations, or to such psychological factors as overcompensation for inner doubts about sexual adequacy or masculinity, an attempt to prove sexual prowess, or compensation for failures or shortcomings in other areas of life. Technical terms are nymphomania and satyriasis.

overt homosexuality homosexuality that is consciously recognized and expressed in sexual behaviour, as distinguished from unconscious homosexual impulses or desires, or conscious wishes that are held in check.

oviduct an alternative term for the fallopian tube, which, in mammals, carries an ovum from the ovary to the uterus. In egg-laying animals, the oviduct transports the ova, or eggs, to the outside of the female's body.

oviferous pertaining to a woman who is capable of producing ova.

ovotestis a gonad associated with hermaphroditism and containing both male and female germinal tissues or substances.

ovulation the once-a-month discharge of a mature ovum from an ovary (usually in alternate order month by month). After ovulation, the cell is carried into a uterine, or fallopian, tube where it may or may not be fertilized by a sperm.

ovulum a Latin term meaning a small egg, or small ovum.

ovum the female reproductive cell (gamete, egg cell). About 400,000 immature ova are stored in the two ovaries from birth, and about 400 to 500 mature and are ovulated during the woman's reproductive lifetime. Plural: ova.

oxytocin a hormone secreted by the pituitary gland that results in muscle contractions in some organs of the body, particularly the uterus. It is also involved in the 'let-down' reflex of lactation in which human milk is released in the mammary gland. Natural or synthetic oxytocin may be injected into a pregnant woman at term to stimulate uterine contractions. In lactation, the stimulus of the infant sucking on the nipple causes a release of oxytocin from the posterior pituitary. The oxytocin causes contraction of the breast alveoli, forcing milk into the ducts leading to the nipple.

oxytocin challenge test one of several tests of the ability of a foetus to withstand the stress of childbirth. The pregnant woman is given an intravenous infusion of oxytocin, and the foetal heart is monitored during a series of uterine contractions triggered by the oxytocic drug. If it appears that the foetal heart cannot take the stress, the foetus may be delivered by caesarean section.

oysters molluscs that are among the most popular alleged aphrodisiacs. The Romans probably were the first to see a link between oysters and sex. Juvenal claimed in the 1st century A.D. that oysters were a favourite food of 'shameless and lascivious women.' Roman legionnaires rushed oysters from Briton to Rome, packed in ice, perhaps to keep their women in an erotic mood. Nutritionists note that oysters contain more zinc than any other type of food, and zinc is a mineral associated with a healthy sex life.

paederosis a synonym for paedophilia.

paedication an uncommon term for pederasty. Also called *paedicatio*. A man who indulges in this practice is called a *paedicator*.

paedomania an obsolescent term for a man's obsessive, uncontrolled passion for boys or very young men.

paedophilia a psychosexual disorder, or paraphilia, in which an adult (the *paedophile*) desires, engages in, and persistently prefers sexual activity with children who are usually, but not always, of the opposite sex. The sexual activity may consist of heterosexual intercourse, fellatio, or anal intercourse, but may also be limited to looking and touching.

paedophthoria in ancient Greece, the sexual seduction of boys by adult men (*phthoria*, 'corruption').

paedotribes in ancient Greece, an adult man who loves a boy and, usually, teaches him not only about sex but also about life in general (*tribein*, 'to rub').

painful intercourse pain that occurs during or immediately after sexual intercourse. Pain associated with initial attempts at intercourse is usually classified as primary dyspareunia while pain that occurs with subsequent intercourse may be identified as secondary dyspareunia. Examples of primary dyspareunia include pain stemming from rupture or tearing of the hymen. Secondary dyspareunia is often identified with atrophy of the vaginal tissues during menopause. Women may also experience pain from bruising of the urethral meatus (the opening of the urethra) during coitus, injury to the labia, or because of irritation or an allergic reaction to contraceptive devices and materials. In some cases, plastic surgery to repair the vagina or an episiotomy during childbirth may be a source of pain. Painful coitus can be psychogenic in nature or the result of inadequate foreplay that fails to stimulate the natural lubrication of the vagina. Vaginismus, a spastic contraction of the vaginal muscles, is generally regarded as a psychological cause of painful intercourse and is related to an unconscious desire by the woman to prevent access to her vagina. Some women are so protective of the vagina that an anaesthetic must be used to permit a routine pelvic examination.

pair bonding development of a close and mutual attachment between two persons, such as mother or father and infant, lover and lover, or husband and wife. It is particularly important that bonding take place as soon as the child is born, by such means as holding the baby on the mother's abdomen, nursing, stroking, close body contact with the father as well as the mother, gazing into the baby's eyes, and anticipating the baby's bodily needs.

palimony an allowance made by court decree to a woman out of the estate or income of a man she lived with as though, but not actually, married to him (from *pal* and *alimony*).

palingenesis a genetic theory that humans transmit through successive generations various characteristics that have not been apparent in intermediate generations. The theory is an attempt to explain certain human abnormalities.

palinogenetic a trait or physical characteristic of an individual that originated in a previous generation.

palmate folds a number of small tissue columns on the walls of the uterine cervix. They contain glands that secrete a mucus substance. The folds are arranged so that they can dovetail together to effectively close the cervix.

pampiniform plexus a group of three veins

that drain deoxygenated blood from the testicles. Any obstruction of one or more of the veins, particularly the internal spermatic vein, can result in formation of a varicocele.

panderer a person who supplies clients for prostitutes or prostitutes for clients; a procurer. If he is a so-called 'business manager' for prostitutes, he is called a pimp. In a more general sense, a panderer is a person who caters to or profits from the weaknesses and vices of others.

pangenesis a Darwinian concept that every cell and particle in a parent is reproduced in the child and is represented in the gametes of the next generation.

panhypopituitarism a form of anterior hypopituitarism, usually caused by a tumour, with the signs and symptoms of lessening of secondary sexual characteristics, but with an additional complication of diabetes insipidus. Diabetes insipidus is often the first effect of the pituitary disorder because the general shutdown of endocrine function involves a deficiency of antidiuretic hormone secretion. Regression of male or female sex organs and characteristics follows.

panmixia the sexual association of persons of different 'races,' or the indiscriminate and unselective crossbreeding of strains of a species (Greek *pan*, 'all,' and *mixis*, 'intercourse').

pansexualism a doctrine that all human behaviour can be explained in terms of the sex drive. The view that 'everything is sex' has been attributed to Freud by many of his critics and opponents, but is a complete misrepresentation. Although he traced the development of sexuality from birth to maturity, and described the libido, or sex instinct, as a basic source of energy, he also recognized the importance of other drives such as hostility, hunger, thirst, and, towards the end of his life, the 'death instinct.'

pantagamy a type of marriage, in some societies, in which every man is considered to be the husband of every woman, and vice versa. An example is the Oneida community.

papilloma a type of tumour that is commonly found in and around the urethra, developing from polyps. Like warts of the urethra, papillomas are usually noncancerous, but they can cause urinary difficulties and interfere with normal sexual activity.

pappus the first downy facial hair that appears on the male during adolescence (Greek *pappos*, 'down').

Pap test a test of cervical mucus for the presence of cancerous cells (named after George N. Papanicolaou). Although this test, also called *Pap smear*, is an important part of the standard gynaecological examination, it usually does not detect uterine cancer. See also SMEAR TEST.

paracyesis a synonym for an ectopic pregnancy.

paradidymis a vestige of the mesonephros, consisting of a few convulated tubules on the spermatic cord, slightly above the head of the epididymis.

paradoxia sexualis sexual activity that is not considered appropriate for the chronological age of the individual, such as a 90-year-old man fathering a child or a 5-year-old girl becoming a mother.

paradoxical incontinence urination that occurs as a result of intraabdominal pressure, a complication of prostatic hypertrophy (overgrowth). In untreated prostatic hypertrophy, the bladder wall becomes thicker and capacity is reduced, resulting in increased urinary frequency. However, the bladder also becomes dilated and loses its muscle tone, resulting in a large amount of residual urine and difficulty in completely emptying the bladder in a single urination.

paradoxical refractory period a phenomenon observed in older men who require 12 or more hours to attain another erection if foreplay or love play is interrupted before orgasm.

paramour a mistress or lover of either sex involved in a love affair, often adulterous. The term is derived from the French, *par amour*, which may be translated as 'by the way of love.'

para I an indication, when applied to a particular mother, that she has carried a pregnancy to term resulting in the birth of one viable offspring. The term is derived from the Latin *parere*, meaning 'to bear,' with the Roman numeral indicating the number of successful pregnancies. Also called primipara.

paraphilias deviant or distorted forms of sexuality in which sexual excitement is achieved in unusual or bizarre ways. They include coprophilia, exhibitionism, fetishism, frotteurism, klismaphilia, misophilia, necrophilia, paedophilia, sexual masochism, sexual sadism, telephone scatalogia, transvestism, voyeurism, and zoophilia.

paraphimosis of the tube a complication of salpingitis, or inflammation of the fallopian tube, in which the tube becomes constricted just before the fimbriated open end. The tube may be completely closed by the constriction, thereby prohibiting the movement of an ovum, or it can be partially closed. For male paraphimosis, see PHIMOSIS.

parasexuality abnormal or 'perverted' sexual behaviour, as in paederasty, sadomasochism, and voyeurism.

parasympathetic nerves the part of the autonomic nervous system that is involved in dilatation of the blood vessels serving the clitoris and labia minora and the erection of the penis.

paravaginitis an inflammation of the tissues around but not including the vagina, such as an infection of the labia.

parenchyma the functional part of an organ or tissue, as distinguished from structural units.

parenchyma testis the functional part of the testis including the seminiferous tubules.

parenchymatous neurosyphilis syphilis that affects the functional parts of the nervous system, such as the nerve cells of the brain and spinal cord. Parenchymatous neurosyphilis is responsible for such neurological signs as tabes dorsalis, which makes coordination of the leg muscles in walking difficult, and general paresis. The first signs of parenchymatous neurosyphilis usually appear 10 to 30 years after infection.

parental behaviour activities performed by parents to insure the health, growth, and development of their children. According to current cultural standards, both parents should share in the responsibilities involved in child rearing, such as providing them with adequate living facilities, nourishment, and medical care as needed and—just as important—giving them a full measure of love, encouragement, emotional security, as well as opportunities to develop interests, relationships, and stimulating activities with their peers.

parental perplexity incapacity of parents to provide the kind of guidance, communication, and emotional support their children need, because of their own confusion, indecisiveness, and lack of empathy. As a result, one or more children in the family become disoriented and disorganized, sometimes to the point of developing schizophrenic tendencies.

parental rejection constant expressions of disapproval directed to one or more children in a family, often to a point where they feel unwanted and unloved. Parental attitudes of this kind tend to undermine the child's self-

confidence, corrode the child's self-image, make it difficult for the child to form attachments and develop feelings of love, including sexual love, towards others as he or she matures.

paresis a partial paralysis. The term is sometimes used interchangeably with paralysis, particularly with a modifying word to indicate a specific type of neuromuscular deficit, such as general paresis caused by cerebral syphilis or paresis sine pareses, an early stage of neurosyphilis.

pareunia an alternative term for sexual intercourse (Greek *pareunos,* 'lying beside').

pareusia the early Christian belief in a Second Coming of Christ and the end of the world. Some authorities have traced the practice of celibacy to this belief, which carried the implied mandate that marriage and procreation would be inappropriate if the end of the world was approaching. A similar expression of uselessness of bringing children into the world has accompanied the two World Wars and the threat of a nuclear holocaust.

parous introitus a vaginal opening in which the hymen has been stretched to its maximum by the delivery of a child.

parthenogenesis a form of reproduction that occurs in an egg-laying animal without fertilization by a male member of the species. Artificial parthenogenesis is induced by chemical or mechanical techniques. It may occur naturally in some lower animals.

parthenophobia a morbid fear of girls, especially of virgins (Greek *parthenos,* 'maiden, virgin').

partialism a paraphilia characterized by an intense sexual interest in one part of the body, sometimes termed a 'part object.' One man may be 'turned on' by contact with nipples, another by a leg or a foot, and a woman may be 'turned on' by a hairy chest.

partial septate vagina a vaginal malformation in which the mullerian ducts failed to fuse completely at the lower end, with the result that a part of the vagina is divided by a wall of tissue.

particular friendship a euphemism for a lesbian relationship. The term reportedly has been used within orders of Roman Catholic nuns in the context that 'particular relationships' among nuns are prohibited.

partner swapping an exchange of sexual partners, within or outside marriage. Within marriage it may be called mate swapping or wife swapping. The practice is frequently found among 'swinging' couples, who are constantly looking for new forms of sexual excitement. Partner swapping may be either an erotic game played at a party, with partners chosen at random, or it may be practiced by a couple, or a small group of couples, or members of a special club which meets regularly for this purpose.

part object a part of the body that persistently elicits sexual excitement. See PARTIALISM.

partousse (pätōōs') a French term meaning (almost literally) an orgy or group sex.

partunate period the neonatal period when a newborn must rapidly adjust to survival in a new environment, such as obtaining nourishment by mouth and oxygen by breathing, instead of depending upon a parasitic existence in which oxygen and food are received via the umbilical cord. The neonate also must quickly adapt to room temperatures after spending all of its early life in a moist warm womb.

parturition the process of giving birth; labour. Childbirth is divided into four stages of labour: (a) dilatation of the cervix, to allow the foetus to pass out of the uterus into the vaginal barrel (takes 15 to 20 hours for firstborns, and 6 to 10 hours thereafter); (b) 'bearing down,' to propel the foetus through the birth canal by rhythmic contraction of the uterine muscles (takes from 10 minutes to 2 hours); (c) emergence of the baby; and (d) expulsion of the placenta about 15 minutes after the baby is born.

party a euphemism meaning to have sex, used particularly by prostitutes.

passion killers a humorous British slang term for voluminous or otherwise impenetrable female underwear that frustrates male attempts at intimacy.

passion mark an older term for a mark made by a love bite.

passive algolagnia an alternative term for masochism.

passive-congenial relationship a heterosexual relationship characterized by a pleasant stability. Both partners have similar attitudes towards sex, even though their sex life may be less exciting than in a conflict-habituated relationship.

passive role the relatively inactive, receptive role in either heterosexual or homosexual intercourse. Studies show that partners may at times switch from the passive to the active role and vice versa.

passive scopophilia a form of exhibitionism in which an individual obtains sexual pleasure by having other persons view his or her body or genitalia.

passivism a pattern of submissiveness, particularly in sexual relations; also, a sexual variation in which the individual, usually male, submits to the will of a dominant partner in such practices as anal intercourse and fellatio.

paternal nondisjunction a failure of the father's X and Y chromosomes to divide evenly during mitosis or meiosis, resulting in one daughter cell with no sex chromosomes and one with both the X and Y sex chromosomes. If the gamete with both sex chromosomes fertilizes a normal female ovum with a single X chromosome, the result will be an XXY karyotype, or individual with Klinefelter's syndrome. If the daughter cell with no sex chromosomes as a result of paternal nondisjunction unites with a normal female X chromosome ovum, the individual will be born as an XO karyotype person with Turner's syndrome. Klinefelter's syndrome or Turner's gonadal dysgenesis can result from either maternal or paternal nondisjunction. But only maternal nondisjunction can result in a superfemale karyotype with an XXX sex chromosome combination.

paternity blues transient feelings of mild depression experienced by a new father, particularly if he is unprepared for a radical change in everyday routines, as well as the shift of the mother's attention from himself to the newborn infant. Fathers who involve themselves in the care of the child—as many do today—are not likely to feel rejected or displaced. Also called new-father blues.

paternity suit a legal proceeding undertaken to establish the paternity of an alleged father. The general purpose is to compel him to contribute to the child's support. Evidence may be presented that the couple were living together at the time of conception, also evidence that the child and the alleged father are of the same blood type. This, however, is not conclusive proof of paternity because theoretically any man of the same blood group could be the father.

paternity test blood-grouping tests of the mother, child, and alleged father conducted to establish or disprove paternity in a paternity suit.

pathicism a form of homosexuality in which the passive (or 'pathic') partner undergoes a role change and is often a transvestite or in some other way does not play a sexual or social masculine role. Examples of pathicism are found throughout the world, but they usually involve only a handful of homosexuals in each society.

pathological deviance deviant sexual behaviour that violates local laws and mores and is likely to be prosecuted because it is not commonly practised. An example is paedophilia.

patriarchal family a family in which the father is the final authority, sole provider, and decision maker, and in which descent and kinship are patrilineal, that is, reckoned through the father's line. In this type of family the wife plays a subservient role as full-time mother and housewife.

patriophobia a morbid fear of inheriting a defect or disease.

pausimenia an alternative term for menopause.

Pautrier's giant lichenification a condition of thick warty-appearing lichenification of the genital area. The thickening and hardening of the skin may stem from a variety of causes ranging from scurvy to syphilis.

pc an abbreviation for pinky cheater, a term used by doctors for the rubber gloves worn when performing gynaecological examinations.

PDA a colloquial American abbreviation for 'public display of affection,' which may include necking and petting.

peak day a day in the ovulation method of the family-planning system of birth control when ovulation is most likely to occur. The cervical mucus becomes clear, slippery, and elastic. To reduce the risk of pregnancy, the woman avoids sexual intercourse on the peak day and the four following days, which, like wet days, are considered 'unsafe' days.

peak mucus sign the appearance of slippery, cloudy to white mucus in the female cervix at the time of ovulation. The mucus sign is also interpreted as an indication of a peak level of oestrogen secretion.

peccatophobia a morbid fear of committing a sin, usually coupled with an exaggerated moral sense and a tendency to see evil where there is no evil. This type of attitude may lead to sexual inhibitions and, in extreme form, to delusions of sin.

pecker a euphemism for the penis. In present-day usage it occurs virtually only in the phrase 'keep one's pecker up,' meaning to remain cheerful in spite of discouragement.

pederasty anal intercourse between a man (*pederast*) and a boy or young man.

pediculosis pubis another term for CRAB LOUSE. See this entry.

pedigree a table or chart showing the lineage of a person or animal (horse, dog). The study of a family's history and genealogy is used as one method of tracing traits or disorders, and determining if they are inherited.

pee a euphemism for urine, an act of urinating, and to urinate.

peepee a children's term for the penis. It is also a childish alternative for *pee*.

peeping sentinel an older euphemism for clitoris.

Peeping Tom a colloquial term for a voyeur, derived from the name of a tailor who peeped at Lady Godiva as she rode naked through the streets of Coventry in the 11th century. According to the legend, her husband had promised tax relief to the people if she committed this sacrificial act.

peep show another term for sex show.

peer pressure a force that contributes to teenage sexual experimentation. In male groups, particularly, it is important to demonstrate to one's peers that the individual is capable of seducing a girl.

peg house a slang term for a homosexual brothel. The name derives from such establishments in Southeast Asia where between clients the prostitutes sat on pegs to keep their anuses suitably distended.

pelvic abscess a pus-filled cavity accompanied by fever and lower abdominal pain as a result of pelvic inflammatory disease. The disorder may also occur as a complication of acute appendicitis or diverticulitis of the colon. The abdomen is tender, and the examining physician can usually locate the abscess by palpation. The pelvic abscess is usually drained through the vagina or through the rectum.

pelvic arch either of two curved bony structures of the pelvis. The anterior pelvic arch is formed by the pubic bones. The posterior pelvic arch is formed by the sacral vertebrae and the ilium.

pelvic axis the curved central line of the pelvic canal formed by the two hip bones and the sacrum.

pelvic cavity the space at the bottom of the abdomen. It is bounded by two sets of muscles, the levator ani and the coccygeus, which stretch like a hammock across the lower abdominal cavity, restraining the abdominal contents from compressing the urogenital structures.

pelvic-floor exercises another term for Kegel exercises.

pelvic inflammatory disease (PID) an inflammation of the uterine lining and fallopian tubes caused in many cases by untreated chlamydial infection and in some cases by gonorrhoea and long-term use of intrauterine devices, and accompanied by chronic pain and fever. In women this condition can cause blocking of the fallopian tubes with scar tissue, not infrequently resulting in infertility, premature delivery, or life-threatening ectopic pregnancy. The condition can often be cured in its early stages by a course of tetracycline or erythromycin. See also SALPINGITIS.

pelvic minilaparotomy an operation in which a small incision is made in the female abdomen above the pubic area to diagnose certain reproductive disorders or to perform tubal ligations. It is usually performed on an outpatient basis so that overnight hospitalization is not required.

pelvic muscles the two major sets, of muscles that form the true pelvic muscles (the levator ani and the coccygeus) and the muscles of the pelvic wall (the obturator internus and the piriformis). The levator ani is a broad thin hammocklike muscle that forms a floor of the pelvis. The coccygeus stretches from the pubic bones to the base of the spinal column. With the piriformis, it closes the back of the pelvic outlet. The obturator internus and piriformis are extensions of thigh muscles.

pelvic thrusts thrusting movements of both male and female during intercourse, controlled by rhythmic contractions of the pelvic muscles, and culminating in orgasm. The initial thrusts tend to be slow and shallow, but as coitus progresses they become more rapid and vigorous.

pelvic wall the inner surface of the pelvis, which is lined with muscle and connective tissue. The pelvic wall includes the pelvic diaphragm and the levator ani muscles, which stretch across the floor and up the walls of the pelvic cavity.

pelvis the bottom part of the trunk of the body bounded generally by the hip bones on either side, the sacrum and coccyx at the back, and the pubic area in the front. The pelvis is often described in terms of the shape of the hollow portion of the pelvic bone structure through which the foetus must pass during labour. They are gynaecoid, or oval; android, or wedgeshaped; anthropoid, mar-ked by an elongated oval or heart shape; and platypelloid, or wide and short (from front to back). An unusually large pelvis is called justo major, with all dimensions above average.

pendulant breasts sagging or hanging breasts—a physical feature that is frequently considered unattractive among women in Western countries, but far less so in Africa and Eastern countries. The condition can be corrected to some extent by exercises that develop the pectoral muscles, by improved posture, and, superficially, by wearing a brassiere.

pendulous urethra an alternative term for the penile segment of the male urethra.

penetration entrance of the penis into the vagina. The question whether penetration actually occurs is often raised in cases involving rape or child molestation. The legal interpretation varies somewhat, but often depends on whether the glans of the penis has passed beyond the labia majora. Also called immissio penis. See also FULL PENETRATION.

penile pertaining to or relating to the penis. Also called *penial*.

penile bone a bone that occurs naturally within the penile shaft of most male animals, humans being the exception. The bone is located above the corpus spongiosum and between the corpora cavernosa.

penile cancer and circumcision a relationship based on studies indicating that among patients treated for cancer of the penis, men who had been circumcised accounted for only 3 percent of the cases.

penile clamp a clamp designed to fit over the penis as an aid in the control of urinary incontinence. The clamp is released periodically to allow urine to flow through the urethra.

penile implant any of several types of silicone or other plastic devices that can be inserted into the shaft of the penis to allow a man with organic impotence to maintain an erection during intercourse.

penile meatus an alternative term for the urethral meatus of the male, or the opening at the end of the glans penis.

penile piercing the practice of making holes in the foreskin, the glans, or the rim of the glans, and inserting a ring or stud which is believed to increase the pleasure and excitement of intercourse. Historically, this process was described in the *Kama Sutra* as an apadravyas, or 'penis enhancer,' and it is still practised in some quarters today.

penile plethysmograph an instrument designed to analyse the ability of a male to achieve a normal erection by measuring blood flow and tissue-size changes in the penis. It may be used in the diagnosis of impotence or other reproductive disorders.

penile prosthesis an artificial device used to produce a partial or full erection in cases of male impotence because of illness or disability. One type consists of a plastic rod implanted in the penis. A more complex type consists of tubes that are connected to a reservoir of fluid implanted in the abdomen and drawn into the penis by means of a manually operated pump placed in the scrotum. They are both last-resort measures, used only after careful medical and psychiatric evaluation.

penile splint a sexual aid for men who have difficulty getting or maintaining an erection. It consists of a soft rubber cylinder reinforced with plastic plates. The sensitive head of the penis (the glans) is exposed, and there are gaps in the sides for contact with the vagina. The device is sometimes used as a treatment aid, and is said to reduce the anxiety associated with impotence.

penile urethra the portion of the male urethra that is carried in the shaft of the penis.

penile vein of the bulb a tributary of the internal pudendal vein of the pelvic areas. It is the vein that drains the blood from the penis after an erection. A similar vein in the female anatomy, the vein of the vestibule, drains erectile tissue blood from the clitoris.

penile size the size of the penis, for which the average has been calculated to range from 2.5 to 4.0 inches in length and 1 inch in diameter when flaccid. During erection, the average sizes have been measured at 5.5 to 6.5 inches in length and 1.5 inches in diameter. As a general rule, there is more variation in the sizes of the flaccid penis than in the erect state. However, Masters and Johnson have reported penile sizes in erection varying from 2 to 10 inches in length.

penilingus another term for fellatio.

penis the cylindrical male organ of intercourse. The penis consists of three parallel shafts of spongy tissue bound together with fibrous tissue and covered with skin. Two of the columns of spongy tissue are the corpora cavernosa, which form the top of a somewhat triangular prism of the three cylinders, and the corpus spongiosum penis, which contains the male urethra. The corpus spongiosum lies within a groove beneath the septum, or tissue dividing the corpora cavernosa, and contains at its terminal end the usually mushroom-shaped glans penis, which fits over the terminal ends of the corpora cavernosa. At the opposite end of the corpus spongiosum is a conical enlargement, the bulbus penis, at its attachment to the perineal tissues at the base of the pelvis. The urethra enters the corpus spongiosum at the bulbus penis. Each of the shafts of the corpora cavernosa contains a central artery which carries blood to the spongy tissue, enabling it to fill rapidly in reaction to sexual stimulation, which may be cerebral or spinal, or both, resulting in an erection. The blood is returned by a series of veins, some of which have valves that help prevent the immediate return of blood from the spongy tissue as long as the penis is in the erectile state. The skin covering the penis is thin, usually dark, somewhat loose, and lacking in fatty tissue. At the neck of the penis the skin becomes folded to form the prepuce, or foreskin.

See also ABLATIO PENIS; ARTIFICIAL PENIS; FRACTURED PENIS; GLANS PENIS; IMMISSIO PENIS; KRAUROSIS PENIS; OS PENIS.

penis amputation the partial or total surgical excision of the penis, a procedure that may be performed in the control of cancer.

penis captivus retention of the penis within the vagina because of vaginismus or painful spasm of the vagina. The condition is more likely to occur in animals—in those that possess a penile bone—than in humans. Although it is possible for a penis to become trapped within a vagina during human intercourse, documented cases in the medical literature are rare. Psychoanalysts attribute most anecdotal reports of human penis captivus to male castration fantasies.

penis enhancers devices such as 'extenders,' French ticklers, or special condoms designed to increase the size or stimulating capacity of the male organ.

penis envy the Freudian doctrine that every female feels 'handicapped and ill-treated' when she discovers that she does not possess a penis. According to this theory the little girl first becomes aware of this lack during the phallic stage of psycho-sexual development, between the ages of 3 and 7, and reacts by blaming her mother for the loss. Normally the wish for a penis is transformed into the wish for a child, but in some cases a young woman may deny that she lacks a penis and will behave like a man.

penis fear an equivalent of the technical term phallophobia.

penis holding the ritual act of placing the penis in another man's hand. The custom has been traced to the early Hebrews, who performed this act while swearing an oath. The 'phallic oath' has also been found among the Walbiri of Central Australia, who also hold the penis of a visitor as a form of greeting equivalent to shaking hands.

penis muliebris a Latin term meaning literally 'female penis'—that is, the clitoris (*mulier,* 'woman').

penis pride the feeling of superiority and power generated by possession of the male genital organ, as experienced especially by young boys when they realize they have a penis and girls do not.

penis sheath a protective 'phallocrypt' (penis hider) worn in various native societies of South America and Papua New Guinea, although the rest of the body, including the testicles, is completely exposed. Sheaths of this kind are usually made of gourds, cloth, or metal and decorated with feathers, fur, or flowers. Also called *penis wrapper.*

penitis any inflammation of the penis.

penoclitoris a term sometimes used in defining the sex of an infant born with ambiguous genitalia, including a penis the size of a clitoris, or a clitoris the size of a penis.

penoscrotal raphe a fused edge of the embryonic urethral groove fold that persists into adult life as a scarlike line running along the underside of the penile shaft to the anus, marking the margins of the folds. It is colloquially called the Great Divide.

pentamidine isethionate a drug used in the treatment of pneumocystis carinii, a form of pneumonia caused by an AIDS infection. Like suramin, pentamidine drugs were developed originally for the treatment of protozoal infections in Africa but were found in the 1980s to be helpful in treating patients who had lost their natural immunity against the AIDS virus. See also AIDS.

perforated hymen a hymen that is neither ruptured nor intact but which contains an opening, such as an annular hymen.

performance anxiety a fairly widespread fear among young or older men that they will be sexually inadequate or unable to arouse a girl or woman effectively. Fear of failure may produce an inability to achieve or maintain erection (impotence). It may also be intense enough to obliterate any sense of pleasure in a sexual relationship for both the man and

his partner. The same sort of situation may occur in reverse if the female partner has trouble reaching orgasm—and in many cases each partner may feel that the other is 'to blame.'

perinatal herpes-virus infection a genital herpes infection of a newborn infant, who acquires the virus during vaginal birth. Ordinarily, if it is known that a pregnant woman has genital herpes, it is recommended that the foetus be delivered by caesarean section. The virus can cross the placental barrier and is often fatal. If the infant survives, there is a grave risk of visual or neurological damage from the infection.

perineal pertaining to the perineum, the region between the anus and the scrotum of the male, or between the anus and vagina of the female. The region is used for an approach in treating the male prostate. It also is used in obtaining prostate tissue samples for biopsy studies; and if the biopsy results indicate the presence of cancer, the prostate gland and neighbouring tissues can be removed through the same incision.

perineal body a mass of muscle and connective tissue between the vagina and anus of the female and between the scrotum and anus of the male.

perineal coitus intercourse in which the penis is rubbed against the area between the woman's vulva and anus. Also called external coitus.

perineal testicle a testicle that descends from the abdomen but becomes lodged in perineal tissues under the bulb of the penis, instead of in the scrotum.

perineum the perineal area. See PERINEAL.

period a colloquial term for menstruation; a shortening of 'menstrual period.'

periodic leukorrhoea a discharge of whitish mucus from the vagina that may occur during the menstrual period or just before the onset of menstruation.

peripheral androgen blocker a class of drug used to treat symptoms of hirsutism in women. A drug with peripheral androgen blocker effects is spiralactone. Some women also use hormonal drugs derived from oral contraceptive medications.

peritonitis an inflammation of the peritoneal membranes that line the walls of the abdomen, marked by backache, pain during excretion, and discomfort during intercourse. A common cause is drainage of an infection from the fallopian tubes into the peritoneal cavity.

P

permissiveness a parental approach in which the child is encouraged to express his or her thoughts and feelings and assume responsibility for personal behaviour. The child is also allowed a considerable latitude in his or her actions. Punishment is avoided wherever possible, and replaced by explaining reasons why certain rules and limitations are necessary. Some parents, however, cross the line to overpermissiveness and refrain from giving their children the positive guidance they need in sexual as well as other areas of life.

permissiveness with affection the attitude that premarital sex between males and females is acceptable if they are in love or engaged. The attitude has generally prevailed in North America in recent years, replacing the alternatives of abstinence or the traditional double standard. Intercourse between males and females on the basis of mere physical attraction is suggested in films and television shows but was not generally accepted by young men and women in the 1980s.

pernicious vomiting of pregnancy an alternative term for hyperemesis gravidarum.

persistent puberism arrested development of secondary sex characteristics such as breasts or beard, usually because of undersecretion of sex hormones. In many cases development may be so retarded that the individual gives the appearance of an eternal adolescent.

personal ads newspaper and magazine columns that present brief advertisements containing personal data designed to attract potential companions, or marriage or sex partners. In some cases these advertisements appear to be inserted by individuals who are having difficulty making social contacts, such as the divorced or widowed, single parents, or individuals suffering from loneliness or timidity. In other cases, they are a cover for unnamed companies that deal in sexual or pornographic materials.

perversion a culturally, morally, and often legally unacceptable form of behaviour, particularly in the sexual sphere. Some psychiatrists still apply the term to practices that deviate most widely from the norm, such as sadomasochism, necrophilia, coprophilia, zoophilia, and paedophilia, but sexologists tend to avoid the terms perversion and perverted, as well as deviant, deviation and 'unnatural,' preferring the less judgmental and more neutral descriptive terms variation and variant.

pessary a contraceptive consisting of a spermicidal suppository inserted in the vagina a few minutes before intercourse to give it time to dissolve. Pessaries are usually used with a contraceptive of the barrier type (diaphragm, condom) for maximum protection. When used alone, they are only fairly effective. The technique dates back to ancient Egypt (but the term derives from a Greek word for pebble).

pester an obsolete term used by women in referring to sexual intercourse (often but by no means always with negative connotations), as in 'My master pesters me all the time.'

peter a slang term for penis.

Peter Panism a compulsion to keep 'forever young' by such means as ignoring birthdays, constantly proving one's athletic ability, dyeing one's hair, and undergoing cosmetic surgery. The term is based on the name of the hero of Sir James M. Barrie's play *The Boy Who Never Grew Up* (1904).

Petri papyrus an Egyptian papyrus (around 1850 B.C.) containing the earliest known medical prescription for a contraceptive. It consisted of a piece of lint impregnated with a paste made of crocodile dung and honey, to be placed in the vagina to prevent the sperm from entering the cervix.

petticoat punishment punishing a child by forcing him or her to dress in the clothes of the opposite sex (cross-dressing).

petting sexual activity short of intercourse, consisting of fondling, caressing, deep kissing, and, in general, exploring and stimulating the erogenous zones. Petting prepares the way to intercourse and may itself culminate in orgasm for one or both participants. A distinction is often made between light petting (necking) and heavy petting, which cannot be distinguished from foreplay.

Peyronie's disease an abnormal condition involving the sheets of connective tissue that surround and also divide the three fleshy cylinders that form the shaft of the penis. The tissues become fibrous and thickened, usually on one side, resulting in a contracture so that during erection the penis is pulled to one side. The condition not only makes an erection painful but often makes it difficult or impossible to achieve penetration of the vagina. If the condition spreads into the corpus cavernosum, erection may not be possible at all. The disease may disappear without treatment, or one or more of several therapies may be applied. They include surgical removal of the offending tissues, injections of steroid hormones, and ultrasonic treatment. The disease affects mainly men beyond middle age.

Phaedra complex sexual love of a mother for her son, or, also a nonpathological attraction between stepparent and stepchild, based on the Greek myth in which Phaedra, the wife of Theseus, was in love with her stepson, Hippolytus; but when he rejected her, she accused him of violating her, and hanged herself.

phallanastrophe an abnormal condition in which the penis is twisted upwards.

phallic aggression a form of sexual behaviour observed in some male animals who make an aggressive display against an opponent with the erect penis. The analogous situation in human terms is seen in the rapist, whose victim may be either female or male, and in the 'flasher' who uses the penis to shock and frighten others.

phallicism another term for phallic worship, in which ikons of the penis are considered sacred.

phallic love love of the penis in boys and love of its equivalent, the clitoris, in girls. This form of love develops in the phallic period of psychosexual development. It is a source of penis pride, or phallic pride, and is also manifested in an interest in masturbation.

phallic mother a psychoanalytical term based on the belief among boys that their mother possesses a penis. Freud believed this notion can be so entrenched that the discovery that it is false may produce such a feeling of disappointment and disgust that in some cases it may lead to impotence, homosexuality, or misogyny. Interestingly, some ancient maternal deities are depicted as possessing both breasts and phallus.

phallic-narcissistic character in psychoanalytical theory, the classical outcome of an unresolved Oedipus complex among men: a narcissistic, exhibitionistic, seductive Don Juan with an insatiable drive for more and more sexual conquests. A constant demonstration of potency is interpreted as a defence against castration anxiety.

phallic oath the ritual act of a man's touching another man's penis to solemnize an oath. See also penis holding.

phallic pride a psychoanalytical term for penis pride, which gives young boys a feeling of superiority and helps them master their castration anxiety.

phallic primacy in the psychoanalytical scheme, the phase of psychosexual development that follows the pregenital oral and anal stages, when libidinal (sexual) energy is focussed on the penis in the boy and the clitoris in the girl.

phallic sadism a psychoanalytical term for sexual fantasies during the phallic stage, in which intercourse is pictured as a violent, painful act, and the penis as an instrument of aggression.

phallic stage according to psychoanalysis, the phase of psychosexual development when sexual feeling is first focussed on the genital organs, and masturbation becomes a major source of pleasure. During this period, which extends from the age of 3 to the age of 6 or 7, the Oedipus complex develops, and the boy experiences sexual fantasies towards his mother and rivalry towards his father. At about the same time, girls discover the pleasure-giving possibilities of their clitoris, and experience erotic desire for their father and hostility towards the mother. Also called phallic phase.

phallic symbol any object that suggests or represents the penis in dreams or realistic observations, such as a telegraph pole, steeple, cigar, snake, sword, or knife. Though the term is psychoanalytical in origin. Freud himself is said to have remarked 'But sometimes a cigar is just a cigar.'

phallic worship reverence for the lingam, or penis. Among ancient and modern Hindus and Buddhists, sacred phalluses are made of various materials such as stone and wood. They are the principal ikons of the god Shiva, and in some cases are used as dildos during religious rites. Phallic shrines and ceremonies were also an integral part of the ancient Greek Dionysian rites and modern Shintoism. Also called phallicism; phallism.

phallitis an inflammation of the penis.

phallocampsis an abnormal condition in which the penis is curved, as in the abnormality known as chordee in which an inflammation affecting one side prevents a symmetrical erection. As a result the penis turns downwards or to one side in an erection which also may be quite painful.

phallocentric culture a society in which the phallus, or penis, is worshipped as the source of life and a symbol of fertility and power. In such a culture, the phallus is represented in art forms such as pictures and sculptures which play an essential part in religious rituals and ceremonies. Special deities also represent the phallus, such as Priapus among the Greeks and Shakti among the Hindus.

phallocrypsis the retraction of a penis to a point at which it is almost invisible.

phallocrypt another term for penis sheath, which is worn in many primitive societies to hide, protect, and decorate the male genital organ.

phallodynia a pain in the penis.

phalloid shaped like a penis.

phalloncus a swelling of the penis (Greek *phallos,* for 'penis,' and *onkos,* for 'swelling').

phallophobia a morbid fear of the penis especially when it is erect. Among the causes are fear of intercourse (coitophobia), revulsion stemming from parental attitudes towards sex, or fear of venereal disease. Also called penis fear.

phallus the penis, especially when in a state of erection. The term is used by Freud for the penis during the period of infantile sexuality.

phallus girl a term referring to the fantasy of a male transvestite that he is a girl with a penis hidden beneath his clothes.

phanermania an irresistible impulse to touch or stroke some part of one's own body repeatedly, especially a part that protrudes, such as the nose or breast. The compulsion usually has a sexual meaning for the individual.

phantom-lover syndrome a form of erotomania in which a poorly integrated schizophrenic woman suffers from a delusion that an unknown man is in love with her.

Pharaonic circumcision the stitching together of the labia majora to prevent sexual intercourse. The foreskin or labia also may have a metallic device, such as a ring, inserted between the folds of tissue to make coitus unlikely. These steps are believed to be taken to insure fidelity on the part of the wife. The practice is said to have originated in ancient Egypt and is still occasionally found in East Africa. The term circumcision, however, appears to be a misnomer.

Pharaonic mutilation a practice found in parts of Africa, in which the genitals of women are mutilated by ripping the vulva. The object appears to be to reduce sexual responsiveness and thereby make them 'safer' wives.

pharmacogenic orgasm a pleasurable orgasmic sensation reported by some individuals from the use of certain drugs of abuse. The effect of the drug use is reported to account for the diminished sex drive of the user, who substitutes drug effect for sexual orgasm.

pheromone a hormonal substance that is secreted by one individual to stimulate and attract another member of the species, usually of the opposite sex. Pheromones are released by a wide variety of nonhuman animals, from insects to rodents, inciting reproductive behaviour in the other members of the species. They are usually olfactory in nature, and have been synthesized for insect control.

philanderer today, a colloquial term referring to a man who makes love without serious intentions, often a married man who strays. However, the meaning that used to be the common one in English referred to a woman, namely a woman who loves men—the literal meaning of the Greek word being 'man lover.' (What we call a philanderer today should actually be called—to coin a term—a *philogynist,* a lover of women.)

philoboupaes in ancient Greece, an adult man who is sexually interested in boys that are big or bulky (*bous,* 'ox').

philomeirax in ancient Greece, a mature man who loves boys in their prime. The great tragedian Sophocles was called a philomeirax, which was considered to be a title of honour. (*Meirax,* 'beautiful.')

philtrum the verical groove in the centre of the upper lip. The term is derived from the Greek *philtron,* meaning 'philter, charm,' referring to the fact that this feature is usually considered attractive. Plural: *philtra.*

phimosiotomy a surgical procedure for relieving a condition of phimosis, or constriction of the foreskin.

phimosis a narrowing of the opening of the penile foreskin so that it cannot be retracted easily. The condition may be congenital or the result of an inflammation leading to fibrosis. In severe cases, phimosis may interfere with urination. If uncorrected, smegma accumulation can result in further inflammation and formation of gravel under the foreskin. Paraphimosis is a condition in which a tight foreskin may become swollen from fluid accumulation in the tissue cells after it has been retracted so that it will not return to its normal position over the glans penis. The swelling may hinder the circulation to the glans so that the glans also becomes swollen. The usual procedure for correcting paraphimosis is to massage the swollen area of the foreskin while pulling on the shaft of the penis. An alternative procedure is a surgical incision to release the foreskin.

phimosis of the tube an abnormal condition of the fallopian tube that may follow an inflammation which results in the fimbriae at the opening of the tube becoming inverted, thereby sealing the opening. See also PARA-PHIMOSIS OF THE TUBE.

phimosis vaginalis a congenital narrowing of the vagina. In some cases, the vaginal opening may be obstructed.

phony an American slang term for a person, usually a man, who makes obscene telephone calls.

phosophonoformate an antiviral drug tested in Europe as a possible treatment for AIDS, marketed under the Swedish trademark Foscarnet. See also AIDS.

photoplethysmograph a plethysmograph for measuring the physiological response to sexual arousal in a female. In consists of a transparent plastic cylinder containing a photocell and a light source.

phthirus pubis the scientific term for CRAB LOUSE. See this entry.

physical characteristics of homosexuals a term referring to the fact that physical traits associated with homosexual men and women rarely fit the stereotype. Studies show that—despite the popular conception by the general public that passive, frail males and robust, aggressive women are likely to be homosexual—only 15 percent of practising homosexual men and 5 percent of lesbians could be identified as such on the basis of their physical appearance.

physical stimulation the sexual arousal that results from physical contact with another person or from self-contact with sensitive parts of the body. Though usually effective, direct physical contact is not necessary to produce erection and ejaculation in a normal male, as is commonly demonstrated by instances of nocturnal emissions that are stimulated only by erotic dreams.

physique and sexuality the relationship, or alleged relationship, between body type and sexual activity. According to W.H. Sheldon, whose typologies are widely cited, the thin, fragile ectomorph is periodically overwhelmed with sexual desire and experiences the most intense ecstasy; the round, soft endomorph has a great need for companionship and a lesser need for sex; while the strong, muscular mesomorph tends to be matter-of-fact and rather unimaginative about sex. Sheldon did not apply these distinctions to women, but Indian love manuals describe four female types: The heavenly lotus woman

is beautiful, soft, and full-breasted and likes to make love in the daytime; the artistic woman is also heavenly, beautiful and full-breasted, but is proficient in the '64 arts' and likes to make love at night; the conch woman emanates from the earthly rather than the heavenly realm, has a large body but small breasts and is subject to sudden fits of amorous passion; and the elephant woman is short, stout, and slow in movement and likes prolonged love making under any and all circumstances.

piblokto an acute hysterical state in which an Eskimo woman suddenly screams, tears off her clothing, and runs about naked in the snow emitting the sounds of animals or birds. The episode is followed by unconsciousness and amnesia for the incident. The cause of the disorder is believed to be frustration and sexual abuse, stemming from the fact that Eskimo women are considered the property of men.

picket-fence injury medical jargon for a type of injury to the vagina that results from insertion of foreign objects during masturbation. Sharp or breakable objects can rupture the wall of the vagina, producing the kind of impalement that would occur if the woman fell astride a picket fence. Depending upon the angle of insertion of an object, it may puncture the urinary bladder or bowel as well as the vagina, which shares walls with those organs.

pictophilia a sexual obsession with erotic pictures.

PID an abbreviation for pelvic inflammatory disease. See this entry.

piece a British slang term for a woman, especially used in the phrases *piece of arse* and *piece of tail*.

piercing the practice of perforating various parts of the body and inserting rings or studs either for ornamentation or for enhancement of sexual pleasure. The use of earrings and nose rings for adornment is widespread; far more rare is the insertion of metal rings or rods in the nipples of both sexes, in the head of the penis (the glans), the prepuce, the scrotum, the perineum, the labia, or the hood of the clitoris—all of which are said to be erotically stimulating.

pili microscopic hairlike appendages of gonococcal bacteria cells. The pili enable the bacteria to attach themselves to cells lining the urogenital tracts of humans. An experimental antigonorrhoea vaccine is designed to prevent the gonorrhoeal pili from becoming attached to the human cells, which is the first step required by gonococcal cells to establish a colony in human tissues.

pill, the a birth control drug containing synthetic oestrogen and progesterone in dosages that alter normal menstruation so that ovulation does not occur. Available only by prescription, the pill must be taken by mouth according to exact directions. If correctly used, it is said to be close to 99 percent effective.

pillow books early bedside manuals in which sexual activities such as coital positions were explicity depicted and described. Their purpose was apparently both to instruct the uninitiated and to be sexually provocative. Examples are Ovid's *Art of Love* in the 4th century, the Hindu 4th-century classic known as *Kama Sutra,* Aretino's Renaissance sonnets, the 15th-century *Ananga Ranga,* the 16th-century Arabic *Perfumed Garden,* the Japanese bridal rolls, and the Chinese erotic handbooks.

pillow talk subjects discussed by couples during lovemaking. Studies show that common, if not popular, subjects in bed include sex and death. A subject apparently rarely discussed during lovemaking is money.

pills a rather dated British slang term for testicles. 'Pill' derives ultimately from Latin *pila,* 'ball.'

pill tumour a popular term for a hepatic adenoma, a rapidly growing liver tumour that is associated with the use of oral contraceptives.

pimp a procurer for prostitutes who presents himself as their 'business manager' and protector. His major functions are usually to manage their money (which they give to him), to provide living quarters for them, to supply them with sexy clothes, to get them medical attention when needed, and to protect them from police and from brutal clients. They also give them a degree of superficial kindness when they feel lost. Their interest in these women evaporates quickly if they do not 'turn' enough 'tricks,' and they may be replaced or punished by beatings or sexual harassment. The 'profession' of the pimp is illegal, and much time is spent in dodging or paying off the police, and in paying petty fines.

pimples and penetration a slang term referring to extreme close-up shots for pornographic photos or films—close enough to see the pimples on the skin, and unobstructed enough to see the actual penetration. More

commonly used is the abbreviation, P&P.

pinafore punishment punishing a child by forcing him or her to dress in the clothes of the opposite sex (cross-dressing).

Pincus, Gregory an American medical researcher credited as 'father of the Pill,' for his work in the 1950s in developing the first oral contraceptive pills.

pineal body a pinecone-shaped organ less than 1 centimetre in length located in a pocket of the forebrain near the thalamus. Tumours of the pineal body have been associated with cases of precocious puberty.

pinealoma a tumour of the pineal gland that can affect the rate of sexual maturity in a male or female. Girls with tumours of the pineal gland tend to have a delayed menarche, whereas in boys a pinealoma results in sexual precocity.

ping-pong infection a venereal infection, such as candidiasis, gonorrhoea, or syphilis, that is transmitted back and forth between a couple who engage in intercourse, each infecting and reinfecting the other.

pinup a photograph of an attractive young woman with shapely sexual features, especially breasts and legs, fastened to a wall in a dormitory, workplace, etc.

piss a vulgar slang term meaning to urinate or urination. It is also used in various metaphorical ways, especially in British English: *pissed* means drunk; a *piss-up* is a bout of heavy drinking; *pissed off* means annoyed or fed up; the expletive *piss off* means go away; *it's pissing down* means it's raining heavily; and a *piss artist* is a useless or contemptible person. The term piss ranks number 18 in the TABOONESS RATING OF DIRTY WORDS. See this entry.

pissproud a slang term for having a penile erection caused by an overfull urinary bladder. It is a condition typical of the early morning.

pituitary gland an endocrine gland near the base of the brain and a source of a number of hormones, including the gonadotropic hormones. The pituitary actually is three glands in one. The anterior lobe is the source of the thyroid-stimulating hormone, adrenocorticotropic hormone, follicle-stimulating hormone, luteinizing hormone, prolactin, and growth hormone. The intermediate lobe secretes some growth hormone and two forms of melanocyte-stimulating hormones. The posterior lobe secretes oxytocin and vasopressin. The pituitary gland in turn is under the influence of the neighbouring hypothalamus, which secretes eight neurohormones. An example of the effect is the negative-feedback mechanism whereby secretion of the follicle-stimulating and luteinizing hormones can be turned off by the hypothalamus when the levels of oestrogen or progesterone in the bloodstream reach a certain critical point. There is evidence that control of the pituitary secretions also involves emotional, physical, or environmental influences. A woman who is worried about becoming pregnant, for example, may actually develop amenorrhoea through the stress effect that induces the hypothalamus to stop pituitary release of hormones needed for a successful pregnancy. At the other extreme, a tumour or other disorder of the hypothalamus can cause an excessive release of pituitary hormones, resulting in precocious puberty.

placenta an organ of pregnancy that is attached to the inner wall of the uterus and connected to the foetus by an umbilical cord. The blood vessels in the umbilical cord provide all the nutrients for the growth and maturation of the foetus and carry away the waste of its metabolism. The placenta develops from the implantation of the finger-like chorionic villi of the trophoblast, near the end of the first week of a human pregnancy. During implantation, an enzyme opens small arteries and veins in the lining of the uterus, producing small ponds of blood which stimulates the growth of additional villi to form the foetal portion of the placenta. The umbilical cord develops from tissues of the primordial body stalk, the amniotic membrane, and evolving blood vessels. They become a single stalk that links the embryo to the placenta. As the placenta grows, it divides into 15 to 20 separately functioning units called cotyledons. The placenta reaches its maximum thickness of slightly more than 1 inch by the 20th week of pregnancy, but continues to grow in diameter to a size of 6 to 8 inches. The weight of the placenta is about 1 pound, give or take a few ounces. The umbilical cord grows to a length of 20 to 22 inches and a thickness of almost 1 inch. In a multiple pregnancy there may be more than one placenta, or there may be two placentas that become fused so that they appear to be a single placenta. Blood flows between the mother and the foetus appears to be controlled by a kind of pumping action in which uterine contractions cause blood to flow from the uterus into the blood lakes within the placenta. The uterus then relaxes and blood

drains from the foetal side back towards the maternal circulation. The uterus moves about 1 pint of blood per minute into the placenta, and a slightly smaller amount returns during uterine relaxation. The foetus thus gains a small amount of blood materials in each exchange, the increase being contributed toward its parasitic growth. The so-called *placenta barrier* consists of two layers of cells through which the blood exchange must flow. During the second trimester, the inner layer of cells degenerates as a barrier because the cells become fewer and more widely separated as the placenta grows. As a result, only one cell layer eventually separates the maternal and foetal blood supplies and it, too, tends to develop gaps that diminish the integrity of the placental barrier.

placental hormones hormones that are produced by the foetoplacental portion of the uterus during pregnancy. The hormones are synthesized from substances supplied by the maternal bloodstream and those produced by the developing embryo and include oestrogens, oestrone and oestradiol, human chorionic gonadotropin, human chorionic somatomammotropin, and human chorionic thyrotropin. Human chorionic somatomammotropin is also known as placental lactogen.

placental immunity a protection given to the developing foetus by immunoglobulins that cross the placental barrier. The foetus thus shares in the mother's supplies of antibodies against certain infectious disease organisms until its own immune system matures, usually a few months after birth.

placental infection involvement of the placenta and foetus in infectious diseases that may invade or cross the placenta during pregnancy. Although the placental barrier is capable of protecting the foetus against most bacteria, viruses are small enough to slip through the tiny openings in the membrane, causing foetal death or damage. Among the most notorious of the viruses that may attack the foetus are rubella and genital herpes. Syphilis is a bacterial disease that can slip through the protective membrane after the barrier begins to lose its integrity, around the 16th week of pregnancy. The placenta itself can acquire infections from bacteria, viruses, protozoa, or other disease organisms, causing placentitis.

placenta previa a placenta that is located in the lower area of the uterus so that it either blocks the birth canal or encroaches upon it. A placenta previa is sometimes graded according to the extent that it covers the cervical os, or opening into the vagina. A first-degree placenta previa is one in which only a placental edge reaches the lower uterine segment while most of the placenta is higher in the uterus. A fourth-degree (or total) placenta previa is one that completely covers the cervical os, even when it is fully dilated, thereby preventing a normal delivery of the foetus ahead of the placenta.

placentitis an inflammation involving the placenta. It is usually a disorder that affects the tissues on the foetal side of the membranes, particularly the cells separating the amnion from the chorion. However, the inflammation may spread to the umbilical vessels.

Planned Parenthood the shortened name of Planned Parenthood-World Population, a family-planning organization with affiliates throughout the world as part of the International Planned Parenthood Federation. The organization provides information and guidance on unwanted pregnancies, abortion, overpopulation, contraceptive methods, infertility, and spacing of children, all on a confidential basis.

plasma proteins proteins in the bloodstream that transport male and female sex hormones to various organs and tissues. Female oestrogens are generally carried on molecules of albumin, a plasma protein.

plaster caster a female fan of male stars, especially rock stars, who makes and collects plaster of Paris replicas of the stars' penises.

plastic surgery a surgical speciality that encompasses the repair, transfer, or removal of body organs and tissues, such as reconstruction of the female breast or facial features. Plastic surgery may also be used to reconstruct a penis after amputation or to construct a vagina. Although plastic surgery has been a recognized medical speciality in the West for only 50 years, it has been practised in India and Egypt for thousands of years.

plateau phase a stage of preorgasmic sexual activity which in men is marked by the emission of several drops of fluid from Cowper's glands while the testes continue to be elevated until they are close to the body to increase ejaculatory pressure. In women, the plateau phase is more complex and includes retraction of the clitoris as a protective measure against injury from direct intense pressure of the male, enlargement of the labial gap to form a funnel into the vagina, and a change in colour of the labia minora to bright red in a woman who has never been pregnant or to a burgundy red in a woman who has borne children. Orgasm usually follows within 3 minutes after the labial colour change unless stimulation ceases. The skin and breasts of the woman may develop what is known as a sexual flush, characterized by a mottling or rash. The breasts may increase as much as 25 percent in size and there is areola enlargement. The orgasmic platform develops in the vagina. The phase may last 30 seconds to 3 minutes.

platonic love a type of relationship between man and woman, two women, or two men, which was idealized by the Greek philosopher Plato (427-347 B.C.). Though intimate, this relationship is essentially spiritual in nature, based on common ideas, interests, and ideals, but devoid of overt sexual content. In adulthood the persistent search for this 'ideal' love may be a form of escape from sexuality and marriage.

Playboy Survey a 1970s sex survey sponsored by the Playboy Foundation in the U.S.A. A total of 982 men and 1,044 women in 24 cities were interviewed by questionnaire about sex histories and attitudes. The survey was more representative of the total population than the Kinsey Report conducted about 30 years earlier (Kinsey, for example, did not interview blacks), and many new trends had developed in the intervening years: more variety in intercourse positions; more orogenital contact; more premarital sex; more marital sex; more extramarital sex among women under 25; a decline in the double standard; and less sex with prostitutes.

player a slang term, mainly in black American English, for pimp.

play solitaire a euphemism meaning to masturbate.

play the flute a slang term meaning to perform fellatio.

play with oneself a widely used colloquial term meaning to masturbate.

pleasure centres brain areas that control the experience of pleasure. Rats and other animals that have been conditioned to press a lever producing electric stimulation of portions of the thalamus, hypothalamus, and mesencephalon (midbrain) experience such intense pleasure that they will repeat the manoeuvre as many as 5,000 times an hour, and will not take time to eat even when starving. Similar centres in human beings have not yet been precisely identified, though it is believed that they exist in the same general area.

pleasure principle the psychoanalytical theory that we are governed by the impulse to seek pleasure and avoid pain. When our instinctual, or libidinal, drives such as sex, hunger, thirst, or elimination are unsatisfied, we are in a state of tension and discomfort, but when they are fulfilled, the reduction in tension evokes the feeling of pleasure. The pleasure principle dominates the early life of the child, but is gradually 'tamed' and modified by the reality principle. Also called pleasure-pain principle.

pleasuring a current term for activities other than actual intercourse that yield erotic pleasure. Though pleasuring is usually identical with foreplay (that is, kissing, caressing, stroking), and usually an indispensable preliminary to intercourse, it can also be enjoyed for its own sake, for the sake of comforting one's partner, or as an expression of intimacy and love.

Until last century, pleasuring meant having sexual intercourse, as in 'He pleasured his wife twice a week.'

plethysmograph an instrument used to measure changes in the size of organs or the amount of blood flow in a part of the body. A penile plethysmograph may be employed to record blood flow and other changes that occur when a penis undergoes secretion. Similarly, a vaginal plethysmograph is used to record changes in the vaginal walls during sexual arousal.

plicamycin the generic name of an antineoplastic drug that is prescribed for the treatment of cancer of the testicles.

plonker a British slang term for penis. It comes from *plonk*, meaning to copulate, and like most of its synonyms is also used as a term for a foolish man.

plum a Shakespearean (and once general) euphemism for vagina.

plural marriage polygamous marriage; a marriage in which there is more than one permanent spouse (wife or husband).

pneumocystis carinii pneumonia a major form of AIDS disease. It is a lethal lung infection marked by air- or gas-filled cysts in the lung tissue. The disorder also occurs in children with gamma-globulin deficiency. See also AIDS.

pneumogynaecography a method of studying the ovaries and uterus by making an x-ray film of the female pelvic area after carbon-dioxide gas has been injected into the peritoneal cavity.

podophyllotoxin a substance derived from the mandrake root and a source of podophillin, a remedy prescribed for the treatment of genital warts.

point of no return during intercourse, the moment when ejaculation, or orgasm, becomes inevitable. In men the tension involved in thrusting, has reached a point where reflexes take over, producing waves of contraction leading to an overpowering feeling of approaching climax. Progress then proceeds in a breathless rush culminating in ejaculation, which brings with it a peak of sexual excitement. Women's experience is similar in reaching orgasm.

point percy at the porcelain a humourous euphemism meaning to urinate.

poke a slang term meaning to copulate. It is generally used of a man.

polar body a nonfunctional cell produced during the meiotic division process of the development of the female gamete. Polar bodies are produced during divisions of the primary and secondary oocytes. Although the polar body of the secondary oocyte division has the right number (23) of chromosomes for mating with a spermatozoon, it does not take part in the reproductive process and is discarded.

polyandry a form of plural marriage in which one woman has two or more husbands at the same time. In fraternal polyandry the husbands are brothers. Polyandrous societies are rare, the best known occurring in Tibet and other areas of the Himalayas.

polycyesis a term meaning a multiple pregnancy, such as twins or triplets (Greek *poly*, 'many,' and *kyesis*, 'pregnancy').

polygamy a form of marriage in which there is more than one wife or husband (polygyny or polyandry), although the term usually refers to a plurality of wives, as in Mormonism. Polygamous societies are found throughout the world, especially in 'tribal' cultures and in developing countries.

polygene any of the nonallelic genes that may represent neither dominant nor recessive traits but which may interact in a synergistic manner to produce a characteristic that is a blend of maternal and paternal traits, such as skin colour.

polygyny a form of plural marriage in which a man has more than one legal wife at the same time. In general polygyny, as contrasted with the sororal type, the co-wives are of no particular relationship to each other. The practice is found throughout the world and is usually an indicator of superior status or wealth, although among the Mormons (Church of Jesus Christ of Latter-Day Saints) it was (and still is in some areas) based on religious belief. In parts of the Islamic world the Koran is interpreted as permitting a man to have up to four wives. The reason for polygyny may also be economic. Among the Cayapa of Ecuador, it is regarded as sinful but accepted de facto because the wives provide assistance with the banana crop.

polymastia a condition which in humans is characterized by more than two distinct mammary glands, a normal feature of some animals. Also called supernumerary breasts.

polymorphous perverse Freud's term for the capacity to respond to many types of sexual stimulation, such as fondling, sucking, viewing, masturbating, smelling, defecating, and inflicting or suffering pain. This capacity originates in infancy and is expressed to some degree in normal sexual activity, but may also take the form of practices that are characterized as perversions, deviations, or paraphilias.

polyoestradiol phosphate a drug commonly prescribed for the treatment of cancer of the prostate. The drug is a form of oestrogen that also results in impotence, gynaecomastia, and loss of sex drive in men.

polyoestrous having two or more reproductive cycles in each mating season or each year. Examples include birds that may ovulate once a day until a certain number of eggs has been produced.

polyorchid a person with one or more supernumerary testes.

polyps benign tumours that are pedunculated, or grow from stalks, in the uterus or cervix. Cervical polyps are likely to bleed after intercourse or even as a result of douching. Large cervical polyps may protrude from the cervix into the vagina. Like myomas, uterine polyps tend to cause abnormal bleeding and also may acquire an infection resulting in a vaginal discharge.

polythelia a medical term for supernumerary nipples. The extra nipples may develop anywhere along the so-called milk line, a ridge of embryonic tissue that runs from near the armpits to the thighs. The supernumerary nipples are easily removed by plastic surgery.

Pomeroy, Wardell Baxter (born 1913) American psychologist, academic dean of the Institute for Advanced Study of Human Sexuality, and past president of SIECUS (Sex Information and Education Council of the United States). Dr Pomeroy is coauthor with Alfred Kinsey of *Sexual Behavior in the Human Male* and *Sexual Behavior in the Human Female* and author of many other works in the field of sex research.

pompadour fantasy a variation of the courtesan, or hetaeral, fantasy in which a woman imagines that she is the mistress of a king or emperor. The fantasy is named after the mistress of King Louis XV of France, Madame de Pompadour.

poof a derogatory slang term for a male homosexual. It is also spelt *pouf*.

poofter a derogatory slang term for a male homosexual.

poontang a common slang term, especially black American English, for (a) sexual intercourse and (b) a woman. (The term may be derived from the French *putain*, meaning 'prostitute'.)

porn burnout a form of boredom reported by persons who are more or less continuously exposed to films, photos, or literature featuring explicit sexual activity. Eventually, pornographic material loses its erotic appeal and is no longer of prurient interest.

pornographomania a compulsion to write sexually obscene material, especially letters.

pornography explicit erotic material presented in pictorial or written form for the express purpose of sexual arousal or of satisfying sexual curiosity or interest. The emphasis is usually on anatomical details, the more unusual forms of sexual activity, and material that is frequently considered obscene. A distinction is sometimes made between soft pornography, typified by 'girlie' magazines and albums depicting nudes, and hard (or hard-core) pornography, typified by sadomasochistic sequences and close-up shots of various types of intercourse. (Greek *porne*, 'prostitute,' and *graphein*, 'to write.')

porno-hypnosis a form of stage entertainment in which hypnotized subjects are induced to engage in suggestive or erotic acts.

pornolagnia (Greek, 'lust for prostitutes') an extreme attraction to prostitutes and to sexual activity with prostitutes.

positive nuclear sex a term pertaining to the general rule that only one X chromosome of a female tissue cell is active, allowing the second X chromosome to take the tissue stain that reveals the cell's chromatin material as a Barr body. In a superfemale, with three X chromosomes, a tissue cell would normally show the extra chromosomes as two Barr bodies. Exceptions include cells of some Turner's-syndrome patients who have only one X chromosome per cell but test as positive nuclear sex, or chromatin-positive.

positive signs of pregnancy physical changes in a woman that are more definitive evidence of a pregnancy than presumptive or probable signs. They include detection of movement within the uterus, detection of foetal heartbeats, and x-ray or ultrasonic images of the foetus within the uterus.

positive transference a psychoanalytical term for transference to the therapist of feelings of attachment, love, and idealization originally experienced towards the patient's parents.

POSSLQ (pos'əlkyoo) an abbreviation for 'partners of the opposite sex sharing living quarters,' a category established by the U.S. Census Bureau for unmarried male and female cohabitants. The abbreviation has been used in its plural form (POSSLQs), and as an alternative term for a person who may participate in cohabitation, as in the question, 'Will you be my POSSLQ?'

postambivalent phase the final stage of psychosexual development characterized by full 'object love' and the ability to obtain complete gratification from genital orgasm. Earlier stages are described as ambivalent because they involve not only positive feelings, but hostile feelings as well, because of the fact that satisfaction can only be achieved by destroying the object, as in biting or swallowing.

postcoital semen test a laboratory examination of semen collected from the vagina and cervix after intercourse. The test is performed as part of a diagnosis for possible male infertility. Failure to find spermatozoa in the semen samples may indicate a condition of azoospermia or an inflammation or hostile secretion in the cervical area.

post coitum triste (Latin, 'sad after coitus') depressive feelings after sexual intercourse resulting, in some cases at least, from inability to attain a full orgasm.

postconsummatory behaviour behaviour in the postorgasmic phase of the sexual response cycle, characterized by relaxation of the entire musculature, and overwhelming need to rest, a heavy head, a generally quiescent state in which the heart and breathing rates revert to normal, and a profound sense of gratification, peace and satiation, which may be followed by sleep.

posterior urethritis an infection of the lining of the male urogenital system from the testes to the end of the prostatic urethra, including the urinary bladder.

posthon in ancient Greece, a boy loved by a man (*posthe*, 'penis').

postillionnage a French word for the practice of inserting and manipulating a finger in the partner's anus during foreplay or intercourse, or in one's own anus during masturbation. The practice appears to be more common among men than among women, and usually has a powerful erotic effect when it is done just before or during orgasm. A small vibrator is sometimes used in place of the finger.

postmenopausal muscular-dystrophy syndrome a condition of progressive weakness of the muscles of the hips and shoulders after menopause. Unlike menopausal myopathy, there is no evidence of muscle atrophy. However, the woman experiences difficulty in stretching her arms above her head, climbing stairs, or even rising from a chair. The disorder is progressive, leading to a waddling gait and eventual inability to use stairs.

postorgasmic phase an alternative term for postconsummatory phase or postconsummatory behaviour.

postovulatory pertaining to the phase of the menstrual cycle that follows the release of an ovum from an ovary.

postpartal eclamptic symptoms high blood pressure, severe headache, dizziness, visual disturbances, abdominal pain, vomiting, and muscle twitching that usually precede an attack of convulsions. The symptoms may occur within 48 hours after labour and are usually accompanied by mental confusion, fluid accumulation, and the presence of proteins in the urine. The attack of convulsions may include a state of rigidity and muscle contractions and relaxations with noisy breathing. The skin may turn a bluish colour because of an oxygen deficiency in the blood. The patient then enters a comatose state that lasts for an indefinite period and finally regains consciousness with no memory of the events surrounding the attack. Although the condition has been observed for generations, its cause is still unknown. It has been theorized that a toxic product of metabolism accounts for the symptoms, but no toxic substance has ever been identified in connection with the disorder.

postpartal period the period immediately after the birth of an infant. Also called postnatal period.

postpartum blues a synonym for maternity blues and baby blues.

postpartum emotional disturbances a term that embraces relatively mild and transient emotional disorders after childbirth, such as maternity blues, feelings of anxiety, insomnia, and indifference or hostility towards the child or the father.

postpartum intercourse resumption of intercourse after delivery. Gynaecologists usually recommend refraining from vaginal intercourse for 6 weeks, or possibly for a shorter time if healing has taken place and the flow of lochia has ended.

postpartum psychosis an episode of mental illness after childbirth. The symptoms are usually either severe depression or schizophrenic reactions such as delusions or hallucinations. Many causative factors have been suggested: endocrine disturbances, emotional stresses during the puerperium, and various psychological factors such as marital problems, financial burdens, lack of desire for the baby on the part of the wife or husband—any of which may be aggravated by preexisting personality defects and maladjustments. Also called puerperal psychosis.

postpartum taboos several types of taboos after childbirth, including a taboo against sex during breast feeding (common in Africa); a taboo against adultery during ritual seclusion of the father of a newborn child (among certain African societies, such as the Mongo-Nkundu); and a taboo against intercourse between husband and wife for very long periods among Muslims, and for shorter periods in other societies such as North, Central and South American Indians.

postpill amenorrhoea a failure of normal menstrual cycles to resume after the use of oral contraceptives has been discontinued. The absence of menses rarely is permanent. The cause of the phenomenon is not well understood. Normally, menstrual cycles resume within 3 months after use of the pill has stopped.

postpubertal panhypopituitarism a disorder caused by disease or injury to the pituitary gland that develops after puberty, resulting in loss of sex drive, amenorrhoea and failure to lactate in women, and loss of pubic and axillary hair in both men and women. A common cause is an obstruction

in the blood flow to the pituitary gland, as by thrombosis.

potency the ability of the male to achieve and maintain an erection, and to ejaculate—to perform sexual intercourse.

potential fertility the chance that a woman or group of women will become pregnant in a normal married situation when no method of birth control is used to prevent conception.

Prader-Willi syndrome an abnormal condition of cryptorchism and hypogonadism combined with short stature, obesity, small hands and feet, muscular weakness, and mental retardation. When diabetes mellitus is associated with the other conditions, it is known as Royer's syndrome. The condition is believed to affect both males and females, but it is more easily diagnosed in men because of the abnormalities of the external genitalia.

preadolescence the period of psychosexual development preceding the onset of puberty, comprising approximately the 2 years before the age of 12 in girls and the age of 13 in boys. This developmental phase is characterized by rapid change and growth during which the sex glands begin to mature and the physical differences between the sexes become more marked. Also called prepubescence; prepubertal stage; prepuberty.

precocious birth the natural termination of a pregnancy in less than the usual length of gestation.

precocious breast enlargement enlargement of the female breast at a time in childhood significantly earlier than normal thelarche. Medical records include cases of female infants born with enlarged breasts, and in at least one case the girl was born with milk in the breasts. The mother of the child had enlarged breasts at the age of 10 and menstruated at 12 years of age. See also WITCHES' MILK.

precocious menstruation menstruation that begins before the average or normal age of menarche. A 1939 medical report cites a case of a girl who began menstruating at the age of 8 months and became the mother of a boy at the age of 5 years. A 1955 medical report cites a case of a girl who had a bloody vaginal discharge at the age of 2 months but did not begin regular menstrual periods until she was 16 months old.

precocious parenthood a term referring to males or females who were able to become fathers or mothers at an extremely early age because of precocious puberty. The youngest mothers on record were 5 and 6 years old; one had begun menstruating at the age of 3. Boys at the ages of 7 and 9 have become fathers, according to medical records. In a 19th-century report, a boy was reported to have semen emissions at the age of 4.

precocious pubarche the appearance of pubic hair at an age significantly earlier than normal. A British medical report of the 1950s noted in a case of precocious male puberty that pubic hair began growing at the age of 5 months. Pubic hair was observed in a 6-month-old girl who had a bloody vaginal discharge when only 5 weeks old; the vaginal discharge was followed by an enlargement of the breasts. In the 19th century, a girl was reportedly born with pubic hair present.

precocious puberty the premature development of functioning gonads in girls and boys. In true precocious puberty, girls ovulate and boys produce mature spermatozoa. The young people also have adult levels of sex hormones and the secondary sexual characteristics of their gender. Precocious puberty may occur as early as the age of 8 in girls and the age of 10 in boys.

precocity earlier-than-usual or premature development. See CEREBRAL-TYPE SEXUAL PRECOCITY; COMPLETE PRECOCITY; ENDOCRINE-TYPE SEXUAL PRECOCITY; HETEROSEXUAL PRECOCITY; INCOMPLETE PRECOCITY; ISOSEXUAL PRECOCITY; PSEUDOSEXUAL PRECOCITY; SEXUAL PRECOCITY; UNILATERAL SEXUAL PRECOCITY.

precoital fluid the alkaline fluid secreted by the Cowper's glands of the male. The Cowper's or bulbourethral glands are located on both sides of the urethra just below the edge of the prostate. The thin fluid of the glands usually precedes ejaculation, the alkalinity helping to neutralize the acidity of the lining of the urethra (which could kill sperm). It may contain a small amount of spermatozoa, enough to induce a pregnancy. But it lacks the major portion of spermatozoa and the seminal substances needed to support passage to the uterus.

pre-Columbia theory of syphilis a scientifically based concept that syphilis was not introduced to Europe by members of the crew of Christopher Columbus in the late 15th century. The pre-Columbia evidence indicates that the syphilis organism is merely a different form of treponematosis which may have always been present in humans. Other variations include yaws, which infects monkeys and apes as well as humans, and pinta. Syph-

ilis, according to the theory, may be a mutant form of yaws.

predatory rapist an alternative term for an impulse rapist, a man who commits rape simply because he finds himself in an opportunistic position for the sexual crime, such as finding himself alone in a bedroom with a strange woman.

preeclampsia a hypertension syndrome accompanied by the presence of proteins in the urine or a fluid accumulation in the tissues, or both, that may develop during pregnancy or immediately after pregnancy. The blood circulation is altered, there is sodium retention, increased central-nervous-system activity, and reduced kidney function. The symptoms usually develop in the second trimester of pregnancy with a rise in blood pressure and a weight gain of more than 3 pounds per week. The woman may complain of headache, blurred vision or other visual problems, nausea and vomiting, abdominal pain, and irritability or emotional tension. The condition can be dangerous, particularly if the oedema, or fluid accumulation in the tissues, involves the brain or lungs. The victim is often a young mother, in her teens or early 20s, and experiencing her first pregnancy. If the early symptoms cannot be controlled, the condition may progress to convulsions and coma.

preemptive abortion a precautionary measure in which the contents of the woman's uterus are removed by suction before her next expected menstrual period, to avoid pregnancy.

preformism the archaic theory that the characteristics of the individual already exist in the germ cell and that embryonic development consists of the gradual emergence of these preexisting characteristics. This hypothesis contrasts with epigenesis, the theory that new characteristics, not determined by the fertilized egg, can develop as a result of prenatal environmental influences. See also HOMUNCULUS.

pregenital love a psychoanalytical term for the first signs of caring for another person, usually the mother. Pregenital love makes its appearance during the infantile sucking and biting stages that precede the stage of genital love, which is focussed on the genital organs.

pregenital phase in psychoanalysis, the first stages of psychosexual development, when the libido, or sex instinct, is focussed on the mouth, anus, and urethra rather than the genital organs.

pregnancy the period between conception and the complete delivery of the foetus and the other products of conception, that is, the afterbirth and foetal membranes; or the period between conception and an interruption of pregnancy, as by abortion. The average human pregnancy lasts 280 days or 9 calendar months. See also ABDOMINAL PREGNANCY; ADOLESCENT PREGNANCY; CERVICAL PREGNANCY; ECTOPIC PREGNANCY; EXTRAUTERINE PREGNANCY; FALLOPIAN-TUBE PREGNANCY; HYSTERICAL PREGNANCY; INTERSTITIAL PREGNANCY; INTERSTITIAL TUBAL PREGNANCY; MALE PREGNANCY; MARIJUANA AND PREGNANCY; MASK OF PREGNANCY; MOLAR PREGNANCY; OVARIAN PREGNANCY; PSEUDOPREGNANCY; TEENAGE PREGNANCY; TUBAL PREGNANCY; UNWANTED PREGNANCIES.

pregnancy fantasies mental images involving misconceptions about pregnancy such as the notion that the baby will be born through the anus, mouth, or umbilicus, or that it will be a gift from the father. Revival of such early fantasies may lead to various neurotic symptoms during pregnancy, such as uncontrolled vomiting, fear of mutilation, or fear of being devoured by the foetus.

pregnancy urine test a variation of the chorionic-gonadotropin-hormone test in which a sample of urine is used instead of blood. The hormone is present in both blood and urine whenever there is living placental tissue in the woman. The hormone is measured in the urine about 10 to 14 days after likely conception, and preferably 2 weeks after the first missed menstrual period. The test is usually performed with the first urine of the morning. An excess of protein in the urine can give incorrect results.

pregnanediol-urine test a pregnancy test that measures the level of pregnanediol in the female urine. Pregnanediol is the main excretion product of progesterone produced in the ovaries and placenta; it is not produced from progesterone in drugs, such as oral contraceptives. The levels of pregnanediol in the urine rise steadily during pregnancy, rise rapidly and briefly just after ovulation, and fall when spontaneous abortion threatens.

pregnanetriol test a laboratory test for androgenital syndrome, in which excessive levels of male sex hormones are produced as a result of adrenal gland disorders. The test is based on the presence of pregnanetriol, an adrenal gland hormone, in the urine.

premarital counselling a counselling process conducted by a trained professional with a couple who are planning to be married. The object is to help them to know each other better and share their concerns, and to obtain information as needed on such questions as birth control, family planning, and ways of dealing with marital problems.

premarital sex intercourse between two unmarried people, whether or not they intend to be married.

premature ejaculation a male sexual dysfunction in which ejaculation consistently occurs before or immediately after penetration, and before the partner has had a chance to reach orgasm. Such methods as the squeeze and stop-start techniques are frequently effective in treating this condition.

premature labour the termination of a pregnancy before the usual or normal time but at a phase of gestation when the foetus is capable of surviving outside the uterus. Technically, it is labour that occurs before the 37th week of gestation and results in the birth of an infant weighing less than 2,500 grams (about 5.5 pounds).

premature pubarche the development of pubic hair in a girl before any other signs of puberty occur. The girl may have pubic hair throughout childhood as the only feature suggesting advanced adolescence.

premature thelarche a condition in which the female breasts become enlarged at an early age but other reproductive features remain at the prepubertal stage. There is no pubic hair and no evidence of maturation of the ovary or uterus.

prematurity the relatively undeveloped state of a child who has been born before the normal foetal processes of development have been completed. A newborn is usually considered premature if it weighs less than 5 pounds 8 ounces (2,500 grams). After about 20 weeks of gestation, the foetus has usually matured fully enough to survive, especially if it is placed in an incubator.

premenstrual congestion the accumulation of fluid in the mucous membranes and other tissues of a woman during the luteal phase of the menstrual cycle. The fluid retained during this phase can amount to more than 2 quarts and a weight gain of as much as 5 pounds.

premenstrual disorders disturbances associated with glandular imbalance during the 4 to 7 days before menstruation, especially irritability, tension, headache, fatigue, pain in the lower back, bloating, and heaviness in the pelvic region.

premenstrual sex drive a period of increased sexual desire among some women during the luteal phase of the menstrual cycle. Studies indicate a correlation between premenstrual tension in certain women and a heightened sex drive at the same time.

premenstrual tension (PMT) one of several disorders that frequently occur a few days before menstruation.

prenatal developmental anomaly a congenital defect that develops during the prenatal period. Examples are clubfoot, cleft palate, hydrocephalus, hypertelorism (wideset eyes), osteogenesis imperfecta (brittle bones), arthrogryposis (crooked joints), and phocomelia (absence of limbs).

prenatal influence any influence on the developing organism between conception and birth. Among the factors that may have a harmful effect are maternal diseases such as German measles, x-rays of the abdomen, alcoholism, drug abuse, excessive smoking, gonorrhoea, blood incompatibility, nutritional deficiencies, and severe emotional stress. Influences of this kind should not be confused with the discredited doctrine of 'maternal impression,' which held that the mother could transmit the effects of her experiences to the unborn child—for example, that a red birthmark could be caused by fright experienced in watching a conflagration.

prenatal period the period preceding birth, or the combined germinal, embryonic, and foetal periods that occur successively between conception and labour.

prenatal sensorineural lesion a congenital disorder of the inner ear or auditory nerve, resulting in hearing loss, that is a result of infection or other effect of maternal illness while the individual was an embryo. The condition is often caused by a rubella-virus infection that crosses the placental barrier.

prenatal sexual development a process that begins with conception and determination of gender by the sex chromosome (X or Y) carried by the sperm. The sex chromosome in the egg is always X, and if the sperm that fertilizes it is also an X, the baby will be XX, or female, and will eventually develop a uterus, fallopian tubes, vagina, clitoris, labia, and ovaries that manufacture the female hormone, oestrogen. But if the fertilizing sperm carries a Y, the baby will be XY, or male, and will develop a penis, testes, and the male hormone, testosterone. In either case

the development of the sex organs begins to occur between the sixth and 12th weeks after fertilization.

preoedipal period in psychoanalysis, the early stages of psychosexual development (especially the oral and anal phases), when children of both sexes focus their love on the mother, and the father is not yet considered either a rival or a love object.

preorgasmic characterizing the stages of the sexual response cycle before orgasm, and extending over a period of 30 seconds to 3 minutes. During this period, foreplay produces such changes as increased heart rate, breathing rate, and blood pressure, as well as muscle contractions and increase in the size of the penis, testes, and upper vaginal walls. The term preorgasmic has also been adopted by women's therapy groups as a replacement for frigid, because it implies that a woman who has yet to experience orgasm may be helped to reach one through therapy or other means.

preorgasmic emission discharge of two or three drops of a mucoid substance from the glans penis during the plateau phase of the sexual response cycle. The emission is believed to come from Cowper's glands, but its function is unknown. Although it normally contains active sperm, it is not known whether the number is sufficient to produce fertilization.

preovulatory pertaining to the period of the menstrual cycle that precedes the release of a mature egg from an ovary.

prephallic masturbation equivalent a psychoanalytical term for autoerotic activities occurring before the genital organs become the focus of sexuality. In these activities the child derives pleasure from the mouth, anus, urethra, skin, motor activities, sensation, and perception.

prepubertal panhypopituitarism a failure of the anterior lobe of the pituitary gland to secrete adequate levels of gonadotrophic hormones because of disease or injury to the gland during childhood. The disorder may be reflected in subnormal sexual development and in an individual with normal body proportions but less than normal size body.

prepubertal sexual activity erotic behaviour before puberty. Erections in male infants immediately after birth are probably reflexive and not evidence of sexual arousal. However, infants of both sexes appear to respond to genital stimulation and self-manipulation in a way that strongly suggests erotic pleasure, as early as 4 months of age, and a few of Kinsey's subjects have reported that their children, male or female, appear to reach orgasm through masturbation at about 3 years of age. Between 5 and 10 nearly all boys and about 20 percent of girls engage in autoerotic activities (fondling of the penis and manual stimulation of the clitoris) as well as exhibiting and handling their genitals in the presence of companions and, in some instances, homosexual play. Also called prepubescent sexuality.

prepubertal stage another term for the approximately 2 years of preadolescence.

prepuberty an alternative term for preadolescence.

prepuberty growth spurt an alternative term for pubescent growth spurt.

prepubescence a synonym for preadolescence, prepubertal stage, and prepuberty.

prepuce a fold of thin, hairless skin that covers the neck of the penis and may overhang the glans penis. A corresponding fold overhangs the glans of the clitoris.

prepuce of clitoris a fold of tissue formed by the union of parts of the labia minora that overhangs the glans of the clitoris. Also called preputium clitoridis.

prepuce of the penis the preputium penis, or foreskin of the neck of the penis.

preputial glands the sebaceous glands on the corona of the glans and the neck of the penis, generally on the underside of the prepuce, that secrete an oily substance. The oil may become mixed with discarded skin cells to form smegma. Also called Tyson's glands.

preputium a fold of skin that covers a body area, such as the prepuce of the penis.

preputium clitoridis the Latin term for prepuce of the clitoris.

preputium penis the Latin term for prepuce of the penis.

preservative an alternative term for condom.

presumptive signs of pregnancy physical effects that are associated with pregnancy but which are not necessarily evidence of a pregnancy. They may include a missed menstrual period, nausea in the morning, changes in the size or coloration of the breasts and nipples, and an increased urge to urinate.

presymphysial node a lymph node in front of the symphysis pubis and the lymph node closest to the penis, with lymphatic vessels that communicate with inguinal lymph nodes. Most of the lymphatic drainage from the penis follows ducts leading directly to the inguinal lymph nodes, on the inner thighs next to the genitalia. Thus, the inguinal lymph nodes are generally the first to become involved in microorganisms of sexually transmissible diseases.

prevalence model a term used in contraceptive studies to estimate the number of pregnancies averted by using a particular birth-control technique. Survey data containing questions about types of contraceptives and sources of supply are used for building a prevalence model.

previously married women a category of women who have been married but are separated, divorced, or widowed. Previously married women were surveyed by Kinsey researchers to determine their sexual behaviour. Although they were expected to fall in a range between single and married women, their sexual behaviour actually was closer to that of married women, with coitus as the primary source of orgasms. The percentage of coitus ranged from 80 percent by the youngest previously married women to about 50 percent for those over the age of 45. Nocturnal orgasms, masturbation, and homosexual contacts were reported by previously married women in all age groups. Masturbation and nocturnal orgasms were major noncoital sources of orgasms for older women, whereas homosexual contacts were important secondary sources of orgasms for women in their 20s and 30s.

priapism persistent penile erection, often painful and usually unaccompanied by sexual desire. The condition is rare and has nothing to do with virility. The cause is either unknown, or the condition may be associated with a disorder such as leukaemia, sickle cell anaemia, tumour, or infection. The term is also used as a synonym for satyriasis, and is derived from the name of the Greek and Roman god of procreation, Priapus.

priapitis an obsolescent term for inflammation of the penis.

prick a slang term for the penis, also used for a contemptible or ineffectual male person. It ranks number 6 on the TABOONESS RATING OF DIRTY WORDS. See this entry.

prick teaser another term for cock teaser.

primacy zone an erogenous area that plays a dominant role in sexual life. According to Freud, one primacy zone succeeds another in the course of psychosexual development, in the following order: oral, anal, phallic, and finally, genital.

primal anxiety in psychoanalysis, the most

basic form of anxiety, first experienced when the infant is separated from the mother at birth, and is suddenly overwhelmed by stimuli that did not exist in the protective envelope of the womb.

primal fantasies figments of a child's imagination concerning various aspects of sexual experience, such as parental intercourse, conception, and birth. According to psychoanalysis, fantasies of this kind are formed in the unconscious and expressed most clearly in dreams and daydreams.

primal-horde theory Freud's hypothetical concept of the original human family in which a powerful male held sway over a subordinate group of females and probably younger men.

primal scene the child's first mental picture of parental intercourse or seduction, which may be based on actual observation or fantasy, or a mixture of the two. This recollection, or alleged recollection, frequently plays a role in neuroses, and may be a factor in voyeurism.

primary amenorrhoea an absence of menses, usually caused by a congenital defect or a hormonal dysfunction, such as a pituitary disease.

primary erectile dysfunction the technical term for primary impotence.

primary follicle a tiny vesicle about 35 microns in diameter containing a primordial ovum about 20 microns in diameter and located in the stroma, or soft tissue, of the ovary. During maturation, the ovum will increase fivefold in size, and the follicle will evolve into a graafian follicle nearly one-half inch in diameter.

primary homosexual a person who has manifested distinct homosexual tendencies in early childhood or youth, as contrasted with a person who has become homosexual as a response to circumstances or outside influences. The latter is sometimes called a secondary homosexual.

primary hypogonadism testicular dysfunction that results from a defect in the testes rather than a disease. The condition has resulted in abnormally low testosterone levels and impotence, particularly in aging men.

primary impotence extreme sexual impotence in which a man has never been able to achieve erection sufficient for intercourse. The condition is technically known as primary erectile dysfunction.

primary masochism according to Freud, the basic form of masochism in which a 'lust for pain' and physical or psychological abuse are a prerequisite to sexual gratification. Also called erotogenic masochism.

primary motivation drives or impulses originating in basic body needs, that is, hunger, thirst, sex, urination, and defecation.

primary narcissism a psychoanalytical term for the earliest form of self-love, in which the libido, or sex drive, is directed at the infant's own body and its needs. The fact that these needs are satisfied the moment he or she cries induces a feeling of omnipotence which, together with increasing abilities, leads to formation of a 'narcissistic ego ideal.' This holds sway until the libido is directed towards the formation of 'object relations' with persons in the environment.

primary need a basic, unlearned need stemming from biological processes and leading to physical satisfaction. The need for sex falls into this category, along with the need for air, food, water, rest, sleep, urination, and defecation.

primary oocyte an immature ovum that still contains the diploid number of chromosomes (46 for a normal human) and which must undergo meiotic division to produce a secondary oocyte with the haploid number (23) of chromosomes needed before it can undergo further maturation towards becoming an ovum.

primary orgasmic dysfunction a condition in which a woman or man has never been able to reach orgasm through any method of stimulation.

primary sex characteristics physical features directly involved in sexual behaviour and reproduction: the gonads (testes and ovaries) and the external sex organs (penis and vagina).

primary testicular failure a gonadal deficiency resulting from a defect involving the testicles, such as testicular atrophy. The male receives normal levels of follicle-stimulating and interstitial-cell-stimulating hormones from the pituitary gland, but there is a deficiency of androgenic hormones. Also called primary hypogonadism.

primiparous (primip'ərəs) pertaining to a woman who is giving or who has given birth to a child for the first time. Technically, the term is applied to any first-time pregnancy that is carried to term, regardless of whether the child is dead or alive when born.

prior learning a previous experience, somewhere between childhood and adulthood, that may shape one's sexual behaviour. Examples of prior learning include punishment as a child for masturbating. Failure to achieve an erection may become a prior-learning situation that results in psychogenic impotence for a man.

privacy the idea in Western society that one's sex life should be conducted in private, especially when children are at home. Children are usually taught that privacy is expected when the bedroom door is closed, and that they should knock before entering. It is enough to explain that sometimes daddy and mummy want to be alone. 'Swinging' couples may, however, get extra excitement by engaging in group sex or by frequenting semipublic 'clubs'.

private property a jocular, male-chauvinist term for one's wife's or girlfriend's vagina.

privates the external genital organs of the male or female. Also called private parts; privy parts.

probable signs of pregnancy physical changes in the body of a woman that are usually positive signs of pregnancy. They include enlargement of the abdomen, distention of the uterus so that it can be felt through the abdominal wall, occasional contractions of the uterus, and a softening of the tissues of the cervix.

processus vaginalis a medical term for the sac that descends into the scrotum during the seventh month of gestation and which will eventually form a sheath around the testis when it descends. After the testis enters the processus vaginalis, the structure is called the tunica vaginalis, one of several tissue layers protecting the testis.

procreation the act of producing offspring.

procreational behaviour behaviour that is associated with sexual reproduction. In human sexology, such behaviour includes not only repeated intercourse without the use of contraceptive measures, especially during the woman's fertile days, but also recognition of a mutual desire to have children, planning for this eventuality, and medical treatment of any condition that might interfere with reproduction.

procreation fantasy a dream or daydream concerned with reproduction. For example, a woman who develops a false pregnancy may imagine that she has had intercourse, or a man may imagine himself playing the role of a father who begets a famous offspring.

proctalgia a learned euphemism for the literal translation of this Greek term—a pain in the arse.

proctophobia a morbid fear of anything related to the rectum, such as enemas, rectal examinations, or anal intercourse.

procurer a person who induces or coerces women and sometimes men, to engage in sexual acts for money or other advantages, and who shares in their earnings. Procurers usually operate out of houses of prostitution. Also called panderer.

productive love the term applied by Eric Fromm to a healthy, constructive form of love in which the emphasis is on interdependent relationships without curtailment of individuality, as well as mutual respect and responsibility and an active effort to develop a rewarding relationship.

progeria an abnormal condition, usually congenital, in which the person shows signs of premature aging. One of the physical characteristics of the disorder is a loss of pubic hair.

Progestasert a medicated intrauterine contraceptive device available in some countries. It is impregnated with progesterone that is slowly released over a period of one year. Its effectiveness has been challenged by experts who contend it is less effective than the non-medicated IUDs.

progestational compounds hormonal medications administered to mothers with habitual or threatened abortions. Because some of the drugs contain synthetic progestins that have androgenic effects, female foetuses of the mother may be virilized in the uterus and be born with masculinized female genitalia.

progesterone a hormone produced by the corpus luteum and the placenta. Its role is to prepare the endometrial lining of the uterus for implantation of the zygote after fertilization and to develop the mammary glands and help maintain the pregnancy. It also has an effect on the tissues of the vagina, as cells of the surface are lost and replaced during the menstrual cycle.

progesterone block an abnormal condition of male sexuality caused by the lack of an enzyme needed to convert pregnenolone, a cholesterol derivative, into progesterone. Because normal production of progesterone is blocked and androgenic hormone synthesis is restricted, the individual with this genetic defect usually develops as a male pseudohermaphrodite.

progesterone test the injection of a synthetic form of progesterone or the administration of progesterone pills for 5 to 10 days in the diagnosis of possible causes of amenorrhoea. If the women's oestrogen levels are normal, menstruation will follow after the end of the test, thus indicating that amenorrhoea is probably the result of a progesterone deficiency.

progestin any of several natural or synthetic progesterone-type substances or agents with progestational (feminizing) effects. Progestin was the name originally assigned to a hormone produced by the corpus luteum and now called progesterone.

progestogen any substance, natural or synthetic, that has a pharmacological action similar to that of the female hormone progesterone. Many oral contraceptives contain a synthetic progestogen.

projected jealousy the tendency of a person who has been unfaithful to accuse his or her spouse or lover of the same behaviour.

prolactin a hormone secreted by the anterior lobe of the pituitary gland to stimulate the production of milk. Prolactin secretion is regulated by two substances in the hypothalamus, a prolactin-inhibiting hormone (PIH) and a prolactin-releasing hormone (PRL). PIH inhibits the release of prolactin, and PRL allows the pituitary to release prolactin in response to stimulation such as by the infant sucking on a nipple.

prolan a hormone produced by the chorionic villi. It is the same substance as human chorionic gonadotropin (HCG) and is used in certain pregnancy tests.

prolapse the sinking or collapse of an organ or part of an organ, which may protrude through an opening. Common types of prolapse include prolapse of the vagina, marked by collapse of the vaginal walls, and prolapse of the uterus, usually after childbirth. Uterine prolapse may range in severity from first degree to third degree, depending upon descent of the uterus to the opening of the vagina, partial descent of the uterus to the outside of the vagina, and descent of the entire uterus outside the vagina. Uterine prolapse often is accompanied by hernias of other organs, such as the rectum or bladder.

proliferative phase the stage of the menstrual cycle, lasting about 14 days, when the lining of the uterus (the endometrium) thickens and becomes enriched with blood in anticipation of implantation by a fertilized ovum. If this does not occur, the endometrial lining, along with its blood and blood vessels, are shed as menstruation occurs.

promiscuity casual and in some cases unselective sexual relations with a variety of partners, often without attaining full sexual satisfaction. Promiscuous behaviour may be associated with many factors: feelings of insecurity or inadequacy, parental rejection or neglect, emotional conflicts, lack of impulse control, a delinquent subculture, or psychosexual disorders such as impotence, frigidity, nymphomania, or satyriasis.

promised land an older euphemism for vagina.

proof of pregnancy a term sometimes applied to laboratory tests for pregnancy, which actually may not be any more positive than the physical signs that appear in the first weeks or months of pregnancy. They include the chorionic gonadotrophic hormone, agglutination, and progesterone laboratory tests.

prophylaxis the prevention of disease. The term or a variation, such as *prophylactic*, may be used as synonyms for condom. (Greek *prophylax*, 'advance guard.')

proposition to suggest or propose sexual intercourse, sometimes directly but more often indirectly ('let's go to my place').

prostaglandins a group of fatty acids found in semen and in many body tissues. They were originally isolated from semen and prostate gland tissue, which explains the name, but have since been discovered in a wide range of animal tissues. More than a dozen forms of prostaglandins are known, each with specific physiological effects. One prostaglandin, PGEF2, for example, lowers blood pressure while PGF_2 raises blood pressure. Prostaglandins also stimulate smooth muscle of the uterus and are used as an agent to induce abortions. Because prostaglandins are rapidly metabolized, they are injected locally to achieve a desired effect; and in triggering a first- or second-trimester abortion, doses of PGE_2 or PGF_2 are usually administered directly into the uterus or amniotic tissues. Prostaglandins may also be used to induce or assist true labour, but produce adverse side effects of severe nausea and diarrhoea. The substances have been found in the uterine lining and menstrual fluid of women suffering from dysmenorrhoea, although the role of prostaglandins in the disorder is not clear.

prostatectomy the excision or surgical removal of all or part of the prostate gland. The procedure, usually undertaken to remove a benign or malignant tumour or correct a problem of prostatic hypertrophy (overgrowth), may involve an incision through the lower abdominal wall, through the perineal

P

tissues between the scrotum and anus, or through the urethra.

prostate enlargement prostatic hyperplasia or hypertrophy (overgrowth), a condition commonly occurring in men over the age of 50 who experience bladder-outlet obstruction because of an overgrowth of prostate-gland tissue round the urethra.

prostate gland an organ of musculature and glandular tissue attached to the male urinary bladder. It is about the shape and size of a chestnut and is located in the pelvic cavity immediately in front of the rectum. It can be felt through the wall of the rectum, particularly when it is enlarged. As the prostate gland is immediately below the urinary bladder, the urethra passes through it. Immediately above are the seminal vesicles and the terminal end of the ductus deferens from either side; they terminate in the ejaculatory ducts, which in turn terminate in the urethra, within the body of the prostate. The glandular portion of the prostate consists of numerous follicles, or pouches, that open into a series of ducts leading to the urethra. The glands secrete an alkaline fluid that protects the spermatozoa from the acidic environment of the male urethra and the vagina. The secretion of the prostate probably accounts for more than half of the substance in seminal fluid. Disorders of the prostate can alter the quality of the seminal fluid and may reduce the number and motility of the spermatozoa. Because of the location of the prostate with regard to the urinary bladder and urethra, enlargement of the prostate after middle age may obstruct normal urine flow, requiring surgical removal of the prostate.

prostate massage a technique employed by physicians for the relief of prostatitis. The massage is performed with a gloved finger through the rectum. Using slow firm strokes, the finger works from the outside towards the centre of each lobe of the prostate, ending with firm midline strokes to force prostatic fluid through the urethra. The massage may be performed once a week to remove excess prostatic fluid as long as symptoms persist.

prostatic cancer the second most common cause of cancer of males in the United States and the third leading cause of cancer deaths. It affects between 30 and 40 percent of men by the age of 80. Surgery and radiation are among the primary therapeutic techniques. The condition also may be treated with various chemotherapies, including the use of oestrogen to counter the presence of testoster-

one, a contributing factor.

prostatic fluid the secretions from the prostate produced by massage of the prostate gland through the rectum. The physician usually examines samples obtained by massage to determine whether an excessive number of white blood cells, indicating an infection, may be present.

prostatic pouch a minute pouch in the floor of the prostatic segment of the urethra. It evolves from ends of the embryonic mullerian ducts.

prostatic urethra the portion of the male urethra that passes through the prostate gland after leaving the urinary bladder immediately above the prostate.

prostatic utricle a blind sac extending into the prostate gland for a distance of about one fourth of an inch. The openings of the ejaculatory ducts are on either side of the cul-de-sac. It is a vestige of the lower ends of the embryonic paramesonephric ducts and is said to be homologous with the female uterus and vagina.

prostatitis an inflammation of the prostate gland.

prostitute a woman, or man, who engages in sexual activity for financial reward. People become prostitutes for a variety of reasons other than easy money: rebellion against parents and society; a high degree of sexual need; a neurotic urge to punish and degrade themselves; mental deficiency; inability to find regular work; or a desire to find a partner. Men visit prostitutes for such reasons as shyness in establishing other outlets, a monotonous or inadequate sex life at home, a need to gratify variant sex urges, the search for sex activity without incurring obligations, or sexual deprivation.

prostitution an occupation based on providing sexual services in exchange for money or other valuables. The services may be heterosexual or homosexual, and performed by males or females. They may include not only standard coitus and masturbation, but acts involving various paraphilias such as flagellation and bondage. See also CHILD PROSTITUTION; MALE PROSTITUTION; SACRED PROSTITUTION; TEMPLE PROSTITUTION.

prudishness excessive modesty or priggishness, especially in regard to sexual matters such as wearing revealing clothes or telling risqué stories. The line between prudery and hypocrisy is often blurred, especially among zealots who express their own obsessive interest in sex by overconcern for the 'morality' of others. Also called *prudery*.

prurient interest 'a shameful and morbid interest in nudity, sex, or excretion'—according to a 1984 decision of the U.S. Court of Appeals for the Ninth Circuit. (Latin *prurire*, 'to itch.').

pseudocopulation bodily contact between a male and female producing sexual excitement and orgasm but without actual intercourse.

pseudocyesis a false or phantom pregnancy. The woman may have a number of the usual signs of pregnancy, such as morning sickness, enlarged abdomen, weight gain, and absence of menses, but simply is not pregnant. The condition tends to occur in immature women as a hysterical reaction to a conflict about childbearing.

pseudoexhibitionism a psychological condition in which a person (usually a man) under stress exhibits himself as a substitute for the normal sexual intercourse he prefers, unlike the true exhibitionist who may expose himself with the intention of shocking a viewer.

pseudofamily a foster family, or similar which acts as a substitute for a biological family and which provides for the physical and emotional needs of one or more children.

pseudohermaphroditism a congenital condition in which a person has either testes or ovaries but also the external genitalia of the opposite sex. The individual also may have a mixture of male and female characteristics. However, sexual classification is usually based on the gonadal gender, regardless of the external genitalia.

pseudohomosexuality homosexuality motivated by nonsexual feelings of dependence and power in addition to the basic desire for sexual gratification and pleasure.

pseudomucinous cystadenoma an ovarian tumour of mucus-producing cells. It may be the most common type of ovarian cyst. It generally begins as a tiny tumour but may grow to 10 to 12 inches in diameter before producing symptoms. Untreated, the pseudomucinous tumour may eventually fill the pelvic cavity, causing the woman to have the physical appearance of an advanced pregnancy.

pseudoprecocious puberty a condition in which a hormonal disturbance, such as an endocrine gland tumour, results in premature development of the secondary sexual characteristics of a person without also stimulating early maturation of the gonads.

pseudopregnancy a condition created in the female reproductive system by oral contraceptives. The contraceptives create through their content of female sex hormones a simulated pregnancy that suppresses ovulation, just as natural female sex hormones help suppress further ovulation when a woman is already pregnant.

pseudosexual precocity an effect of untreated juvenile hypothyroidism in girls. The girls, who also show signs of a pituitary tumour, develop enlarged breasts with milk production and menstruation. However, they do not acquire pubic hair, and bone development is retarded. Treatment with thyroid hormone causes the signs of precocious puberty to regress.

pseudovoyeurism a mild form of voyeurism in which the act is a substitute for normal heterosexual intercourse, which is preferred, as contrasted with true voyeurism in which the individual prefers looking to participating in coitus.

psoriasis of the vulva a type of skin disease that may affect the female external genitalia with red, dry skin surfaces covered with patches of silvery scales. The disease tends to occur in members of families who are affected by psoriasis in other areas of the body.

psychic impotence functional incapacity of the male to perform satisfactory sexual intercourse in spite of desire and intact genital organs. The condition may take the form of premature or retarded ejaculation, or of inability to achieve or maintain erection, to expel seminal fluid, or to reach a full orgasm. Psychoanalysts trace this disorder to such factors as persistence of castration fears, unresolved attachment to the mother, and association of sexuality with dirt or filth.

psychic masturbation sexual gratification through erotic images and fantasies without physical manipulation of the genital organs (penis, clitoris) or other erogenous zones.

psychic vaginismus a painful vaginal spasm severe enough to prevent sexual intercourse. The condition stems from psychological factors such as inhibitions instilled by parents, fear of being hurt, or association of intercourse with disease.

psychogender psychological or emotional sex orientation as distinguished from anatomical sex.

psychogenic aspermia a form of functional impotence in which ejaculation of semen does not occur. The condition may stem from a variety of factors, such as fear of failure, homosexual conflict, religious inhibitions, or, in psychoanalytical terms, an unresolved attachment to the mother. Also called ejaculatory impotence.

psychogenic impotence another term for psychic impotence.

psychopathia sexualis Krafft-Ebing's term for psychosexual disorders; also, the title of his celebrated work.

psychopathia transsexualis a term introduced in 1949 to describe a distinct syndrome exhibited by persons who wanted to change their sexual identities.

psychoprophylaxis method an alternative term for the Lamaze technique of natural childbirth, based on Pavlov's concept of the conditioned reflex. Also called *psychoprophylactic method*.

psychose passionnelle an alternative term for DE CLÉRAMBAULT'S SYNDROME. See this entry.

psychosexual development a psychoanalytical term for the sequence of sexual maturation as it affects personality development. Freud viewed this sequence as a stage-by-stage expression of a single source of energy, the libido. In the first, or oral, stage, the mouth is the prime erotic zone, and sucking and biting are the characteristic expressions; next comes the anal stage, characterized by pleasure in expelling or retaining the faeces; then comes the phallic stage, in which the libido is focussed on the genital organs, with masturbation the major source of pleasure, as well as the development of the Oedipus complex; this is followed by the latency stage, in which overt sexual interest is repressed and sublimated into peer activities; and finally comes the genital stage, which is reached in puberty, when erotic interest and activity are focussed on a sexual partner. Each of these stages leaves its mark on personality and sexuality; for example, the pleasure of biting in the oral stage may lead to biting or other sadistic behaviour during intercourse, especially if sexual development is arrested, or 'fixated,' at this stage. Also called libidinal development.

psychosexual disorders a group of sexual disorders stemming from psychological rather than organic factors, and comprising gender-identity disorders, paraphilias, psychosexual dysfunctions, ego-dystonic homosexuality, Don Juanism, and nymphomania.

psychosexual dysfunctions a group of sexual disorders characterized by inadequate functioning in one or more phases of the total sexual response cycle, and resulting from psychological factors. The cycle comprises the excitement phase, the plateau phase, the orgasmic phase, and the resolution phase.

psychosexual neutrality the concept that an individual is neither male nor female in gender identity at birth and that actual gender identity is the result of learning and environment.

psychosexual trauma a terrifying, degrading or otherwise disturbing sexual experience that is causally related to a current psychosexual dysfunction such as inhibited sexual desire or functional vaginismus. Examples are forcible rape, incest, or child sexual abuse.

PT an abbreviation for prick teaser.

pubarche the first appearance of pubic hair in a person (Latin *pubes*, 'youth,' and Greek *arche*, 'beginning').

puber a little-used term for a boy or girl who has arrived at the stage of puberty.

puberism a term occasionally used as a synonym for puberty; also for retarded development of secondary sexual characteristics, technically termed persistent puberism.

pubertal sexual recapitulation the psychoanalytical concept that at the beginning of puberty the individual regresses to the successive stages of sexuality (oral, anal, phallic) which he or she has passed through during the first 5 years of life. Many of the problems encountered by adolescents are attempts to resolve conflicts that occurred in this earlier period.

pubertas plena a Latin term for the attainment of full sexual maturity.

pubertas praecox the Latin term for precocious puberty.

puberty the developmental stage during which the genital organs reach maturity and secondary sex characteristics begin to appear. The period extends from about 11 to 13 in females and 12 to 14 in males, and is marked by the first ejaculation of semen for the boy and the first menstruation for the girl. Increasingly intense interest in the opposite sex occurs in both, and though neither boys nor girls are ready for the responsibilities of parenthood, it is usually possible for the boy to impregnate the girl and for the girl to carry a child. Also called puberism.

puberty rites ceremonies performed in 'undeveloped' societies to celebrate the arrival of puberty and the beginning of adulthood. The formal rites usually include teaching of 'tribal' legends and laws, as well as sexual practices and responsibilities expected of an adult in the particular society. In many cultures the rites for boys involve circumcision (and sometimes subincision), as well as severe physical tests such as flogging, body scarring, and teeth pulling. Coming-of-age ceremonies for girls are usually less elaborate and more private, and may involve deflowering, introcision, and clitoridectomy. Also called initiation rites.

pubes the technical term for either the pubic area in general, or for the pubic hair.

pubescence the period when puberty is reached; also, the process of development that takes place during puberty.

pubescent growth spurt the period before the appearance of secondary sexual characteristics as the body begins to respond physically to hormonal influences. Boys may suddenly add height and weight to their bodies, and muscle growth appears. Similar changes occur in the female body before the onset of menstruation or other signs of approaching sexual maturity. Also called pubic growth cycle.

pubic arch an arch formed below the articulation, or joint, between the pubic bones. It forms an opening for the deep dorsal vein of the penis which helps drain the blood from the erectile tissues after an erection.

pubic growth curve a period of adolescence lasting from 4 to 7 years, but averaging 6 years, during which full sexual maturity develops from the onset of pubescence.

pubic growth cycle an alternative term for pubescent growth spurt.

pubic hair a patch of hair of varying size, texture and colour which first appears at the onset of puberty just above the penis in males and the vulva in females, It is a secondary sex characteristic.

pubic rite a puberty ceremony performed in various societies in which the genitals may be scarified or mutilated, as in the practice of subincision or superincision.

pubic wig a hair piece worn by women over the pubic area, especially in 17th-century England, when these wigs were in fashion. Also called a merkin and, later, a bowser.

pubiotomy a rare surgical procedure in which part of the pubic bone, usually on one side of the pubic symphysis, is removed to enlarge the pelvic outlet for passage of a foetus during childbirth.

public copulation intercourse performed in public or semipublic situations. Among the Mangaians and other Polynesian groups, mar-

ried couples have been reported to perform ritual intercourse in sacred enclosures before battles; and public outdoor nonritual copulation has been reported from contemporary Yapese, Formosan, and Aleutian aborigines and, historically speaking, among the Incas. In some Polynesian and European peasant societies, couples have intercourse in the same room with others who are sleeping or presumed to be asleep.

pubococcygeal pertaining to a muscle or other anatomical feature that extends between the pubis on the front of the body and the coccyx on the back and circumventing the anus.

puboprostatic ligaments ligaments that extend from the pubic bones and hold the prostate gland in place. In an accident resulting in a fracture of the pelvis, the puboprostatic ligaments are likely to become separated from their attachment resulting in a dislocation of the prostate gland. Such a severe injury also tends to tear apart the portion of the urethra below the prostate. Blood may flow from the penile urethra, but urination is not possible, and a catheter cannot be inserted as far as the bladder.

puboscrotal testicle a testicle that descends from the abdomen but fails to reach the bottom of the scrotum, lodging instead in a position approximately level with the shaft of the penis.

pudenda the plural of PUDENDUM. See this entry.

pudendal nerve a branch of the sacral nerve plexus that extends into the perineum, innervating the skin and muscle tissues of the area between the pubis and the anus.

pudendal plexus a network of sensory and motor nerves originating in the sacral portion of the spinal cord. The nerve plexus lies in the pelvis and supplies the nerves for the bladder, uterus, prostate, and seminal vesicles, and the external genitalia of both sexes.

pudendum the Latin term for vulva, meaning 'something to be ashamed of.' The term is sometimes applied to the external genitalia of the male as well as the female. It is usually used in the plural: pudenda.

puella publica (Latin, 'public girl') an obsolete term for prostitute.

puer aeternus (Latin, 'eternal boy') a term applied by Jung to the archetype, or universal concept, of eternal youth.

pueri in ancient Rome, teenage boys who were the passive partners in anal intercourse, usually in male brothels. (*Pueri* is the plural of *puer*, 'boy.')

puerilism immature behaviour characteristic of the stage of development between early childhood and puberty; also, childish behaviour in an adult.

puerperal disorders mental disorders occurring during the period between the termination of labour and the return of the uterus to its normal condition, including depressive and schizophrenic psychoses, and in some cases manic or delirious episodes, resulting from haemorrhage, exhaustion, infection, or toxaemia.

puerperium the period of approximately 6 weeks after childbirth, during which the woman's reproductive system and body contours gradually return to their normal condition, usually followed by the return of menstruation.

pulling out a slang term for coitus interruptus, or withdrawal of the penis before ejaculation.

punch biopsy a method of taking small samples of tissue from the uterine cervix for microscopic examination in cases of suspected cancer or other disorders. A special scissorslike instrument with coneshaped tips is used to punch tissue samples from several different areas of the cervix for study.

puppy love a transient, highly romanticized form of infatuation occurring during the late adolescent or young adult stage of psychosexual development. Also called calf love.

purdah (Hindu, 'curtain') the Muslim (and later, Hindu) practice of concealing women from the sight of men and strangers by means of long hooded robes (the chadar), the veil, screens, curtains, and high enclosures. This custom is both an expression of male dominance and a way of controlling women.

puritan complex adherence to a rigid set of moral standards regarding obscene or 'impure' thoughts, feelings, or behaviour, accompanied by a persistent dread of violating these standards. Also called obscenity-purity complex.

puritanism conformity to a rigid moral code with regard to sex, usually coupled with an attempt to hold others to similar standards. This approach originated with members of a Protestant sect who protested against dominance of the Church of England, and emigrated to New England in the 16th and 17th centuries in search of religious freedom.

H. L. Mencken called puritanism 'the impulse to punish the man with a superior capacity for happiness' and 'the haunting fear that someone, somewhere, may be happy.' He also wrote: 'Moral certainty is always a sign of cultural inferiority. The more uncivilized the man, the surer he is that he knows precisely what is right and what is wrong. ... The truly civilized man is always sceptical and tolerant, in this field as in all others.'

pussy a vulgar slang term for (a) the vagina, and the vulva, or (b) a woman. The term ranks number 4 in the TABOONESS RATING OF DIRTY WORDS. See this entry.

pussy-whipped a vulgar slang term referring to a female-dominated man.

pus tube a fallopian tube that is distended with pus.

pygal relating to the buttocks (Greek *pyge*, 'rump').

pygalgia a medical term meaning, literally, a pain in the buttocks. See also PROCTALGIA.

pygalopubic pertaining to the buttocks and pubic region.

pygmalionism a sexual variance in which a person falls in love with his or her own creation. The concept is based on the Greek myth of Pygmalion who carved the statue of Aphrodite which, with Athena's assistance, came to life and became his bride.

pygomania sexual obsession with large female buttocks. See also ARSE MAN.

pyosalpinx an inflamed fallopian tube that may become distended with pus, assuming the shape of a sausage. The pyosalpinx may rupture, spilling its contents into the peritoneal cavity and causing peritonitis.

pyrimidinones a family of drugs that increases the production of interferon, a natural antiviral agent. Pyrimidinone is being used experimentally as a treatment for genital herpes.

pyrolagnia sexual arousal produced by observation of large fires or conflagrations. 'Fire buffs' often follow fire engines and even assist firefighters for sexual reasons. Also called erotic pyromania.

pyromania a persistent, pathological impulse to set fires, and to achieve sexual excitement and gratification during the act of fire setting or while watching the early stages of the conflagration. Arsonists are generally young men, some of whom are psychotic or mentally defective. Those closer to normal tend to feel guilty and may help to extinguish the fire.

quality of motility the ability of spermatozoa to swim forwards, a factor considered in studies of male fertility.

queen a slang term for a male homosexual who voluntarily plays the female role in a gay relationship. A queen is also a male homosexual who conforms to the stereotype of the homosexual as effeminate in speech and mannerisms (colloquially termed a fairy). This stereotype is dying out because most male homosexuals today look and act like other ordinary people.

queer an offensive slang term for homosexual. The term ranks number 20 in the tabooness rating of dirty words. See this entry.

quickie a colloquial term for hurried sexual intercourse, especially if it leads to a fast climax.

quim an obsolete slang term for vagina.

quince on oriental fruit now grown throughout the world and noted for its presumed aphrodisiac qualities, particularly when made into jellies or preserves. The quince was believed to 'guarantee' that a woman would produce sons of remarkable energy and ability.

Q

rabbit test an obsolete pregnancy test: The women's urine is injected in a female rabbit, which will show signs of ovulation within hours or days if the woman is pregnant.

Racine's syndrome a phenomenon in which some women experience a swelling of the salivary glands before menstruation. Enlargement of the salivary glands begins about 5 days before the onset of menstruation, and the swelling diminishes as the menstrual flow begins. The breasts may undergo swelling and retraction in a similar cyclic pattern.

racist genocide a political issue in birth control raised by nonwhite activists who claim that Third World population-control campaigns are designed to reduce the birth rate of blacks and others while white populations are allowed to increase.

Raggedy Android a male homosexual term for a poor and poorly dressed homosexual hustler.

raincoat a slang term for condom.

rajasic foods foods that induce passion, according to practitioners of yoga. The category includes foods related primarily to salty and pungent tastes, such as most fish, red meat, chicken, root vegetables, spices, and salt. Indian philosophy contends that such foods result in semen that is thick and slimy, with the characteristics of the yoni. (Sanskrit *rajas*, 'darkness.')

ram job a slang term for anal intercourse.

randy a slang term meaning horny, wanting to have sex.

ranges of variation the various differences among individual humans in physiological tolerances and performances. Examples include the narrow range of heat that spermatozoa can endure and survive and the wide range of spermatozoa that may be contained in the ejaculate of different men.

Rank, Otto (1884-1939) an Austrian psychoanalyst who broke with Freud in emphasizing short-term therapy and the concept of the birth trauma, which he believed to be at the root of neurosis. To eliminate the ill effects of the birth experience—especially separation anxiety and dependence—he sought to help his patients achieve full independence and constructive relationships.

rape forcible intercourse against the will of the victim, who is usually a woman but may be a boy or man. Occasionally men rape babies, and adult women have been known to force sex upon adolescent boys. Authorities claim that only about one tenth to one twentieth of cases of rape are reported, because of shame, fear, ignorance, and insensitive dealing with rape cases by the police.

rape counselling provision of guidance, support, and psychotherapy as needed for victims of rape. Counselling may be on an individual or group basis, and is conducted at rape crisis centres in a growing number of communities.

rape of the penis a slang term for circumcision, used mainly by critics of this practice.

rape prevention recommended steps to be taken by women to avoid situations that might result in rape. Among them are avoidance of dark, lonely streets or parks as well as other areas where rapes have already occurred; keeping alert to anyone who appears to follow them; keeping doors and windows locked, and finding out for certain who is at the door before opening it; refraining from acting or dressing in a sexually provocative manner in unprotected situations; thinking in advance, and discussing with others, how to handle a rape threat; preparing for such an emergency by taking a self-defence course; and becoming acquainted with a nearby rape crisis centre and rape-hotline number and joining a community organization that takes active steps towards a safer environment. Groups such as Women Reclaim the Night are working towards the provision of better street lighting and safer public transport to make the streets safer at night and reduce the risks of rape.

rape-trauma syndrome a reaction pattern composed of feelings of shame, humiliation, rage, fear, and confusion experienced by a rape victim. The trauma may also result in a lasting fear of being alone, feelings of being followed, a compulsion to wash the body, sexual phobias, vaginismus, and a haunting sense of guilt.

raphe of the penis (raf'ē) an alternative term for penoscrotal raphe.

rapist an individual who commits a rape. According to recent studies, the typical rapist is a young man (averaging 25 years of age) whose life is oriented towards crime and violence as a result of environmental influences or psychological disorder (psychosis or sociopathic personality). Many rapists have experienced emotional deprivation in childhood, and most of them have an animus against society as a whole and women in particular because of early experiences that have instilled feelings of fear, anger, and sexual inadequacy. See also IMPULSE RAPIST; PREDATORY RAPIST; SEX-AGGRESSION-FUSION RAPIST; SEXUAL-AIM RAPIST.

read braille a slang term meaning to feel someone up; also, to caress.

Read method a method of natural childbirth designed by Dr. Grantly Dick-Read, who promoted the concept that childbirth is a normal function and the pain of labour is the result of a fear-tension pain syndrome of psychological origin. Read is credited with introducing the term 'natural childbirth.'

real girl a homosexual slang term for a real female (used because the term girl is also applied to a male homosexual).

reality principle in psychoanalysis, the force that enables us to control our sexual impulses and meet the demands of the external world by dealing rationally and effectively with the situations of life. The reality principle represents the ego rather than the id, and runs counter to the pleasure principle and its demand for immediate gratification of instinctual impulses.

real thing a slang term referring to the vagina.

ream a slang term meaning to perform anilin-

gus, to do a *ream job*. An alternative expression is 'to rim.'

rear admiral a nurses' slang term for proctologist. An alternative slang term is COMPREHENSIVE PHYSICIAN. See this entry.

rebellion a psychological force that frequently leads to adolescent sexuality. A teenager may engage in sex as a way of expressing independence.

rebirth fantasy the mental image of being born again, usually experienced in dreams in which an individual emerges from water. The fantasy is variously interpreted as an unconscious wish to return to the tranquillity of the womb, an attempt to deny death, an expression of the religious belief in resurrection, or, in psychoanalysis, an incestuous desire for the mother.

recreational sex a colloquial term for nonprocreative sex, especially if it includes swinging or, generally, a pleasure-oriented attitude.

recruitment of eggs the stimulation of ovaries by artificial means to produce ova. Egg recruitment is utilized in fertilization in vitro. The procedure yields from two to six human ova at a time, compared with a normal release of one ovum per menstrual cycle. Recruitment involves injections of follicle-stimulating hormone. The eggs are removed surgically from the follicles when they have reached maturity but before the follicle ruptures to release the ova into the fallopian tubes.

rectalgia another term for proctalgia, with the same literal meaning.

red degeneration a condition in which a haemorrhage develops in a fibroid tumour in the uterus, leading to the death of the tissues involved. If the condition occurs during pregnancy, it becomes a serious threat to the foetus and mother. Not all fibroid tumours are so incompatible with pregnancy, and some small fibroids exist side-by-side with the foetus and placenta.

red-light district a neighbourhood containing many houses of prostitution, which are traditionally marked with a lighted red lamp in the window or above the door when 'open for business.'

reduction division the process of meiosis, in which a primary spermatocyte divides into two smaller secondary spermatocytes, each with a haploid number of 23 chromosomes. The reduction division is necessary for the spermatocyte to become a mature gamete. Theoretically, half of the secondary spermatocytes will contain one X chromosome, and the other half will contain one Y chromosome.

Ⓡ

redundant prepuce a prepuce that contains an excessive amount of skin.

referred pain of testicles a phenomenon in which stimulation of testicular tissues sometimes is perceived as pain in the lower abdomen, above the internal inguinal ring. However, stimulation of the parietal or visceral tunica vaginalis is perceived as originating in the scrotum. The cause is a sharing of autonomic nerve fibres by various structures in the lower abdomen.

reflex arc the nervous-system circuit that routes impulses associated with sexual arousal to the centres that control erection. While the brain may play a role in sexual arousal, as with sexual fantasies, the vasoconstrictor and vasodilator centres of the spinal cord can function independently to cause an erection. Men who have suffered a severed spinal cord, breaking that connection between the brain and the genitalia, can still, in most cases, achieve erection and ejaculation.

refractory period the period immediately after orgasm during which sexual response does not occur, regardless of the nature and intensity of sexual stimulation. The refractory period occurs in almost all males (and to a lesser extent, if at all, in females), and lasts from a few minutes to a few hours, depending on the man's age, state of health, interest, and response level.

regional fibrosis a type of testicular failure resulting from the effects of noxious agents on developing spermatozoa. The agent, which may be associated with a feverish infection of other disease, results in fibrosis of the seminiferous tubules. Fibrosing of the tubules leads to germinal-cell arrest and a lowered sperm count, the reduction in sperm being more or less in proportion to the number of tubules inactivated.

regression of secondary characteristics an effect of disease or injury to the anterior pituitary gland resulting in destruction of a major portion of the pituitary tissue. In women, the ovaries become small and fibrous, the vagina and uterus shrink to infantile proportions, and the breasts regress. In males, the penis and testes shrink, as does the prostate gland. Shrinkage of other glands, such as the thyroid and adrenals, also accompanies the condition.

Reich, Wilhelm (1897-1957) an Austrian-American psychoanalyst. Reich first was a student of physics, but after World War I, he joined the Psychoanalytical Association in Vienna. He broke with Freud, however, after refusing to accept the theory of the death instinct and Freud refused to analyse him. Reich became an active Marxist for 5 years, during which he tried to combine this social theory with psychoanalysis and sought to change the laws on sexual behaviour through the German Association for Proletarian Sexual Politics. His political activities brought him expulsion from both the communist party and from the Psychoanalytical Association. From there on, he concentrated on orgastic potency as the single measure of psychological well-being as well as the source of both a psychic and physical force which he dubbed 'orgone energy.' He moved to America and sought to tap this energy by various means, especially through the orgone box, which the U.S. Food and Drug Administration declared a fraud. For defying a court decision, he was put in prison, and died while under psychiatric care.

Reiter's disease a form of arthritis with abacterial urethritis and conjunctivitis. The disease tends to occur in males after a sexual contact within the previous 2 weeks. It may be complicated by cystitis or prostatitis. A manifestation may be a puslike drainage from the urethra that is similar to but less painful than gonorrhoea. There also may be skin lesions and ulcers on the mucous membranes of the mouth and penis. Although a specific disease organism is not found as a causative agent, most patients carry an antigen that is associated with certain diseases that may be transmitted sexually, such as chlamydia. It is theorized that males affected are those who have inherited a susceptibility to the disease.

rejection the withholding of love, interest, attention, or approval, especially on the part of the parent; also, an antagonistic or discriminatory attitude towards a minority group. Childhood feelings of rejection often interfere with the development of a positive self-image and a sense of self-worth. As a result, it may be hard for the person to form attachments, including sexual relationships, to other people.

rejection fear another term for fear of rejection.

rejuvenants medications, aphrodisiacs, or other substances alleged to produce sexual rejuvenation or to restore youth in general.

relaxin a hormone that relaxes the pelvic ligaments during pregnancy. It is produced by the ovary in humans and is present in the blood of pregnant animals. It is also believed to stimulate breast growth and prevent premature labour.

relieve oneself a common colloquial term meaning to masturbate (besides to urinate and to defecate).

religion and breast cancer a statistical relationship between religious practices and breast cancer. Studies have found that the incidence of breast cancer is lower among women members of the Mormon and Seventh Day Adventist Churches. However, the reason is not clear. Both religious groups prohibit the use of caffeine, and the Seventh Day Adventists are generally vegetarian in their dietary practices.

religious orthodoxy an important factor in cases of sexual inadequacy. Studies indicate that Western religious beliefs, regardless of which of the major religions is involved, can have an inhibiting effect on normal sexual activity. The data conforms with a Masters and Johnson study showing that religious beliefs prevented many women from participating in coitus during menstruation even though a significant proportion of women found intercourse more pleasurable at that period.

renewable marriage an alternative to traditional marriage vows. Instead, marriage is regarded as a limited-term contract which the partners have an opportunity to renew or cancel upon mutual consent at the end of a specified period such as every 3 years. This type of marriage was advocated by Margaret Mead and others.

renifleur (rəniflœ′) a person who is sexually aroused by body odours, as in smelling urine, faeces, or sexual secretions (French *renifler*, 'to sniff').

rent boy a young male homosexual prostitute.

reorganization phase a period of time, which may be lengthy, in which a woman who has been raped undergoes appropriate rehabilitation. A woman who has been raped at work may stop working altogether or change jobs. Sexual phobias commonly develop, and the woman may require years to be able to return to her prerape sexual lifestyle. She may panic in the presence of men. If the rape occurred outdoors, she may acquire a phobia about going outdoors again.

reproduction the creation by an individual or pair of individuals of other individuals that possess the same genetic components. The offspring may be a simple cell or a complex plant or animal. Sexual reproduction generally requires the fusion of male and female gametes to form a zygote, although parthenogenesis is classified as a form of sexual reproduction even though it requires only the gamete of one sex. Asexual reproduction is a method of producing a new generation of like individuals without the need for production of gametes. Spores, fission, gemmation, and vegetative reproduction represent asexual processes. Somatic reproduction is a form of reproduction by the budding-off of multicellular-fragments. Gametic reproduction may be unisexual, as in parthenogenesis, or bisexual, requiring the fusion of two gametes, such as a spermatozoon and an ovum.

reproductive behaviour any activity that leads to intercourse or the propagation of the species. The term also may be extended to cover activities associated with protection and supervision of offspring until they have matured sufficiently to survive and reproduce themselves.

reproductive instincts unlearned drives related to reproduction in animals, as in courtship behaviour, mating, nest building, and caring for the young. Among human beings the urge to reproduce is rarely considered an instinct because it is so dependent upon learning.

reproductive period the period during which human beings are able to produce offspring. This period extends from puberty (from 11 to 13 years of age in girls, and 12 to 14 in boys) to the climacteric (40 to 55 years of age in women, and about 65 to 75 in men).

resolution phase the last of the four phases of sexual response as outlined by Masters and Johnson. It follows the orgasmic phase and is marked in women by perspiration that tends to cover the sexual flush areas, return of the breasts to normal size, return of the shaft of the clitoris to its normal position, and return of the colour of the labia minora to its preexcitement hue. The labia majora, which decrease in size in the nulliparous woman and increase in size in the multiparous woman before orgasm, return to normal size. In the man, the resolution phase is characterized mainly by a loss of most, but not all, of the preorgasmic erection. The testicles return to their normal position in the scrotum, which loses its congestion, and the glans penis is retracted within the foreskin, if that was the position in its flaccid state. The male position also includes a refractory period, or the time necessary to begin another cycle of sexual response. This can range from a few minutes to a few days.

respectable deviant a person who may be a sexual deviant but because of wealth or political influence is able to manage an appearance of being a respectable straight individual. A colonial governor of New York and New Jersey, Edward Hyde, enjoyed dressing as a woman, a behaviour that would have been condemned in a person of less influence. Some authorities argue that most studies of deviant behaviour are inaccurate because the respectable deviants are seldom included or are not identified in police records.

respiratory changes breathing effects of the sexual response, which usually lag behind cardiovascular effects of sexual excitement. Normally, breathing becomes faster and deeper during the plateau and orgasmic phases of sexual response, increasing from about 15 respirations per minute to about 40. Most sex partners hold their breath momentarily during orgasm, then take a deep breath at the end of the orgasmic phase.

respiratory eroticism a psychoanalytical term for sexual pleasure achieved through the respiratory apparatus, as in smoking.

retarded ejaculation an English equivalent of the Latin medical term ejaculatio retardata.

retention cyst a cyst produced by abnormal retention of secreted substances, such as a milk cyst of the breast, a seminiferous cyst of the male reproductive tract, a bulbourethral gland cyst, or a cyst in the prostatic urethra.

rete testis (rē'tē) a network of tubules in the part of the testis where the seminiferous tubules converge towards the head of the epididymis. The 800 to 1,000 seminiferous tubules empty into a dozen efferent ducts leading into the highly convoluted head of the epididymis.

retifism an erotic obsession with women's shoes, which are believed to represent the female genital organs because of their hollow shape. The term is derived from the name of an 18th century French educator and novelist, Rétif de la Bretonne, who was famous for this deviation. Shoe fetishists (usually men) achieve sexual excitement and gratification from observing, wearing, licking, smelling, kissing, or masturbating with women's shoes.

retractile testis a testicle that is pulled away from the scrotum by spasms of the cremasteric muscle. A retractile testis often can be coaxed into a permanent location in the scrotum by the gentle application of heat and manipulation by a physician. Retractile testes account for a significant proportion of cases of cryptorchidism in adolescents.

retroglandular sulcus a constriction in the shaft of the penis, between the neck of the penis and the corona of the glans penis.

retrograde ejaculation the ejaculation of semen into the urinary bladder rather than from the glans penis. The abnormal effect may result from diabetes or from surgery of the prostate gland, which is located immediately below the urinary bladder. Semen ejaculated into the bladder is excreted with the urine. Retrograde ejaculation can be caused by squeezing the penis just before normal ejaculation, a practice used by some men who mistakenly believe it will prevent pregnancy. See also COITUS SAXONICUS.

retropubic pertaining to a type of surgical approach in the treatment of prostatic disorders: An incision is made through the lower abdominal wall, after which the prostate is reached and opened directly, that is, without going through the urinary bladder as in suprapubic surgery.

retrovirus a type of virus with a specific assortment of genes with two RNA molecules and reverse transcriptase molecules. Both the LAV and HTLV viruses that have been associated as possible causes of acquired immune deficiency syndrome (AIDS) are members of the retrovirus category and fit the same basic description of genetic makeup, a factor that made early identification of the AIDS organism difficult. See also AIDS.

return naked to the womb a slang term meaning a man's committing incest with his mother.

Rh blood-group incompatibility an inherited antigen condition that can effect the life of a foetus carried by a mother who has become sensitized to the antigen. A person who has inherited the Rh (for rhesus, a monkey species used in the original studies) factor is said to be Rh positive. One who lacks the factor is called Rh negative. If an Rh positive foetus is carried by an Rh negative mother, the mother's blood will develop antibodies against the foetal blood antigen, a condition similar to a severe allergy or rejection of an organ transplant from a person with an incompatible blood type. The reaction by the mother's antibodies results in a gradual destruction of the red blood cells produced by the foetal body, a condition called erythroblastosis foetalis. The sensitivity reaction generally increases with each pregnancy because the response of the mother's immune system grows with each exposure to a foetus whose blood is incompatible with her own. The situation develops from the marriage of persons with incompatible Rh factors. The chances of a marriage between an Rh positive man and Rh negative woman are about 1 in 10 among whites and 1 in 20 among blacks. The condition is rare among Orientals. Since the early research into Rh incompatibility, it has been found that there may actually be 36 different variations of the Rh factor, each with a different risk of severe antibody reaction. Treatment for the condition can include transfusion and immunization of the mother with Rh immunoglobulin.

rhinoceros horn the horn of the rhinoceros, usually taken internally in powdered form, as an alleged aphrodisiac. Its effect on the sex drive, if any, would not result from its natural properties but from expectation based very probably on the association between the horn and the erect penis, and between the rhinoceros itself and masculinity, because the rhinoceros is seen as a symbol of power, and a prime example of the Chinese yang force.

rhinosporidosis a fungal infection that results from bathing in infected water. Females may develop a fungal infection of the vagina from swimming in water contaminated by the organism *Rhinosporidium seeberi*, which may be carried by domestic animals.

rhythm method a technique of birth control based on the regularity of a woman's menstrual cycle. By carefully recording the phases of her own cycle, she may be able to predict when she will ovulate, and refrain from intercourse just before, during, and just after that time. The method is only 80 percent effective because of difficulty in making predictions of the precise time of ovulation.

ribavirin an antiviral drug that has been found to be effective in the treatment of a variety of viral infections. Although human clinical trial data had not been completed in 1985, ribavirin was reported to be effective in combatting the AIDS virus in laboratory experiments. See also AIDS.

ride bareback a slang term referring to a man's having intercourse without a condom (or, by way of extension, without the couple using any contraceptive).

right of the first night an alternative term for DROIT DU SEIGNEUR. See this entry.

right to life a term used by antiabortion groups and individuals who assert that the fertilized ovum is a person and has an absolute right to be born. In opposing abortion, they claim that there is no more right to 'kill' an embryo or a foetus for 'social convenience' than to kill any other person for this reason. They usually advocate natural family planning and oppose the use of mechanical devices, pills, and other chemicals for contraception.

rimming a slang term for oral-anal sexual activity.

ring around the rosey another term for 'daisy chain.'

rites of passage ceremonies performed to mark an individual's change in status at critical points in life, especially at the onset of puberty, entry into marriage, having a first baby, or acceptance into a clan.

ritual abstinence temporary abstention from intercourse during certain holy days as, for example, in the Muslim world where all believers are required to abstain not only from intercourse but also from passionate kissing during the daylight hours of Ramadan, the month of fasting.

ritual baths ceremonial bathing (showers, shared hot baths, washing the sex organs) prescribed as a religious ritual to be performed before intercourse or after menstruation. Water is regarded as a purifying and erotic agent for both the body and the mind in many cultures such as Christianity, Judaism, and Hinduism and in China and Japan.

ritual dancing dance as an integral part of religious rites and ceremonies. Though common throughout the world, some societies use the dance in unique ways; for example, among one aboriginal Australian group, the Aranda, the purpose is to arouse the sexual interest of women for strange men, after which their husbands arrange rendezvous for them with the men of their choice. Among the Mandan Plains Indians of America, the Buffalo Dance required the women to have intercourse, which was viewed as a means of drawing power from the primal bison, to insure large herds and prosperity.

ritual defloration another term for ceremonial defloration.

ritual mutilation a term usually referring to the removal of the clitoris (clitoridectomy) as a custom among certain cultures of Latin America, Africa, and the Middle East. Although the euphemism 'circumcision' may be used in describing the procedure, it is the clitoris itself, corresponding to the glans of the penis, that is removed, rather than the foreskin. Historically, a similar procedure had been used in America by puritanical subcultures in the belief that a woman without a clitoris would be less likely to be promiscuous.

ritual rape forced intercourse associated with the custom of bride capture, especially in Polynesia.

ritual sex sexual acts performed as an aspect of religious devotion. In Africa, the Ila forced their boys to masturbate and to imitate sexual intercourse with one another during initiation training; the Ashanti of Ghana required a widow to cleanse herself of the spirit of her dead husband by having intercourse with a stranger; and the Kikuyu required circumcised boys to have sex with a married woman who is a stranger to them. The Lepcha of Southern Asia required a man to have intercourse with his wife, 3, 7, or 21 days after the birth of a baby, to rid her of the pains of childbirth.

ritual wife exchange a rare custom found mainly among aborigines of Australia, in which a ceremonial exchange of wives is performed after defloration (usually with a special boomerang), as a means of preventing sickness for both partners. The woman may boast of the number of men with whom she has had intercourse during the ceremony.

rocks an American slang term for testicles.

rod an American slang term for penis.

roger an archaic word meaning to copulate.

role confusion distorted sex-role identity, especially masculine behaviour in a female or feminine behaviour in a male. Confusion may result from different factors, such as cross-dressing in early childhood, separation of the mother from the father during infancy, mistaken assignment of sex roles in infants with ambiguous genitalia, or favouritism shown by one or both parents towards a sibling of the opposite sex. Feminine behaviour in boys after the age of 3 is usually harder to change than tomboyishness in girls. Also called identity confusion.

Roman culture a colloquial term for orgies and swinging—used, for example, as a code term in 'personal' ads.

romantic love a highly emotional, 'starry-eyed' relationship based largely on idealization, physical attraction, adoration, and a large dash of fantasy—but it usually ignores practical, down-to-earth realities of life. Anthropologists have found that the ideal of romantic love grew mainly out of medieval concepts of chivalry, and is rare in all cultures except those of Europe and (European-settled) America.

root a term sometimes applied to the attachment of the bulb of the penis, designating the portion embedded in the pelvis. Root is also a slang term for penis; and in Australia the word may mean to have sexual intercourse.

rough trade a slang term for a vicious and dangerous male homosexual, usually said of a hustler.

round vesicle an alternative term for an ovarian follicle. A follicle may reach a size of 10 to 12 millimetres in diameter when mature, growing from a microscopic dot called a primary follicle.

round eye a slang term for anus, especially in the context of anal intercourse.

rousing the dead a colloquial expression sometimes used to describe the stimulation of the male penis after intercourse to produce a second erection.

rubber a colloquial American term for condom; also, a popular term for a person who practises frottage.

rubberites a slang term for the fetish of wearing garments made of rubber or rubberized fabrics. Some rubberites insist that the rubber product must not only be made of rubber but must also have the odour of rubber.

rubber johnny a colloquial term for condom. Unlike 'rubber' it is used in British as well as American English, although it is now rather dated.

Rubin test a test of the condition of the fallopian tubes in which carbon-dioxide gas is injected via the uterus. If the tubes are open, as for the passage of an ovum, the gas will pass through the open ends of the tubes into the peritoneal cavity, where it can be detected by x-rays. If the tubes are blocked, pressure will build up from the injected gas. The degree of pressure is translated into the amount of patency, or opening, in the tubes.

rudeness in many English-speaking countries, for example, throughout the Caribbean, sexual intercourse or overt sexual behaviour. A girl may be admonished not to 'do rudeness' or to 'be rude.' Also expressions such as 'He rudenessed me' are common.

rudimentary testis a developmental anomaly in which one or both of the testes fail to mature beyond the embryonic stage. In such cases of primordial gonadal arrest, examination of the germinal tissue may show only testis cords and interstitial cells similar to those found in the male embryo. Because the genital organizing substance that influences development in the embryo acts locally and unilaterally, the testis on one side may develop normally while the testis on the opposite side remains in the rudimentary state.

rule of abstinence an alternative term for the psychoanalytical term abstinence rule.

ruptured hymen a hymen that is no longer intact, usually because it has been penetrated by a penis during initial intercourse. However, the hymen may be ruptured for other reasons, as by an examining physician during a gynaecological examination, or by bicycle or horse riding. Or a hymen may simply appear ruptured as a result of a congenital condition.

rut periodically recurring sexual excitement and activity in deer, sheep, goats, and other mammals. It is a phase of oestrus behaviour.

Sacher-Masoch, Leopold von (1836-1895) an Austrian lawyer and writer whose sexual interest was focussed on his compulsive desire for pain and humiliation, which Krafft-Ebing later termed masochism. He also developed a fetish for furs. Both tendencies apparently originated in his childhood when he experienced sexual excitement from watching his aunt and her lover play bondage and whipping games in a fur closet. In his adult life, he reenacted these games and described them in detail in a celebrated novel, *Venus in Furs*, which culminated not only in masochistic but also sadistic scenes—that is, sadomasochism. Like Sade, he was committed to an asylum; he died shortly afterwards.

sack coitus an unusual technique in which one partner has placed himself or herself in a rubber or other sack.

sacral area a segment of the spinal cord in the lower back where nerve centres that control penile erection and ejaculation are located. Because sexual stimulation is controlled in part by the brain, men who have suffered spinal injuries are frequently able to achieve partial or complete erections, and many are able to have successful intercourse.

sacred prostitution an early religious custom in which prostitutes dedicated themselves to the service of fertility gods or goddesses. These women performed sexual acts with priests or, in some instances, with worshippers, inside the temple. The practice has been traced as far back as the 5th century B.C. and was at one time common in Babylonia, Arabia, Greece, India, and West Africa. It has been conjectured that prostitution itself may have started as a sacred rite and only later became secularized. Also called temple prostitution.

sacred triangle the triangular mound above the vulva; the mons veneris or mons pubis.

sacrum the bones of the sacral vertebrae, which in adult life are a fused mass of separate vertebrae. The sacrum forms a smooth concave surface below the small of the back and represents the back of the pelvis.

sadism a psychosexual disorder, or paraphilia, in which sexual excitement is obtained by inflicting pain on the sexual partner. Sadistic acts may consist of physical cruelty, such as flogging or bondage, or mental cruelty, as in humiliating the partner. The suffering may be inflicted on either a consenting or a nonconsenting person, and may range from mild injury to raping, torturing, or even killing the victim. See DE SADE; ANAL SADISM; PHALLIC SADISM.

sadomasochism a complementary relationship in which one person derives pleasure and usually sexual gratification from inflicting pain while the other becomes sexually aroused by experiencing that pain. Also called sadomasochistic relationship, and S/M.

safe a slang term for condom.

safe period a popular term for the days of the menstrual cycle when conception is least likely to result from intercourse without use of a contraceptive device.

saint's delight a colloquial term for vagina.

saliromania a compulsive need to obtain sexual gratification through preoccupation with filth, ugliness, or deformity. Examples are soiling one's partner or oneself, watching mud-wrestling bouts between women, viewing grotesquely deformed persons at fairs, getting a 'kick' out of anal or urinary odours, or, more mildly, using obscene, 'dirty' words during sexual foreplay. The most extreme form of this paraphilia is coprophagia. Many Freudians trace saliromania to an unsatisfied urge to play with faeces at about 2 years of age.

salpingectomy the surgical removal of a uterine, or fallopian, tube. An incision into a fallopian tube is a salpingotomy. A salpingectomy accompanied by surgical removal of an ovary is termed a salpingo-oophorectomy.

salpingitis an inflammation of the fallopian tubes. The condition may be marked by pain on one or both sides, infrequent episodes of nausea, excessive menstrual flow, and a fever that may rise to 104° F. Causes may include hypersensitivity to an IUD, or an infection, such as gonorrhoea or tuberculosis. Salpingitis from gonorrhoea often is associated with an abnormal discharge or painful or difficult urination, particularly just before the start of a menstrual period.

salpingitis isthmica nodosa a disorder of the fallopian tubes marked by the development of nodules and abnormally thickened walls in the portion of the tube that is attached to the uterus.

salpingotomy a surgical procedure in which an incision is made into a fallopian tube.

saltpetre a common name for potassium nitrate, a substance that has been used as a diuretic and to induce sweating. It is an ancient medication, included in prescriptions on Sumerian tablets of 4,000 years ago, but potentially harmful as a precursor of nitrosamine carcinogens, as a destroyer of red blood cells, and as a lethal poison, despite its legendary application as an anaphrodisiac.

same-sex sex play the tendency of children to adopt, in play with other children of the opposite sex, roles identified with older members of their own sex. A boy and girl may agree to 'play house,' a game in which the boy plays the father role and the girl the role of the mother. The game may include coital play in which the boy lies on top of the girl in imitation of scenes from their own home or in films or television.

Samoans inhabitants of a group of islands in Western Polynesia. Monogamy is the rule except for chiefs, who usually have several wives. Other practices include sex hospitality (which seems to be prevalent throughout Polynesia); adolescent homosexuality, which is regarded as an innocent form of play; decorating the bodies with tattoos, a custom that is on the decline today; and night-crawling by unpopular and desperate young men—a practice that Margaret Mead called 'surreptitious rape', and which led to outright shunning by other girls if they were caught.

Sanger, Margaret (1883-1966) an American leader of the birth-control movement. Building on wide experience as an obstetrical nurse for underprivileged families and single mothers, Sanger decided that the high infant-and-adult-mortality rates, especially found in self-induced abortions, could only be combatted by liberating women from unwanted pregnancies. Accordingly, and in defiance of the Comstock Act, she began publicizing contraceptive methods in a magazine she founded in 1914, the *Woman Rebel* (later renamed *Birth Control Review*); she published a widely read pamphlet, *Family Limitation*, and in 1921 founded the American Birth Control League. In 1927 she organized the first World Population Conference in Geneva, and in 1936 was instrumental in modification of the Comstock Act to permit doctors to prescribe contraceptives. Her work then spread to overpopulated countries, and in 1953 she was elected first president of the International Planned Parenthood Federation.

sanitary towel a disposable pad made of cellulose or cotton designed to absorb the menstrual flow when held in place along the opening of the vagina by panties, a belt, or adhesive backing that sticks to the panties. In American English it is called a *sanitary napkin*.

sapphism an alternative for lesbianism based on the fact that the Greek poetess *Sappho* lived on the island of Lesbos and wrote lyrical poems about love and sex, generally assumed to be between women.

sarcoma botyroides a type of vaginal cancer that may appear as grapelike clusters of tissue. Untreated, the growth may eventually protrude from the opening of the vagina. It also is likely to be accompanied by bleeding.

sarcoma of the prostate a rare form of prostatic tumour that may affect men at any age but occurs most often in infants and small boys. In infant boys, the treatment usually is surgical removal of the prostate, seminal vesicles, and urinary bladder. The urinary system is rebuilt so that urine is diverted through the intestinal tract.

Sarcoptes scabiei a mite that burrows between the layers of skin to deposit eggs, resulting in a skin rash that itches and may produce pimples and pustules. The condition, called scabies, can be transmitted by sexual contact in the same manner as crab lice.

sard the oldest English term for having sexual intercourse, from around 950 A.D.

sathon in ancient Greece, a boy loved by an

older man (*sathe*, 'penis').

satiation a state of complete satisfaction or gratification of sexual or other drives, such as hunger or thirst.

sattvic foods foods that, according to practitioners of yoga, stimulate the creative and erotic senses. They include milk, butter, honey, nuts, grains, most fruits, and the vegetables that grow above ground. Sattvic foods are related to the sweet taste, and reportedly result in a sweet, nonirritating semen that is best for a healthy offspring. (Sanskrit *sattva*, 'existence.')

satyriasis a male psychosexual disorder characterized by an obsessive, insatiable desire for sexual gratification. The condition is not the result of being physically 'oversexed,' but stems from unconscious emotional needs, such as the need for reassurance of potency, an attempt to deny homosexual tendencies, a means of alleviating anxiety, or a need to compensate for failures or inadequacies in other areas of life. The term itself is derived from the satyrs of Greek mythology, who were alleged to be part human and part animal, and to have an unlimited sex drive. Also called Don Juan syndrome.

saucer edge medical jargon for the breasts of women with adenosis, a lymph-gland disorder. The breasts tend to be small, dense, and filled with tiny nodules which give them the feel of the edge of a saucer when palpated.

sauna club often a euphemism for massage parlour (which itself is a euphemism).

scabies a contagious disease caused by the itch mite SARCOPTES SCABIEI. See this entry.

scarification the process of producing a scar, or cicatrix, as in making superficial cuts in the surface of the skin. Scarification is found among many African societies, where it is used as a means of beautifying the skin and making the individual more sexually desirable.

scarlet woman an obsolete euphemism for loose woman.

scatography the practice of writing any kind of material, including graffiti, relating to eliminative functions, as a means of expressing or arousing sexual interest.

scatology the study of or interest in excrement, filth, and obscenity. Scatological language is sometimes used as a stimulant during sexual encounters, especially those involving anal eroticism. Also called *scatologia*.

scatophobia another term for coprophobia.

schlong an American slang term for penis.

schmuck a Yiddish colloquialism for penis.

The term is also used figuratively, referring to someone who is considered to be stupid or silly.

school of Venus an older term for brothel (17th to 19th century).

Schrenck-Notzing, Albert von (1862-1929) a Viennese psychiatrist who helped pave the way for acceptance of Freud's theories, but was particularly noted for his attempts to modify the sexual orientation of homosexuals through hypnotic suggestion and visits to brothels, where they might be reconditioned to heterosexual relationships.

scirrhus a form of cancer of the prostate that is identified by its hardness when palpated through the rectum by an examining doctor. A scirrhus cancer may also occur in the breast.

sclerosing lymphangitis of the penis an inflammation of the lymphatic vessels of the shaft of the penis. The condition is characterized by an enlargement and hardening of the lymph vessels resulting in a cordlike thickening of the lymph ducts near the corona glandis.

Scold's bridal an alternative term for brank, a gag used for taming shrews and, more recently, for bondage games.

scopophilia a sexual variance in which gratification is achieved by viewing the sexual activities or sexual organs of others. Freud distinguished between an active and a passive form of scopophilia—that is, pleasure in looking and pleasure in being looked at. If this deviation is a persistent or exclusive source of gratification, it is essentially equivalent to voyeurism. Also called scoptophilia; scotophilia.

scopophobia a morbid fear of being looked at. It is an extreme form of shyness usually occurring in adolescence and resulting from sexual self-consciousness.

scoptolagnia sexual excitement produced by looking at nude persons or exposed genitalia.

scoptophilia an alternative term for scopophilia.

score a slang term meaning to achieve sexual success, particularly in persuading a woman to have sex with one—thus a man might be asked 'Did you score last night?'

scotophilia an alternative term for scopophilia.

scrape an Australian slang term meaning to copulate.

screw a slang term used either as a verb, meaning to copulate, or as a noun, meaning sexual intercourse or partner in intercourse (as in 'he was a great screw'). In addition it is used metaphorically in phrases like *screw you!*, an expletive, and *screw up*, meaning to botch.

scrotal angioma a type of tumour of the scrotum marked by wartlike growths associated with a disorder involving dilated blood vessels of the skin.

scrotal erysipelas an infection of the scrotal skin and subcutaneous tissues caused, as in most other types of erysipelas, by a streptococcal organism. It results from wounds and abscesses, and as secondary disorders is associated with chancroid or other diseases, such as lymphatic infections. The scrotum becomes smooth, swollen, and warm, with small blisters on the surface.

scrotal hypospadia a congenital malformation in which the outlet of the male urethra is between the testicles. The scrotum in such cases is usually associated with imperfectly descended testes.

scrotal pouch the pocket of membrane that precedes the descent of the testes into the scrotum during the seventh month of gestation. The membranous pouch leaves the abdominal cavity and migrates into the primitive skin sac that will become the scrotum, to serve as one of the inner layers of the scrotum.

scrotal sac an alternative term for scrotum.

scrotal temperature the temperature of the scrotum, which normally is slightly lower than body temperature. The lower temperature is necessary for the production of viable spermatozoa. The scrotum is quite temperature-sensitive, tending to move farther away from the body in a warm environment such as a hot bath but moving closer to the body in cold temperatures.

scrotal xanthomata a type of eruptive xanthomata, or skin lesions, that may appear on the surface of the scrotum and other genital and perineal areas in cases of hypertriglyceridaemia, a condition of extremely excessive blood fats. The lesions resemble the skin sores associated with chicken-pox.

scrotitis an inflammation of the scrotum. The causes may include a number of infections, such as mumps, gonorrhoea, typhoid fever, scarlet fever, influenza, syphilis, leprosy, tuberculosis, or brucellosis. Other possible causes include injury, a hernia with a segment of the intestine incarcerated in the scrotum, undescended testicle with referred pain, a tumour, gout, rheumatic fever, hydrocele, or torsion of the spermatic cord. The

scrotum also could be the site of referred pain from appendicitis or a kidney stone. The scrotal pain may be mild or excruciating.

scrotopexy a surgical procedure in which a portion of the scrotum is removed to correct a defect. The operation is usually combined with *scrotoplasty*, or the use of plastic surgery to refashion the scrotum.

scrotum a pouch of skin and related supportive tissues containing the male testis, epididymides, and portions of the spermatic cord. It is located near the bulb of the penis and in the pubic area of the perineum. The scrotum is divided by a wall of tissue (a septum), and because the left spermatic cord is longer, the left side is normally lower than the right side. The scrotum is generally translucent, meaning a beam of light from one side will illuminate the scrotal contents in a darkened room.

scrubber a British derogatory slang term for a prostitute, or more generally for any woman with accommodating sexual morals.

seafood a male homosexual slang term for a homosexual sailor.

seasonal sex a term referring to the idea that human sexual activity, like mating in 90 percent of the animal kingdom, is a seasonal function. There is, however, little if any evidence for a biologically based human 'rutting season,' but there are variations caused by other factors. Among the Eskimos more intercourse takes place during long winter nights than during the summer, and among Westerners, as a whole, more children are conceived in the summer when holidays occur.

seated sex sexual intercourse with one or both partners in a sitting position. Usually the man sits in a chair or on the edge of a bed, and the woman lowers herself on him; his pelvic movements are restricted, but his hands are free. The woman usually faces the man but may have her back to him; she may also sit on him as he lies on his back.

sebaceous cyst a sebum gland cyst, similar to an acne swelling, that can develop in the labia majora or minora (or in other parts of the body). The labia are well supplied with the sebaceous oil glands. If one or more become blocked by skin-cell debris, a tender, painful furuncle (boil) will develop at the site. Untreated, a sebaceous cyst of the labia can grow to the size of a walnut.

secondarism the seeking of sexual arousal through relations with a person who has just participated in a sex act.

secondary amenorrhoea a cessation of

menses after they have become established. The cause may be an illness, change of environment, or surgical removal of the ovaries or uterus before menopause.

secondary erectile dysfunction a form of impotence in which a man is not able to produce or maintain an erection to perform intercourse, although he was previously able to produce a satisfactory erection. A major causal factor is psychological stress or conflict.

secondary hypogonadism a condition of male sexual dysfunction that is related to a malfunction of brain-regulated testosterone production, as distinguished from a hormonal disorder caused by a defect in the testes.

secondary impotence a condition in which a male has been able to achieve a normal erection and ejaculation in intercourse but is not able to repeat the performance. Technically, secondary impotence can occur after the first act of coitus, and nearly all men eventually encounter a time when they cannot repeat a sexual activity they may have performed thousands of times without failure. As a rule of thumb, secondary impotence is considered a problem only when a man fails to achieve an erection in 25 percent of attempts.

secondary oocyte a female gamete produced by meiotic division of a primary oocyte. The primary oocyte contains the diploid (46) number of chromosomes and in dividing produces the secondary oocyte and one polar body, each with 23, or half the diploid number. The secondary ooctye undergoes mitosis to produce a mature ovum and a second polar body, each with the haploid (23) number of chromosomes.

secondary orgasmic dysfunction a condition in which a woman or man has managed to achieve orgasm at least once, whether by coitus, masturbation or some other form of stimulation, but can no longer do so. Also called situational orgasmic dysfunction.

secondary sex characteristics physical characteristics other than the external sex organs that distinguish between male and female: texture of facial, body, and underarm hair; voice quality; size of the breasts and nipples; pattern of pubic hair; and body contours (for example, wider hips among women).

secondary testicular failure a male gonadal deficiency that results from failure of the pituitary gland to secrete gonadotropic hormones. Because the testes fail to receive the stimulating hormones, they remain in an infantile state. Secondary hypogonadism, or secondary testicular failure, accounts for more than three fourths of males afflicted with hypogonadism.

secondary wives in a polygynous society, women who serve as additional wives beyond the original or primary wife. These wives, or concubines, are recognized as sexual partners but not as managers of the household or even as mothers of the children, even though they may actually be the mothers.

second-stage orgasm the phase of ejaculation of semen by the male after the prostate, seminal vesicles, and ductus deferens have released their semen components into the dilated urethral bulb. Contractions of the muscles at the base of the penis and peristaltic action of the genital ducts combine to expel the semen forcefully from the urethral meatus during this phase of orgasm.

second testicular hormone a term applied to a speculative source of oestrogens found in the urine of men. Because male oestrogen occurs only in males with functionally active Leydig cells, it has been assumed that the cells produce a testicular hormone in addition to testosterone and that it is a form of oestrogen.

secret service a slang term for the work of a prostitute (the *secret-service agent*) whose sexual services are clandestine, known only to her regular clients, but otherwise unknown even among her close acquaintances.

secret vice an older euphemism for masturbation.

seduction the enticing or inducing of a female (sometimes a male) into sexual intercourse without the use of force—for example, by promising marriage or by bribery. Seduction is considered a criminal act in some countries, usually when it involves an unmarried girl or woman. See also INFANTILE SEDUCTION.

seductive behaviour a form of unconscious incestuous behaviour, according to many psychotherapists, in which parental attitudes towards a child may be seductive. The parental behaviour may never culminate in overt incest, but it may condition the child to accept the role playing because of the implicit approval of the parents. The child may have little or no guilt until later in life when he or she learns from others that incest is forbidden.

segmentation the process of mitotic division of the zygote, or fertilized ovum, into 2, then

4, 8, 16, and so on daughter cells. The process, however, follows a pattern of cleavage planes whereby the second division, from 2 to 4 cells, occurs at right angles to the first phase of division. The third division occurs in a third plane, and so on, until the mass of small cells, called a morula, is ready for implantation into the wall of the uterus.

selective gonadotropic failure a condition caused by mild anterior-pituitary-gland insufficiency in the male and characterized by a penis, scrotum, and prostate that fail to grow to mature sizes. The body type of the individual is eunuchoid, with arms and legs of abnormal proportions.

self-abuse an archaic, moralistic term for masturbation based on the antiquated notion that it is injurious or sinful.

self-castration another term for self-emasculation.

self-control the ability to exert restraint over one's impulses, especially to inhibit the sex urge, or delay orgasm until the partner is 'ready.'

self-emasculation a form of self-mutilation in which an individual castrates himself, usually as a religious or ascetic practice. Self-emasculation is extremely rare today although it is occasionally found among psychotic patients who are suffering from a delusion of guilt. In the past there have been many cases in ancient Egypt, among the priests of Atzis in Greece, among medicine men in Asia and North America, among certain dervish sects, and in the Skoptsy sect of 18th-century Russia. The best known Christian example is Origen, a theologian who lived in the 3rd century.

self-induced abortion abortion deliberately brought on by the pregnant woman, for example, by removing the embryo or foetus through the use of an instrument such as a corkscrew. Such methods are extremely dangerous and may result in serious illness or even death from blood poisoning.

self-mutilation a self-destructive act in which the individual severely injures or disfigures himself or herself as a form of expiation for real or fancied misdeeds, religious excess, or an extreme form of masochism. Examples are repetitive wrist cutting ('slashing'), burning the skin with a cigarette or flame, self-castration, or scarification.

self-pleasuring a recently adopted term for masturbation, or manipulation of the sex organs or other body areas for pleasure and for release of sexual tension.

self-pollution an obsolete term for masturbation (17th to 19th century).

self-stimulation a synonym for masturbation, manipulation of the sex organs for the purpose of sexual excitement and gratification.

semen the fluid containing spermatozoa that is ejaculated by the male during intercourse. The fluid is produced by the prostate gland and seminal vesicles and contains substances that tend to increase the survivability of the spermatozoa in the female reproductive tract, such as an alkaline substance to neutralize the acidity of the vagina.

semen analysis laboratory examination of a sample of semen obtained in a wide-mouthed glass bottle after masturbation or coitus reservatus has been performed to produce an ejaculate. The patient abstains from sexual activity for 3 to 5 days before producing the semen sample. The semen is never collected in a rubber container because rubber is usually impregnated with chemicals that destroy spermatozoa. A sample of 3 to 5 millilitres should contain 100 to 120 million spermatozoa, of which 80 to 85 percent should be highly motile. And at least 80 percent of the spermatozoa should be normal in appearance. When fewer than 40 percent of the spermatozoa are actively motile and more than 20 percent are of abnormal shapes and sizes, the risk of subnormal fertility can often be explained. Abnormal spermatozoa may include microsperm, megalosperm, aplastic head, double head, double tail, and other forms. Spermatozoa of a normal healthy male usually contain a few abnormally shaped spermatozoa. See also SEMEN CONTENT.

semen content a term usually referring to the total content of semen (whereas the term semen analysis usually refers to the analysis of sperm). The question of semen content arises especially among persons who regularly swallow semen, as in fellatio, and who are concerned about calorie intake and nutritional substances. The average ejaculate of about 4 cubic centimetres, weighing about 4 grams, contains less than 35 calories, mainly in proteins and fats (weightwatchers don't have to worry). In all, semen contains tiny amounts of over 30 substances, none of which is harmful—including ammonia, ascorbic acid, blood-group antigens, calcium, chlorine, cholesterol, choline, citric acid, creatine, deoxyribonucleic acid (DNA), fructose, glutathione, hyaluronidase, inositol, lactic acid, magnesium, nitrogen, phosphorus, potassium, purine, pyrimidine, pyruvic acid, sodium, sorbitol, spermidine, spermine, urea, uric acid, vitamin B_{12}, zinc... For analysis of sperm, see SEMEN ANALYSIS.

semen fear an alternative term for spermatophobia.

semen myths fictitious beliefs and superstitions concerning semen, for example, the Hindu belief that the semen is the basis of health, strength, and long life, and should be conserved through periodic abstinence and through avoiding masturbation and nocturnal emissions as far as possible. Somewhat similarly, the early Chinese held that ejaculation diminished the yang, or male, element and therefore reduces the man's strength and may even shorten his life. Various methods were therefore used to retain as much semen as possible even during intercourse. A third example is the belief among the Etoro, in Oceania, that boys have no semen at birth but acquire enough semen for sexual activity through oral insemination by older men.

semen retention in early Taoist and Tantric treatises, the use of various techniques (especially breath and thought control) to regulate the emission of semen so that a portion of it will 'ascend and nourish the brain'. Some Taoist masters recommend that ideally semen should be released only two or three times in ten sessions, and that certain lovemaking postures such as sitting, squatting, and having the man lie flat on his back, are especially effective in helping to control the semen, and in directing sexual energy upwards to the brain.

semenuria the presence of semen in the urine. The condition may result from semen reflux, or retrograde ejaculation, in which semen is forced into the urinary bladder as a result of effects of prostate surgery or a urethral defect, such as a stricture.

seminal cyst a cyst caused by retention of the sperm in the testis or epididymis.

seminal discharge the discharge of semen, during intercourse, masturbation, or nocturnal emission.

seminal duct an alternative name for the ductus deferens or vas deferens.

seminal vesicles a pair of membranous pouches embedded in the prostate gland and united with the ductus deferens at the ejaculatory ducts. The vesicles secrete a fluid that is combined at the ejaculatory ducts with the spermatozoa from the ductus deferens and added to the akaline secretions of the prostate gland. The seminal vesicles do not store sper-

matozoa as was previously believed. Each vesicle is actually a blind tube that coils upon itself so that its internal length is actually several times that of its external size of approximately 3 inches.

semination the deposition of semen in the vagina or uterus, either during intercourse or by artificial insemination.

seminiferous tubules the straight or convoluted tubes in the lobes of the testes. A testis is estimated to contain more than 800 of the tubules, each of which may be 30 inches in length. In the walls of the convoluted tubules are spermatozoa in various stages of development and maturation.

seminoma a common type of testicular tumour with a cellular pattern that resembles the germinal cells in the seminferous tubules. Most of the tumours that develop in undescended testicles are seminomas.

senile ovary the ovary of the postmenopausal woman. It contains few follicles and consists mainly of old corpora albicantia and corpora atretica cells. Most of the functional tissue has been replaced by connective-tissue fibres.

sensate-focus-oriented therapy the Masters and Johnson approach to sexual difficulties, which involves training sessions in which both partners learn to think and feel sensually by progressively touching, stroking, fondling, kissing, and massaging all parts of their mate's body, with special attention to the erogenous zones. The purpose is to arouse the most exciting possible sensations in their partner and themselves. The therapy also includes a detailed history of each patient's attitudes and patterns, improvement in communication between the partners, reassurance and support, and prescribed practice at home.

sensitive spot a euphemism for clitoris.

sensuality unrestrained indulgence in the pleasures of the senses, particularly food and sex; gratification of the 'carnal appetites.'

sensuous appealing to the senses, as in sensuous music, poetry, or painting. The term is also applied to a person who appreciates and enjoys experiences that involve the senses, including erotic stimulation.

separate ova two or more ova released at the same time. Fertilization of separate ova results in dizygotic, or fraternal, twins. About 70 percent of twins are the result of multiple ovulation. Triplets or other multiple births also can result from separate ova. Studies indicate that the tendency to release separate ova at the same time is an inherited trait.

septate hymen a hymen that has an opening blocked only by a vertical fold of tissue in the middle.

septum a partition. The septum of the brain is associated with sexuality. It is part of the limbic system of the brain. Stimulation of the limbic system, and particularly the septum, results in erections and orgasms for monkeys and humans.

sequential pills a system of administering oral contraceptives in which pills containing only oestrogen are taken for 15 days. On the following 5 days, the woman takes pills containing both oestrogen and progestagen. The manufacturers note that this routine follows the natural pattern of female sex hormones more closely than in taking only pills containing both types of hormones.

serial monogamy a sequence of monogamous marriages; consecutive marriages, with divorce or annulment between, so that the individual is married to only one partner at a time. Also called *serial marriage*.

The term serial monogamy also applies to a form of courting behaviour in which young men and women remain faithful to each other as long as the relationship lasts. However, the relationship may be of short duration. One survey indicated that serial monogamists maintained a relationship for an average of a year or more but each had averaged four partners. Nearly half had experienced premarital sex as part of the relationship.

serosa an alternative term for the serous coat, which covers the uterus. It is derived from the peritoneum, a membrane that covers many of the pelvic structures.

serous cyst a large fluid-filled cyst of the ovary. It is grey to amber in colour and is named after the type of fluid, which resembles blood serum. A serous cyst of the ovary may grow to the size of an orange.

Sertoli cells the supporting cells of the seminiferous tubules in the testes. They are found between germinal cells and contain spermatids (immature sperm cells) in their cytoplasm.

Sertoli-cells-only syndrome an alternative term for an abnormal condition of the testes in which only Sertoli cells are present and there is no germinal epithelium in the tubules.

sessile nodule a partial extrusion of sex chromatin material from the nucleus into the cytoplasm of a white blood cell (neutrophil) of a female. The phenomenon, which is peculiar to females, is associated with the presence of Barr bodies in the white cells. If the chromatin material is completely extruded, it is called a drumstick appendage. The patterns of sex chromatin extrusion are representative of the sex chromosomal complements of the individuals, as XX, XXY, XXXX, etc.

17-ketosteroids substances produced in the adrenal cortex of both males and females. The 17-ketosteroids play an important role in sexual development and function as they are able to divert amino acids, the building blocks of proteins, into muscle mass and sex organs. The ketosteroids stimulate pubic-hair growth in adolescence, contribute to the enlargement of the penis and clitoris at puberty, and are responsible for much of the adolescent problem of acne. Abbreviation: 17-KS.

sex the physical and psychological characteristics that distinguish between males and females; attributes that determine one's gender; also, the functions and processes involved in intercourse and procreation. In addition *have sex* means 'to have sexual intercourse, copulate.' The term is derived from the Latin word *sexus*, which appears to be related to *secare*, meaning to cut or to divide.

sex act any form of copulation or sexual intercourse; coitus.

sex addiction another term for sexual addiction.

sex after childbirth another term for postpartum intercourse.

sex-aggression-fusion rapist a rapist who associates violence and sadism with sex. He usually has a history of antisocial and aggressive behaviour and may be impotent in sexual encounters with a woman unless the woman fights back. The violence itself is needed for his sexual arousal. Although the sex-aggression-fusion rapist is relatively rare, attacks by this type of person tend to be well publicized and result in more common forms of rape being overlooked or unreported.

Sexaholics Anonymous an American organization of individuals who consider themselves addicted to sex and who conduct periodic meetings to discuss their preoccupation with sexual matters. Patterned after Alcoholics Anonymous, Sexaholics Anonymous is organized into local chapters. Members include persons who have risked jobs, family, and friends to maintain expensive contacts with prostitutes, massage parlours, and pornographic shops.

sex aids another term for erotic aids.

sex and alcohol intake of alcoholic drinks as a means of increasing the sex drive or enhancing sexual performance. Studies show that modest amounts may help people overcome anxiety, fear or inhibition, and enable them to 'relax and enjoy it.' Large amounts, however, have been found to decrease or even eliminate the man's capacity to achieve or maintain an erection, and the woman's ability to have an orgasm. Alcohol may also impair judgment and open the way to sexual activity that may be later regretted; under its influence, contraceptives may be forgotten and unwanted pregnancy may result.

sex and disability the view that individuals affected by severe physical disability such as cerebral palsy, paraplegia, and multiple sclerosis, have the right to and, in most cases, the capacity for sexual gratification—and in some instances can have children of their own. Even in cases where they cannot achieve full orgasm, they are almost always capable of some form of sexual pleasure and excitement, provided they have the opportunity to experiment with every possible form of stimulation: masturbation, oral sex, and homosexual relationships where desired, plus any variation in position that works, or any artificial aid such as a vibrator, or even a third party acting as an assistant.

sex and social class general differences in sexual attitudes and behaviour observed on different socioeconomic levels. Using education as an indicator, Kinsey found that single males with some higher education relied more heavily on masturbation, deep kissing, petting, and nocturnal emissions, and less heavily on relations with prostitutes and homosexual contacts than males with less education. Highly educated men are also generally more responsive to the sexual needs of their wives than are the less well-educated, and more likely to believe that a woman's sexual gratification is as important as a man's.

sex apparatus the internal and external sexual organs (especially the labia, clitoris, vagina, penis, and testicles) as well as the glands that produce the sexual products (androgen, oestrogen, progesterone, testosterone) or that stimulate or control the functions of the sexual organs or the development of secondary sex characteristics.

sex appeal the capacity to arouse sexual interest and desire. This is largely a matter of personal taste and cultural pattern. However, generally speaking (and judging by film and TV idols in the 80s), people in Western society are particularly responsive to athletic, muscular, somewhat aggressive men, and relatively slim women with slightly oversized breasts, shapely legs and buttocks, careful makeup, flowing hair, and revealing or provocative clothes. In certain non-Western societies the sources of sex appeal are extremely varied, including such features as gigantic buttocks, pendulous breasts, flattened heads, protruding navels, crossed eyes, blackened teeth, artificially stretched necks, and scarred or tattooed bodies.

sex-appropriate behaviour behaviour that is considered suited to one's sex. See also SEX-TYPING.

sex assignment identification of an individual as male, female, pseudohermaphrodite, or hermaphrodite, on the basis of physical characteristics (anatomy, hormone production). Transsexuals do not accept their sex assignment, feeling that they are victims of a mistake of nature, and some of them may request sex-change operations.

sex-blind a term applied to US state laws that prohibit discrimination between the sexes, such as insurance laws that prohibit differences in rates based on sex.

sex centre of the brain a term sometimes applied to a small area at the base of the brain which is believed to control the sex drive and various sexual functions, including the ovulation cycle in the female and ejaculation in the male. Its principal component is the pituitary gland, the 'master gland' that programs not only the sex glands but every other gland in the body. Studies have also suggested that damage in this area may be one of the causes of nymphomania and satyriasis on the one hand, and impotence and diminished sex interest on the other.

sex change the alteration of a patient's external sex organs through surgery and hormone treatments with the aim of making them conform as closely as possible to the physical structures of the opposite sex. The procedure is typically performed on male transsexuals, and occasionally on female transsexuals. Both male and female transsexuals are convinced that they have been trapped in the wrong body, and insist that they are meant to be members of the opposite sex physically, emotionally, and mentally.

The male-to-female operation is usually preceded by a year of psychiatric evaluation and counselling, accompanied by hormone injections and cross-dressing. During the surgical procedure, the penis and testes are removed and labia and vagina are constructed. In the female-to-male procedure, skin from the abdomen and labia are used to construct a penis and scrotum. The requests for male-to-female sex changes average about 20 to 1 in frequency over requests by females to be changed into males.

sex characteristics visible features associated with gender identity and reproduction. See PRIMARY SEX CHARACTERISTICS; SECONDARY SEX CHARACTERISTICS.

sex chromatin a dark mass representing the X chromosome that can be observed in a human cell that has been stained with a particular dye for study under a microscope. The X chromosome must be inactive to absorb the stain. Therefore, only cells of a female will reveal the chromatin presence by this test. A normal male, with one X and one Y chromosome will not have body cells with one extra, inactive X chromosome and thus will not have cells that show the stain. Although the female has two X chromosomes, only one will be active. A male body cell showing sex chromatin would suggest that the male had a chromosome abnormality, such as Klinefelter's syndrome, with an XXY or XXYY chromosome complement. A female with a multiple X chromosome abnormality, such as an XXX or XXXX complement, probably would have body cells that would show sex chromatin in two or more areas when stained for the test. Also called Barr body.

sex chromosomes the chromosomes that determine the gender of an individual. A normal human female possesses two X chromosomes, although only one of the X chromosomes is active. The normal human male has one X and one Y chromosome. The function of the Y chromosome apparently is to code the embryonic molecules necessary to produce male sex hormones. A normal female complement of sex chromosomes is identified as XX, and the normal male set is indicated as XY. It is difficult if not impossible to determine precisely which of the human sex chromosomes is actually an X or a Y chromosome. The X chromosome bears an almost exact resemblance to any of the 14 chromosomes in the second row of a standard karyotype, and the chromosome used to represent the Y sex chromosome may be interchangeable with either chromosome 21 or 22, which have the same size and shape. (For animal sex chromosomes, see W CHROMOSOME and Z CHROMOSOME.)

sex-chromosome aberrations any variation from the normal male complement of an XY set of sex chromosomes or deviation from the normal female complement of an XX set of sex chromosomes, in addition to the 22 pairs of autosomes. One of the most common aberrations is Klinefelter's syndrome, in which a male has one, two, or three extra X chromosomes. The extra chromosomes alter the individual's sexual characteristics in varying degrees, but the usual manifestations include hypogenitalism and infertility. The person with Klinefelter's syndrome also may have a deficiency of some male secondary sexual characteristics. But in many cases, the condition is not revealed until the person has married and his infertility has resulted in a visit to a medical specialist in an effort to find the reason for being sterile. An extra X chromosome in a female is even more likely to go unnoticed because fertility would not be affected. There is a possibility that the female with extra X chromosomes might be mentally retarded, the only consistent manifestation in sex-chromosome disorders. In fact, a female with as many as five X chromosomes could appear quite normal in so far as secondary sexual characteristics are concerned. The woman with three or more X chromosomes often is identified as a 'superfemale' or 'metafemale.' A male with extra Y chromosomes, similarly might appear physically as a 'supermale' with normal sexual development and a body size above average. Except for possible mental retardation and aberrant behaviour, the only noticeable defect could be a lack of good muscular coordination. A female sex-chromosome aberration that is characterized by abnormal physical features is Turner's syndrome, a condition in which the individual receives only one sex chromosome, an X chromosome. See also KLINEFELTER'S SYNDROME; TURNER'S SYNDROME; SUPERFEMALE; SUPERMALE.

sex counselling guidance provided to an individual or couple by a sex therapist, social worker, psychiatrist, or doctor on such questions as conception, family planning, infertility, fear of failure in performance, unresponsiveness, sexual anatomy and physiology, and techniques of intercourse.

sex determination the random sorting of male gametes, or spermatozoa, containing either an X sex chromosome or a Y sex chromosome as they approach a female gamete, or ovum, which always will contain only an X chromosome. The spermatozoon that finally merges with the ovum will determine the sex of the new individual by forming either an XX, or female, combination of sex chromosomes, or an XY, or male, combination. Regardless of external sexual characteristics, the sex of the individual in adult life will be determined by the type of gonad that develops in the person. Genetically, a person with ovaries will be classified as female, and an individual with testes will be considered a male.

sex differences overall differences, or alleged differences, between males and females (as well as hermaphrodites and pseudohermaphrodites) on primary sex characteristics, secondary sex characteristics, personality characteristics, social roles, type and level of intelligence, motor-development skills and aptitudes, interests and values, emotional adjustment, and life expectancy, as well as differences in sexual development and behaviour, including sexuality in infancy and childhood, age for entering puberty, frequency of masturbation, frequency of orgasm, and the comparative ages for the peak and diminution of sexual activity.

sex differentiation the process of developing anatomical features (especially testes and ovaries) typical of male or female sex, or, in rare cases, hermaphroditism. These characteristics are genetically determined at the time of fertilization, but do not begin to appear externally until the seventh or eighth week.

sex discrimination discrimination against an individual or group of individuals (usually women) on the basis of sex, especially in regard to the type of job, remuneration, and opportunities for tenure or promotion. Currently the term also applies to discrimination against male and sometimes female homosexuals not only in the job market but in holding public office, membership in social or political organizations, and clubs. See also SEXISM.

sex doll a life-sized, inflatable doll with somewhat exaggerated sexual features, including large breasts, an open mouth, a full head of hair, and a relatively realistic vagina and anus as well as pubic hair. Typically, these dolls are sold to men who suffer from shyness, loneliness, or physical handicap or to sailors or others who have no immediate access to women. For women, sex dolls such as a male torso with an inflatable penis have also become available.

sex dreams an alternative term for nocturnal emissions, which usually occur during erotic male dreaming. Sex dreams also occur among women, but are less common. A Kinsey study found about 4 percent of women experience nocturnal orgasms while dreaming and most such events happen among older single women. The term sex dreams is usually distinguished from SEXUAL DREAMS. See this entry.

sex drive the primary, probably instinctual, urge for sexual gratification. On the average, the impulse reaches its peak in the late teens among males and in the 30s among females. Although both sexes maintain an interest in sexual activity throughout their lives, by the age of 50 the average man is satisfied with two orgasms per week, and beginning in the 50s and 60s the average woman experiences a slight decline in sex drive, and is usually less preoccupied with sex than in her earlier years. Unlike other primary drives such as hunger and thirst, survival of the individual does not depend on the sex drive, though survival of the species does. Also, in contrast to lower species, the human sex drive is less seasonal, less dependent upon an oestrous cycle, more varied in expression, and aroused by a wider range of stimuli.

sex during menstruation intercourse during menstrual flow. Although the practice is discouraged by some cultures and individuals, a Masters and Johnson study found that only 10 percent of women object to sexual activity during menstruation, mainly for religious or aesthetic reasons. Of those approving of the practice, it was indicated that orgasm during menstruation helped expel the menstrual fluid at a rapid rate, thereby reducing the pain and discomfort often associated with menstruation. In most societies intercourse is forbidden or frowned upon during menstruation, for example, among Hindus. The Naayar of India go farther and believe that man who has intercourse with a menstruating woman is likely to become impotent.

sex during pregnancy a term referring to the advisability of continuing intercourse during pregnancy. Specialists usually allow their patients to continue sex relations until approximately the seventh month if there is no discharge or pain. As pregnancy advances, some modification of coital position will be necessary. They also assure their patients that intercourse will not harm the baby or cause a miscarriage.

sex education instruction on the physical, psychological, and behavioural aspects of sex, given in a classroom setting, but also through books and other publications. Formal sex education is designed to supplement or correct information and misinformation imparted by parents, peers, and the mass media. See also SIECUS.

sex experimentation among children, the tendency to explore each other's bodies, to imitate intercourse before being capable of achieving it, or in some cases to fondle, kiss, masturbate, or perform fellatio or cunnilingus. Among teenagers all forms of foreplay (necking, petting) and many forms of intercourse may be tried, as well as variations they have seen or read about in magazines, such as erotic bondage, flagellation, bestiality, and experimenting with the effects of drugs of various kinds. Among adults all these may be tried, also other variations such as group sex, partner swapping, trial marriage, and open marriage.

sex fiend a colloquial term for a sex offender who commits sadistic acts of the most extreme kind, such as a series of rapes, mutilation of the sex organs of victims, or homicide after sexual assault. Many of these offenders are psychotic.

sex hormones chemical 'messengers' that control the sexual and reproductive processes. The primary sources are the pituitary gland, the ovaries, the testes, and the adrenal cortex.

sex hospitality a sexual practice in which a man's wife (or sometimes daughter) is placed at the disposal of a male guest as a gesture of friendship and hospitality. The custom has been found in many parts of the world, including Africa, Siberia, Polynesia, Alaska, and the Aleutian Islands. Also called wife lending.

sex hygiene measures taken to insure clean, healthy, well-functioning sexual organs. These include washing with water (avoiding the use of scented soap or sprays just before intercourse, because they destroy exciting sexual odours) and precautions for the prevention of venereal disease. Women need to take special precautions to maintain cleanliness during menstruation, and also need periodic smear tests and gynaecological examinations, with attention to discharges, lumps, and bleeding. In addition, good sex hygiene involves general fitness, because sexual activity requires considerable expenditure of energy, especially if it is vigorous and prolonged.

Sex Information and Education Council of the United States a nonprofitmaking health organization—usually abbreviated SIECUS. See this entry.

sexing piece an older term for penis.

sex initiative taking the lead in suggesting intercourse or other sexual activity, either openly or indirectly. In Victorian times men were generally expected to take the initiative, although women might sometimes take the lead by using their 'wiles.' However, because women have achieved a greater measure of social equality in the present era, they are far more likely to take the sexual initiative than in the past.

sexism a pattern of discrimination against an individual (usually a female) or group stemming from prejudicial beliefs and attitudes. Examples are 'A woman's place is in the home,' 'Women can't stand up to competition,' 'Women are the weaker sex,' 'Women should not engage in body-contact sports,' or 'Women are too emotional for executive positions.' See also SEX DISCRIMINATION.

sexless gonad the embryonic gonad at 6 weeks after conception. The sex has been determined genetically at conception, but at 6 weeks the structure is an indifferent sex gland that could be either a male or female gonad.

sex-limited character a trait that is normally expressed in only one sex, for example, the tendency to balding among men.

sex-linked character a characteristic that is determined by genes of one of the sex chromosomes. The term applies mainly to recessive traits located on the X chromosome. For this reason, men are more likely to be affected than women. In women, the trait will be masked by a dominant gene for the characteristic in most instances, whereas the Y chromosome will lack a dominant gene for the trait.

sex maniac a popular term for an individual who is preoccupied with sexual satisfaction and sexual exploits, including such variations as voyeurism, exhibitionism, a history of seducing a maximum number of men or women, as well as more malignant behaviour such as murder, mutilation, and intercourse with corpses for sexual gratification.

sex manuals handbooks written for the explicit purpose of imparting sex information and promoting sex education. The first handbooks were probably the early 'pillow books,' but the first manuals that could be called modern were Dr. Albutt's *The Wife's Handbook* (1866) and Marie Stopes' *Married Love* (1918). These were followed by hundreds of manuals of sex adjustment, techniques, and physiology, such as *Ideal Marriage* by T.H. Van de Velde (1926), *The Marriage Manual* by Hannah and Abraham Stone, and *The Joy of Sex* by Alex Comfort (1974).

sex-negative a term referring mainly to social institutions, to a society's rituals, religions, and so on that restrict sexual expression. For example, Christianity has often been called the most sex-negative of all religions.

sex object a person, animal, or inanimate object (such as a fetish) towards which sexual impulses are directed. The term is often used in a derogatory sense, because many women (and sometimes men) resent being treated primarily as objects for stimulation and gratification. Also called sexual object.

sex offender an individual who commits sex offences that are punishable by law. The term includes milder offences stemming from neurotic trends, such as voyeurism, as well as more severe offences such as forcible rape, stemming from a severe personality disturbance and possibly from a chromosomal disorder. Contrary to popular opinion, the typical convicted sex offender is undersexed and severely inhibited rather than oversexed. The majority are in their late teens or early twenties, and 50 to 60 percent are unmarried.

sexologist a professional worker who has been trained to engage in research, therapy, or educational programmes in the field of human sexuality.

sexology the scientific study of sexuality and sexual behaviour, including sexual relationships, sexual practices, sexual disorders, sexual anatomy and physiology, and sex education. The field draws its content from studies of human and animal behaviour, psychology, psychiatry, anthropology, medicine, sociology, education, and the law.

sex play an expression referring to (a) children's exploratory activities such as the doctor game; (b) children's play that has a sexual tinge, such as hair pulling and wrestling; (c) foreplay preceding intercourse; (d) erotic activities short of intercourse, such as necking and petting; and (e) masturbatory activities, or 'playing with oneself.'

sex prediction the ability to forecast or select in advance the gender of an offspring. A number of techniques are used, including intercourse before ovulation to increase the likelihood that a girl will be conceived or immediately after ovulation to increase chances for a boy, or use of an acid douche

before intercourse to increase the chances of producing a female offspring or an alkali douche to improve the likelihood of conceiving a boy. Amniocentesis can be used to find out the sex of a child before delivery; however, the results are usually not available until the 17th or 18th week of a pregnancy. Physicians in China reported a technique of accurately predicting the sex of an unborn child 47 days after conception by scraping cells from the cervix of the mother. Many Old Wives' tales have been used over the centuries to explain predetermined sex selection. One of the oldest is the notion that one testicle contains sperm producing only girls and the other holds sperm that produces only boys. See also SEX SELECTION.

sex ratio the proportion of male and female infants born in a given population. The usual frequency is about 106 males to 100 females. Later in life, the rate of premature male deaths usually exceeds that of female so that eventually the ratio shifts and women outnumber men of the same age group.

sex reannouncement an announcement to members of the family and community that a child first identified in birth announcements as a boy has now been correctly identified as a girl, or vice versa. Because external genitalia at birth are sometimes misidentified as to gender, resulting in an incorrect birth announcement, a later announcement is made to correct the information.

sex reassignment change in sex assignment resulting from a sex-change operation. If the operation is a success, the male may feel more comfortable as a female, and perform sexually as a female, though he will not be able to conceive and reproduce. Females may become, to all intents and purposes, male except that it will not be possible to impregnate a woman.

sex-reassignment operation an alternative term for sex-change operation, or surgery in which a male is transformed into a female, or vice versa.

sex relations a broad term for any physical relationship between two or more people that serves the purpose of arousing or satisfying the sexual impulse, ranging from necking and petting to all forms of intercourse. Sex relations include the exploratory sexual behaviour of children as well as premarital, extramarital, and marital sex (and may be heterosexual, homosexual, or bisexual).

sex research studies of sexual behaviour that can be documented in large populations, as distinguished from anecdotal information based on observations of a few individual subjects. Because of widely varied sexual behaviour of individuals, data based on observations of a few cases can be misleading.

sex reversal the procedures involved in transforming a man into a woman or a woman into a man, with appropriate surgery, administration of sex hormones, and psychological counselling.

sex rituals rites and ceremonies prescribed by various societies and religions as a means of celebrating or controlling sex activities. Examples are ritual baths required by the Hindus and Hebrews after menstruation; ritual intercourse performed by the Asian Lepchas in a special position (rear entry) 3, 7, and 21 days after the birth of a baby; exchange of wives conceived as a purification rite among the Murngin of Australia; and the requirement, in several African societies, that the boy have sex with a married woman as part of his initiation ceremony.

sex-role inventory any psychological test in which the individuals rate themselves on personality characteristics indicative of their sex role. A widely used test is the BEM Sex Role Inventory, which yields four types of scores: feminine, masculine, androgynous, undifferentiated.

sex-role stereotypes fixed, oversimplified patterns of sexual behaviour and attitudes as defined in a given society, such as the traditional concepts of males as relatively unemotional, rational, decisive, strong, and brave; and of females as highly emotional, illogical, weak, dependent, and unfit for participation in the rough-and-tumble world outside the home. An example of a nontraditional stereotype is that of the androgynous sex role, which combines features of both male and female.

sex selection the process of determining before coitus the sex of the offspring. It is claimed by Landrum Shettles of Columbia University that an alkaline douche (made with baking soda) before intercourse will increase the chances that a boy will be conceived, while an acid douche, made with vinegar, will increase the odds for conception of a girl. Professor Shettles also recommends coitus before ovulation for couples hoping for a girl and sexual intercourse after ovulation for those wishing for a boy. See also SEX PREDICTION.

sex shop an alternative term for 'porn shop.'

sex shows live performances that feature nudity or sexual activities. Such performances are said to date from the days of the Roman emperors Tiberius and Caligula, and have been associated with many royal courts since that time. In India travelling entertainers performed almost incredible feats of sexual gymnastics. Private erotic theatres existed in the Western world from time to time, and during the 19th century scenes of copulation, lesbian acts, and bestiality were enacted in brothels. Many modern Western performances such as striptease and several theatrical productions (*Hair, Oh Calcutta!*) belong in this general category.

sex skin the minor lips (labia minora) of the sexually excited woman, which become progressively more pink and red during the plateau phase of the sexual response cycle. If erotic stimulation continues, the lips become more swollen and engorged with blood, orgasm is usually inevitable. The term is also applied to the sexually sensitive area of the skin adjacent to the female genitals.

sex statistics the quantified data of sex research. Although statistics are an accepted research device, the interpretation of results can be misleading, particularly when expressed in terms such as 'average' or 'percent' or 'normal.' Many persons tend to confuse 'average' with 'normal' and regard sexual behaviour that is not average as 'abnormal,' which is not the intention of the statistical report.

sex-stereotyped play childhood games and play activities that are traditionally associated with either male or female sex roles, such as boys playing with action toys or in competitive sports while girls play with dolls.

sex stereotyping the development of a sexual typology based on behaviour and attitudes that are considered by society to be appropriate for males and females, such as the expectation (now questioned) that all girls and women have a special interest in homemaking activities, or for boys and men to be more interested in muscular activities than women (which is also being questioned). Also called sex typing.

sexual aberrations any deviations from normal or typical sexual behaviour, especially those associated with mental or emotional disorders. Examples are sexual sadism, sexual masochism, paedophilia, fetishism, exhibitionism, voyeurism, transvestism, zoophilia, coprophilia, and necrophilia.

sexual ability the capacity to become sexually excited and, in particular, to achieve orgasm. In the male, sexual ability depends on the capacity to achieve and maintain erection, and in the female, the capacity to become aroused when the erogenous zones are stroked or manipulated. Most people of both sexes are also capable of becoming sexually excited by dreams, fantasies, films, or pictures, without physical contact of any kind.

sexual abnormality sexual behaviour that does not conform to the accepted expressions of sexuality within a given culture or community. It is important for an individual to understand what is considered as normal sexual behaviour to avoid feelings of guilt about his or her own fantasies and practices, which may not actually deviate from those of other persons in the culture or community even though they are not openly sanctioned by the more conservative members of the group.

sexual abstinence refraining from sexual activity temporarily or permanently. Examples of temporary abstinence are during menstruation or late pregnancy, before marriage, or during certain religious celebrations. Lifelong abstinence is required as a means of expressing holiness among Catholic nuns and priests.

sexual abuse physical injury administered for the purpose of sexual arousal or gratification in the abuser or, in some cases, in the victim. Milder forms are pinching, slapping, and squeezing; more extreme forms are whipping, beating, cutting, biting, and, in rare instances, mutilation of the sex organs or other parts of the body.

sexual activity a general term covering any kind of behaviour, such as petting, flagellation, masturbation, and intercourse, whose purpose is to produce sexual excitement.

sexual addiction according to recent sex therapists, a pattern of excessive, repetitive sexual activity that resembles addiction to alcohol or drugs in providing relief from feelings of anxiety or worthlessness. For some individuals, possibly one in 12, sex becomes an all-consuming compulsion pursued at the expense of marriage, career, or family life. An increasing number of sex therapists are dealing with this problem, and a number of self-help groups modelled after Alcoholics Anonymous have been formed. See SEXAHOL-ICS ANONYMOUS.

sexual advances any deliberate attempt to arouse sexual interest or response in another individual. Sexual advances vary widely, and include indirect approaches such as smiling, winking, firmly holding the other person's hand when introduced, inviting the other person to share drinks, as well as more direct approaches, such as stroking, caressing, suggesting 'Let's go to my place,' and making a direct 'proposition.'

sexual affinity a strong sexual attraction between two individuals of the opposite or the same sex.

sexual-aim rapist a rapist who is truly sexually motivated and uses only as much force as is necessary to achieve intercourse. He may have fantasies of his victims falling in love with him after he has demonstrated his sexual prowess.

sexual anaesthesia an inability to experience sexual feeling; frigidity.

sexual analism sexual intercourse in which the penis is inserted into the anus of the partner. Except for occasional experiments, the practice, also known as sodomy, is seldom performed in heterosexual contacts.

sexual apathy a negative attitude towards sexual relations, ranging from indifference and listlessness to active revulsion, for an extended period—despite propitious circumstances and a willing partner. The precise reasons may be hard to fathom, but apathy is often based on a distasteful or painful experience, a monotonous and unimaginative approach on the part of one or both partners, the pressure of business or home responsibilities, preoccupation with other interests and events, excessive demands by the partner, chronic fatigue, general depression, or unconscious conflicts over sex.

sexual appetite the need, or the desire, for sexual gratification. The sex urge has been found to vary greatly from person to person and time to time.

sexual athlete a man or woman whose sex life is governed by quantity more than quality, and who engages in practically every conceivable coital position and variation, even the most outlandish. To sexual athletes, sex is more of a game or sport than an expression of affection.

sexual attitudes attitudes towards sex and sexual behaviour as influenced by such factors as family relationships and upbringing, and the demands, expectations, and sexual ethics of the particular culture and subculture in which one lives. There are wide cultural differences around the world; for example, in a study of 158 societies, 70 percent were tolerant of premarital intercourse, but not of adulterous relationships; in societies where sexual expression among women is approved or encouraged, they are as uninhibited and active as men; and in American society, attitudes towards virginity at marriage have changed dramatically in the past generation.

sexual attraction the capacity to elicit sexual interest through a provocative manner or exciting physical features, such as full lips and shapely breasts, legs and buttocks in women, and an athletic build in men. In many cases reputation as a skilled lover also increases attraction. Various societies have developed unique ways of increasing sexual attraction. See also SEX APPEAL.

sexual awakening a period of psychological change that accompanies pubescence. It is usually marked by changes in attitudes, emotions, and interests that are more appropriate for this stage of approaching sexual maturity. It also is a period in which physical experimentation, including increased masturbation, occurs.

sexual behaviour the sexual activity of an individual as observed by others, as distinguished from a subjective or inner perspective on one's own sexual acts. Other characteristics of sexual behaviour may include conscious, unconscious or innate, or socially determined components, with biological, psychological, and developmental influences.

sexual conditioning the development of a positive mental attitude towards sexual activity as a normal human function, as opposed to the negative concept that anything sexual is wicked or nasty and may be tolerated only in certain situations, such as producing an offspring.

sexual cord a strand of cells in the embryo that give rise during foetal development to the follicles of the ovary and the seminiferous tubules of the testis.

sexual cosmetics cosmetics as a means of enhancing sexual attractiveness. Eye and face makeup are common in Western societies, but this form of ornamentation reached a peak in Eastern societies, particularly in ancient Egypt, China, and India. In particular, Tantric rites specify that a symbolic Third Eye be painted on the forehead to represent awakened consciousness; that body makeup consist of crushed marijuana, opium, and other intoxicating substances mixed with oils and pigments; and that the hands and feet of the woman be completely painted with designs.

sexual deprivation denial of an opportunity to obtain full sexual gratification, as in pri-

son, long sea voyages of males (in tankers, submarines, or navy ships), and POW camps. One of the effects is 'deprivation homosexuality'; another is increase in emotional tension that cannot be adequately relieved by masturbation.

sexual desire an urgent need for sexual activity and gratification. According to Kinsey, this need reaches a peak among males during adolescence, and somewhat later among females. Though the urgency of the drive tends to decrease with age, it is usually present in some degree throughout life. Many couples, however, seek sex therapy or counselling when one member of the pair exhibits considerably less desire for sexual activity than the other. Many other couples consider themselves happily married even though they do not have a strong sexual desire and do not engage in frequent sexual activity. Also called sexual appetite.

sexual disorders any physical or psychological impairment of the ability to perform intercourse or produce offspring, because of such conditions as disease, injury, anatomical defect, internal conflict, or unconscious inhibition. Examples are impotence, frigidity, inhibited male or female orgasm, inhibited sexual excitement, dyspareunia, vaginismus, venereal diseases, cystitis, and cancer of the cervix or prostate.

sexual display the endless ways of exhibiting sexual features to enhance sexual attractiveness. In our culture, women rely largely on cosmetics, hair fashions, deep necklines, slit skirts or miniskirts, designer jeans, long boots, and revealing bikinis. Many men rely on body-hugging trousers, shirts, and extremely small bathing suits. In some 'super masculine' groups, men artifically enlarge their muscles by 'pumping iron' or wear leather clothing and studded belts to arouse sexual fantasies. Societies in 'underdeveloped' countries have their own means of sexual display such as tattooing, scarification, large penis sheaths, body piercing, and depilation.

sexual dreams dream sequences involving sexual activities, attractive members of the opposite sex, images of sexual features, and sexual symbols. Sexual dreams are frequently a key to the individual's sexual desires, concerns, and frustrations. Such dreams may be accompanied by erection and ejaculation in boys and men, and by vaginal lubrication and orgasm in women. The term sexual dreams is usually distinguished from

SEX DREAMS. See this entry.

sexual dwarf a misleading term for a dwarf who is an adult with normally developed adult genitalia.

sexual dysfunction a sexual malfunction that interferes with adequate sexual performance and gratification, because of psychological or physiological factors or both. Masters and Johnson maintain that some form of sexual inadequacy or dysfunctioning is found in at least 50 percent of American marriages. Examples are dyspareunia, impotence, premature ejaculation, retarded ejaculation, vaginismus, retrograde ejaculation, ejaculatory incompetence, inhibited sexual desire, inhibited sexual excitement, inhibited female orgasm, and inhibited male orgasm.

sexual ecstasy the peak of pleasure, excitement, and euphoria experienced at the moment of orgasm, or climax.

sexual excitement the first phase of the sexual response cycle, in which sexual stimuli of various kinds—fondling, kissing, tonguing, looking, and sometimes sucking—produce a state of tension and arousal. During this state, vaginal lubrication, swelling of the labia, and erection of the nipples and clitoris occur in the female, and erection of the penis and contraction of the scrotum take place in the male, while increased blood flow and heart rate occur in both. Sexual excitement can also be produced by fantasies, masturbation, sex dreams, dancing, and the rhythmical movements of a vehicle.

sexual exploitation taking advantage of another person or persons for sexual purposes, either as a source of financial gain or for personal gratification. Major forms of sexual exploitation are enticing boys and girls into heterosexual or homosexual prostitution, using them as subjects for pornographic films and magazines, and forcing them into pederasty and sodomy.

sexual failure in the male, failure to achieve or maintain erection, premature ejaculation, or failure to ejaculate; in the female, failure to be aroused, painful intercourse, or failure to reach orgasm; in both, failure to derive pleasure from sexual activity.

sexual fantasies erotic images of either standard lovemaking or, in about 25 percent of instances, such variations as homosexual encounters, group sex, or sadomasochism. Recent studies indicate that most people have seven or eight such fantasies every day, and that replacement of the established partner, forced sexual encounters, and observation of the sexual activities of others are three of the most common. They are not necessarily a key to one's basic sexual orientation (though many psychoanalysts disagree), but they may reveal a need for psychotherapy, as in cases where there are problems of intimacy, or an obsession with rape and sadistic images. Also called erotic fantasies.

sexual favours an obsolescent term for sexual 'privileges,' including intercourse and other activities, granted by women, usually freely but sometimes for remuneration. Men, too, may grant sexual favours to women or other men.

sexual fears various fears that affect sexual performance and gratification, including fear of inadequacy; fear of not arousing or satisfying one's partner, fear of pregnancy, fear of injury, fear of discovery, fear of contracting a venereal disease, and, in psychoanalytical theory, an unconscious castration fear among men.

sexual fetish a fetish that involves part of the body associated with reproduction, such as the breasts or genitals.

sexual flush suffusion of skin areas with blood during sexual excitement, particularly in women. Flushing begins with a rashlike discoloration of the lower chest, and spreads to the breasts and the rest of the chest and neck, reaching a peak in the late plateau phase just before orgasm, rapidly subsiding during the resolution phase of the sexual response cycle.

sexual frustration thwarting of the sexual impulse in greater or lesser degree, by such internal forces as parental admonitions, the demands of religion, feelings of insecurity or anxiety, and such external circumstances as confinement to prison, rigid social rules, or lack of opportunity to meet members of the opposite sex or a partner with a lower sex drive.

sexual fulfilment the sense of completion and gratification that follows a successful sexual encounter. Fulfilment is experienced in the orgasmic and resolution phases of the sexual response cycle.

sexual functioning the performance of sexual intercourse, or the ability to perform intercourse.

sexual gratification satisfaction of the sex urge, usually implying orgasm. The term is a broad one covering any form of intercourse and any other means of achieving sexual excitement and release, such as flagellation, masturbation, or sadistic activities.

sexual gymnastics a term applied to extreme, highly athletic forms of sexual activity, such as copulation on or in a chariot, as illustrated in early Egyptian, Hindu, and Japanese manuscripts.

sexual harassment unwanted sexual attentions usually from men towards women.

sexual history a compilation of detailed information on a patient's sexual behaviour and experiences throughout his or her past and present life. A sexual history is usually an integral part of a psychological case history assembled for purposes of diagnosis and prognosis in psychiatry or clinical psychology, because many cases of mental disorder involve disturbed sexual relationships. It is also an important first step in sex therapy, as recognized by Masters and Johnson.

sexual humour riddles, songs, tall tales, limericks, jokes, and other comic material that involve a reference to sexual anatomy or sexual activity. Psychologically, laughter at such humour is believed to arise not only from the display of wit, but from an urge to defy social conventions or a need to release inner repressions, or what Freud has called 'letting the cat out of the bag.' Also called erotic humour.

sexual identity a person's biologically determined sex orientation; the internal sense of maleness or femaleness. In cases of ambiguous genitalia, as in hermaphroditism, the individual may be confused about his or her sexual identity.

sexual inadequacy inability to achieve a satisfactory level of sexual satisfaction, and to help one's partner to achieve a similar level. Masters and Johnson have estimated that at least 50 percent of marriages are afflicted with some form of sexual inadequacy or dysfunctioning, such as lack of desire, inability to reach or enjoy orgasm, impotence, or frigidity. Other specialists (psychiatrists, psychologists, social workers) have reported that as many as 75 percent of their patients have sexual problems severe enough to require professional help. Also called sexual failure.

sexual incompatibility inability of sexual partners to adjust to each other's needs, stemming from such factors as differences in sexual desire or timing, impotence or frigidity, physical disability, anatomical incongruity, inhibitions or other emotional 'hangups' on the part of one or both partners. Sexual incompatibility is grounds for divorce in some countries.

sexual infantilism the tendency to avoid forms of sexual expression characteristic of adults, especially intercourse, and to limit oneself to activities that were appropriate during the years of childhood, such as stroking, biting, and kissing. Many psychosexual disorders, including fetishism and voyeurism, are considered basically infantile.

sexual inhibition an unconscious, involuntary suppression of the sexual impulse, especially the inability to feel sexual desire, to perform adequately, or to experience orgasm. The condition results from such factors as fear of failure or injury, or negative feelings ('Sex is ugly and dirty') implanted by the parents.

sexual instincts a psychoanalytical term for all erotic drives, anal, oral, and genital. Freud held that these instincts not only afford pleasure and lead to preservation of the species, but may also be 'sublimated' into creative activities such as artistic and scientific pursuits. Sexual instincts is also a biological term for all unlearned behaviour involved in sexual activities and reproduction, such as nest building, courtship behaviour, and copulation in animals.

sexual intercourse the commonly used expression for the more technical term coitus (usually shortened to 'intercourse').

sexuality the capacity to behave sexually, that is, to respond to erotic stimuli and to obtain pleasure from sexual activities such as foreplay, intercourse, and masturbation. Sexuality involves not only the genital organs but all the erogenous zones of the body, as well as all wishes, desires, and fantasies associated with sex.

sexualization the process of endowing various parts of the body (the mouth, breasts, anus, genital organs) and various activities (dancing, joking, dressing according to one's sex) with sexual energy, which Freud termed the libido. Psychoanalysts would also include all types of behaviour into which sexual energy is 'sublimated,' such as creative art and scientific research.

sexualization of society the preoccupation with sex in various cultures; the pervasive effects of sexual interests, customs, and behaviour on a given culture, as exemplified by the influence of sex-oriented films and magazines in Western society and the influence of sexual mysticism in Eastern societies.

sexual liberation a trend towards (a) greater freedom of sexual expression, which had hitherto been hampered by the repressive morality of the Victorian era, and (b) greater freedom in sexual research, which had hitherto been hampered by prejudice, ignorance, and reliance on folklore and superstition. Among the great liberators on both counts are Havelock Ellis, Hirschfeld, Krafft-Ebing, Freud, Margaret Sanger, Marie Stopes, Kinsey, and Masters and Johnson. Also called sexual emancipation.

sexual life-style the particular pattern of sexual expression developed by each individual on the basis of his or her experience with sexual relationships, individual sexual needs and desires, and male or female sex role. Sexual life-styles vary all the way from the prudishness of the Puritan to the licentiousness of the libertine.

sexually mature female from the anatomical point of view, a woman whose primary sex organs (vagina, clitoris, uterus, ovaries, fallopian tubes) and secondary sex characteristics (breasts, pubic hair, underarm hair) are fully developed.

sexually mature male from the anatomical point of view, a man whose primary sex organs (testes, epididymis, vas deferens, seminal vesicles, Cowper's glands, urethra, and penis) and secondary sex characteristics (pubic hair, underarm hair, facial hair, and deepening of the voice) are fully developed.

sexually transmitted disease (STD) any disease that may be acquired by sexual contact with another person, including AIDS; balanitis gangraenosa (gangrenous balanitis); candidiasis; chancroid; chlamydia; crab louse (pediculosis pubis); cytomegalovirus (CMV); genital herpes (herpes genitalis); genital (venereal) warts (condylomata acuminata); gonorrhoea; granuloma inguinale (Donovan's disease); group B streptococcal infection; hepatitis B (serum hepatitis); herpes simplex I; herpes simplex 2; lymphogranuloma venereum (or inguinale); molluscum contagiosum; (some cases of) nongonococcal (and nonspecific) urethritis (NGU, NSU); Reiter's disease; scabies; syphilis (lues); trichomoniasis (trichomonas vaginitis); and (some cases of) yaws.

The term venereal disease (or VD) is more popular but less precise than sexually transmitted disease. Also called *sexually transmissible disease.*

sexual maladjustment any condition of failure to achieve normal sexual relations with another person, as manifested in impotence, frigidity, vaginismus, or other sexual problems.

sexual marketplace a general term for the group of individual enterprises that make a business of sex, including houses of prostitution, massage parlours, 'adult' book shops, shops that specialize in sex aids, pimping, pornographic films, and magazines that specialize in sexually explicit articles and photographs.

sexual masochism the term used by the American Psychiatric Association for a psychosexual disorder in which sexual arousal is repeatedly or exclusively sought through being beaten, flogged, bound, verbally abused, or otherwise maltreated, or through voluntary participation in an activity that involves being subjected to physical harm or threat to life.

sexual maturation the development of the reproductive system to the point where intercourse and reproduction are possible. Also called *sexual maturity.*

sexual mechanisms the physical structures and functions involved in sexual activity, including the internal and external sex organs, reflexes, muscles that control coital postures and movements, and the sex hormones involved in erection, ejaculation, vaginal secretions, and orgasm.

sexual melancholia a mentally depressed state, often part of a bipolar disorder, in which a male is convinced that he is impotent.

sexual myths misconceptions and fallacies arising out of hearsay, superstition, bigotry, or faulty sexual education. Examples are the beliefs that alcohol is a sexual stimulant; that women who have multiple orgasms tend to be oversexed; that hormonal imbalance is the major cause of homosexuality; that a seventh-month baby has a better chance for survival than an eight-month baby; that sexually frigid women are less likely to conceive than responsive women; that a prostatectomy reduces sexual capability; or that masturbation produces debility and mental disorder.

sexual need an internal condition of tension generated by an unsatisfied desire for sexual gratification. The basis for this need is threefold: biological, psychological, and social. Even though sexual need has a physical basis and is sometimes called metaphorically sexual 'hunger,' and although at times people as well as animals may prefer copulation to eating, sexual activity is not necessary to sustain life except in a broad sense of species preservation. Moreover, the need is conditioned by such factors as opportunity, the attractiveness and willingness of the partner, the social situation (parties, 'swinging'), and the desire for release of tension created by work or worry.

sexual negativism a term applied by Magnus Hirschfeld to a lack of interest in sex that might stem from a deficit of sexual hormones.

sexual neuroses neurotic trends and symptoms that have a sexual basis. Among these are inordinate sexual desire (erotomania), sexual anxiety, excessive sexual submissiveness or timidity, extreme prudishness stemming from feelings of guilt instilled in childhood, compulsive sex activity as a compensation for feelings of inferiority, extreme preoccupation with sexual fantasies, phobias related to sex (for example, a morbid fear of pointed objects), and sexual dysfunctions (impotence, frigidity, satyriasis, nymphomania) resulting from deep-seated emotional conflicts and tensions.

sexual nightmare a vivid dream depicting an acutely disturbing anxiety-provoking sexual encounter. Typically, the dreamer is caught in a threatening situation such as being attacked by a rapist, experiences agonizing dread, makes futile attempts to escape, and awakens in a cold sweat.

sexual normality sexual behaviour that is considered acceptable within a particular culture or population. See also SEXUAL NORMS.

sexual norms the accepted standards of sexual attitudes and behaviour. These standards vary widely from society to society and from time to time. In one society sex may be regarded as a marital duty (especially by the wife); in another, sexual gratification is considered a right for the woman as well as the man. In one social group, 'recreational sex' (including swinging) is the norm; in another, any departure from traditional behaviour (for example, from the missionary position) is considered taboo.

sexual novelty sexual activity with new partners, or in untried ways, usually as a means of satisfying curiosity or escaping from boredom or monotony. The search for novelty is most likely to occur when the established partner is unimaginative, inhibited, or uninterested in experimentation. See also COOLIDGE EFFECT.

sexual oralism a type of sexual activity in which partners obtain pleasure by applying the mouth, lips, or tongue to the sex organs of the other individual. Studies indicate an association between a desire for sexual oralism and a sensitivity for certain aromas

associated with the genitalia. The activity is not considered deviant if it is not performed to the exclusion of other forms of sexual pleasure.

sexual orientation an established pattern of sexual interest and in most cases sexual activity directed towards members of the other sex (heterosexuality), the same sex (homosexuality), or both sexes (bisexuality). The orientation pattern usually becomes fixed during the first few years of life.

sexual-orientation disturbance an older psychiatric category comprising individuals whose sexual interests are directed towards persons of the same sex, and who are emotionally disturbed by this orientation. In the current classification of mental disorders by the American Psychiatric Association, this category has been replaced by the term ego-dystonic homosexuality.

sexual outlet any form of behaviour that results in the release of sexual tension, especially through the achievement of orgasm. Examples are 'heavy' petting, masturbation, nocturnal emissions, and all forms of intercourse including fellatio, cunnilingus, and anal coitus.

sexual pathology sexual aberrations and disorders, such as those described in Krafft-Ebing's monumental work, *Psychopathia Sexualis*. Major examples are sadism, masochism, syphilis and other venereal diseases, impotence, frigidity, genital mutilation, coprophilia, necrophilia, satyriasis, and nymphomania.

sexual permissiveness the view that sexual activity should be as free as possible from restrictions or regulations, based on the conviction that sexual expression and experimentation are natural and good. The permissive attitude countenances such practices as orogenital contact and 'recreational sex' among adults, and usually favours legalization of abortion and recognition of homosexual relationships among consenting adults. It rarely if ever favours elimination of controls on such practices as paedophilia, rape, extreme sadomasochism, and incest, nor does it favour sexual irresponsibility and exploitation.

sexual perversion a culturally unacceptable deviation from prevailing norms of sexual behaviour.

sexual phobias intense, morbid fears stemming from sexual inhibitions, neuroses, or traumatic experiences. They include fear of sex after rape, or injury (traumatophobia), of women (gynaephobia), of homosexuals (homophobia), or bearing a monster (teratophobia), of being touched (haptephobia), of childbirth (maieusiophobia), of female genitals (eurotophobia), of girls (parthenophobia), of men (androphobia), of marriage (gamophobia), of naked bodies (gymnophobia), of pleasure (hedonophobia), of pointed objects including penises and penis symbols (aichmophobia), of semen (spermatophobia), of sex generally (genophobia), of sexual intercourse (coitophobia), of snakes (ophidiophobia), of syphilis (syphilophobia), and of venereal disease generally (cypriphobia).

sexual pleasure the sense of pleasure experienced through sexual stimulation or gratification, as in necking and petting, foreplay, masturbation, any type of intercourse, viewing sexual films and photographs, watching other people engaged in sexual activity, reading erotic books and articles, using devices designed to enhance sexual response (vibrators, dildos, dydoes, vaginal balls, French ticklers), and engaging in unusual practices that stimulate sexual response, such as bondage and flagellation.

sexual precocity premature development of primary and secondary sex characteristics. In boys, sexual precocity may stem from early development of centres in the hypothalamus (cerebral type), or from dysfunctions of the adrenal cortex or the interstitial cells of the testes (endocrine type). In girls, neoplasms (growths) in or on the ovaries may affect hormonal output and produce rapid and premature enlargement of the breasts, premature development of the genitalia, and early growth of pubic hair.

sexual preference preference for sexual activity with males, females, or both (heterosexuality, male or female homosexuality, bisexuality), or for specific forms of sexual gratification such as oral sex, anal sex, rear entry, woman-above, man-above, mutual masturbation, as well as for particular forms of sexual stimulation such as biting, whipping, and bondage.

sexual preoccupation a strong, sometimes obsessive, interest in or concern about sex. An obvious example is the large role played by sex in Western clothing styles, novels, art, films, and the mass media. But any examination of Eastern cultures, such as Hindu and Polynesian societies, indicates an equal or even greater preoccupation with sex. Moreover, sexual preoccupation is also exemplified by negative attitudes, such as those

expressed in Christianity, in Victorian society, in cultures like Inis Beag, and among prudes and other sexual zealots.

sexual primordial reaction a term introduced by Wilhelm Stekel to describe the normal behaviour of appraising any other person in terms of 'sexual worth.' Stekel related the human behaviour to that observed in lower animals, such as dogs sniffing each other at their first meeting. Stekel commented, 'Consciously or unconsciously we disrobe every stranger with whom we become acquainted and form an image of the stranger's genitalia.'

sexual problems a wide range of difficulties, dysfunctions, and psychosocial disorders associated with sexual adjustment. Typical male problems include impotence, feelings of inadequacy, premature ejaculation, priapism, inhibited sexual desire, inhibited orgasm, incest, sexual sadism, child molestation, fetishism, voyeurism, bestiality, exhibitionism, transvestism, necrophilia, rape, confusion over sexual orientation or gender identity, and satyriasis. Typical female problems include frigidity, inhibited orgasm, dyspareunia, vaginismus, nymphomania, confusion over sexual orientation or gender identity, inhibited sexual desire, exhibitionism, transvestism, child molestation, sexual masochism, and fetishism.

sexual proceptivity the female's tendency to be attracted to males and to act as a sexual stimulus for males. Studies show that secretion of the hormone oestrogen produces proceptive behaviour ranging from merely approaching, investigating, and staying near the male, to explicit invitations or solicitations of copulation. This has been shown to occur in animals such as dogs, rodents, and monkeys, and may occur in women as well.

sexual prodigies a term sometimes applied to individuals who display or are reputed to display a high level of sexual activity. Among the most celebrated are the Roman Empress Valeria Messalina and Emperor Nero in the 1st century, and Catherine II of Russia and the Venetian Casanova in the 18th century. Also Goethe, greatest of German writers, almost certainly made many thousands of sexual conquests; and in our time, Georges Simenon asserts he made love to at least 10,000 women (or about three women per week on average in six decades of sexual pursuit)—besides writing over 500 novels. However, frequent sexual activity is also found among ordinary people (who generally just don't talk about it). Kinsey's studies reveal that 7 percent of (white American) males averaged seven orgasms per week, and one man averaged 33 per week over 30 years. Kinsey also found that generally women were as active as males.

sexual prowess unusual skill and endurance in the physical art of lovemaking, with particular emphasis on frequency of intercourse. Display of sexual prowess is the major motive among satyriasists and nymphomaniacs, as well as in certain primitive societies, such as the Chaga of Tanzania, where it is not unusual for men to have intercourse as often as 10 times a night.

sexual psychopath an individual with an antisocial personality whose characteristic offences take the form of repeated sexual aggression such as rape, child molestation, or sexual mutilation, as well as nonviolent activities such as exhibitionism, bestiality, and incest.

sexual receptivity the readiness of females to be receptive to the sexual advances of males. In female animals, receptivity is highest during the oestrus; in human females it tends to be highest just before and just after menstruation, although responsiveness is not wholly determined by physiological mechanisms. Among the other factors involved are the attractiveness of the male and his skill as a sexual partner, as well as the setting in which his advances are made.

sexual reflex the erection of the genitalia (penis or clitoris) and orgasm or ejaculation as a result of physical or psychic erotic stimulation, or both.

sexual reflexes any of a number of spontaneous physical responses to a stimulus that may have an erotic effect. Included are the abdominal reflex, produced by stroking the skin overlying the abdominal wall; the bulbospongiosus reflex, produced by tapping the top of the penis; the cremasteric reflex, caused by stimulating the skin on the inside of the male thigh; and Geigel's reflex, in which stroking the skin of the female thigh causes a response similar to the cremasteric reflex in the male.

sexual regression an event in embryonic life that follows the first sign that the indifferent sex organs will become either male or female genitalia. Until the time that sexuality is determined, the embryo exhibits sex ducts that may become either male or female organs. During the seventh week of gestation, one set of sex ducts will advance beyond the indifferent state, and the complementary set of ducts, either male or female, will undergo regression.

sexual rehabilitation restoration of the ability to function sexually by treating a sexual dysfunction such as impotence, vaginismus, or rape-trauma syndrome. The term applies also to measures taken to enable a disabled person, such as a quadriplegic, to function sexually as well as possible.

sexual rejuvenation the restoration of youthful sexual vigour among the aging. An untold number of substances, exercises, and treatments have been tried and found wanting. Among them are downright frauds such as radioactive water, x-ray lamps, and various pills and lotions, as well as substances that might, just might, have aphrodisiac effects, such as palmetto seeds, soma-plant extract, and Spanish fly. Various pseudomedical treatments are also prevalent including gland transplants of goat and monkey testes; unilateral vasectomy; the cellular therapy of Paul Niehans, a Swiss physician; and a procaine-containing drug developed by Professor Anna Aslan of Rumania, which may have a greater tranquillizing than rejuvenating effect.

sexual relations a colloquial term for SEX RELATIONS. See this entry.

sexual repression in psychoanalysis, a defence mechanism in which unacceptable sexual impulses are banned from consciousness because they produce anxiety; also, deliberate attempts to curb sexual activity and sexual interest, as in extremely Puritanical or other sexually inhibited societies.

sexual response reaction to sexual stimulation such as fondling or kissing. Initial responses of females include vaginal lubrication and erection of the nipples. In males, the most obvious response is erection of the penis. Responsiveness is determined by such factors as sexual desire and readiness, environmental circumstances, the skill of the partner, and the use of stimulants.

sexual-response cycle the generalized pattern of sexual response as reported by Masters and Johnson, which is applicable not only to heterosexual intercourse, but to homosexual and masturbatory activities as well. The four stages of this cycle are excitement, plateau, orgasm, and resolution.

sexual response time the amount of time required for the average man or woman to reach orgasm. Some studies indicate that a man needs between 2 and 4 minutes to reach orgasm while, despite the general belief that a woman requires more time, some women have been found to reach orgasm in as little as 15 to 30 seconds while the average is less than 4 minutes.

sexual revolution the widespread shift in sexual attitudes and behaviour in the direction of greater permissiveness, more liberal attitudes towards premarital sex, assertion of women's sexual rights and needs, revolt against the double standard, frank and open sex education, more varied sexual relations, and sexual activity at earlier ages than at the start of this century. These changes may be characterized as a revolution when compared with the Victorian era, but studies show that the change is often more in attitudes than in actions, and that extremes like group sex and 'swinging' have not become standard sexual behaviour.

sexual rights as used in cross-cultural studies, a term that usually refers to the exercise of sexual privileges with women other than a man's wife—for example, the right to intercourse with the wife's sister, the right of brothers to sexual access to each other's wives, or the right of the father of a newly married man to initial intercourse with his son's wife.

sexual script an individual's unique pattern of attitudes and expectations concerning sexual behaviour responses, roles, feelings, and relationships. The 'script' reflects not only individual experiences, but the influence of the person's family, culture, and subculture.

sexual selection the Darwinian concept that the choice of a mate is based on attractive features such as the coloration or song of birds. This process, which has its counterpart in human beings, tends to favour reproduction of individuals with similar attractive traits.

sexual senescence the gradual decline in sexual functions during the later years of life, especially in women after menopause, when the reproductive cycle is slowly extinguished, and after the climacteric among men when potency and fertility slowly diminish. However, sexual *interest* may continue indefinitely.

sexual sorcery attempts of witch doctors and shamans to enlist supernatural powers by the use of spells, incantations, black magic, and drugs, for such purposes as enforcement of sexual taboos, sexual rejuvenation, and cure of sexual ills such as impotence.

sexual standards norms of sexual behaviour as set by a particular society or subculture, or by particular influences such as parental teachings, moral or religious beliefs and dicta, civil laws, superstitions, the mass media (including television, magazines, and advertising). It is often said that almost every form of sexual behaviour has been condemned or condoned in some place at some time. Kinsey has pointed out that most people desire many outlets for their sexuality, that virtually everyone behaves sexually in some manner condemned by society or probably by laws as well.

sexual stimulation any form of stimulation that produces sexual excitement: tactile (as in masturbation and foreplay), visual (pictures of nudes, sexually explicit films), psychological (images and fantasies, as in day and night dreams), orogenital contact (cunnilingus, fellatio, anilingus), anal penetration, and various other forms of heterosexual and homosexual intercourse.

sexual synergism the collaboration of different, and sometimes contradictory, stimuli to produce sexual excitement. Freud maintained that these stimuli may include unpleasant as well as pleasant stimuli (fright, horror, or pain), or even a combination of love and hate, provided these do not exceed a certain limit.

sexual taboo a sexual act, word, or symbol that is prohibited in a particular society on religious or social grounds. Most common, though not universal, are incest taboos, followed by prohibitions against sexual intercourse during menstruation, pregnancy, and nursing. In various parts of Africa, intercourse is prohibited during daylight hours, before going to war, during a thunderstorm, and for up to a year after birth of a child. Elsewhere there are taboos against sex between grandparents (a Taiwan society), on birthdays of the gods (traditional Chinese), after planting narcotic plants (Ivaro Indians), against intercourse out of doors (among the Yucatec and Mayan Indians) and indoors (in Papua New Guinea), as well as during certain phases of the moon (Hindu societies). In Western society, adultery, anal intercourse, sex with animals, and the use of certain gestures (the 'finger') and certain slang words for sex organs and activities are frequently considered taboo.

sexual techniques activities that enhance or inhibit sexual arousal in one's partner. Sex educators generally agree that there has recently been an overemphasis on 'technique' in the sense of specific behaviour that is bound to produce a maximum response. Instead, they say that the emphasis should be on experimenting with various approaches, discovering what both partners like, and communicating special desires to each other. Any number of activities can be either positive or negative in their effect on a particular relationship: deep or light kissing, lightly biting different parts of the partner's body, deep or shallow penetration, cuddling and fondling, making love silently or expressing one's feelings openly, or emphasizing or deemphasizing simultaneous orgasm. In any case, there are no set rules and recommendations, except to be imaginative, spontaneous, and to focus on one's partner's pleasure as well as one's own.

sexual tension a condition of restlessness and strain resulting from an acute desire or need for sexual gratification and release, usually relieved by experiencing orgasm.

sexual trauma an emotionally disturbing sexual experience such as rape, sexual child abuse, incest, or forced anal intercourse. Experiences of this kind are psychologically injurious and may result in marked feelings of anxiety, sexual phobias, inhibited sexual desire, or inability to reach orgasm.

sexual underactivity the level of sexual activity that is at the lower end of the frequency.

sexual vandalism a compulsion to destroy sexual features depicted in statues, painting, or other art forms.

sexual variance sexual behaviour that varies from what is considered conventional or usual. It may be manifested in the choice of a sex partner or object, in the degree and strength of the sexual drive, and in the method of functioning and quality of sexual striving.

sexy erotically provocative, suggestive, or stimulating, as applied to a person, film, novel, photograph, or play. It can also mean aroused, horny or randy.

shack up a colloquial term meaning to live like husband and wife without being legally married.

shaft a slang term meaning to copulate with a woman.

shag a slang term meaning to copulate. By extension *shagged out* means extremely tired.

shagbag a derogatory slang term for a woman of loose sexual morals, particularly

one whose activities in this area over the years have left their mark on her appearance.

shagger's back a humorous Australian slang term for bad backache.

Shakespearean terms with sexual meanings an extraordinary number of terms— over 1,500—with direct or implied sexual meanings that occur in the works of the greatest author of the English language. Most of these terms were common 400 years ago, but many were coined by Shakespeare. His sexually most risqué works include *Much Ado about Nothing, The Merry Wives of Windsor, Hamlet, Measure for Measure, Othello*, and *Henry the Fifth*; and in *Romeo and Juliet* there is a passage of 23 lines (II, iv, lines 93-115) that includes no fewer than 12 different sexual terms, mainly for male and female genitalia and for intercourse. Many of Shakespeare's sex-related terms and puns are still in active use today. For examples, see the entries ACTION; BALLS; COME; DILDO; DOING IT; EAT; HARD; HOLLAND; HORN; IT; MAKE LOVE; NETHERLANDS; PRICK; TAIL.

shaman a 'medicine man,' priest, or 'witch doctor' who uses 'sorcery' to cure mental or physical illness. In many Native American and Asian societies, shamans enforce sexual taboos such as intercourse in a cornfield, or abstention from intercourse for a year after taking a scalp. They themselves frequently abstain from sexual activity, particularly when they are in training, and in the Siberian cultures many shamans are transvestites.

shame feelings of humiliation associated with exposure of one's faults and short-comings; also, acute embarrassment experienced by some individuals over exposure of their genitals (even during intercourse), or self-consciousness about menstruation or skin disorders during puberty. Psychoanalysts claim that feelings of shame may be a defence against exhibitionist impulses.

shame-aversion therapy a form of behaviour therapy in which an undesirable activity, usually sexual in nature, is enacted before a neutral audience as a means of creating a sense of shame in the patient. The final objective is to encourage the patient to avoid such behaviour because of the shameful feelings it produces.

sheath a colloquial term for condom.

sheepshagger a British slang term for someone who sodomizes a sheep, particularly in the absence of any other sexual outlet. It came into vogue during the Falklands War as a derogatory term for the islanders, among whose scattered population sheep-farming is a major occupation.

sheet-smell a slang term referring to a private eye's tailing someone to intimate situations to obtain evidence (usually of adultery).

she-male a recent synonym for a butch, especially in prison slang.

shirtlifter a derogatory term of Australian origin for a male homosexual.

shit a vulgar slang term meaning (a) to defecate or (b) excrement; also popularly used as an expletive. The term ranks number 16 in the TABOONESS RATING OF DIRTY WORDS. See this entry.

shoe fetishism an obsession with shoes as sexual objects or symbols, as in retifism.

shoot a colloquial term meaning to ejaculate.

short-eyes an American prison-slang term for a child molester.

short hairs a colloquial term for pubic hairs. When used in the phrase of 'having somebody by the short hairs,' the connotation is that one has another person under one's control or power.

shotgun perineum medical jargon for a congenital abnormality in some women in which the anus and vagina appear side by side.

shotgun wedding a slang term for a marriage necessitated by a pregnancy; a forced wedding. Also called military wedding.

show, the the plug of mucus in the neck of the womb of a pregnant woman which, when dislodged, can indicate the onset of labour.

shower cap an American slang term for condom.

showering in a raincoat an American slang term meaning intercourse with a condom.

shrimping an American slang term for sucking the partner's toes for one's own and/or the partner's sexual turn-on.

shut-eyes an American prison-slang term for a sex offender generally.

sibling one of two or more children who have a common parent. Siblings may be brothers, sisters, or both.

sibling rivalry competition among siblings for the attention, affection, or approval of one or both parents, or for recognition at school or on the playing field.

side girl a married man's girlfriend. The term is popular throughout the English-speaking Caribbean but also in parts of the southeastern United States, especially in black English.

SIECUS (sē'kəss) Sex Information and Education Council of the United States, a nonpro-fitmaking health organization with headquarters in New York City. Founded in 1964, SIECUS is primarily concerned with imparting information on all phases of human sexuality to students and professionals, based on the work of specialists in sexology, psychiatry, psychology, anthropology, sociology, education, and religion. Its monthly Report contains articles on current books, audiovisual aids, and training opportunities. It also maintains one of the most comprehensive libraries in the field.

silent beard an older term for a woman's pubic hair.

silent rape reaction a psychiatric syndrome that evolves from a rape that has not been reported to anyone. The symptoms are similar to those of the rape-trauma syndrome but often expressed as psychosomatic complaints, anxiety, or depression. Researchers believe that many women do not report rapes and as a result suffer from the symptoms of silent rape reaction.

Simmond's disease a chronic progressive hormonal disorder marked by signs and symptoms that include decreased sexual function and atrophy of the genitalia. The disease, which may affect both men and women, results in a loss of pubic and axillary hair, loss of facial hair in men, weight loss, emaciation, hypoglycaemia, and signs of premature aging. The symptoms reflect failure of the anterior lobe of the pituitary gland.

Sim's position a posture in which a patient lies on the left side with the right knee and thigh drawn upwards towards the chest. It is one of several positions used for a medical examination of the male prostate gland.

simulsex a colloquial term for bisexuality. Also called *simulsexuality* or *simulsexualism.*

simultaneous fertilization the fertilization of more than one ovum at approximately the same time by the spermatozoa of one or more males. The simultaneous fertilization will result in dizygotic twins, or in some instances triplets or quadruplets, depending upon the number of ova released at the same time. The tendency to release more than one ovum at the same time is an inherited trait of some women, but may also result from fertility drugs.

simultaneous orgasm an alternative term for mutual orgasm.

singles bar a bar that caters to unmarried men and women who are seeking entertainment, companionship, and, in many instances, sexual contacts.

sinning fear an intense, sometimes morbid fear of committing or having committed an unpardonable sin. In its pathological form, this phobia (or delusion) may be a symptom of mental illness. However, it may also be instilled by parents or others as a means of controlling sexual impulses, particularly the urge to masturbate. In psychiatry, sinning fear of the pathological sort has several names: peccatophobia, hamartophobia, and enosiophobia.

sister a male homosexual slang term for a fellow homosexual.

sister of the night a colloquial term for prostitute.

sit on the fence a colloquial term meaning to be bisexual.

situational homosexuality male or female homosexuality undertaken in an environment in which the opposite sex is inaccessible for a more or less extended period, such as in a boarding school, in a prison, aboard ship, or at a military outpost. Homosexuality of this kind may only be temporary, and heterosexual contacts may be resumed soon after release from the situation. Similarly used terms are accidental homosexuality, faute de mieux, and occasional inversion.

situational orgasmic dysfunction a term applied by Masters and Johnson to nonorgasmic women who have managed to reach orgasm at least once in their lives, whether by masturbation, coitus, or some other form of stimulation, but no longer do so.

69 a colloquial term for mutual oral sex: The partners assume a head-to-feet position (side by side or with either partner above the other) and perform fellatio and cunnilingus simultaneously. The technique may be a prelude to intercourse, or may itself be a means of achieving orgasm. Also spelled out—*sixty-nine*—or called by its French name—soixante-neuf.

66 a slang term for anal intercourse (patterned on '69'). Also written *sixty-six*. A synonymous term is '99'.

size queen a slang term used by male homosexuals to refer to a partner with large genitalia.

Skene's glands paraurethral glands located on either side of the urethral meatus (orifice) of the female. They are believed to be vestiges of tissues that would have developed into the prostate gland if the individual had differentiated into a male instead of a female. Skene's glands are often the site of inflammation if the person acquires gonorrhoea.

skin an American colloquial term for condom.

skin brassiere medical jargon for the skin tissues of the breast that hold the breast in an appropriate position with aesthetic forward projection.

skin colour the colour of the skin as a component of sexual attractiveness. In the white 'race,' light-coloured skin is not universally prized, though alabaster sculpture may give that impression. In Victorian times, Western ladies carried parasols to avoid a suntan, but today a suntanned face and body are considered highly sexy. Attitudes vary greatly: Some Polynesians attempt to bleach their skin, but Trobrianders find both albinos and very dark people equally distasteful. Among dark-skinned people, many societies, countries, or individuals value the darkest shades as especially beautiful.

skin decoration in sexology, the decoration of the skin for sexual attractiveness. The almost universal use of makeup—heavy or light—in both Eastern and Western societies attests to the fact that skin decoration has sexual overtones, particularly among women. In non-Western societies, such as Zaïre and Samoa, extensive tattoos, elaborate scars, and painted designs on the bodies of both men and women are considered highly erotic.

skin-dive a slang term meaning to perform cunnilingus.

skin eroticism sexual excitement derived from caressing, rubbing, or licking the skin, especially during foreplay. Also, exposure of large areas of the skin can be stimulating in itself. It is no accident that pornographic films are called 'skin flicks.' The skin is regarded as a secondary sex organ, and Freud saw it as the erotogenic zone par excellence.

skin flick a colloquial term for a pornographic film; also, for a sexually explicit film that is not entirely pornographic.

skirt a slang term for women in general, considered as objects of sexual pursuit. It is used in such contexts as *a piece of skirt* (a woman) and *a skirt-chaser* (a man always on the look-out for sexual conquests).

Skoptsy an ascetic religious sect dating from the 18th century and composed of dissenters from the Russian Orthodox Church. The name itself is derived from the Russian *skopets*, meaning eunuch, which aptly befits the cult's ritual of castration in which the scrotum and testicles are first removed, and afterwards the penis itself. This practice is based on their interpretation of a passage in the Book of Matthew (19:12): 'And there be

S

eunuchs, which have made themselves eunuchs for the kingdom of heaven's sake.' Some Skoptsy women participate in the ritual by having their ovaries and even their breasts excised.

slap and tickle a British colloquial term for petting.

slash a British slang term for urination, usually in the phrase 'have a slash.'

slaughterhouse an older slang term for brothel, especially a mass brothel. See also TÔLES D'ABATTAGES.

sleep around to be promiscuous in one's sex life; have sex with many partners.

sleeping together a euphemism for nonmarital sex. Some studies show, however, that a significant percentage of young males and females may live together for several months before having intercourse.

sleep with a euphemism meaning to have intercourse with (someone). This euphemism has been in use for a thousand years.

slice a slang term for the external female genitals.

Slim a name used for AIDS in East Africa, where the disease is rife. It is derived, with macabre irony, from the emaciation the disease causes.

slit a slang term for the external female genitals.

sloughing a condition in which immature male germ cells are released into the tubules leading to the epididymis. The immature cells are unable to progress normally and eventually clog the tubules. Because only a reduced number of mature spermatozoa are actually produced and released from the testes, the patient is usually diagnosed as lacking normal fertility because of oligospermia.

slut a dirty or immoral woman; also, a prostitute.

S/M abbreviation for sadomasochistic, that is, sadism with masochism. Also abbreviated as S&M (which is sometimes interpreted to stand for submission and mastery—with the variant SM&M, for sexual mastery and masochism).

smallest baby the smallest infant reported to have survived after birth. According to the *Guinness Book of Records* the tiniest viable infant weighed 10 ounces, delivered without the help of a doctor in England in 1938.

small-penis complex an emotional concern by some men that they possess a penis that is abnormally small, a concern based in part on the individual's visual perspective when looking downwards towards a flaccid penis,

a viewpoint that distorts the true size. The complex may also be supported by the emphasis in literature and other art forms as well as folklore and pornographic material on male genitalia that are unusually large.

smear test another term for PAP TEST. See this entry.

smegma a fatty or oily substance secreted by sebaceous glands of the prepuce and the neck and glans of the penis of most men. It has a distinctive odour and may accumulate in the absence of personal hygiene, mixing with exfoliated tissue cells to form an irritating pebble-like calculus. A similar substance is secreted by glands of the clitoris and labia minora.

SNAFU (snafoo') an American abbreviation for 'situation normal: all fucked up.' The expression originated among soldiers in World War II, and was 'cleaned up' later for civilian use to stand for 'situation normal: all fouled up.'

snake phobia an intense, morbid fear of snakes. Evidence from the biblical Garden of Eden, as well as from dreams, fantasies, artistic productions and primitive rituals indicates that the snake represents the penis and fear of snakes symbolizes fear of intercourse. The psychiatric term for snake phobia is ophidiophobia.

snake symbol the representation of a snake as found in dreams, primitive rites, sculptures, and ceramics. The snake is believed to represent the penis as well as fertility.

snatch a slang term for female genitals.

snatch purser a slang term for pimp.

snog a colloquial British term meaning to pet.

snuff movies pornographic films of the worst kind, in which sexual excitement is linked intimately to torture and in which the victim gets actually killed in front of the camera.

S.O.B. an abbreviation for son of a bitch.

social disease a euphemistic expression for venereal, or sexually transmissible, disease.

social hygiene preventive measures for the control of venereal, or sexually transmissible, diseases (also euphemistically known as social diseases), including dissemination of information on these conditions and their social effects as well as promotion of sex education and information on community conditions that serve as a breeding ground for prostitution and other forms of sexual delinquency. The term social hygiene is being replaced by *social health*, as in the title American Social Health Association.

socialization of sex social customs and characteristics derived from primary male-female differences essential to reproduction. The most prevalent and enduring social differences are those related to functions essential to survival and reproduction—for example, child rearing and homemaking. Beyond these are behaviour patterns characteristic of the particular culture, such as sex hospitality among the Eskimos, partner swapping among suburban 'swingers,' and the various taboos found in restrictive societies.

sodomia imperfecta a medieval Christian term for 'unnatural' sexual intercourse, particularly anal intercourse among homosexuals. The crime was distinguished from other sexual offences as one that would be handled by ecclesiastical courts rather than civil courts—which were responsible for adultery and similar crimes. In the 12th century, punishment for homosexuality among members of the priesthood included confinement in a monastery.

sodomy a group of sexual variations that are illegal in many jurisdictions, including intercourse of any kind with animals, as well as anal intercourse and mouth-genital contact between human beings. The name is derived from the ancient city of Sodom where corruption was so rampant that it was destroyed, according to the Book of Genesis. A person who practises sodomy is a sodomite.

soft chancre the genital ulcer associated with an infection of *Haemophilus ducreyi*. It begins as a small reddish pimple that fills with pus and becomes a punched-out sore that discharges pus profusely. Unlike the hard chancre, the soft chancre can be quite painful and tends to occur in multiple lesions.

soft media fetish objects that are soft, frilly, or fluffy, such as lingerie. Unlike hard-media objects, soft-media fetish materials can be loose-fitting. While black is a popular colour, soft-media garments can be in other colours, as demonstrated by the colours of garments purchased by men for their wives or girlfriends. Furs are usually considered an example of soft media.

soft-tissue metastases cancers that develop in various body organs and tissues, excluding bones, as a result of the spread of cancer cells from the prostate gland. The most common sites include the lymph nodes of the lower abdomen, the lymph nodes of the bronchial area, the liver, the lungs, the adrenal glands. Because cancer of the prostate tends to be painless, men generally are unaware of the disease until other organs or body areas have become involved in the spread of cancer cells.

soixante-neuf (sô-äsäNt' nœf') the French term for sixty-nine.

solicitor general a slang term for penis.

somatic sex the sex chromosome complement of the somatic, or body, cells of a person.

son of a bitch an offensive and vulgar address, with no relation to the literal meaning. The term ranks number 9 in the TABOONESS RATING OF DIRTY WORDS.

Soranos of Ephesus (98-138 A.D.) a Greek physician believed to be one of the first gynaecologists who described abortifacients and contraceptives in detail, maintaining that it is far more advisable not to conceive than to destroy the embryo.

Sorensen Report a report of a nationwide US survey of young people's sexual activities published in 1973 by the social psychologist Robert C. Sorenson, entitled *Adolescent Sexuality in Contemporary America*. The study reveals among other things that 75 percent of boys and 60 to 70 percent of girls between 13 and 15 masturbate; and that between the ages of 13 and 19, 59 percent of boys and 45 percent of girls had experienced sexual intercourse.

sororate marriage between a man and two or more sisters (sometimes successively: after the death of the first sister or the discovery that she is infertile). The custom is widespread and is often the preferred form of polygyny, as it is in many parts of Africa, in many Native American nations, and in the Caucasus, Papua New Guinea, New Hebrides, northeastern Asia, and the Solomon Islands. Also called *sororal polygyny*.

soul kiss another term for 'French kiss.'

spacing of pregnancies the use of birth-control measures such as abstinence and contraception to regulate the period of time between one pregnancy and another. Pregnancies that follow each other too closely have been found to be injurious to the health of both mother and child—for example, it has been found that when births are only 1 year apart the death rate for babies is about 50 percent higher than when births are 2 years apart.

Spanish collar a condition in which the foreskin, or prepuce, becomes too tight, producing irritation of the penis, frequent erections, and painful swelling. The condition can be corrected by circumcision.

Spanish fly a powder known as cantharides made from a species of dried beetles (*Cantharis vesicatoria*) that is native to France and Spain. The substance is a powerful irritant that has been used to stimulate the sex organs, producing priapism in men, but so dangerous that it can be lethal. De Sade was accused of poisoning prostitutes by giving them the substance as an aphrodisiac. See also CANTHARIDES.

spanking and sex a term referring to spanking as a form of sexual stimulation. Studies have shown that children can be aroused by spanking—which may be one reason many of them 'invite' punishment. The buttocks and anal area are erogenous zones, and this form of stimulation may implant masochistic or sadistic tendencies.

spare a collective male slang term for women available for sexual activity. It is most commonly used in 'a bit of spare,' meaning a woman with no male escort.

spatter one's boots a humorous British euphemism meaning to urinate—also as *splash one's boots.*

speak Low Genitalese an American slang term meaning to have oral sex.

spectatoring a term introduced by Masters and Johnson to describe the behaviour of an individual who likes to observe his own sexual performance as if he were a spectator. The researchers suggested that the compulsion to rate one's own performance in the sex act is self-defeating because it is assumed that a 'full sexual response' does not allow room for the person to simultaneously evaluate the response because the assessment inhibits experiencing the total erotic feeling.

spectrophilia a morbid attraction to ghosts or evil spirits; also, the fantasy, or illusion, of having sexual relations with phantoms. This disorder, or paraphilia, was far more common during the Middle Ages and early modern era than today, particularly in monasteries and nunneries, where it probably arose from extreme sexual repression and possibly from guilt over masturbation or other sexual activity. See INCUBUS; SUCCUBUS.

speculum an instrument used for examining a body opening, particularly the vagina. A vaginal speculum, sometimes called a bivalve speculum, contains two smooth blades that can be separated by turning a small knob on the handle of the instrument. With the blades open, the examining physician can see rather clearly the inside of the vagina and the cervix of the uterus.

spend a slang term meaning to ejaculate.

spend a penny a British euphemism meaning to urinate.

sperm the spermatozoa; also, the seminal fluid containing spermatozoa. See also FEMALE SPERM; MALE SPERM.

sperm agglutination the immobilization of sperm because of a blockage of the ductus deferens. The occlusion results in the production of antibodies against the man's own sperm. The antibodies immobilize or agglutinate the sperm so that they lose their motility when ejaculated. The condition can also be the result of orchitis.

sperm analysis another term for semen analysis.

sperm aster a pattern that appears in the newly fertilized ovum characterized by cytoplasm granules radiating from the head of the sperm. Also called aster of fertilization.

spermatemphraxis any obstruction to the normal passage of semen.

spermatic canal the inguinal canal of the male. The term is sometimes used to distinguish the opening from the similar structure in the female.

spermatic-cell arrest a condition in which the spermatogenic process of the male reproductive system does not undergo the reduction-division stage leading to production of secondary spermatocytes. This is a common cause of azoospermia.

spermatic cord a cordlike structure composed of connective tissue, blood and lymphatic vessels, and nerves, and containing the ductus deferens. It extends from the deep inguinal ring of the abdomen to the upper pole of the testis on each side.

spermatic duct an alternative term for the ductus deferens, or vas deferens.

spermatid an immature form of a spermatozoon in the lining of a seminiferous tubule. It usually appears as a spherical cell embedded in a Sertoli cell, having derived from the division of a secondary spermatocyte. During the spermatid stage, its nucleus evolves into the head of a spermatozoon, the cell protoplasm becomes the middle piece, and the centrioles becomes the tail. The spermatid receives its haploid number of chromosomes in dividing from a secondary spermatocyte.

spermatocelectomy a surgical procedure for removal of a spermatocele, a cystic dilatation of the ducts of the upper part of the epididymis.

spermatocyte an early stage in the development of a spermatozoon from a primitive gamete. A primary spermatocyte derives from the division and enlargement of a spermatogonium and contains the diploid (46) number of chromosomes. By meiotic division, the primary spermatocyte divides into two secondary spermatocytes, each with the haploid (23) number of chromosomes. In the next division, it becomes two spermatids.

spermatogenesis the process of formation and development of spermatozoa from primordial male germ cells in the walls of the seminiferous tubules through a complex series of mitotic amd meiotic cell divisions.

spermatogenic cells one of the two types of cells in the germinal tissue of the seminiferous tubules. The second type of cell is the Sertoli or sustenacular cell.

spermatogonia the basic male germ cells located in the lining of the walls of the seminiferous tubules of the testes. Through repeated mitotic divisions, spermatogonia evolve into primary spermatocytes.

spermatolysin a substance found in the vagina of some women who are hypersensitive to semen or spermatozoa. The substance destroys the spermatozoa.

spermatophobia a morbid fear of semen.

spermatorrhoea a copious emission of semen, which may occur without orgasm. A nocturnal emission may be termed *spermatorrhoea dormientum*. False spermatorrhoea is a form of the condition in which only seminal fluid, without spermatozoa, is discharged.

spermatozoon a single mature male gamete consisting of a conical head, a nucleus, a middle piece of cytoplasm, and a flagellate tail or end piece that helps propel the spermatozoon towards fertilization of an ovum in a fallopian tube. A human spermatozoon is about 5 microns long and 2 to 3 microns thick. Plural: *spermatozoa*.

spermaturia an alternative term for semenuria, or seminuria, indicating the presence of semen or spermatozoa in the urine.

sperm bank a storage depot for frozen sperm to be used in artificial insemination.

sperm cell a spermatozoon or one of its precursors, such as a spermatid.

spermicide any agent that may be used to kill spermatozoa and therefore may serve as a contraceptive. Many spermicides contain one of the nonoxinol chemicals, each of which is identified by a following number indicating its particular molecular structure, such as nonoxinol-10.

sperm life the length of time that a spermatozoon may remain viable after being ejaculated. Studies show that under ideal conditions an ejaculated sperm may live up to 14 days. In the vagina, however, sperm seldom remain viable for more than 2 days. Sperm longevity before ejaculation can be measured in weeks and months, as evidenced by conceptions produced by men who have undergone vasectomies but remain fertile long after the operation.

sperm morphology the shapes and sizes of various spermatozoa in a sample. In fertility studies, the percentage of abnormal spermatozoa forms is considered. At least 80 percent should be within the limits of shapes and sizes considered normal. Particular attention may be paid to the proportions of certain abnormal forms.

sperm-producing tubules an alternative term for the seminiferous tubules of the testis, where primitive spermatogonia are spawned and nurtured until they are ready to enter the epididymal pipeline as mature spermatozoa.

sperm speed the forward progress of spermatozoa after ejaculation. Human spermatozoa have been recorded moving at an average rate of 1.5 millimetres per minute, a speed that is comparable to the speed of a human swimmer when the relative size of a spermatozoon is taken into consideration. At this rate of speed, spermatozoa should be able to travel approximately 1 inch every 15 minutes. Various other species apparently receive help from muscular contractions of the cervix or uterus; for example, spermatozoa of a dog have been found in the fallopian tubes 1 minute after ejaculation. For a rabbit, about 4 hours are required to complete the trip from copulation to the end of the fallopian tube; the timetable for ram sperm is about the same. Human spermatozoa usually reach the 'lover's lane' portion of the fallopian tube within a few hours after ejaculation.

sperm vitality the longevity of spermatozoa in the female reproductive tract. Of the estimated 300 million spermatozoa in a single male ejaculation, it is believed that no more than a few thousand survive for as long as 3 days. By comparison, human sperm have been kept alive outside the body for 2 weeks. Among other animals, experiments indicate rabbit sperm loses its ability to fertilize within 30 hours and is usually dead within 2 days. The sperm of male domestic fowl have been found alive and well in the oviducts of a hen after 3 weeks. Unusual is the bat, which copulates in the autumn even though fertilization does not occur until after hibernation in the following spring.

sphincter a ringlike voluntary or involuntary muscle that surrounds an opening of the body, expanding to open it and contracting to close it—as the anal sphincter. See also EXTERNAL SPHINCTER; INTERNAL SPHINCTER.

sphincter control the ability to voluntarily open or close the openings of the body that depend upon contraction or relaxation of circular bands of muscle fibres, such as the anal and urinary sphincters, and, in some women, the sphincter cunni. The development of this ability is considered an important step in psychosexual maturation.

sphincter cunni the bulbospongiosus muscle which in the male completely encircles the back of the penis including the corpora cavernosa and corpus spongiosum and in the female surrounds the orifice of the vagina. Also called bulbocavernosus muscle.

spider bite a relatively common cause of oedema of the scrotum. The scrotum tissues are quite sensitive to any inflammatory reaction. The scrotum becomes filled with fluid and greatly swollen, requiring bed rest with the scrotum elevated to help drainage of the lymph vessels and veins.

spinnbarkeit (shpin'bäkīt; German, 'weavability') the formation of a stretchable thread of mucus from the uterine cervix, an effect that is possible only at the time of ovulation when the cervix is under the influence of increased oestrogen secretion. The ability of the mucus to be formed into thin strands several inches in length results from a chemical effect on the mucus. It is believed that the chemical change enhances the ability of spermatozoa to move quickly to the cervix along the strands of mucus at the precise time that the woman is/at the fertile peak of the menstrual cycle. The spinnbarkeit filaments therefore become a temporary express route to the uterus.

spinster an outmoded and now insulting term for a woman who remains unmarried beyond the 'usual' age for marriage, and seems unlikely ever to be married. Today many 'spinsters' have an active sex life, and some adopt children or give birth to illegitimate children.

Spirochaeta pallida the Treponema pallidum species of spiral-shaped bacteria that causes syphilis and possibly some nonvenereal forms of spirochaetal infections.

split-beaver shot an extremely close BEAVER SHOT. See this entry.

sponge contraceptive a polyurethane-foam sponge designed to be inserted into the vagina as a means of preventing conception. In contrast to the use of ordinary sea sponges, which dates back to ancient times and is extremely unreliable, today's sponges contain a spermicide that is continually released for about 24 hours. Many authorities consider these sponges to be safe and highly reliable.

spontaneous abortion the medical term for miscarriage, or premature expulsion of the foetus when this occurs without intention on the part of the pregnant woman, and without the use of any artificial method. Most spontaneous abortions take place before the third month of foetal life, and are most likely to occur when the mother is below the age 20. Risk of losing the child is about twice as high in a fourth pregnancy as in a first. In many cases the cause is not known, although hormonal imbalance, illness, trauma, malnutrition, or a defective foetus may be factors. A woman who has had a spontaneous abortion can usually conceive again, and have a normal pregnancy.

spontaneous urethral rupture the sudden failure of the wall of the urethra, sometimes occurring at a point previously weakened or damaged by a catheter. The pressure of urine release during routine urination may break through the weak spot, resulting in inflammation of surrounding tissues. Spontaneous urethral rupture also can be a result of obstruction stemming from a stricture in the urethra.

sport an organism that has undergone mutation and has become obviously different in appearance from its parents or ancestors. The term is used in genetics.

sport of Venus a 19th-century euphemism for intercourse.

spousal rape a synonym for marital rape.

spunk a slang term for semen (which has subsequently come to mean also 'courage, pluck').

squash preparation an assortment of the chromosomes taken from a body tissue cell of a male or female before the chromosomes are arranged in a karyotype. The chromosomes are 'captured' during the metaphase stage of cellular division by the injection of a chemical that freezes the structures in their typical patterns and sizes. The chromosomes are photographed, and the photo images are cut from the print for use in a karyotype.

squeeze technique a method for treating premature ejaculation, preferably under the guidance of a sex therapist. The female partner stimulates erection, then squeezes or pinches the head of the man's penis with her fingers as soon as he signals that ejaculation is about to take place. Repetition of this manoeuvre conditions him to achieve a normal delay in ejaculation. Also called pinch technique.

stacked a slang term of male approval meaning 'having large breasts.'

stag films short films in which sexual acts are explicitly depicted. Generally speaking, these films are not exhibited in standard cinemas but in private showings at clubs and parties. The audience was at one time confined to men, but today women may be included.

standing coitus intercourse with one or both partners in a standing position. Variations include both partners standing face to face (the shorter partner may stand on a stool); the knee-and-elbow position in which the man places his two arms under the women's knees, supporting her on his elbows and raising her as high as his waist; face-to-face with the man raising one of the woman's legs while the other remains on the floor to support her body; face-to-face with the woman clasping her hands behind the man's neck and clasping his waist with her legs; and, most difficult of all, a position in which the man stands while the woman is upside down with her legs around his neck, performing fellatio while he performs cunnilingus.

status orgasmus a term sometimes applied to a rapid series of orgasms experienced by some women while enjoying the third stage, or orgasm stage, of the sexual response cycle. Typically, these orgasms are experienced as a single sustained climax followed by a more or less protracted resolution phase.

statutory rape in the USA, sexual intercourse with a female who is below the age of consent.

staying power a slang term for the ability of a man to delay ejaculation after penetration of the vagina until both sex partners are ready for orgasm.

STD abbreviation for sexually transmitted disease.

steatopygia an extreme accumulation of fat in the female buttocks, especially among Hottentots and Bushmen in southern Africa. In these and other cultures, huge buttocks are considered a mark of beauty and sexual attraction. Also called Hottentot bustle.

Steinach, Eugen an Austrian physician who pioneered sex-change medicine in the 1920s. Steinach claimed to have changed the sex of a patient with surgery and hormone injections. Steinach also consulted with psychiatrist Sigmund Freud about the role of sex hormones in certain emotional disorders.

sterility infertility; inability to produce offspring. Sterility that is voluntary is called facultative sterility. Relative sterility is a form in which fertility is theoretically possible but in which one or more factors such as a low sperm count reduce the chances of normal fertilization. Revocable sterility is a form in which an obstacle to fertility can be removed, as in reconnecting the vas-deferens or fallopian-tube portions previously severed as a means of contraception.

sterilization rendering an individual incapable of reproduction. A female is sterilized by a process of interrupting the sequence of steps necessary to conceive, such as surgical removal of the ovaries, fallopian tubes, or uterus, or a combination of those organs, or by ligating (tying off) the tubes so that an ovum released during ovulation cannot be fertilized. A male is sterilized usually by surgical vasectomy in which the ductus deferens is severed so that spermatozoa cannot be ejaculated during intercourse. Male sterilization also may be produced by castration, or surgical removal of the testes, as in the treatment for testicular cancer. A vasectomy or tubal ligation can in certain cases be corrected surgically so that fertility may be restored.

steroidogenesis the process whereby steroid hormones, particularly the sex hormones, evolve in biosynthetic steps from cholesterol molecules.

steroids a category of chemical substances that includes the sex hormones. Steroids have in common a specific molecular structure, although they do not all produce the same or similar effects. Besides sex hormones, steroids include cholesterol, vitamin D, bile acids, and toad poisons.

stigma a physical or mental trait that distinguishes an individual from others and is usually considered a mark of disgrace. An unconventional sexual preference or sexual activity may be a stigma in a particular community or culture. The term is also used to refer to a spot on the surface of an ovary that indicates the site of a future rupture of a graafian follicle (also called follicular stigma).

stillbirth birth of a dead child. In contrast to

a miscarriage, which usually occurs very early in pregnancy, the stillborn foetus is beyond the sixth month of pregnancy and fully recognizable as a dead baby. Though the cause of a particular stillbirth may be obscure, some of the factors that are commonly involved are immaturity of the foetus, syphilis, protracted labour, water in the lungs, and strangulation by the umbilical cord.

stinginess extreme penuriousness or miserliness. In psychoanalysis, it is a character trait believed to stem from fixation at the anal-retention stage when the child derives pleasure and power from withholding the faeces.

stone baby a foetus that dies within the uterus without being aborted and is instead preserved by a bonelike layer of calcium salts. The calcium shroud presumably develops to protect the mother from the toxic effects of the dead foetus. A stone baby may remain undetected in a uterus for many years. In one recorded case, a stone baby was removed surgically after 61 years in the womb of a woman.

stones a slang term for testicles.

Stopes, Marie Carmichael (1880-1958) a British scientist who proclaimed women's right to personal fulfilment and sexual satisfaction in marriage. She opened the first British birth-control clinic in 1921, advocated the use of the diaphragm or *Stopes cap* for contraception, and founded the Society for Constructive Birth Control. Her books, *Married Love and Wise Parenthood*, were widely read and contributed greatly to the sexual liberation of women.

stop-start technique a two-step sex-therapy method used in overcoming premature ejaculation. In the first step, the man stops all stimulation, whether by himself or by his partner, just as he approaches the moment of inevitable ejaculation. When that moment has passed, he starts again, and by repeating this process will gradually gain control over the timing of his ejaculation. The same procedure can be followed during masturbation.

storge (stô'gē) a Greek term for a form of love that is generally interpreted as synonymous with affection, as distinguished from erotic or passionate love, or philia or agape. Storge is sometimes defined as a nondiscriminating type of love that one may show to parents, children, or pets.

stork a bird invoked in old wives' tales, or in explaining childbirth to young children, as the bringer of babies into the world. See also GOOSEBERRY BUSH.

stork bites a fanciful name for pink or purple marks found on the face and scalp of some infants at birth. The lesions, which resemble birthmarks, gradually fade and usually have disappeared by the end of the first year. Also called telangiectatic naevi.

straddle injury an injury to the penis, urethra, or adjacent structures as a result of falling astride a hard blunt or sharp object. One of the serious effects is a rupture of the urethra at a point behind the scrotum. The corpora cavernosa and corpus spongiosum are usually damaged at the same time.

straight a colloquial term meaning (a) heterosexual, or (b) proper, conforming to the norms of the establishment—'square.'

Straight Partners an American organization to help straights who have married homosexuals.

strangulation a type of phimosis that occurs mainly in young boys who insert the penis through a metal ring or other hard metal object, after which swelling occurs so that the penis cannot be withdrawn. If the device is not removed, usually with a jeweller's saw, gangrene can develop, requiring amputation of the affected part of the penis.

streaking the practice of running around in the nude in public places in order to shock others present. Occasionally a means of political protest, it is more often done simply for a dare. Sports matches are popular targets for streakers. It was particularly prevalent in the early 1970s, but it has not entirely died out.

street hustlers teenage practitioners of male homosexual prostitution who solicit clients in the street.

stretch marks a popular term for the lines that appear on the abdomen and other body areas of women as a result of pregnancy. The marks also may be caused by obesity and certain illnesses, such as Cushings syndrome. Also called *striae albicantes; striae atrophica.*

streetwalker a euphemism for a prostitute, particularly one who solicits on the streets.

strictures any abnormal narrowing of a passageway, such as the urethra, that can interfere with normal functioning of the reproductive system. Strictures may result from scarring, tears, punctures, or other injuries, such as damage to the lining of the urethra from insertion of a urinary catheter. The symptoms include pain and difficulty in urination and a nonvenereal discharge. The stricture can be a cause of impotence. In a woman, a stricture can develop in the urethra, from similar causes such as improper use of a urinary catheter during medical treatment. Strictures also can develop in the fallopian tube or the cervical os, thereby blocking the passage of spermatozoa en route to the fertilization of an ovum. Strictures of the fallopian tubes or cervical os are more easily corrected than strictures of the urethra.

striptease a sexually provocative performance in which women, or in some instances men, parade or dance fully clothed, and then slowly expose more and more of their body by removing one article of clothing after another. Striptease is especially appealing to voyeurs.

stroll an American slang term for streetwalking, a practice used by some prostitutes to make themselves available to the local male population.

stroma the fibrous framework surrounding the ovaries.

stud a slang term meaning (a) any male, (b) a male who is young and carefree, and (c) a male whose masculinity is beyond doubt, especially if it is proven through many sexual conquests.

subfecundity a fertility level that is below normal for a female, as in relative sterility or one-child sterility, a type of female infertility that follows the birth of the first infant.

subincision a form of genital mutilation consisting of a slitting of the underside of the penis with permanent opening of the urethra. It is part of the puberty rites of certain Australian and Fijian societies.

sublimation a psychoanalytical term for the unconscious process of channelling sexual or aggressive drives into acceptable expression; for example, an exhibitionistic urge may gain an approved outlet in ballet training, or a voyeuristic impulse may be expressed in the use of a microscope for scientific research.

submission compliance of one individual (usually a woman) with the sexual wishes and demands of another person (man or woman). Some women play a passive, submissive role, waiting for their husband or lover to initiate sexual activity. Extreme submission is exemplified by the Romans, who subjected female slaves to every form of sexual indignity; and by the practice of erotic bondage and discipline in some areas of society today.

substitute sex partner an especially trained surrogate used in sex therapy.

substitution the replacement of one type of

satisfaction with another, as in 'raiding the refrigerator' when disappointed in love; also, the replacement of unacceptable impulses with socially acceptable activities, as in cleaning the house from cellar to attic as a substitute for the 'unclean' impulse to be promiscuous.

subtotal hysterectomy a hysterectomy that involves removal of the uterus at or above the level of the cervix, the isthmus of the uterus. Also called supracervical hysterectomy.

succubus a medieval term for a demon who assumes the shape of a woman and has intercourse with a sleeping man. See INCUBUS; SPECTROPHILIA.

suck a vulgar slang term meaning mainly to perform fellatio. The term ranks number 11 in the TABOONESS RATING OF DIRTY WORDS. See this entry.

sucking impulse the impulse to apply suction with the lips, which first appears in early infancy when the nipple is grasped in the feeding process. According to Freud, sucking is the earliest form of autoerotic gratification. It later takes the form of thumb sucking and sucking the partner's tongue, nipples, vulva, clitoris, or penis during sexual relations.

sugar daddy an older man who provides financially for a woman, usually in return for sexual favours.

suicidal sex an alternative term for EROTIC HANGING or AUTOEROTIC ASPHYXIA. See these entries.

suigenderism the tendency of boys to associate with boys and girls with girls without sexual involvement. This occurs primarily during the 'latency' years before puberty. The term derives from Latin 'of one's own sex.' After puberty, relationships cease to be exclusively with one's own sex.

summa libido the highest point, or summit, of erotic pleasure, reached during the orgasmic phase of the sexual response cycle. Also called acme.

superego in psychoanalytic theory, the body of conscious and unconscious principles and value judgments that help control our conduct. Popularly known as conscience, the superego stems primarily from our parents and secondarily from our culture. When its demands are not met, as may happen in our social or sexual life, we usually feel a sense of guilt.

superego anxiety in psychoanalytic theory, an anxiety that is frequently experienced when ethical principles, social codes, or parental behests are violated.

superfecundation fertility that is well above what is considered normal; also, the fertilization of two separate ova released in the same menstrual cycle during separate acts of sexual intercourse with the same male or different males. See also SIMULTANEOUS FERTILIZATION.

superfemale a term sometimes applied to a female born with more than the normal XX complement of female chromosomes. In some rare cases of sex-chromosome aberrations, females have been found with as many as five X chromosomes. Women born with three or more X chromosomes occur at a frequency slightly greater than one per thousand. However, the additional X chromosomes are often associated with mental retardation, sterility, and, despite the term superfemale, underdeveloped female sexual characteristics. See also SEX-CHROMOSOME ABERRATIONS.

superfoetation the conception of a second foetus by a woman already pregnant, as a result of the fertilization of an ovum released in a later ovulation—an extremely rare occurrence.

superincision a form of genital mutilation performed on adolescent boys among the Mangaians and other Polynesian societies as part of their puberty rites. The foreskin is pulled over an object called an anvil, the purpose of which is to protect the glans during the incision which runs the entire length of the penis. No anesthetic is used, and there is much bleeding. The boy runs into the sea for relief, shouting, 'Now I am really a man!' The penis is treated with poultices as it heals.

superior-kneeling position an intercourse position in which one partner kneels above the other. Masters and Johnson recommend that the woman use this position if her male partner tends to be impotent. It gives her maximum control over the insertive process, and enables her to avoid pelvic thrusting, which is very demanding for the male. Men suffering from partial impotence find insertion difficult and may lose their erection at this point.

supermale a term sometimes applied to a male born with more than the normal complement of male chromosomes. Early study findings suggested that men with XYY chromosome sets were large and aggressive because of the extra male chromosome. However, the first cases were discovered in prison inmates; and further study showed that normal, average men in the general population may also have an extra male chromosome. See also SEX-CHROMOSOME ABERRATIONS.

supernumerary breasts an alternative term for polymastia.

supernumerary chromosome a chromosome that is in addition to the normal complement of the individual, does not match any of the normal chromosomes for the species, and apparently has little if any effect on the physical appearance of the individual. Supernumerary chromosomes are found occasionally in wild populations of some animals.

supernumerary tube a congenital anomaly consisting of an extra fallopian tube that runs alongside a normal functioning tube. It may or may not be associated with a supernumerary ovary.

superovulate to produce a number of mature ova from the ovary at the same time. This frequently happens as a result of treatment with fertility drugs.

supersex a superfemale or supermale possessing extra female or male chromosomes. A supersex male would have a complement of 47,XYY, or a total of 47 chromosomes including two Y, male, chromosomes, as compared with the normal 46 chromosome total, including one X and one Y sex chromosome for a male individual. A supersex female would have a chromosome complement of 47,XXX, with one extra female, X, chromosome. See also SUPERFEMALE; SUPERMALE.

superstraight a latent homosexual who exhibits an antihomosexual attitude as a reaction formation. Thus, a person who persecutes homosexuals may actually be expressing anxiety about his own homosexual feelings.

suprapubic pertaining to a surgical procedure in which the pelvic cavity is entered through the lower abdomen. The approach is used in some treatments of prostate difficulties, such as obstruction of the urethra. After an incision through the lower abdominal wall, the urinary bladder is opened so that a tumour or other abnormal growth can be removed through the bladder.

suprasellar disease any disorder caused by a tumour or other lesion, including an injury, to the hypothalamus or the stalk connecting the hypothalamus and the pituitary gland. A suprasellar disease may be hypogonadism or precocious puberty. The term suprasellar refers to the location of the hypothalamus, which is above the sellar turcica level of the skull, a depression in the sphenoid bone that contains the pituitary gland.

suramin a drug used in Africa to treat protozoal infections and in Europe as an experimental therapy for AIDS infections. Suramin, also called naganol, interferes with the activity of an enzyme that AIDS viruses must use in order to reproduce. See also AIDS.

surface papilloma a type of ovarian tumour in which the growth appears as a mass of tiny warts on the surface of an ovary. It is formed by wildly growing fibrous tissue with multiple branches, each covered with clusters of the minute warts. Untreated, the surface papilloma may continue growing until it fills the pelvic cavity.

surrogate a person who acts in the place of another—for example, a sister, aunt, or uncle who substitutes for the mother or father. In sex therapy, an experienced professional may act as a surrogate partner in helping the patient overcome inhibitions, resistances, and faulty behaviour patterns that stand in the way of satisfactory intercourse.

surrogate mother a woman who takes the place of a sterile wife for the purpose of insemination by the husband. This form of impregnation is unusual. Surrogate motherhood is the subject of legal dispute as to the rights of the surrogate mother over the child she bears.

surrogate partner a substitute sex partner who has been especially trained to participate in sex therapy.

surrogate therapy treatment of sexual problems through the use of professionally trained and supervised substitute sex partners. Through sympathetic and skilful cooperation, these partners—male or female, as the case may require—help the patient overcome the hindrances to sexual performance, such as tension, anxiety, fear of failure, and lack of confidence. Through a step-by-step procedure, at least one half of male patients suffering from premature ejaculation or impotence, and female patients afflicted with vaginismus or frigidity, can be effectively treated, according to Masters and Johnson, the originators of this technique.

suspensory ligament a strong fibrous triangle of tissue that extends from the linea alba of the belly to the top of the penis, with attachments also to the symphysis pubis.

sustenacular cells the cells of the seminiferous tubules of the testis, which have the function of nurturing the spermatozoa at various stages of their production and maturation.

suttee a Hindu custom in which a widow demonstrated her devotion to her husband by cremating herself on his funeral pyre. The practice was outlawed by the British in 1829. Also called satii.

sweating response the production of a mucoid lubrication fluid directly from the walls of the vaginal barrel and to a lesser extent from Bartholin's glands during the excitement phase of the female sexual-response cycle. The biological function of this secretion is to prepare the vagina for entry by the penis.

sweetmeat a slang term for woman.

swing both ways a slang term meaning to be bisexual.

swinging a euphemistic term for partner swapping or mate swapping, though sometimes more widely applied to individuals or couples (*swingers*) who engage in a wide variety of sexual practices with a wide variety of partners (for example, group sex, or homosexual activities) in their search for exciting sexual experiences. See also CLOSED SWINGING; OPEN SWINGING.

swish a slang term meaning to walk in an effeminate manner, including 'feminine' hip movements. The term is usually applied to the *swishy* type of male homosexual.

switch hitter an American slang term for a bisexual man or woman.

swive a once-common term meaning to have intercourse. (The other common term was the 10th-century word 'to sard.') Swive was popular since the 14th century, but by the 18th century it had become almost as vulgar as 'to fuck,' and soon fell into disuse.

Swyer's syndrome a form of male pseudohermaphroditism in which the individual is genetically a male, with an XY set of chromosomes, but has the internal and external sexual organs of a female. The person is usually raised as a girl, possesses a vagina, uterus, and fallopian tubes, but does not menstruate and fails to develop breasts and other adult female characteristics.

symbiotic marriage a marriage characterized by an extreme degree of mutual dependence, similar to the relationship between mother and infant. In many instances a marital relationship of this kind is based upon neurotic needs, and becomes so close that the partners cannot function without each other.

symbolic masturbation various acts that are believed to substitute for manipulation of the genital organs (penis or clitoris), such as rubbing the nose, pulling the ear lobes,

S

twisting strands of hair, constantly playing with one's watch or adjusting one's tie.

symphysis pubis the foremost portion of the pubic bone on either side, or more specifically the joint formed by the meeting of the right and left pubic bones, an area that usually is covered with pubic hair.

symptothermal method a birth-control technique that depends upon a combination of basal-body-temperature monitoring and examination of cervical mucus to determine which days of the menstrual month are

symptothermal method a birth-control technique that depends upon a combination of basal-body-temperature monitoring and examination of cervical mucus to determine which days of the menstrual month are days when intercourse is most likely to result in a pregnancy. Like other birth-control techniques that avoid the use of synthetic hormones, IUD's, condoms, spermicides, and similar 'unnatural' methods, the symptothermal method requires a great deal of self-motivation and self-discipline and the ability to make accurate observations of physiological changes. Also called the Billings method.

synergic marriage a marriage in which the partners work together and reinforce each other in their effort to achieve common goals and the satisfaction of their individual needs.

synorchidism the complete or partial fusion of both testes.

synoscheos (sinos′kē·əs) a congenital male abnormality in which the penis is a part of the scrotum (Greek *syn-*, 'together,' and *osche*, 'scrotum').

syphilis a systemic infection caused by the spiral-shaped bacterium *Treponema pallidum* that is usually transmitted by sexual contact. Although the disease has been well known for hundreds of years, the disease organism was not identified until early in the 20th century. For centuries it was known in Europe and Asia as the 'great pox,' which distinguished the lesions from the disease still called 'smallpox.' (Perhaps because of their venereal nature, syphilis, gonorrhoea, and chancroid were at one time believed to be manifestations of the same infection, a concept that received tangible but erroneous support from an 18th-century physician who developed syphilis after injecting himself with gonorrhoea pus.) Because of public-health measures and the development of diagnostic tests and antibiotics, the incidence of primary syphilis has fallen dramatically since the 1940s. But the number of new cases reported is nearly 90,000 per year in the United States, and the true rate is believed to be higher because many cases are treated privately and are not reported. It takes about 3 weeks after a sexual contact with an infected partner for a primary lesion to appear. During the incubation period, the concentration of Treponema organisms increases by tens of millions. The initial lesion is a chancre, a painless pimple that quickly erodes into an ulcer. In heterosexual men, the chancre is usually on the penis. In homosexual men, it is usually on the genitalia, in the mouth, or the anal canal. In women, the chancre may appear on the labia or cervix. Lymph glands in the area of the chancre become firm and swollen within a week. The chancre heals within 2 to 12 weeks, but the lymph-gland effects persist. Secondary lesions can apppear before the chancre heals or several months later. The lesions appear as a skin rash or pink-to-red macules or pimples, some of which may contain pus. The skin lesions may pop up anywhere from the soles of the feet to the scalp. (Some victims develop mucous patches, erosions on the lips, tongue, pharynx, vagina, glans penis, or foreskin.) The lesions may be accompanied by fever, loss of appetite, weight loss, and general discomfort. Headaches are common, and the person may experience neuritis and visual problems. After the first 2 years, a syphilis infection may follow a number of courses, but some 50 percent of those untreated are likely to develop inflammation of the aorta and other large blood vessels, or neurosyphilis leading to paralysis or other debilitating physical damage and mental degeneration.

The term syphilis comes from the thus infected hero of a 16th-century play by Girolamo Fracastero, a shepherd named Syphilis (which in Greek means 'lover of swine').

See also ASYMPTOMATIC NEUROSYPHILIS; CONGENITAL SYPHILIS; MENINGEAL NEUROSYPHILIS; MENINGOVASCULAR SYPHILIS; NEUROSYPHILIS; PARENCHYMATOUS NEUROSYPHILIS; PRE-COLUMBIAN THEORY OF SYPHILIS; GREAT IMITATOR.

syphilis innocentum a syphilis infection that was acquired by accidental contact with the disease organism rather than through intercourse.

syphilitic adenopathy a disease of the lymph glands resulting from an infection of syphilis. The lymph glands in the area of the original syphilis lesion, whether inguinal, cervical, or occurring elsewhere, become swollen and hard. The symptom commonly persists for some time after the primary syphilis lesion has disappeared.

syphilitic arteriosclerosis a degenerative condition of the arteries, marked by a loss of elasticity of the artery walls, resulting from syphilis.

syphilitic chancre a hard chancre that develops at the site of contact with a person infected with *Treponema pallidum* spirochaetes, particularly during the stage in which the disease organisms are multiplying rapidly in an exposed sore. The point of contact is usually an area of the genitals or mouth. Over a period of about a week, the initial lesion, a painless pimple, evolves into an ulcer—the hard chancre.

syphilitic conjunctivitis a form of conjunctivitis caused by an infection of syphilis and characterized by a variety of lesions of the eye, ranging from conjunctival chancres to gummas (soft tumours).

syphilitic vitiligo an acquired loss of skin pigmentation, especially around the neck, that is a sign of a second stage of syphilis. Also called vitiligo acquisita.

syphilization the development of a relative immunity to syphilis. According to some authorities, repeated exposure to syphilis over several generations in a community may lead to a relative immunity to the disease. There also have been some serious attempts to develop immunity to syphilis by inoculation with the disease organism, *Treponema pallidum*.

syphiloma a tumour that is related to a syphilis infection, such as a gumma.

syphilophobia a morbid fear of syphilis.

sypho an Australian colloquialism for syphilis.

S

tabetic curve a reaction pattern that occurs in the Lange-colloidal-gold test when a sample of cerebrospinal fluid from a patient suffering from meningovascular syphilis or tabes is added to a test tube containing the reagent. A statistical curve is derived by comparing results of a series of 10 different test tubes, each containing a different concentration of the test substance.

taboo a Polynesian term for an object, act, word, gesture, or person that is prohibited by social custom or religious belief in a particular society. Freud describes a taboo as follows: 'On the one hand it means to us sacred, consecrated; but on the other hand it means uncanny, dangerous, forbidden, and unclean.' Taboo examples are father-daughter-incest taboo, mother-son-incest taboo, and virginity taboo. Also spelled tabu and tapu. See also INCEST TABOO; SEXUAL TABOO; VIRGINITY TABOO; TABOONESS RATING OF DIRTY WORDS.

tabooness rating of dirty words a briefer term for a study conducted by Timothy B. Jay at Kent State University, USA in 1976 (*Maledicta*, Vol. I, No. 2). Twenty-eight words were ranked in the following order of offensiveness, or 'tabooness' (disregarding here the ranking for frequency, for male versus female responses, and for other criteria): (1) motherfucker, (2) cocksucker, (3) fuck, (4) pussy, (5) cunt, (6) prick, (7) cock, (8) bastard, (9) son of a bitch, (10) asshole, (11) suck, (12) nigger, (13) tits, (14) whore, (15) goddam, (16) shit, (17) bitch, (18) piss, (19) slut, (20) queer, (21) bullshit, (22) ass, (23) spic, (24) blow, (25) jesus christ, (26) damn, (27) hell, (28) pig.

(Unrelatedly, the US Supreme Court, on July 3, 1978, found seven of these terms to be 'indecent'; they were cocksucker, cunt, fuck, motherfucker, piss, shit and tits—numbers 2, 5, 3, 1, 18, 16, and 13 above.)

tactile stimulation sexual stimulation through the sense of touch during the state of foreplay preceding intercourse. A large proportion of the activities of both partners are tactile, including handholding and kissing and caressing any or all parts of the body, with special attention to the breasts and nipples, and to the buttocks, inner thighs, and genital organs. Licking, sucking, and biting are all tactile, as are tight embraces in which arms and legs are intertwined. All these tactile stimuli increase sexual excitement and prepare the way for intromission.

Tahitians inhabitants of Tahiti, one of the Society Islands in the South Pacific. The island has been called a 'sexual paradise,' based largely on the oft-quoted tale that Tahitian girls would swim out to passing boats in the nude offering themselves to the sailors. That reputation was perpetuated for a time by a religious group known as the Arioi Society, whose members worshipped the goddess of fertility by travelling from island to island as dancers, singers, and sexual exhibitionists. Today there is probably less promiscuity among Tahitians, because of colonialization, but other sexual customs have developed, such as institutionalized transvestites, called Mahu, who act as servants in the chief's household and frequently enter into homosexual relations with non-transvestite men.

tail a Shakespearean euphemism for (a) the vagina, (b) the penis, and (c) the buttocks. These meanings are still current in slang use, as well as the further meaning of tail as (d) sexual intercourse (for example, a man saying, 'I'd like to get some tail').

tail dater an American term referring to a system for meeting persons of the opposite sex by obtaining their identity through the registration number of their car. The technique was introduced in southern California where several commercial dating services provide bumper or windowstickers for men or women who, for a fee, supply their names and telephone numbers to be made available to tail daters.

taint an American slang term for the perineum, the area between the anus and the scrotum of a male or between the anus and the vagina of the female—'taint' because 'it ain't' the one or the other.

take it from behind a slang term meaning to be the passive partner in anal intercourse.

take the sheet a homosexual slang term meaning to be the passive partner in anal intercourse.

talent a collective informal term for the sexually attractive woman especially in the phrase 'eyeing up the local talent'.

tampon a roll of cellulose material designed to absorb the menstrual flow when inserted into the vagina.

Tantric love rite a Hindu sexual rite in which there is a gradual progression of physical and spiritual activities culminating in orgasm. The rite begins with enhancement of the environment with flowers, fruit, incense, music, and candlelight; next come bathing, then oiling and massaging each other, a period of meditation and alternate-nostril breathing, followed by humming a Mantra during which both partners envisage themselves as Shiva and Shakti, the Supreme Couple. The woman then places herself to the right of the man, and the man proceeds to kiss and stroke her entire body, from toes to head and back again. She then slowly arouses her male partner with her hands and lips in a similar order. Finally, the woman moves to the left of the man for the last stage of sexual fulfilment, in which various prearranged intercourse positions are employed until each of them experiences the 'transcendental power of love' during the climax.

taphophilia a morbid attraction for cemeteries. The term is related to necromania and necrophilia.

tart an obsolescent colloquial term for prostitute.

tattooing the tattoo-marking of various parts of the body—as for the purpose of enhancing physical attraction and sex appeal. The designs usually express sexual symbolism—for example, snakes, tigers, daggers, or the name of the loved one—and are applied to arms, legs, buttocks, breasts, back, and even the sex organs themselves. Tattoos are prevalent in the United States and Britain, but also in Japan, Africa and Oceania.

T-Cell a lymphocyte that is influenced in some way by the thymus gland, usually by passing through the thymus as it circulates through the body. Various kinds of T-cells can suppress or stimulate antibody production in responding to infectious organisms and the formation of tumours, and are capable of destroying some cells. T-cells are involved in natural resistance to sexually transmissible diseases, but in a case of AIDS may be overwhelmed by the infection. See also AIDS.

T-cell helper depletion a diagnostic factor in cases of AIDS. Because the HTLV-III virus destroys the helper T-cells that ordinarily engulf and devour microorganisms in the body, the human system gradually loses the battle as its T-cells are depleted. See also AIDS.

tear-drop prosthesis a female breast implant that produces the contour of a normal pendulous breast. It is recommended for women with abnormally small breasts and a minimum of 'feminine contour' to the rest of the body.

tearoom trade an American slang term for male homosexual activity that is based in public lavatories (the *tearooms*), where a sexual encounter may be conducted in a cubicle.

teasing in sexual behaviour, deliberate acts designed to provoke sexual interest or suggest availability for sexual activity. Teasing ranges from wearing revealing clothes to smiling and flirting, touching, kissing, and sex play short of intercourse. A vulgar slang term for a woman who keeps men dangling in this manner is 'cock-tease' or 'cock teaser'.

teddy-bear syndrome the tendency to form attachments in order to ensure a childlike emotional security rather than on the basis of the sort of compatibility appropriate to an adult relationship. It is often cited as a major reason for the breakdown of many marriages.

teenage pregnancy pregnancy that occurs in females under the age of 20, for whom the majority of births would be out of wedlock and presumably unintended. In 1985, the United States led nearly all developed nations of the world in teenage pregnancies, abortions, and births. The maximum difference in birthrates between the United States and other countries occurred among girls under the age of 15. The United States also was the only country where teenage pregnancy was increasing. The rate of pregnancies among girls 15 to 19 years of age was 96 per 1,000, compared with 14 per 1,000 in the Netherlands, 35 per 1,000 in Sweden, 43 per 1,000 in France, 44 per 1,000 in Canada, and 45 per 1,000 in England and Wales. The U.S. rate of abortions among teenagers ranged from about 10 per 1,000 at the age of 15 to over 60 per 1,000 at the age of 18. (The figures are from the Alan Guttmacher Institute).

teenage runaways teenage boys and girls who run away, usually to the 'big city', as a gesture of independence or an escape from an unhappy home or school situation. Many of them can be enticed into prostitution by pimps or the equivalent because of a desperate need for money and someone to care for them—and because they are unaware of the consequences of their sexual activities in terms of disease, drugs, beatings, involvement with the law, and, in general, a sordid life.

teenage sex the introduction of persons to sexual experience before adulthood.

teenybopper a slang term for a female teenager, especially one who identifies with the counterculture.

telegony the erroneous theory that a 'previous sire' exerts an influence on a later conception. As applied to humans, the theory holds that the offspring of a second husband might be affected by the wife's previous impregnation by her first husband, or simply by having had intercourse with him. However, any resemblance between the child and the first husband has to be regarded as purely coincidental. In the case of animals, the theory gains superficial credence from observations of female dogs, but here the resemblances can probably be explained from the fact that they remain in heat for several days and may mate with several males, making it possible to have a litter in which one or more puppies appear—falsely—to be a carryover from previous matings. Also called the previous-sire myth.

telephone scatalogia a psychosexual disorder in which a man achieves sexual gratification by making obscene, provocative telephone calls, usually to women chosen at random.

temperature eroticism the erotic pleasure of feeling warmth, especially being 'hot' as an accompaniment of sexual desire, fantasy, or activity. The immediate cause is probably increased flow of blood during sexual excite-ment, and the ultimate cause is the pleasure of warmth experienced when the individual was cuddled by the mother.

temple prostitution another term for sacred prostitution.

temptation the act of tempting, or a thing that tempts, especially into doing something one should not do. (But Oscar Wilde found that 'The only way to get rid of a temptation is to yield to it.')

tenderness feelings of warmth, closeness, affection, and caring associated with gentle expressions of love such as stroking, hugging, cuddling and kissing.

tenting effect a term applied to the dilatation of the inner end of the vagina during the plateau phase. It is during this phase that full vaginal expansion occurs.

teratocarcinoma a tumour, such as a testicular tumour, that contains trophoblastic or other embryonic tissues. Teratocarcinomas account for more than one third of all testicular cancers.

teratogen any agent, such as a chemical, virus, or radiation, that can cause foetal malformations or diseases. A teratogen usually disrupts some stage of normal development in an embryo or foetus, with the damage occurring in the first trimester. The classic teratogen, thalidomide, a tranquilizer, disrupts the normal development of arms and legs of a foetus if the mother takes the drug during the fourth week of a pregnancy, when the embryonic arm and leg buds first appear. Hearing and vision, which also first appear then, may be affected as well.

teratological effect a malformation found in a newborn infant that was probably induced by exposure of the mother to a teratogen during the early weeks of the pregnancy and which cannot be attributed to a genetic defect or injury inflicted during labour. Teratological effects may include abnormal vision, hearing deficits, mental retardation, and missing body parts.

teratomatous rest a tumour that evolves from misplaced embryonic tissue and secretes large quantities of chorionic gonadotropin hormone. The effect is sexual precocity, particularly in the male who may show true sexual maturity in childhood. However, the tumour is cancerous and usually spreads throughout the body before the cause of the sexual precocity can be corrected.

teratophobia a morbid fear of monsters; also, fear of giving birth to a monstrously deformed or disfigured child.

terebinth a member of the turpentine tree family, one variety of which is the source of an aromatic resin called mastic. Mastic is mixed with salep, a starch made from dried orchid tubers, to produce an alleged aphrodisiac used in India.

term the end of the normal gestation period of between 38 and 42 weeks. The word may refer to the infant born alive during the span of 38 to 42 weeks. (It has also been used to refer to the menses, as in menstrual term.) An infant born before the 38th week is described as preterm, and one born after the 42nd week may be called postterm.

tertiary sex characteristics a term sometimes applied to personality (as contrasted with physical) characteristics of the sexes. These characteristics are now being questioned, but many people associate masculinity with greater physical confidence and endurance, aggressiveness, emotional self-control, and economic competitiveness; and femininity with greater altruism, tenderness, emotionality, and interest in child rearing and homemaking.

testes the plural of TESTIS. See this entry.

testicle an alternative term for TESTIS. See this entry.

testicular agenesis a congenital absence of normal testicular tissue in a male, resulting in a lack of secondary male sexual characteristics. The individual possesses vestigial wolffian ducts terminating in nodules that represent primitive testes that failed to develop normally.

testicular atrophy a loss of function and degeneration of a testis because of disease or injury. Atrophy of a testis may result from an interruption of the blood supply, an infection such as syphilis, the mumps, or filariasis. Congenital syphilis can be the cause of a condition known as 'pigeon's-egg testicle', which may appear large but defective. Interruption of the blood supply, which can occur during surgery, may cause the testis to become both small and functionless.

testicular biopsy a method of obtaining a small sample of a male testicle for study of possible causes of infertility or other problems. A local anesthetic is used to deaden the feeling of the testes, and a small incision is made until the tunica albuginea is visible. Unless there is evidence of a problem elsewhere, such as the vas deferens, a sample of a single testis is usually representative of the condition of the general contents of the scrotum. The single testis sample should show the condition of the Sertoli cells, seminiferous tubules, and other structures. The biopsy is usually coordinated with a semen analysis. The scrotal incision can in most cases be sealed with a couple of sutures after the biopsy sample is taken.

testicular cord an alternative term for spermatic cord.

testicular elevation the involuntary lifting of the testes within the scrotum during excitement. The lifting of the testes, by automatic action of the muscle fibres within the scrotum, is a necessary step towards male orgasm.

testicular failure any dysfunction of the various parts of the testes, resulting in infertility. Causes can include failure of the interstitial cells to produce testosterone, blockage of the vas deferens, or a similar disorder.

testicular feminization an abnormal condition in which a male has the normal complement of an XY set of chromosomes but his body fails to respond to the stimulation of androgenic hormones. As a result, he may develop some feminine characteristics.

testicular tumour a cause of sexual precocity in boys. The features usually are unique in that the child may have pubic hair and an enlarged penis, because of male-sex-hormone production by the testicular tumour, but only one testis is involved. Thus, the scrotum on the side containing the tumour may appear mature, but the testis on the unaffected side remains infantile. The asymmetry of the testicles is a diagnostic sign of the cause of the apparent sexual maturity.

testis the male gonad, which is suspended in the scrotum by the spermatic cord. In foetal life, the testes (which is the plural) are located in the abdominal cavity and normally descend into the scrotum before birth, becoming covered in their passage through the inguinal canal with various layers of muscle and connective tissue. The layers include fibres of the cremasteric muscle, and internal and external spermatic fascia, and the tunica vaginalis. Blood vessels and nerves are found in the tissue layers surrounding each testis. The tunica vaginalis is a membrane pouch derived from tissues of the peritoneum, which covers the visceral organs. The tunica vaginalis actually forms in the scrotum before the arrival of the testes from their prenatal location in the abdomen. Each testis contains hundreds of coneshaped lobules—experts differ on the precise number—which in turn contain the seminiferous tubules in which the spermatozoa are produced. The tubules are supported by the interstitial cells which are the source of the male sex hormone testosterone. The lobules have openings that merge as they approach the ductus deferens so that the mature spermatozoa leave the seminiferous tubules by one of the several dozen relatively large ducts feeding into the head of the epididymis. Although each testis is about 1.5 inches long, the left testicle may appear larger because it usually hangs lower. (The reason is that the left spermatic cord is longer.) Also called testicle.

See also ABDOMINAL TESTICLE; APPENDIX TESTIS; ARRESTED TESTIS; CONGESTED TESTICLES; ECTOPIC TESTIS; FEMORAL TESTICLE; HYPERMOBILE TESTES; MALPOSITION OF TESTES; MEDIASTINUM TESTIS; PARENCHYMA TESTIS; PERINEAL TESTICLE; PUBOSCROTAL TESTICLE; RETRACTILE TESTIS; RUDIMENTARY TESTIS; WOLF TESTICLES.

testis cords the embryonic structure of the male reproductive system that will evolve into the seminiferous tubules.

testolactone an oestrogen inhibitor administered to infertile men whose low sperm count is associated with excessive levels of the female sex hormone.

testosterone the male sex hormone secreted by the interstitial cells of the testis. It is the most potent of all the natural male sex hormones. Variations of the hormone include ethinyl testosterone, which has some of the pharmacological activity of the female sex hormone progesterone; methyl testosterone, a derivative that can be administered orally; testosterone phenylpropionate; and testosterone propionate, a long-acting version of the hormone that can be administered by injection.

testosterone cypionate an injectable form of testosterone supplement for men with sexual dysfunction resulting from abnormally low levels of the male sex hormone. Injection every 3 to 4 weeks reportedly restores potency in many cases of impotence.

testosterone deprivation the effects of castration of the male, whose testosterone hormone is produced in the testes. The effect is observed in birds and other animals, in addition to male humans.

test-tube baby an infant whose conception was produced outside the human body. A test-tube baby is conceived by fertilizing an ovum extracted from the woman with spermatozoa obtained from the man under carefully controlled conditions in a laboratory dish.

The fertilized ovum is then implanted in the uterus of the woman.

TFR abbreviation for total fertility rate.

Thai beads an alternative name for vaginal balls. Also called *Thailand beads*, and by a variety of other names.

thalidomide a tranquilizer developed in Germany, in 1953 and marketed as a 'safe' sedative. In animal tests it was found that the drug had virtually no toxic effects in massive doses and therefore would be a suitable substitute for barbiturates because it would be virtually impossible for a patient to take a lethal overdose. In 1960, however, it was discovered that pregnant women who took thalidomide were delivered of deformed children with a variety of defects. The most common birth defect was phocomelia, or arms and legs that were extremely short or with parts missing. In retrospective research, it was found that thousands of women with children so afflicted had taken doses of thalidomide during the fourth week of pregnancy, when the embryonic limb buds were forming. Those who took the drug on days when the eyes or ears were forming gave birth to infants with visual or hearing difficulties. Thalidomide was taken off the market. One important test that had not been performed on the drug was one that would demonstrate the safety of thalidomide during pregnancy. Since the thalidomide tragedy, women have been advised to use extreme caution in taking *any* drug during pregnancy because medical studies now indicate that many drugs, including alcohol, can cause birth defects. (Ironically, thalidomide is now known to have beneficial effects in the treatment of leprosy, a disease which itself can have disfiguring effects. However, thalidomide is never given to female leprosy patients with child-bearing potential.)

theca externa a layer of thick, dense connective tissue fibres that forms an outer protective layer around the ovarian follicle. It is adjacent to the theca interna layer, with which it forms a double-layered envelope.

theca interna a layer of tissue cells round the ovarian follicle. It is rich with blood capillaries and lymph vessels interspersed with connective tissue. After the rupture of the follicle releasing the ovum, the theca interna provides the capillaries that support the formation of the corpus luteum.

thecoma a functioning tumour of the ovary that secretes female sex hormones. The tumour is generally found in a postmenopausal woman. It causes irregular menstrual bleeding, breast enlargement, and increased sex drive.

thelalgia a pain experienced in the breast nipple.

thelarche a form of premature puberty in which the female breasts develop in childhood. The cause is usually benign and not the effect of a tumour or other serious disorder. (Greek *thele*, 'nipple', and *arche*, 'beginning.')

thelasis a medical term for suckling, or breast feeding.

thelerethism an erection of the nipple as a result of stimulation, as in sexual foreplay, which causes contraction of the muscle fibres of the nipple (Greek *thele*, 'nipple,' and *erethisma*, 'stirring').

thelitis an inflammation of the breast nipple.

thelyblast the nucleus of a zygote, or fertilized ovum (Greek *thelys*, 'female').

thelygenic pertaining to a pattern of giving birth only to female offspring.

thelygonia the production of ova containing only the female (X) sex chromosome. Technically, the term applies to all ova because only the male gametes contain the male, or Y, chromosome.

thelymania an obsolete term for satyriasis.

thelyplasm the portion of a gamete, male or female, that contains the female (X) sex chromosome material.

theoretical failure rate the failure rate of a contraceptive under hypothetical conditions in which nothing goes wrong.

theory of ovum viability the concept that the survival of an individual is related to the viability of the fertilized egg from which he or she develops. The theory is based on experiments with nonhuman mammals in which viability varied according to the amount of time elapsing between ovulation and fertilization of the ovum. Extrapolated to humans, the theory suggests that—excluding environmental factors such as accidents—the quality of the egg cell at fertilization influences the survival of the person.

therapeutic abortion an induced abortion performed to protect the life or physical or mental health of the mother. A therapeutic abortion also might be performed if prenatal evidence indicates that the foetus if born would suffer a severe physical or mental handicap.

therapeutic lovemaking a term referring to Oriental sexual practices based on the Taoist and Tantric doctrine that specific coital postures and rhythms can have a healing effect

by enabling the body to correct imbalances; for example, some positions enhance circulation of the blood, and others strengthen the bones, rest the spirit, increase the production of marrow, or adjust the whole system. Each of these benefits is believed to be achieved not only by its special 'love posture', but by a specific number of 'strokes of love' by the man, as well as a specific amount of daily practice.

thigh sandwich another term for femoral intercourse.

third sex a mythological tribe living north of the Black Sea who were reputed to be ambisexual. Writings of Plato and Herodotus referred to the tribe, and Plato suggested that the third-sex people eventually died out.

Today, the term may be applied to homosexuals when viewed as a sex that is separate and distinct from male or female.

Thonga an agricultural society in Mozambique, organized along polygynous lines, with the sororal type preferred. In this society, kissing is regarded as revolting because of the contact with another person's saliva. Elongated labia minora are considered sexually exciting, and attempts are made to stretch them. Ritual copulation is commonly practised, and widows are required to perform ritual intercourse to cleanse themselves of the spirit of the dead husband; and the headman must have ritual intercourse with his principal wife on the site chosen for a new village.

three F's, the a 19th-century male bragging phrase meaning 'fuck, fun, and a footrace.' A similar attitude is reflected in the FOUR-F METHOD. See this entry.

three-inch fool a Shakesperean term for a man with a short penis, as in *The Taming of the Shrew* (IV, 1, lines 25-27): '*Curtis*: Away, you three-inch fool! ... *Grumio*: Am I but three inches? Why, thy horn is a foot, and so long am I at the least.'

thrush a disease of the mucous membranes, characterized by white patches, or plaques, in the mouth and vagina, and caused by infection by a fungus, *Candida albicans*. See CANDIDA INFECTION.

thyme a small grey-green shrub that has been the source of medicines and food flavourings since at least the days of Theophrastus, in the 4th century B.C. One of its virtues was said to be its aphrodisiac quality. It also was grown as a plant that attracted honey bees, and honey was always an ingredient of aphrodisiacs.

T

Tikopia inhabitants of a small island in the Pacific Ocean east of the Solomons. Their characteristic sexual customs include coitus interruptus as a means of birth control; adoption of a side-by-side facing position during intercourse; a taboo among males against touching their own genitals or those of their female partners; and the use of bananas and roots as dildos. In this society bride capture was practised at one time: A young woman was abducted from her father's house and taken to the house of her future husband, where a proclamation of marriage was made at a ritual feast.

timing of intercourse preferred times for intercourse. In Western cultures most couples make love during the quiet of the night, though fatigue may interfere with full pleasure if the hour is late. For the sake of variety, they may also change the time to the morning or midday, with an occasional spontaneous 'quickie' at other times, especially on holiday.

tinea cruris a ringworm infection of the genital area caused by any of several fungal organisms, including *Epidermophyton floccosom, Trichophyton interdigitàle,* or *Trichophyton rubrum.* The infection is named after its location, being derived from the Latin *crus* which is sometimes used to refer to the genital area of the leg or thigh.

tinkle a British euphemism for urination, used particularly in the phrase 'have a tinkle'.

titillatione mammarum a Latin term for coitus intra mammas, once used by prostitutes who specialized in that form of sexual activity and employed the term in advertising their availability.

tits a vulgar slang term for the female breasts. The term, in use for at least 300 years, ranks number 13 in the TABOONESS RATING OF DIRTY WORDS. See this entry.

tits man a man who is attracted by the female breasts as primary turn-on, also called a 'breast man', as distinguished from the ARSE MAN and the LEG MAN. See these entries.

titties a colloquial term for the female breasts.

T.L.C. a common abbreviation for tender loving care.

T-mycoplasma a type of bacteria responsible for a genital tract disease called ureaplasma urealyticum. A related species, *F. mycoplasma,* is believed responsible for many cases of infertility. It has been found in the cervical mucus of infertile women and on the middle piece of the spermatozoa of infertile men.

tobacco stains brown endometrial cysts that are found on the peritoneal membranes of the pelvis. They are caused by the presence of misplaced endometrial tissue, which normally lines the uterus. They are generally noncancerous and cause few if any symptoms. But like endometrial tissue elsewhere, they are under the influence of female sex hormones and react to menstrual cycles like the endometrium of the uterus.

tocoergometry a measurement of the expulsive force of the uterus in childbirth.

tocomania a mental disturbance that sometimes follows childbirth (Greek *tokos,* 'birth', and *mania,* 'madness').

tocopherol the generic chemical name for vitamin E, an essential nutrient in maintaining a normal pregnancy. Tocopheryl acetate is used in the treatment of habitual abortion. Because of its role in reproduction, it was given its chemical name at the time the substance was first isolated, in 1936.

tocophobia a morbid dread of childbirth.

Todas buffalo herders of southern India whose society is organized along polyandrous lines, usually of the fraternal type, with brothers sharing the same wife. Wives may also have several officially recognized lovers, just as men in other societies have several concubines. In selecting these lovers, one of the major qualifications is strength and skill, especially in catching buffalo for ritual feasts.

tôles d'abattage (tôl' däbätäzh'; French, 'slaughter tables' or 'demolition tables') the cheapest kind of mass brothels in Paris in the mid-19th century. It appears that tables were used instead of beds.

tom a British slang term for prostitute.

tomboy a girl who behaves in a manner commonly associated with boys, preferring rough-and-tumble play and the company of boys to pursuits and companions that are ordinarily considered feminine. Such girls are usually going through a stage of rebellion against the restrictions involved in being a 'little lady', as expected in many homes and schools. They usually outgrow their tomboy tendencies (unless they have a high androgen level), and a few become female homosexuals.

tongue kiss another term for 'French kiss'.

tool a slang term for penis.

tooth alteration filing, blackening, reddening, drilling, pulling, or knocking out teeth for purposes of enhancing sexual attractiveness. These practices are not uncommon among some African societies and Australian aborigines, especially in connection with initiation ceremonies.

topless a colloquial term meaning (a) bare-breasted, especially when referring to dancers, waitresses, and other women in service or entertainment functions, (b) featuring such women, when referring to restaurants, nightclubs, and other places serving the public, or (c) tailored in such a way that the breasts are exposed, when referring to a garment. The term is also used as a noun in American English, as in 'She works as a topless,' 'Let's go to a topless,' or 'All her toplesses were designed in Paris.'

topless radio in American English meaning a phone-in programme in which callers can air their sexual problems, and *topless TV* is a programme that may feature a topless or entirely nude hostess, sometimes with a nude male, and which is usually, but not always, a phone-in show.

top man the active male homosexual partner in anal intercourse—the opposite of the 'bottom man'.

topos (Greek, 'place') a euphemism for lavatory in the 19th century.

TORCH an acronym for remembering the types of infectious organisms that can cause congenital defects in an embryo or foetus. The initials stand for *T*oxoplasmosis, *O*ther, *R*ubella, *C*ytomegalovirus, and *H*erpes simplex. The 'other' is generally a euphemism for syphilis.

torsion of the testicle an abnormal rotation of a testicle, resulting in interruption of the blood supply. The condition must be corrected by surgical incision into the scrotum to straighten the spermatic cord. If not corrected early, the interrupted blood flow can result in gangrene, requiring castration to save the life of the man.

TOSOS abbreviation for The Other Side Of Silence, a U.S. homosexual group founded by the playwright Doric Wilson. The term may also refer to the homosexual community in general.

toss off a British slang term meaning to masturbate.

total fertility rate (TFR) the average number of children that would be born alive to a woman during her lifetime if she conformed to an age-specific fertility rate of a given year for her entire childbearing span of life. Unlike the crude birthrate, the TFR is independent of the age structure of a population.

total hysterectomy the removal of the entire uterus, usually through an abdominal wall incision, but sometimes vaginally. The total hysterectomy removes the cervix as well as the body of the uterus, as compared with the subtotal hysterectomy, in which the cervix remains after the body of the uterus is excised.

totem an animal, plant, or natural force such as rain that is revered as the tribal ancestor, symbol, tutelary spirit, or protector of a clan. Members of the clan are forbidden to destroy the totem and often may not have sexual relations with each other—which Freud interpreted in terms of prevention of incest (*Totem and Taboo*, 1913).

touching tactile contact with another person as a way of expressing affection or as a means of stimulating erogenous zones during sexual foreplay.

touch up a slang term meaning to touch someone in a sexually sensitive place as a form of furtive sexual advance. For example, a man trying to put his hand up a woman's skirt might be said to be 'touching her up'.

Tourette's syndrome a lifelong disorder starting in childhood, characterized by episodes of involuntary muscle spasms in various parts of the body, vocal tics such as barks, yelps, grunts, and an uncontrollable urge to utter obscenities (coprolalia). The condition was first described by the French physician Georges Gilles de la Tourette, in 1885. Also called Gilles de la Tourette's syndrome.

toxaemia of pregnancy any of a series of conditions that may affect a pregnant woman, such as eclampsia, preeclampsia, gestational hypertension, gestational oedema, gestational proteinuria, or hyperemesis gravidarum.

toxic-shock syndrome (TSS) a combination of symptoms of fever, headache, confusion, vomiting, diarrhoea, and rapidly falling blood pressure caused by an infection of *Staphylococcus aureus*, a bacterium commonly found on the skin and the lining of the genitals. An outbreak of 850 cases of the disease in the USA in 1980 was attributed to the use by some women of superabsorbent menstrual tampons. The effects were caused by a toxin produced by the bacterium.

toy boy a derogatory term for a woman's younger male lover. It usually carries the implication that the woman is providing for the man financially, and that he is regarded as little more than a sex object. See also CRADLE SNATCHING.

TPAL letters used in a system of classifying women who have been pregnant or have borne children. The letters indicate the *total* number of pregnancies, *p*remature infants, *a*bortions, and number of *l*iving children.

transcervical uterine aspiration the removal of fluid, products of conception, or abnormal endometrial tissue by suction. The procedure is commonly used in firsttrimester abortions, a technique sometimes identified as vacuum curettage. The cervix is dilated approximately 1 millimetre per week of gestation, and a vacuum tip of about the same diameter is inserted and rotated around the uterine cavity. A local anaesthetic is used, and the procedure usually lasts less than 3 minutes.

transference love a Freudian term for feelings of strong affection and attachment experienced by the patient towards the analyst during the process of therapy. Because psychoanalysis involves the transference, or 'projection,' of unconscious feelings originally directed towards the parents, and the process of 'working through' these feelings, the patient temporarily directs feelings of love (as well as anger) towards the analyst. This is an artifact of the process, because it is a reenactment of infantile feelings unrelated to the character or even the sex of the analyst as a person. Also called positive transference.

transgenderism a gender-identity disorder in which a person strongly identifies with the opposite sex and may cross-dress, yet does not wish to undergo sex-change surgery. The confusion of sex roles usually stems from a failure of one or both parents to provide adequate sex-role models.

transitional double standard a variation in the traditional or orthodox double-standard concept regarding premarital sex. While the traditional double standard accepts premarital sex for males but not for females, transitional double-standard rules accept the notion that premarital sex for females is acceptable if they are in love or engaged.

transsexualism a gender-identity disorder characterized by a persistent sense of discomfort and inappropriateness with one's anatomical sex, as well as an obsessive need to change one's sex organs and live and dress as a member of the other sex. According to the American Psychiatric Association, the diagnosis is made only if the condition has been continuous for at least 2 years and does not stem from other mental disorders, such as schizophrenia, and is not associated with physical intersex or genetic abnormality.

transurethral referring to a method of examining and treating disorders of the prostrate gland through the urethra. Electroscopic instruments are inserted through the urethral opening at the end of the penis, through the penile and other segments of the urethra, and into the prostate gland and bladder, if necessary. The lighted instruments allow the surgeon to see into the prostate and manipulate devices within the shaft of the instrument for cutting away bits of offending tissue.

transverse birth a 'presentation' occurring once in 200 births, in which the foetus lies crosswise with the arm, shoulder or hand entering the birth canal first. During labour the foetus must be turned, or a caesarean section may be indicated.

transvestism a psychosexual disorder usually characterized by a persistent, often compulsive, urge to wear clothes of the opposite sex as a means of achieving sexual excitement. Cross-dressing, as it is also called, is usually observed among basically heterosexual males whose sexual experience with women is limited, and who may have occasionally engaged in homosexual acts. In many cases their mothers dressed them as girls in childhood because their mother (or father) wanted a girl child. In some instances cross-dressing was used as a 'petticoat (or pinafore) punishment.'

traumatic avulsion an injury to the male genitalia in which the skin of the scrotum and occasionally the penis is torn away in an accident involving powerful machinery. Traumatic avulsion is a hazard of mechanized farming. The mishap leaves exposed the testicles, which must be surgically reimplanted under the skin of the thigh unless enough skin remains to generate a new scrotum. A skin graft may be needed to speed the healing of the scrotum.

traumatic epididymitis a form of epididymitis that often develops after strenuous physical activity in a young man. It is believed to result from a backflow of urine or prostate secretion from the prostatic portion of the urethra during physical effort, rather than from direct injury to the epididymal tissues.

travail an archaic term for labour pains.

treatment of impotence a therapeutic process in which the primary objective is that of overcoming the 'fear-of-failure' factor in impotence. The therapy requires the active participation of the sexual partner and the creation of an atmosphere in which the male does not feel any pressure to perform, but instead is allowed to relax and enjoy body-contact pleasures and the emotional interaction of lovemaking. The process may involve stimulating the penis to an erection several times without requiring coitus.

trial marriage an informal marriage arrangement in which a couple agree to a trial period in which they live together and test their relationship more deeply and comprehensively than is possible during the courting process. They also try to resolve any difficulties they encounter and thereby reduce the possibility of divorce after actual marriage. They usually agree not to have children during the trial period.

tribadism a lesbian practice in which one partner lies on top of the other and simulates coitus by rubbing the genitals together. The partner who plays the 'male' role usually has an especially large clitoris and is called a *tribade*. (Greek *tribein*, 'to rub'.)

TRIC agents a group of chlamydia disease organisms that are strains of *Chlamydia trachomatis* and are responsible for such sexually transmissible disorders as lymphogranuloma venereum; nongonococcal urethitis, pelvic inflammatory disease, and Reiter's syndrome. TRIC agents were originally believed to be viruses but have now been classified as bacteria.

Trichomonas vaginitis an infection of the vaginal tract by a protozoon, *Trichomonas vaginalis*. The effects of the infection include irritation, redness caused by an increased blood flow, swelling of the vulva, and painful intercourse. The condition is also marked by a profuse white discharge, and painful or difficult urination. The Trichomonas organism can be present in the urogenital tract of the male, who may not feel any symptoms although he is capable of reinfecting a female sex partner and should be treated with an antifungal drug, such as metronidazole (Flagyl), at the same time as the female patient.

trichomoniasis an infection by a flagellate (whiplike) protozoon which often occurs in the human vagina. It may produce a copious white fluid but does not invade the uterus. However, it can be transmitted by sexual contact, causing urethritis in men and vaginitis in women.

trick a slang term for a prostitute's client. The word also is used by homosexual males to distinguish a temporary sex partner from a 'lover'.

trick baby a slang term for a prostitute's child who was fathered by a client.

trilobular pertaining to three lobes, a term that may be applied to the presence of three lobes of prostate tissue that have overgrown the base of the urinary bladder so as to obstruct normal flow of urine. It is one of several variations of prostatic hypertrophy.

trim a slang term for sexual intercourse.

triolism a triadic (or triangular) relationship in which a man engages in sexual relations with a woman and then looks on while she has relations with another man or woman. Similarly, a woman may have intercourse with a man then watches him have relations with another woman or man. The term is also applied by some sexologists to a simultaneous sexual relationship involving three persons (one male and two females or the reverse); in this case they usually engage in a combination of coitus with oral-genital stimulation. Also called troilism.

triorchid a male with three testicles.

triple-X condition a congenital abnormality of some women who have a normal female body but whose body cells contain an extra X, or female sex, chromosome. Fertility is not affected, but the incidence of mental retardation is higher among triple-X females than in the general population. A woman with this condition is called a superfemale, metafemale, or poly-X female.

Trobrianders inhabitants of a Melanesian island in the western Pacific who engage in fishing, gardening, woodcarving, and basket making. Marriage is primarily monogamous although polygyny is permitted. Among their sexual customs are sex expeditions by women as well as men; nose rubbing without kissing; no prostitution, though gifts are given to sex partners; erotic festivals; no punishment for rape; and no attempt at contraception (linked to the belief that men are not necessary for conception).

troilism an alternative term for triolism.

TSS abbreviation for toxic shock syndrome. See this entry.

Tswana a large society living in Botswana in which subsistence is dependent on products of animal husbandry and farming. Marriage is generally polygamous, with the sororal form preferred. Sex is performed frequently (usually two or three times a night); in contrast to most primitive societies, foreplay includes sucking and kissing the woman's breasts; co-wives may engage in homosexual acts, especially when the husband is away; and prominent labia minora are considered a major sexual attraction, and from the onset of puberty, girls pull at them, and may even resort to killing a bat, burning its wings, and smearing the ashes on cuts made around the labia so that they will become 'as big as the wings of a bat.'

tubal abortion the termination of an ectopic pregnancy within a fallopian tube. Tubal abortions usually occur spontaneously when the pressures of the developing embryo cause the tube to rupture.

tubal abscess an abscess that can form in one or both fallopian tubes of a woman as a complication of a gonorrhoeal infection. The condition may be marked by fever, colicky pain, and menstrual irregularity and discomfort.

tubal insufflation a method of testing the patency (opening) through the fallopian tubes by injecting a gas, such as carbon dioxide, into the uterus. If the gas can pass through the fallopian tubes, a wavy pattern is recorded on an instrument attached to the tube leading into the uterus. If the fallopian tube is obstructed, the pattern will be recorded as a flat curve. The test is used in establishing a cause for infertility.

tubal ligation a surgical sterilization procedure for females in which both fallopian tubes are blocked by applying ligatures, or sutures, that constrict the opening through the tube. Among the various techniques used are the following. In the Irving operation the tubes are ligated (tied off), then severed, with one end buried in the muscle tissue of the uterus and the other end buried in a nearby ligament. The Madlener operation involves crushing of the middle section of the tube, which is tied with a nonabsorbable suture material. The Pomeroy operation is one in which the tube is ligated with absorbable material in the middle, then severed. Other techniques are the Uchida operation, the Kroener fimbriectomy procedure, and laparoscopic tubal fulguration. The Madlener, Pomeroy, and Kroener tubal ligations can be performed through the vagina so that an incision through the abdominal wall is not necessary. Abdominal approaches, such as laparoscopic tubal fulguration, can be relatively simple, requiring only a local anaesthetic. The woman is admitted in the morning and sedated. A small incision is made through the abdomen just below the umbilicus, and the tube is lifted through the incision, to be ligated. The operation itself is usually painless and requires less than a half hour. The woman is observed for several hours for

possible side effects or complications and usually returns home the same day. Any abdominal discomfort can usually be treated with aspirin-type drugs.

tubal pregnancy an ectopic pregnancy that occurs in a fallopian tube. It is the most common form of ectopic pregnancy. The tube is likely to rupture as the pregnancy develops, causing the placenta and embryo, or foetus, to drop into the abdominal cavity, where it becomes a tuboabdominal pregnancy. It may also result in a spontaneous abortion.

tubectomy the surgical excision of a fallopian tube.

tuberculosis prostatitis a form of tuberculosis that involves the prostate gland, replacing the normal prostate tissue with fibrous growth and calcification. The condition is generally painless; it is found in about 12 percent of all terminal cases of tuberculosis.

tuberculous endosalpingitis a disease of the fallopian tubes caused by tuberculosis. The disease is insidious and difficult to diagnose because the woman may experience only menstrual difficulty and a dull pain in the pelvic area. Meanwhile, the fallopian tube may become inflamed and filled with cheese-like pus. The disease is often discovered only during examination to determine a cause of infertility.

tubular testicular adenoma a type of tumour that is found in the gonads of hermaphrodites, the undescended testicles of otherwise normal males, and the ovaries of otherwise normal females who suffer only from amenorrhoea. Because of the frequency of occurrence of the tissue in several genital anomalies, some authorities have attempted to find a correlation. The tissue of the tubular testicular adenoma also is similar to that of the masculinizing-adrenal-gland tumours.

tufting a complication of salpingitis in which the ampullary, or open, end of the fallopian tube is changed so that only a small tuft of fimbriae extends from a closed or partly closed opening. It is, for practical purposes, an obstruction to fertility.

Tukano a Native American society in Brazil whose members believe a pregnant woman should avoid intercourse altogether to keep the number of foetuses from piling up to a point where she may explode. Among the Tukano practices are insertion of a finger into the vagina of girls by an impotent old man as a means of defloration; the requirement that a boy have intercourse with his mother in the presence of his father as part of his coming-of-age ritual; and extreme sexual aggression among women, to a point where seduction of men is a common occurrence and many husbands seek relief by giving their wives anaphrodisiacs.

tumescence a swelling or engorgement that causes enlargement, as in the erection of the penis or clitoris during sexual stimulation.

tunica albuginea a covering of white collagenous fibres that forms a sheath over each of the testes.

Tupinambá a Native American society of hunters and farmers living around Rio de Janeiro. The most prevalent form of marriage is monogamy, though polygyny is permitted. The men wear penis sheaths, and at one time let poisonous animals bite their penises so that they swelled to such a size that women could hardly stand them. Both men and women believe that 'the woman is simply the greenhouse in which a man's seed grows to become a child,' as the anthropologist Edgar Gregersen puts it.

Turkish culture a colloquial term for anal intercourse.

Turner-Ombredanne orchidopexy a surgical procedure for correcting an undescended testicle by suturing it into a compartment on the opposite side of the scrotum, between the septum (middle wall) and the normal testis.

Turner's syndrome a condition in which the gonads fail to develop, usually occurring in females who also manifest a webbing of the neck, short stature, scoliosis, and other physical abnormalities. The cause is a sex-chromosome aberration in which the woman acquires only one X chromosome. She usually has 'streak ovaries' instead of functioning gonads and does not ovulate. Also called ovarian agenesis of Turner; XO monosomy.

TURP an abbreviation for transurethral resection of the prostate—a procedure to correct an obstruction of the urinary flow in a male that is caused by an overgrowth of prostate-gland tissue. The obstruction is removed via the urethra (transurethral) and by cutting away a portion (resection) of the prostate. The procedure is performed with the aid of an endoscope inserted through the urethra for visual control of the resectioning. Also called TUR.

tush a colloquial American term for (a) the buttocks or (b) the vagina.

TV an abbreviation sometimes used for transvestite, particularly by members of the transsexual subcultures. A transvestite will use the abbreviation in classified advertisements of underground newspapers to attract persons interested in having sexual contacts with a transvestite.

TV style a slang term for intercourse in 'doggie fashion'. Both can watch TV.

twat a vulgar term for vagina, used since the 17th century.

21-hydroxylase deficiency a congenital defect resulting in the inability of the body's steroid-hormone processes to synthesize desoxycorticosterone from progesterone, one of the steps toward the synthesis of aldosterone hormone. Progesterone is converted instead into 17-ketosteroids, leading to an excessive accumulation of the adrenal hormone. It is the most common congenital defect in the body's steroidogenesis system and may be either partial or complete.

21:7 pill programme a method of administering oral contraceptives to women who take a pill containing the female sex hormones each day for 21 days, then stop for 7 days to permit menstruation to begin. The woman begins the next cycle of 21 pills after 7 days regardless of when menstruation actually begins. The ritual helps the woman remember the routine because she always starts taking the contraceptive pills on the same day of the week. An alternative approach is to include 7 placebo pills to be taken between the 21-day contraceptive pills.

twins either of two general types of twins: fraternal, also called dizygotic or biovular; or identical, also called monozygotic or uniovular. See BIOVULAR; BOY-GIRL IDENTICAL TWINS; DIZYGOTIC TWINS; FRATERNAL TWINS; IDENTICAL TWINS; MONOZYGOTIC TWINS; UNIOVULAR TWINS.

twixter an obsolete term for (a) a boyish girl or (b) a girlish boy.

two-backed beast, to do the an old literary term meaning to have face-to-face intercourse. See BEAST WITH TWO BACKS, TO MAKE THE.

two-digit system a classification system for recording the number of times a woman has been pregnant and the number of viable offspring. The system uses the symbols 0 and i (ii, iii, etc.) separated by a solidus. Thus, a woman who is pregnant for the first time is recorded as 0/i; if the pregnancy ends with a viable infant, the record is changed to i/i. A second pregnancy is recorded as i/ii whether or not it is successfully carried to term. The system simply records parity/gravidity.

Type A and Type B the commonly identified

psychological types of personality, with Type A representing the uptight, deadline-orientated individual and Type B the 'laid-back,' easy-going person. In tests of sexual behaviour by psychologists, it was found that Type A men could perform mathematical problems requiring concentration while listening to an erotic audiotape while Type B men were unable to concentrate on sexual and nonsexual events at the same time.

Tyson's glands the oil-secreting glands on the inner surfaces of the foreskin and the corona of the glans penis. The glandular secretion contributes to the formation of smegma; a lubricating substance.

Tzanck test a laboratory test for genital herpes, utilizing tissue scraped from a lesion. The tissue sample is stained with a dye that helps identify the herpes virus under a microscope.

u/c a common abbreviation meaning 'uncut' (that is, uncircumcised)—as a code word in 'personal' ads.

ultimate kiss a colloquial term for 'deep throat' fellatio.

umbilical cord the cord that connects the foetus with the placenta and provides a means for the flow of nutrients from the maternal blood supply to the foetus and for the removal of waste products from foetal metabolism. The umbilical cord is about 20 inches long and 1 inch thick and contains two arteries and one vein. The vein carries oxygenated blood to the foetus, and the arteries return the deoxygenated blood to the placenta. At birth, the umbilical cord is clamped or ligated and severed. The stump atrophies and falls off in about a week, leaving the navel, or belly button. Also called funis.

Ugandan a euphemistic adjective coined by the satirical magazine *Private Eye* denoting sexual activity—thus 'Ugandan negotiations' are sexual intercourse.

unconsummated marriage marriage in which the husband and wife have not had intercourse. In a study of 1,000 verified virgin wives, who had been married between 1 and 21 years, it was found that the largest proportion cited fear of pain as a reason for avoiding intercourse (20 percent). The second most common reason (18 percent) was that sex was considered to be nasty or wicked. About 12 percent reported their husbands were impotent, 5 percent said that they were lesbians, and 9 percent expressed a general dislike of men or the penis or had a fear of semen. Nearly 14 percent indicated a lack of knowledge about sex anatomy, either misbelieving that the vagina was too small to accommodate an erect penis or claiming ignorance about the exact location of the female genit-

alia. Other reasons given by the women was a desire to be only a 'mother' to the husband or that submitting to intercourse with a man would be interpreted as a loss of female equality or independence. When asked why they married a man in the first place, the virgin wives explained that they believed it was the proper thing to do, that they wanted to avoid being identified as an 'old maid', or that they did it for financial security. One quarter of the women admitted to participating in mutual masturbation with their husbands.

undersexed a colloquial term referring to a man or woman whose sex drive appears to be unusually weak. Though commonly attributed to an unspecified physical defect, the actual cause may be psychological—that is, inhibitions, inner conflicts, or distaste instilled during the individual's upbringing. In many cases, a person who is labelled undersexed may be normally responsive if he or she finds the right partner. Technical terms are inhibited sexual desire, inhibited sexual excitement, inhibited female orgasm, and inhibited male orgasm.

undinism a rarely used term for a pathological interest in urine—as in urolagnia or urophilia.

unilateral sexual precocity a condition in which genitalia on one side of the body develop prematurely while the corresponding body parts on the opposite side develop at the normal rate. Thus, a girl may have an enlarged breast and mature labia with pubic hair on one side with no signs of precocity on the other. A corresponding type of condition is seen in cases of rudimentary testes.

uninhibited free from inhibitions, usually sexual or moral.

uniovular twins twins that develop from a

single ovum. About 30 percent of all twins are uniovular although the manner in which they develop in the uterus can vary. A single fertilized ovum may separate into two blastomeres, resulting in two implantations with two placentas and two sets of membranes. The blastomeres may remain fused with two inner cell masses that implant with one chorion and one placenta but two separate amnions. Or, one blastomere with two inner cell masses may become implanted with a single placenta and shared amnion and chorion. Triplets or quadruplets also could develop from a single ovum, or from two, three, or four ova.

uniparous (yōōnip′ərəs) pertaining to a woman who has given birth only one time. The term has also been used to describe a delivery resulting in only one infant.

unisex an androgynous life-style in which men and women wear similar clothes, adopt similar hair styles, perform similar types of work, and share the same child rearing and other home responsibilities.

unisex toys toys that are neither male-nor female-oriented, such as building bricks, crayons or puzzles. They avoid the problem of sex-stereotyped toys for boys and girls.

unnatural acts a term sometimes applied by lawyers, legislators, or the public to sexual activities that they condemn, such as orogenital sex, anal intercourse, and homosexuality. The term is avoided by sexologists because it is moralistic rather than scientific, and because it implies that nature has intentions that can be known and understood.

unpleasure a psychoanalytical term for the feelings of tension, discomfort, and frustration that occur when instinctual impulses, such as hunger and sex, are denied gratification. The German synonym, *Unlust,* is sometimes used by psychiatrists.

Ⓤ

unsexed by failure a term introduced by Margaret Mead to describe a loss of sexual drive that often occurs in men who have failed to succeed at some endeavour. Being fired or retired from a job may have an effect of psychological emasculation. The effect may be related to the so-called male menopause.

unwanted pregnancies a term referring to the number of undesired and usually unplanned children per couple. In the United States at present the number of children unwanted by at least one parent has been conservatively estimated at over one million per year, and the number born to poor parents has

been estimated at double the number born to the more affluent.

unwed chic a colloquial term referring to a young unmarried mother who is economically and socially able to become pregnant and support a child without the benefit of legal ties to a husband.

unwed father the father of the child of an unmarried mother.

unwell a traditional euphemism for menstruating.

upper lip according to Tantric and Japanese doctrines, one of the most erogenous areas of the female body. Hindu treatises claim there is a 'secret nerve' connecting the clitoris to the upper lip, and that a woman can enhance the pleasures of lovemaking both for herself and her partner by stimulating this nerve through deep alternate-nostril breathing. See also PHILTRUM.

uranism an obsolete term for homosexuality, especially in the male, coined by Karl Heinrich Ulrichs in 1862, and derived from Aphrodite Urania, the goddess of heavenly love in Greek mythology. Two other terms were derived from the same source: urning, applied to a male homosexual who plays the female role with other males; and urninde, applied to a female homosexual who plays the passive role with other females.

ureaplasma urealyticum a species of very small bacteria that cause genital-tract infections in both men and women.

urethra the channel through which urine passes from the urinary bladder. The female urethra is relatively short, a little more than 1 inch in length. It exists in front of the vaginal orifice. The male urethra is about 8 inches long and is divided into three segments. The first, the prostatic portion, runs more or less vertically for a bit more than 1 inch through the prostate gland. In the prostatic segment, the male urethra is perforated by openings from the prostate-gland ducts and the seminal vesicles. Next is a short membranous portion of less than 1 inch between the prostate and the bulb of the penis. In the membranous portion the urethra passes through the urethral sphincter. The third segment is within the corpus spongiosum of the penile shaft. Congenital defects found occasionally in the corpus spongiosum portion are clefts that direct the urine from the undersurface (hypospadias) or upper surface (epispadias) of the shaft of the penis.

urethral abscess an abscess in the submucosal layer of tissue lining the urethra as a result of an infection such as gonorrhoea. In the male urethra, an abscess frequently develops in the midportion of the penis (in Littre's follicle), producing a visible swelling.

urethral character a Freudian term for a personality pattern characterized by a long history of bed-wetting and a set of traits stemming from feelings of shame associated with incontinence as well as the fear of urethral eroticism—namely, overambitiousness and boastfulness. These character traits are interpreted as an attempt to reestablish the bed wetter's self-esteem.

urethral chill a chill experienced by persons as a result of the entry of bacterial or other foreign products into the circulation via the corpus spongiosum. The urethral chill is often associated with the insertion of catheters of instruments into the penile urethra. It also may be a sign of damage to the lining of the urethra, permitting urine, pus, or other substances to infiltrate the surrounding tissues.

urethral eroticism a psychoanalytical term for sexual pleasure accompanying urination. A person who remains fixated at the urethral stage of psychosexual development may develop fantasies or wishes concerning urinating on other people, or being urinated on. See UROLAGNIA.

urethral groove the lower surface of the embryonic penis which normally closes to form the penile segment of the urethra. If the groove fails to close, it results in the congenital defect of hypospadias.

urethral insertion introduction of an object such as a pin or match stick into the urethra during masturbation or as a form of masturbation. The practice is occasionally found among boys and girls but is highly dangerous. Medical assistance and possibly surgery may be required.

urethral stage the phase of psychosexual development that occurs between the anal and phallic stages, when the urethra becomes the prime erogenous zone and sexual pleasure is derived from urinating. At this stage the child frequently comes into conflict with the parents over bladder training, and feels humiliated when he or she cannot exercise control or wets the bed.

urethritis an inflammation of the urethra, usually producing pus cells that indicate infection by bacteria (such as gonococcus, Escherichia coli, or ureaplasma), Chlamydia trachomatis, fungi (especially *Candida albicans*) viruses (such as *Herpes simplex*), chemi-

cals (such as certain spermicides), protozoa (such as trichomonas vaginalis), or objects inserted in the urethra for purposes of masturbation. See also NONGONOCOCCAL URETHRITIS; NONSPECIFIC URETHRITIS.

urethrovaginal meatus an anomaly associated with some cases of hermaphroditism in which a well-developed clitoris resembles a penis with hypospadias. The opening of the urethra is at the base of the clitoris. Because of the similarity between the labia and a scrotum, some females born with this congenital defect have been judged hypospadiac males at birth.

urinary responses the reactions of the urinary system to sexual excitement. In women, the urethra may undergo a few feeble contractions during orgasm. The urethra of the male is an important part of the penis and is quite sensitive to sexual activity. The urge to urinate after orgasm is common and may be aggravated in some cases because of irritation to the bladder during the body pressures and frictions of sexual intercourse.

urinary-tract infection any infection involving all or a portion of the urinary system, from the kidneys to the urethra. Urinary-tract infections are generally bacterial in origin and in adults are likely to enter the body through the urethra. In children, the infection usually enters the urinary tract from the blood vessels or lymphatic system. Kinds of urinary-tract infections include miliary tuberculosis, vesical mycoses, gonorrhoea, group A streptococcus, Escherichia coli, staphylococcus, Candida, and Chlamydia. Urinary-tract infections are relatively rare in men, except for those with spinal-cord injuries, but women are frequently at risk from such infections. Surveys indicate that 15 percent of all women suffer from urinary-tract infections at one time and 10 percent of all pregnant women are likely to experience a urinary-tract infection.

urination and sex a term referring to the observing of urination (in male or female)—an early, and usually surreptitious, expression of interest in sex and the sex organs. In some instances this interest may develop into a paraphilia known as urolagnia, characterized by a morbid preoccupation with urine and urination, especially as a means of sexual excitement.

urinism a sexual practice in which urine or urination plays a part in the sexual act, as in urinating on one's partner, watching the partner urinate during foreplay, urinating during intercourse (women only), or smelling urine on the body or clothes of the partner. See UROLAGNIA.

urninde and urning two terms for types of homosexuality derived from the name of the goddess Aphrodite Urania. See URANISM.

urogenital chamber a structure in the embryonic stage of human development in which the primitive genital and urinary organs share a common opening.

urogenital diaphragm a layer of tissue that forms a floor at the bottom of the pelvic cavity within a triangular area consisting of the lower edges of the pelvic bones, from the ischial tuberosities on either side of the anus to the symphysis pubis beneath the bulb of the penis. The deep transverse perineal muscle lies between layers of connective tissue of the diaphragm.

urogenital-floor muscles a group of five muscles in the male that participate in the clonic spasms of semen ejaculation. They include the bulbocavernosus, the sphincter urethrae, erector penis, transversus perineiprofundus, and transversus perinei superficialis. A similar group of urogenital muscles are found in the female, where the bulbocavernosus is known as the sphincter vaginae, and the ischiocavernosus is identified as the erector clitoridis.

urogenital sinus a primordial structure in the embryo that later develops into either male or female genital features. In the male, the urogenital sinus evolves into the prostate, the prostatic utricle, and the Cowper glands. In the female, the same structure develops into the lower vagina, the paraurethral glands, and Bartholin's glands.

urolagnia a sexual deviation, or paraphilia, characterized by a morbid attraction for the urine or the urinary processes of the sex partner or other individuals. Sexual stimulation may be experienced by watching the partner urinate, by sniffing garments smelling of urine during intercourse or masturbation, by drinking the partner's urine, or by yielding to one's desire or the partner's desire to be urinated upon (also called by the vulgar terms 'cunt pissing' or 'golden showers of rain').

urophilia a psychosexual disorder consisting of an obsessive interest in urine and urination as a source of sexual excitement. See UROLAGNIA.

uterine angle the portion of the uterus surrounding the openings of the fallopian tubes.

uterine axis a hypothetical line running through the longest diameter of the uterus.

uterine cavity the hollow portion of the uterus, including the cervical canal.

uterine displacement a shift from the normal position of the uterus in the pelvic cavity, usually because of failure of the ligaments to maintain the womb in the normal position— at right angles to the vagina and horizontal when the woman is standing. Displacement of the uterus can result in painful menstruation, pelvic congestion, backache, and discomfort during coitus.

uterine-hernia syndrome a condition in which a person with normal male sexual characteristics, including the ability to produce sperm, also possesses a uterus and fallopian tubes. In most cases, the condition is not discovered until surgery is required or an inguinal hernia or other disorder develops that involves an incision into the pelvic area.

uterine sinus a blood-filled space in the pregnant uterus.

uterine tube an alternative term for fallopian tube.

uteroplacental insufficiency any disorder of the placenta that renders it incapable of supporting foetal life. Causes may be hormonal insufficiency, an infection, or an interference with the blood supply. Placentitis may result from a bacterial, viral, rickettsial, or protozoal infection. Deposition of fibrin around the villi can inactivate the villi, thereby eliminating the maternal blood circulation.

uterosacral ligaments strong cords of fibrous tissue that follow a curved course from the uterine cervix to the sacrum, at the lower end of the spinal column, along the wall of the pelvis. The ligaments help support the uterus.

uterovaginal canal a structure in the embryo that evolves into vagina, uterus, and fallopian tubes of the female. In the male, the canal atrophies but leaves vestiges of tissue on the testis and the prostate.

uterus a hollow muscular organ with thick walls located in the pelvic region of the female; the structure in which a fertilized ovum is nurtured into a viable individual. In a nonpregnant woman, the uterus is a small pear-shaped organ, about 3 inches in length, which protrudes at the cervical end into the vault of the vagina. Two fallopian tubes, or oviducts, are attached to the uterus at both sides less than 1 inch from the top, or fundus. The portion below the level of the tubes is the body of the uterus, except for the cervix, and round neck of the womb that extends into the vagina. The proportions of corpus, or body, and cervix, change between childhood and motherhood. In a female child, the cervix represents about two thirds of the uterus. In a nonpregnant young woman, the uterus is divided so that about half is body and half cervix. After pregnancy, one third is cervix and two thirds are uterine body.

uterus bicornis unicollis a congenital anomaly in which a single uterine cervix leads into two adjacent uterine organs. Each side of the duplex uterus is attached to one of the fallopian tubes.

uterus didelphys a congenital anomaly in which two normal uteruses develop. Each uterus receives a fallopian tube from its side of the pelvic cavity. And each fallopian tube is attached to one ovary. The separate uteruses function independently and each is capable of supporting a pregnancy.

uterus duplex bicornis a congenital anomaly in which a pair of uteruses develop side by side, each attached to one of the fallopian tubes. However, unlike the uterus didelphys, which consists of completely separate reproductive organs, the uterus duplex bicornis consists of a uterus on either side of a thick wall of myometrium that is shared by both uteruses.

uterus masculinus an alternative term for the male prostatic utricle, which is believed to be homologous with the uterus and vagina of the female.

uterus septus a pair of fused uteruses with a single cervix but divided by a wall of muscle tissue. The wall, or septum, extends to the cervical opening.

uterus subseptus a uterus that is partly divided down the centre by a wall of tissue. Unlike the septum in the uterus septus, the uterus subseptus contains a dividing wall that extends from the fundus to a point about halfway through the uterine cavity.

uterus unicornis a congenital anomaly in which a normal functioning uterus develops with only one fallopian tube attached.

U

vacuum aspiration the most common method of performing an abortion, possible only in the first trimester of pregnancy. A tube is inserted through the cervical canal into the uterus, and attached to an aspirator, or suction machine. Also called uterine aspiration; vacuum curettage. See also TRANSCERVICAL UTERINE ASPIRATION.

vagina a musculomembranous tube that is a passageway between the uterine cervix and the vaginal orifice. It develops from early in the foetal period through puberty into a thin-walled tube about 4 inches in length and less than 2 inches in width, with the cervix extending nearly 1 inch into the vault of the tube. The vagina is located anatomically between the bladder and the rectum and is supported by ligaments and muscles of the pelvic floor. Its walls are formed by an internal mucous membrane lining and a muscular coat, with a layer of erectile tissue between them. The mucous membrane lining is continuous with that of the uterus. It is not a smooth surface but rather one that is marked by ridges and furrows. The ridges are sometimes identified as the columns of the vagina, and also as rugae. It contains a number of mucous crypts, but there are no glands within the vagina. The muscular coat consists of an external layer of longitudinal fibres that are continuous with the muscles of the uterus and an internal layer of circular fibres. The erectile tissue is provided by fibres of the bulbocavernosus muscle. The main functions of the vagina are to provide a passageway for spermatozoa from the penis, an outlet for the menstrual flow from the uterus, and a birth canal for the foetus at term. The vaginal lining responds to stimulation by the female sex hormones oestrogen and progesterone. As a result, there is some proliferation and exfoliation of the mucosa during the menstrual cycle. Because the mucosal lining of the uterus is continuous with that of the vagina, a sample of vaginal tissue is regarded as a reliable source for information about the condition of the endometrium of the uterus, particularly with regard for effects of the sex hormones. A scraping of vaginal mucus is often included with the cervical scraping when a sample of tissue is required for a smear test for cancer. But the vagina itself is rarely a source of cancer. It is, however, a potential source for parasitic and pathogenic organisms, particularly those associated with sexually transmissible diseases.

See also DOUBLE VAGINA; DRY VAGINA; PARTIAL SEPTATE VAGINA; RUDIMENTARY SECOND VAGINA.

vagina dentata (Latin, 'vagina with teeth') in psychoanalysis, the fantasy—more unconscious than conscious—that the vagina contains teeth that can castrate the male partner. In males, this fantasy is believed to be based on castration anxiety; and in females it is believed to stem from penis envy and a desire to castrate the male as an act of revenge.

vaginal adhesions a condition associated with the postmenopausal senile vagina in which firm fibrous growths descend from the upper vagina, forming attachments across the lumen (opening) of the vagina, and eventually obscuring and obstructing the vaginal canal.

vaginal ballottement a method of examining the condition of a pregnancy by producing a movement in the amniotic fluid through the walls of the vagina. By initiating movement of the amniotic fluid, the examiner can obtain information about the foetus whose movements respond to the fluid activity because the foetus is of about the same specific gravity as the fluid in which it is suspended.

vaginal balls a sexual device for women that consists of two weighted plastic spheres, each about 1 inch in diameter attached to a cord joined to a waist belt. The balls are inserted in the vagina (and in some cases in the rectum), and the woman derives sexual pleasure, usually to the point of repeated orgasm, by walking back and forth or rocking in a chair. The device is said to have originated in Japan. It is also known as geisha balls, Ben-Wa, Rinno-Tama, Burmese bells, and Thai Beads, and by other names.

vaginal barrel an alternative term for vagina.

vaginal bulb the embryonic tissue mass that forms at the end of the uterovaginal canal. It is usually visible in the foetus during the seventh week of gestation.

vaginal canal the tubular structure formed by the walls of the vagina. Also called vulvouterine canal.

vaginal columns the transverse ridges of mucosal tissue on the walls of the vagina.

vaginal creams medicated ointments containing female hormones that may be applied to the vagina to act as a lubricant, thereby reducing the discomfort of dyspareunia.

vaginal discharge the flow of any substance from the vagina, usually excluding the natural menstrual flow. The term is commonly applied to irritating discharges that are associated with infections. Leukorrhoea, a whitish discharge consisting of mucus and discarded cells of the vaginal lining, may be normal if it occurs during pregnancy, just before menstruation, or during ovulation, unless the flow is copious. Abnormal vaginal discharges are associated with trichomonas vaginitis, a leukorrhoea that is irritating and causes swelling of the vaginal tissues and painful intercourse; monilial vaginitis, which also is irritating and a cause of painful intercourse; and gonorrhoea. Lochia is a normal vaginal discharge that occurs after child delivery and may persist for several weeks, changing in colour from red to brown to a yellowish white during the first two weeks after labour.

vaginal envy a form of envy experienced particularly by male transsexuals who not only have a persistent desire to be rid of their own genitals, but also to possess the sexual organs of the female, including the vagina.

vaginal epithelioma a type of vaginal cancer that begins as a small ulceration or pimply growth on the wall of the vagina. Untreated, it tends to spread wildly through the vaginal walls to invade other organs and tissues of the pelvic cavity.

vaginal examination the study of the vagina for the possible presence of anomalies, infections or other diseases, and to determine its role as a possible infertility factor. A routine digital examination of the vagina often is not feasible before puberty because of the presence of the hymen. A long, thin, lighted vaginoscope may be inserted through a perforation in the hymen, allowing a superficial prepubertal examination. At puberty, the hymenal opening is usually larger and the vaginal wall more distensible so that a finger or thin vaginal speculum can be inserted. After puberty, the vaginal examination is performed as part of a complete pelvic examination for evidence of infections, tumours, vaginismus, infertility, and dyspareunia. The presence of an infection, such as *Trichomonas vaginalis* can cause the vagina to be too alkaline for the male spermatozoa to survive. The study of the vaginal canal may indicate whether a healthy male ejaculate would likely be deposited in the area of the vagina next to the opening of the cervix. A narrow vagina, for example, could prevent the penis from reaching the optimum portion of the vagina and that problem could be compounded if the male happened to suffer from erectile dysfunction or premature ejaculation. A malpositioned uterus or a cervix that is too high in the vagina could also be obstacles to fertilization of an ovum and would be detected by a vaginal examination. The examination might reveal the presence of a polyp or other lesion that could obstruct the passage of spermatozoa. Other observable factors may be signs of an infection and excessive mucus production, which can be a cause of infertility. A cervix that is tapered with a tiny opening is a sign of an undeveloped uterus and would be noticed during a vaginal examination.

vaginal father a psychoanalytical term for a male who dreams or fantasizes that he has a vagina. This notion is believed to stem from an unconscious identification with the man's own mother, and is associated with motherly, unaggressive behaviour, intense rivalry with women, and a predilection for homemaking and child rearing in marriage.

vaginal fistula an abnormal passageway that develops through the vaginal wall so that it connects directly with neighbouring organs, such as the rectum or the urinary bladder. The fistula may be congenital or may result from a tumour or injury related to surgery or child delivery.

vaginal fluid another term for vaginal lubrication.

vaginal hypoaesthesia a form of partial frigidity in which sexual sensitivity is limited to the clitoral area.

vaginal insertions the insertion of fingers or objects into the vagina during masturbation. Kinsey found that one in five women reported such insertions—most frequently the fingers, but also easily available objects such as pencils, bananas, or candles and in some cases artificial penises (dildos, vibrators).

Vagina Littlefinger a male homosexual slang term for a snob.

vaginal lubrication secretion of lubricating fluid by the vaginal walls and Bartholin's glands situated on each side of the vaginal orifice. The process is also known as 'sweating' and occurs during the excitement stage of the sexual-response cycle making coitus easier to perform. Also called vaginal fluid.

vaginal melanoma a particularly dangerous type of pigmented tumour that may develop in the vagina. It is a lethal type of cancer and one that is always secondary to a melanoma that first appeared in some other body area. But it is distinctively out of place in the vagina, because of its dark, molelike appearance, and easy to detect in its earliest stages.

vagina loquens (Latin, 'speaking vagina') in ancient folklore, a vagina that is forced, through a charm, to speak and thus reveal its lack of chastity (telling all about her lovers).

vaginal orgasm a climax reportedly experienced by the woman through stimulation of the vagina alone, without any clitoral stimulation. According to Freud, only a vaginal orgasm, as distinguished from a clitoral orgasm, can be called 'mature' and 'real'. This view, as well as the view that there is a separate and distinct vaginal orgasm, has been challenged by Kinsey and by Masters and Johnson.

vaginal plethysmograph a device that measures the sexual arousal in a female by data obtained from changes in blood flow and erectile-tissue changes in the vagina.

vaginal sarcoma a type of cancer of the vagina that may develop in the muscle or subcutaneous layers of the posterior vaginal wall. It grows so rapidly that portions may slough off because of a lack of blood supply.

It may spread by metastasis to the lungs or other parts of the body.

vaginal secretion a clear fluid secreted by the vaginal barrel during sexual excitement. Contractions of the vaginal muscles often bring the walls together so sharply that the secretions spurt out of the vagina. This is the source of the mistaken notion that women ejaculate like men.

vaginal suppository a cone-shaped medical preparation that is melted by the body heat when introduced into the vagina before intercourse. Though suppositories of this kind provide a barrier against sperm, and contain a spermicide, they are not regarded as an effective contraceptive.

vaginal sweat another term for vaginal lubrication.

vaginismus a painful spasm of the vagina, usually of emotional origin. It can interfere with satisfactory intercourse or with a routine pelvic examination. It involves an intense contraction of the muscle fibres surrounding the vagina. See also FUNCTIONAL VAGINISMUS; PSYCHIC VAGINISMUS.

vaginitis any inflammation of the lining of the vagina resulting from atrophy, infection, or physical injury. Infectious agents may include *Haemophilus vaginalis,* primarily a parasitic organism but one that produces a malodorous leukorrhoea. Amoebic vaginitis is caused by *Entomoeba histolytica,* an organism that causes ulcerations of the vagina and cervix. Vaginitis may result from *Listeria monocytogenes,* which is harboured in the vagina of a significant percentage of women, particularly in the summer and autumn. Simple vaginitis may be caused by *Escherichia coli,* one of several disease agents that alter the acidity of the lining of the vagina to produce symptoms of burning, itching, and swelling, with pain or urination. Monilial vaginitis is associated with *Candida albicans,* a fungal infection that causes a thick discharge that produces itching and irritation and usually results in dyspareunia, or pain during intercourse. Trichomonas vaginitis is a protozoon that also produces a discharge and irritation and causes dyspareunia. Some other forms of vaginitis are caused by *Pediculosis pubis,* the crab louse, and by the use of clothing and cosmetics, mainly deodorants, that create an allergic reaction. Adhesive vaginitis is caused by walls of the vagina that stick together. Atrophic vaginitis is an effect of the menopause when decreased oestrogen levels result in a thinning and increased sensitivity of the mucosal lining.

valerian a herb generally associated with sexual stimulation, also known as 'drunken sailor'. This alleged aphrodisiac was administered by witches; and as 'cetwale' in Chaucer's *Canterbury Tales* it was a herb to be added to ale to cause 'lovelonging.' The herb, whose name is derived from the Latin *valere*, meaning 'to be well,' was known to ancient Greeks and Romans and was used as a source of medicines by monks in the Middle Ages.

vampirism belief in the existence of preternatural beings who arise from the ground and fly around like bats (or like Count Dracula), sucking the blood of sleeping persons. Drawing, and drinking, blood is believed to be a means of achieving sexual gratification. Some writers regard the practice of biting the partner during sexual activity as a form of vampirism. See LOVE BITE.

vanilla a plant that is related botanically to the orchid and which, for that reason, has been thought to be an aphrodisiac. Next to celery soup and chocolate, Madame Pompadour recommended the use of vanilla, in fact, she flavoured her chocolate with vanilla extract.

variant sexual behaviour a recently coined expression used by sexologists and sex educators for sexual behaviour (such as cunnilingus) that is not engaged in by most people. It is a purely descriptive term, not implying right or wrong or abnormality, in contradistinction to older terms like deviant, perverted, or unnatural. Also called sexual variance.

varicocele a large varicose vein in the scrotum that is associated with as many as 40 percent of cases of male infertility. Surgical correction of a varicocele reportedly increases the sperm count in half the cases.

varicose vulva an abnormal condition in which the vulva becomes swollen because of an impeded return flow of blood. The condition stems from or is aggravated by repeated pregnancies that cause increased pressure of blood vessels in the lower pelvis. Varicose veins of the vulva may appear only when a woman is standing and subside when she lies on her back. There are hazards of a rupture of one of the varicose veins or formation of blood clots in the vulva.

vas an alternative term for vas deferens, or ductus deferens. Plural: *vasa*.

vasa efferentia an alternative term for the efferent ducts of the rete testis, through which the mature spermatozoa move into the epididymis.

vas deferens (vas def'erens) an alternative term for ductus deferens, a long muscular tube that carries spermatozoa from the epididymis to the urethral portion of the prostate gland.

vasectomy a male sterilization procedure in which the vas deferens (ductus deferens) is divided within the male scrotum. The procedure takes less than 15 minutes in most cases and requires a local anaesthetic. The genital area is cleaned and shaved to reduce the risk of infection. An anaesthetic is injected into the scrotal skin and again into each vas deferens after it has been located within the scrotal tissues. The vas may be simply severed or a small section may be excised. Some doctors irrigate the opened vas to decrease the postoperative sperm count using xylocaine or another substance, such as a salt solution. Studies indicate that *vasectomized* men treated with xylocaine irrigation of the vas are azoospermic within 6 weeks after the procedure, whereas untreated vasectomized men required up to 10 weeks to produce semen free of motile spermotozoa. After irrigation, the vas ends may be sealed by one of three standard methods: by ligation, or tying the open ends with sutures; by coagulation with electricity or heat; or by applying tantalum clips. Some doctors apply clips without severing the vas while others sever the vas, irrigate, and cauterize before applying clips. The patient is advised to rest for a couple of hours after a vasectomy and to avoid strenuous physical work or exercise for several days. For postoperative discomfort, doctors may recommend wearing a scrotal support for a week and taking aspirin or other easily available analgesics. Because some doctors perform a vasectomy with a single incision into the scrotum whereas others make a separate incision for each vas deferens, plus other individual factors, the rate of healing varies somewhat. However, the man is allowed to resume intercourse as soon as he feels comfortable in that activity. Unlike female sterilization, a vasectomy does not have immediate results. Spermatozoa stored anywhere along the reproductive tract beyond the point of the vas division can result in a pregnancy. Pregnancies have occurred more than 1 month after a vasectomy, and whereas 95 percent of vasectomized men are azoospermic after 10 weeks, the other 5 percent may still ejaculate spermatozoa. In the United States, doctors performing vasectomies frequently request a sperm sam-

V

ple 7 or 8 weeks after the operation for examination. In other countries, men are advised to continue using other forms of contraception for a period of 3 months after the vasectomy. A vasectomy is usually permanent, but some surgeons report a 50 percent success in reversing the procedure.

vasocongestion the engorgement of the spongy erectile tissues of the penis and clitoris with blood. By automatic manipulation of the blood flow by spinal nerve tracts, arteries allow blood to move into the spongy tissues faster than it is allowed to drain through the veins, as occurs when the penis is flaccid. Valves in the veins also retard the return flow of blood, which is required to produce turgidity in the erectile tissues.

vasoconstrictor centres a part of the sympathetic nervous system, located in the lumbar area of the spinal cord. The vasoconstrictor centres prevent blood entering the penis or clitoris from leaving during the erection phase of sexual stimulation. By allowing an inflow of blood while preventing an outflow, the penis can remain turgid and still during intercouse.

vasodilator centres a part of the parasympathetic nervous system, located in the sacral-nerve areas of the spinal cord, that controls the flow of blood into the penis or clitoris during the erection phase of sexual arousal.

Vatican roulette a colloquial term for the rhythm method of birth control, which depends upon avoiding intercourse around the time of ovulation. It is the only method permitted by the Roman Catholic Church.

VD a common abbreviation for venereal disease.

vegetarian a slang term for a person who does not like to perform fellatio or cunnilingus.

veil wearing the practice of covering the face of women with a cloth or veil as a sexual shield and a means of keeping them in seclusion and subservience. Once common in Muslim societies, the veil is slowly disappearing, although it has been retained or reintroduced by fundamentalists, as in Iran. In Chad, some non-Muslim women wear an elaborate beaded veil, but wear nothing else; and among the Tuareg of the Sahara only the men wear veils.

vena cava syndrome a condition that occurs in a normal pregnant woman during the third trimester when she lies on her back so that the bulk of the uterus passes on the inferior vena cava, the major vein of the lower part of the body. The inferior vena cava is compressed against the spinal column, reducing the return flow of blood to the mother's heart. This condition, in turn, results in falling blood pressure so that less blood can reach the placenta, causing foetal distress.

venereal disease (VD) a popular term for sexually transmitted disease.

venereal-disease phobia a more common term for cypridophobia.

venereal warts another term for genital warts.

venery an obsolete term for indulgence in sexual intercourse.

venetian blinds a homosexual slang term for foreskin.

ventral-dorsal a coital position in which intercourse is performed with one partner facing the back of the other.

ventral-ventral an alternative term for the coital position in which the partners face each other.

Venus the ancient Roman goddess ('Aphrodite' to the Greeks) associated with love. Born of the sea, she has often been linked with the belief that fish are a powerful erotic aid. So deeply rooted is the association between Venus and the aphrodisiac value of seafood that the eating of seafood was prohibited by religious leaders on several occasions in history, including the beginning of the Christian era, when church officials tried to eradicate ties with the Roman past.

Venus' highway an older euphemism for vagina, especially a prostitute's.

verbal masochism a form of masochism in which a person seeks or actually achieves sexual excitement by imagining he or she is a target for insults and other forms of verbal abuse. Some mental patients dwell on the same masochistic fantasies and dialogues for years because they find them sexually exciting.

version a change in the lie, or position, of the foetus in the uterus. The change is usually manipulated by the physician to make the delivery easier. Three basic types of version are cephalic, podalic, or combined. A cephalic version is one in which the foetus in a breech or transverse position across the cervical outlet is manoeuvred so that the feet and buttocks are at the top of the uterus and the cephalic, or head, portion is pointed downwards into the birth canal. A cephalic version is manipulated externally by gently pushing the buttocks upwards and the head downwards through palpation of the foetal body through the mother's abdominal wall. The manoeuvre reduces the risk of a foetal loss from 15 to 3 percent. The podalic version accomplishes a similar objective, but the manipulation is performed internally, usually by reaching into the uterus and grasping the feet of the foetus. The combined version, as the name suggests, involves both external and internal manipulation of the foetus within the uterus. Because of improved techniques and safety, a caesarean section is preferred by most modern obstetricians to the internal or combined forms of version.

verumontanitis an inflammation of the verumontanum, located on the floor of the urethra near the prostate. Among causes are excessive sexual activity (including masturbation), prostatitis, and seminal vesculitis. If the swelling blocks the ejaculatory ducts, the man may experience pain radiation to the lower back, perineum, and scrotum. Urinary frequency and premature ejaculation are sometimes caused by verumontanitis.

verumontanum an elevated portion of the back wall of the prostatic urethra, at the point where the ejaculatory ducts and the prostatic utricle open into the urethra.

vestibular glands a pair of small glands located on both sides of the vaginal orifice, or opening. The term may also be applied to numerous small mucous glands that open into the vestibule of the vagina.

vestibule a space leading to an entrance, such as the vestibule of the vagina, the space enclosed by the labia minora (Latin *vestibulum,* 'forecourt'). Also called vestibulum vaginae.

vestibulovaginal bulb a long mass of erectile tissue on both sides of the orifice of the vagina. Also called bulb of the vestibule.

vibrator a motor-driven plastic cylinder used mainly to transmit vibrations to the clitoris directly or through the hand. A penis-shaped vibrator is used—and often recommended by sex therapists—to produce an orgasm in women (also men) who have not had this experience, or who are having difficulty reaching orgasm through other forms of stimulation. Some women, however, find the instrument too mechanical for their taste. A smaller version is sometimes used for anal stimulation.

vicarious menstruation an unusual condition in which bleeding from the nose or other parts of the body, such as the eyes, occurs during the menstrual flow, presumably caused either by psychological factors

or by a vasospasm that results in a sudden decrease in the size of the blood vessels of the endometrium (lining of the uterus).

vice a term referring to any practice that a particular society considers to be depraved or immoral—often used with another word, as in 'secret vice,' which was probably the most common 19th century euphemism for masturbation. (Latin *vitium,* 'defect,' 'crime,' or 'flaw in the god's auspices.') Ogden Nash wrote: 'Vice is nice / But virtue / Won't hurt you.'

vice allemand, le (ləvis'älmäN'; 'the German vice') a French slang term for anal intercourse.

vice anglais, le (ləvis'äNglä'; 'the English vice') a French slang term for masochism.

vice versa a slang term referring (a) to the 69 position (b) to mutual cunnilingus (that is, between two women).

Victorianism stereotyped attitudes prevalent in Western nations during the age of Queen Victoria, who reigned from 1837 to 1901. The term includes the notion that sex itself is ugly or 'beastly,' that only loose women enjoy it, that nice women must avoid getting sexually excited, that they tolerate sexual relations only as a necessary evil and a duty to their husbands ('lie back and think of England'), and that sex is something one doesn't talk about in polite society or even behind closed doors. As a result, prudery (and hypocrisy) were triumphant, books and plays (even Shakespeare) were censored, children were kept in complete ignorance of sexual matters, lovers were chaperoned, and women wore bathing attire that covered their legs down to their ankles. Also called *Victorian ethic.*

viraginity a term pertaining to a woman with the physical characteristics of a man. (Latin *virago,* 'female warrior,' from *vir,* 'adult male'.)

virgin an individual, male or female, who has not engaged in sexual intercourse. Virginity, or premarital chastity, is regarded as essential in Islamic societies, and is greatly emphasized by many parents and some young people in our own culture. Virginity was regarded as a sacred state by the Romans, who appointed the vestal virgins to deal with the gods. On the other hand, many societies do not consider virginity to be important, and some even require women to prove their fertility by having a child before marriage. (Latin *virgo,* 'maid, virgin.').

Virgin is also a slang term for a couple or

a partner not experienced in group sex or 'swinging'—that is, greenhorns in this practice.

virginal anxiety a state of apprehension experienced by a girl or woman during her first sexual encounter.

virginal tribute an alternative term for DROIT DU SEIGNEUR. See this entry.

virgin birth the concept of human pregnancy and subsequent birth without a union of ovum and sperm after intercourse. The belief in the virgin birth of Jesus appears to be a reflection of the view that equates virginity with purity. The nearest thing to virgin birth is impregnation without penile penetration: This has been known to occur when the man ejaculates near or on a virgin's vulva during sex play, or if he gets semen on his hands and then brings his fingers into contact with her vagina.

virginity the state of being a virgin.

virginity taboo a social prohibition against defloration of the woman before marriage. This taboo is by no means universal; for example, an anthropological study of 141 non-Western societies conducted by Broude and Greene has shown that these societies were about evenly divided on the question of premarital virginity. In Western societies a woman was expected to be virginal before marriage until the 1950s (and Kinsey's statistics indicate that all but 3 percent obeyed the taboo against premarital sex). Since that time, the number of nonvirgins at marriage has rapidly risen and appears to be well over 50 percent at present.

virilescence the gradual appearance of male characteristics, such as facial hair and a deeper voice, in a woman, particularly after menopause.

virilism a condition of women possessing masculine characteristics, such as an enlarged clitoris, deep voice, male hairline, and general masculine body shape, in addition to hirsutism. See also ADRENAL VIRILISM; DISSOCIATED VIRILISM.

virility the capacity for sexual functioning in the male; male potency.

virtue admirable quality or moral excellence. Literally, the term means manliness, a male's strength or merit, from Latin *vir*, meaning 'adult male' (and 'a virtuous woman' would be a contradiction in terms). Ironically, however, the term virtue has come to refer primarily to women—perhaps as an expression of 'male chauvinist' expectations.

vital strength a term referring to the energy

that some men mistakenly believe is discharged along with semen during ejaculation. It is part of a myth that a man is born with a fixed number of possible orgasms in his reproductive system and that he becomes increasingly debilitated in later life because of this loss of 'vital strength'.

voice change the deepening and maturing of the male voice and, less obviously, the female voice during puberty. In boys this occurs during the rapid growth spurt of the whole body; more specifically, the enlargement of the voice box is the result of an increase in male hormone secretion from the testicles. The change usually becomes noticeable (with a few 'voice breaks') several months after the first ejaculation. In the case of castration, the male hormones cease to be produced, and voice pitch increases. On the other hand, neoplasms of the ovaries may result in a masculine lowering of the female voice.

voluptas sexualis a Latin term meaning sexual pleasure, found mainly in 19th century literature.

von Fernwald's sign a pregnancy sign noted during the eighth week of gestation by a bulge on a side of the top of the uterus, the site of implantation of the embryo.

Voronoff, Serge one of several experimenters in rejuvenation techniques based on the transplantation of animal gonads into humans. Voronoff, a Russian doctor, worked in the 1920s at implanting ape testicles in humans to increase or restore male potency—but was not successful.

voyeurism a sexual disorder in which an individual, usually a male—a *voyeur*—derives sexual satisfaction from secretly observing people (95 percent are strangers) in the nude, or in the act of undressing or engaging in sexual activity. If this is the preferred or exclusive method of achieving sexual excitement, it is classified as a paraphilia. Also called inspectionalism.

voyeuse a female voyeur.

vulcanization the discovery in 1843 of a method for processing flexible rubber products. The new process made possible the large-scale manufacture of rubber condoms, replacing the traditional types made of linen, animal intestines, or other substances. The first rubber condoms were moulded from crepe rubber and carried a seam lengthwise. It was not until the end of the 19th century that seamless rubber condoms became available.

vulva (Latin, 'covering') the external female sex organs, or genitalia, comprising the mons veneris, the labia majora and minora, the clitoris, the vestibule or opening of the vagina, and Bartholin's glands. In addition to many colloquial terms for vulva, the formal terms cunnus and pudendum are used.

wallflower a colloquial term for someone who gets excluded from social activity between the sexes, particularly a *young woman* who fails to get asked to dance.

wallflower week a colloquial term for the time of a woman's menstrual period, viewed as excluding her temporarily from social activity.

wand a male homosexual slang term for penis.

Wanda Wandwaver a male homosexual slang term for someone who brags about his penis size or performance.

wandering uterus a term applied to variations in the position of the uterus, which is normally at right angles to the axis of the vagina. A shift to an unusual position may cause painful menstruation, backaches, and pelvic congestion, and may also make intercourse uncomfortable. See HYSTERIA.

Wandervogel movement an early 20th century youth movement in Germany in which nudism was practised. Wandervogel groups, which resembled the Scouts, denied charges of licentiousness and homosexuality that were levelled at them. (The literal meaning of the German word *Wandervogel* is 'migratory bird.').

wank a slang term meaning to masturbate or masturbation In addition to being a masturbator, a *wanker* is a dilettante and also more generally a useless incompetent person.

warfarin a coumarin-type of anticoagulant drug sometimes prescribed for the treatment of coronary thrombosis and related cardiovascular disorders. Its use is contraindicated in women who are pregnant or capable of becoming pregnant because of its teratogenic effects on the offspring, including blindness and mental deficiency.

Wasserman test an obsolete test for syphilis.

watering-can perineum medical jargon for a urethral abnormality in which strictures of the urinary pathway have led to multiple fistulas that permit the urine to spray from several openings at once.

waters a euphemism for the amniotic fluid within a pregnant woman's uterus, used particularly in the phrase 'breaking of the waters,' referring to the rupture of the membranes containing this fluid. See also BAG OF WATERS.

water sports a slang term referring to sexual fascination with urine and urination, often abbreviated as w/s.

W chromosome a female sex hormone of certain animals, particularly birds, fishes, and insects. Unlike human females who possess duplicate (XX) sex chromosomes, females with a W chromosome received only one sex chromosome which must be paired with a Z chromosome, the male sex chromosome of the species. The WZ letters were assigned to such animals to distinguish their sex chromosomes from the XY or XX sets of human sex chromosomes.

weapon an older slang term for penis.

wedding depression feelings of dejection and loss of initiative experienced by prospective brides and bridegrooms while plans for the wedding are in progress. This condition is presumably caused by such factors as apprehensiveness about taking on new responsibilities and the prospect of leaving the security of the family home. The depressed mood usually clears up spontaneously, but if it persists and is accompanied by insomnia and weight loss, professional assistance will generally be required.

wedding night the night after the marriage

ceremony, when the couple are 'alone at last.' Traditionally, this night marks the beginning of sexual adjustment between the bride and groom. If one or both are virginal, the wedding night may be disappointing or stressful, particularly if they expect to 'reach the stars' immediately. But if they are mature enough to recognize that the sexual relationship takes time to develop—and is intertwined with their total relationship—they will be as realistic as they are romantic. Even those who have already experienced sexual relations with each other, or with other persons, usually find that marriage brings with it new circumstances and new responsibilities from the wedding night on.

wedding tackle a humorous euphemism for the male genitals.

wee-wee a euphemism meaning urine or to urinate, used by or to children. The shorter *wee* is used similarly.

Weinberg and Williams Survey a large scale study of male homosexuals conducted in the 1970s in the United States and Europe under the sponsorship of the Kinsey Institute. Male homosexuals in the United States were contacted through mailing lists of the Mattachine Societies of New York and San Francisco. European homosexuals were interviewed in Amsterdam and Copenhagen. Data were obtained from more than 1,000 male homosexuals.

well hung an appreciative slang term describing a man with large genitalia or a woman with large breasts.

Westphal's sign a diagnostic sign of tabes dorsalis in advanced cases of syphilis, as manifested by the loss of the patellar (knee-jerk) reflex.

wet day a day in the menstrual cycle when cervical mucus secretion has increased and has become less clear and less sticky than in previous days that were still considered relatively free of risk of pregnancy. For women who use the ovulation method of family planning, wet days may indicate that ovulation is about to occur and intercourse should be avoided unless the woman wants to become pregnant.

wet dream an alternative term for nocturnal emission, a seminal discharge that accompanies an erotic dream by a male.

wet nurse a woman who breast-feeds an infant that is not her own child.

wet kiss a sexually stimulating kiss performed with wet lips and wet tongues.

whackapohane the Maori practice of exposing the buttocks as a sign of contempt or protest.

wham-bang-thankyou-ma'am a derogatory term for the male attitude towards sexual intercourse as something to be indulged in for speedy and selfish gratification, with no thought for affection towards or the feelings of one's partner.

whipping lashing another person (or being lashed) with a whip, belt, thong, or other object, especially for the purpose of sexual arousal and gratification, as in dippoldism, flagellation, flagellantism, and flogging.

white-oak leaves leaves with alleged erotic properties. Women in 18th century England were advised to place two white-oak leaves on their pillow on the evening of Saint Valentine's Day. The leaves presumably would help the woman see her lover in her dreams that night.

whites a slang term for leukorrhoea.

white slave a young woman (regardless of 'race') who has been forced into prostitution. The term is apparently derived from a 19th-century drama entitled *The White Slave*, a story about a woman who was kidnapped and forced to be a prostitute. Because the story was set in the 1850s, it was necessary to distinguish *white slavery*, an illegal practice then, from black slavery which was legal in many states of the United States.

white tunic an alternative term for tunica albuginea, the whitish fibrous sheath that encloses each testis.

whore a prostitute. The term has been used with this sense since the 12th century, but it is derived from the Latin word *carus*, meaning 'dear, beloved.' Whore ranks number 14 in the TABOONESS RATING OF DIRTY WORDS. See this entry.

widdle a euphemism meaning to urinate, used particularly by or to children.

widow inheritance a practice found in many African societies: A man inherits all his dead father's wives except for his own mother. The object seems to be to carry on the family. In some parts of East Africa, the heir must go through the ritual of having intercourse with each of the wives in a single night on penalty of being required to renounce his father's property. See also WIFE INHERITANCE.

wiener children's (and sometimes an adult) euphemism for penis in American English. Also called *wienie*.

wife beating a common term referring to the battered-wife syndrome.

wife inheritance a custom in which a man may be the principal heir of his mother's brother, including the mother's brother's wife or wives. The custom is found in many African societies; in some cases the inherited rights over the wife or wives may only be domestic, not sexual, though in other cases both sexual and domestic rights are inherited. See also WIDOW INHERITANCE.

wife lending another term for sex hospitality.

Wilde, Oscar (1856-1900) Irish-English dramatist, poet, aphorist, and wit—the most famous homosexual of the 19th century. His love affair with Lord Alfred Douglas became a cause célèbre when it led to a slander trial in which Wilde was sentenced to 2 years in prison. 'To oscarize' came to mean to have homosexual intercourse, to be an 'oscar.'

willing an erection an aspect of the fear-of-failure process in secondary impotence in which a man who has failed to achieve an erection believes he should be able to produce an erection simply by 'will power,' even though he may have unintentionally obstructed the physiological requirements for an erection by an excessive intake of alcohol. The approach usually results in another failure, thereby reinforcing the problem.

willy a euphemism for penis, used particularly by or to children.

wimp an alternative term for cissy, or a male who lacks traditional masculine behavioural traits or who displays submissive or retiring characteristics.

wings of the vulva a colloquial term for the labia majora and labia minora.

winkle a euphemism for penis, used particularly by or to children.

wish fulfilment the realization of desires and goals—in psychoanalysis, one of the major mechanisms in dreams and fantasies; also the drive to find relief from tension produced by instinctual needs such as sex and hostility.

Witches' Hammer the English translation of the Latin title *Malleus maleficarum*, a manual of witchcraft published by two German theologians, Heinrich Krämer and Johann Sprenger, in 1487. The work argued for the existence of witches who practiced sorcery in league with the devil, and described how they could be identified by pigment spots and anaesthetic areas of their bodies. These women were blamed and put to the stake for all natural catastrophes and for criminal behaviour and sexual excesses.

witches' milk a thin yellowish fluid resembling colostrum secreted by the breasts of newborn infants of both sexes. The secretion is normal, harmless, and transient.

withdrawal bleeding the discharge of blood from the uterus after a woman stops using a hormonal medication taken to evaluate the cause of her amenorrhoea symptoms. By taking progesterone for several days, then discontinuing the hormone, a discharge resembling a menstrual flow is a sign that the cause of the amenorrhoea is not the result of a uterine disorder. The process is similar to the progesterone test for pregnancy.

withdrawal method a contraceptive method in which the male withdraws the penis from the vagina just before ejaculation. This technique is not reliable because the penis often releases semen containing sperm even before ejaculation, and because many men find it difficult to withdraw near the peak of sexual excitement. If possible, withdrawal should be delayed until the woman reaches a climax, otherwise it might interfere with her gratification. Also called coitus interruptus; withdrawal.

Witkop an Africaans term for the white skullcaplike crusts that form on the scalps of some black Africans who have acquired syphilis. The white crusts are caused by syphilitic lesions. The term means, literally, 'white head.'

witness a term referring to the origin of the term 'to testify,' because in ancient times it was customary for a man to place his hand on his testicles when taking an oath. Thus, the term, 'testify' is derived from 'testes,' and the testicles were 'witnesses' to the man's oath.

wolf an obsolescent slang term for a sexually aggressive male.

wolffian duct a paired mesonephric tube that appears in the embryo and in the male evolves into the vas deferens and a portion of the epididymis. In the female, the wolffian duct usually, but not always, degenerates and disappears.

wolf testicles an ingredient of alleged aphrodisiac formulations of the ancient Romans.

woman an adult human female. The term comes from Old English *wifeman*, or 'female man;' nevertheless, woman has become the term preferred in the women's liberation movement, over other terms such as girl or lady (although the latter would seem to have more dignity, etymologically speaking—coming from Old English *hlaefdige*, 'loaf kneader, kneader of bread,' thus the indispensable provider of the family). But, then, usage has always been more important than literal sense. Willard R. Espy muses: 'The very word *woman* has become offensive in some circles; *lady* has come down to where *woman* was a hundred years ago, and in two thousand years, *carus*, Latin for 'dear,' has degenerated to *whore*. A *courtesan* was once a lady at court; a *wench* any young girl; *tart*, a term of endearment. Even *housewife*, that most respectable of appellations, becomes opprobrious when pronounced *hussy*. *Dame* is now a slang term of dubious implications; *madam* makes us think of someone running a house of prostitution, and *queen* (properly *quean*) is a homosexual.' (*An Almanac of Words at Play*, 1975.)

womandrake a counterfeit version of mandrake once offered in England. It actually was carved from the roots of a bryony vine and decorated with 'pubic hair' made from grass or wheat stalks.

womanizer a colloquial term for a man who habitually chases women; also, for a philanderer.

woman-year a statistical term used in determining the comparative effectiveness of various kinds of birth-control methods. A woman-year represents 12 months in the life of a sexually active woman of an age between menarche and menopause, or who is at risk of becoming pregnant.

womb a common synonym for uterus.

womb envy a form of envy experienced by male transsexuals who identify themselves so completely with the female sex that they have a persistent desire to possess a womb.

womb fantasy the fantasy of returning to the womb, usually in response to the wish to escape from the world and its pressures. According to Freud, this wish is usually expressed in symbolic form as a dream about living in a cave, being alone on an island, or being confined to an empty room.

women at risk women who are exposed to the risk of pregnancy, such as low-income women, teenage girls, and others who for various reasons do not have access to contraceptive methods or services.

women with penis the psychoanalytical concept that some children between the ages of 2 and 5 believe that all women once possessed a penis. Among girls this idea is a denial of reality stemming from the discovery of the anatomical differences between males and females. Among boys the discovery that girls lack a penis reinforces their anxiety about castration.

woodruff a small perennial herb that is used in the production of medicinal drugs. It has also been claimed over the centuries as a 'mild aphrodisiac'; or, as one natural scientist noted in the 17th century, woodruff is 'provocative to venery.'

working girl a euphemism for prostitute.

wrong door a slang term for anus, used in the context of anal sex.

wrongful birth the birth of an unwanted child, a situation that has been the basis of lawsuits against doctors, hospitals, clinics, and other health-care workers or facilities. The action may result from a failed vasectomy or tubal ligation leading to a pregnancy. See WRONGFUL-LIFE ACTION.

wrongful-life action a type of US civil lawsuit that may be brought against a doctor or hospital or other health facility on the grounds that their negligence resulted in the birth of an unwanted child. Such legal actions have been brought in cases of failed tubal ligations, abortions, or vasectomies. Similar suits have been based on failure to diagnose a pregnancy in time for an abortion or incorrect medical advice resulting in the birth of a physically or mentally deformed child. Plaintiffs have filed claims for repayment of medical expenses of pregnancy and delivery, for pain and suffering, and for the expenses of education and care of an unwanted child.

W

X chromosome the female sex chromosome. It is present in all ova and in half of all spermatozoa; the other half of the spermatozoa contain the Y, or male, sex chromosome. Female somatic (body) cells normally contain two X chromosomes, although one is inactivated.

X-linked abnormality any genetic disorder that is transmitted by a gene on an X chromosome. X-linked abnormalities are always manifested in the male whose sex-chromosome counterpart, the Y chromosome, has no matching genes for those on the female sex chromosome. The male may express an X-linked abnormality even though it is carried as a recessive gene. Examples are Haemophilia A and Duchenne's muscular dystrophy.

X deletion a loss or deletion of part of the X chromosome of a female karyotype. It is not unusual for a portion of a chromosome to be lost during the cell divisions of meiosis or mitosis. The event often results in an offspring being born with an abnormality if the lost portion is not required for survival of the embryo. Authorities estimate that 75 percent of all such chromosomal defects involve the sex chromosomes, resulting in such abnormalities as Turner's syndrome effects.

XXXXX syndrome a rare condition marked by the presence of three extra X chromosomes in a superfemale. The woman is generally normal in female physical characteristics, and fertile, but may exhibit some degree of mental retardation, ocular disorders, or limb abnormalities. Also called 49,XXXXX.

XXXXY syndrome one of the genetic expressions of Klinefelter's syndrome, usually characterized by a tall male with long legs but with poorly developed male genitalia, a deficiency of normal male secondary sexual characteristics, an absence of fertility, and in some cases mental retardation. Such individuals often are discovered after adulthood when they undergo medical tests to determine the reason for their infertility.

XXXY syndrome a variation of the Klinefelter syndrome in which the male possesses three X chromosomes, or a total of 48 chromosomes. The features of the Klinefelter individual who is trisomic for the X chromosome are similar to those of the 49,XXXXY male.

XXY syndrome a condition that is the most common form of Klinefelter's syndrome. With a chromosome count of 47, as compared with the normal total of 46, the individual usually possesses enough Y chromosome influence to acquire the basic male features although disomic for the X chromosome. The additional X chromosome is generally not detected or expressed until after puberty. The XXY complement occurs about once in every 500 male births.

XXYY syndrome a male who is disomic for both the X and Y chromosomes. He may have some of the features found in Klinefelter's syndrome, particularly testicular dysgenesis and sterility. He may also display some of the psychological traits observed in individuals with the XYY-sex-chromosome combination, such as a tendency towards aggressiveness.

Yakút a reindeer-breeding polygynous society in northeastern Siberia. The Yakúts are unique on two counts: Unlike practically all other aborigines, they prefer women who are slim, and they require their daughters to wear a 'chastity girdle' in the form of heavy leather trousers to preserve their virginity until marriage.

yang and yin according to ancient Chinese doctrine, two fundamental forces that pervade the universe and control human life. They represent such opposites as masculine-feminine, active-passive, moon-sun, and earth-heaven. Sexually speaking, the yang force of Heaven is dominant in men and determines the outer shape of the male sex organ, and the yin force of Earth is dominant in women and determines the inward shape of the female sex organ. These two forces complement each other during sexual contact, and a balanced, cosmic harmony is believed to result.

yantra in the Hindu tradition, a mystic sixpointed diagram composed of two superimposed triangles that symbolize the harmonious balance between the five senses (touch, sound, sight, taste and smell), the mind, and the male and female functions. The diagram is used as a meditation device in creating a harmony of emotions, as an aid in performing rituals, and as a protective talisman.

Yapese inhabitants of a large island in the Carolines whose diet depends on fishing. The society is mainly monogamous, though polygyny is permitted. Their customs and beliefs include insistence that a man is unnecessary for procreation; an intercourse position in which a man is seated and the woman squats on top facing him and urinates as she reaches orgasm; blackening of the teeth as a form of beautification; the view that incest is some-

thing that animals do, not human beings, and that a woman who has committed incest cannot bear children; erotic festivals involving sexual licence and public outdoor copulation; the practice of coitus interruptus, possibly for birth control; a taboo against intercourse during menstruation; a unique taboo against bathing in the ocean after intercourse; and a practice known as GICHIGICH. See this entry.

yard an old euphemism for penis.

yarrow a common herb that grows in much of the world between the tropics and the Arctic Circles. It is also known by its common name of staunch-wound, which reveals its links to medieval witchcraft. Yarrow was traditionally used at weddings to ensure 7 years of true love. Young women in Europe and America used to believe that if tickling their nostrils with yarrow caused a nosebleed it meant their lovers were faithful.

yaws a tropical disease occurring primarily in parts of Africa, South America, Indonesia, Australia and the West Indies. It is caused by infection with Treponema pertenue, a corkscrew-shaped organism similar to Treponema pallidum (which causes syphilis). The first symptoms are lesions on the legs or feet, later giving rise to papules over the entire body, including the anogenital area, and still later affecting the bones and joints. Some cases seem to be sexually transmitted.

Y chromosome the male sex chromosome, which is present in half of all spermatozoa while none is found in a female gamete or a normal female body cell. The main function of the Y chromosome is believed to be the synthesis of molecules that lead to production of male sex hormones, which in turn result in the physical characteristics of the male sex. All males require an X chromosome in addition to the Y chromosome.

yellow body the corpus luteum of the ovary.

Y-linked pertaining to the genes or traits carried by the male sex chromosome. Certain characteristics, such as hair on the external ear, are Y-linked and are expressed only in males.

yohimbine an alkaloid obtained from the bark of the yohimbe tree (*Pausinystalia yohimba*), which grows in west central Africa. It is used as an alleged aphrodisiac. Yohimbine has been discovered to be identical with quebrachine, obtained from white quebracho bark. The name is western African in origin.

yolk sac an embryonic structure formed by cells that extend into the cavity of the blastocyst. In lower animals, the yolk sac contains nutrients that sustain life and growth of the embryo. In humans, the yolk sac is a rudimentary bit of tissue that provides little or no nourishment to the beginning embryo which obtains its nutrients by osmosis from the blood lakes in the walls of the uterus.

yolk stalk a threadlike structure that connects the embryo to the yolk sac. It also is known as the vitelline duct.

yoni the Hindu name for the female sex organ (vagina), which is worshiped in Tantric rites throughout India. The yoni is depicted in sculpture placed at Hindu shrines, and its likeness is frequently worn as an amulet.

Zande an African people, living in the Congo-Sudan region, who differ from most other societies in idealizing long, pendulous breasts. The Zande also delay marriage until the 30s or 40s, making pederasty a common custom. Other customs are prohibiting marriage of a man with the midwife who assisted at his birth; punishing a woman's adultery by killing both the wife and her lover, or mutilating the lover by cutting off his ears, upper lip, hands, and penis; permitting harems for selected men, thus creating a scarcity for others; and encouraging the use of bananas and roots as dildos.

Z chromosome a male sex chromosome of some birds, fishes, and insects with male disomic sex chromosomes. In such species it is the male that possesses the duplicate (ZZ) sex chromosomes while the female sex characteristics are determined by a combination of one W and one Z sex chromosome.

Zina a Muslim category for all forbidden sex acts, including bestiality, prostitution, anal sex, and lesbianism. The penalty for Zina violations is death.

zinc deficiency a condition resulting from a lack of zinc in the diet. Effects include a loss of taste and smell sensitivity, fatigue, and delayed sexual maturity. There also is evidence that zinc contributes to normal sexuality. Because oysters and other seafood can be a good source of zinc, it has been suggested that its presence may be the basis for claims that seafoods may have aphrodisiac qualities.

zip injury of the penis a painful injury caused by catching the excess skin of the penis in the zip of a trouser fly. The recommended treatment is to sedate the victim, then deaden the sensitivity of the penis with a generous amount of Nupercainal ointment.

If necessary, the zip is cut away from the trousers to manipulate it away from the skin without causing added injury.

zipper ring an intrauterine contraceptive device made of coils of nylon thread. Its claimed advantage is that it can be inserted without prior mechanical dilation of the cervix.

zona fasciculata a layer of the adrenal gland cortex in which androgenic sex hormones are produced.

zona pellucida a thick, transparent, protective membrane that is secreted round the ovum during its maturation in an ovary. The membrane is produced by the cytoplasm of the ovum and remains with the ovum until after fertilization.

zooerasty (zō′ə·iras′tē) sexual excitement or gratification through contact with an animal (from Greek *zoon,* 'animal,' and *erastes,* 'lover'). Also called zoophilia.

zoolagnia (zō′əlag′nē·ə) sexual pleasure from contacts with animals.

zoophilia (zō′əfē′lyə) a psychosexual disorder in which farm animals or household pets are persistently preferred or exclusively used to achieve sexual excitement. Also called zooerasty.

zoosadist (zō′əsā′dist) a person who derives sexual pleasure from injuring animals. Also called *zoo sadist.*

Zovirax a brand name for the drug acyclovir approved by the US Food and Drug Administration in 1985 as a medication for the treatment of genital herpes.

Zulu a South African society in which polygyny is (or was) the general rule, preferably the sororal type. Among their customs is (or was) the removal of all hair in the pubic and armpit regions by both men and women; rituals in which unmarried women dance

Z

bare-breasted and wearing nothing but beads, to show that their bodies are not flabby, which would be an indication of sexual immorality; punishment for adultery by flogging the offenders with thorny branches, and in some cases thrusting cacti into the women's vagina; a taboo against daylight intercourse—otherwise people would 'behave like dogs'; and various other taboos such as avoidance of sex during a storm, after a bad dream, or after the husband has killed a python, crocodile, or hyena.

zygote the fertilized ovum, containing both sets of chromosomes from the male and female gametes, before it begins to divide.